Financial Reporting for Managers
A Value-Creation Perspective

JAMIE PRATT
Indiana University

D. ERIC HIRST
University of Texas at Austin

WILEY

JOHN WILEY & SONS, INC.

VP AND EXECUTIVE PUBLISHER	Donald Fowley
ASSOCIATE PUBLISHER	Christopher DeJohn
EXECUTIVE MARKETING MANAGER	Amy Scholz
SENIOR MARKETING MANAGER	Julia Flohr
SENIOR DESIGNER	Kevin Murphy
SENIOR PRODUCTION EDITOR	Nicole Repasky
PRODUCTION MANAGEMENT SERVICES	Aptara Corporation
SENIOR PHOTO EDITOR	Lisa Gee
EDITORIAL ASSISTANT	Kathryn Fraser
SENIOR MEDIA EDITOR	Allie K. Morris
COVER PHOTO	Bruno Ehrs/Corbis
COVER DESIGN	David Levy

This book was set in Times Roman by Aptara Corporation and printed and bound by Hamilton Printing. The cover was printed by Phoenix Color.

The book is printed on acid-free paper. ∞

To order books or for customer service, please call 1-800-CALL WILEY (225-5945).

Library of Congress Cataloging-in-Publication Data:
Pratt, Jamie.
  Financial reporting for managers / Jamie Pratt, Eric Hirst.
      p. cm.
  Includes index.
  ISBN 978-0-471-45749-7 (cloth)
1. Financial statements.   2. Business enterprises—Finance.   I. Hirst, Eric.   II. Title.
  HF5681.B2P724 2009
  658.15'12—dc22

                                                          2007043721

Printed in the United States of America

10   9   8   7   6   5   4   3   2   1

Preface

We wrote this book to fill what we consider to be a huge void in the supply of texts that bring together financial reporting and management decision making, aimed at thoughtful MBAs and the fast-growing executive education market. The concept of shareholder value creation is fundamental to management performance and performance evaluation, and certainly it is not new. Yet, no one has combined this valuable concept and the financial reporting process—the primary provider of the measures of shareholder value creation and its determinants—into a relatively short and intuitive management-based textbook. Existing textbooks seem to realize that managers need to know how to use and interpret financial accounting statements, and occasionally—not in the accounting area however—you see some work on value creation; but our text is clearly the first and only to bring the two together in a thoughtful, creative, and easy-to-understand manner. In addition, our text goes further by linking shareholder value creation and the financial accounting statements to the market value of the firm in a way that can easily be understood by practitioners. To date, this link has only been made in the academic literature. It's simple. Our text lays out the pathways leading from good decisions by management to strong financial statements, and higher shareholder value and stock prices.

Our text is designed for business students and managers, with little prior exposure to financial reporting, who wish to understand how financial statements can help them—and encourage others—to make decisions in the long-run interest of the firm's shareholders. On the first page of the first chapter, the text describes what it means to create shareholder value, a primary management goal, and then proceeds to link the measurement and achievement of shareholder value creation to the financial statements. It then carefully develops the economic context in which financial statements are prepared and used, focusing on corporate governance, and relying heavily on real-world examples, anecdotes, and situations.

Chapter 2 explores the financial statements more closely. Rather than discussing each statement separately, however, this coverage uses current DuPont financial statements to show how information about operating, investing, and financing activities—available on the balance sheet, income statement, statement of cash flows, and statement of shareholders' equity—can be used to assess firm performance and shareholder value creation.

Chapter 3 covers the measurement principles underlying the primary performance evaluation metrics provided by financial statements, and then applies these principles by demonstrating—via the basic accounting equation—how the statements can be constructed. Journal entries and T-accounts are briefly covered in an appendix.

The text then moves into analysis mode beginning with Chapter 4, which is devoted exclusively to the return on equity (ROE) (DuPont) framework and its value drivers—again organized in terms of operating, investing, and financing activities. Here, the shareholder value creation of Nordstrom and Saks are compared and contrasted. Chapter 5 then demonstrates how Nordstrom's value drivers, through their influence on ROE, can be linked to its market value. The point here is that managers can use the value-driver metrics, available on the financial statements, to manage toward increased shareholder value creation and higher firm market values.

The first five chapters of this text represent a package, showing how performance metrics available from the financial statements, shareholder value creation, and the firm's market value are all tied together. When viewed in this manner, the financial statements can indeed be considered an essential management tool.

Chapter 6 offers a thoughtful coverage of earnings management: the use of discretion by management in the preparation of the financial statements to cast a favorable picture of the financial performance and condition of the firm. We describe and illustrate various earnings management strategies, provide a framework of the use of discretion in the preparation of the financial statements, and comment on the relative effectiveness of these strategies. We do not condone earnings management, but we do realize that savvy financial statement readers need to understand where, how, and to what extent it occurs. Similarly, analysts need to be able to recognize the extent and direction of earnings management, as well as adjust for it when they analyze the financial statements.

The final three chapters delve more deeply into the methods used to account for operating (Chapter 7), investing (Chapter 8), and financing (Chapter 9) transactions. The bulk of Chapter 7 comprises receivables, inventories, and current liabilities; equity investments, and fixed and intangible assets are covered in Chapter 8; and long-term liabilities and shareholders' equity are the subjects of Chapter 9. The coverage of these items considers the effects of the various accounting methods on the income statement, balance sheet, statement of cash flows, and statement of shareholders' equity. Again, the theme here is how to account for and manage these transactions toward shareholder value creation and increased firm value. The remainder of the text consists of an appendix on the time value of money, and an extensive glossary of key accounting terms.

This package of material strikes an effective balance among the mechanics underlying the preparation of the statements, the measurement issues behind the mechanics and, most importantly, the economic context in which the statements are prepared and used, which includes analysis of the financial statements, and construction and interpretation of the metrics necessary to manage businesses toward shareholder value creation and increased firm value. This text is targeted at thoughtful business students and managers who wish to learn how financial statement use and analysis can be a path to business success.

A number of distinctive features separate this text from others that cover introductory financial reporting.

Shareholder Value Theme
The shareholder value creation theme is unique. The text begins by making the point that the goal of management is long-run shareholder value creation and then proceeds to explain how the financial reports can be used to measure, identify, and encourage value creation. This theme pervades the entire text—from the first to the last chapter.

ROE Focus
In Chapter 1, the text explains that to create long-run shareholder value, management must generate ROEs that exceed the cost of equity. The text, therefore, is organized around ROE, its determinants, and its relationship to the market value of the firm. Chapter 4 introduces the ROE model of analysis, Chapter 5 links ROE and shareholder value creation to the value of the firm, and much of the remainder of the text is organized in terms of accounting for and managing operating, investing, and financing transactions—the determinants of ROE, shareholder value creation, and the value of the firm.

Real-World Cases
Each chapter contains a set of real-world cases, requiring the student to identify and use the concepts covered in the chapter. These relatively short cases have been extensively class tested and well received, and involve a selection of both U.S. and non-U.S. companies and settings.

Integrated Global Coverage

In addition to the cases devoted to international companies and settings, each chapter contains a section on global accounting issues and a number of international examples and references sprinkled throughout the reading. Indeed, global accounting coverage is not treated as a separate afterthought. It is integrated throughout the discussion. In light of the recent move toward International Financial Reporting Standards (IFRS) the text frequently points out differences between IFRS and U.S. GAAP.

Boxed-In Features

Each chapter contains a large number of boxed-in items, each of which is identified by a particular icon. These items provide commentary that is separated from—but related to—the text discussion, and the icons signal the content of the commentary. The content of the boxed-in items includes short "test your knowledge" review exercises, as well as issues related to analysis of financial statements, definitions of key terms, insights on real-world situations, globalization, and IFRS performance measurement, the ROE model, "red flags" to watch out for, and corporate governance. A large number of these commentaries involve current, real-world settings.

Flexibility of Mechanics Coverage

The text offers flexibility with respect to the nature and order of the mechanics coverage. Chapter 3 is devoted to the mechanics of preparing the financial statements, and it is important that it be covered prior to Chapters 6–9. The early chapters are designed, however, so that Chapter 3 could be covered at any time before Chapter 6, depending on the preference of the user. Furthermore, the preparation of the statements, as well as the effect of transactions on the statements, can be covered with or without the aid of journal entries and T-accounts. Chapter 3 covers the basic accounting equation, and an understanding of how transactions are recorded to maintain its equality and how these transactions affect the financial statements is critical for an understanding of the material in Chapters 6–9. However, journal entries and T-accounts are introduced in Appendix 3A, and throughout the remainder of the text, journal entries and T-accounts are separated (boxed-in items) from the text discussion.

All of this is offered in a very efficiently written package (440 pages), and all of the chapters have been extensively class tested in both executive education programs and MBA classrooms. The end-of-chapter cases, all of which raise any of a number of key issues in real-world contexts, have already been discussed by a variety of students, and any "bugs" are long since gone. Enough mechanics to ensure that the student learns the fundamentals and develops an appreciation for where the numbers come from, a number of different frameworks to aid perspective, analysis and interpretation, and a timeless theme (the links among financial reports, shareholder value creation, and firm value) make for an excellent and extremely useful introduction to financial reporting for interested business persons. The approach is effective, unique, and ahead of its time.

Acknowledgments

This text has benefited significantly from the constructive and insightful comments provided by the individuals listed below.

Al Hartgraves, Emory University; James A. Schweikart, Boston University; Michael F. Van Breda, Southern Methodist University; Thomas Dyckman, Cornell University; Sanjeev Bhojraj, Cornell University; Tim Fogarty, Case Western Reserve University; Donna Rapaccioli, Fordham University; William Knowles, University of New Hampshire.

In addition, the John Wiley editorial, design, and marketing staffs deserve thanks and recognition for their contributions. Finally, a special, heartfelt and sincere thank you goes to my wife, Kathy, and children, Jason, Ryan, and Dylan, all of whom have sacrificed and supported me as I have pushed forward on this project. Now that the text is complete, it will be nice to return to being a more available husband and father.

J.P.

Special thanks to my family (Patty, Kevin, and Matt) for their patience and understanding throughout this project. I'm blessed to have their support.

E.H.

About the Authors

Jamie Pratt is KPMG Professor of Accounting at the Kelley School of Business at Indiana University. He received his doctoral degree from Indiana in 1977 and has held faculty positions at the University of Washington–Seattle, University of Zurich, Northwestern University, and INSEAD—returning to Indiana in 1991. He served as chair of the Accounting Department from 1998–2004, and chair of Graduate Accounting Programs from 2006–2007. He teaches financial accounting and financial statement analysis at both the undergraduate and graduate levels, and he has received teaching awards at each of the institutions listed above. In addition, he has taught in executive education programs all over the world. His research interests primarily include financial reporting and auditing issues, and he publishes frequently in the top academic accounting journals, including *The Accounting Review, Journal of Accounting Research, Contemporary Accounting Research, Accounting, Organizations & Society, Auditing: A Journal of Practice and Theory*, as well as journals devoted to educational issues such as *Issues in Accounting Education and Journal of Accounting Education*. He has served as Associate Editor of *The Accounting Review*, program chair for the American Accounting Association (AAA) annual meeting, and he has received a number of AAA awards and recognitions. Professor Pratt is sole author of a popular textbook now in its 7th edition (*Financial Accounting in an Economic Context*), and he has co-authored a number of other educational materials, including casebooks, spreadsheet exercises, and state-of-the-art interactive CD-ROM products. He lives with his wife (Kathy) and three boys (Jason, Ryan, and Dylan) in Bloomington, Indiana, where he enjoys sports, landscaping, and playing the piano.

   D. Eric Hirst is Associate Dean for Graduate Programs, Professor, and the Ernst and Young Faculty Fellow in accounting at the McCombs School of Business at the University of Texas at Austin. He received a BA in Economics and Master of Accounting from the University of Waterloo (Waterloo, Ontario) and a Ph.D. in Management from the University of Minnesota. At UT, he teaches the MBA core course in financial reporting and an elective course in financial statement analysis. In addition, Eric teaches in UT's MBA Programs in Mexico City and Houston. Eric has been recognized numerous times for Teaching Excellence in the MBA Core at the McCombs School and was recognized as Outstanding Teacher of Core Classes at INSEAD (Fontainebleau, France). He has developed and taught programs for KPMG, Dow Chemical, 3M, Texas Instruments, USAA, Motorola, Freescale Semiconductor, and other major companies. His research interests center on the role of financial reporting in investor and professional analyst judgment and decision making. He has published articles in scholarly journals including *Journal of Accounting Research Research, The Accounting Review, Contemporary Accounting Research*, and *Organizational Behavior and Human Decision Processes*. He was awarded the College of Business Administration Award for Research Excellence for Assistant Professors in 1997 and the Award for Research Excellence in 2003. His monograph, *Earnings: Measurement, Disclosure and the Impact on Equity Valuation,* was distributed to over 32,000 members of the Association for Investment Management and Research. He was awarded the American Accounting Association Financial Reporting Section's 1999 "Best Paper Award" and received the AAA Auditing Section's "Notable Contributions to The Auditing Literature Award" for 2000–2001. Outside of work, he spends time with his wife (Patty) and two sons (Kevin and Matthew) and plays in-line hockey and golf.

Contents

Value Creation, Financial Statements, and the Environment of Financial Reporting

ANALYSIS CHALLENGE: SHOULD THE CHAMPAGNE FLOW?

Your company made $1,000,000 this year. Should the champagne flow? If your company owns the rights to operate a single McDonald's restaurant, the answer is likely a resounding "yes." If your company is McDonald's Corporation, the owner and franchiser of more than 31,000 restaurants in over 100 countries on five continents, the answer is certainly "no."

Why? Would the answers change if the company made $100 million? $1 billion?

This book describes how financial reports can help investors, directors, employees, suppliers, regulators—indeed all of the firm's stakeholders—assess whether, to what extent, and how a firm's managers have created value for the firm's owners. In this chapter, we define value creation and illustrate how it can be measured. We also introduce the major financial statements and discuss the economic context in which they are produced and used. We delve more deeply into the financial statements in Chapter 2 and the measurement principles that underlie them in Chapter 3. Chapter 4 describes a powerful model for analyzing financial statements, and we discuss the relationship between value creation and a company's market value in Chapter 5. Chapter 6 discusses how managerial discretion can influence the numbers reported on the financial statements, and Chapters 7, 8, and 9 examine how operating, investing, and financing activities are reflected on the financial statements.

▶ VALUE CREATION AND SUCCESSFUL MANAGEMENT

Orlando Owner invests in real estate. He hired Mike Manager to manage his real estate operations in South Carolina. Mike identifies an old home that he believes could be purchased for $100,000, remodeled, and sold for a profit. He recommends the project to Orlando, who agrees to pay Mike $50,000 to remodel and sell the home. Orlando also gives Mike $300,000 to finance the project—$100,000 of his own money and $200,000 borrowed from a bank (at a 10% annual interest rate). Mike uses the money to purchase the home and complete the project, and one year later sells the remodeled home for $325,000. He repays the bank loan, and then presents Orlando with a check for $103,000 and a financial report (Figure 1-1). Review the report and consider whether the project was a success and whether Orlando should be pleased with Mike's work.

You probably noted that the project netted a $3,000 profit, repaid the $200,000 bank loan, and returned Orlando more money ($103,000) than he originally invested ($100,000). On that basis, perhaps you concluded that the project was a success and Orlando should be pleased with the outcome. Unfortunately, that may not be the case. The $103,000 payment does show that the proceeds from the sale more than covered the costs of purchasing the home, materials and supplies, labor, interest, and taxes, but the payment was not large enough to provide Orlando with a reasonable return on his $100,000 investment. Specifically, Orlando's annual return on the project was only 3.0% ([$103,000 − $100,000] / $100,000). In essence, Orlando received only $3,000 in exchange for giving up the use of $100,000 for an entire year.

How large a return is necessary to make Orlando happy? Consider first that Orlando could have earned 5% ($5,000) by simply investing his $100,000 in a no-risk certificate of deposit at a local bank. After taxes, that would amount to the same 3% return as on the real estate investment. However, real estate investments are inherently risky, suggesting that a reasonable return for this kind of investment would be well above the risk-free 5%, perhaps as high as 20% after taxes. Why else would Orlando be willing to put his $100,000 at risk unless he could expect a return large enough to make taking such a risk worthwhile? Thus, Orlando likely entered the project expecting a payment at the end of the year somewhere around $120,000. Surely, $103,000 is a disappointment—far below what he probably would have received had he chosen other investments of equal or even lesser risk. In Orlando's view, was Mike a successful manager? Maybe not. Is Mike's job in jeopardy? Perhaps.

The major point of this illustration is that simply creating "profits" is not enough to compensate owners for the investments they make in firms. Value is only created for the owners if profits are large enough to compensate them adequately for the risks they bear. One way to improve the financial report in Figure 1-1—to reflect value creation—is to add the payment to the owner that is necessary to compensate him for risk, as shown at the bottom of Figure 1-1a. This format clearly shows that the project did not create, but in fact lost, value for Orlando, the owner.

Sources of financing:		
Investment by owner	$ 100,000	
Bank loan	200,000	$ 300,000
Profit on remodeling project:		
Sale of remodeled home	$ 325,000	
Cost to purchase home	(100,000)	
Cost of materials and supplies	(150,000)	
Labor expense (Mike's fee)	(50,000)	
Profit before tax and cost of debt financing	$ 25,000	
Interest expense (10% × $ 200,000)	(20,000)	
Profit before tax	5,000	
Income tax payments (40% × $ 5,000)	(2,000)	3,000
Cash available at completion of project		$ 303,000
Repayment of bank loan		(200,000)
Payment to owner		$ 103,000

Figure 1-1. Remodeling Project Financial Report

Sources of financing:		
Investment by owner	$ 100,000	
Bank loan	200,000	$ 300,000
Profit on remodeling project:		
Sale of remodeled home	$ 325,000	
Cost to purchase home	(100,000)	
Cost of materials and supplies	(150,000)	
Labor expense	(50,000)	
Profit before tax and cost of financing	$ 25,000	
Interest expense	(20,000)	
Profit before tax	5,000	
Income tax payments	(2,000)	3,000
Cash available at completion of project		$ 303,000
Repayment of bank loan		(200,000)
Payment to owner		$ 103,000
Repayment of owner's investment		(100,000)
Payment necessary to compensate owner for risk (20% × $ 100,000)		(20,000)
Value created (lost) for owner		$ (17,000)

Figure 1-1a. Remodeling Project Financial Report *(adjusted to reflect value creation)*

What then is successful management? The simple answer is management that creates value for the owners of the firm. Value creation involves finding and managing projects that provide returns greater than the cost of financing the projects. In other words, managers create value when they invest in assets (e.g., buildings, equipment, other companies, and inventories) and oversee day-to-day operations that create returns for the firm's owners that exceed the costs of the debt and equity capital used to finance the investments and operations. In the example earlier, on the investment in the home and the operating activites involved in remodeling it, Mike Manager did generate $25,000, an amount large enough to cover the cost (interest) associated with the $200,000 loan. However, as Figure 1-1a shows, the $3,000 in profit generated after interest and taxes was not large enough to adequately cover the cost of the $100,000 in equity capital provided by the owner—the $20,000 (20% annual return) that Orlando expected to earn on his $100,000 investment, given the level of risk he faced.

It is easy to see that financing with debt (borrowing) has a cost because the interest rate is an important—and normally clearly identified—term in the debt contract. In the remodeling example, the interest expense for the year was easily computed (10% × $200,000) and, therefore, figured prominently in Figure 1-1. On the other hand, the cost of equity, while equally significant, is much less explicit and unfortunately often ignored. It was not even mentioned in Figure 1-1. In the remodeling example, we estimated it at roughly 20%. Despite the fact that the cost of equity is difficult to estimate, it is key to determining management's success and value creation, and we return to it later in this chapter and its appendix, and throughout the text.

Because value creation is such an important goal, it is crucial that both management and the owners have timely and accurate measures of the returns generated by management's investing and operating activities, the amount of capital invested by the owners, and the cost of the invested capital. Financial accounting reports—the balance sheet, income statement, statement of cash flows, statement of changes in owners' equity, and related footnotes—provide many of these measures. Although imperfect, these measures play a critical role in management's attempt to attract capital at low rates, and when used and interpreted correctly, numbers from the financial reports can help to indicate whether, and the extent to which, management's decisions create value for the firm's owners. Furthermore, using these measures in performance-based compensation contracts can encourage management (and the firm's employees) to engage in value-creation activities.

► VALUE CREATION THROUGH OPERATING, INVESTING, AND FINANCING ACTIVITIES

Figure 1-2 illustrates the flow of capital through the firm, highlighting a number of concepts that we rely upon heavily throughout the text. In the figure, management must attract money, often called capital, from two sources: from shareholders by selling ownership (equity) in the firm and from debtholders (creditors) through borrowings (1). Management normally attracts this capital by presenting to these potential investors historical and prospective information explaining how it expects to use the capital to create returns for the investors. Shareholders (equity investors) expect returns in the form of price appreciation of their investments and/or dividends. Debtholders (debt investors) expect returns in the form of interest.

Management invests the capital in both producing assets (e.g., property, plant, and equipment; other companies; intangible assets; and ideas) and operating assets (e.g., inventory), often referred to as working capital (2). Producing assets typically provide benefits for the firm over many periods by supporting the operating activities—the management of the assets used in day-to-day operations. Managing the producing and operating assets generates revenues (e.g., sales of inventories or services), which are matched against the expenses incurred to generate them (e.g., wages and salaries), including interest on the outstanding debt (3). The difference between revenues and expenses is called net income, profit, or earnings (4), and represents a measure of the wealth created by management for the shareholders during a given time period. The shareholders, normally through the board

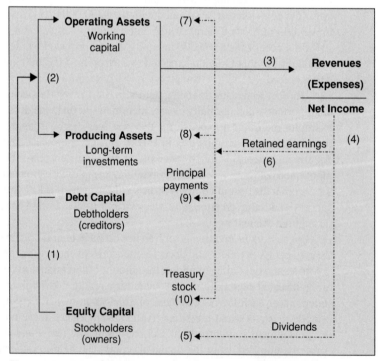

Figure 1-2. Flow of Capital

of directors, decide whether to take the created wealth out of the firm in the form of dividends (5), or reinvest it in the firm (6). The reinvestment is called retained earnings—a measure of the resources that management can use to purchase working capital (7), producing assets (8), pay off loans (9), and/or buy back ownership interests (shares of stock) from the shareholders in the form of treasury stock (10).

This process highlights three fundamental activities involved in managing a business: (1) operating activities, (2) investing activities, and (3) financing activities. Operating activities involve managing the operating assets, which includes activities related to the production and sale of goods and services (e.g., sales, receivables, inventory, and payables management). Investing activities involve acquiring and disposing of producing assets—the assets used to produce and support the goods and services provided (e.g., buildings, equipment, and know-how). Financing activities involve raising capital through equity or debt issuances and the related payments to capital providers such as debt payments, dividends, and share repurchases.

Return on Equity (ROE)

Value creation occurs when the operating and investing activities produce a return for the shareholders that exceeds the cost of the financing activities. It can be determined by first computing the return created by management for the shareholders on their equity investment—the return on equity or ROE.

DEFINITION: RETURN ON EQUITY (ROE)

Net Income / (Equity Capital + Retained Earnings − Treasury Stock)

The numerator of ROE is net income, a measure of the wealth created for the shareholders during the period; the denominator is a measure of the *net* investment provided by the shareholders, defined by their original capital investment (equity capital), plus the capital they have chosen to reinvest in the firm (retained earnings), less capital the firm has returned to the shareholders (treasury stock). ROE by itself is not a measure of value creation because net income—the numerator—reflects only the cost of debt; it does not reflect the cost of equity. Consequently, to determine whether ROE is large enough to create value, it must be compared to the cost of equity. If ROE is greater than the cost of equity, value has been created and management has succeeded. Management has used the shareholders' investment to generate a return that exceeds what the shareholders could have reasonably expected given the risk level of the firm. If ROE is less than the cost of equity, value has been lost.

Recall, for example, the illustration at the beginning of the chapter where Orlando Owner invested $100,000 and hired Mike Manager to remodel and sell an old home, receiving $103,000 at year end. The ROE on Orlando's investment was 3.0% ($3,000/$100,000).[1] In that example, we estimated the cost of equity to be 20%, the

---

[1] In the example, which illustrated only a single period, both retained earnings and treasury stock purchases were zero.

return Orlando could have reasonably expected, given the relatively high risk level associated with real estate investments. In this case, therefore, Mike Manager failed to create value for Orlando, the owner; the ROE (3%) was well below the cost of equity (20%).

A Caution About Measures of Value Creation

We defined and illustrated value creation in terms of the return (ROE) in a single period, and we noted that management success in a single period is determined by whether value is created (ROE > cost of equity) in that period. This description is oversimplified in the sense that value creation is actually a long-run concept, and that sometimes what appears to be value loss (ROE < cost of equity) in a given period can underlie greater value creation over time. It is not unusual, for example, for management to incur large start-up costs in the early years of a project, which drive down ROE temporarily, giving rise to what may appear to be loss of value. However, this apparent loss of value may serve as the foundation for greater value creation in the future. Similarly, if expenses incurred in year 1 increase a firm's market share, creating substantial value in year 2 and beyond, then a loss of value in year 1 need not indicate that management failed. Internet retailer Amazon.com, for instance, generated massive losses in its early years as it invested in infrastructure and brand recognition. In recent years, the company has reported considerable profits.

Furthermore, the available measures of value creation are imperfect, containing both error and bias, which can further complicate the conclusions one can draw from a value-creation computation in a given year. Net income may be misstated because revenues and/or expenses are misstated; the measure of the investment provided by the stockholders may be in error; and estimating the cost of equity is difficult and subjective. It is important, therefore, that value-creation measures be used thoughtfully and with an understanding of the nature of their components and the context in which they are prepared. In later chapters, we discuss how the implementation of accounting rules can sometimes obscure the measurement of value creation, and how analysts and other financial statement users can adjust and interpret financial reports to better measure value creation. We now introduce and briefly discuss the primary measures of value creation: the cost of equity and the financial statements.

Estimating the Cost of Equity—An Intuitive Approach

Value is created if ROE is greater than the cost of equity, the return an investor can reasonably expect given the risk level of the investment. The higher the risk level, the higher the cost of equity. In concept, this idea makes sense—investors need to be compensated for the risks they bear, or they will not invest in risky projects; in reality, however, the cost of equity is very elusive and even the best economists have been unable to agree on how it should be computed. The cost of equity is not disclosed on the financial statements or related footnotes because it is simply too subjective. It must be estimated. Some companies discuss their cost of capital estimates in their annual reports, but it remains relatively rare.

Recall the remodeling example at the beginning of the chapter where we discussed what rate of return would be necessary to make Orlando happy. We settled upon 20% by first noting that he could have earned 5% by investing in a no-risk certificate of deposit at a local bank, and then added to that a risk premium associated with risky real estate investments. Similarly, most economists agree that the cost of equity contains two components: a risk-free rate of return, which is shared by the entire economy, and a risk premium, which is unique to the particular investment. That is,

$$\text{Cost of equity} = \text{Risk-free rate of return} + \text{Risk premium}$$

The rate of return on 10-year government treasury bills as of a particular date is often used to estimate the risk-free rate. Historically, it has ranged from around 3 to 8%, averaging about 6%. The more difficult part of estimating the cost of equity is the risk premium, which varies significantly across firms and industries. In Appendix 1A, we describe the capital asset pricing model (CAPM), a popular method used to estimate the cost of equity, and below we list estimates of the cost of equity for selected firms as of the end of 2006. The 10-year government treasury bill rate was approximately 5 percent.

Firm	Industry	Risk-Free Rate	Risk Premium	Cost of Equity
Cisco Systems	Internet hardware and software systems	5%	12%	17%
DuPont	Science	5%	6%	11%
General Motors	Auto manufacturing and financial services	5%	13%	18%
Lowe's Companies	Retail home improvement	5%	5%	10%
McDonald's	Fast food	5%	8%	13%
Nordstrom	Retail clothing	5%	8%	13%
Walt Disney	Entertainment and Media	5%	7%	12%

ANALYSIS CHALLENGE: SHOULD THE CHAMPAGNE FLOW? (REVISITED)

If the equity capital invested in McDonald's Corporation was $2 million and it earned $1 million in profit during 2006, its 50% return on equity ($1 million / $2 million) for 2006 would surely exceed any reasonable estimate of its cost of capital. In reality, McDonald's Corporation had equity capital of $15.5 billion as of December 31, 2006. Had the company earned only $1 million, its ROE would be miniscule and certainly less than its cost of capital. *The Wall Street Journal* reported that McDonald's, in fact, had an average ROE of close to 16% for the five-year period 2002–2006. Over that period, estimates of McDonald's cost of equity capital were in the 12%–14% range (see chart above), suggesting that McDonald's did create shareholder value over the period 2002–2006.

▶ THE FINANCIAL STATEMENTS—AN INTRODUCTION

Figure 1-3 presents a general overview of the financial statements published by Lowe's Companies, Inc., a world leader in the home improvement industry. Note the four statements indicated by the numbers: (1) balance sheet (February 3, 2006), (2) statement of cash flows, (3) statement of stockholders' equity, and (4) income statement. An additional balance sheet, dated February 2, 2007, is included on the right side of the figure.

Briefly, the two balance sheets represent snapshots of the financial condition of Lowe's as of February 3, 2006 and February 2, 2007—its assets and the financing of those assets *as of* the beginning and end of the fiscal year. The remaining statements reflect activities occurring *during* the year. The statement of cash flows is a record of the cash inflows

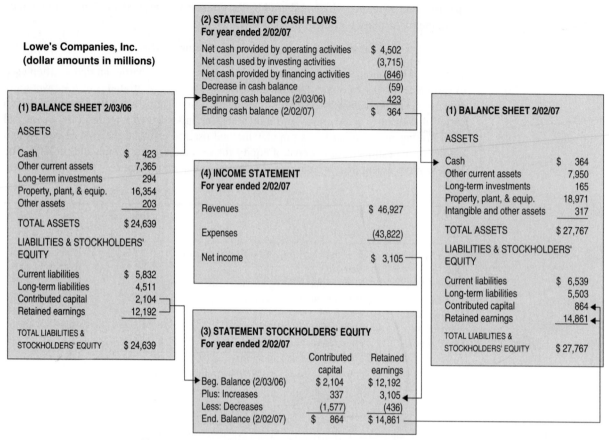

Figure 1-3. Overview of Financial Statements

and outflows associated with operating, investing, and financing activities; the statement of shareholders' (or stockholders') equity is a record of the exchanges with shareholders; and the income statement is a measure of the net assets created by Lowe's management primarily through its operating activities.

Note also how the financial statements relate to each other. The change in the cash amounts reported on the two balance sheets is explained by the statement of cash flows; the changes in the contributed capital and retained earnings amounts on the two balance sheets are explained by the statement of shareholders' equity; and the net income amount on the income statement increases retained earnings, which appears on both the balance sheet and statement of shareholders' equity.[2]

The Balance Sheet

The balance sheet includes assets, resources expected to create future benefits, and the financing of those assets at a given point in time. The assets are divided into two categories: (1) current assets (cash, receivables, inventory, and other) and (2) non-current assets (long-term investments; property, plant, and equipment; and other assets). The sources of financing are divided into three categories: (1) borrowings from creditors (current and long-term liabilities), (2) contributions from owners (contributed capital), and (3) previous profits not

---

[2]In Chapter 3, we will see the algebraic relationships that tie these statements together.

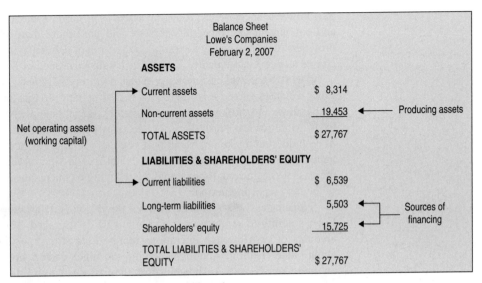

Figure 1-4. Operating, Investing, and Financing

paid to the owners in the form of dividends (retained earnings). The balance sheet always balances because the resources at Lowe's disposal (current and non-current assets) must equal the financing sources of those resources (current liabilities + long-term liabilities + owner investments, which includes contributed capital and retained earnings).

As illustrated in Figure 1-4, the Lowe's Companies' balance sheet can also be viewed in terms of operating, investing, and financing activities. Working capital (current assets less current liabilities) or net operating assets represents the resources available to support management's operating activities; non-current assets represent the current state of the producing assets, the result of management's investing activities; and long-term liabilities (debt) and shareholders' equity, the owners' accumulated investment in the firm, together provide a current "snapshot" of the status of management's financing activities.

Refer back to Figure 1-3 and note that the amounts of Lowe's working capital, non-current assets, and shareholders' equity all changed from February 3, 2006, to February 2, 2007. Lowe's appears to have grown (total assets increased by more than $3 billion), but did it create value for its shareholders? In terms of the balance sheet, value is created if the return generated from managing the working capital (net operating assets) and producing assets during the year exceeds the cost of the long-term liabilities and the owners' investment (shareholders' equity). The remaining statements, each of which explains changes in the balance sheet amounts, help answer that question.

Statement of Cash Flows

The statement of cash flows explains the change in Lowe's cash balance during the year. At the beginning of the year, the cash balance was $423 million. Operating, investing, and financing activities combined to bring the balance to $364 million as of year end. During the year, operating activities produced more than $4.5 billion in cash. The management of Lowe's working capital—including cash receipts from customers and clients less cash payments to suppliers and for operating expenses (e.g., employee wages and salaries, advertising, research and development, insurance, and rent)—appears to have netted a huge amount of cash for the company. How was this cash used? Lowe's used more than

$3.7 billion to increase its producing assets (e.g., cash payments to acquire property, plant, and equipment, and other businesses), and paid more than $846 million to its capital providers (debt and equity investors) in the form of debt repayments, dividends, and repurchased shares. Consequently, Lowe's cash balance dipped by $59 million during the year.

The statement of cash flows provides no direct information about the extent to which Lowe's created value for its shareholders during the year. It is limited to information about cash inflows and outflows, and cash is merely one of many ways in which wealth manifests itself. More (or less) cash does not necessarily mean more (or less) wealth. A wallet full of cash does not make you wealthy if you carry a large balance on your credit card. A big increase in cash flow from operations is not a clear sign of value (wealth) creation if the increase was achieved, for example, by delaying payments to suppliers until the beginning of the next reporting period.

Nonetheless, the statement of cash flows does provide important information about Lowe's ability to produce cash and how cash is managed. The ability to generate large amounts of cash through operations represents a strong positive, albeit indirect, signal about value creation. Although carrying too much cash is not desirable because cash is an unproductive asset, cash balances are necessary and useful. Debts are paid in cash and available cash can both allow management to more quickly take advantage of investment opportunities and serve as a buffer against uncertain future business downturns. Consequently, although the statement of cash flows provides no direct information about value creation, it provides important information about activities that lead to value creation. Note also that the statement discloses cash changes associated with operating, investing, and financing activities—the three areas where management must perform to create shareholder value.

INSIGHT: "KING" CASH FLOW AND VALUE CREATION

Is value creation all about cash flow? Not really. To run a business, the liquidity that cash affords is necessary and valuable. In that sense, "cash is king." But cash creation and value creation are not the same. Assume, for example, that at the beginning of the year, you own a tract of land with a market value of $250,000. By year end, the market value jumps to $310,000. You received no cash, but your wealth grew by $60,000. Did you create value? Assume further that investments in real estate typically earn 10% in a year. At that rate, your investment would have grown to $275,000 ($250,000 × 1.1). Because your investment grew to more than $275,000, you created value of $35,000 ($310,000−$275,000) even though your cash position was unaffected.

Income Statement

The income statement measures the change in Lowe's net assets (total assets less total liabilities) available to the shareholders during the year. Revenues, which reflect asset increases (or liability decreases) associated with the sale of inventory or the provision of services, totaled almost $47 billion. Expenses, which measure the costs required to generate the revenues (e.g., cost of sold inventories, employee salaries and wages, research and development, rent, advertising, depreciation of producing assets, interest on outstanding debts, and income taxes), totaled almost $44 billion. The difference—referred to as net income, net earnings, or net profit—of approximately $3 billion is one measure of the wealth created by Lowe's operating and investing activities (less the cost of debt financing) during the year.

Three points about net income are particularly important. First, the net income amount ($3.105 billion) differs from the amount of cash provided by operating activities reported on the statement of cash flows ($4.502 billion) even though both measures reflect operating performance. Recall that the statement of cash flows reflects only changes in cash, and the income statement reflects changes in assets and liabilities, which include, but are not limited to, changes in cash. Net income, therefore, is a broader performance measure, designed to capture the change in the firm's wealth.

Second, as we discuss in more detail in later chapters, not all revenue and expense items are equally meaningful. They differ on two important dimensions: (1) the extent to which they reliably measure an actual change in the firm's wealth, and (2) the extent to which they can be expected to persist in the future. Some revenue and expense items are the result of very subjective estimates, raising questions about how well they measure actual increases or decreases in the firm's wealth. Furthermore, some revenue and expense items are the result of one-time events, often not closely related to the firm's normal business activities. These events are less likely to occur again in the future.

Finally, although net income represents a measure of wealth creation, it is not a measure of value creation for the owners. It captures only two of the three key components of value creation: the net return from operating and investing activities and the cost of debt (interest expense). It ignores the cost of equity.

Statement of Changes in Shareholders' Equity

Like the statement of cash flows, the statement of changes in shareholders' equity explains changes in balance sheet amounts. In this case, instead of cash, the amounts refer to the components of the shareholders' equity section of the balance sheet. These components are divided into two categories: (1) contributed capital and (2) earned capital. Contributed capital represents the net contributions from the shareholders—proceeds from prior share issues less prior payments to shareholders to buy back outstanding shares (treasury stock). Earned capital (or retained earnings) is the accumulation of prior profits retained in the business and not paid to the shareholders in the form of dividends.

Together, contributed capital and retained earnings (earned capital) represent the shareholders' net investment in the firm—capital they have chosen to contribute plus profits they have chosen (normally through a decision by the board of directors) to reinvest. By choosing to invest their capital in the firm, shareholders forfeit the opportunity to invest in *other* potential return-producing investments. Consequently, for management to be successful in the eyes of the shareholders—the owners of the firm's resources—it must generate a return that equals or exceeds the return available to the shareholders if they had chosen instead to place their capital in other equally risky investments—the cost of equity. In terms of the financial statements, therefore, value creation takes place when the income amount reported on the income statement leads to a return on the shareholders' total investment (shareholders' equity) that exceeds the cost of equity.

DEFINITION: VALUE CREATION

Shareholder value is created when, over the life of the enterprise, return on equity exceeds the cost of equity capital.

▶ DID LOWE'S CREATE VALUE IN 2007?

First, we need to estimate the cost of equity for Lowe's. Using a risk-free rate of 5% and a risk premium of 5%, we come to 10% as the estimate of Lowe's cost of equity:

$$0.10 = 0.05 + 0.05$$

Given a cost of equity of 10%, there are two equivalent methods to ascertain whether Lowe's created value for the shareholders in 2007. Consistent with how we discussed the value creation computation so far, we can simply compare the ROE generated by Lowe's during the year to 10%. If ROE exceeds 10%, value has been created; if not, value has been destroyed. This method expresses value creation as a percent return to the shareholders.

A second method is to first compute the average shareholders' equity amount outstanding during the year ([beginning amount + ending amount] / 2) and multiply this average by the cost of equity (10%). This computation creates an estimate of the net income necessary to cover the cost of Lowe's equity financing. This estimate can then be compared to Lowe's reported net income to determine whether management created value for its shareholders. This method expresses value creation as a monetary amount.

 DEFINITION: DOLLAR (MONETARY) AMOUNT OF SHAREHOLDER VALUE CREATED

The dollar amount of value created is Net Income − (Average Equity Capital × Cost of Equity Capital). If this figure is negative, value has been lost.

Did Lowe's create shareholder value in 2007? According to the analyses in Figure 1-5, they did. The actual ROE was 20.7%, which far exceeds the estimated required return of 10%. In essence, the shareholders gave management about $15.011 billion to work with during 2007, and Lowe's needed to earn approximately $1.5 billion to provide a sufficient return given the level of risk associated with that investment. The managers actually earned more than $3 billion for the shareholders, creating $1.6 billion of additional shareholder value. Lowe's can report that it had a good year.

So far, we have discussed the meaning of value creation, linked it to the financial statements, and used this framework to assess the performance of Lowe's Companies during the period of February 3, 2006, to February 2, 2007. Although this analysis is very useful and we rely on it heavily throughout the text, it only provides a starting point for the understanding of the financial statements and how they relate to firm performance. For example, we have used dollar amounts from the financial statements with no regard for their reliability, relevance, or completeness. How are assets, liabilities, shareholder investments, revenues, and expenses measured? Do all the firm's assets and liabilities appear on the financial statements or are some ignored? How useful is a measure of past value creation in a world where the value of any firm has more to do with the future than the past? These important questions are addressed in subsequent chapters. In the remainder of this chapter, we describe the economic context in which the financial statements are prepared and used.

(dollar amounts in billions)

Method 1:
ROE = Net Income / Average Shareholders' Equity (Beg. Balance + End. Balance / 2)
20.7% = $ 3.105 / $ 15.011

Percent amount of value created by Lowe's during 2007: 20.7% − 10.0% = 10.7%

Method 2:

Shareholders' equity (2/03/06)	$ 14.296
Shareholders' equity (2/02/07)	15.725
Total	$ 30.021
Average shareholders' equity for 2007 [$30.021 / 2]	$ 15.011
Net income reported by Lowe's on 2007 income statement	$ 3.105
Net income necessary to cover cost of equity financing [$15.011 × 10%]	(1.501)
Estimate of dollar amount of value created by Lowe's	$ 1.604

Figure 1-5. Did Lowe's create value for its shareholders during fiscal 2007?

▶ THE ECONOMIC CONTEXT IN WHICH FINANCIAL REPORTS ARE PREPARED AND USED

Financial statements provide measures of firm performance that support decisions by a wide variety of individuals and entities leading to massive resource transfers each year. Indeed, the world economy depends on the reliability and validity of financial statements. Recent and significant financial meltdowns (e.g., Enron, WorldCom, Ahold, Parmalat, and others) perpetrated by fraudulent financial statements underscore the importance of credible financial reporting for the United States and world economies.

Figure 1-6 illustrates the key elements of the financial accounting environment. The figure shows that providers of capital (people with money—debt investors and equity investors) invest in companies operated by managers (people with ideas). In return, creditors (debt investors) expect to receive interest and principal payments, and equity investors expect to receive returns in the form of dividends and/or share price appreciation. Company managers enter into debt and/or compensation contracts that often are based on amounts from the financial statements. These contracts either protect the interests of creditors or are structured to encourage management to act in the interest of the company's owners—the shareholders. Managers also hire auditors to attest to the financial information. Auditors add credibility to the financial statements by attesting to whether they were prepared in conformance with financial reporting standards and fairly present the company's financial performance and position. Auditors pledge (as Certified Public Accountants and members of the American Institute of CPAs) to have the proper expertise and to act independently from management, and are legally liable to the capital providers to do so.

In this environment, financial reporting information plays two fundamental and important roles. First, it helps debt and equity investors evaluate management's past business decisions and predict future performance. In this sense, financial reporting information helps to guide debt and equity investment decisions. That is, it helps the people with money allocate that scarce resource to the people with the best ideas and to do so at an appropriate price. Second, financial reporting information includes numbers (e.g., working capital and net income) used in debt and compensation contracts designed to encourage management to act in the interest of the capital providers. In this sense, financial reporting information

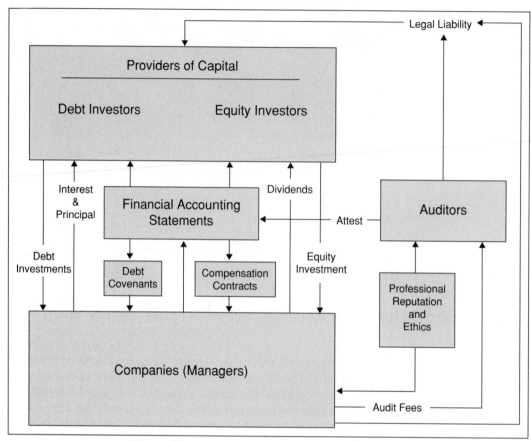

Figure 1-6. Financial Reporting Environment

helps in the management and control of business activities. In the sections that follow, we discuss each of the elements of Figure 1-6 in greater detail.

INSIGHT: CONTRACTS AND FINANCIAL STATEMENT DATA

Compensation contracts are commonly based on revenues, revenue growth, net income, or ROE. Debt covenants are often specified in terms of financial statement ratios such as the debt-to-equity ratio or working capital.

DuPont pays its officers 20% of after-tax net income in excess of 6% of shareholders' equity, and Nordstrom recently reported that its debt contracts require that working capital be at least $50 million or 25% of current liabilities, whichever is greater.

▶ REPORTING ENTITIES AND INDUSTRIES

Financial statements are prepared by reporting entities called companies, businesses, or firms—referred to as "Companies (Managers)" in Figure 1-6. These profit-seeking entities are often further divided into segments and subsidiaries, each of which provides its own financial statements. For example, in the annual report of The Limited, Inc., the financial statements are referred to as consolidated financial statements, which means that the total dollar amounts in the accounts on the financial statements include those of other companies, such as Victoria's Secret, Express, and Bed & Body Works, which The Limited owns. These companies, called subsidiaries, prepare their own separate financial statements. Furthermore, The Limited is divided into 12 retail divisions, and financial reports on each of these are compiled.

Financial statements are also prepared by entities not established to make profits, including counties, cities, school districts, other municipalities, charitable organizations, and foundations. In this book, we limit our coverage to financial reports prepared by profit-seeking entities.

Companies can be grouped into industries based on the nature of their operations. Although there are many industry classifications, they can be summarized into three basic categories: manufacturing, retailing, and services (general and financial). Manufacturing firms like Toyota, Dell, and PepsiCo acquire raw materials and convert them into goods sold either to consumers, usually through retailers, or to other manufacturers who use them as raw materials. Retail firms like Wal-Mart, Home Depot, Lowe's Home Improvement, Kohl's, Carrefour, and Amazon.com purchase goods from manufacturers and sell them to consumers. The service industry includes firms like Telefonos de Mexico, Verizon Wireless, FedEx, and H&R Block, which provide general services, as well as firms like Citicorp, HSBC, and Prudential Insurance, which provide financial services. Internet firms, such as Google, eBay, and Yahoo!, are also part of the service industry. Specific industry classifications are provided by the well-known Standard Industrial Classification (SIC) Index, which assigns a 1- to 4-digit code to industries—the more digits in the code, the more specific the industry classification.

Knowledge of industries is important when analyzing financial statements because the relative importance of different aspects of financial performance and condition vary across firms in different industries. Managing outstanding loans, for example, is very important for lending institutions (banks), but less important for retailers such as Wal-Mart that extend limited credit to customers. Furthermore, it is difficult to assess management's performance without knowledge of the overall performance of the company's industry, and without benchmarking management's performance against the performance of companies facing similar economic environments.

► CORPORATE GOVERNANCE

Figure 1-6 also highlights the key elements of a firm's corporate governance, which refers to mechanisms that encourage management to act in the interest of, and report in good faith to, the shareholders. Effective corporate governance is necessary because management has incentives to act and report in its own interest at the expense of the shareholders, and auditors face conflicting goals—they are responsible to capital providers to perform independent and objective audits, but their fees are paid by management, who can attempt to replace them. A firm's corporate governance environment includes a variety of features, including (1) the variety of parties that use the financial statements to evaluate management's performance and the capital markets in which the firm operates (debt and equity investors); (2) contracts between management and debt and equity investors designed to encourage management to act properly; (3) the financial accounting statements, as well as the regulations and standards underlying their preparation; (4) the board of directors, elected by the shareholders to oversee management; (5) the audit process, which involves the independent auditor, the audit committee (part of the board of directors) and the auditor's legal liability, professional reputation, and ethics; and (6) regulations such as the Sarbanes–Oxley Act—federal legislation designed to improve the effectiveness of corporate governance in U.S. firms. There is no one-size-fits-all recipe for effective corporate governance. These features act as complements and substitutes and interact with factors such as the regulatory environment, the legal system, and other factors. However, each of these components is part of the financial reporting environment and somehow involves the financial statements.

Financial Information Users and Capital Markets

Financial statements are used by a variety of groups. We divide them into three categories: equity investors, debt investors, and others (including management).

INSIGHT: WHAT KINDS OF QUESTIONS DO DIFFERENT FINANCIAL STATEMENT USERS ASK?

Equity Investors: Is management creating value?

Debt Investors: What terms are appropriate for this debt?

Security Analysts: What is this company worth?

Managers: Are we creating as much value as our competitors are?

Employees: Will this company be around next year?

Unions: Are we getting our fair share of the profits?

Suppliers: Will this customer be able to pay its bills?

Directors: Are the managers acting in the best interest of the shareholders?

Audit Committees: Do the financial statements accurately portray the performance of the firm?

Competitors: Where and how does the firm make its profits?

Government Agencies and Regulators: Is the company meeting regulatory requirements?

Potential Acquirers: If we acquire this company, will it help us create value?

Equity Investors

Equity investors (often referred to simply as investors) purchase shares of stock, which represent ownership interests in a company. Ownership of an equity security entitles the holder to two basic rights: (1) to vote for company directors at the annual shareholders' meeting and (2) to receive dividends if paid and to sell their shares. Equity investors can be classified into two groups. The first owns a substantial amount of the company's shares, and uses the voting rights associated with that ownership to exert influence on the activities of the company. The majority of equity investors, however, fall into a second group, where the ownership interest is too small to exert significant influence on the company through voting power. These investors have little direct influence over management, so their main concern is the returns (dividends and price appreciation) associated with holding the equity security.

Equity investors and their representatives, such as financial and security analysts and stockbrokers, are interested in financial information because it helps them ascertain whether management is creating value. Value creation should lead to higher equity values. If the financial statements indicate that management has failed, investors holding large equity interests can use voting power to replace management and investors with relatively small equity interests can sell their ownership interests. Indeed, management's performance as depicted by the financial statements plays an important role in monitoring and enforcing management's accountability to the shareholders. Simply put, the financial statements tell shareholders how well their capital is being managed.

Debt Investors (Creditors)

Creditors provide capital (funds) to companies through loans. These investments involve loan contracts that normally specify (1) a maturity date (the date when the loan is to be repaid); (2) an annual interest payment (the amount of interest to be paid each year); (3) collateral (assets to be transferred to the creditor in case the loan payments are not met (default)); and (4) additional debt restrictions (debt covenants) generally designed to reduce default risk.

Creditors have limited influence over the company other than through the terms of the debt contract. They use financial information because it helps them assess the likelihood of default (the company is unable to make the loan payments), which, in turn, helps to establish the terms of the debt contract. Normally, if the financial statements indicate that the risk of default is increasing, the terms of the debt contract become more onerous—the interest rate and need for collateral increases, and additional restrictions may be imposed by the creditor to further limit management's behavior. Consequently, a company's financial condition and performance, as indicated by the financial statements, is directly linked to how much it costs to borrow funds from creditors, an important determinant of value creation.

Management and Other Financial Statement Users

Management uses its own financial statements to determine dividend payments, set company policies, and, in general, to help guide business decisions. Internal financial statements are used to evaluate business unit performance, reward managers, and allocate capital. Management also uses the financial statements of other firms to assess the financial strength and strategies of competitors, and determine whether to enter into business relationships with other firms (e.g., suppliers and customers).

Other users include government bodies, such as the Federal Trade Commission, who often base regulatory decisions on information disclosed in the financial statements, and public utilities, which base their rates (the prices they charge their customers) on financial accounting numbers such as net income. Labor unions have also been known to use accounting numbers to argue for more wages or other benefits.

Capital Markets

Equity and debt securities are held by both individuals and entities. Billions of shares of stock are held in large U.S. corporations that, in turn, hold shares in each other. Debt securities in the form of loans are held primarily by banks. Debt securities in the form of bonds issued by large corporations are held by individuals and institutions.

Equity and debt securities are traded on public exchanges in the United States and in other countries. The New York Stock Exchange (NYSE) is by far the largest; however, active exchanges exist in most of the major cities throughout the world. Large U.S. companies normally have their shares listed on several exchanges, and many non-U.S. firms are listed in New York. More information about the NYSE, and the firms listed on it, can be found on the Internet at http://www.nyse.com.

The prices at which equity and debt securities trade on the financial markets vary from day to day based largely on changes in investor expectations about the issuing company's future performance. Good news about the company leads to increases in the market prices of its outstanding equity and debt securities and bad news is associated with price declines. Price changes are considered by many to be a measure of management's performance, although they are determined by a variety of factors, only some of which are under management's control. Financial statements are an important source of the information used by those who invest in capital markets in setting expectations about a company's future prospects, and consequently help to determine the market prices of the company's equity and debt securities. In Chapter 5, we show how value creation, as depicted by the financial statements, links to the value of the firm's equity securities.

INSIGHT: SHARE VALUATION

The process of valuing a share of stock is complex. Yet it is intuitive that—other factors being equal—an investor will pay more for a share of a company whose future performance is expected to be better than that of some other company. How are expectations about future performance formed? In large part, expectations come from disclosures that management makes about its future plans, along with evidence about how they have done in the past. That past performance is reported in the financial statements and it provides insight into the likelihood that management will be able to achieve its future plans.

Contracts—Debt Covenants and Management Compensation

Capital providers (debt and equity investors) normally require management to enter contracts designed to manage risk and encourage business decision making consistent with capital-provider interests. Such contracts take two general forms: debt covenants and management compensation.

Debt covenants are included in many debt contracts, and often require management to maintain certain levels of financial performance or position to help ensure that the debt payments are made when they come due. Violating these requirements (technical default) normally gives the debtholder the right to demand that the entire debt be paid immediately. Typically, rather than being repaid, the debt contract is renegotiated with more costly terms (e.g., higher interest rates or more collateral). Management compensation contracts typically base management pay on certain net income or share price goals, which can encourage desirable management decision making. Debt covenants and management compensation contracts provide examples where numbers taken from the financial statements are used in contracts written by capital providers to shape management behavior.

ALSTOM, A FRENCH ENGINEERING FIRM

The *Financial Times* (April 28, 2004) reported that "Alstom's banks have given the French engineering group five month's breathing room to renegotiate the terms of last year's €3.2bn government-backed bail-out. The maker of high-speed TGV trains, power turbines, and cruise ships warned last month that results for the year would be worse than expected, which could put it in violation of covenants governing €1.5bn in loans granted as part of its bail-out. The company claimed to have won the approval of at least two-thirds of its banks to suspend the covenants requiring minimum earnings and consolidated net worth amounts, which it was in danger of breaching."

Financial Reporting Regulations and Standards

In 1934, the U.S. Congress created the Securities and Exchange Commission (SEC) to implement and enforce the Securities Act of 1933 and the Securities Exchange Act of 1934. The Securities Act of 1933 requires companies that raise capital through public equity and debt exchanges (e.g., the New York Stock Exchange) to file a registration statement (Form S-1) with the SEC. The SEC Act of 1934 states that, among other requirements, companies with equity and/or debt securities listed on the public security markets (called "listed companies") must (1) annually file a Form 10-K (audited financial reports), (2) quarterly file a Form 10-Q (unaudited quarterly financial statements), and (3) annually provide audited financial reports (on Form 10-K) to the shareholders. The Forms 10-K and 10-Q contain a wealth of publicly available information, and can be obtained by accessing the Electronic Data Gathering, Analysis, and Retrieval (EDGAR) system at http://sec.gov. Annual reports for individual companies are sent directly to shareholders, but generally can be obtained by anyone through the investor relations section of a company's Web site (e.g., http://www.homedepot.com).

Annual reports published by major U.S. companies include audited balance sheets for the two most recent years and audited statements of income, shareholders' equity, and cash flows for the three most recent years. They also include

- a letter to the shareholders from a high-ranking officer;
- a description of the business;
- management's discussion and analysis of the company's financial condition and performance (known as MD&A);
- notes that describe the estimates, assumptions, and methods used to produce the numbers on the financial statements;
- selected quarterly data;
- summaries of selected financial information for at least the last five years;
- information about each of the company's major segments;
- a letter from management stating its reporting responsibilities;
- a letter from the company's outside (external) auditors stating whether the financial statements were prepared according to acceptable standards; and
- a listing of the members of the board of directors and executive officers;

Generally Accepted Accounting Principles

Generally accepted accounting principles (GAAP) define the standards for financial reporting to shareholders. The Form 10-K must be prepared in conformance with these standards, and auditors attest to whether these standards have been followed in the preparation of the financial statements. U.S. GAAP is established by a privately financed body called the Financial Accounting Standards Board (FASB). The FASB's pronouncements and current research projects are found at http://fasb.org. A set of widely accepted and consistent standards is useful because it lends credibility to the financial statements and helps to facilitate meaningful comparisons across different companies. However, the standards are sometimes controversial because reporting requirements impose costs on companies required to follow them. Many companies argue with passion that these costs exceed the benefits created by the standards. Consequently, the accounting standard-setting process can be very political, involving controversial input from companies, government regulators (e.g., SEC),

Congress, financial statement users (financial and security analysts), and sometimes even the general public.

INSIGHT: THE POLITICS OF STANDARD SETTING

Two high-profile illustrations of the politics of standard set-ting are the cases of accounting for share-based compensation in the United States (i.e., Statement of Financial Accounting Standards (SFAS) 123R) and the accounting for financial instruments under international accounting standards (i.e., International Accounting Standards (IAS) 32 and 39). Both cases involved major lobbying efforts on the part of compa-nies (the FASB received more than 2,000 comment letters on SFAS 123R) and threats of government intervention into the standard-setting process. Indeed, even former French pres-ident Jacques Chirac waded into the debate over financial instrument accounting.

Independent Auditors

Major U.S. companies incur considerable costs to have their financial statements audited by independent public accounting firms. Four public accounting firms, known as the "Big 4," audit most of the large companies. These firms and a selection of their major clients are listed in Figure 1-7. Many regional and local public accounting firms are located throughout the United States. Their audit clients comprise the thousands of mid-sized and small companies who, for various reasons, have their financial statements audited.[3]

The result of the audit is the audit report or audit opinion. For public companies in the United States, the standard audit report renders an opinion on both the financial statements and the company's system of internal controls, and normally contains four sections. The first section states that the financial statements were audited, but that the responsibility for preparing the reports rests with management; the second section explains that the auditor conducted the audit in accordance with generally accepted auditing standards, established by the Public Company Accounting Oversight Board (PCAOB), and briefly describes what that means; the third section normally indicates that the financial statements present the company's financial position and performance fairly and in accordance with GAAP; and the final section renders an opinion on the effectiveness of the company's internal control over the final reporting system, normally stating that the company's system is consistent with established criteria for effective controls. A standard audit opinion, however, is not always rendered. Sometimes auditors find that they are unable to reach a conclusion, the financial statements are not in conformance with GAAP, some concern exists about the company's viability as a going concern in the foreseeable future, and/or there are certain deficiencies in the company's internal control system. Departures from the standard audit opinion can signal problems that cause great concern to management and capital providers.

Board of Directors and Audit Committee

The board of directors, elected annually by the shareholders, oversees management to ensure that it acts in the interest of the shareholders. Such oversight involves periodic

---

[3] The main purpose of the external audit is, of course, to enhance the credibility of the financial statements. Research evidence indicates that this enhanced reliability lowers firms' cost of capital.

Accounting Firm	Major Clients
Deloitte & Touche	Microsoft, Boeing, Merrill Lynch
Ernst & Young	Wal-Mart, Intel, Hewlett-Packard
KPMG Peat Marwick	JCPenney, PepsiCo, Xerox
PricewaterhouseCoopers	eBay, Cisco Systems, DuPont

Figure 1-7. "Big 4" Accounting Firms and Major Clients

(at least quarterly) meetings where company policies are set, dividends are declared, and the performance and compensation of the company's officers are reviewed. The board, normally composed of both company officers and non-management representatives, has the power to hire and fire the officers, as well as determine the form and amount of their compensation.

Figure 1-8 illustrates that the shareholders elect the board of directors, which appoints a subcommittee of outside directors, called the audit committee. This committee works with management to choose an auditor, and monitors the audit to ensure that it is thorough, objective, and independent. Despite these controls, management still pays the audit fee and has considerable influence over whether the auditing firm is hired again. Such influence can threaten the auditor's independence.

Legal Liability

Management is legally responsible to the shareholders to act in their interest and to report in good faith. Auditors are legally responsible to the shareholders to conduct a thorough

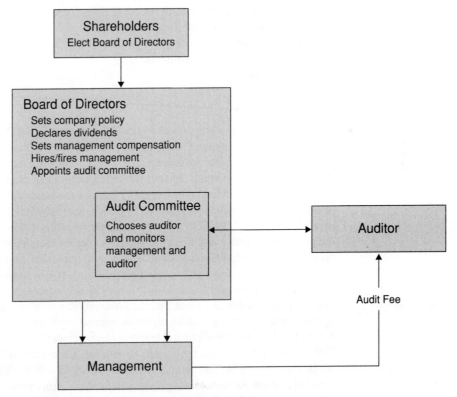

Figure 1-8. Board of Directors and Audit Committee

and independent audit. These responsibilities create a legal liability for those who rely on the financial statements. If management or the auditors fail in these responsibilities and as a result investors and others suffer financial losses, management and the auditors can be sued to recover those losses. Litigation brought against management and auditors by shareholders is common, very costly, and seems to increase each year in the United States. Legal liability plays a critical role in corporate governance, creating a powerful economic incentive for managers and auditors to act professionally and ethically.

Professional Reputation and Ethics

The many aspects of corporate governance (e.g., capital markets, contracts, SEC and FASB reporting regulations, independent auditors, boards of directors and audit committees, and legal liability) suggest that a large amount of mistrust exists among shareholders, managers, and auditors. This observation is difficult to question, given the cases of management fraud and embezzlement that have arisen in recent years and given that audit firms have increasingly been found guilty of misconduct. Some even suggest that U.S. business is suffering from an ethics crisis.

Notwithstanding these developments, little doubt exists that a high-quality reputation is a major business asset and that ethical behavior is in the long-term best interests of managers, shareholders, and auditors. Indeed, the American Institute of Certified Public Accountants (AICPA), the professional organization of CPAs, has a strong professional code of ethics, designed to instill higher ethical standards in the members of the accounting profession. Such efforts are not only moral, they are driven by sound economic logic. Companies and auditors with reputations for quality, service, and ethical business practices are valued highly by investors and creditors, partially because their financial statements can be trusted. That trust can lead to a lower cost of capital. Such companies and their managers are sued less frequently. Not surprisingly, the most successful companies and audit firms enjoy the best reputations for high ethical standards.

Sarbanes–Oxley Act and Internal Controls

The **Sarbanes–Oxley Act**, passed by the U.S. Congress in 2002 in response to a series of corporate financial statement frauds leading to billions of dollars in investor losses, is an attempt to bolster corporate governance and restore confidence in the U.S. financial reporting system. It enacted sweeping changes in the responsibilities of management, financial disclosures, independence and effectiveness of auditors and audit committees, and oversight of public companies and auditors. The Act—which established the Public Company Accounting Oversight Board (PCAOB), a government organization that oversees auditors—requires the principal executive and financial officers to certify that the financial reports have been reviewed, do not contain untrue statements or omit important information, and fairly present the company's financial condition and performance. It also places additional responsibilities on management and the auditor to ensure that adequate internal controls are in place to provide reasonable assurance that the financial records are complete and accurate. Management must also file an annual report on internal control over financial reporting, and the external auditor must attest to and report on management's assessment of internal controls. Finally, public firms must have audit committees composed of independent members of the board of directors. The audit committee is charged with the hiring and oversight of the external auditor. As such, the auditors' independence from management can be enhanced. In summary, this Act places heavy emphasis on the quality of a company's internal control system, and significantly increases the auditor's role in ensuring that the control system meets high standards.

► GLOBAL PERSPECTIVE: MOVEMENT TOWARD A GLOBAL FINANCIAL REPORTING SYSTEM

For many years the different histories, economies, political systems, and cultures of countries throughout the world gave rise to vastly different financial reporting systems. In North America, the United Kingdom, and Australia, for example, the financial reporting systems were oriented toward the decision needs of equity investors and designed to measure management performance in a true and fair manner. In European countries and Japan, the financial reports were heavily influenced by government requirements (e.g., tax law) and the statements were targeted more toward the needs of creditors, giving management much more discretion in the preparation of the reports. In these settings, financial reporting also tended to be intentionally conservative instead of designed to report management's true performance. In today's fast-moving, global marketplace, this situation is quickly changing.

Although most countries have their own accounting standards, two primary financial reporting systems currently exist in the world: U.S. Generally Accepted Accounting Principles (U.S. GAAP) and International Financial Reporting Standards (IFRS). IFRS are established by the International Accounting Standards Board (IASB) (http://www.iasb.org). The IASB is the successor to the International Accounting Standards Committee (IASC), which was formed in 1973 to develop worldwide accounting practices. The IASC's pronouncements are known as International Accounting Standards (IAS) and are currently being revised and updated by the IASB. The IASB, representing well over 100 countries, has issued a number of international financial reporting standards recognized as acceptable reporting by many of the major stock exchanges (e.g., London, Tokyo, Frankfurt, and Paris) in the world. Indeed, since 2005 all public companies in the European Union (EU) are required to report using IFRS and IAS.

Many substantive differences still exist, but ongoing efforts are moving IFRS and U.S. GAAP closer together. Furthermore, the SEC already allows non-U.S. companies whose securities trade on the public U.S. equity and debt markets to file their financial statements using IFRS (with no reconciliation to U.S. GAAP). It is likely that very soon U.S. companies that list their securities on the U.S. exchanges will be allowed to report under IFRS. Although this landscape is quickly changing, it is very possible that within the next few years a single financial reporting system (most likely based on IFRS) will emerge, and be required by all the major security exchanges in the world. Such a change may lead to the eventual demise of the FASB in favor of a single global standard setting board—perhaps a modified form of the IASB. Consequently, in the remainder of the text we comment frequently on differences between U.S. GAAP and IFRS.

► SUMMARY

We began this chapter with an illustration that introduced the concept of value creation, the goal of management. We then formally defined value creation and described how it can be measured for a firm that conducts operating, investing, and financing activities. The financial statements (balance sheet, income statement, statement of cash flows, and statement of shareholders' equity) were introduced and linked to the operating, investing, and financing activities of a firm and the measurement of value creation. We then briefly analyzed the financial statements of Lowe's Companies, concluding that it created value for its shareholders during 2007. The second part of the chapter covered the economic environment in which financial statements are produced, used, and audited. Here, we focused on the notion of corporate governance, explaining it in terms of capital markets, contracts, regulations, auditors, legal liability, and ethics—paying close attention to the important role of financial statements. We concluded by briefly describing the relationship between U.S. GAAP and international accounting standards. In the next chapter, we take a closer look at the content of the financial statements.

▶ APPENDIX 1A: ESTIMATING THE COST OF EQUITY

The cost of equity represents the return an investor can reasonably expect on an equity investment in a firm. More specifically, it is the return (expressed as a percentage) foregone by a firm's shareholders, who have chosen to invest their funds in the firm instead of other equally risky investments. To the extent that, over the long run, the ROE exceeds this minimum required return, value is created for the shareholders. If the cost of equity for Firm A is 15%, for example, management must generate an ROE of at least 15% before value is created for the shareholders. The cost of equity varies significantly across firms and industries. As the risk associated with an investment increases, the cost of equity in that firm also increases.

The cost of equity is not disclosed on the financial statements or notes. It cannot be measured objectively enough to meet the reliability requirements for financial statement disclosure. However, it can be estimated—albeit subjectively—using the following formula, called the capital asset pricing model (CAPM):

$$E(R) = E(R_f) + \beta \times [E(R_m) - E(R_f)]$$

where

$E(R) =$ expected return on investment in a firm's common stock (cost of equity);

$E(R_f) =$ expected risk-free rate of return (e.g., return on government securities);

$\beta =$ covariation between the market return and returns on the firm's common stock; and

$E(R_m) =$ expected overall market return.

The CAPM expresses the return an investor can reasonably expect on an equity investment (cost of equity) as a function of two factors: (1) the expected risk-free rate of return $E(R_f)$, and (2) the expected risk premium associated with an investment in the firm itself ($\beta \times [E(R_m) - E(R_f)]$).

The expected risk-free rate $[E(R_f)]$ is the return an investor can expect on investments in securities with guaranteed returns (e.g., 10-year government treasury bill). Historically, it has ranged from around 3 to 8%, averaging about 6%. Recently, it has been closer to 4 to 5%.

The risk premium depends on the difference between the overall market return and the risk-free rate $[E(R_m) - E(R_f)]$ multiplied by β (beta)—the extent to which the returns on investments in the firm's common stock covary with changes in the overall market return. Historically, the overall market return (the rate of return on a portfolio of investments containing all publicly traded equity securities) has averaged between 9 and 13% and is normally based on returns computed from overall market indexes, such as the S&P 500 or the Dow Jones Industrial Average. Over long periods, the difference between the overall market return and the risk-free rate $(R_m - R_f)$ historically has been around 3 to 6%.

Beta (β) is a direct measure of the variance in price across time (risk) associated with an investment in the firm's common stock; it can range from more than 2.0 (high-risk firms) to well below 1.0 (low-risk firms). To illustrate, when overall market prices increase (decrease) by 10%, the market price of a firm with a beta of 2.0, on average, will increase (decrease) by 20%, while the market price of a firm with a beta of 0.50 will only increase (decrease) by 5%. The prices of high-beta common stocks are very sensitive to market changes; the prices of low-beta stocks are not. Estimates of betas for publicly traded firms are published regularly and can easily be accessed. See, for example, http://finance.yahoo.com or http://valueline.com.

In general, the cost of equity for an individual firm $[E(R)]$ increases with increases in the risk-free rate $[E(R_f)]$, increases in the firm's beta (ß), and increases in the difference between the overall market return and the risk-free rate $[E(R_m) - E(R_f)]$. The risk-free rate and the difference between the overall market return and the risk-free rate are the same for all firms; the beta is unique to each firm. Investments in firms with betas of zero are equivalent to investments in risk-free securities with guaranteed returns, and investments in firms with betas of 1.0 are equivalent to investments in market index funds.

To illustrate how the CAPM is used to estimate the cost of equity, consider investments in the common stocks of Microsoft and Cisco Systems. According to Hemscott, Inc., data reported by Factiva (a division of Dow Jones & Company), as of November 25, 2005, Microsoft and Cisco had betas of 0.53 and 1.99, respectively. Using a risk-free rate of 5.0% (10-year government treasury notes) and an expected risk premium of 6% leads to the following cost of equity estimates for Microsoft and Cisco:

Microsoft	$0.08 = 0.05 + 0.53\,(0.06)$
Cisco	$0.17 = 0.05 + 1.99\,(0.06)$

Cisco has a higher cost of equity because it has a higher beta—that is, historically the price of an investment in Cisco common stock has been more sensitive to market changes than the price of an investment in Microsoft. Because Cisco shareholders are bearing more risk holding Cisco stock, they can reasonably expect a higher ROE from Cisco's management. Using these estimates, to create value for its stockholders, Cisco's management must generate an ROE of more than 17%, while Microsoft's management need only generate an ROE that is greater than 8%.

MEASUREMENT CHALLENGE—MEASURING BETA

Although the CAPM is a Nobel Prize–winning innovation in financial economics, it remains controversial. In part, the controversy arises in trying to apply the model. We can calculate historical rates of return and historical betas, but the model calls for inputs of future returns and future betas, which are, of course, unobservable today. Furthermore, even measurement of the historical values is subject to disagreement: What historical period should be used? Daily or weekly returns? And so on. Regardless, accounting reports are often used in estimating these expected future values.

▶ CASE AND REVIEW QUESTIONS

The Home Depot, Inc., Kingfisher plc, and Value Creation

According to the analysis described in Figure 1-5, Lowe's created value for its shareholders in 2006. You would like to know how Lowe's performance compares with its main competitor in the United States, The Home Depot, Inc., and a major home improvement retailer in the United Kingdom, Kingfisher plc. A brief description of each company follows (drawn from their annual reports), along with their balance sheets and income statements. For comparison purposes, Lowe's balance sheets and income statements are also provided.

Home Depot, Inc., was incorporated in 1978 and it is the world's largest home improvement retailer and the second largest retailer in the United States, based on net sales for the fiscal year ending January 28, 2007 (hereinafter fiscal 2006). Home Depot stores sell a wide assortment of building materials and home improvement, lawn, and garden products, and provide a number of services. As of the end of fiscal 2006, Home Depot had 2,147 stores. The stores average approximately 105,000 square feet of enclosed space, with approximately 23,000 additional square feet of outside garden area. As of the end of fiscal 2006, the company had 2,100 Home Depot stores located throughout the United States, Canada, Mexico, and China. In addition, at the end of fiscal 2006, the company operated 34 EXPO Design Center stores, 11 Home Depot Landscape Supply stores, and 2 Home Depot Floor stores. The company's financial statements were audited by KPMG LLP and received a clean (unqualified) audit opinion. The auditors also opined that Home Depot maintained an effective system of internal control over its financial reporting. Home Depot's financial statements are prepared using U.S. GAAP. More information about Home Depot is available at http://www.homedepot.com.

Kingfisher is Europe's leading home improvement retail group and the third largest in the world, with leading market positions in the United Kingdom, France, Poland, Italy, China, and Taiwan. More than 40% of its 2005 sales were generated outside the United Kingdom. Kingfisher operates more than 700 stores in 11 countries in Europe and Asia (under brand names including Castorama, Brico Dépôt, B&Q, and Screwfix Direct) and also has a strategic alliance with Hornbach, Germany's leading do-it-yourself warehouse retailer, which operates more than 120 stores in Germany, Austria, Netherlands, Luxembourg, Switzerland, Sweden, and the Czech Republic. The company's financial statements were audited by PricewaterhouseCoopers LLP and received a clean audit opinion. Kingfishers' financial statements are prepared using EU-endorsed IFRS. More information about Kingfisher is available at http://www.kingfisher.com.

1. Calculate each company's return on equity for fiscal 2006 and compare your results to those for Lowe's.
2. Calculate the value created (or destroyed) by each company. Assume that each firm's cost of equity capital is 12%. The foreign exchange rate on February 3, 2007 for pounds sterling (GBP) to U.S. dollars was 1.96. Why is net income an incomplete measure of value creation? Explain why cash flow is not a measure of value creation.
3. Review the income statements and balance sheets for Home Depot and Kingfisher and speculate on the reasons why their returns and value creation differ.

The Home Depot, Inc., and Subsidiaries
Consolidated Statements of Earnings

	Fiscal Year Ended[1]		
amounts in millions, except per share data	**January 28, 2007**	**January 29, 2006**	**January 30, 2005**
NET SALES	**$90,837**	$81,511	$73,094
Cost of Sales	61,054	54,191	48,664
GROSS PROFIT	29,783	27,320	24,430
Operating Expenses:			
Selling, General and Administrative	18,348	16,485	15,256
Depreciation and Amortization	1,762	1,472	1,248
Total Operating Expenses	20,110	17,957	16,504
OPERATING INCOME	9,673	9,363	7,926
Interest Income (Expense):			
Interest and Investment Income	27	62	56
Interest Expense	(392)	(143)	(70)
Interest, net	(365)	(81)	(14)
EARNINGS BEFORE PROVISION FOR INCOME TAXES	9,308	9,282	7,912
Provision for Income Taxes	3,547	3,444	2,911
NET EARNINGS	**$ 5,761**	$ 5,838	$ 5,001
Weighted Average Common Shares	2,054	2,138	2,207
BASIC EARNINGS PER SHARE	**$ 2.80**	$ 2.73	$ 2.27
Diluted Weighted Average Common Shares	2,062	2,147	2,216
DILUTED EARNINGS PER SHARE	**$ 2.79**	$ 2.72	$ 2.26

[1] *Fiscal years ended January 28, 2007, January 29, 2006, and January 30, 2005, include 52 weeks.*

The Home Depot, Inc., and Subsidiaries
Consolidated Balance Sheets

amounts in millions, except per share data	January 28, 2007	January 29, 2006
ASSETS		
Current Assets:		
Cash and Cash Equivalents	$ 600	$ 793
Short-Term Investments	14	14
Receivables, net	3,223	2,396
Merchandise Inventories	12,822	11,401
Other Current Assets	1,341	665
Total Current Assets	18,000	15,269
Property and Equipment, at cost:		
Land	8,355	7,924
Buildings	15,215	14,056
Furniture, Fixtures, and Equipment	7,799	7,073
Leasehold Improvements	1,391	1,207
Construction in Progress	1,123	843
Capital Leases	475	427
	34,358	31,530
Less Accumulated Depreciation and Amortization	7,753	6,629
Net Property and Equipment	26,605	24,901
Notes Receivable	343	348
Goodwill	6,314	3,286
Other Assets	1,001	601
Total Assets	$52,263	$44,405
LIABILITIES AND STOCKHOLDERS' EQUITY		
Current Liabilities:		
Short-Term Debt	$ —	$ 900
Accounts Payable	7,356	6,032
Accrued Salaries and Related Expenses	1,295	1,068
Sales Taxes Payable	475	488
Deferred Revenue	1,634	1,757
Income Taxes Payable	217	388
Current Installments of Long-Term Debt	18	513
Other Accrued Expenses	1,936	1,560
Total Current Liabilities	12,931	12,706
Long-Term Debt, excluding current installments	11,643	2,672
Other Long-Term Liabilities	1,243	1,172
Deferred Income Taxes	1,416	946
STOCKHOLDERS' EQUITY		
Common Stock, par value $0.05: authorized: 10,000 shares; issued 2,421 shares at January 28, 2007, and 2,401 shares at January 29, 2006; outstanding 1,970 shares at January 28, 2007, and 2,124 shares at January 29, 2006	121	120
Paid-In Capital	7,930	7,149
Retained Earnings	33,052	28,943
Accumulated Other Comprehensive Income	310	409
Treasury Stock, at cost, 451 shares at January 28, 2007, and 277 shares at January 29, 2006	(16,383)	(9,712)
Total Stockholders' Equity	25,030	26,909
Total Liabilities and Stockholders' Equity	$52,263	$44,405

Consolidated Income Statement
For the financial year ended 3 February 2007

Kingfisher plc Annual Report and Accounts 2006/07

£ millions	Notes	2007 Before exceptional items	Exceptional Items (note 5)	Total	2006 Before exceptional items	Exceptional Items (note 5)	Total
Continuing operations:							
Revenue	4	**8,675.9**	—	**8,675.9**	8.010.1	—	8,010.1
Cost of sales		**(5,623.7)**	—	**(5,623.7)**	(5,165.1)	(7.9)	(5,173.0)
Gross profit		**3,052.2**	—	**3,052.2**	2,845.0	(7.9)	2,837.1
Selling and distribution expenses		**(2,207.3)**	—	**(2,207.3)**	(2,005.0)	(181.0)	(2,186.0)
Administrative expenses		**(433.7)**	—	**(433.7)**	(390.7)	(26.4)	(417.1)
Other income		**23.7**	**49.5**	**73.2**	24.2	18.9	43.1
Other expenses		—	—	—	—	(19.0)	(19.0)
Share of post-tax results of joint ventures and associates		**16.9**	—	**16.9**	11.4	—	11.4
Operating profit		**451.8**	**49.5**	**501.3**	484.9	(215.4)	269.5
Analysed as:							
Retail profit before central costs		**503.7**	**49.5**	**553.2**	533.1	(219.1)	314.0
Central costs		**(39.1)**	—	**(39.1)**	(37.8)	3.7	(34.1)
Amortisation of acquisition intangibles		**(0.3)**	—	**(0.3)**	(0.1)	—	(0.1)
Share of interest and taxation of joint ventures and associates		**(12.5)**	—	**(12.5)**	(10.3)	—	(10.3)
Total finance cost		**(75.6)**	—	**(75.6)**	(51.6)	—	(51.6)
Total finance income		**24.8**	—	**24.8**	13.9	—	13.9
Net finance costs	6	**(50.8)**	—	**(50.8)**	(37.7)	—	(37.7)
Profit before taxation	7	**401.0**	**49.5**	**450.5**	447.2	(215.4)	231.8
Income tax expense	9	**(119.4)**	**7.3**	**(112.1)**	(161.6)	68.8	(92.8)
Profit for the year		**281.6**	**56.8**	**338.4**	285.6	(146.6)	139.0
Attributable to:							
Equity shareholders of the parent				**336.8**			139.5
Minority interests				**1.6**			(0.5)
				338.4			139.0
Earnings per share (pence)	11						
Basic				**14.4p**			6.0p
Diluted				**14.4p**			6.0p
Adjusted (basic)				**11.9p**			12.3p

Consolidated Balance Sheet   Kingfisher plc Annual Report and Accounts 2006/07
As at 3 February 2007

£ millions	Notes	2007	2006
Non-current assets			
Goodwill	12	**2,551.5**	2,558.8
Intangible assets	13	**89.5**	101.7
Property, plant and equipment	14	**3,210.5**	3,265.0
Investment property	15	**29.4**	15.3
Investments accounted for using equity method	17	**184.9**	185.0
Deferred tax assets	27	**30.2**	–
Other receivables	19	**46.6**	51.7
		6,142.6	6,177.5
Current assets			
Inventories	18	**1,531.0**	1,355.3
Trade and other receivables	19	**505.4**	570.6
Current tax assets		**14.6**	20.7
Available for sale financial assets	20	**28.4**	–
Cash and cash equivalents	21	**394.5**	234.1
		2,473.9	2,180.7
Total assets		**8,616.5**	8,358.2
Current liabilities			
Short-term borrowings	22	**(241.0)**	(346.8)
Trade and other payables	24	**(1,958.3)**	(1,750.8)
Provisions	29	**(56.3)**	(46.6)
Current tax liabilities		**(86.9)**	(77.0)
		(2,342.5)	(2,221.2)
Net current assets/(liabilities)		**131.4**	(40.5)
Total assets less current liabilities		**6,274.0**	6,137.0
Non-current liabilities			
Long-term borrowings	22	**(1,431.7)**	(1,255.5)
Other payables	24	**(50.8)**	(5.7)
Provisions	29	**(53.2)**	(111.4)
Deferred tax liabilities	27	**(262.7)**	(204.4)
Post-employment benefits	28	**(54.6)**	(239.6)
		(1,853.0)	(1,816.6)
Total liabilities		**(4,195.5)**	(4,037.8)
Net assets		**4,421.0**	4,320.4
Equity			
Share capital	30	**370.7**	369.8
Share premium	30	**2,185.2**	2,175.3
Treasury shares	30	**(81.3)**	(95.1)
Reserves	31	**1,939.9**	1,861.0
Minority interests		**6.5**	9.4
Total equity		**4,421.0**	4,320.4

Lowe's Companies, Inc.
Consolidated Statements of Earnings

(in millions, except per share and percentage data) Fiscal years ended on	February 2, 2007	% Sales	February 3, 2006	% Sales	January 28, 2005	% Sales
Net sales (Note 1)	$46,927	100.00%	$43,243	100.00%	$36,464	100.00%
Cost of sales (Notes 1 and 15)	30,729	65.48	28,453	65.80	24,224	66.44
Gross margin	16,198	34.52	14,790	34.20	12,240	33.56
Expenses:						
Selling, general and administrative (Notes 1, 4, and 9)	9,738	20.75	9,014	20.84	7,562	20.74
Store opening costs (Note 1)	146	0.31	142	0.33	123	0.34
Depreciation (Notes 1 and 3)	1,162	2.48	980	2.27	859	2.35
Interest—net (Note 16)	154	0.33	158	0.37	176	0.48
Total expenses	11,200	23.87	10,294	23.81	8,720	23.91
Pre-tax earnings	4,998	10.65	4,496	10.39	3,520	9.65
Income tax provision (Note 11)	1,893	4.03	1,731	4.00	1,353	3.71
Net earnings	$ 3,105	6.62%	$ 2,765	6.39%	$ 2,167	5.94%
Basic earnings per share (Note 12)	$ 2.02		$ 1.78		$ 1.39	
Diluted earnings per share (Note 12)	$ 1.99		$ 1.73		$ 1.35	
Cash dividends per share	$ 0.18		$ 0.11		$ 0.08	

Lowe's Companies, Inc.
Consolidated Balance Sheets

(in millions, except per value and percentage data)	February 2, 2007	% Total	February 3, 2006	% Total
Assets				
Current assets:				
Cash and cash equivalents (Note 1)	$ 364	1.3%	$ 423	1.7%
Short-term investments (Notes 1 and 2)	432	1.6	453	1.8
Merchandise inventory—net (Note 1)	7,144	25.7	6,635	27.0
Deferred income taxes—net (Note 11)	161	0.6	155	0.6
Other current assets	213	0.8	122	0.5
Total current assets	8,314	30.0	7,788	31.6
Property, less accumulated depreciation				
(Notes 3 and 4)	18,971	68.3	16,354	66.4
Long-term investments (Notes 1 and 2)	165	0.6	294	1.2
Other assets (Notes 1 and 4)	317	1.1	203	0.8
Total assets	$27,767	100.0%	$24,639	100.0%
Liabilities and shareholders' equity				
Current liabilities:				
Short-term borrowings (Note 5)	$ 23	0.1%	$ —	—%
Current maturities of long-term debt (Note 6)	88	0.3	32	0.1
Accounts payable	3,524	12.7	2,832	11.6
Accrued salaries and wages	372	1.3	424	1.7
Self-insurance liabilities (Note 1)	650	2.4	571	2.3
Deferred revenue (Note 1)	731	2.6	709	2.9
Other current liabilities (Notes 1 and 4)	1,151	4.1	1,264	5.1
Total current liabilities	6,539	23.5	5,832	23.7
Long-term debt, excluding current maturities				
(Notes 6, 7, and 13)	4,325	15.6	3,499	14.2
Deferred income taxes—net (Note 11)	735	2.7	735	3.0
Other long-term liabilities (Note 1)	443	1.6	277	1.1
Total liabilities	12,042	43.4	10,343	42.0
Commitments and contingencies (Note 14)				
Shareholders' equity (Note 8):				
Preferred stock—$5 par value, none issued	—	—	—	—
Common stock—$0.50 par value				
Shares issued and outstanding				
February 2, 2007 1,525				
February 3, 2006 1,568	762	2.7	784	3.2
Capital in excess of par value	102	0.4	1,320	5.3
Retained earnings	14,860	53.5	12,191	49.5
Accumulated other comprehensive income (Note 1)	1	—	1	—
Total shareholders' equity	15,725	56.6	14,296	58.0
Total liabilities and shareholders' equity	$27,767	100.0%	$24,639	100.0%

CHAPTER 2

The Financial Statements— A Closer Look

ANALYSIS CHALLENGE: OVERCOMING THE OBSTACLE OF VOCABULARY

What is a provision for income taxes? Deferred revenues? Paid in capital? Debtors—amounts falling due within one year? Accumulated something or other?

Just as engineers, archeologists, poets, and musicians have their own jargon, so do accounting and finance professionals. It is difficult to use financial reports intelligently when the terms are foreign. Reading to gain familiarity helps, as does a good dictionary. An extensive glossary is provided in the back of this text, and many financial glossaries are available online. Good ones can be found at *The Wall Street Journal* (http://online.wsj.com), Yahoo! (http://finance.yahoo.com), and Investopedia (http://investopedia.com).

Chapter 1 introduced the concept of value creation and related it to the three key activities that management must perform effectively and efficiently to create value: operating, investing, and financing. The balance sheet, statement of cash flows, income statement, and statement of shareholders' equity, and the value-creation measures they provide were discussed. In this chapter, we walk through E. I. du Pont de Nemours and Company's (DuPont) financial statements,[1] identify key items, and provide insight into what each line item represents and how it relates to value creation.

Figure 2-1 provides an overview of the 2006 financial statements prepared by DuPont, a world leader in products and services for markets including agriculture, nutrition, electronics, apparel, and more. Take a few minutes to review these statements. In the remainder of the chapter, we discuss DuPont's operating, investing, and financing activities and how they are reflected in the detailed accounts contained on these statements. Recall that value is created for the owners of DuPont if the net return generated from the operating and investing activities exceeds the cost of the financing activities.

---

[1] In several places, we present simplified versions of DuPont's financial statements. The complete statements can be found at http://www2.dupont.com.

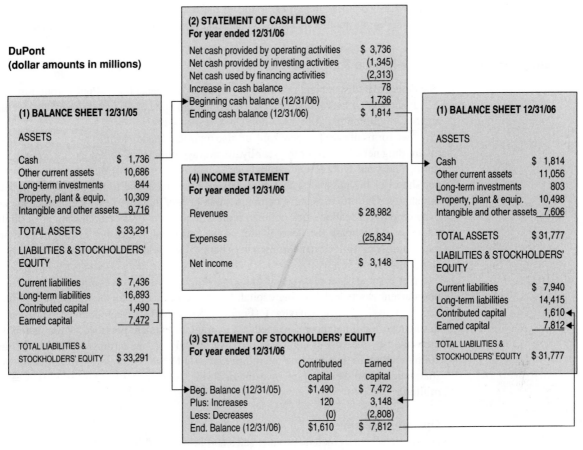

DuPont
(dollar amounts in millions)

(2) STATEMENT OF CASH FLOWS
For year ended 12/31/06

Net cash provided by operating activities	$ 3,736
Net cash provided by investing activities	(1,345)
Net cash used by financing activities	(2,313)
Increase in cash balance	78
Beginning cash balance (12/31/06)	1,736
Ending cash balance (12/31/06)	$ 1,814

(1) BALANCE SHEET 12/31/05

ASSETS

Cash	$ 1,736
Other current assets	10,686
Long-term investments	844
Property, plant & equip.	10,309
Intangible and other assets	9,716
TOTAL ASSETS	$ 33,291

LIABILITIES & STOCKHOLDERS' EQUITY

Current liabilities	$ 7,436
Long-term liabilities	16,893
Contributed capital	1,490
Earned capital	7,472
TOTAL LIABILITIES & STOCKHOLDERS' EQUITY	$ 33,291

(4) INCOME STATEMENT
For year ended 12/31/06

Revenues	$ 28,982
Expenses	(25,834)
Net income	$ 3,148

(1) BALANCE SHEET 12/31/06

ASSETS

Cash	$ 1,814
Other current assets	11,056
Long-term investments	803
Property, plant & equip.	10,498
Intangible and other assets	7,606
TOTAL ASSETS	$ 31,777

LIABILITIES & STOCKHOLDERS' EQUITY

Current liabilities	$ 7,940
Long-term liabilities	14,415
Contributed capital	1,610
Earned capital	7,812
TOTAL LIABILITIES & STOCKHOLDERS' EQUITY	$ 31,777

(3) STATEMENT OF STOCKHOLDERS' EQUITY
For year ended 12/31/06

	Contributed capital	Earned capital
Beg. Balance (12/31/05)	$1,490	$ 7,472
Plus: Increases	120	3,148
Less: Decreases	(0)	(2,808)
End. Balance (12/31/06)	$1,610	$ 7,812

Figure 2-1. Overview of Financial Statements

ANALYSIS CHALLENGE: DID DuPONT CREATE VALUE FOR ITS OWNERS IN 2006? YES.

DuPont's Return on Equity (ROE) was 34.2% ($3,148 / $9,192) in 2006, and a reasonable estimate of this mature firm's cost of equity capital is in the 9%–11% range.

► OPERATING ACTIVITIES, THE FINANCIAL STATEMENTS, AND VALUE CREATION

The central role that ROE plays in value creation suggests that we should understand its components. We start with the numerator: net income or earnings. Net income is a measure of the firm's operating performance for the period. A company's operating performance is reflected in the income statement and is measured after interest and taxes. Net cash provided by operating activities, found in the operating section of the statement of cash flows, represents another measure of operating performance. Both are discussed below.

Operating Performance and the Income Statement

The consolidated statement of earnings (income statement) for DuPont is found in Figure 2-2. It shows that DuPont reported net (earnings) income of $3.148 billion, $2.056 billion, and $1.780 billion in 2006, 2005, and 2004, respectively.

Two forms of earnings per share are also reported. Basic earnings per share is computed by dividing net earnings for the year by the average number of common shares outstanding during the year. Diluted net earnings per share is the result of adjusting basic earnings per share for the possibility that other shares could be added to the number of outstanding shares. Options to acquire common stock at less than market prices owned by company employees (called stock options) represent one of many potential sources of dilution, which could increase the denominator of the ratio and reduce net earnings per share—explaining why diluted net earnings per share (3.38) is lower than basic net earnings per share (3.41).

Net earnings is a measure of the net assets created by the company's investment in non-current assets and working capital, less the cost of debt financing (primarily interest expense). As shown in Chapter 1 (Figure 1-5, Method 2), shareholder value is created during a period if net income exceeds the average investment provided by the shareholders multiplied by the cost of equity. In the case of DuPont, net earnings of $3.148 billion in 2006 much more than covered the return that could have been reasonably expected by the shareholders' on their average investment during the year ($9.192 billion × 10% = $919 million).

Operating Revenues

Operating revenues include product sales and fees earned for services. They represent the inflow of assets (or decrease in liabilities) due to a company's operating activities over a

---

DuPont
Consolidated Statement of Earnings
(dollars in millions)

	2006	2005	2004
Net sales and other income	$ 27,421	$ 26,639	$ 27,340
Cost of products sold	20,440	19,683	20,827
Gross profit	6,981	6,956	6,513
Selling, marketing, and administrative expenses	3,224	3,223	3,141
Amortization of intangible assets	227	230	223
Research and development expenses	1,302	1,336	1,333
Income from operations	2,228	2,167	1,816
Interest expense	460	518	362
Other losses (gains)	(1,576)	(1,877)	3
Provisions for (benefit from) income taxes	196	1,470	(329)
Net earnings	$ 3,148	$ 2,056	$ 1,780
Basic net earnings per share	$ 3.41	$ 2.08	$ 1.78
Diluted earnings per share	$ 3.38	$ 2.07	$ 1.77

Figure 2-2. Consolidated Statement of Earnings for DuPont

period of time. Operating revenues lead to value creation when they exceed the operating expenses required to generate them by enough to cover the costs of financing the company's non-current assets and working capital.

Sales is the most common revenue account. It represents a measure of asset increases (usually in the form of cash or customer receivables) due to selling a company's products or inventories to customers. DuPont reported relatively flat sales from 2004 to 2006, ranging from $26.64 billion in 2005 to $27.42 billion in 2006. If a company provides a service (e.g., a law firm or accounting firm) instead of selling a product, the revenue account reflecting such activity is called fees earned or service revenue.

Operating Expenses

Operating expenses include the cost of goods (products) sold and expenses related to wages, rent, selling, marketing, administration, and depreciation and amortization—expenses related to the use of property, plant, and equipment and intangible assets (e.g., patents). They represent the periodic outflow of assets (or creation of liabilities) required to generate operating revenues. Effective control of operating expenses helps create value by increasing net income, or by reducing the level of operating revenues necessary to create a net income amount sufficient to cover the costs of financing.

Cost of Goods (Products) Sold. Cost of goods sold represents the original cost (i.e., the purchase price or cost of manufacturing) of the inventory items sold to generate sales revenue. For retail and manufacturing companies, this expense is normally separated from other operating expenses because it is comparatively large, and comparing it to sales revenue indicates the relationship between the inventory's cost and selling price—that is, gross profit. Gross profit expressed as a percentage of sales is called gross margin, and for DuPont, it was not very consistent across the three-year period: 0.238 (2004), 0.261 (2005), and 0.255 (2006). Gross profit (margin) can be increased by decreasing the cost of the sold inventory or increasing the selling price mark up over cost. Consequently, another useful way to view gross margin is in terms of markup; that is, in 2006, DuPont's average product's selling price was about 1.34 (1.00/[1.00–0.255]) times its cost, or its average markup over cost was 34%.

Other Operating Expenses. The remaining operating expenses differ based on the nature of a company's operations. For retailing companies, which purchase finished goods and then sell them (e.g., Wal-Mart, Burberry), this expense category contains such items as commissions to salespersons, salaries, wages, insurance, advertising, rentals, utilities, property taxes, equipment maintenance, depreciation of buildings and equipment, and amortization of intangible assets. Manufacturing companies (e.g., General Motors), on the other hand, typically include only selling and administrative expenses in this category. DuPont reports selling, general, and administrative expenses of more than $3 billion, and its reliance on research and development is illustrated by its huge, annual $1.3 billion plus investment in that area.

Operating revenues less operating expenses leads to income from operations (before taxes)—the earnings generated from items considered normal and recurring in the business. DuPont reports increasing income from operations from 2004 to 2006: $1.816 billion (2004), $2.167 billion (2005), and $2.228 billion (2006). Operating income is a widely followed number because it reflects the portion of the company's profits due to its normal operating activities.

ANALYSIS CHALLENGE: ANALYZING TERSE REPORTS

DuPont is a complex company, yet it boils its income statement down to a few highly aggregated line items. Other companies provide more detail. For example, Southwest Airlines (see below) provides a considerably more detailed picture of both revenues and expenses. To analyze DuPont's income statements, you need to examine the notes to the financial statements and management's discussion and analysis of the company's results.

SOUTHWEST AIRLINES CO.

CONSOLIDATED STATEMENT OF INCOME

| | Years Ended December 31, | | |
	2006	2005	2004
	(In millions, except per share amounts)		
OPERATING REVENUES:			
Passenger	$8,750	$7,279	$6,280
Freight	134	133	117
Other	202	172	133
Total operating revenues	9,086	7,584	6,530
OPERATING EXPENSES:			
Salaries, wages, and benefits	3,052	2,782	2,578
Fuel and oil	2,138	1,341	1,000
Maintenance materials and repairs	468	446	472
Aircraft rentals	158	163	179
Landing fees and other rentals	495	454	408
Depreciation and amortization	515	469	431
Other operating expenses	1,326	1,204	1,058
Total operating expenses	8,152	6,859	6,126
OPERATING INCOME	934	725	404
OTHER EXPENSES (INCOME):			
Interest expense	128	122	88
Capitalized interest	(51)	(39)	(39)
Interest income	(84)	(47)	(21)
Other (gains) losses, net	151	(90)	37
Total other expenses (income)	144	(54)	65
INCOME BEFORE INCOME TAXES	790	779	339
PROVISION FOR INCOME TAXES	291	295	124
NET INCOME	$ 499	$ 484	$ 215

Other Revenues and Expenses

Companies also report revenues and expenses not central to their normal operating activities and, in some cases, non-recurring. Other revenues include such items as interest income on bank accounts, rent collected on the rental of excess warehouse space, and gains recognized when assets other than inventory are sold for amounts greater than their book values. Other expenses include interest on outstanding loans (debt financing) and losses recognized when assets other than inventory are sold for amounts less than their book values. Finally, companies report the income tax expense (or benefit) associated with each year.

Two points about other revenues and expenses are important. First, one of the most important non-operating expenses—interest expense—is a measure of the pre-tax cost of debt financing. Because it is included on the income statement, net income already reflects a measure of the cost of debt.

Second, income statement items that reflect the results of unusual and/or infrequent transactions should be examined carefully. Does the item represent a change in the company's wealth, and can it be expected to repeat in the future? Items that represent a change in wealth and are expected to repeat in the future should be given more weight in the assessment of operating performance than those that do not.

For example, in "other items, net," DuPont includes interest income in each of the past three years. Although interest income is not part of the company's core business activities (DuPont is not a financial institution), it does represent an increase in the company's wealth and it can be expected to repeat in the future. As a result, interest income should play a role in the assessment of management's past and future performance. In contrast, in 2004, DuPont sold its Textiles and Interiors division and recorded a $667 million loss associated with the sale. This charge reduced reported net income considerably. Many analysts, however, would discount this loss in their assessments of management's 2004 performance because, although it may represent a loss of company wealth, it is doubtful that the loss should be associated only with 2004. The loss of value in the division likely occurred over several of the prior years.

ANALYSIS CHALLENGE: OPERATING? RECURRING? PREDICTABLE?

Manchester United PLC is one of England's most well-known football (soccer) clubs. Its income statement lists "(loss)/profit on disposal of players" as a line item excluded from operating profits. Is this a normal, recurring operating item for Man United? Though it may be tough to predict, buy-ing and selling players—and the resulting gains and losses—seems like one of the core activities of the business. The moral of the story—sophisticated financial statement readers ignore labels and focus on the underlying economics.

Operating Performance and Cash Provided by Operating Activities

The income statement measures performance in terms of revenues and expenses. As we see in the next chapter, revenues and expenses are measured on an accrual basis, not a cash flow basis. In brief, accrual accounting measures economic events as they occur regardless of when the related cash flow takes place. Suppose, for example, that Taiwan Semiconductor

Manufacturing Company (TSMC) produced and delivered semiconductors to Texas Instruments (TI) billing them $25 million for the sale. Under accrual accounting—even though no cash had been exchanged—at delivery, TSMC would record both a $25 million revenue, which would appear on the income statement, and a $25 million receivable, while TI would record both a $25 million asset and a $25 million payable. Later, when the $25 million cash payment is made, TSMC will increase its cash balance and remove the receivable, and TI will reduce its cash balance and remove the payable. Clearly, accruals and cash flows are related. Often they occur in the same period. But in any given period, they may differ, sometimes substantially. The income statement reflects the accruals; the statement of cash flows reflects the cash flows.

Cash provided by operating activities (often called net cash from operating activities) represents the net amount of *cash* generated (or consumed) from the acquisition and sale of the company's goods and/or services. Under Generally Accepted Accounting Principles in the United States (U.S. GAAP), it also includes payments for interest expense and income taxes. It is a narrower measure of operating performance than net income because cash represents just one of many different kinds of assets. However, cash generation is very important because cash pays debts; it is used to pay owners in the form of dividends and treasury stock purchases; it allows companies to react quickly to investment opportunities without worrying about outside financing; and it provides a buffer against negative effects on the company related to unexpected business downturns.

Figure 2-3 shows that cash provided by operating activities for DuPont is computed by adjusting net income from an accrual basis to a cash basis. These adjustments explain the differences between these two measures of operating performance, and all involve transactions where the timing of the revenue and expense recognition does not coincide with the timing of the cash receipt or payment. Recall the example earlier where TSMC recorded $25 million in revenue before it received the cash for the sale. We illustrate the mechanics underlying these differences in the next chapter.

For mature companies, like DuPont, operating activities are normally the major source of cash. DuPont's operations generated $3.736 billion in cash in 2006, $2.542 billion in 2005, and $3.231 billion in 2004. Young and fast-growing companies, on the other

	2006	2005	2004
Cash from operating activities			
Net income	$ 3,148	$ 2,056	$ 1,780
Adjustments to reconcile net income (loss) to cash provided by operating activities:			
Depreciation	1,157	1,128	1,124
Amortization of intangible assets	227	230	223
Contributions to pension plans	(280)	(1,253)	(709)
Other special charges	(428)	(341)	1,020
Increase (decrease) in operating assets:			
Accounts and notes receivable	(194)	(74)	(309)
Inventories and other operating assets	(61)	211	569
Decrease in operating liabilities:			
Accounts payable and other operating liabilities	526	(406)	57
Accrued interest and income taxes	(359)	991	(524)
Cash provided by operating activities	$ 3,736	$ 2,542	$ 3,231

Figure 2-3. Operating Section of DuPont's Statement of Cash Flow (dollars in millions)

hand, often show negative balances in cash from operating activities because operations are not yet well-enough developed to support growth and substantial investments in operating working capital. The cash they need to expand normally comes from financing activities.

Operations are the central activity of the firm. Operations, however, require investments and investments require financing—the activities to which we now turn our attention.

INSIGHT: DEPRECIATION AND OPERATING CASH FLOW

Depreciation involves recording an expense in each year of an asset's useful life for an amount that reflects that portion of the original cost of the asset used up during that period. Consequently, the annual depreciation amount reflects neither a cash inflow nor a cash outflow in that period; indeed, the cash outflow was made when the asset was acquired and paid for. Why, then, is depreciation added to net income in calculating operating cash flow (see Figure 2-3)? The reason is straightforward. Net income is measured after depreciation expense has been subtracted, but as stated, depreciation ex-

pense does not involve a cash outflow or payment. This means that the depreciation expense causes net income to understate the amount of cash provided by operations. Adding back the depreciation expense to net income adjusts net income to more accurately reflect cash provided by operating activities. The add-back completely offsets the reduction in net income associated with the non-cash depreciation expense. The cash payment associated with acquiring the depreciated asset appears in the investing section of the statement of cash flows, discussed in the next section.

TEST YOUR KNOWLEDGE: RESEARCH IN MOTION

Research in Motion (RIM), a Canadian company, designs, manufactures, and markets wireless communication devices, including the popular BlackBerry®. RIM's financial statements are found at the end of the chapter.

Refer to RIM's income statements for 2005–2007. What is the total amount of revenue the company reports each year? Why is revenue reported on more than one line of the statement of operations? RIM reports an item called "income from

operations." Comment on the items included and excluded from income from operations.

Refer to RIM's Consolidated Statements of Cash Flows for 2005–2007. Explain why net income is not the same as net cash provided by operating activities. Are operating cash flows positive at RIM? Why does RIM add amortization (which is similar to depreciation) to net income in the Consolidated Statements of Cash Flows?

► INVESTING ACTIVITIES, ASSET MANAGEMENT, THE FINANCIAL STATEMENTS, AND VALUE CREATION

We turn now to the denominator of ROE—shareholders' equity. Algebraically, shareholders' (owners') equity is simply assets less liabilities. Accountants treat owners' equity as a residual figure. That is, they measure assets and liabilities and then equity simply "drops out." By analogy, think about one's investment in a home. The home owner's equity is the value of the home less the outstanding mortgage balance. Rather than measuring the equity directly, it is viewed as the difference between the asset and liability values—just like shareholders' equity on the balance sheet.

What do assets and liabilities represent? Assets appear on the balance sheet and represent future economic benefits—what managers use to operate the business and generate returns. They represent the investments made by management—both operating and long term. Liabilities are one of the vehicles used by management to finance (pay for) these investments.

Figure 2-4 depicts two forms of the balance sheet. Traditional U.S.-format balance sheets look like the top part of Figure 2-4. Assets are listed first (or on the left side of the balance sheet) and the liability (current and long-term debt) and shareholders' equity accounts are listed next (or on the right side of the balance sheet).

In the bottom part of the figure, we rearrange the balance sheet by netting the current assets and current liabilities, creating a section called working capital. This format presents management's investments on one side and how they are financed on the other. It also clarifies the two basic categories of investments that managers need to manage: (1) working capital (net operating assets) and (2) long-term (producing) assets. Investing in both categories is costly; the greater the level of investment—whether in working capital or long-term (producing) assets—the greater the need for debt or equity capital to finance it. More debt capital means more interest to be paid; more equity capital means that higher income needs to be generated to achieve an ROE greater than the cost of equity.

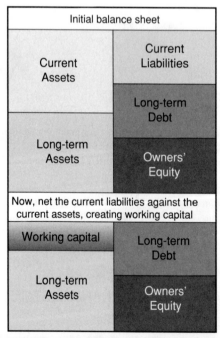

Figure 2-4. Rearranging the Balance Sheet to Highlight Investing and Financing Activities

INSIGHT: BALANCE SHEET FORMAT—KINGFISHER PLC

Refer to the case at the end of Chapter 1 and note the way Kingfisher presents its balance sheet. Rather than following an Assets = Liabilities + Owners' Equity format (as The Home Depot did), it structures the balance sheet as follows:

$$\text{Fixed Assets} + (\text{Current Assets} - \text{Current Liabilities}) - \text{Long-Term Debt} = \text{Owners' Equity}$$

It is the same algebra, but rearranged to highlight the net investments and how they are financed.

We now turn to the left side of the balance sheet—the result of management's investing activities in working capital accounts and long-term (producing) assets.

Working Capital Management

A company's operating activities are conducted primarily by managing its assets, which can be divided into working capital (current assets less current liabilities) and long-term assets. DuPont's working capital accounts are included in Figure 2-5.

Current Assets

Assets categorized as current are expected to be realized or, in most cases, converted into cash in the near future, usually within one year. They are grouped into a separate category because they are considered highly liquid. The amount of highly liquid assets held by a company is one indication of its ability to meet debt payments as they come due. Current assets include cash (and cash equivalents), short-term marketable investments, accounts receivable, inventory, and other current assets, and they often represent a significant portion of a company's total assets. For DuPont, current assets typically represent about 40 percent of total assets.

	2006	2005
Current assets		
Cash and cash equivalents	$ 1,814	$ 1,736
Marketable debt securities	79	115
Accounts and notes receivable	5,198	4,801
Inventories	4,941	4,743
Other current assets	838	1,027
Total current assets	$ 12,870	$ 12,422
Current liabilities		
Accounts payable	$ 2,711	$ 2,670
Short-term borrowings	1,517	1,397
Income taxes	178	294
Other accrued liabilities	3,534	3,075
Total current liabilities	$ 7,940	$ 7,436
Total working capital	*$ 4,930*	*$ 4,986*

Figure 2-5. Working Capital Accounts from DuPont's Balance Sheet (dollars in millions)

Cash and Cash Equivalents.   Cash represents the currency a company has access to as of the balance sheet date. It may be in a bank savings account, a checking account, or perhaps on the company premises in the form of petty cash. Cash amounts that a company can use immediately should be separated on the balance sheet from restricted cash (e.g., required compensating balances). Such a distinction can be useful when assessing how much cash is available to meet outstanding debts. Cash in and of itself generates no return, so overly large cash balances make value creation more difficult. As illustrated in Figure 2-4, more cash makes the left side of the balance sheet bigger, requiring more debt or equity to finance it.

Short-Term Investments.   Short-term investments, also called marketable securities, include shares (equity investments in other companies), bonds (debt investments in the government or other companies), and similar investments. These securities are both readily marketable (i.e., able to be sold immediately) and intended by management to be sold within a short period of time, usually less than one year. Companies normally purchase these securities to earn income with cash that otherwise would be idle and unproductive. Marketable securities are usually reported on the balance sheet at their market value.

Accounts Receivable.   Accounts receivable represents the amount of money a company expects to collect from its customers. Receivables arise from sales of products or services for which customers have not yet paid. These sales are often referred to as credit sales or sales on account. The amount appearing on the balance sheet is computed by taking the total amount of the receivables owed and subtracting an estimate for uncollectibles—the amount not expected to be received. For DuPont, net receivables for 2006 totaled $5.198 billion, which consisted of gross receivables (before expected uncollectibles) of $5.431 billion less estimated uncollectibles of $233 million (disclosed in the footnotes to the financial statements). The uncollectibles estimate is highly subjective, and financial statement users must be careful not to conclude that all reported receivables will necessarily lead to cash receipts.

The accounts receivable balance represents management's investment in providing financing for its customers. Because interest normally is not charged on outstanding balances, accounts receivables, in and of themselves, produce no return for the shareholders. Accordingly, carrying large balances can inhibit value creation. Offering financing may be necessary to acquire and maintain important customers, but management must realize that accounts receivable balances increase the need for costly financing.

Inventory.   Inventory, often called merchandise (or stocks in the United Kingdom), represents items or products intended for sale to customers. This account is very important to retailers and manufacturers because inventory involves a significant investment, and inventory sales are their primary method of producing shareholder returns. Although the sales value of a company's inventory would be very useful information, the balance sheet reflects the *cost* of acquiring (purchasing or producing) inventory or the cost of replacing it as of the balance sheet date, whichever is lower.

Like accounts receivable, large investments in inventory can require large amounts of costly financing, which inhibits value creation. Accordingly, management must be careful not to carry more inventory than is necessary to adequately serve its customers or production processes.

Other Current Assets.   Other current assets consist of a variety of items. The most common is called prepaid expenses—amounts paid by a company before the corresponding service or right is used. Insurance and rent payments are common examples. Prepaid expenses are considered assets because they represent future benefits for the company. However, they also represent investments that require costly financing, so they create shareholder value only if the benefits they help generate exceed the cost of financing.

Current Liabilities

Current liabilities are obligations expected to be paid (or services expected to be performed) within the next year. Often, current liabilities are satisfied with the assets listed as current on the balance sheet. Examples include accounts payable, wages payable, interest payable, short-term notes payable, income taxes payable, current maturities of long-term debt, and deferred revenues.[2]

Accounts payable are obligations to a company's suppliers for merchandise purchases made on account. Wages payable are obligations to a company's employees for earned but unpaid wages as of the balance sheet date. Interest payable represents unpaid interest owed to financial institutions and other creditors. Income taxes payable are amounts owed to the government for taxes assessed on a company's income. Deferred (unearned) revenues represent services yet to be performed by a company for which cash payments have already been collected—the opposite of prepaid expenses.

A key feature of short-term liabilities is that many of them are non-interest bearing, meaning that management is using someone else's money to finance its operating activities. For example, suppliers willing to carry outstanding receivables, which appear as accounts payable on the purchaser's balance sheet, are helping to cover the cost of financing the purchased inventory. Figure 2-5 shows that as of December 31, 2006, DuPont reported $4.941 billion in inventory and $2.711 billion for accounts payable. The company's suppliers, therefore, were financing 55% ($2.711 / $4.941) of its inventory investment, leaving only $2.23 billion ($4.941 − $2.711) to be financed by DuPont.

Long-term (Producing) Assets

Management's investments in long-term assets are also listed on the left side of the balance sheet. Figure 2-6 reproduces the long-term asset section of DuPont's balance sheet. As of December 31, 2006, DuPont had long-term investments, property, plant, and equipment, and intangible assets valued on the balance sheet at $18,907 billion (59% of total assets). These assets, called producing assets, support the earnings process and operations. Again, to create value for the shareholders, these assets, together with working capital, must generate a return that exceeds the total cost of DuPont's debt and equity financing.

Long-term Investments

Long-term investments include notes receivable and other long-term investments in debt securities, long-term investments in equity securities, and any other assets held as investments. Notes receivable include company receivables evidenced by promissory notes—contracts (formal, legally enforceable documents) stating the face value of the receivable, the due date (normally longer than one year), and the periodic interest payments. Notes receivable often arise because companies receive notes in exchange for the sale of high-priced items (i.e., they provide vendor financing). They can also result from direct company loans to employees, and customers with large, overdue outstanding accounts are sometimes asked

---

[2]We could refine the current liability category to distinguish between operating and financing components. For example, we could exclude the current portion of long-term debt on the basis that it represents a financing activity. We discuss refinements in later chapters.

	2006	2005
Long-term investments	$ 803	$ 844
Property, plant, and equipment (net)	10,498	10,309
Intangible and other assets (net)	7,606	9,716
Total non-current assets	$ 18,907	$ 20,869

Figure 2-6. Long-term (Producing) Assets Section of DuPont's Balance Sheet (dollars in millions)

to sign promissory notes. Management must also provide an estimate—often quite subjective—for the amount of the notes receivable balance expected to be uncollectible.

Long-term investments in bonds and equity securities not intended to be sold in the near future are also included in the long-term investment section of the balance sheet. Most major U.S. companies, for example, invest in the equity securities of other companies, intending to exert long-term influence over the management of these companies. When a company holds an equity interest from 20% to 50% in another company (called an affiliate), the investment is considered a long-term investment on the balance sheet. When the level of investment exceeds 50%, it is not reflected in the long-term investment section. Rather, the investee's (subsidiary's) assets and liabilities are consolidated (included) with those of the investor (parent) on the parent's balance sheet.

Property, Plant, and Equipment

The property, plant, and equipment section of the balance sheet includes assets acquired for use in the day-to-day operations of the business. For many companies, especially manufacturers, this is the largest asset category on the balance sheet. Property, plant, and equipment for DuPont is the company's largest single asset category, representing about 33 percent of total assets.

The property (or land) account represents the land on which the company conducts its operations, and is carried on the balance sheet at its original cost. Plant and equipment represent the physical structures used in the company's operations. The plant account includes, for example, factory and office buildings and warehouses, and the equipment account includes machinery, vehicles, furniture, computers, and similar items. For these items, the amount on the balance sheet is the original cost at the time the assets were purchased, reduced by an amount, called accumulated depreciation, which loosely approximates the asset's lost usefulness over time. Subtracting accumulated depreciation from the acquisition cost results in the net value or net book value of the assets. The following excerpt is from the footnotes of the DuPont 2006 annual report (dollars in millions):

	2006	2005
Buildings	$ 4,081	$ 3,982
Equipment	20,058	19,457
Land	417	442
Construction in progress	1,163	1,082
	25,719	24,963
Less accumulated depreciation	15,221	14,654
	$ 10,498	$ 10,309

Intangible Assets

Intangible assets are so-called because they have no physical substance. In many cases, they represent legal rights to the use or sale of valuable names, items, processes, or information. Many companies, such as Coca-Cola, have patents on certain formulas that grant them the sole legal right to produce and sell certain products. In a similar way, a company's trademark (e.g., the golden arches of McDonald's) or its name (e.g., Bridgestone, Michelin, or Goodyear Tire & Rubber) can also be valuable. Perhaps the most common intangible asset, called goodwill, represents the cost of purchasing another company over and above the total market price of that company's identifiable individual assets and liabilities. The goodwill account is prominent on the balance sheets of many major U.S. companies.

Intangible assets are divided into two categories: those with definite lives (e.g., patents and purchased technology) and those with indefinite lives (e.g., acquired brand names and goodwill). Like property, plant, and equipment, intangibles with definite lives are carried on the balance sheet at net book value, which is equal to the cost of acquiring the intangible asset, reduced by an amount, called accumulated amortization that loosely approximates the asset's reduction in usefulness over time. Intangible assets with indefinite lives are not amortized, but are subject to an impairment test each year, where management subjectively assesses whether their book values can be recovered. If they cannot, the accounts and earnings are reduced. The excerpt below was taken from the 2006 annual report of DuPont (dollars in millions):

	2006	2005
Goodwill	$ 2,108	$ 2,087
Other intangibles not subject to amortization	1,155	1,158
Intangibles subject to amortization	2,829	2,982
Less accumulated amortization	(1,505)	(1,456)
	$ 4,587	$ 4,771

Figure 2-7 summarizes the cash effects of DuPont's investing transactions during 2006, 2005, and 2004. These transactions represent the acquisitions and sales of the company's producing assets (long-term investments; property, plant, and equipment; and intangibles).

Over the three-year period, DuPont invested approximately $4 billion in property, plant, and equipment, and approximately $548 million to establish significant ownership in affiliates and to purchase other companies. Importantly, DuPont sold off a major subsidiary in 2004 (Textiles and Interiors division), collecting almost $4 billion in cash. Recall earlier that this transaction resulted in a $667 million loss on DuPont's 2004 income statement. This transaction likely highlights a shift in DuPont's strategic direction. The "other" category represents cash payments primarily devoted to the acquisition and sale of financial investments.

	2006	2005	2004
Cash flows from investing activities			
Purchases of property, plant, and equipment	$ (1,532)	$ (1,340)	$ (1,232)
Investments in affiliates	(31)	(66)	(66)
Payments for businesses	(60)	(206)	(119)
Proceeds from sales of assets	148	312	3,908
Other	130	698	(555)
Cash provide by (used for) investing activities	$ (1,345)	$ (602)	$ 1,936

Figure 2-7. Investing Section of DuPont's Statement of Cash Flows (dollars in millions)

TEST YOUR KNOWLEDGE: RESEARCH IN MOTION

Refer to the Research in Motion (RIM) consolidated balance sheets for 2006 and 2007. What is the balance of shareholders' equity at the end of each fiscal year? What are RIM's major assets and liabilities? How much working capital did the company have at the end of fiscal 2007? How does that compare with 2006?

Refer to the investing section of RIM's consolidated cash flow statements. Overall, did the company generate or use cash from investing activities? What major investments did RIM make in 2007? Where do those appear on the balance sheet?

In later chapters, we explore in more detail how working capital and producing assets are measured and managed to create value. We now turn to how they are paid for.

▶ FINANCING ACTIVITIES, THE FINANCIAL STATEMENTS, AND VALUE CREATION

Financing activities include transactions with debt and equity holders. Recall that estimating the costs of both debt and equity financing is key to determining whether management created value for the shareholders. Financing transactions are reflected in three areas of the financial statements: (1) the financing section of the statement of cash flows (Figure 2-8), (2) the long-term debt and shareholders' equity sections of the balance sheet (Figure 2-9), and (3) the statement of changes in shareholders' equity (Figure 2-10).

Take a few minutes to review these three figures. Cash transactions and account balances associated with debt financing are reflected in the top half of both Figures 2-8 and 2-9, and cash transactions and account balances associated with equity financing are reflected in the bottom half of Figures 2-8 and 2-9, and summarized for 2006 in Figure 2-10.

Transactions with Debtholders

Borrowing is an important form of financing for most major corporations. Companies issue notes payable to banks in exchange for cash; they issue bonds to collect large cash amounts from bondholders; and companies acquire properties by entering into lease contracts that create obligations to make lease payments in the future. Borrowed funds can be used to create value by generating returns that exceed the interest cost associated with the borrowing. This concept is called leverage. For example, if a company borrows $10,000 at a 5% annual

	2006	2005	2004
Financing activities			
Net (decrease) increase in short-term borrowings	$ (263)	$ (494)	$ (3,853)
Long-term and other borrowings			
Receipts	2,611	4,311	1,601
Payments	(3,139)	(2,045)	(1,555)
Dividends paid to shareholders	(1,378)	(1,439)	(1,404)
Acquisition of treasury stock	(280)	(3,530)	(457)
Proceeds from exercise of stock options	148	359	197
Other	(12)	(13)	(79)
Cash (used for) provided by financing activities	$ (2,313)	$ (2,851)	$ (5,550)

Figure 2-8. Financing Section of the DuPont Statement of Cash Flows (dollars in millions)

	2006	2005
Long-term debt		
Long-term borrowings and capital lease obligations	$ 6,013	$ 6,783
Other liabilities	8,402	10,110
Shareholders' equity		
Preferred stock	237	237
Common stock	303	302
Additional paid-in capital	7,797	7,678
Retained earnings	9,679	7,990
Accumulated other comprehensive income (loss)	(1,867)	(518)
Less common stock held in treasury	(6,727)	(6,727)
Total long-term debt and shareholders' equity	**$ 23,837**	**$ 25,855**

Figure 2-9. Financing Section of DuPont's Consolidated Balance Sheet (dollars in millions)

DuPont
Consolidated Statement of Stockholders' Equity
(dollars in millions)

	Preferred stock	Common stock	Additional paid-in capital	Retained earnings	Accumulated comprehensive income	Treasury stock	Total stockholders' equity	Total comprehensive income
Balance (12/31/05)	$ 237	$ 302	$ 7,678	$ 7,990	$ (518)	$ (6,727)	$ 8,962	
Net income				3,148			3,148	$ 3,148
Other comprehensive income					206		206	206
Total comprehensive income								$ 3,354
Common dividends				(1,368)			(1,368)	
Preferred dividends				(10)			(10)	
Treasury stock								
Acquisition			(180)			(100)	(280)	
Retirement		(1)	(18)	(81)		100	0	
Common stock issued		2	142				144	
Compensation plans			175				175	
Pension adjustment					(1,555)		(1,555)	
Balance (12/31/06)	$ 237	$ 303	$ 7,797	$ 9,679	$ (1,867)	$ (6,727)	$ 9,422	

Figure 2-10. Consolidated Statement of Shareholders' Equity in DuPont

interest rate, and invests the funds in a project that provides a return of 10%, the company has used leverage to produce a pre-tax $500 ([$10,000 × 10%] − [$10,000 × 5%]) return for the shareholders without requiring any investment from them, which would boost ROE.[3] However, borrowing cannot be relied upon too heavily because it increases a company's risk by obligating it to contractual future cash payments and other restrictions. Interest payments must be met before dividends can be paid; in the event of liquidation, outstanding payables must be satisfied before shareholders are paid; and debt covenants often place restrictions on management's investment options.

Figure 2-8 shows that over the three-year period, DuPont reduced its reliance on short-term borrowing by approximately $4.6 billion. Over the same period, it increased its reliance on long-term debt by about $1.8 billion, boosted mostly by the $2.3 billion increase in long-term debt during 2005. Overall, DuPont paid off more debt than it borrowed from 2004–2006. A reduction in long-term debt financing is also reflected on the balance sheet (Figure 2-9) from 2005 to 2006.

---

[3]Whether leverage is a value-creation activity is subject to debate. Finance theory argues that shareholders can choose whatever leverage level they want by borrowing to buy the shares. It follows that markets do not reward firms for borrowing unless managers have better access to debt than shareholders do (which is often the case). Furthermore, debt adds risk to the firm and that could increase the cost of equity.

Transactions with Equityholders

Transactions with shareholders (equityholders) involve contributed capital or earned capital. Transactions involving contributed capital include stock issuances where shareholder funds are contributed to the company in exchange for ownership interests (e.g., shares of stock). When a company buys back its own stock from shareholders and holds it "in treasury" (treasury stock), contributed capital is reduced because company funds are being returned to the shareholders. The financial statement accounts that reflect these transactions include preferred stock, common stock, and additional paid-in capital. The amount of contributed capital can be computed by totaling the amounts in these accounts and subtracting the amount of treasury stock. The dollar amount of contributed capital for DuPont as of the end of 2006 and 2005, for example, was $1.610 billion (0.237 + 0.303 + 7.797 − 6.727) and $1.490 billion (0.237 + 0.302 + 7.678 − 6.727), respectively. These dollar amounts can be computed from Figures 2-9 and 2-10.

Earned capital represents wealth earned primarily through operations in prior periods that the shareholders have chosen (via the Board of Directors) to leave in the company and not pay to themselves in the form of dividends. Retained earnings, profits from past years not distributed to the owners, is normally the major component of earned capital, but earned capital also includes the effect of transactions that lead to increases or decreases in the company's wealth not reflected on the income statement. The financial effects of these transactions are reflected in "other comprehensive income" on the statement of changes in stockholders' equity and "accumulated other comprehensive income (loss)" on the balance sheet. The dollar amounts of earned capital for DuPont as of the end of 2006 and 2005 were $7.812 billion (9.679 − 1.867) and $7.472 billion (7.990 − 0.518), respectively. These dollar amounts can also be computed from Figures 2-9 and 2-10.

Most of DuPont's equity financing (about 83 percent) comes from earned, rather than contributed, capital. This phenomenon is common among mature, successful companies because over the years they tend to reduce contributed capital by purchasing treasury stock at prices that exceed the amounts at which the stock was originally issued. Relying heavily on earned capital, and especially retained earnings, as a source of financing normally signals financial strength because it indicates that the company's growth has been financed by profitable operations.

The total dollar amount of contributed capital and earned capital, reflected on the balance sheet as shareholders' equity, represents the total investment by the shareholders in the company as of a given point in time (for DuPont, $9.422 billion and $8.962 billion as of December 31, 2006 and 2005, respectively). The average of these two amounts ($9.192 billion) represents the average investment by the shareholders during 2006.

Figures 2-8 (financing section of the statement of cash flows) and 2-10 (statement of shareholders' equity) report the activity in the shareholders' equity accounts during the year. Consider 2006, for example, and note in Figure 2-10 that net income increased earned capital by increasing retained earnings. Dividend payments (common and preferred) are reported on both statements and totaled $1.378 billion. Figure 2-10 shows that these dividends reduced earned capital by reducing retained earnings. DuPont also paid $280 million to repurchase outstanding shares of common stock in the form of treasury stock (Figure 2-8), which served to reduce contributed capital via additional paid-in capital ($180 million) and treasury stock ($100 million), reported in Figure 2-10. Finally, a stock issuance in 2006 produced $148 million in cash (Figure 2-8), which increased contributed capital by increasing the common stock ($2 million) and additional paid-in capital ($142 million) accounts.

Finally, Figure 2-10 includes other comprehensive income, a component of earned capital. This measure of the company's performance is broader than net income because it reflects certain transactions affecting the company's wealth not considered part of net income. Changes in the market prices of certain assets, for example, clearly represent changes in the company's wealth, but in some cases are not considered part of net income. Such changes are considered other comprehensive income, and we discuss various examples as they arise later in the text.

TEST YOUR KNOWLEDGE: RESEARCH IN MOTION

Refer again to the Research in Motion (RIM) balance sheets for 2006 and 2007. How did the company finance its assets? Has the nature of the financing changed from 2006 to 2007?

Refer to the company's cash flow statements. What were the major financing cash flows over the past three years?

Refer to RIM's Statements of Shareholders' Equity. Describe the information on that statement and explain how it differs from the information reported on the other financial statements? Does RIM pay cash dividends or purchase its own shares?

▶ FINANCIAL STATEMENT DIFFERENCES ACROSS INDUSTRIES

Using financial information from 2004 financial statements, Figure 2-11 compares the relative size of key balance sheet and income statement accounts across a group of well-known companies from different industries. Balance sheet accounts are expressed as a percentage of total assets, and income statement accounts are expressed as a percentage of total revenues.

Note the wide variance across companies. Some companies, such as Wal-Mart, carry large amounts of inventory, while others (H&R Block, Verity, and BankAmerica) carry none. Current liabilities are a key source of financing for BankAmerica, but relatively unimportant for Verity. Some companies rely exclusively on selling products (Wal-Mart, 3M, and Bristol-Myers Squibb), and for these companies, cost of goods sold is a critical figure; others rely almost exclusively on selling services (H&R Block and BankAmerica) and show no cost of goods sold. Others sell both products and services (Hewlett-Packard, Verity, and General Electric).

These differences highlight the diversity in the way in which these companies conduct business. Wal-Mart, a retailer, places most of its investment in inventory and facilities, and carries little customer credit. Its past success is illustrated by the size of retained earnings relative to shareholders' equity. Hewlett-Packard, 3M, and Bristol-Myers Squibb are manufacturers that carry some inventory (though not as much as Wal-Mart), but also carry significant amounts of receivables and property, plant, and equipment. As a professional service firm, H&R Block's primary investment is in people, who do not appear on the balance sheet. BankAmerica provides financial services and carries huge amounts of receivables, cash, and short-term investments, financed almost exclusively by current liabilities—e.g., customer bank deposits.

Verity is a special case. Like many other companies that relied on the Internet explosion, Verity—a leader in providing knowledge retrieval solutions—was not profitable until recently; note the small retained earnings number. General Electric is also an interesting case.

Account	Wal-Mart	H&R Block	Hewlett Packard	3M	Bristol-Myers Squibb	Verity	General Electric	Bank America
Income Statement:								
Sales	1.00	0.05	0.81	1.00	1.00	0.58	0.36	0
Service revenue	0	0.95	0.19	0	0	0.42	0.64	1.00
Cost of goods sold	0.77	0	0.76	0.50	0.31	0.16	0.41	0
Research and development	0	0	0.04	0.06	0.13	0.16	0.02	0
Other expenses	0.20	0.76	0.15	0.30	0.44	0.58	0.46	0.78
Net income	0.04	0.24	0.04	0.15	0.12	0.09	0.11	0.22
Balance Sheet:								
Cash and short-term investments	0.05	0.30	0.17	0.13	0.25	0.34	0.20	0.41
Receivables	0.01	0.18	0.17	0.13	0.14	0.09	0.44	0.46
Inventory	0.24	0	0.09	0.09	0.06	0	0.01	0
Current assets	0.32	0.55	0.56	0.42	0.49	0.45	0.66	0.87
Property, plant, and equipment	0.54	0.05	0.09	0.28	0.19	0.01	0.08	0.01
Other assets	0.14	0.39	0.35	0.29	0.32	0.53	0.26	0.12
Current liabilities	0.36	0.46	0.38	0.29	0.32	0.14	0.27	0.82
Long-term liabilities	0.23	0.19	0.13	0.21	0.34	0	0.58	0.09
Retained earnings	0.36	0.52	0.21	0.76	0.65	0.10	0.12	0.05
Shareholders' equity	0.41	0.35	0.49	0.50	0.34	0.86	0.15	0.09

Figure 2-11. Financial Statement Differences across Companies

The large receivables balance and its heavy reliance on liabilities indicate that GE is not only a manufacturer, but also a financial institution. Many of the products purchased by GE customers are financed through its financial subsidiary (GE Capital Services), which—like all financial institutions—consists primarily of receivables, investments, and liabilities.

Finally, note that for H&R Block, 3M, and Bristol-Myers Squibb, the retained earnings balance is larger than the total shareholders' equity balance. While it may seem strange, it is quite common, occurring because these companies have repurchased portions of their outstanding stock at prices that exceed the original issuance price. The balance sheet value of this treasury stock, which is subtracted from shareholders' equity, is greater than the value of the capital originally contributed by the shareholders—normally a sign of financial strength.

Regardless of the nature of the business, all companies can only create value for their shareholders by generating a return on their investments in non-current (producing) assets and working capital that exceeds the cost of financing those investments. The nature of the investments may differ and companies may rely on different forms of financing, but the fundamental goal of value creation is the same for all managers.

TEST YOUR KNOWLEDGE: FINANCIAL STATEMENTS AND ACCOUNTS

Test your knowledge of financial statements and the accounts that appear on them with the following exercises.

- Listed below are accounts that may appear on either the balance sheet or the income statement:

a. Equipment
b. Fees earned
c. Retained earnings
d. Wage expense
e. Patent
f. Cost of goods sold
g. Common stock
h. Dividend payable
i. Accumulated depreciation
j. Prepaid expense

k. Gain on sale of short-term investments
l. Rent revenue
m. Supplies inventory
n. Accounts receivable
o. Land
p. Insurance expense
q. Interest payable
r. Deferred revenue

For each account, indicate whether a company would ordinarily disclose the account on the balance sheet or the income statement.

- Presented below are the main section headings of the balance sheet:

a. Current assets
b. Long-term investments
c. Property, plant, and equipment
d. Intangible assets
e. Current liabilities
f. Long-term liabilities
g. Contributed capital
h. Retained earnings

Classify the following accounts under the appropriate headings and prepare a balance in proper form without account balances.

1. Dividend payable
2. Payments received in advance
3. Allowance for uncollectible accounts
4. Inventories
5. Capital stock
6. Accumulated depreciation—building
7. Bonds payable
8. Machinery and equipment
9. Accounts receivable
10. Short-term investments
11. Buildings
12. Patents
13. Property
14. Investment fund for plant expansion
15. Wages payable
16. Cash
17. Accumulated depreciation—equipment
18. Prepaid rent
19. Trademarks
20. Land held for investment
21. Current portion due of long-term debt
22. Accounts payable
23. Short-term notes payable

- Presented below are the main section headings of the income statement:

a. Sales
b. Fees earned
c. Other revenues
d. Cost of goods sold
e. Operating expenses
f. Other expenses

(continues)

▶ GLOBAL PERSPECTIVE: FINANCIAL STATEMENTS AND ANALYSES IN OTHER COUNTRIES

We commented in Chapter 1 that much of the world outside the United States is moving toward International Financial Reporting Standards (IFRS). The 2006 balance sheet of Novartis AG, a Swiss-based global pharmaceutical company, appears in Figure 2-12. PricewaterhouseCoopers conducted an audit and concluded, "In our opinion, the consolidated financial statements present fairly, in all material respects, the financial position of the Novartis Group, the results of operations and its cash flows in accordance with International Financial Reporting Standards (IFRS) and comply with Swiss law." The balance sheet is expressed in U.S. dollars because that is the company's functional currency, but Novartis does not follow U.S. GAAP.

Two fundamental differences exist between balance sheets based on U.S. GAAP and the IFRS-based balance sheet provided by Novartis: (1) financial statement format and (2) the measurement of assets, liabilities, equity, and earnings. Concerning format, Novartis lists long-term (non-current) assets ($46.604 billion) before current assets ($21.404 billion) and, in general, assets are listed in reverse order of liquidity. Similarly, equity ($41.294 billion) is listed before liabilities ($26.714 billion). Total equity is divided into three main categories: (1) share capital ($990 million), (2) reserves ($40.261 billion), and (3) treasury shares (a reduction of $140 million). A further balance, called minority interests, rounds out the equity section. Share capital represents funds contributed by the shareholders (contributed capital), and reserve accounts include, but are not limited to, what U.S. firms call retained earnings. Still, total assets ($68.008 billion) equal total equity ($41.294 billion) plus total liabilities ($26.714 billion).

Although not obvious from simply examining the balance sheet, many differences exist between U.S. GAAP and IFRS concerning the measurement of revenues, expenses, assets, liabilities, and equities. The reserve account, for example, contains several different categories, some of which include discretionary adjustments to earnings made by management. Although such adjustments are not allowed under U.S. GAAP, we discuss in Chapter 6 how U.S. managers use discretion to influence the measurement of earnings, assets, liabilities, and equities.

Consolidated Balance Sheets (at December 31, 2006 and 2005)

	Note	2006 USD millions	2005 USD millions
Assets			
Non-current assets			
Property, plant & equipment	8	10 945	8 679
Intangible assets	9	21 230	13 294
Associated companies	10	6 111	7 086
Deferred tax assets	11	3 903	3 401
Financial and other non-current assets	12	4 415	3 829
Total non-current assets		**46 604**	36 289
Current assets			
Inventories	13	4 498	3 725
Trade accounts receivable	14	6 161	5 343
Marketable securities & derivative financial instruments	15	4 140	4 612
Cash and cash equivalents		3 815	6 321
Other current assets	16	2 054	1 442
Total current assets from continuing operations		**20 668**	21 443
Assets related to discontinuing operations	23	736	
Total current assets		**21 404**	21 443
Total assets		**68 008**	57 732
Equity and liabilities			
Equity			
Share capital	17	990	994
Treasury shares	17	−140	−146
Reserves		40 261	32 142
Issued share capital and reserves attributable to shareholders of Novartis AG		**41 111**	32 990
Minority interests		183	174
Total equity		**41 294**	33 164
Liabilities			
Non-current liabilities			
Financial debts	18	656	1 319
Deferred tax liabilities	11	5 290	3 472
Provisions and other non-current liabilities	19	4 534	4 449
Total non-current liabilities		**10 480**	9 240
Current liabilities			
Trade accounts payable		2 487	1 961
Financial debts and derivative financial instruments	20	6 643	7 135
Current income tax liabilities		1 161	1 253
Provisions and other current liabilities	21	5 736	4 979
Total current liabilities from continuing operations		**16 027**	15 328
Liabilities related to discontinuing operations	23	207	
Total current liabilities		**16 234**	15 328
Total liabilities		**26 714**	24 568
Total equity and liabilities		**68 008**	57 732

The accompanying notes from an integral part of the consolidated financial statements.

Figure 2-12. Novartis AG balance sheet.

► SUMMARY

In this chapter, we described the content of the four major financial statements, linking the accounts on each statement to value creation through the operating, investing, and financing activities of the firm. In so doing, we conducted a brief analysis of the performance, financial condition, and financial activities of DuPont. We introduced a number of terms and showed how relationships on the financial statements and vocabulary can differ across companies and industries. In Chapter 3, we temporarily depart from our value creation theme and focus on how financial statements are prepared from the transactions entered into by management. This coverage of the mechanical process linking transactions to the financial statements is crucial for an understanding of the financial statements, and provides a firm foundation for the analyses we cover in Chapters 4 and 5.

Research in Motion Financial Statements

RESEARCH IN MOTION LIMITED
Consolidated Statements of Operations
(United States dollars, in thousands, except per share data)

| | For the Year Ended | | |
	March 3, 2007	March 4, 2006 (Restated—note 4)	February 26, 2005 (Restated—note 4)
Revenue			
Devices and other	$ 2,303,800	$ 1,526,268	$ 983,621
Service and software	733,303	539,577	366,826
	3,037,103	2,065,845	1,350,447
Cost of sales			
Devices and other	1,265,251	840,549	555,034
Service and software	114,050	85,049	81,276
	1,379,301	925,598	636,310
Gross Margin	1,657,802	1,140,247	714,137
Expenses			
Research and development (note 15)	236,173	158,887	102,665
Selling, marketing and administration (notes 18(d) and 19)	537,922	314,317	193,838
Amortization	76,879	49,951	35,941
Litigation (note 13(b))	—	201,791	352,628
	850,974	724,946	685,072
Income from operations	806,828	415,301	29,065
Investment income	52,117	66,218	37,107
Income before income taxes	858,945	481,519	66,172
Provision for (recovery of) income taxes (note 10)			
Current	123,553	14,515	1,425
Deferred	103,820	92,348	(140,865)
	227,373	106,863	(139,440)
Net income	$ 631,572	$ 374,656	$ 205,612
Earnings per share (note 16)			
Basic	$ 3.41	$ 1.98	$ 1.10
Diluted	$ 3.31	$ 1.91	$ 1.04

See notes to the consolidated financial statements.

RESEARCH IN MOTION LIMITED Incorporated under the Laws of Ontario
Consolidated Balance Sheets
(United States Dollars, in thousands)

	As at	
	March 3, 2007	March 4, 2006 (Restated—note 4)
Assets		
Current		
Cash and cash equivalents (note 5)	$ 677,144	$ 459,540
Short-term investments (note 5)	310,082	175,553
Trade receivables	572,637	315,278
Other receivables	40,174	31,861
Inventory (note 6)	255,907	134,523
Other current assets (note 19)	41,697	45,453
Deferred income tax asset (note 10)	21,624	96,564
	1,919,265	1,258,772
Investments (note 5)	425,652	614,309
Capital assets (note 7)	487,579	326,313
Intangible assets (note 8)	138,182	85,929
Goodwill (note 9)	109,932	29,026
Deferred income tax asset (note 10)	8,339	—
	$ 3,088,949	$ 2,314,349
Liabilities		
Current		
Accounts payable	$ 130,270	$ 94,954
Accrued liabilities (notes 14, 18(c), and 19)	287,629	150,457
Income taxes payable (note 10)	99,958	17,584
Deferred revenue	28,447	20,968
Current portion of long-term debt (note 11)	271	262
	546,575	284,225
Long-term debt (note 11)	6,342	6,851
Deferred income tax liability (note 10)	52,532	27,858
	605,449	318,934
Shareholders' Equity		
Capital stock (note 12)		
Authorized—unlimited number of non-voting, cumulative, redeemable, retractable preferred shares; unlimited number of non-voting, redeemable, retractable Class A common shares and an unlimited number of voting common shares		
Issued—185,871,144 voting common shares (March 4, 2006—186,001,765)	2,099,696	2,068,869
Retained earnings (deficit)	359,227	(100,174)
Paid-in-capital	36,093	28,694
Accumulated other comprehensive loss (note 17)	(11,516)	(1,974)
	2,483,500	1,995,415
	$ 3,088,949	$ 2,314,349

Commitments and contingencies (notes 11, 13, 14, 15, and 19)
See notes to the consolidated financial statements.

On behalf of the Board:
Jim Balsillie   Mike Lazaridis
Director   Director

RESEARCH IN MOTION LIMITED
Consolidated Statements of Shareholders' Equity
(United States dollars in thousands)

	Capital Stock	Paid-in Capital	Retained Earnings (Deficit)	Accumulated Other Comprehensive Income (Loss)	Total
Balance as at February 28, 2004—as previously reported	$ 1,829,388	$ —	$ (119,206)	$ 11,480	$ 1,721,662
Adjustment to opening shareholders' equity (note 4)	172,062	60,170	(233,005)	—	(773)
Balance as at February 28, 2004—as restated (note 4)	2,001,450	60,170	(352,211)	11,480	1,720,889
Comprehensive income (loss):					
Net income	—	—	205,612	—	205,612
Net change in unrealized gains on investments available for sale	—	—	—	(18,357)	(18,357)
Net change in derivative fair value during the year	—	—	—	8,446	8,446
Amounts reclassified to earnings during the year	—	—	—	(4,340)	(4,340)
Shares issued:					
Exercise of stock options	54,151	—	—	—	54,151
Transfers to capital stock from stock option exercises	25,269	(25,269)	—	—	—
Share-based payment	—	2,899	—	—	2,899
Excess tax benefits from share-based compensation (note 12(b))	—	3,777	—	—	3,777
Deferred income tax benefit attributable to fiscal 2004 financing costs	8,727	—	—	—	8,727
Balance as at February 26, 2005—as restated (note 4)	$ 2,089,597	$ 41,577	$ (146,599)	$ (2,771)	$ 1,981,804
Comprehensive income (loss):					
Net income	—	—	374,656	—	374,656
Net change in unrealized gains on investments available for sale	—	—	—	(5,888)	(5,888)
Net change in derivative fair value during the year	—	—	—	18,029	18,029
Amounts reclassified to earnings during the year	—	—	—	(11,344)	(11,344)
Shares issued:					
Exercise of stock options	23,269	—	—	—	23,269
Transfers to capital stock from stock option exercises	18,984	(18,984)	—	—	—
Share-based payment	—	2,551	—	—	2,551
Excess tax benefits from share-based compensation (note 12(b))	—	3,550	—	—	3,550
Common shares repurchased pursuant to Common Share Repurchase Program	(62,981)	—	(328,231)	—	(391,212)
Balance as at March 4, 2006—as restated (note 4)	$ 2,068,869	$ 28,694	$ (100,174)	$ (1,974)	$ 1,995,415
Comprehensive income (loss):					
Net income	—	—	631,572	—	631,572
Net change in unrealized gains on investments available for sale	—	—	—	11,839	11,839
Net change in derivative fair value during the year	—	—	—	(13,455)	(13,455)
Amounts reclassified to earnings during the year	—	—	—	(7,926)	(7,926)
Shares issued:					
Exercise of stock options	44,534	—	—	—	44,534
Transfers to capital stock from stock option exercises	18,055	(18,055)	—	—	—
Share-based payment	—	19,454	—	—	19,454
Excess tax benefits from share-based compensation (note 12(b))	—	6,000	—	—	6,000
Common shares repurchased pursuant to Common Share Repurchase Program	(31,762)	—	(172,171)	—	(203,933)
Balance as at March 3, 2007	**$ 2,099,696**	**$ 36,093**	**$ 359,227**	**$ (11,516)**	**$ 2,483,500**

See notes to the consolidated financial statements.

RESEARCH IN MOTION LIMITED
Consolidated Statements of Cash Flows
(United States dollars in thousands)

	For the Year Ended		
	March 3, 2007	March 4, 2006	February 26, 2005
		(Restated—note 4)	(Restated—note 4)
Cash flows from operating activities			
Net income	$ 631,572	$ 374,656	$ 205,612
Items not requiring an outlay of cash:			
Amortization	126,355	85,873	66,760
Deferred income taxes	101,576	77,154	(144,642)
Share-based payment (note 4)	19,063	2,551	2,899
Other	(315)	507	(137)
Net changes in working capital items (note 18(a))	(142,582)	(390,650)	(147,490)
Net cash provided by operating activities	735,669	150,091	277,982
Cash flows from financing activities			
Issuance of share capital	44,534	23,269	54,151
Excess tax benefits from share-based compensation (note 12(b))	6,000	—	—
Common shares repurchased pursuant to Common Share Repurchase Program (note 12(a))	(203,933)	(391,212)	—
Repayment of long-term debt	(262)	(229)	(199)
Net cash provided by (used in) financing activities	(153,661)	(368,172)	53,952
Cash flows from investing activities			
Acquisition of investments	(100,080)	(103,179)	(615,098)
Proceeds on sale or maturity of investments	86,583	61,495	18,385
Acquisition of capital assets	(254,041)	(178,732)	(109,363)
Acquisition of intangible assets	(60,303)	(23,702)	(17,061)
Business acquisitions (note 9)	(116,190)	(3,795)	(3,888)
Acquisition of short-term investments	(163,147)	(199,194)	(227,072)
Proceeds on sale or maturity of short-term investments	242,601	514,431	76,022
Net cash provided by (used in) investing activities	(364,577)	67,324	(878,075)
Effect of foreign exchange loss (gain) on cash and cash equivalents	173	(57)	76
Net increase (decrease) in cash and cash equivalents for the year	217,604	(150,814)	(546,065)
Cash and cash equivalents, beginning of year	459,540	610,354	1,156,419
Cash and cash equivalents, end of year	$ 677,144	$ 459,540	$ 610,354

See notes to the consolidated financial statements

► CASE AND REVIEW QUESTIONS

Exploring the Nike, Inc., and Manchester United PLC Financial Statements

1. Review the 2006 statements of Nike, Inc. Based on the account titles and the discussion in the chapter, which accounts are likely to incorporate significant subjective estimates made by management? What forces prevent managers from making completely self-serving estimates?

2. In this chapter, we reviewed the content of each of the four financial statements. Explain how each statement represents the operating, investing, and financing activities of the firm.

3. Using Figure 2-4 as a guide, reformat Nike's balance sheet. Comment on the firm's portfolio of investments and how those assets have been financed. That is, net the current operating assets and current operating liabilities to arrive at a net working capital figure. Add that to long-term (producing) assets and compare the total to the debt and equity used to finance the assets.

4. Did Nike create value for its shareholders in 2006? Explain. (Assume a cost of equity of 9%.)

5. Retained earnings represent the cumulative profits of the firm that have not been paid out to shareholders in the form of dividends. If a company has a large retained earnings balance, does it have a large cash balance? Why or why not?

6. Nike sponsors a variety of athletes and sports teams. One of its major sponsorships is of the Manchester United football club, one of the soccer world's best-known teams. What sorts of assets would you expect a professional soccer club to own? How would you expect those assets to be financed? What sorts of revenues and expenses would you expect Manchester United to report? Review the 2004 Manchester United income statement (profit and loss account) and consolidated balance sheet. Are your expectations confirmed? Where do transactions with Nike likely appear? Where do transactions with Manchester United likely appear on the Nike statements?

7. In this chapter, we commented, "H&R Block's primary investment is in people, who do not appear on the balance sheet." Manchester United fields an all-star cast of athletes. Are those people reflected on the Man United balance sheet? If so, where? If not, why not?

NIKE, INC.
Consolidated Statements of Income

	Year Ended May 31,		
	2006	**2005**	**2004**
	(in millions, except per share data)		
Revenues	$14,954.9	$13,739.7	$12,253.1
Cost of sales	8,367.9	7,624.3	7,001.4
Gross margin	6,587.0	6,115.4	5,251.7
Selling and administrative expense	4,477.8	4,221.7	3,702.0
Interest (income) expense, net (notes 1, 6, and 7)	(36.8)	4.8	25.0
Other expense, net (notes 5 and 16)	4.4	29.1	74.7
Income before income taxes	2,141.6	1,859.8	1,450.0
Income taxes (note 8)	749.6	648.2	504.4
Net income	$ 1,392.0	$ 1,211.6	$ 945.6
Basic earnings per common share (notes 1 and 11)	$ 5.37	$ 4.61	$ 3.59
Diluted earnings per common share (notes 1 and 11)	$ 5.28	$ 4.48	$ 3.51
Dividends declared per common share	$ 1.18	$ 0.95	$ 0.74

NIKE, INC.
Consolidated Balance Sheets

	May 31,	
	2006	**2005**
	(in millions)	
ASSETS		
Current assets:		
Cash and equivalents	$ 954.2	$1,388.1
Short-term investments	1,348.8	436.6
Accounts receivable, less allowance for doubtful accounts of $67.6 and $80.4	2,395.9	2,262.1
Inventories (note 2)	2,076.7	1,811.1
Deferred income taxes (note 8)	203.3	110.2
Prepaid expenses and other current assets	380.1	343.0
Total current assets	7,359.0	6,351.1
Property, plant, and equipment, net (note 3)	1,657.7	1,605.8
Identifiable intangible assets, net (note 4)	405.5	406.1
Goodwill (note 4)	130.8	135.4
Deferred income taxes and other assets (note 8)	316.6	295.2
Total assets	$9,869.6	$8,793.6
LIABILITIES AND SHAREHOLDERS' EQUITY		
Current liabilities:		
Current portion of long-term debt (note 7)	$ 255.3	$ 6.2
Notes payable (note 6)	43.4	69.8
Accounts payable (note 6)	952.2	775.0
Accrued liabilities (notes 5 and 16)	1,286.9	1,053.2
Income taxes payable	85.5	95.0
Total current liabilities	2,623.3	1,999.2
Long-term debt (note 7)	410.7	687.3
Deferred income taxes and other liabilities (note 8)	550.1	462.6
Commitments and contingencies (notes 14 and 16)	—	—
Redeemable Preferred Stock (note 9)	0.3	0.3
Shareholders' equity:		
Common stock at stated value (note 10):		
Class A convertible — 63.9 and 71.9 shares outstanding	0.1	0.1
Class B—192.1 and 189.2 shares outstanding	2.7	2.7
Capital in excess of stated value	1,451.4	1,182.9
Unearned stock compensation	(4.1)	(11.4)
Accumulated other comprehensive income (note 13)	121.7	73.4
Retained earnings	4,713.4	4,396.5
Total shareholders' equity	6,285.2	5,644.2
Total liabilities and shareholders' equity	$9,869.6	$8,793.6

NIKE, INC.
Consolidated Statements of Cash Flows

	Years Ended May 31,		
	2006	2005	2004
		(in millions)	
Cash provided (used) by operations:			
Net income	$ 1,392.0	$ 1,211.6	$ 945.6
Income charges not affecting cash:			
Depreciation	282.0	257.2	255.2
Deferred income taxes	(26.0)	21.3	19.0
Amortization and other	8.9	30.5	58.3
Income tax benefit from exercise of stock options	54.2	63.1	47.2
Changes in certain working capital components:			
(Increase) decrease in accounts receivable	(85.1)	(93.5)	97.1
Increase in inventories	(200.3)	(103.3)	(55.9)
(Increase) decrease in prepaids and other current assets	(37.2)	71.4	(103.6)
Increase in accounts payable, accrued liabilities, and income taxes payable	279.4	112.4	255.6
Cash provided by operations	1,667.9	1,570.7	1,518.5
Cash provided (used) by investing activities:			
Purchases of short-term investments	(2,619.7)	(1,527.2)	(400.8)
Maturities of short-term investments	1,709.8	1,491.9	—
Additions to property, plant, and equipment	(333.7)	(257.1)	(214.8)
Disposals of property, plant, and equipment	1.6	7.2	11.6
Increase in other assets	(30.3)	(39.1)	(53.4)
(Decrease) increase in other liabilities	(4.3)	11.1	(4.1)
Acquisition of subsidiary, net of cash acquired	—	(47.2)	(289.1)
Cash used by investing activities	(1,276.6)	(360.4)	(950.6)
Cash provided (used) by financing activities:			
Proceeds from long-term debt issuance	—	—	153.8
Reductions in long-term debt including current portion	(6.0)	(9.2)	(206.6)
Decrease in notes payable	(18.2)	(81.7)	(0.3)
Proceeds from exercise of stock options and other stock issuances	225.3	226.8	253.6
Repurchase of stock	(761.1)	(556.2)	(419.8)
Dividends—common and preferred	(290.9)	(236.7)	(179.2)
Cash used by financing activities	(850.9)	(657.0)	(398.5)
Effect of exchange rate changes	25.7	6.8	24.6
Net (decrease) increase in cash and equivalents	(433.9)	560.1	194.0
Cash and equivalents, beginning of year	1,388.1	828.0	634.0
Cash and equivalents, end of year	$ 954.2	$ 1,388.1	$ 828.0
Supplemental disclosure of cash flow information:			
Cash paid during the year for:			
Interest, net of capitalized interest	$ 54.2	$ 39.9	$ 37.8
Income taxes	752.6	585.3	418.6
Dividends declared and not paid.	79.4	65.3	52.6

NIKE, INC.
Consolidated Statements of Shareholders' Equity

	Common Stock				Capital in Excess of Stated Value	Unearned Stock Compensation	Accumulated Other Comprehensive Income (Loss)	Retained Earnings	Total
	Class A		Class B						
	Shares	Amount	Shares	Amount					
					(in millions, except per share data)				
Balance at May 31, 2003	97.8	$0.2	165.8	$2.6	$ 589.0	$ (0.6)	$ (239.7)	$ 3,639.2	$ 3,990.7
Stock options exercised			5.5		284.9				284.9
Conversion to Class B Common Stock	(20.2)	(0.1)	20.2	0.1					—
Repurchase of Class B Common Stock			(6.4)		(7.6)			(406.7)	(414.3)
Dividends on common stock ($0.74 per share)								(194.9)	(194.9)
Issuance of shares to employees			0.4		23.2	(7.5)			15.7
Amortization of unearned compensation						2.6			2.6
Forfeiture of shares from employees					(1.7)			(0.3)	(2.0)
Comprehensive income (Note 13):									
Net income								945.6	945.6
Other comprehensive income (net of tax expense of $69.0):									
Foreign currency translation							27.5		27.5
Adjustment for fair value of hedge derivatives							125.9		125.9
Comprehensive income							153.4	945.6	1,099.0
Balance at May 31, 2004	77.6	$0.1	185.5	$2.7	$ 887.8	$ (5.5)	$ (86.3)	$ 3,982.9	$ 4,781.7
Stock options exercised			4.4		273.2				273.2
Conversion to Class B Common Stock	(5.7)		5.7						—
Repurchase of Class B Common Stock			(6.9)		(8.3)			(547.9)	(556.2)
Dividends on common stock ($0.95 per share)								(249.4)	(249.4)
Issuance of shares to employees			0.5		32.1	(10.2)			21.9
Amortization of unearned compensation						3.9			3.9
Forfeiture of shares from employees					(1.9)	0.4		(0.7)	(2.2)
Comprehensive income (Note 13):									
Net income								1,211.6	1,211.6
Other comprehensive income (net of tax expense of $40.2):									
Foreign currency translation							70.1		70.1
Adjustment for fair value of hedge derivatives							89.6		89.6
Comprehensive income							159.7	1,211.6	1,371.3
Balance at May 31, 2005	71.9	$0.1	189.2	$2.7	$ 1,182.9	$ (11.4)	$ 73.4	$ 4,396.5	$ 5,644.2
Stock options exercised			4.0		254.0				254.0
Conversion to Class B Common Stock	(8.0)		8.0						—
Repurchase of Class B Common Stock			(9.5)		(11.3)			(769.9)	(781.2)
Dividends on common stock ($1.18 per share)								(304.9)	(304.9)
Issuance of shares to employees			0.5		33.0	(6.1)			26.9
Amortization of unearned compensation						11.5			11.5
Forfeiture of shares from employees			(0.1)		(7.2)	1.9		(0.3)	(5.6)
Comprehensive income (Note 13):									
Net income								1,392.0	1,392.0
Other comprehensive income (net of tax benefit of $37.8):									
Foreign currency translation							87.1		87.1
Adjustment for fair value of hedge derivatives							(38.8)		(38.8)
Comprehensive income							48.3	1,392.0	1,440.3
Balance at May 31, 2006	63.9	$0.1	192.1	$2.7	$ 1.451.4	$ (4.1)	$ 121.7	$ 4,713.4	$ 6,285.2

Manchester United PLC
Consolidated Balance Sheet At 31 July 2004

	Note	2004 £'000	2003 £'000 Restated (note 1)
Fixed assets			
Intangible assets	11	78,233	55,299
Tangible assets	12	125,093	125,526
Loan to joint venture	13	1,000	1,000
Investment in associate	13	178	189
		204,504	182,014
Current assets			
Stocks	14	216	208
Debtors—amounts falling due within one year	15	39,487	30,756
Debtors—amounts falling due after more than one year	15	1,760	13,219
Intangible asset held for resale	31	1,382	11,941
Cash at bank and in hand		36,048	28,576
		78,893	84,700
Creditors—amounts falling due within one year	16	(44,635)	(50,202)
Net current assets		34,258	34,498
Total assets less current liabilities		238,762	216,512
Creditors—amounts falling due after one year	17	(8,795)	(2,391)
Provision for liabilities and charges			
Deferred taxation	19	(5,330)	(5,506)
Other provisions	19	(1,550)	—
Investment in joint venture:	19		
—Share of gross assets		260	375
—Share of gross liabilities		(4,760)	(4,641)
		(4,500)	(4,266)
Accruals and deferred income			
Deferred grant income	20	(856)	(1,011)
Other deferred income	21	(44,377)	(46,920)
Net assets		173,354	156,418
Capital and reserves			
Share capital	22	26,219	25,977
Share premium account	23	4,013	—
Other reserves	23	600	500
Profit and loss account	23	142,522	129,941
Equity Shareholders' funds	24	173,354	156,418

The financial statements on pages 54 to 78 were approved by the Board of Directors on 27 September 2004 and signed on its behalf by:

David Gill Director   Nick Humby Director

The accompanying notes on pages 59 to 78 are an integral part of these financial statements.

Manchester United PLC
Consolidated Profit and Loss Account For the Year Ended 31 July 2004

	Note	2004 £'000	2003 £'000
Turnover: Group.and share of joint venture		171,500	174,936
Less: Share of joint venture		(2,420)	(1,935)
Group turnover	2	169,080	173,001
Operating expenses—other	3	(139,170)	(144,033)
Operating expenses—exceptional costs	4	—	(2,197)
Total operating expenses		(139,170)	(146,230)
Group operating profit before depreciation and amortisation of intangible fixed assets		58,340	55,072
Depreciation		(6,591)	(7,283)
Amortisation		(21,839)	(21,018)
Group operating profit		29,910	26,771
Share of operating loss in:			
—Joint venture		(147)	(407)
—Associates		(11)	(47)
Total operating profit: Group and share of joint venture and associates		29,752	26,317
Profit on disposal of associate		173	409
(Loss)/profit on disposal of players	11c	(3,084)	12,935
Profit before interest and taxation		26,841	39,661
Net interest receivable/(payable)	5	1,066	(316)
Profit on ordinary activities before taxation		27,907	39,345
Taxation	7	(8,486)	(9,564)
Profit for the year		19,421	29,781
Dividends	9	(6,974)	(10,391)
Retained profit for the year	23	12,447	19,390
Basic and diluted earnings per share (pence)	10	7.4	11.5
Basic and diluted adjusted earnings per share (pence)	10	14.1	14.3

CHAPTER 3

Measurement Framework and Mechanics of Financial Accounting

ANALYSIS CHALLENGE: WHERE DO THE NUMBERS COME FROM?

The numbers reported in financial statements are used in contracts and in many different analyses. Bonus plans and debt covenants, anti-trust cases, security valuation, and competitive intelligence analyses all rely on financial statement numbers. Savvy users realize that these numbers are a product of a process that imperfectly reflects the underlying economic events—imperfect because the financial effects of these events are often very difficult to measure and management may be biased. Consequently, understanding this process is at the heart of effectively using the numbers on the financial statements.

This chapter is divided into two parts. Part 1 describes the framework underlying the measurement of the financial statement elements—the"building blocks" of measuring value creation. Part 2 covers the mechanics of how the framework is implemented and the financial statements are prepared.

Understanding the measurement framework and mechanics of financial accounting is crucial for effective management. Managers constantly choose and structure transactions, and such choices should not be made without considering the impact on value creation and how it is measured. Managers must also understand how to read, interpret, and analyze financial statements when they attempt to assess the extent to which other parties (e.g., potential investments, subsidiaries, affiliates, suppliers, customers, and competitors) are creating value. In Chapter 4, we provide a comprehensive framework for financial statement analysis. In Chapter 5, we show how numbers from the financial statements map into the value of the firm. The "building blocks" and mechanics you learn in this chapter will determine how well you understand what follows.

PART 1: MEASUREMENT FRAMEWORK FOR THE FINANCIAL STATEMENTS

Figure 3-1 describes the organization of the chapter. It illustrates that financial statements result from a process based first on a set of objectives—the goals of financial statements. The second level identifies the key elements of the financial statements and the qualitative

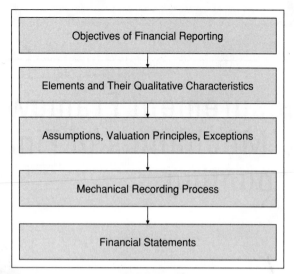

Figure 3-1. Measurement Framework of Financial Accounting

characteristics of those elements necessary to achieve the objectives. The mechanical recording process leading to the financial statements, or the implementation of the objectives, is based on a set of assumptions about the real world, valuation principles, and exceptions.

▶ OBJECTIVES OF FINANCIAL REPORTING

In Statement of Financial Accounting Concepts (SFAC) No. 1, the Financial Accounting Standards Board (FASB) maintains that the objectives of financial reporting are to provide information that is (1) useful to investors and creditors with a reasonable understanding of business and economic activities; (2) helpful to present potential investors, creditors, and other users in assessing the amounts, timing, and uncertainty of future cash flows; and (3) about economic resources, the claims to those resources, and the changes in them. Thus, the goal of the financial reports is to provide useful measures of the company's financial performance and position—information that can be used to assess the extent to which management has created value in the past and will create value for the shareholders in the future. In the next section, we discuss the elements in the financial reports and the characteristics that they must have to achieve these objectives.

▶ ELEMENTS AND THEIR QUALITATIVE CHARACTERISTICS

SFAC No. 6, "Elements of Financial Statements," identifies 10 interrelated elements necessary to provide useful information to investors, creditors, and others: assets, liabilities, equity, investments by owners, distributions to owners, comprehensive income, revenues, expenses, gains, and losses. We introduced these elements in Chapters 1 and 2. Assets, liabilities, and equity are important parts of the balance sheet. Revenues, expenses, gains, and losses are the essential elements of the income statement. Comprehensive income includes both net income—the "bottom line" of the income statement—and the change in the "other comprehensive income" account, which is disclosed with contributions from and distributions to owners on the statement of shareholders' equity. The cash flow statement provides details about the change in an important asset: cash.

Figure 3-2 provides definitions of the key elements. These definitions are important because they provide guidance for managers as they consider how to account for new

Assets are probable future economic benefits obtained or controlled by the company as a result of past events or transactions.

Liabilities are probable future economic sacrifices arising from present obligations to transfer assets or provide services to another entity as a result of past events or transactions.

Owners' equity is the residual interest in the company—the difference between assets and liabilities.

Revenues are increases in assets or decreases in liabilities due to the firm's performing activities (delivering goods or performing services) that are considered central to the firm's operations.

Expenses are decreases in assets or increases in liabilities that result from performing the activities (delivering goods or performing services) that are considered central to the firm's operations.

Gains are increases in assets or decreases in liabilities that are peripheral or incidental to the firm's central operations.

Losses are decreases in assets or increases in liabilities that result from transactions that are peripheral or incidental to the firm's central operations.

Comprehensive income is the change in the firm's equity during the period from all transactions except those with owners.

Figure 3-2. Definitions of Key Elements of Financial Statements

transactions or economic events. Most accounting rules are based on the logic of these definitions, but in the absence of a specific rule, which occurs quite frequently, financial managers rely on these definitions. Pay special attention to the definition of an asset, which is considered the most fundamental element because all other elements can be defined in terms of assets or changes in assets.

SFAC No. 2, "Qualitative Characteristics of Accounting Information," provides guidance on how to measure these elements—one of the central activities of financial reporting. It describes the characteristics that the measurements must possess to achieve the objectives of financial reporting. Understanding these characteristics is helpful to understanding the tradeoffs underlying financial statement data. SFAC No. 2 is summarized in Figure 3-3.

The most fundamental objective of financial reports is to provide useful information, so focus first on decision usefulness. Figure 3-3 shows that to be decision useful, financial statement elements should reflect certain qualitative characteristics, the most important of which are relevance and reliability. To be relevant, accounting information must be timely

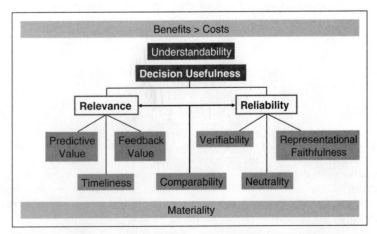

Figure 3-3. Qualitative Characteristics of Accounting Information

and capable of making a difference to a decision in terms of predicting future events or providing useful feedback. To be reliable, accounting information must faithfully represent the underlying economics and be neutral and verifiable. Relevance and reliability are both enhanced when data are comparable and consistent across time and across firms.

Figure 3-3 also recognizes that financial reporting should be practical, meaning that the costs of financial reporting information should not exceed their benefits. A good example is the concept of materiality, which is discussed in more detail later. It states that if the monetary value of a transaction is too small to affect a decision, it should be accounted for in the most expedient way.

▶ ASSUMPTIONS, VALUATION PRINCIPLES, AND EXCEPTIONS

Measuring the 10 elements in a way that helps to ensure decision usefulness (relevance and reliability) requires a set of assumptions, valuation principles, and exceptions. The assumptions establish a foundation for relevant and reliable measures; the valuation principles describe how relevant and reliable measures are constructed; and the exceptions identify situations where practical (cost–benefit) considerations are especially important.

Assumptions of Financial Accounting

There are four basic assumptions of financial accounting: (1) economic entity, (2) fiscal period, (3) going concern, and (4) stable dollar. Some are reasonable representations of the real world, others less so. To the extent that certain assumptions fail to capture the real world, the financial statements are limited, as are any of the value-creation measures based upon them. Savvy financial statement users recognize these limitations and adjust their analyses and inferences as needed.

Economic Entity Assumption

A fundamental assumption of financial accounting involves the definition of the entity, or reporting unit, which in this text we define as individual, profit-seeking companies. Included are consolidated entities, which comprise a parent company and its subsidiaries, as well as subsidiaries or other profit-seeking reporting units that prepare separate financial statements. Here, the measurement framework focuses primarily on constructing relevant and reliable measures of net income or profit, an important part of assessing value creation. Financial statements are prepared for non-for-profit entities (e.g., municipalities), but these statements, as well as their elements and objectives, are quite different.

INSIGHT: ECONOMIC VS. LEGAL ENTITIES

Modern businesses regularly involve groups of legal entities interrelated by contract, ownership interests, partnerships, joint ventures, and other arrangements. Consolidated financial statements focus on the *economic entity* and not the legal entities. Under current U.S. practice, the economic entity notion groups companies on the basis of ownership control, which means that when a company owns more than half the interest (shares or otherwise) in a second entity, the financial statements of the two companies are consolidated. As we see later in the text, ownership control can be very difficult to determine, leading to a variety of controversial practices in the area.

Fiscal Period Assumption

To be relevant, financial measures of performance must be available on a timely basis. Financial statement users need periodic feedback to monitor management's performance, as well as control and direct its decisions. The fiscal period assumption addresses this need by assuming that the operating life of a profit-seeking entity can be divided into time periods over which such measures can be developed and applied. Most corporations, for example, prepare annual financial statements, providing yearly feedback and performance measures to their shareholders. The Securities and Exchange Commission (SEC) requires that publicly traded companies provide financial statements (called a Form 10-Q) to their shareholders on a quarterly basis. For internal purposes, most well-run companies produce monthly financial statements. Advances in information technology enable companies to prepare financial reports even more frequently, continually boosting the feedback value associated with the reporting system.

Although frequent feedback is valuable, it becomes more difficult to produce reliable and objective performance measures as the time period over which performance is measured decreases. As the time period shrinks, more and more transactions remain incomplete as of the balance sheet date. For example, contracts to provide bundles of "solutions" to customers may not have run their course. Splitting bundled contracts into components is a subjective task and one that can lead to considerable differences in when the revenue associated with the bundle should be recorded on the books. If the reporting period is sufficiently long, then all elements of the bundle are complete and the splitting becomes a moot issue. The quarterly accounting reports published by major U.S. corporations are unaudited and are generally more subjective than audited annual reports.

Another consequence of the fiscal period assumption is that companies must choose the dates of their reporting cycles. Most major U.S. corporations report on the calendar year, publishing annual reports each year as of December 31, and quarterly statements for periods ending March 31, June 30, September 30, and December 31. However, a number of companies report on 12-month periods, called fiscal years, ending on dates other than December 31. In most cases, a company chooses a fiscal reporting cycle because its operations are seasonal, and the financial statements are more meaningful if the reporting period includes the entire season.

FISCAL YEAR ENDS AROUND THE GLOBE

Manchester United has a July 31 year end, which allows the annual financial statements to capture the transactions from a complete football (soccer) season. U.S. retailers generally have January 31 year ends, allowing them to capture the most recent holiday season results. Given the busy time of year and issues with post-holiday returns, this timing makes sense. Mexican firms are required by law to have December 31 year ends. Japanese firms have March 31 year ends.

Going Concern Assumption

The going concern assumption follows logically from the fiscal period assumption. If we assume that a profit-seeking entity's life can be divided into fiscal periods, we must further assume that its life extends beyond the current period. In other words, we assume the entity will not discontinue operations at the end of the current period over which its performance is being measured. In the extreme, this assumption states that the life of the entity will continue indefinitely.

FASB invoked the going concern assumption when, in SFAC No. 3, it defined assets as "probable future economic benefits obtained or controlled by a particular entity as a result of past transactions or events." As such, the going concern assumption is fundamental to the definition of an asset. The cost of equipment, for example, is placed on the asset side of the balance sheet because the equipment is expected to provide benefits in the future.

The going concern assumption is important when it comes to measuring assets and liabilities. Consider, for example, how to measure the value of an office building. If a company is a going concern, it may be able to recover the cost of its investment over future periods. On the other hand, if the company was forced to liquidate, the company might not be able to recover the investment. The real estate market at that time might be weak. Potential buyers, sensing the weakness of the company, might not offer favorable prices. Investments in customizing the building might be of little value to other companies.

Stable Dollar Assumption

To measure the dimensions, quantity, or capacity of anything requires a unit of measurement. Height and distance, for example, can be measured in terms of inches, feet, centimeters, or meters; volume can be measured in gallons or liters; and weight can be measured in pounds or kilograms. The unit of measurement for the financial performance and condition of a company is the monetary unit used in the economic transactions entered into by that company. In the United States, for example, the monetary unit is the dollar, so the financial statements of U.S. companies are expressed in dollars.

Mathematical operations, such as addition or subtraction, require that the unit of measurement maintain a constant definition. The measures of financial performance and position on the financial statements all involve the addition, subtraction, or division of dollar amounts. Total assets on the balance sheet, for example, represent the sum of the dollar values of all the individual assets held by a company at a particular time. The return to the shareholders (return on equity [ROE]) is computed by dividing net income by the total dollar amount of shareholders' equity. Valid use of these mathematical operations requires that the definition of all dollar values involved in these computations is constant. Thus, a stable dollar assumption is implicit in the measures of financial performance.

However, a dollar's value is defined in terms of its purchasing power—the amount of goods and services it can buy at a given point in time. During inflation—a fact of life—the purchasing power of the dollar decreases steadily. In reality, therefore, the unit used to measure the elements of the financial statements is not stable, because the value of the dollar changes over time. Asset dollar values on the balance sheet are actually the result of the addition of assets acquired at different times, measured in dollars with different purchasing power.

The stable dollar assumption is one case where the financial statements are based on an unrealistic assumption, which can cause serious misstatements and reduce their relevance, especially in highly inflationary economies. Fortunately, inflation in the United States has not been significant recently, but financial statement users should at least recognize that this limitation exists and, in some cases, they must deal with financial statements that have been, or should be, adjusted for inflation. Indeed, in some countries, inflation is a significant problem, and financial statements need to be restated periodically.

INSIGHT: INFLATION ACCOUNTING

A number of years ago, U.S. financial accounting standards required certain large companies to disclose in their footnotes inflation-adjusted values for inventories and property, plant, and equipment. After financial managers complained that estimating these values was costly and far too judgmental, and analysts noted that the estimates were not considered very useful, the requirement was rescinded.

Markets and Valuation Bases

The monetary values attached to the accounts on a company's financial statements are largely determined by the markets in which the company operates. To understand these markets, it is helpful to view a business entity as in Figure 3-4.

Businesses operate in two general markets: input markets, where they purchase inputs (materials, labor, and overhead) for operations, and output markets, where they sell outputs (services or inventories). Input market values (prices) are normally less than output market values (prices). For example, prices paid for automobiles by dealers in their input market are generally less than the prices paid by consumers in the output market. Moreover, one entity's output market may be another entity's input market.

Viewing a business entity in terms of both its input and output markets introduces a number of different ways to value the elements of the financial statements. Should assets, for example, be valued in terms of prices from the input market or prices from the output market? Is there a way to reflect both input and output prices in their valuations? For example, should the value of an automobile on the dealer's balance sheet be expressed in terms of the dealer's input cost or the expected selling price in the output market?

Financial reporting in the United States today follows a mixed attribute measurement model in that four different valuation bases are used to determine the dollar amounts attached to the financial statement elements: (1) present value, (2) fair market value, (3) replacement cost, and (4) original cost. Present value, the computation of which is discussed and illustrated in the appendix at the end of the text, represents the discounted expected future cash flows associated with a particular financial statement item. The present value of a long-term note receivable, for example, is calculated by determining the amount and timing of its future cash inflows and then adjusting the dollar amounts for the time value of money. Fair market value (FMV), or sales price, represents the value of goods and services in the output market. Replacement cost, or current cost, is the current price paid in the input

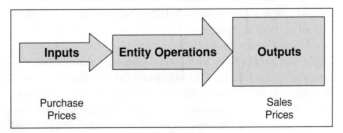

Figure 3-4. Entity Operations and Markets

market. Original (historical) cost represents the input price paid when the item was originally acquired.

MEASUREMENT CHALLENGE: VALUATION BASES

On the balance sheet, the valuation base for notes receivable and payable is present value; the valuation base for short-term investments is fair market value; and the valuation base for property, plant, and equipment is historical cost. These differences in valuation bases reflect tradeoffs between data relevance and reliability.

Valuation Principles of Financial Accounting

There are four valuation principles of financial accounting: (1) objectivity, (2) matching, (3) revenue recognition, and (4) consistency. These principles identify the conditions under which each of the four valuation bases (present value, fair market value, replacement cost, and original cost) are used.

Principle of Objectivity

The principle of objectivity, which is perhaps the most important and pervasive principle of accounting measurement, helps to ensure reliable financial statements by stating that financial accounting information must be verifiable and neutral. It requires that the values attached to the elements of the financial statements be as objectively determined as possible and backed by documented evidence. Although it ensures that the amounts disclosed on the financial statements are reasonably reliable, the principle of objectivity also precludes much relevant and useful information from appearing on the financial statements on a timely basis.

For example, to provide useful information, financial accounting statements must provide information about value: the value of entire companies, the value of company assets and liabilities, and the value of the specific transactions entered into by companies. As described in the appendix, the economic definition of value is present value, which reflects both the future cash inflows (output market) and outflows (input market) associated with the valued item, as well as the time value of money. One problem inherent in the present value calculation is that it assumes that future cash flows and discount rates are reliably predictable. This requirement limits the situations where present value is objective enough to be used as the basis for valuing financial statement elements. In fact, present value is generally used as the primary valuation base for financial statement elements only in cases where future cash flows are contractually determined because the underlying contracts remove much of the subjectivity associated with cash flow prediction. Examples include assets and liabilities related to notes receivable and payable, mortgages, bonds, leases, and pensions.

Market values existing in a company's output and input markets represent attractive candidates for purposes of financial element valuation because they can be viewed as estimates of present value. Unfortunately, like present value, market values are normally too subjective to meet the requirements imposed by the principle of objectivity, limiting the use of market value to cases where market prices are well developed and objective. Examples include short-term investments in publicly traded markets and, in some limited cases, the valuation of inventories.

MEASUREMENT CHALLENGE: INTANGIBLES AND KNOWLEDGE

Many companies are valuable because they have knowledge not possessed by other companies, often referred to as intellectual property rights. While most believe that these intangible assets have value, the principle of objectivity keeps internally developed intangibles from appearing on the balance sheet because their value cannot be objectively measured. Intangibles acquired in an exchange between independent parties are reported at their purchase price (less any subsequent amortization) because objective evidence of value exists at the time of the exchange.

The need for reliable financial statements imposes significant constraints on the use of present value, output market value, and input market value in the valuation of the financial statement elements. Monetary assets and liabilities backed by contracts and short-term investments are basically the only cases where these valuation bases are used, leaving original (historical) cost as the primary valuation base. The advantage of original cost within a framework that places much importance on objectivity is that it can be objectively verified and supported by documented evidence. Historical costs are reliable and can be audited at a reasonable cost. Consequently, the primary measurement attribute of the financial statement elements is original (historical) cost. The principles of matching, revenue recognition, and consistency, discussed next, describe how income can be measured within a system that relies primarily on historical cost.

INSIGHT: A RECENT MOVE TO FAIR VALUE REPORTING

Despite the need for reliable financial statements, recent accounting standards, both in the United States and globally, increasingly require fair value measurements. Not everyone is comfortable with the change as the following passages from an October 2004 article ("A Fairwell to History") in *CFO Europe* explains.

Martin Cubbon, group finance director of Hong Kong-based Swire Pacific, notes: "Fair value isn't just creeping into accounting, it's marching headlong. It seems to be the avowed intent of the IASB [International Accounting Standards Board] to pretty much standardise on fair value."

"As an old-fashioned 25-year qualified accountant, I think the move to greater fair value is very dangerous," says Cubbon. For one, he doesn't believe the volatility that fair-value accounting introduces to earnings is useful. But more than that, he worries that fair-value accounting is too subjective. "Where liquid markets exist, determining the fair value of an asset or liability is simple enough. But when companies must make their own assessments of fair value ... then room for error, or even abuse, opens up. Historical cost accounting may be flawed, but at least it's objective; you know what you're getting," he observes.

Others share Cubbon's view. "Logically, all assets should go on the balance sheet," notes Robert Kirk, a professor of financial reporting at the University of Ulster in Ireland, "but assigning a value to assets that aren't bought or sold regularly—such as intellectual property—can't be an exact science."

Yet Rebecca McEnally, from the CFA Institute in Virginia, counters that accountants have been using estimates ... for years. What's more, she points to a deeper issue. "If management finds such difficulty in determining the values of its assets, then what sort of decisions are they making in the absence of such relevant and useful information?" she asks.

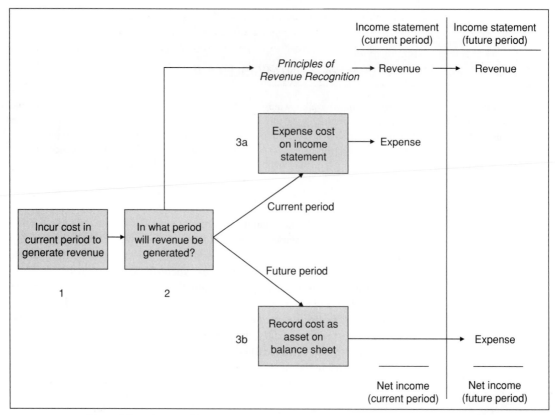

Figure 3-5. Matching Process and Principles of Revenue Recognition

Principles of Matching and Revenue Recognition

The matching principle states that company performance in a given period is measured by matching efforts expended in the period against benefits generated in the period. As illustrated in Figure 3-5, the process is initiated when a company incurs a cost (e.g., pays wages, purchases equipment, and invests in a security) to generate benefits in the form of revenues. If the revenues are generated immediately, the cost is treated as an expense, appearing on the income statement of the current period. If the revenues are expected to be realized in future periods, the cost is considered an asset and appears on the balance sheet. In future periods, as the revenues are realized, the assets are converted to expenses appearing on the income statements of the future periods. Thus, costs incurred to generate revenues are matched against those revenues in the time periods when the revenues are realized.

The most critical question in the matching process occurs at Point 2: In what period will revenue be generated? The proper accounting for the cost incurred at Point 1 cannot be determined, and the matching principle cannot be applied, until this question is answered. The answer is not always obvious because many possibilities exist. The principle of revenue recognition provides the guidelines for answering this question.

To understand the principle of revenue recognition, the selling of a good or a service can be viewed as involving four events. A good or service is (1) ordered, (2) produced, (3) transferred to the buyer, and (4) payment is received by the seller. Although these events often occur in the sequence order–production–transfer–payment, exchanges between sellers and buyers can take many forms, and they can occur in almost any order.

The revenue recognition principle determines when the revenue from the sale of a good or service should be recognized on the income statement. Revenue is recognized most commonly when a good is transferred or service is rendered to a buyer. At this point, the selling company has normally completed the earning process, generating an asset (e.g., receivable) or extinguishing a liability (e.g., obligation for which payment was previously received). Yet, situations exist where each of the other events may be the point at which revenue should be recognized. Determining exactly when revenues should be recorded has proven challenging. In Staff Accounting Bulletin (SAB) No. 104, the SEC ruled that revenue should not be recognized until it is realized or realizable and earned, as evidenced by all four of the following:

- There is persuasive evidence that an arrangement exists.
- Delivery has occurred or services have been rendered.
- The seller's price to the buyer is fixed or determinable.
- Collectibility is reasonably assured.

While these guidelines are helpful, defining the point when all four criteria are met still requires much judgment and can be very important because it can dramatically affect the amount of revenue (sales or fees earned) reported on the income statement. Recall also that, according to the matching principle, once the revenue is recognized, the costs associated with generating the revenue must be converted to expense and matched against the revenues on the income statement.

MEASUREMENT CHALLENGE: MULTIYEAR CONTRACTS

MicroStrategy, a prominent software company, provides software services for clients on contracts that extend over several years. At first, the company recorded the entire amount of revenue from these multiyear contracts in the first year. Later, its auditors forced the company to spread the recognition of the revenue over the lives of the contracts, which significantly reduced MicroStrategy's reported net income (in fact, it turned to a loss position). The SEC determined that certain officers of the company had violated accounting standards for revenue recognition and deliberately misled investors. They were fined more than $11 million. You can read the SEC press release at http://www.sec.gov/news/press/2000-186.txt. The company's stock price fell from more than $300 to less than $20 as this debacle unfolded.

Principle of Consistency

Generally accepted accounting principles(GAAP) allow a number of different methods to be used to account for the assets, liabilities, revenues, expenses, and dividends on the financial statements. For example, several acceptable methods may be used to account for each of the following assets: accounts receivable, inventories, long-term investments, and fixed assets. Such variety exists for two reasons: (1) no method is general enough to apply to all companies in all situations, and (2) GAAP is the result of a political process in which interested parties who face widely different situations are allowed and encouraged to provide input.

The principle of consistency states that when there is choice among methods, companies should choose a set of methods and use them from one period to the next. Its primary economic rationale is that consistency helps investors, creditors, and other interested parties to compare measures of performance and financial position over time. Comparability, a qualitative characteristic, is important for effective financial analysis—if a company does not change its accounting methods, outside parties can more easily identify trends. In addition, management rarely wishes to change accounting methods; it had reasons for choosing the existing methods in the first place, and changing from one method to another could be viewed by outsiders as an attempt to manipulate the financial statements, reducing their credibility.

The principle of consistency does not, however, preclude companies from changing accounting methods. If management can convince its independent auditor that the environment it faces has changed to the point that an alternative accounting method is appropriate, the company is allowed to switch. However, such changes are not easily granted, and when approved, the effects of the change on the financial statements are clearly disclosed. The change is usually described in the footnotes and mentioned in the auditor's report, and its effect on income is disclosed in a separate category on the income statement.

ANALYSIS CHALLENGE: CUSTOMER ACQUISITION COSTS

During AOL's period of tremendous growth, the company capitalized (treated as assets) all costs associated with acquiring new customers. The company subsequently changed its treatment to expense these costs. This accounting change made it more difficult for analysts to compare the company's performance across time.

Exceptions in Financial Accounting

Under certain circumstances, the costs of applying the valuation principles of accounting exceed the benefits. In these situations, management is allowed (and, in some cases, required) to depart from the basic principles. All rules have exceptions, even the valuation principles of financial accounting. Two important exceptions are materiality and conservatism.

Materiality

The monetary amounts of some transactions are so small that the method of accounting has virtually no impact on the financial statements and, thus, no effect on the conclusions that a user may come to based on an analysis of the statements. In such cases, the least costly method of reporting is chosen, regardless of the method suggested by the principles of accounting measurement. The amounts of these transactions are referred to as immaterial, and management is allowed to account for them as expediently as possible.

For example, the matching principle indicates that the cost of a wastebasket should be included on the balance sheet and converted to expense over future periods because its usefulness is expected to extend beyond the current period. That is, it meets the definition of an asset. However, the cost of an individual wastebasket is probably immaterial, and it is costly in terms of management's time and effort to carry such items on the books. For practical reasons, therefore, the purchase price is immediately treated as an expense. Granted, such treatment misstates reported net income for both current and future periods over the wastebasket's useful life, but the misstatement is extremely small (i.e., immaterial), having no bearing on the decisions of financial statement users. In this case, the costs of properly accounting for the wastebasket simply exceed the benefits such accounting would provide.

Although materiality is a practical concept, it can be a challenge to implement because it requires judgment that can differ considerably among investors, creditors, managers, auditors, and others. What exactly is too small to make a difference and to whom? Unfortunately, few useful guidelines exist for what is, and is not, material, leaving the decision largely in the hands of management and the auditor. Regulatory oversight, the threat of litigation, and other formal and informal forms of corporate governance (see Chapter 1) help to ensure that judgments of materiality are kept within reason.

INSIGHT: MATERIALITY JUDGMENTS

For many years, companies used *quantitative* methods to determine the materiality of a financial statement item (e.g., 5% of net income). In 1999, the SEC eliminated that practice, requiring instead the use of *qualitative* analysis when determining whether an item is large enough to affect a user's decision. The guidance appears in SAB No. 99, "Materiality," which can be found at http://www.sec.gov/interps/account/sab99.htm. Of course, qualitative analysis relies heavily on judgment. Is an amount material if it affects EPS (earning per share) by a single penny? A penny seems minor if the comparison is between $10.00 and $10.01 per share. Is that same penny material if the comparison is between a loss of a penny per share and breaking even? Between flat profits and increased profits?

Conservatism

Another important exception to the valuation principles is conservatism. Like materiality, conservatism is practical and has evolved over time in response to cost–benefit considerations. In its simplest form, conservatism states that, *when in doubt*, financial statements should understate assets, overstate liabilities, accelerate the recognition of losses, and delay the recognition of gains.

Conservatism does not suggest, however, that the financial statements should be intentionally understated. When objective and verifiable evidence exists about a material transaction, the principles of accounting measurement should be followed, and no attempt should be made to intentionally understate assets or overstate liabilities. Only when there is significant uncertainty about the value of a transaction should the most conservative alternative be chosen.

The economic rationale for conservatism is partially driven by the liability associated with overstating the financial condition and performance of a company. When stock prices go down and investors lose money, they often attempt to recover their out-of-pocket losses by filing lawsuits against management and auditors, claiming that financial performance and position were overstated. Such litigation can be very costly, creating an economic incentive for management and auditors, when in doubt, to favor understatement over overstatement because understatement rarely results in out-of-pocket investor losses that lead to litigation.

MEASUREMENT CHALLENGE: CONSERVATISM

Many examples of conservatism exist in the financial statements. An obvious one, mentioned in Chapter 2, is the rule to value inventory on the balance sheet at the *lower* of its cost or market value. We return to the topic of conservatism in Chapter 6 where we discuss hidden reserves.

TEST YOUR KNOWLEDGE: PEET'S COFFEE & TEA

Peet's Coffee & Tea, Inc., is headquartered in the state of Washington. They sell fresh roasted coffee, tea, and merchandise in grocery stores, via home delivery, and through company-operated retail stores. Peet's financial statements and selected notes are found at the end of the chapter.

Refer to the financial statements and notes to their 2006 annual report and describe how Peet's applies the assumptions and measurement principles that underlie U.S. GAAP. What valuation bases does the company use to measure key assets and liabilities? Provide examples of how they apply the matching principle in measuring assets, liabilities, revenues, and expenses.

PART 2: MECHANICS OF FINANCIAL ACCOUNTING

The framework of financial accounting measurement establishes the *conceptual* basis for how transactions are recorded. We now cover the recording process and the preparation of the financial statements.

▶ BASIC ACCOUNTING EQUATION AND FINANCIAL STATEMENTS

The four financial statements are based on a mathematical equation, which states that the value of a company's assets equals the value of its liabilities (the creditors' investment in the company) plus the value of its shareholders' equity (the owners' investment in the company). The balance sheet itself is a statement of this equation, and the mechanics of financial accounting are structured so that this equality is always maintained. That is,

$$\text{Assets} = \text{Liabilities} + \text{Owners' Equity}$$

Assets are items and rights acquired by a company through objectively measurable transactions that can be used to generate future economic benefits. The right side of the equation (liabilities and owners' equity) represents the three sources of assets: borrowings, contributed capital, and earned capital. Liabilities consist primarily of a company's debts or payables, existing obligations for which assets must be used in the future. Contributed capital is the value of the assets contributed by shareholders, and earned capital (primarily retained earnings) is the value of the assets generated through operating activities and retained in the business (i.e., not paid to the shareholders in the form of dividends).

As illustrated in Figure 3-6, the financial statements can be expressed in terms of the basic accounting equation. The balance sheet is a statement of the basic accounting equation. Changes (Δ) in the balance sheet accounts lead to the other statements. The left side of Figure 3-6 shows that changes in the cash account (ΔCash) can be expressed in terms of operating cash flows ($\text{NI} - \Delta\text{OCA}$),[1] investing cash flows (ΔNCA), and financing

---

[1] We define OCA as current operating assets less current operating liabilities, or working capital.

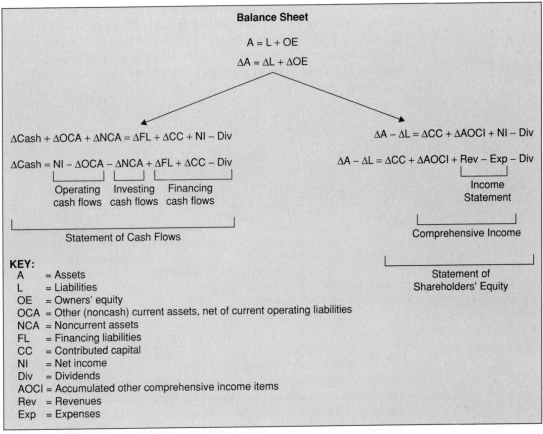

Figure 3-6. Basic Accounting Equation and the Financial Statements

cash flows (ΔFL + ΔCC – Div)—the statement of cash flows.[2] The right side of Figure 3-6 shows that changes in the owners' equity section of the balance sheet (ΔA – ΔL) can be expressed in terms of the income statement (Rev – Exp), comprehensive income (ΔAOCI + Rev – Exp), and the statement of shareholders' equity (ΔCC + ΔAOCI + Rev – Exp – Div). Note also that Figure 3-6 expresses the key elements of financial statements (see Figure 3-2) in terms of the basic accounting equation.[3]

Transactions, Accounts, and the Accounting Equation

Companies conduct operations by exchanging goods, services, assets, and liabilities with other entities (e.g., individuals and businesses). These economic events are referred to as business transactions. Exchanging cash for equipment, for example, is a transaction representing the purchase of equipment. Borrowing money is a transaction where a promise to pay in the future (i.e., loan payable) is exchanged for cash. The sale of a service on

---

[2]Some refinements to this general overview are needed to construct the statement of cash flows. For example ΔNCA includes purchases of fixed assets (an investing cash outflow) and depreciation expense (an adjustment made to arrive at operating cash flow). We discuss the refinements in later chapters.

[3]Gains and losses, as defined in Figure 3-2, can be found in both comprehensive income (CI) and revenues (Rev) and expenses (Exp).

account is a transaction where the service is exchanged for a receivable. The passage of time may also give rise to the creation of an asset or liability. Interest owed as of year end, for example, leads to the recognition of a liability. In each of these cases, and in all business transactions, something is received and something is given up, and all such exchanges are recorded so that the value of a company's assets always equals the value of its liabilities and owners' equity.

MEASUREMENT CHALLENGE: TRANSACTIONS VS. REMEASUREMENTS

Much of what is reported in the financial statements is the result of transactions between independent parties. These transactions typically provide evidence of values exchanged and thus help provide relevant and reliable measurements. Remeasurement of assets and liabilities poses a measurement challenge. For example, when new competitors enter a market or when regulators or technologies change, the value of assets and liabilties might also change. The lack of specific transactions makes measurement of the assets and liabilties more subjective. We discuss many such situations in later chapters.

To record transactions and prepare financial statements, the main components of the accounting equation (assets, liabilities, and shareholders' equity) can be further subdivided into separate accounts and categories of accounts. Accounts serve as "storage units," where the monetary values of business transactions are initially recorded and later compiled into the financial statements. The accounts that appear on the financial statements are a balance between enough detail to provide meaningful breakdowns of assets, liabilities, and shareholders' equity, but not so much as to overwhelm the user. There is no preferred number of accounts that a company must keep. Managers use enough accounts so that they have the information they need to effectively run their business, meet regulatory and other required reporting needs, and create value.

Figure 3-7 illustrates how the fundamental accounting equation can be broken down into categories and accounts. Assets are divided into current and noncurrent assets; liabilities are divided into current and noncurrent liabilities. Shareholders' equity is divided into contributed capital and retained earnings. These categories are further divided into accounts, the actual "storage units" for the monetary effects of the transactions.

Mechanics of Financial Accounting: An Illustration

The balance sheet (December 31, 20X1) for Illustration, Inc., is provided in Figure 3-8. Review the individual accounts and their balances. As of December 31, 20X1, the company reported working capital of $3,100 ($5,800 − $2,700), comprising cash, outstanding accounts receivable, and merchandise inventory reduced by accounts payable and accrued payables (miscellaneous payables owed at year end), and investments in noncurrent assets of $6,500. The $9,600 total ($3,100 + $6,500) was financed by $1,000 of outstanding long-term debt, contributed capital of $4,500 (Capital stock of $5,000 less Treasury stock of $500), and retained earnings of $4,100. Typical of U.S. balance sheets, the company does not display the net working capital number ($5,800 − $2,700 = $3,100). The balance

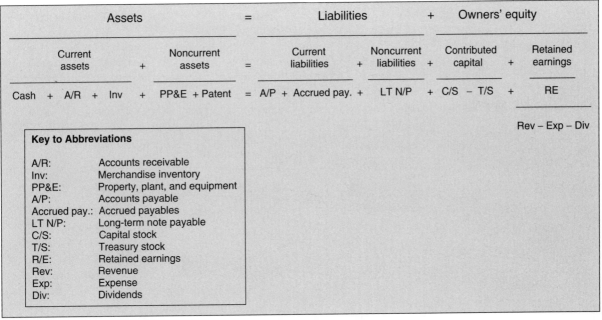

Figure 3-7. Basic Accounting Equation and Accounts

sheet, however, does balance: total assets ($12,300) equal total liabilities and shareholders' equity ($12,300).

During 20X2, the company entered into transactions and recorded the 17 entries described below. The effect of each entry on the basic accounting equation is illustrated in Figure 3-9. Note that in each of the 17 cases, the entry is recorded in a manner that maintains the equality of the equation.

Illustration, Inc.
Balance Sheet
December 31, 20x1

Assets		Liabilities and Shareholders' Equity	
Current assets:		Current liabilities:	
Cash	$ 3,000	Accounts payable	$ 500
Accounts receivable	2,000	Accrued payables	2,200
Inventory	800		
Total current assets	5,800	Total current liabilities	2,700
Noncurrent assets:		Noncurrent liabilities:	
Property, plant, and equipment (net)	6,000	Long-term note payable	1,000
Patent (net)	500		
		Capital stock	5,000
		Retained earnings	4,100
		Less treasury stock	(500)
		Total liabilities and	
Total assets	$12,300	shareholders' equity	$12,300

Figure 3-8. Balance Sheet for Illustration, Inc.

	Assets					=	Liabilities			+	Shareholders' equity		
	Current assets			Noncurrent assets		=	Current liabilities		Noncurrent liabilities	+	Contributed capital		Retained earnings
	Cash	+ A/R	+ Inv	+ PP&E	+ Patent	= A/P	+ Accrued pay.	+ LT N/P		+ C/S	– T/S	+	RE
BB.	3,000	2,000	800	6,000	500	500	2,200	1,000		5,000	500		4,100
													Rev – Exp – Div
1.	10,000 (F)									10,000			
2.	8,000 (F)							8,000					
3.	–2,200 (O)					–2,200							
4.	–5,000 (I)			5,000									
5.	–1,000 (I)				1,000								
6.			3,000			3,000							
7.		6,000											6,000
			–1,500										–1,500
8.	4,000 (O)												4,000
9.	–4,000 (O)												–4,000
10.	4,500 (O)	–4,500											
11.	–1,200 (F/O)							–1,000					–200
12.	–3,500 (F)										–3,500		
13	–1,800 (O)						–1,800						
14.							2,500						–2,500
15.				–1,000									–1,000
16.					–100								–100
17.	–500 (F)												–500
EB.	10,300	3,500	2,300	10,000	1,400	1,700	2,500	8,000		15,000	4,000		4,300
		27,500				=				27,500			

Figure 3-9. Basic Accounting Equation—An Exercise

INSIGHT: CASH BASIS VS. ACCRUAL BASIS ACCOUNTING

As you read through the transactions for Illustration, Inc., pay careful attention to how the focus is not on cash flows. Cash flows are recorded, to be sure, but net income is measured on an accrual basis. Accrual-basis accounting records economic events as they occur, which may or may not coincide with the related cash flows. For example, when inventory is purchased, it is recorded as an asset regardless of whether it has been paid for. When it is paid for, there is a cash outflow, but not an expense. Only when the inventory is used up, normally at the time that it is sold to a customer, does the cost of the inventory become an expense. Though it involves more judgment, accrual accounting better reflects the underlying economics of the events in question. We return to this point many times in the coming chapters.

Entry 1

The company issued new shares of capital stock to shareholders, receiving $10,000. This financing activity increased the cash balance, and increased the investment of the shareholders in the company (contributed capital).

Entry 2

The company borrowed $8,000 from creditors (e.g., financial institutions or bondholders). This financing activity increased the cash balance, and required the company to enter into a debt contract, specifying future obligations associated with interest and principal payments. This transaction increased long-term notes payable, increasing the company's leverage. To effectively use this leverage, management must use the borrowed funds to generate a return that exceeds the cost of the debt (interest).

Entry 3

The company paid the short-term accrued liabilities outstanding as of the end of the previous year, reducing both cash and accrued payables (obligations associated with wages, interest, taxes, warranties, and other short-term operating liabilities). This operating activity had no effect on working capital or income because it simply exchanged cash—a current asset—for a current liability.

Entry 4

The company invested $5,000 in property, plant, and equipment. This investing activity exchanged cash—a nonproducing asset—for producing assets, and reduced the company's working capital position. The company now has fewer liquid assets, but more assets are now producing returns. The investment is considered an asset because it is expected to generate future revenues, and the cost of this investment will be converted to expense (matched) as those revenues are recognized.

Entry 5

The company invested $1,000 in a patent—an intangible asset. Similar to Entry 4, this investing activity exchanged cash for a producing asset, and reduced working capital. Again, this investment is considered an asset and its cost will be matched against future revenues as they are generated.

Entry 6

The company acquired $3,000 of merchandise inventory on account. This operating activity increased both current assets and current liabilities, having no effect on working capital or income. The company is now obligated to pay the supplier and bears the risks of selling the inventory. The inventory is considered an asset because it is expected to generate a future benefit (revenue) when it is sold. At that time, the cost of the inventory will be converted to an expense and matched against the sales revenue on the income statement.

Entry 7

In this operating activity, the company sold merchandise inventory with a cost of $1,500 for a sales price of $6,000. The sales amount is recorded as revenue because the four criteria of revenue recognition must have been met. The company generated an account receivable, and now bears the risk of collectibility. The cost of the inventory is removed from the balance sheet (the asset is used up), and reflected as an expense (cost of goods sold) on the income statement in the measure of net income. Note that by simultaneously creating an asset (the receivable) and removing an asset (the inventory), we are matching benefits (revenues) and costs (expenses). Consistent with accrual accounting, the measure of income is unaffected by whether Illustration, Inc., received payment for the sale or paid for the inventory. Settlement of the receivable and liability is unrelated to the timing of the revenue or expense recognition.

Entry 8

The company provides a service with a sales price of $4,000, collecting cash. This operating activity is recognized as revenue because the four criteria of revenue recognition must have been met. The entry will increase net income and retained earnings. In this example, cash flow and revenue recognition occurred at the same time. But the key to revenue recognition was performing the work, not the fact that the cash was received the same day (though the fact that the customer paid might be considered evidence that the work was done satisfactorily).

Entry 9

The company pays operating expenses in cash ($4,000). These expenses covered such operating activities as wages, rent, advertising, and utilities. The costs associated with these items are considered expenses because they are considered to have supported the operations of the company in the current period. As there is no future benefit associated with those costs, they are not considered assets. Their usefulness has expired; they are matched against the revenues recognized in the current period.

Entry 10

The company received $4,500 cash from customers, reducing outstanding accounts receivable. This operating cash inflow does not affect the income statement because the revenue was recognized previously when the accounts receivable were created. This is another example of accrual accounting. Revenues are recorded when the asset is generated, not when the company is paid. This transaction has no effect on working capital because it represents an exchange of one current asset for another. However, the company is now more liquid than before, and fewer assets are at risk.

Entry 11

The company pays $1,200 cash to the creditor holding the long-term note payable. One thousand dollars reduced the principal of the note, and $200 covered the interest obligation. The principal payment is considered a financing activity, but the interest payment is treated as interest expense because there is no future benefit (i.e., no asset was purchased). The interest was a cost of borrowing money. Hopefully, the borrowed funds were used to invest in assets that create value, but the interest is considered a cost, not a benefit.[4]

Entry 12

The company purchased outstanding shares from its own shareholders for $3,500, reducing the cash balance and reducing contributed capital via treasury stock. This financing transaction returned cash to the shareholders, reducing the shareholders' investment in the company. It also increased the company's leverage (relative reliance on debt), increasing risk because the company now has less cash to cover future debt obligations. Note that purchasing treasury stock, which reduces the shareholders' investment, reduces the amount of net income required to create value for the remaining shareholders.

Entry 13

The company paid suppliers $1,800 for prior merchandise inventory purchases, reducing both cash and outstanding accounts payable. Like Entry 10, this operating activity had no effect on either the income statement or working capital.

---

[4]U.S. GAAP defines interest payments as operating cash flows. Many analysts treat them as financing cash flows.

Entry 14

At the end of the year, the company determined that it owed $2,500 in miscellaneous operating costs. Items include unpaid wages, interest owed, and warranty obligations; $500 of the total represents income taxes on current-year profits yet to be paid. These items are expected to be paid early the next year. These are obligations of the firm at year end resulting from past events and transactions—that is, they are liabilities. There is no corresponding asset; the company has already received whatever benefits were associated with the wages, interest, warranties, and taxes. As such, the unpaid costs are expenses on the 20X2 income statement. Note in Entry 3 that accrued payables, recognized as expenses on the prior year's (20X1) income statement, were paid early in 20X2, and this transaction was not reflected on the 20X2 income statement. This series of entries represents an example of the timing differences between operating accruals, recognized on the income statement, and operating cash flows, recognized on the statement of cash flows.

Entry 15

At the end of the year, the company depreciated its property, plant, and equipment, reducing the balance sheet value by $1,000 and recognizing a depreciation expense for the same amount. This entry represents a cost expiration—the asset is being used up over time. When property, plant, and equipment is acquired, it is considered an asset (see Entry 4) because it is expected to generate future economic benefits (revenues). As those revenues are generated in future periods, the asset's cost is converted to an expense via a depreciation entry. Cost expiration refers to the mechanical process of converting an asset to an expense. Matching the cost of the assets with the revenues they help generate provides financial statement users with useful information about the firm's profitability. Later in the text, we discuss how the amount of depreciation is determined.

Entry 16

At the end of the year, the company amortized its patent by $100. Amortization is the term used to describe the cost expiration of an intangible asset. When the intangible is originally acquired, it is considered an asset (see Entry 5). As the benefit from using the intangible occurs and revenues are recognized, the asset is converted to an expense via a cost expiration entry. Later in the text, we discuss how the amount of amortization is determined.

Entry 17

The company's board of directors declared and paid a cash dividend of $500. This financing transaction reduces both cash and retained earnings, and represents a return of cash to the shareholders. Normally, companies (the board of directors) consider the amount of net income during the period before they determine the amount of the dividend. The amount by which net income exceeds the dividend (i.e., the net increase in retained earnings) represents an increase in the shareholders' investment in the company, increasing the net income amounts necessary in the future to create value for the shareholders.

After the entries have been recorded, the financial statements as of December 31, 20X2, can be prepared directly from Figure 3-9. They appear in Figures 3-10 through 3-13.

The balance sheet (Figure 3-10) contains the ending balances in the asset, liability, and shareholders' equity accounts. Note that total assets ($27,500) is equal to total liabilities plus shareholders' equity ($27,500) because each entry was recorded in a way that maintained the equality of the fundamental accounting equation.

The income statement (Figure 3-11) consists of the revenue and expense accounts listed under retained earnings. Operating revenues less operating expenses produces net operating income, a measure of the company's pre-tax operating performance during 20X2 ($1,400).

Illustration, Inc.
Balance Sheet
December 31, 20x2

Assets		Liabilities and Shareholders' Equity	
Current assets:		Current liabilities:	
Cash	$10,300	Accounts payable	$ 1,700
Accounts receivable	3,500	Accrued payables	2,500
Inventory	2,300		
Total current assets	16,100	Total current liabilities	4,200
Noncurrent assets:		Noncurrent liabilities:	
Property, plant, and equipment (net)	10,000	Long-term note payable	8,000
Patent (net)	1,400		
		Capital stock	15,000
		Retained earnings	4,300
		Less treasury stock	(4,000)
Total assets	$27,500	Total liabilities and shareholders' equuity	$27,500

Figure 3-10. Balance Sheet for Illustration, Inc.

Bottom-line after-tax net income ($700) reflects the cost of debt (interest expense of $200), but does not reflect the cost of equity.

Recall that dividing net income ($700) by the average balance in shareholders' equity ($11,950 = [$8,600 + $15,300] / 2) provides an estimate of the return to the shareholders generated by management during 20X2 (5.9% = $700 / $11,950), and this return must be compared to the cost of equity to ascertain the extent to which management created value for the shareholders.

Illustration, Inc.
Income Statement
Year Ending December 31, 20x2

Operating revenues:	
Fees earned	$ 4,000
Sales of goods	6,000
Cost of goods sold	(1,500)
Gross profit	8,500
Operating expenses:	
Selling and administrative expenses	(4,000)
Accrued expenses	(2,000)
Depreciation of property, plant, and equipment	(1,000)
Amortization of patent	(100)
Net operating income before taxes	1,400
Non-operating revenues and expenses:	
Interest expense	(200)
Net income before taxes	1,200
Income tax expense	(500)
Net income	$ 700

Figure 3-11. Income Statement for Illustration, Inc.

Illustration, Inc.
Statement of Shareholders' Equity
Year Ending December 31, 20x2

	Capital stock	Retained earnings	Treasury stock
December 31, 20x1, balance	$ 5,000	$ 4,100	$ (500)
Issuance of capital stock	10,000		
Net income		700	
Dividends		(500)	
Treasury stock purchases			(3,500)
December 31, 20x2, balance	$15,000	$ 4,300	$(4,000)

Figure 3-12. Statement of Shareholders' Equity for Illustration, Inc.

Illustration Inc.
Statement of Cash Flows
Year Ending December 31, 20x2

Operating cash flows:	
Cash receipts from customers on account	$ 4,500
Cash receipts from services rendered	4,000
Cash payments for operating expenses	(4,000)
Cash payments for accrued expenses	(2,200)
Cash payments to suppliers	(1,800)
Cash payments for interest	(200)
Net cash provided by operating activities	300
Investing cash flows:	
Cash payments for property, plant, and equipment	(5,000)
Cash payment for patent	(1,000)
Net cash used for investing activities	(6,000)
Financing cash flows:	
Cash receipts from issuance of stock	10,000
Cash receipts from issuance of long-term note	8,000
Cash payments for principal on long-term notes	(1,000)
Cash payments to purchase treasury stock	(3,500)
Cash payments for dividends	(500)
Net cash provided by financing activities	13,000
Increase in balance of cash	7,300
Beginning balance of cash (December 31, 20x1)	3,000
Ending balance of cash (December 31, 20x2)	$ 10,300

Indirect Form of Presentation:
Operating Section of the Statement of Cash Flows

Operating cash flows:	
Net income	$ 700
Plus:	
Depreciation of property, plant, and equipment	1,000
Amortization of patent	100
Adjustments for working capital items:	
Less increase in accounts receivable	(1,500)
Less increase in inventory	(1,500)
Plus increase in accounts payable	1,200
Plus increase in accrued payables	300
Net cash provided by operating activities	$ 300

Figure 3-13. Statement of Cash Flows for Illustration, Inc.

The statement of shareholders' equity (Figure 3-12) summarizes the changes in the shareholders' equity accounts during 20X2. The stock issuance increased the capital stock account; retained earnings was increased by reported net income and reduced by dividends; and treasury stock, a reduction to shareholders' equity, was increased by $3,500.

The statement of cash flows (Figure 3-13) discloses the cash inflows and outflows during 20X2, organized into three categories: operating activities, investing activities, and financing activities. Each line item can be traced directly to the cash column in Figure 3–9, where all cash transactions were indicated as operating (O), investing (I), or financing (F). In short, the company collected a net amount of $300 from operating activities and $13,000 from financing activities, and used these funds to invest in property, plant, and equipment ($5,000); acquire a patent ($1,000); and increase its cash balance ($7,300). The $13,000 generated from financing activities consisted of $10,000 from stockholders plus $7,000 ($8,000 − $1,000) in net borrowing, less $4,000 paid to the shareholders in the form of treasury stock purchases ($3,500) and dividends ($500). As you can see, the statement of cash flows provides a clear summary of how the company generated and used its cash during the year.

There are two acceptable ways to present the operating section of the statement of cash flows and both are illustrated on Figure 3-13. The **direct form** of presentation, illustrated above, lists the actual cash inflows and outflows associated with the company's operating activities. It is called the direct form of presentation because the cash amounts can be traced directly to the cash column, and these amounts can be linked to actual cash transactions. This form of presentation is very straightforward, but it is rarely the form used by companies.

Much more common is the **indirect form** of presentation, which is illustrated at the bottom of Figure 3-13. This form of presentation computes the same dollar value as the direct form for cash provided by operating activities ($300), but does so in a different way. It begins with the net income amount (which appears on the income statement) and then lists the adjustments that convert the accrual-basis net income number to a cash-basis "net cash provided by operating activities" number. Depreciation and amortization, for example, are added back to net income because they both represent expenses that reduced net income, but did not involve cash outflows. Each of the adjustments for the working capital items (receivables, inventory, accounts, and accrued payables) represent a case where the timing of the revenue or expense recognition was different from the timing of the cash receipt or payment. For example, the $1,500 increase in accounts receivable (from $2,000 on the 20X1 balance sheet to $3,500 on the 20X2 balance sheet) indicates that sales revenues ($6,000) exceeded cash receipts from customers ($4,500), meaning that the $6,000 sales number used in computing net income overstates by $1,500 the amount of cash collected from customers. Thus, the $1,500 increase in accounts receivable is subtracted from net income in the calculation of net cash provided by operating activities.

While the indirect form of presentation is less straightforward than the direct form, it does provide a useful reconciliation between accrual-basis net income and cash-basis net cash provided by operating activities. Both numbers tell us something important about operating performance, and as we suggest later in the text, understanding why they are different can provide useful insights into the analysis of the firm.

▶ GLOBAL PERSPECTIVE: MEASUREMENT FUNDAMENTALS AND INTERNATIONAL REPORTING STANDARDS

The assumptions, principles, and exceptions in this chapter that form the basis for U.S. GAAP also underlie International Financial Reporting Standards (IFRS). Economic entity, objectivity, matching, revenue recognition, consistency, and conservatism as well as the others are all important in the preparation of financial reports under IFRS. Differences currently exist between the two systems, however, in how these concepts are applied in individual situations.

In general, compared to U.S. GAAP, IFRS tends to allow management more alternatives when choosing accounting methods in a given circumstance. Many have used the term "principles-based" to described IFRS and "rules-based" to describe U.S. GAAP. This distinction suggests that when applying IFRS one looks to achieve general principles of measurement, while when applying U.S. GAAP one looks for specific rules. Since principles tend to be more general than rules, IFRS allows managers more discretion when making reporting choices. For example, in some cases IFRS allows management to somewhat subjectively restate the value of fixed assets to market value, representing a more flexible interpretation of the principle of objectivity than has been practiced in the United States. The rules-based U.S. system also imposes more disclosure requirements on companies than are necessary under IFRS. More discretion and fewer disclosure requirements make IFRS relative attractive to managers, another reason why IFRS has gained great favor in the global financial community.

Peet's Coffee and Tea, Inc., Financial Statements and Selected Notes

PEET'S COFFEE & TEA, INC.
Consolidated Balance Sheets
(in thousands, except share amounts)

	December 31, 2006	January 1, 2006 (as restated, see Note 2)
ASSETS		
Current assets:		
Cash and cash equivalents	$ 7,692	$ 20,623
Short-term marketable securities	19,511	32,453
Accounts receivable, net	6,838	5,152
Inventories	19,533	17,001
Deferred income taxes—current	1,888	1,514
Prepaid expenses and other	3,852	3,372
Total current assets	59,314	80,115
Long-term marketable securities	5,989	16,890
Property and equipment, net	82,447	46,313
Deferred income taxes—noncurrent	1,315	–
Other assets, net	3,940	5,434
Total assets	$ 153,005	$ 148,752
LIABILITIES AND SHAREHOLDERS' EQUITY		
Current liabilities:		
Accounts payable and other accrued liabilities	$ 11,046	$ 8,553
Accrued compensation and benefits	6,389	5,563
Deferred revenue	4,625	3,415
Total current liabilities	22,060	17,531
Deferred income taxes—noncurrent	–	1,806
Deferred lease credits and other long-term liabilities	3,506	2,537
Total liabilities	25,566	21,874
Shareholders' equity:		
Common stock, no par value; authorized 50,000,000 shares; issued and outstanding: 13,516,000 and 13,902,000 shares	93,246	100,562
Accumulated other comprehensive loss, net of tax	(15)	(76)
Retained earnings	34,208	26,392
Total shareholders' equity	127,439	126,878
Total liabilities and shareholders' equity	$ 153,005	$ 148,752

PEET'S COFFEE & TEA, INC.
CONSOLIDATED STATEMENTS OF INCOME
(In thousands, except per share amounts)

	2006	2005 (as restated, see Note 2)	2004 (as restated, see Note 2)
Retail stores	$ 141,377	$ 118,030	$ 100,444
Specialty sales	69,116	57,168	45,239
Net revenue	210,493	175,198	145,683
Cost of sales and related occupancy expenses	98,928	80,837	67,806
Operating expenses	72,272	57,879	47,645
General and administrative expenses	20,634	13,341	11,439
Depreciation and amortization expenses	8,609	7,293	5,787
Total costs and expenses from operations	200,443	159,350	132,677
Income from operations	10,050	15,848	13,006
Interest income	2,458	1,771	1,009
Interest expense	(2)	(2)	(87)
Income before income taxes	12,506	17,617	13,928
Income tax provision	4,690	6,842	5,218
Net income	$ 7,816	$ 10,775	$ 8,710
Net income per share:			
Basic	$ 0.57	$ 0.78	$ 0.65
Diluted	$ 0.55	$ 0.74	$ 0.62
Shares used in calculation of net income per share:			
Basic	13,733	13,801	13,308
Diluted	14,202	14,469	13,949

Peet's Coffee & Tea, Inc.
Notes to Consolidated Financial Statements

1. Summary of Significant Accounting Policies

Organization

Peet's Coffee & Tea, Inc., a Washington corporation (the "Company"), sells fresh roasted coffee, hand-selected tea, and related merchandise in several distribution channels, including grocery, home delivery, food service and office accounts, and company-operated retail stores. At December 31, 2006, and January 1, 2006, the Company operated 136 and 111 retail stores, respectively, California, Colorado, Illinois, Oregon, Massachusetts, and Washington.

Principles of Consolidation—The consolidated financial statements include the accounts of the Company and its subsidiaries. All significant intercompany transactions have been eliminated in consolidation.

Year End—The Company's fiscal year end is the Sunday closest to December 31. The fiscal year ended December 31, 2006, included 52 weeks. The fiscal year ended January 1, 2006, included 52 weeks, and the fiscal year ended January 2, 2005, included 53 weeks.

Use of Estimates—The preparation of financial statements in conformity with accounting principles generally accepted in the United States of America ("GAAP") requires management to make estimates and assumptions that affect the reported amounts of assets and liabilities and disclosures of contingent assets and liabilities at the date of the financial statements and the reported amounts of revenues and expenses during the reporting period. Actual results could differ from those estimates.

Reclassifications—Certain reclassifications have been made to prior years' financial statements in order to conform with the current year's presentation. See Note 2, Restatement of Consolidated Financial Statements and Reclassifications.

Cash and Cash Equivalents—The Company considers all liquid investments with original maturities of three months or less to be cash equivalents.

Inventories—Raw materials consist primarily of green bean coffee. Finished goods include roasted coffee, tea, accessory products, spices, and packaged foods. All products are valued at the lower of cost or market using the first-in, first-out method, except green bean and roasted coffee, which is valued at the average cost.

Property, plant, and equipment—Property, plant, and equipment are stated at cost. Depreciation and amortization are recorded on the straight-line method over the estimated useful lives of the property and equipment, which range from 3 to 10 years. Leasehold improvements are amortized using the straight-line method over the lesser of the estimated useful life or the term of the related lease, consistent with the period used for recognizing rent expense and deferred lease credits, which range from 3 to 10 years.

Intangible and other assets—Intangible and other assets include lease rights, contract acquisition costs, deposits, and restricted cash. Lease rights represent payments made to lessors and others to secure retail locations and are amortized on the straight-line method over the life of the related lease from 5 to 10 years. Intangible assets, primarily lease rights, subject to amortization were $358,000 and $614,000, net of accumulated amortization, at December 31, 2006, and January 1, 2006, respectively. The related accumulated amortization was $2,103,000 and $2,117,000 at December 31, 2006, and January 1, 2006, respectively. Amortization expense for 2006, 2005, and 2004 was $121,000, $135,000, and $156,000, respectively. Future amortization expense for 2007 through 2011 is estimated at $96,000, $96,000, $96,000, $70,000, and $0, respectively. Restricted cash of $3,085,000 and $2,941,000 as of December 31, 2006, and January 1, 2006, respectively, represents collateral for the Company's high-deductible workers' compensation policy and is classified in intangible and other assets, net on the consolidated balance sheets.

Investments—Marketable securities are classified as available for sale and are recorded at fair value. Any unrealized gains and losses are recorded in other comprehensive income (loss). Gains and losses are due to fluctuations in interest rates and are considered temporary impairments as management has the intent and ability to hold the securities to recovery.

Impairment of Long-Lived Assets—When facts and circumstances indicate that the carrying of long-lived assets may be impaired, an evaluation of recoverability is performed by comparing the carrying values of the assets to projected future cash flows in addition to other quantitative and qualitative analyses. Upon indication that the carrying values of such assets may not be recoverable, the Company recognizes an impairment loss by a charge against current operations for an amount equal to the difference between the carrying value and the assets' fair value. The fair value of the retail net asset is estimated using the discounted cash flows of the assets. Property, plant, and equipment assets are grouped at the lowest level for which there are identifiable cash flows when assessing impairment. Cash flows for retail net assets are identified

(continues)

Peet's Coffee & Tea, Inc.
Notes to Consolidated Financial Statements (*continued*)

at the individual store level. Impairment losses for underperforming stores of $0, $311,000, and $280,000 were recorded during 2006, 2005, and 2004, respectively, which were classified as operating expenses on the consolidated statements of income.

Accrued Compensation and Benefits—The Company records an estimated liability for the self-insured portion of workers' compensation claims. The liability is determined based on information received from the Company's insurance adjuster, including claims paid, filed, and reserved for, as well as using historical experience and other actuarial assumptions. As of December 31, 2006, and January 1, 2006, we had $2,616,000 and $2,048,000, accrued for workers' compensation.

Revenue Recognition—Net revenue is recognized at the point of sale at our Company-operated retail stores. Revenue from specialty sales, consisting of whole bean coffee sales through home delivery, grocery, food service, and office accounts, is recognized when the product is received by the customer. Revenue from stored value cards, gift certificates, and home delivery advanced payments is recognized upon redemption or receipt of product by the customer. Cash received in advance of product delivery is recorded in "Deferred revenue" on the accompanying consolidated balance sheets. All revenues are recognized net of any discounts. Sales returns are insignificant. The Company establishes an allowance for estimated doubtful accounts based on historical experience and current trends.

A summary of the allowance for doubtful accounts is as follows (in thousands):

	Balance at begining of year	Additions charged to expense	Write-offs and other	Balance at end of year
Allowance for doubtful accounts:				
Year ended December 31, 2006	$ 145	$ —	$ (78)	$ 67
Year ended January 1, 2006	89	57	(1)	145
Year ended January 2, 2005	54	37	(2)	89

The Company records shipping revenue in net revenue. The Company recorded shipping revenues of $2,532,000, $2,090,000, and $2,029,000 related to home delivery sales in 2006, 2005, and 2004, respectively.

Cost of Sales and Related Occupancy Expenses—Cost of sales and related occupancy expenses consist primarily of coffee and other product costs. It also includes plant manufacturing (including depreciation), freight, and distribution costs. Occupancy expenses include rent and related expenses such as utilities.

Operating Expenses—Operating expenses consist of both retail store and specialty operating costs, such as employee labor and benefits, repairs and maintenance, supplies, training, travel, and banking and card processing fees.

Preopening Costs—Costs incurred in connection with the start-up and promotion of new store openings are expensed as incurred.

Fair Value of Financial Instruments—The carrying value of cash and equivalents, receivables, and accounts payable approximates fair value. Marketable securities are recorded at fair value.

Advertising Costs—Advertising costs are expensed as incurred. Advertising expense was $2,237,000, $1,793,000, and $1,546,000 in 2006, 2005, and 2004, respectively.

Operating Leases—Certain of the Company's lease agreements provide for tenant improvement allowances, rent holidays, scheduled rent increases, and/or contingent rent provisions during the term of the lease. For purposes of recognizing incentives and minimum rental expenses, rent is expensed on a straight-line basis, and we record the difference between the recognized rental expense and accounts payable under the lease to deferred lease credits and other long-term liabilities, over the lease term, which may or may not coincide with the commencement of the lease. Tenant improvement allowances are amortized as a reduction in rent expense over the term of the lease. If the original lease term is less than the Company's anticipated rental period, one or more stated option terms are included in the straight-line computation. Certain leases provide for contingent rents, which are determined as a percentage of gross sales in excess of specified levels. The Company records a contingent rent liability in accounts payable on the consolidated balance sheets and the corresponding rent expense when specified levels have been achieved or when management determines that achieving the specified levels during the fiscal year is probable. During 2004, the Company corrected certain errors with respect to its interpretation of GAAP, resulting in an additional cost of sales and occupancy expense of $768,000, of which the amount related to prior years, $719,000, was determined to be immaterial and previously reported financial statements have not been restated. The error resulted primarily from the use of the lease commencement date, rather than the date the Company had the right to occupy the space, and the original lease term, without renewals, in computing the period over which to apply straight-line rent payments.

Gift Cards—We sell gift cards to our customers in our retail stores and through our Web sites. Our gift cards do not have an expiration date. We recognize income from gift cards when: (1) the gift card is redeemed by the customer, or (2) the likelihood of the gift card being redeemed by the customer is remote (gift card breakage) and we determine that we do not have a legal obligation to remit the unredeemed gift cards to the relevant jurisdictions. We determine the gift card breakage rate on the basis of our historical redemption patterns. We apply an estimated gift card breakage rate after the card has been dormant for 24 months, when based on historical information, we determine the likelihood of redemption becomes remote. Gift card breakage income is included in operating expenses in the consolidated statements of income.

Income Taxes—Income taxes are accounted for using the asset and liability method, under which deferred tax assets and liabilities are determined based on the difference between the financial statements and tax bases of assets and liabilities using enacted tax rates currently in effect.

Stock-Based Compensation—On January 2, 2006, we adopted the fair value recognition provisions of Statement of Financial Accounting Standards No. 123(R), "Share-Based Payment," (SFAS 123(R)), using the modified-prospective-transition method. Under this transition method, compensation cost recognized for the year ended December 31, 2006, includes (1) compensation cost for all stock-based payments granted, but not yet vested as of January 1, 2006, based on the grant-date fair value estimated in accordance with the original provisions of SFAS 123, "Accounting for Stock-Based Compensation," and (2) compensation cost for all stock-based payments granted subsequent to January 2, 2006, based on the grant-date fair value estimated in accordance with the provisions of SFAS 123(R). Such amounts have been reduced by our estimate of forfeitures of all unvested awards. Results for prior periods have not been restated. The fair value of each stock award is estimated on the grant date using the Black–Scholes option-pricing model based on assumptions for volatility, risk-free interest rates, expected life of the option, and dividends (if any). The expected term of the options represents the estimated period of time from date of option grant until exercise and is based on the historical experience of similar awards, giving consideration to the contractual terms, vesting schedules, and expectations of future employee behavior. For grants prior to July 3, 2006, expected stock price volatility was estimated using only the historical volatility of the Company's stock. Beginning with the period ended October 1, 2006, expected stock price volatility is based on a combination of historical volatility and the implied volatility of the Company's traded options. The risk-free interest rate is based on the implied yield available on U.S. Treasury zero-coupon issues with an equivalent term. The Company has not paid dividends in the past and does not plan to pay dividends in the near future. Additional disclosure requirements of SFAS 123(R) are set forth in Note 9, Stock Options, Employee Purchase, and Deferred Compensation Plans.

Stock-based compensation expense recognized in the consolidated statements of income related to stock options was $4,022,000, $44,000, and $212,000 for 2006, 2005, and 2004, respectively. The related total tax benefit was $1,641,000, $19,000, and $84,000 for 2006, 2005, and 2004, respectively. Stock-based compensation expense was recognized as follows in the statements of income (in thousands):

	2006	2005	2004
Cost of sales and related occupancy expenses	$ 466	$ 2	$ 12
Operating expenses	1,292	19	82
General and administrative expense	2,264	23	118
Total	$4,022	$ 44	$212

The net effect of the adoption of SFAS 123(R) on net income was $2,381,000, or $0.17 per basic share and $0.17 per diluted share, for 2006. The adoption of SFAS 123(R) resulted in a decrease of cash flows from operations and an increase in cash flows from financing activities of $724,000 for 2006. Prior to January 1, 2006, the Company accounted for stock-based awards to employees and non-employee directors using the intrinsic value method in accordance with Accounting Principles Board (APB) No. 25, "Accounting for Stock Issued to Employees." The following table shows the effect on net income and net

(*continues*)

Peet's Coffee & Tea, Inc.
Notes to Consolidated Financial Statements (*continued*)

income per share for 2005 and 2004 had compensation cost been recognized the basis of the estimated fair value on the grant date of stock options and ESPP awards (in thousands, except net income per share):

	2005 (as restated, See Note 2)	2004 (as restated, See Note 2)
Net income—as reported	$ 10,775	$ 8,710
Stock-based employee compensation included in reported net income, net of tax	25	128
Stock-based compensation expense determined under fair-value-based method, net of tax	(4,085)	(4,411)
Net income—pro forma	$ 6,715	$ 4,427
Basic net income per share—as reported	$ 0.78	$ 0.65
Basic net income per share—pro forma	0.49	0.33
Diluted net income per share—as reported	0.74	0.62
Diluted net income per share—pro forma	0.46	0.32

The fair value of each option grant and ESPP award is estimated on the date of grant using the Black–Scholes option-pricing model with the following assumptions:

	Stock Options			ESPP		
	2006	2005	2004	2006	2005	2004
Expected term (in years)	5.4	3.8	3.2	0.5	0.5	1.2
Expected stock price volatility	34.1%	37.8%	42.8%	27.8%	26.6%	45.8%
Risk-free interest rate	5.0%	3.9%	3.3%	5.0%	3.3%	1.6%
Expected dividend yield	0%	0%	0%	0%	0%	0%
Estimated fair value per option granted	$11.83	$9.03	$7.56	$7.16	$6.86	$5.93

Net Income per Share—Basic net income per share is computed as net income divided by the weighted average number of common shares outstanding for the period. Diluted net income per share reflects the potential dilution that could occur from common shares issued through stock options. Anti-dilutive shares of 578,424, 28,828, and 268,606 have been excluded from diluted weighted average shares outstanding in 2006, 2005, and 2004, respectively.

The number of incremental shares from the assumed exercise of stock options was calculated by applying the treasury stock method. The following table summarizes the differences between basic weighted average shares outstanding and diluted weighted average shares outstanding used to compute diluted net income per share (in thousands):

	2006	2005	2004 (as restated)
Basic weighted average shares outstanding	13,733	13,801	13,308
Incremental shares from assumed exercise of stock options	469	668	641
Diluted weighted average shares outstanding	14,202	14,469	13,949

Recently Issued Accounting Standards—In July 2006, the FASB issued Financial Interpretation (FIN) No. 48, "Accounting for Uncertainty in Income Taxes," an interpretation of FASB Statement No. 109, which clarifies the accounting for uncertainty in tax positions. FIN 48 requires that we recognize in its financial statements the impact of a tax position, if that position is more likely than not to be sustained on audit, based on the technical merits of the position. The Company is currently evaluating the provisions of FIN 48 and has not yet completed its determination of the impact of adoption on our financial position or results of operations.

▶ CASE AND REVIEW QUESTIONS

Weis Markets—Interpreting Events and Preparing Financial Statements

1. In this chapter, we discussed the concepts underlying modern financial reporting. Explain what qualities enhance the relevance and the reliability of financial reports. What is more important, relevance or reliability? Explain your position.

2. Weis Markets operates 157 retail food stores and 33 SuperPetz pet supply stores in the Eastern and Southern United States. Weis Markets' financial statements through fiscal 2003 are provided on the following pages. Use the fiscal 2003 ending balances from the balance sheet as the opening balances for fiscal 2004. Based on the following description of transactions and events that took place in fiscal 2004, prepare the December 25, 2004 balance sheet and the fiscal 2004 income statement. For each cash flow, determine whether it should be categorized as an operating, investing, or financing cash flow. All figures are in thousands of dollars. You can use the example from the chapter as a guide, as well as the prior years' financial statements. The 2004 statement of cash flows and statement of shareholders' equity are provided.

Transactions and events in fiscal 2004. All figures are in thousands of dollars.

a. The company purchased $1,539,702 of groceries on account.

b. The company made $2,000,000 in cash sales to customers. The cost of these groceries was $1,480,000.

c. The company made $97,712 in credit sales to large institutional customers. The cost of these groceries was $68,210.

d. The company collected $95,765 of accounts receivable.

e. The company paid $1,539,197 of accounts payable.

f. The company paid cash for wages and other operating, general, and administrative expenses totaling $395,000. The wages and other costs were incurred in fiscal 2004.

g. During fiscal 2004, Weis Markets incurred an additional $23,000 of operating, general, and administrative expenses. Of that total, $22,519 was paid in cash and the remainder was added to accrued expenses (a balance sheet account).

h. Weis Markets' management signed a new labor agreement with its employees. The 2-year agreement takes effect on December 26, 2004, and calls for total wage increases of $50,000 per year.

i. An analysis of prepaid insurance policies in effect at the beginning of the fiscal year showed that policies costing $3,190 had expired by December 25, 2004.

j. On December 24, 2004, the company paid $4,173 for a 1-year casualty and property insurance policy that covers the following fiscal year.

k. The company is self-insured for various workers' compensation, general liability, vehicle accidents, and other obligations. The estimated cost of accidents and other events that occurred during fiscal 2004 is $8,592.

l. During fiscal 2004, Weis Markets made payments of $6,130 under its self-insurance plan to settle claims for events and incidents that occurred prior to fiscal 2004.

m. A year-end review of the obligation under the employee benefit plans revealed that an additional $1,200 had been earned but not yet paid.

n. During fiscal 2004, the company had rental income, coupon-handling fees, store service commissions, cardboard salvage, and various other income of $15,239, all of which was received in cash.

o. The company purchased property and equipment for $82,766 in cash.

p. Weis Markets disposed of property with a book value of $10,524 for cash proceeds of $9,086. The difference is considered other income on the income statement.

q. The company recorded $40,614 of depreciation on its property and equipment in fiscal 2004.

r. The company recorded $5,721 of amortization in fiscal 2004. Of that, $995 relates to its intangible assets. The remainder relates to leasehold improvements that are included in the property and equipment, net account.

s. In fiscal 2004, the company purchased $64,900 of marketable securities.

t. Marketable securities owned by the company paid $1,565 in interest in fiscal 2004.

u. Many of Weis Markets' marketable securities are time deposits. In fiscal 2004, $66,406 of the time deposits matured.

v. Weis Markets issued new shares under its stock options plans. The company received $228 in cash on exercise of the options.

w. The company repurchased shares of its own stock for $4,048 in cash.

x. The company declared and paid $57,438 in dividends.

y. A number of other transactions and adjustments were made in fiscal 2004. They are summarized below in terms of their effects on the accounting equation. This is simply a summary of many unrelated transactions. Use the summary, in addition to the entries you recorded in parts a–x, to complete the fiscal 2004 financial statements.

	Assets =	Liabilities +	Shareholders' equity
1. Cash	− 27,224		
2. Marketable securities	+ 511		
3. Income tax recoverable	+ 1,729		
4. Deferred income tax asset	− 1,790		
5. Income taxes payable		− 1,955	
6. Deferred income tax liability		+ 5,222	
7. Accumulated other comprehensive income			+ 319
8. Investment income			+ 52
9. Provision for income tax expense			− 30,412
Total	− 26,774 =	+ 3,267	− 30,041

z. After all of the transactions and adjustments had been recorded, the company closed all of its income statement accounts to retained earnings. That is, each temporary account was reversed and the net balance in those accounts (which by construction equals net income) was added to retained earnings. (See Appendix 3A for an explanation of the closing process.)

3. Based on the income statement you prepared and the results of prior years, evaluate the company's financial performance in fiscal 2004.

4. Review the Statement of Cash Flows and evaluate Weis Markets' sources and uses of cash over the past three years.

5. Did Weis Markets' managers create value for the shareholders in fiscal 2004? Support your response and explain any assumptions you made.

Weis Markets, Inc.
Consolidated Balance Sheets

(dollars in thousands) December 25, 2004 and December 27, 2003	2004	2003
Assets		
Current:		
Cash and cash equivalents	$	$ 73,340
Marketable securities		17,207
Accounts receivable, net		34,111
Inventories		173,552
Prepaid expenses		3,987
Income taxes recoverable		—
Deferred income taxes		4,793
Total current asset		306,990
Property and equipment, net		414,172
Goodwill		15,731
Intangible and other assets		7,422
	$	$ 744,315
Liabilities		
Current:		
Accounts payable	$	$ 95,238
Accrued expenes		20,156
Accrued self-insurance		17,710
Payable to employee benefit plans		9,626
Income taxes payable		1,955
Total current liabilities		144,685
Deferred income taxes		24,182
Shareholders' Equity		
Common stock, no par value, 100,800,000 shares authorized, 32,997,157 and 32,989,507 shares issued, respectively		7,971
Retained earnings		702,961
Accumulated other comprehensive income		4,428
		715,360
Treasury stock at cost, 5,964,330 and 5,849,589 shares, respectively		(139,912)
Total shareholders' equity		575,448
	$	$ 744,315

See accompanying notes to consolidated financial statements.

Annual Report 2004

Weis Markets, Inc.
Consolidated Statements of Income

(dollars in thousands, except shares and per share amounts)
For the Fiscal Years Ended December 25, 2004,
December 27, 2003, and December 28, 2002

	2004	2003	2002
Net sales	$	$ 2,042,499	$ 1,999,364
Cost of sales, including warehousing and distribution expenses		1,505,926	1,471,479
Gross profit on sales		536,573	527,885
Operating, general, and administrative expenses		465,952	448,478
Income from operations		70,621	79,407
Investment income		1,220	879
Other income		16,363	14,400
Income before provision for income taxes		88,204	94,686
Provision for income taxes		33,628	35,537
Net income	$	$ 54,576	$ 59,149
Weighted average shares outstanding, basic		27,186,277	27,201,170
Weighted average shares outstanding, diluted		27,186,277	27,202,435
Cash dividends per share	$	$ 1.10	$ 1.08
Basic and diluted earnings per share	$	$ 2.01	$ 2.17

See accompanying notes to consolidated financial statements.

Weis Markets, Inc.
Consolidated Statements of Shareholders' Equity

(dollars in thousands, except shares) For the Fiscal Years Ended December 25, 2004, December 27, 2003, and December 28, 2002	Common Stock		Retained Earnings	Accumulated Other Comprehensive Income	Treasury Stock		Total Shareholders' Equity
	Shares	Amount			Shares	Amount	
Balance at December 29, 2001	32,978,037	$7,630	$648,522	$6,479	5,774,830	$(137,267)	$525,364
Net income	–	–	59,149	–	–	–	59,149
Other comprehensive income, net of tax	–	–	–	(2,334)	–	–	(2,334)
Comprehensive income							56,815
Shares issued for options	8,300	252	–	–	–	–	252
Treasury stock purchased	–	–	–	–	17,970	(622)	(622)
Dividends paid	–	–	(29,377)	–	–	–	(29,377)
Balance at December 28, 2002	32,986,337	7,882	678,294	4,145	5,792,800	(137,889)	552,432
Net income	–	–	54,576	–	–	–	54,576
Other comprehensive income, net of tax	–	–	–	283	–	–	283
Comprehensive income							54,859
Shares issued for options	3,170	89	–	–	–	–	89
Treasury stock purchased	–	–	–	–	56,789	(2,023)	(2,023)
Dividends paid	–	–	(29,909)	–	–	–	(29,909)
Balance at December 27, 2003	32,989,507	7,971	702,961	4,428	5,849,589	(139,912)	575,448
Net income	–	–	57,191	–	–	–	57,191
Other comprehensive income, net of tax	–	–	–	319	–	–	319
Comprehensive income							57,510
Shares issued for options	7,650	228	–	–	–	–	228
Treasury stock purchased	–	–	–	–	114,741	(4,048)	(4,048)
Dividends paid	–	–	(57,438)	–	–	–	(57,438)
Balance at December 25, 2004	32,997,157	$8,199	$702,714	$4,747	5,964,330	$(143,960)	$571,700

See accompanying notes to consolidated financial statements.

Weis Markets, Inc.
Consolidated Statements of Cash Flows

(dollars in thousands)
For the Fiscal Years Ended December 23, 2004, December 27, 2003, and December 28, 2002

	2004	2003	2002
Cash flows from operating activities:			
Net income	$ 57,191	$ 54,576	$ 59,149
Adjustment to reconcile net income to net cash provided by operating activities:			
Depreciation	40,614	40,196	41,885
Amortization	5,721	6,274	5,095
Loss (gain) on disposition of fixed assets	1,438	122	(3,620)
Gain on sale of marketable securities	(52)	–	–
Changes in operating assets and liabilities:			
Inventories	8,508	9,280	(12,880)
Accounts receivable and prepaid expenses	(2,930)	(3,930)	656
Income taxes recoverable	(1,729)	–	3,395
Accounts payable and other liabilities	4,648	42	9,551
Income taxes payable	(1,955)	(4,157)	6,112
Deferred income taxes	6,786	3,721	(3,561)
Net cash provided by operating activities	118,240	106,124	105,782
Cash flows from investing activities			
Purchase of property and equipment	(82,766)	(35,928)	(46,056)
Proceeds from the sale of property and equipment	9,086	4,271	14,520
Purchase of marketable securities	(64,900)	–	(5,000)
Proceeds from maturities of marketable securities	66,406	1,023	9
Proceeds from sale of marketable securities	86	–	–
Net cash used in investing activities	(72,088)	(30,634)	(36,527)
Cash flows from financing activities			
Payments of long-term debt	–	–	(25,000)
Proceeds from issuance of common stock	228	89	252
Dividends paid	(57,438)	(29,909)	(29,377)
Purchase of treasury stock	(4,048)	(2,023)	(622)
Net cash used in financing activities	(61,258)	(31,843)	(54,747)
Net (decrease) increase in cash and cash equivalents	(15,106)	43,647	14,508
Cash and cash equivalents at beginning of year	73,340	29,693	15,185
Cash and cash equivalents at end of year	$ 58,234	$ 73,340	$ 29,693

See accompanying notes to consolidated financial statements.

► APPENDIX 3A: DEBITS, CREDITS, AND JOURNAL ENTRIES

We did not mention debits, credits, or journal entries in the chapter because they are not necessary to understand the mechanics of financial reporting. However, they are a useful tool and the vocabulary surrounding them is in widespread use. In this appendix, we describe journal entries and illustrate how they can be used to prepare a set of financial statements.

A journal entry is simply a vehicle used to enter a transaction into the financial reporting system—one journal entry is recorded in the journal for each transaction. Each journal entry contains at least two account names and a monetary value, and the structure of the entry indicates whether the accounts are increased or decreased by the monetary value. Each account is also represented in the ledger, where the account balances are maintained. The following illustration shows a journal entry indicating that a cash amount of $100 was received from a customer, who had previously made a purchase on account. The journal entry serves to record the transaction, which is also represented in the ledger where the balances in the cash and accounts receivable accounts are increased and decreased, respectively. The $4,280 balance in the cash account has been increased to $4,380, and the $950 balance in the accounts receivable account has been reduced to $850.

Journal:

Cash	100	
Accounts receivable		100

To record the receipt of cash from a customer

Ledger:

Cash		Accounts receivable	
4,280		950	
100			100
4,380		850	

Note that both the journal entry and the accounts in the ledger have a left (debit) and a right (credit) side. In the above transaction, the cash account was debited (the dollar amount was recorded on the left side), and the accounts receivable account was credited (the dollar amount was recorded on the right side).

► JOURNAL ENTRIES AND THE ACCOUNTING EQUATION

One way to learn journal entries is to view them as shown in Figure 3A-1, which provides a systematic way of converting transactions to journal entries. The top of the box is an expression of the accounting equation. Answers to the three questions shown in Figure 3A-1 identify the three components of each transaction: (1) the accounts affected, (2) the direction of the effect (increase or decrease), and (3) the monetary value of the transaction.

Increases in asset accounts and decreases in liability and shareholders' equity accounts are always represented on the debit (left) side of the journal entry. Decreases in asset accounts and increases in liability and shareholders' equity accounts are always represented on the credit (right) side of the journal entry. Recall that revenue, expense, and dividend accounts are all part of the shareholders' equity account: retained earnings. Thus, revenues, which increase retained earnings, are recorded on the credit side of the journal entry; expenses and dividends, which decrease retained earnings, are recorded on the debit side of the journal entry.

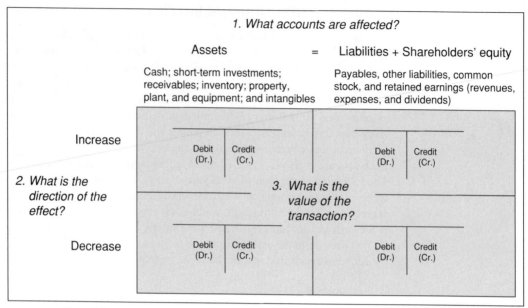

Figure 3A-1. Journal Entry Box

Figure 3A-1 shows that journal entries have been devised so that transactions are recorded in a way that always maintains the equality of the accounting equation. Debits always equal credits, and accordingly, assets always equal liabilities plus shareholders' equity.

▶ PERMANENT AND TEMPORARY ACCOUNTS, AND THE CLOSING PROCESS

There are five categories of financial statement accounts: assets, equities (including liabilities and shareholder equity accounts), revenues, expenses, and dividends. The first two account categories (assets and equities) are called permanent accounts because the balances in these accounts are continually accumulated and maintained from one period to the next. That is, the ending balance for an asset account (say cash) at the close of 20X1 becomes the beginning balance for 20X2. These accounts comprise the balance sheet.

Revenue, expense, and dividend accounts, on the other hand, are maintained only for individual periods, and at the end of each period the account balance is set to zero; that is, values accumulated in these accounts (called temporary accounts) during the period are transferred to retained earnings (a permanent account). This process is called closing, and it is accomplished by recording journal entries in each of the temporary accounts that exactly negate the balances accumulated in those accounts. The opposite sides of those entries are recorded in the retained earnings account. At the beginning of the following period, the balances in the temporary accounts begin again to accumulate the revenue, expense, or dividend activity for that period.

In Figure 3A-2, we illustrate how a set of financial statements can be prepared from a set of transactions using journal entries, a ledger, and the closing process. We use the same information (beginning balance sheet and 17 transactions) used earlier in the text for Illustration, Inc. See Figures 3-8 through 3-12. In this way, you can see that the financial statements can be prepared using either the accounting equation or the journal–ledger process. The two methods are equivalent.

The beginning balances for the balance sheet (asset and equity) accounts in the ledger are the same as those on the 20X1 balance sheet for Illustration, Inc. (see Figure 3-8). The balances for the asset accounts are maintained on the left (debit) side, while the balances for the equity accounts are maintained on the right (credit) side (see Figure 3A-1). The beginning balances in the revenue, expense, and dividend accounts are zero because they are temporary accounts; their previous period balances were closed to retained earnings.

Journal entries 1 through 17 represent how the 17 transactions entered into by Illustration, Inc., during the period were recorded in the journal and the ledger. To understand the structure of each transaction and how it affects the accounting equation, you may wish to refer to Figure 3A-1. Journal entries 18 through 20 comprise the closing process, where the balances in the temporary revenue and expense accounts are transferred to the income summary account (18) and then from the income summary account to retained earnings (19). In journal entry 20, the balance in the temporary dividend account is transferred directly to retained earnings. Although all temporary account balances are transferred to retained earnings, the balances in the revenue and expense are transferred first to the income summary account (itself a temporary account) to highlight the important net income number ($700).

The ending balances of the permanent balance sheet accounts comprise Illustration, Inc.'s 20X2 balance sheet (Figure 3-10); Illustration's income statement (Figure 3-11) can be constructed from closing journal entry 18; the activity in the shareholders' equity accounts in the ledger (common stock, treasury stock, and retained earnings) comprises the statement of shareholders' equity (Figure 3-12); and the entries in the cash ledger account appear on the statement of cash flows (Figure 3-13).

1 Cash (+A) 10,000
    Common Stock (+CC) 10,000

2 Cash (+A) 8,000
    Long-Term Note Payable (+L) 8,000

3 Accrued Payables(–L) 2,200
    Cash (–A) 2,200

4 PP&E (+A) 5,000
    Cash (–A) 5,000

5 Patent (+A) 1,000
    Cash (–A) 1,000

6 Inventory (+A) 3,000
    Accounts Payable (+L) 3,000

7a Accounts Receivable (+A) 6,000
    Sale of Goods (R, +RE) 6,000

7b Cost of Goods Sold (E, –RE) 1,500
    Inventory (–A) 1,500

8 Cash (+A) 4,000
    Fees Earned (R, +RE) 4,000

9 Selling and Administrative (E, –RE) 4,000
    Cash (–A) 4,000

10 Cash (+A) 4,500
    Accounts Receivable (–A) 4,500

11 Interest Expense (E, –RE) 200
    Long-Term Note Payable (–L) 1,000
    Cash (–A) 1,200

12 Treasury Stock (–CC) 3,500
    Cash (–A) 3,500

13 Accounts Payable (–L) 1,800
    Cash (–A) 1,800

14 Accrued Expenses (E, –RE) 2,500*
    Accrued Payables (+L) 2,500
    *Includes income taxes

15 Depreciation Expense (E,–RE) 1,000
    PP&E (–A) 1,000

16 Amortization Expense (E, –RE) 100
    Patent (–A) 100

17 Dividend (–RE) 500
    Cash (–A) 500

18 Sale of Goods 6,000
    Fees Earned 4,000
      Cost of Goods Sold 1,500
      Selling and Administrative 4,000
      Accrued Expenses 2,500
      Depreciation Expense 1,000
      Amortization Expense 100
      Interest Expense 200
      Income Summary 700

19 Income Summary 700
    Retained Earnings 700

20 Retained Earnings 500
    Dividends 500

Note: The effects on the financial statements noted in parenthesis are not included in the closing entries because they were already included in the entries (1–17) to record the original transactions.

A = Asset
CC = Contributed capital, component of shareholders' equity
E = Expense
L = Liability
R = Revenue
RE = Retained earnings, component of shareholders' equity

Cash

Debit	Ref	Credit	Ref
3,000			
10,000	1	2,200	3
8,000	2	5,000	4
		1,000	5
4,000	8		
4,500	10	1,200	11
		3,500	12
		1,800	13
		500	17
10,300			

Accounts Receivable

Debit	Ref	Credit	Ref
2,000			
6,000	7a	4,500	10
3,500			

Inventory

Debit	Ref	Credit	Ref
800			
3,000	6	1,500	7b
2,300			

PP&E

Debit	Ref	Credit	Ref
6,000			
5,000	4	1,000	15
10,000			

Patent

Debit	Ref	Credit	Ref
500			
1,000	5	100	16
1,400			

Accounts Payable

Debit	Ref	Credit	Ref
		500	
1,800	13	3,000	6
		1,700	

Accrued Payables

Debit	Ref	Credit	Ref
		2,200	3
2,500	14		
		2,500	

Long-Term Note Payable

Debit	Ref	Credit	Ref
		1,000	
1,000	11	8,000	2
		8,000	

Common Stock

Debit	Ref	Credit	Ref
		5,000	
		10,000	1
		15,000	

Retained Earnings

Debit	Ref	Credit	Ref
		4,100	
500	20	700	19
		4,300	

Treasury Stock

Debit	Ref	Credit	Ref
500			
3,500	12		
4,000			

Accrued Expenses

Debit	Ref	Credit	Ref
		2,500	14
		2,500	18

Sale of Goods

Debit	Ref	Credit	Ref
		–	
6,000	18	6,000	7a
		–	

Fees Earned

Debit	Ref	Credit	Ref
		–	
4,000	18	4,000	8
		–	

Cost of Goods Sold

Debit	Ref	Credit	Ref
–			
1,500	7b	1,500	18
–			

SG&A Expense

Debit	Ref	Credit	Ref
–			
4,000	9	4,000	18
–			

Income Summary

Debit	Ref	Credit	Ref
–		–	
700	19	700	18
–		–	

Depreciation Expense

Debit	Ref	Credit	Ref
–			
1,000	15	1,000	18
–			

Amortization Expense

Debit	Ref	Credit	Ref
–			
100	16	100	18
–			

Interest Expense

Debit	Ref	Credit	Ref
–			
200	11	200	18
–			

Dividends

Debit	Ref	Credit	Ref
–			
500	17	500	20
–			

CHAPTER 4

Using Financial Statements to Analyze Value Creation

ANALYSIS CHALLENGE: THERE IS SO MUCH TO LOOK AT. WHERE DO I START?

Your executive vice president walks into your office and tosses several thick sets of financial statements and notes onto your desk. "We are streamlining our supply chain and narrowing our list of key suppliers. We need to be sure they are financially sound. The last thing we need is to find ourselves unable to deliver our goods and services because a supplier has shut its doors. I want you to review these documents and rank these companies on the basis of their financial strength. I'll need your report by day's end."

There is a lot to look through. Where do you start? Which numbers help identify performance, profitability, efficiency, leverage, risk, and solvency? What you need is a comprehensive model that links the financial statements to value creation and its determinants.

Management's goal is to generate a return on the owners' investment (return on equity [ROE]) that exceeds the cost of equity (value creation). In this chapter, we describe how the financial statements can be analyzed to identify how operating, investing, and financing decisions affect ROE. Such analysis allows us to assess whether and how management has created value in the past, and establishes a starting point for whether and how management will create value in the future. We use this financial analysis framework to analyze the financial statements of Saks Incorporated and Nordstrom, two high-end retailers, and it plays an important role in the organization of the remaining chapters in this text.

ANALYSIS EXAMPLE: SAKS AND NORDSTROM—OVERVIEW

Before we begin our analysis of Saks' and Nordstrom's financial statements, we review some key figures (all figures are in thousands of U.S. dollars). Saks' and Nordstrom's income statements for the years ending January 29, 2005, and January 31, 2004, and balance sheets at those dates, along with the February 1, 2003, balance sheet are provided in the Appendix to Chapter 4. Some line items have been relabeled and combined to simplify the example. Full financial statements for Saks and Nordstrom are available from their corporate Web sites.

	Saks		Nordstrom	
	2005	2004	2005	2004
Net Income	$ 61,085	$ 82,827	$ 393,450	$ 242,841
Sales	6,437,277	6,055,055	7,131,388	6,491,673
Total assets	4,704,079	4,654,869	4,605,390	4,465,688
Shareholders' equity	2,084,417	2,322,168	1,788,994	1,634,009

The data reveal some very interesting facts. First, the companies are of comparable size—their asset and sales levels are similar and growing. Second, while both companies have positive net income, Saks' profits are considerably lower and on the decline. Furthermore, Saks shareholders' equity is on the decline, whereas Nordstrom's is increasing. We delve into the details as we proceed through the chapter.

► DETERMINANTS OF VALUE CREATION: ANALYZING RETURN ON EQUITY

In Chapter 1, we learned that **return on equity** is calculated as

$$\text{Return on equity} = \frac{\text{Net income}}{\text{Average common shareholders' equity}}$$

The net income number used in this ratio is normally the "bottom line" reported on the income statement. Recall, however, that certain non-operating revenues and expenses on the income statement may not reflect changes in the firm's wealth and/or be expected to persist in the future. Consequently, one may wish to adjust the "bottom line" net income number for these items.[1] Average shareholders' equity is normally computed as the simple average of the shareholders' equity balance during the year.[2]

Because the comparison between ROE and the cost of equity is the indicator of value creation, analysts are very interested in changes in ROE across time for a given firm, as well as ROE comparisons across similar firms (e.g., in the same industry) as of a specific time. The former indicates whether a company's value creation is improving or deteriorating; the latter indicates which companies are creating the most value. Analysis can also include both simultaneously—that is, how does a company's value creation across time compare to that of other companies?

Analysts not only use ROE to track and compare value creation, but they are also interested in *why* value creation changes across time, and *why* one company's value creation exceeds another's. What features about a company's operating, investing, and financing decisions drive changes in value creation or explain why one company creates more value than another? These features are called value drivers, and the identification and analysis of key value drivers is an important objective of financial statement analysis. Managers can use the same tools to predict and explain how their actions will lead to future value creation.

A well-known framework designed to identify value drivers, by analyzing changes in ROE across time and differences in ROE across companies, is called the DuPont (ROE)

[1]Technically, we should use comprehensive income in the numerator. Given current accounting rules, however, many of the differences between net income and comprehensive income are transitory. That is, these differences are due to items not central to performance evaluation. Nonetheless, savvy analysts evaluate these items to ascertain for themselves whether they are central to past and future performance evaluation, and, if so, they belong in the numerator.

[2]A more sophisticated approach would be to compute a weighted average shareholders' equity balance, where balances are be weighted by the amount of time they are outstanding during the year.

model, which is described by the following algebraic expression.[3] That is,

$$
\underset{\text{Average common equity}}{\underset{\text{Net income}}{\text{Return on equity}}} = \underset{\text{Average assets}}{\underset{\text{NI + Interest expense*}}{\text{Return on assets}}} \times \underset{\text{Average common equity}}{\underset{\text{Average assets}}{\underset{\text{leverage}}{\text{Capital structure}}}} \times \underset{\text{NI + Interest expense*}}{\underset{\text{Net income}}{\underset{\text{leverage}}{\text{Common equity}}}}
$$

*After-tax cost of interest = Interest expense × [1−Tax rate]

This expression defines three financial statement ratios (return on assets (ROA), capital structure leverage, and common equity leverage) that when multiplied together equal ROE. This equality means that changes in these ratios lead to changes in ROE. For example, if common equity leverage and capital structure leverage are unchanged, an increase in ROA leads to an increase in ROE. An important goal for managers, therefore, is to increase ROE by taking actions that increase its determinants. Although increasing leverage can increase ROE, the additional reliance on debt associated with increasing leverage also elevates the firm's risk and cost of capital. Consequently, attempts to increase ROE should first be directed at improving operating and investing decisions, which should lead to increases in ROA, the ratio that we discuss next.

ANALYSIS CHALLENGE: AVERAGE BALANCES? ENDING BALANCES?

When computing financial ratios, balance sheet figures are often compared to income statement figures. Because the income statement figures are for a *period of time* (e.g., one fiscal year or a fiscal quarter), it makes conceptual sense to compare them to the average balance sheet figures for that period. We use a simple average ([Beginning balance + Ending balance]/2).

When data are limited—for example, when only one annual report is at hand—analysts typically compare the income statement data with the end of period balance sheet amounts.

Although not as conceptually sound, it represents a pragmatic approach to ratio analysis and allows for more comparisons to be made with a fixed set of data.

In the interest of simplicity, we present many ratios of income statement and balance sheet data without the term "average" in their definition.

For ratios that involve only balance sheet data, averages are seldom used. Those ratios measure financial position and risk at a *point in time*.

Return on assets is defined as

$$
\text{Return on assets} = \frac{\text{Net income} + \text{Interest expense} (1 - \text{Tax rate})}{\text{Average assets}}
$$

The numerator represents the total return generated by the company to both the debt and equity capital providers, and the denominator represents their total investment. Another way to think about the numerator is to consider it the after-tax *operating* profit of the firm. In other words, it represents the after-tax profit that the company would have earned had it been debt-free and thus interest-free. As such, ROA is the overall rate of return generated by management, independent of the firm's financing decisions. According to the model, increases in ROA increase ROE only if the ROA increase exceeds any decreases in common equity leverage and capital structure leverage.

[3]This version of the DuPont model was introduced in Selling, T. I., and C. P. Stickney, "Disaggregating the Rate of Return on Common Shareholders' Equity: A New Approach," *Accounting Horizons* (vol. 4, no. 4, December 1990).

INSIGHT: WHY ADJUST INTEREST EXPENSE FOR TAXES?

Consider two managers. Both are equally talented and manage a set of identical assets for different firms. One firm uses no debt to finance its assets. The other does. Comparing ROA across managers without adjusting for interest expense would unfairly penalize the manager at the debt-financed firm, even though the manager may have had no say in the financing decision. That is, other things being equal, the net income of the debt-financed firm will be lower because it has an additional expense: interest on its debt. However, that interest expense is tax deductible and helps reduce the company's tax bill. The following example demonstrates that a fair comparison of the managers needs to consider both the interest expenses and the associated taxes.

	Equity Inc.	Debt Inc.
Sales	$10,000	$10,000
Operating expenses	6,000	6,000
Earnings before interest and tax	4,000	4,000
Interest expense	—	500
Earnings before tax	4,000	3,500
Tax at 40%	1,600	1,400
Net income	2,400	2,100
Average assets	$10,000	$10,000
ROA = NI / Average assets	24%	21%
ROA = [NI + Interest] / Average assets	24%	26%
ROA = [NI + Interest (1 − 0.4)] / Average assets	24%	24%

Calculating ROA as (Net Income / Average Assets) means that the manager at Equity Inc. reports ROA of 24%, considerably more than the 21% earned by the manager of Debt Inc. Because both managers have generated the same operating profit (i.e., profit independent of the financing of the assets), this comparison unfairly penalizes the manager at Debt Inc.

Simply adding interest back to net income ignores the fact that Debt Inc. lowered its tax costs with the interest. However, when interest is added back net of the taxes it sheltered, the performance of the two managers is now equal.

INSIGHT: ROA AND VALUE CREATION

The firm is not creating value on its investments in assets until the cost of paying for those assets is covered. Net income plus after-tax interest expense represents the profit of the business before considering how the business was financed. This permits analysts to evaluate managers' operating performance across firms that have made different financing decisions.

Value is created when this measure of profit exceeds the cost of both debt and equity. In other words, the firm creates value when ROA exceeds the cost of the debt and equity financing.

Another way to view ROA is in terms of two of the key activities of the firm: operating and investing.

$$\text{ROA} = \frac{\text{(After-tax) Operating profit}}{\text{Assets}} = \frac{\text{Results of operating activities}}{\text{Results of investing activities}}$$

ROA can be decomposed further into the product of two key financial ratios: profit margin (or operating return on sales) and asset turnover. Changes in profit margin and asset turnover lead to changes in ROE through their effects on ROA. Consider a company, for example, that makes a decision that increases profit margin without decreasing asset turnover. This decision would lead to higher ROA and, if the leverage ratios were unchanged, higher ROE and the creation of shareholder value.

$$\textbf{Return on assets} \quad = \quad \begin{array}{c}\textbf{Profit margin} \\ \textbf{(Return on sales)}\end{array} \quad \times \quad \begin{array}{c}\textbf{Asset} \\ \textbf{turnover}\end{array}$$

$$\text{ROA} = \frac{\text{NI} + \text{Interest expense}^*}{\text{Assets}} = \frac{\text{NI} - \text{Interest expense}^*}{\text{Sales}} \times \frac{\text{Sales}}{\text{Assets}}$$

$$^*\text{After-tax cost of interest} = \text{Interest expense} \times (1 - \text{Tax rate})$$

INSIGHT: MANY ROADS TO ROA

A given level of ROA can be achieved in different ways. Consider two retailers: Weis Markets, a grocery store, and Lowe's, a home improvement chain. As illustrated below, grocery stores like Weis generate returns through relatively low profit margins combined with relatively high asset turnovers, while Lowe's operates in a higher margin, lower asset turnover environment.

	Weis Markets (year ended December 25, 2004)	Lowe's (year ended January 28, 2005)
ROA	7.67%	11.43%
Profit margin	2.73%	6.26%
Asset turnover	2.81	1.83

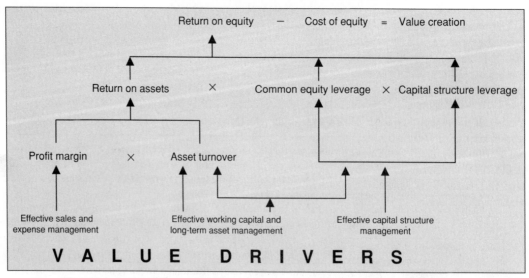

Figure 4-1. Value Drivers and Financial Statement Ratios

Figure 4-1 illustrates the ROE framework and relates it to three important value drivers : (1) effective sales and expense management, (2) effective working capital and long-term asset management, and (3) effective capital structure management. **Effective sales and expense management** creates value by increasing profit margin, which increases ROA, which, in turn, increases ROE. **Effective working capital** and **long-term asset management** creates value by increasing asset turnover, which, in turn, increases ROA and ROE. **Effective capital structure management** can increase ROE by increasing the leverage ratios, but more leverage leads to more interest expense and lower common equity leverage. A close relationship also exists between these three value drivers and operating, investing, and financing activities. Operating activities involve both sales and expense, and working capital management; investing activities involve long-term asset management; and financing activities involve capital structure management. In the next section, we discuss financial statement ratios that measure these value drivers.

ANALYSIS EXAMPLE: SAKS AND NORDSTROM

Saks and Nordstrom are two high-end retailers with operations in the United States. A high-level examination of their ROEs reveals two very different stories. At Saks, ROE is well below any reasonable cost of equity and on the decline. At Nordstrom, ROE is healthy and on the rise. We will look more carefully at the reasons why in the following sections. What is apparent already is that Nordstrom has a healthier ROA (driven by both better return on sales [profit margin] and asset turnover) and a better managed capital structure. Although Nordstrom's capital structure leverage is higher than Saks', its higher common equity leverage shows that the leverage is not as costly as it is to Saks. Nordstrom shareholders keep 88 cents per dollar of operating profit (the other 12 cents are interest expense). Meanwhile, Saks' shareholders keep only 42 cents.

$$ROE = \frac{\text{Net income}}{\text{Common equity}} = \frac{\text{NI} + \text{Interest expense}}{\text{Sales}} \times \frac{\text{Sales}}{\text{Assets}} \times \frac{\text{Assets}}{\text{Common equity}} \times \frac{\text{NI}}{\text{NI} + \text{Interest expense}}$$

	Saks		**Nordstrom**	
	2005	2004	2005	2004
Return on equity	2.77%	3.61%	22.99%	16.16%
Return on assets:	3.07%	3.59%	9.82%	7.05%
Return on sales	2.23%	2.73%	6.24%	4.65%
Asset turnover	1.38	1.31	1.57	1.52
Capital structure leverage	2.12	2.01	2.65	2.85
Common equity leverage	0.42	0.50	0.88	0.80

► MEASURES OF EFFECTIVE SALES AND EXPENSE MANAGEMENT

Costs that generate revenue in the current period are called operating expenses. They are listed on the income statement, and are part of operating activities. Examples include cost of goods sold, selling and administrative expenses, taxes, interest, and other expenses that arise in the normal operations of a business. Effective management of the relationship between operating expenses and revenues is measured by **profit margin**, often called **return on sales**, which indicates the amount of return generated by a dollar of sales in a given period.

For example, a profit margin of 0.05 indicates that a 5-cent operating return was derived from each dollar of sales.

$$\text{Return on sales} = \frac{\text{Net income} + \text{Interest expense} (1 - \text{Tax rate})}{\text{Sales}}$$

The numerator includes the return to both the debt and equity holders, and the denominator represents the revenues recognized during the period. This ratio measures a company's ability to generate and sell products and/or services while controlling expenses. To increase this ratio, management can increase sales at a given level of expenses and/or reduce expenses at a given level of sales. Increasing profit margin increases ROA as long as asset turnover is not decreased by a larger amount, which could occur, for example, if management made a large asset investment to increase sales or reduce expenses.

Like ROA, profit margin is a broad measure that can be broken down into its components, each of which can provide a better understanding of why profit margin has changed across time or differs across companies. Each key operating expense can be expressed as a percentage of sales. Examples are listed below, but one can choose any important expense and analyze it in this manner. For example,

$$\frac{\text{Cost of goods sold}}{\text{Sales}},$$

$$\frac{(\text{Sales} - \text{Cost of goods sold})}{\text{Sales}} \text{ (this ratio is known as the gross margin),}$$

$$\frac{\text{Selling, general, and administrative expenses}}{\text{Sales}}, \text{ or}$$

$$\frac{\text{Research and development}}{\text{Sales}}.$$

DRILLING DOWN—PROFITABILITY AND COMMON-SIZE INCOME STATEMENTS

$$\text{ROE} = \frac{\text{Net income}}{\text{Common Equity}} = \frac{\text{NI} + \text{Interest expense}}{\text{Sales}} \times \frac{\text{Sales}}{\text{Assets}} \times \frac{\text{Assets}}{\text{Common equity}} \times \frac{\text{NI}}{\text{NI} + \text{Interest expense}}$$

A widely used tool for profitability analysis is the *common-size income statement*, which is generated by dividing each line on the income statement by the respective year's net sales. Trends in key expenses across companies and across time are easily seen with this tool. Lowe's Companies, Inc., provides this analysis as a courtesy to readers of its income statement (see the end of chapter case in Chapter 1).

Common-size balance sheets can also be created. Each balance sheet line item is divided by the respective balance of ending total assets. Common-size cash flow statements are seldom seen.

Another important expense is income tax expense. Rather than divide income tax expense by sales, analysts usually focus on the average tax rate—the ratio of tax expense to pretax income. That is,

$$\text{Average tax rate} = \frac{\text{Income tax expense}}{\text{Income before tax}}$$

ANALYSIS EXAMPLE: SAKS AND NORDSTROM—RETURN ON SALES

We observed that Saks' ROA was on the decline while Nordstrom's was on the rise. This is due in part to similar trends in their respective return on sales. Key data from common-size income statements help explain why.

$$\text{Return on sales} = \frac{\text{Net income} + \text{Interest expense } (1 - \text{Tax rate})}{\text{Sales}}$$

	Saks		Nordstrom	
	2005	2004	2005	2004
Return on sales	2.23%	2.73%	6.24%	4.65%
Gross margin	37.93%	37.86%	36.07%	35.09%
SG&A, as stated	25.08%	24.40%	28.33%	29.94%
SG&A, adjusted	34.42%	33.93%	28.33%	29.94%
Tax rate	27.49%	24.62%	39.21%	39.01%

Saks' gross margin is slightly higher than Nordstrom's, but relatively unchanged. Nordstrom's gross margin increased by 98 basis points in 2005. That is a significant increase given that it applies to the entire sales figure for the year.

Taken at face value, Saks seems to have significantly lower selling, general, and administrative (SG&A) costs. However, that is somewhat misleading; Nordstrom's SG&A includes a variety of items that Saks reports on separate income statement lines. When those items are included in the "adjusted" SG&A figure, we see that Saks' advantage in gross margin is completely lost. Saks' SG&A is over 600 basis points higher than Nordstrom's, and it is increasing. Nordstrom, at 28.33% SG&A, reduced expenses in 2005 substantially.

Finally, we observe that Saks' tax rate is substantially lower than Nordstrom's. A large portion of the difference relates to adjustments for prior years' losses and other tax matters that are not likely to recur (these are explained in the notes to Saks' financial statements). Recurring or not, the lower tax rate is not enough to make up for the higher operating costs that Saks incurred. Overall, Nordstrom's return on sales is well over two times greater than Saks'—an important reason for the difference in overall ROE.

▶ MEASURES OF EFFECTIVE ASSET MANAGEMENT

Effective asset management involves two elements: (1) investing in the *appropriate amount* of assets, and (2) finding the *proper balance* between producing assets, which generate returns, and more liquid operating assets, which help to meet debt obligations as they come due and provide a buffer against uncertain future business downturns. Asset turnover and solvency ratios provide valuable information about these two elements.

Asset Turnover Ratios

In general, a company manages its assets effectively when a given level of profit can be earned with fewer assets. A small investment that generates a large amount of revenue is preferred to a large investment that generates a small amount of revenue because the level of asset investment must be financed, via debt or equity, at a cost. This concept can be applied to a company's assets in total or to individual assets (e.g., receivables, inventories, or fixed assets).

Recall that total **asset turnover**, a direct determinant of ROA, is defined as

$$\text{Asset turnover} = \frac{\text{Sales}}{\text{Average total assets}}$$

This ratio indicates how many sales dollars are generated by a $1 investment in total assets. A ratio of 3, for example, indicates that over a given period, on average, a $1 investment in assets generated $3 in sales revenue. Because total assets equal liabilities plus shareholders' equity (the basic accounting equation), total assets represents the total investment of both the debt and equity holders.[4] Consequently, an increase in asset turnover signals that the investments by the debt and equity holders are being managed more efficiently.

Holding leverage constant, increasing asset turnover increases ROA as long as the increase in asset turnover exceeds any decrease in profit margin. Asset turnover, for example, can be increased by increasing revenue, but if the additional revenue is not very profitable, profit margin may decrease. Furthermore, any increase in ROA generated by an increase in asset turnover will result in higher ROE only if the increase in ROA exceeds any decrease in leverage caused by the increase in asset turnover. For example, issuing equity to finance the acquisition of an asset, whose turnover increases ROA, may decrease leverage by more than the increase in ROA, thus reducing ROE.

OUTSOURCING AND ASSET TURNOVER

In recent years, outsourcing has become a popular way to create value. How does it work? How does it relate to asset turnover? Consider Nike, a company examined in a case at the end of Chapter 2, which designs footwear and apparel, but does not produce it themselves. Rather, it uses a number of offshore manufacturers. By doing so, Nike benefits from lower labor costs, leading to potentially higher profit margins, while avoiding an investment in manufacturing assets, leading to potentially higher asset turnover.

Will outsourcing always lead to higher ROA? Not necessarily. If lower labor costs are associated with higher defect rates, then higher sales returns will eat into the profit margin.

If offshore production entails higher shipping costs, again, profit margin may suffer. Understand as well that the offshore manufacturers used by Nike must earn a reasonable return on their asset investment to remain in business, which means that their selling prices to Nike must cover their costs. On the other hand, Nike may be able to take advantage of excess capacity in the offshore manufacturing market or share in the benefits of the offshore manufacturers' economies of scale. Determining whether outsourcing is the proper course of action involves analyzing a complex set of relationships—an analysis in which the ROE decomposition can be quite helpful.

Asset turnover is a relatively broad measure that includes all assets in the denominator—long term and (net) current. Turnover ratios for individual assets can also be computed and analyzed. By analyzing the components of asset turnover, one can better understand changes in overall asset turnover. We discuss fixed-asset turnover, accounts receivable turnover, inventory turnover, and accounts payable turnover next.

---

[4] As we discussed in Chapter 2, total assets represents management's investment in operations. A refined measure of that investment nets the reported operating assets with the operating liabilities (in general, the non-interest bearing liabilities). This allows a cleaner measure of ROA: net operating profit relative to net investment in operating assets.

Fixed-asset turnover indicates how many dollars of sales are generated from each dollar invested in property, plant, and equipment (PPE, i.e., fixed assets).

$$\text{Fixed-asset turnover} = \frac{\text{Sales}}{\text{Average PPE}}$$

This ratio can be interpreted much the same way as the total asset turnover ratio, except that it includes only fixed assets in the denominator. As it increases, it indicates that fixed assets are being used more efficiently. Such a trend can be positive because it puts upward pressure on asset turnover, which can increase ROA. On the other hand, increasing fixed-asset turnover can negatively affect profit margin if the revenue generated from the fixed assets is not very profitable, and the effect on leverage will depend on how the fixed assets are financed and at what cost.

INSIGHT: INTERPRETING FIXED-ASSET TURNOVER

Fixed-asset turnover is a measure of asset efficiency. It can be used to evaluate past performance and predict future performance and capital expenditures. For a given investment in fixed assets, a firm able to generate more sales is more efficient. For example, consider two grocery stores. Assume that the stores cost the same amount. The one that generates more sales is more efficient in its use of assets. Whether it is most profitable depends on the profit margin on those sales. In the retail industry, "same store sales" is a measure akin to fixed-asset turnover. The sales level per equivalent store can be compared across time, across companies, and within companies across regions or sales managers.

As a forward-looking analytic tool, fixed-asset turnover can be used to predict capital expenditures and thus, financing needs. For example, assume that a firm has a stable manufacturing technology where each dollar invested in fixed assets generates, say, $2 of annual revenues (2:1 fixed-asset turnover ratio). That is, to support every additional $1 million in sales, an investment of $500,000 in additional fixed assets should be needed. If sales are forecast to rise from $1 million to $1.75 million, for example, then an additional $375,000 investment in manufacturing assets would be necessary. The firm must then find a way to finance the $375,000 investment.

Working capital, defined as current assets less current liabilities, is another element of operating assets that needs to be effectively managed. We break it down into three major pieces, each of which decomposes total asset turnover more finely.

$$\text{Working capital} = \text{Current assets} - \text{Current liabilities}$$

Accounts receivable turnover reflects the number of times during the period the receivables balance was collected.

$$\text{Accounts receivable turnover} = \frac{\text{Credit sales}}{\text{Average accounts receivable}}$$

This ratio is a close cousin of total asset turnover. The numerator is credit sales (which for many companies will be the same as total sales) and the denominator is the asset related to those credit sales (instead of all of the assets).

ANALYSIS CHALLENGE: CASH SALES? CREDIT SALES?

The accounts receivable turnover ratio calls for sales on account, or "credit" sales in the numerator. Internally, most companies know the proportion of their sales on account. What is an analyst to do if those data are not reported? External analysts have several options.

First, based on industry knowledge, the analyst might make an informed estimate of the proportion of cash and credit sales. That estimate might be informed by an under-standing of the target customers, by business segment practices, and so on.

Second, the analyst can accept that there are errors in the ratio's calculation, but hope that the errors are similar across time and companies. If the proportion of cash sales remains relatively steady, then although the absolute ratio is off, comparisons and trend analyses are still helpful.

By themselves, receivables earn no return, so management would like to collect them as soon as possible to put the cash to good use. High receivables turnover suggests effective credit-granting and collection activities, and low turnover indicates late payments and potential bad debts, probably due to credit being granted to poor-risk customers and/or to ineffective collection efforts. A very high turnover, however, is not always desirable; it may indicate overly stringent credit terms, leading to missed sales and lost profits.

INSIGHT: TURNING TURNOVER INTO DAYS OF SALES OUTSTANDING

The accounts receivable turnover ratio indicates how many times, on average, the receivables balance is turned over. Another way to look at the ratio is in terms of the average time it takes to collect receivables. The **average collection period** or **days sales outstanding (DSO)** is measured by dividing the turnover ratio into the number of days in the credit sales figure. For annual data,

$$DSO = 365 \text{ days} / [\text{Net credit sales} / \text{Average accounts receivable}]$$

The number of days it takes, on average, to collect a receivable can be compared across time, companies, business units, sales persons, and relative to the firm's credit policies and turnover targets.

Managing a large receivables balance can be costly and time consuming in terms of bad debts, collection efforts, financing costs, and related record keeping, but offering customers a financing alternative can increase sales significantly. Management must carefully choose a desirable balance between these costs and the sales potential. Many companies choose not to carry receivables, opting instead to accept credit cards like Visa and MasterCard from customers. In these cases, the receivables are being sold to financial institutions that may be in a better position to manage the receivables. This way, companies can offer customers credit without having to manage large receivables balances. Of course, the financial institutions charge a fee for this service.

ROE, VALUE CREATION, AND RECEIVABLES MANAGEMENT

$$\text{ROE} = \frac{\text{Net income}}{\text{Common equity}} = \frac{\text{NI} + \text{Interest expense}}{\text{Sales}} \times \frac{\text{Sales}}{\text{Assets}} \times \frac{\text{Assets}}{\text{Common equity}} \times \frac{\text{NI}}{\text{NI} + \text{Interest expense}}$$

How does managing receivables create value? We saw that the more assets a company holds, the more debt and equity it needs to finance the assets. That financing is costly and holding receivables does not generate returns. Increasing accounts receivable turnover by collecting receivables faster, by itself, does nothing to reduce assets. It simply changes the composition of the asset balance from receivables to cash. But, if that cash can be used to generate returns, ROA could increase, or the cash could be used to pay down debt, pay dividends, or buy back treasury shares, all of which reduce the cost of financing, affording managers the opportunity to create more value.

Inventory turnover measures the speed with which inventories move through operations.

$$\text{Inventory turnover} = \frac{\text{Cost of sales}}{\text{Average inventory}}$$

This ratio, too, is a close cousin of the total asset turnover ratio. The denominator is inventory (instead of total assets) and the numerator is cost of goods sold—the amount of inventory turned over in the period. Sales is not used in the numerator (as we did with total asset turnover) because the sales figure includes the markup on inventory sold. Cost of goods sold, like inventory, is measured at cost.

The ratio compares the amount of inventory carried by a company to the volume of goods sold during the period, reflecting how quickly, on average, inventories are sold. Because profit (and often cash) is usually realized each time inventory is sold and substantial costs are associated with carrying inventories, increasing inventory turnover is normally desirable. However, high inventory turnover can indicate that inventory levels are too low, leading to stock-outs, and lost sales and profits.

Like receivables, managing large inventory balances can be costly and time consuming. The financing costs can be significant; inventory requires space and insurance; and damaged goods, theft, and obsolescence can be significant. Maintaining control over such costs is important, but inventory levels for retailers must be sufficient to meet customer needs and, for manufacturers, must be adequate to support the manufacturing process.

INSIGHT: TURNING TURNOVER INTO DAYS OF SALES IN INVENTORY

The inventory turnover ratio indicates how many times, on average, the inventory balance is turned over. Another way to look at the ratio is in terms of the average time it takes to sell inventory. The **average inventory holding period** or **days sales in inventory (DSI)** is measured by dividing the turnover ratio into the number of days in the cost of goods sold figure. For annual data,

$$\text{DSI} = 365 \text{ days} / [\text{Cost of goods sold} / \text{Average inventory}]$$

The number of days it takes, on average, to sell inventory can be compared across time, companies, business units, purchasing managers, and relative to the firm's targets.

Accounts Payable Turnover is an important part of working capital management because many companies, especially in the retail industry, use their suppliers as a way to finance their inventory purchases. Accounts payable turnover measures how quickly, on average, suppliers are paid—or the extent to which accounts payable is used as a form of inventory financing. We would like to compute the ratio by dividing inventory purchases by average accounts payable, but normally inventory purchases are not disclosed, so instead we estimate it by computing the following ratio:

$$\text{Accounts payable turnover} = \frac{\text{Cost of sales}}{\text{Average accounts payable}}$$

Slow accounts payable turnover can signal solvency problems in that the company may be having difficulty generating cash to pay its suppliers. On the other hand, it may signal a financially strong company that has the negotiating power with its suppliers to use them as an inexpensive form of financing. Using suppliers to finance operations frees up cash that can be used to pay debts and/or invest in assets that generate returns exceeding the cost of capital. Fast accounts payable turnover can signal financial strength or low negotiating power with suppliers.

INSIGHT: TURNING TURNOVER INTO DAYS OF PAYABLES OUTSTANDING

The accounts payable turnover ratio indicates how many times, on average, the payables balance is turned over. Another way to look at the ratio is in terms of the average time it takes to pay the suppliers. The **average days of payables** or **days payable outstanding (DPO)** is measured by dividing the turnover ratio into the number of days in the cost of goods sold figure. For annual data,

DPO = 365 days / [Cost of goods sold / Average accounts payable]

The number of days it takes, on average, to pay suppliers can be compared across time, companies, business units, sales persons, and relative to suppliers terms and the firm's targets.

INSIGHT: WORKING CAPITAL IN PRACTICE

The following quotes are from Excellence in Working Capital Management, *a report based on a mail survey of executives at 196 companies and interviews with executives at 16 others. CFO Research Services and GE Commercial Finance developed and funded the study.*
http://www.cfo.com/printable/article.cfm/3443013?f=options

At The New York Times Co., days sales outstanding (DSO) and days payable outstanding (DPO) are broken down differently than in other industries: DSO is calculated as advertising DSO, circulation DSO, and other DSO; DPO as trade DPO and raw materials DPO—the latter mostly for the newsprint used in newspaper production.

Reports on all six metrics go out each month to the senior executives and financial officers at all 30 of The New York Times Co.'s operating units. Mention of DSO performance often finds its way into senior management's monthly operations meetings, and even occasionally into presentations to securities analysts.

In other cases, the way the business has grown forces management to think about the impression working capital performance makes on shareholders. At biotech company Invitrogen, "We spend a lot of time talking about how the cash you collected funded the products we just acquired from that new company—products that you're now able to go out and sell, and achieve a higher variable comp payment," says Travis Chester, vice president of finance. "And so we keep repeating that those collections are a direct contributor to shareholder value."

Better metrics make it possible to draw these connections, and in turn to link executives' compensation to their working capital performance, completing the chain of incentives that companies are creating. Indeed, nearly three out of four survey respondents say that they either currently tie compensation to improvements in working capital management or plan to do so in the next two years. The proportion of compensation at risk is usually not large—perhaps 5%–10% of the overall formula, say executives interviewed for this report—but it serves to increase individuals' awareness of their responsibility.

The **Cash Conversion Cycle** is a measure that captures the net result of the receivables days, inventory days, and payables days, and normally the lower the number, the better. It is calculated as

$$\text{Cash conversion cycle} = \text{Days of inventory} + \text{Days of receivables} - \text{Days of payables}$$

Value is created by managing relations with customers and suppliers. Firms buy or produce inventory and hold it until they sell it to customers. Then they wait to be paid. In a perfect world, a manager would hold no inventory and be paid by the customer before paying the supplier. That way, the customer provides cash to the company that can be used to reduce financing needs or to invest in profitable operations. Unfortunately, that is usually not the case. Instead, smart managers have to manage the cash conversion cycle so that they carry enough inventory to attract customers to do business with them; they provide credit terms that maximize profit in light of the cost of holding receivables, and they manage their supplier relations so that they obtain the best input prices, including the implicit financing benefit.

DELL'S SUPPLIERS FINANCE ITS WORKING CAPITAL NEEDS

Dell, Inc., is known for its near obsession with managing the cash conversion cycle. The company realizes that this emphasis helps them minimize inventory risks and financing costs, and provides them with a significant competitive advantage. The data reveal that Dell has a negative cash conversion cycle. That is, its suppliers are financing the company's investment in receivables and inventory.

In their fiscal 2005 Form 10-K, they report:

Dell's direct business model allows the company to maintain a leading asset management system in comparison to its major competitors. Dell is capable of minimizing inventory risk while collecting amounts due from customers before paying vendors, thus allowing the company to generate annual cash flows from operating activities that typically exceed net income. The following table presents the components of Dell's cash conversion cycle for each of the past three fiscal years:

	Fiscal Year Ended		
	January 28, 2005	January 30, 2004	January 31, 2003
Days of sales outstanding (a)	32	31	28
Days of supply in inventory	4	3	3
Days in accounts payable	73	70	68
Cash conversion cycle	(37)	(36)	(37)

(a) Dell defers the cost of shipped products awaiting revenue recognition until the goods are delivered and revenue is recognized. Days of sales outstanding include these product costs, which are classified in other current assets. At January 28, 2005, January 30, 2004, and January 31, 2003, days of sales outstanding included days of sales in accounts receivable and days of in-transit customer shipments of 29 and 3 days, 28 and 3 days, and 24 and 4 days, respectively.

(continues)

DELL'S SUPPLIERS FINANCE ITS WORKING CAPITAL NEEDS (*continued*)

The increase in days of sales outstanding at January 28, 2005, from the end of fiscal 2004, was partially due to an increase in non-U.S. revenues where collection periods tend to be longer. Dell defers the cost of shipped products awaiting revenue recognition until the goods are delivered and revenue is recognized. These deferred costs are included in Dell's reported days of sales outstanding because manage-

ment believes that it illustrates a more conservative and accurate presentation of Dell's days of sales outstanding and cash conversion cycle. These deferred costs are recorded in other current assets in Dell's consolidated statement of financial position and totaled $430 million, $387 million, and $423 million as of January 28, 2005, January 30, 2004, and January 31, 2003, respectively.

ANALYSIS EXAMPLE: SAKS AND NORDSTROM—ASSET TURNOVER

Another reason why Saks' trails Nordstrom in ROA is that it doesn't manage its asset base as well. This shows up in a lower asset turnover ratio, as well as in the sub-ratios.

$$\text{Asset turnover} = \frac{\text{Sales}}{\text{Average total assets}}$$

	Saks		Nordstrom	
	2005	2004	2005	2004
Asset turnover	1.38	1.31	1.57	1.52
Fixed asset (PPE) turnover	3.1	2.9	4.1	3.7
Days of receivables			50.5	46.8
Days of inventory	135.5	133.8	72.8	80.3
Days of payables	31.9	28.8	39.8	40.1
Cash conversion cycle	103.7	105.0	83.5	87.0

Nordstrom's PPE turnover improved in fiscal 2005 and exceeds Saks' by a healthy amount. For every dollar invested in land, stores, and fixed assets, Saks generates $3.1 to Nordstrom's $4.1.

The cash conversion cycle data reveal that Nordstrom is much more efficient in its working capital management. Saks no longer manages its own credit card and consequently holds no receivables. Nordstrom holds about 50 days worth of receivables, up from about 47 days in 2004. The company is involved in a receivables securitization program that accelerates cash flow by, in effect, selling its credit card receivables

to investors. We discuss that in more detail in a later chapter. Whatever working capital edge Saks gains by having no receivables, it gives back by holding its inventory for more than 63 days longer than its competitor. Furthermore, while DSI has fallen at Nordstrom, it is increasing at Saks—not a good sign. Finally, Saks pays its suppliers about a full week sooner than does Nordstrom. Although the suppliers are probably happy, it means that Saks must come up with another source of funds to finance its inventory balance—and those funds are likely to be costly.

Solvency Ratios

Several measures straddle the asset management and leverage domains. Earlier, we discussed the advantages of leverage and how increasing leverage puts upward pressure on ROE and value creation. The major disadvantage of leverage is that it contractually obligates the company to future cash payments, increasing the company's risk and forcing management to ensure that cash is available to meet the contractual debt payments. It is important, therefore, that firms manage their assets in total, but also that they have the liquidity they need to meet their obligations. Effective inventory and receivables management, for example, can help ensure that inventory is sellable and receivables can be collected in a timely manner, producing necessary cash. The inventory and receivables turnover ratios provide useful information here. Management can also maintain adequate cash and short-term investment balances to help meet debt obligations, but cash is not a producing asset, and the cost of maintaining a high cash balance can be significant. Companies that find themselves with excess cash normally look to invest it in short-term securities if the excess is expected to be temporary. Companies that have cyclical cash needs often arrange to have **lines of credit** available to them. They draw on the lines when cash is needed and pay it back when cash is generated.

Two solvency ratios provide information about how a company's liquid assets and current obligations are being managed: the current and quick ratios.

The **current ratio** (sometimes called the working capital ratio) compares current assets to current liabilities as of the balance sheet date. That is,

$$\text{Current ratio} = \frac{\text{Current assets}}{\text{Current liabilities}}$$

It measures solvency in that current assets can be used to meet current liabilities. Often, high levels of leverage are associated with high current ratios because leverage and related debt contracts put pressure on management to hold liquid assets and/or restrict short-term payables and certain investments.

The usefulness of the current ratio as a measure of solvency depends on the liquidity of the current assets. Although cash and short-term investments are normally highly liquid, uncertainty exists about whether inventory and receivables will produce cash in the near future. A high current ratio can signal a solvent company, but it also can signal slow-moving inventories or receivables, perhaps too large an investment in nonproducing assets.

The **quick (or acid test) ratio** is similar to the current ratio, except that it provides a more stringent test of a company's solvency position. Current assets like inventories and prepaid expenses, which are not immediately convertible to cash, are excluded from the numerator.

$$\text{Quick ratio (acid test)} = \frac{\text{Cash} + \text{Marketable securities} + \text{Accounts receivable}}{\text{Current liabilities}}$$

Solvency and liquidity can also be evaluated by analyzing the statement of cash flows. Cash flow from operations provides a measure of the firm's ability to generate cash from operating activities. It is not unusual for firms in a growth stage to have negative operating cash flow, often because as they expand, they need to purchase inventory and generate receivables faster than their payables grow. That working capital needs to be financed through either debt or equity. In the long run, companies need to generate sufficient operating cash flow to cover their investment needs. That is, operating cash flow should exceed capital expenditures—the purchase of property, plant, and equipment (an investing cash flow) needed to keep the business operating. Financial analysts focus on a measure called **free cash flow**. There are several ways to define free cash flow. We focus on equity holders and define it as cash flow from operations less capital expenditures. That is,

$$\text{Free cash flow} = \text{Cash flow from operations} - \text{Capital expenditures}$$

Defined in this way, free cash flow measures the cash generated that is available to pay for expansion and acquisitions, to pay dividends and buy back shares, and to pay down debt.

ANALYSIS EXAMPLE: SAKS AND NORDSTROM—SOLVENCY

When it comes to solvency and liquidity, again, the edge goes to Nordstrom. Saks reports a healthy current ratio of 2.21 at the end of January 2005. However, we see the effect of their large inventory balances when we look at the quick ratio, which plummets to 27 cents per dollar of current liabilities. Saks' ability to sell their inventories is a key factor in their ability to pay their creditors. Nordstrom's current and quick ratios show a healthy solvency position. Their creditors should feel more secure than Saks'.

In terms of cash flow, both firms generate positive operating cash flows—a good sign. Furthermore, both generate sufficient cash flow from operations to fund their capital expenditures, leaving them with positive free cash flow. However, the trend at Saks is negative, while it is positive at Nordstrom.

	Saks		Nordstrom	
	2005	2004	2005	2004
Current ratio	2.21	2.11	1.92	2.34
Quick ratio	0.27	0.38	1.29	1.70
Cash flow from operations	$358,821	$465,562	$606,346	$573,225
Capital expenditures	$(176,472)	$(165,062)	$(241,378)	$(258,314)
Free cash flow	$182,349	$300,500	$364,968	$314,911

A firm's core activities are operations, investing, and financing. We decomposed ROA into operating return on sales (profit margin) and asset turnover, and in doing so introduced the major ratios used to assess operating profit and asset (investment) management. We now turn to financing activities and managing capital structure—capital structure leverage and its cost, common equity leverage.

TEST YOUR KNOWLEDGE: SILICON LABORATORIES INC.

Silicon Laboratories, Inc., of Austin, Texas describes itself as the global leader in innovation of high-performance, analog-intensive, mixed-signal integrated circuit solutions. Silicon Labs is a fabless semiconductor company, meaning it designs semiconductors, but outsources production to large chip foundries. According to the company, its portfolio of both application-specific and general-purpose products includes high-performance, mixed-signal microcontrollers; broadcast audio solutions; ISOmodem® embedded modems; ProSLIC® subscriber line interface circuits; silicon direct access arrangements (DAAs); satellite set-top box receivers; voice codecs; VCXOs and XOs; SiPHY® transceivers, clock and data recovery ICs, and precision clock ICs. These patented solutions serve a broad set of markets and applications, including consumer, communications, computing, industrial, and automotive. Silicon Labs' balance sheets, income statements, and statements of cash flow are found at the end of the chapter.

Refer to the financial statements and calculate Silicon Labs' ROE for 2005 and 2006. Use ending balances of balance sheet figures. Decompose ROE into ROA (return on sales and asset turnover), as well as capital structure leverage and common equity leverage. Comment on the overall levels and trends you observe in profitability and efficiency (we turn later to leverage).

▶ MEASURES OF EFFECTIVE CAPITAL STRUCTURE MANAGEMENT

Managing value through financing activities involves the appropriate management of leverage, using borrowed funds (debt capital) to generate returns for the shareholders. A company that borrows at 8% and invests the funds to generate a 12% return is using leverage effectively. Leverage is desirable because it creates returns for the shareholders without using any of their (equity) capital. However, leverage increases risk, which can increase the costs of both debt and equity. A higher cost of debt puts downward pressure on ROE, and increasing the cost of equity increases the level that ROE must achieve to create shareholder value. Thus, increasing ROE by increasing leverage is normally considered a riskier strategy than increasing ROE by increasing the components of ROA (profit margin and asset turnover). Three ratios, and various sub-ratios, provide information about the effective use of leverage: capital structure leverage, common equity leverage, and the long-term debt ratio.

Recall that a company can meet its financing needs in three ways: (1) borrowings, (2) shareholder contributions, and (3) undistributed profits (retained earnings). **Capital structure leverage**, another direct determinant of ROE, measures the extent to which a company relies on borrowings (liabilities) as a source of financing:

$$\text{Capital structure leverage} = \frac{\text{Average total assets}}{\text{Average common equity}}$$

This ratio equals 1.0 if there are no financing liabilities in a company's capital structure, and increases above 1.0 as liabilities increase. High levels indicate that a company is relying heavily on leverage, which creates large potential earning power and high levels of risk. A company can increase this ratio by borrowing, and ROE will increase if the return generated by the borrowed funds exceeds the after-tax cost of the borrowing. Such a strategy, however, introduces the need to carefully manage the company's available cash to meet the required loan payments. Solvency ratios, discussed earlier, provide measures of this activity.

Capital structure leverage and its relationship to debt can be seen more clearly when one recalls that total assets at a given time is the sum of total liabilities and total equity. That is,

$$\text{Capital structure leverage} = \frac{\text{Total assets}}{\text{Total equity}} = \frac{\text{Total liabilities} + \text{Total equity}}{\text{Total equity}} = \frac{\text{Total liabilities}}{\text{Total equity}} + 1.0$$

There are several sub-ratios that examine capital structure leverage. The ratios generally look at leverage at a specific time and thus use ending balance sheet balances in their calculation. Often they are termed the "debt–equity" ratios and this leads to some confusion, especially when comparing precomputed ratios from different companies or data suppliers. The key is to know how each is computed before making comparisons and drawing conclusions.

The first ratio is the standard **total debt to equity ratio**. It compares liabilities of all sorts to common equity. As we will see later, the "total liabilities" figure can include items that are reported in total shareholders' equity, but that have debt-like characteristics (preferred shares, for example).

$$\text{Total debt to equity} = \frac{\text{Total liabilities}}{\text{Common equity}}$$

Two variants of the total debt to equity ratio are (1) the **long-term debt ratio**, which compares long-term liabilities to total assets, indicating the extent to which a company relies on long-term debt as a source of financing; and (2) the **long-term debt to equity**

ratio, which uses common equity in the denominator.

$$\text{Long-term debt ratio} = \frac{\text{Long-term debt}}{\text{Total assets}}$$

$$\text{Long-term debt to equity} = \frac{\text{Long-term debt}}{\text{Common equity}}$$

Long-term debt is normally considered less risky than short-term debt because the cash obligations are farther in the future. Companies that have large investments in long-term assets tend to finance those investments with long-term debt.

ANALYSIS CHALLENGE: WHAT TO INCLUDE IN LONG-TERM DEBT?

When analysis calls for computing one of the long-term debt ratios, analysts need to decide whether to include the current portion of long-term debt. There is no right or wrong answer and the choice should depend on the reason for the analysis.

If the goal is to understand capital structure (how the assets are paid for), then long-term debt should include the current portion, which is normally reported in the current liabilities section of the balance sheet. On the other hand, if the goal is to understand the relative level of debt payable in the longer term, then it can be excluded. Similarly, the current portion of long-term debt should be included in current liabilities if the goal in calculating a current or quick ratio is to assess the ability to pay obligations due in the short term, but can be excluded if the goal is to analyze operating working capital.

When the focus of analysis is on the returns earned by common shareholders, elements of shareholders' equity that relate to other classes of equity (e.g., preferred shares) need to be reclassified as liabilities for analysis purposes. For consistency, any related preferred dividends should be classified as interest expense.

The arithmetic of the ROE decomposition indicates that more capital structure leverage leads to higher ROE. However, debt comes with a cost—interest expense—and that cost is captured in the decomposition of ROE by **common equity leverage**. Common equity leverage compares the return to the shareholders with the returns to all capital providers (shareholders and debtholders) and is given by

$$\text{Common equity leverage} = \frac{\text{Net income}}{\text{Net income} + \text{Interest expense} \times (1 - \text{Tax rate})}$$

High levels of this ratio indicate that the shareholders are keeping a large portion of the total return generated by the company. For example, a ratio of 0.92 means that 92 cents of every dollar of after-tax operating profit is retained by the shareholders. The remaining 8 cents go to the debt holders in the form of interest. High levels of common equity leverage can result from either of two reasons: using little or no leverage (e.g., low levels of borrowing, and interest expense is very low) or using leverage very effectively (e.g., high levels of borrowing, but net income is still large relative to interest expense). Low levels of this ratio suggest that operating profits are low or a large portion of the return generated by the company is benefiting the debtholders.

A useful way to think about the two leverage ratios (capital structure leverage and common equity leverage) is to consider how they relate. Capital structure leverage measures the *amount* of leverage, while common equity leverage measures *how effectively* that amount of leverage is being used. High levels of both ratios mean that management is relying heavily on debt and the shareholders are the primary beneficiaries of the returns.

ANALYSIS CHALLENGE: NET INTEREST EXPENSE

A quick way to gauge the cost of debt is to compare interest expense and the debt level:

$$\text{Average interest rate} = \frac{\text{Interest expense}}{\text{Average interest-bearing debt}}$$

Many companies report interest expense on a *net* basis by offsetting interest expense against interest and investment income. In such cases, interest expense should be broken out. Normally, the details are found in the notes to the financial statements.

Interest and investment income is an element of non-operating income. In a refined ROA analysis, the non-operating assets (for example, the marketable securities and excess cash) would be excluded from the asset base and the investment earnings would be excluded from the earnings. Separately, we can analyze the return on those investments by comparing interest and investment income with investment levels:

$$\text{Average investment return} = \frac{\text{Interest and investment income}}{\text{Average investments and marketable securities}}$$

The **interest coverage ratio**, sometimes called times interest earned, compares net income before interest and taxes with interest expense:

$$\text{Interest coverage ratio} = \frac{\text{Net income} + \text{Tax expense} + \text{Interest expense}}{\text{Interest expense}}$$

Net income measured before subtracting tax and interest expense (i.e., pretax operating income)—the numerator—represents the earnings generated through investing and operating activities that can be used to pay interest. Increases in this ratio indicate that a company is creating assets through its investing and operating activities that exceed the costs of servicing its debt. The ratio can be large for either of two reasons: (1) a company is profitable with minimal reliance on debt, or (2) a company relies on debt, and is using its leverage effectively. In either case, if the profits eventually create cash, companies with high-interest coverage ratios are likely to be in strong solvency positions.

Financing activities directly affect a company's capital structure and its leverage ratios. Long-term debt issuances, treasury share purchases, and dividend payments tend to increase leverage, while equity issuances and debt repayments decrease leverage. However, management must understand that such transactions also can influence the ROA value drivers—profit margin and asset turnover. How quickly, for example, are the assets generated from a debt issuance turning over (i.e., generating new sales)? It is critical to realize that increasing leverage increases ROE only if the increase in leverage exceeds any decrease in ROA, driven by decreases in profit margin and/or asset turnover.

ANALYSIS EXAMPLE: SAKS AND NORDSTROM—LEVERAGE

Saks and Nordstrom both use long-term debt in their capital structure, but the impact of leverage differs. Saks has less capital structure leverage (2.12 vs. 2.65), but because its profitability is so low, as evidenced by the lower common equity leverage, interest expense takes a larger portion of profit from the shareholders. Indeed, the total effect of leverage on Saks was to reduce ROE in 2005 (the product of the two leverage factors was 0.90). On the other hand, Nordstrom used leverage to its advantage, in effect more than doubling ROA in each year (2.34 and 2.29).

$$\frac{\text{Assets}}{\text{Common equity}} \text{ and } \frac{\text{NI}}{\text{NI} + \text{Interest expense}}$$

	Saks		Nordstrom	
	2005	2004	2005	2004
Capital structure leverage (CSL)	2.12	2.01	2.65	2.85
Common equity leverage (CEL)	0.42	0.50	0.88	0.80
CSL × CEL	0.90	1.01	2.34	2.29
Long-term debt to equity	0.65	0.48	0.52	0.75
Interest coverage	1.70	2.10	6.23	3.32
Average interest expense	8.7%	8.4%	7.8%	7.8%

Nordstrom has a healthy and increasing interest coverage ratio. Saks' is declining and moving close to 1.0—not a good sign. Lenders seem concerned, too; the average interest rate is higher than Nordstrom's and increasing.

TEST YOUR KNOWLEDGE: SILICON LABORATORIES, INC.

Refer again to Silicon Labs' financial statements at the end of this chapter. Earlier, you decomposed ROE and commented on the company's profitability and efficiency. Turn now to leverage (capital structure leverage) and the cost of leverage (common equity leverage).

Does Silicon Labs use leverage to increase its ROE? Estimate the cost of its leverage. That is, compare interest expense to the liabilities that incur it. Estimate the returns that the company earns on its short-term investments. That is, compare interest income to the assets that generate it. Given those returns, speculate on the sorts of investments that the company makes.

▶ USING FINANCIAL RATIOS TO ANALYZE VALUE CREATION: SUMMARY

Figure 4-2 illustrates the complete ROE model. Management's goal is to create value by maximizing the extent to which ROE exceeds the cost of equity. To do so, they must effectively manage three key value drivers: (1) sales and expenses, (2) long-term assets and working capital, and (3) capital structure. Ratios constructed from numbers on the financial statements provide useful measures of these value drivers, and the decomposition of the ROE model shows how managing these measures links to value creation.

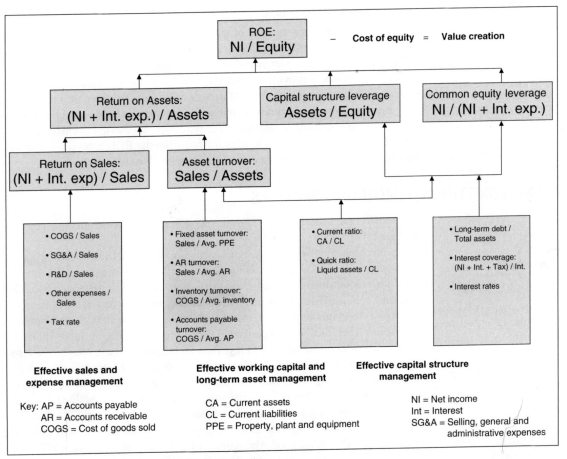

Figure 4-2. Complete ROE Model

Four points should be emphasized. First, the three value drivers and the associated financial ratios can be expressed in terms of the three fundamental management activities: operating, investing, and financing. Operating activities are reflected primarily in the profit margin components (revenues and expenses) and working capital ratios (turnover and solvency ratios); investing activities are reflected primarily in the noncurrent asset turnover ratios; and financing activities are reflected primarily in the leverage and solvency ratios. In later chapters, we cover in greater detail the accounting methods used to produce the financial statement numbers that reflect management's operating (Chapter 7), investing (Chapter 8), and financing (Chapter 9) activities.

Second, the financial statements and the related ratios used to measure the value drivers are imperfect measures. Financial statement numbers are inherently limited because many of these concepts are very difficult to measure, and management, who prepares the financial statements, may provide biased data. That bias may be unintentional (they may see things through rose-colored glasses) or intentional (they may take steps to intentionally influence how the data are perceived). Much of the remainder of the text is devoted to developing a deeper understanding of the strengths and weaknesses of these measures, and the situations where they are more or less useful. Chapter 6 covers earnings management in detail.

Third, any attempt to create value by managing a given ratio must consider effects on other parts of the model. For example, there is no doubt that additional borrowing will increase capital structure leverage, but the ultimate effect on ROE cannot be determined without considering how the use of the borrowed funds affects common equity leverage and ROA.

Finally, no financial statement analysis is complete without an analysis of the statement of cash flows. It provides useful information about the company's cash management strategies, its sources of cash, and its uses of cash—all organized into the three categories that reflect management's fundamental activities: operations, investing, and financing. An analysis of the statement of cash flows not only provides useful information in and of itself, but it also can enrich any conclusions formed from the ROE analysis. In the next section, we discuss the statements of cash flow for Saks and Nordstrom.

► ANALYZING THE STATEMENT OF CASH FLOWS

Excerpts from the statements of cash flows for Saks and Nordstrom are included in Figures 4-3 and 4-4.

Both companies generated a significant amount of cash from operating activities across the 3-year period (2003–2005), although Nordstrom generated quite a bit more and, unlike Saks, the amount increased each year. Also, both companies generated enough cash from operating activities to cover their expansion needs, most of which took the form of purchases of property and equipment, referred to as "capital expenditures" by Nordstrom. Again, Nordstrom seems to have experienced more growth, investing more than $8 billion in capital expenditures, compared to less than $6 billion for Saks. Nordstrom also maintains an active portfolio of short-term investments, indicating excess cash, while Saks does not.

In the financing area, Saks increased its reliance on debt in 2005, boosted by the issuance of $230 million in notes payable, while Nordstrom paid down its long-term debt each year. Interestingly, after paying no dividends in 2003 and 2004, Saks paid a large cash dividend ($283 million) in 2005, a year when net income was only $22 million. Nordstrom, on the other hand, maintained a fairly constant dividend payment, even though net income increased considerably. Both companies bought back common stock from their shareholders—Nordstrom, $300 million (all in 2005) and Saks, about $75 million (spread

	2005	2004	2003
Net cash provided by operating activities	$ 358,821	$ 473,729	$ 281,342
INVESTING ACTIVITIES:			
Purchases of property and equipment	(198,274)	(186,834)	(148,165)
Business acquisitions and investments		(14,012)	
Proceeds from the sale of stores	21,802	14,020	2,434
Net cash used in investing activities	(176,472)	(186,826)	(145,731)
FINANCING ACTIVITIES:			
Proceeds from issuance of notes	230,000		
Payments on long-term debt	(180,565)	(92,055)	(29,393)
Dividends paid	(283,127)		
Purchases and retirements of common stock	(85,397)	(74,537)	(7,111)
Proceeds from issuance of common stock	27,971	36,370	10,590
Net cash used in financing activities	(291,118)	(130,222)	(25,914)
INCREASE (DECREASE) IN CASH	(108,769)	156,681	109,697
CASH AND CASH EQUIVALENTS AT BEGINNING	365,873	209,192	99,495
CASH AND CASH EQUIVALENTS AT END	$ 257,104	$ 365,873	$ 209,192

Figure 4-3. Saks Incorporated and Subsidiaries Consolidated Statement of Cash Flows (in thousands)

	2005	2004	2003
Net cash provided by operating activities	$ 606,346	$ 599,282	$ 390,514
INVESTING ACTIVITIES:			
Capital expenditures	(246,851)	(258,314)	(328,166)
Proceeds from sale of assets	5,473		32,415
Minority interest purchase			(70,000)
Sale of short-term investments	3,366,425	2,090,175	937,521
Purchases of short-term investments	(3,232,250)	(2,144,909)	(1,058,787)
Other (net)	(2,830)	3,451	(2,133)
Net cash used in investing activities	(110,033)	(309,597)	(489,150)
FINANCING ACTIVITIES:			
Principle payments on long-term debt	(205,252)	(111,436)	(88,981)
(Decrease) increase in cash book overdrafts	(2,680)	33,832	(11,908)
Proceeds from the exercise of stock options	87,061	48,598	6,601
Proceeds from employee stock purchase plan	12,892	8,861	8,062
Cash dividends paid	(67,240)	(55,853)	(51,322)
Repurchase of common stock	(300,000)		
Other (net)	(752)	2,341	6,596
Net cash used in financing activities	(475,971)	(73,657)	(130,952)
INCREASE (DECREASE) IN CASH AND EQUIVALENTS	20,342	216,128	(229,588)
CASH AND CASH EQUIVALENTS AT BEGINNING	340,281	124,253	353,841
CASH AND CASH EQUIVALENTS AT END	$ 360,623	$ 340,281	$ 124,253

Figure 4-4. Nordstrom, Inc. Consolidated Statement of Cash Flows (in thousands)

across the three years); both companies raised funds from issuing stock, most of which was to employees who exercised their right to buy stock through their stock option plans. Finally, both companies seem to have built their cash balances since 2002, Nordstrom by almost three times, and Saks by a much smaller amount.

As we observed in our ROE analysis, Nordstrom again outperformed Saks in terms of all key cash flow measures.

TEST YOUR KNOWLEDGE: SILICON LABORATORIES, INC.

Refer again to the Silicon Laboratories financial statements at the end of this chapter. Comment on the how well Silicon Labs has been able to generate cash over the past three years. Has the company generated enough cash to fund its invest-ing needs? That is, have operations generated enough cash to invest in the company's future? Is the company in a position to pay its creditors?

▶ FINANCIAL STATEMENT ANALYSIS—A WRAP-UP AND INDUSTRY COMPARISON

Figures 4-5 and 4-6, based on the format of Figure 4-1, summarize the financial ratios for Saks and Nordstrom, respectively, for 2005 and 2004 in a format consistent with the ROE framework. Figure 4-7 compares selected ratios from Saks and Nordstrom to those ratios computed across the members of their primary industry group—retail apparel and accessories.

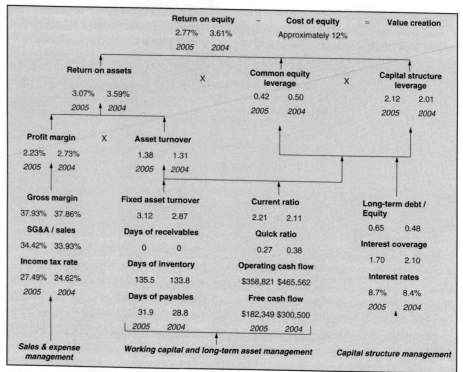

Figure 4-5. Saks ROE Analysis

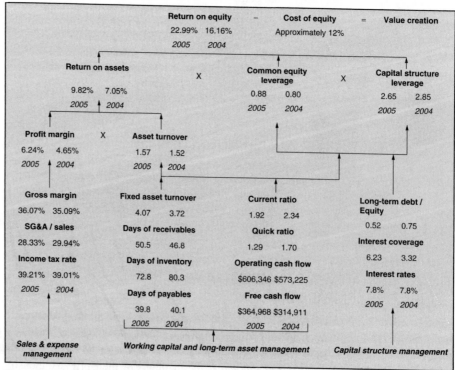

Figure 4-6. Nordstrom ROE Analysis

	Saks	Nordstrom	Industry Median*
Return on Equity	0.028	0.230	0.112
Return on Assets	0.031	0.098	0.047
Profit Margin	0.022	0.062	0.021
Gross Profit Margin	0.379	0.361	0.342
Asset Turnover	1.38	1.57	2.20
Days of Inventory	135	73	88
Long-Term Debt/Equity	0.65	0.52	0.28
Current Ratio	2.21	1.92	1.77
Quick Ratio	0.27	1.29	0.50
Interest Coverage	1.70	6.23	11.48

*Financial ratios provided by Hoover's, Inc.

Figure 4-7. Saks and Nordstrom—Industry Comparison

A reasonable estimate for the cost of equity for each firm is 12%. With an ROE under 4% each year, Saks has been destroying shareholder value. Nordstrom, on the other hand, created value in both years. Furthermore, Nordstrom's ROE was on the rise, and when we look at the determinants of ROE, we see that Nordstrom outperformed Saks on virtually all dimensions—management of sales and expenses, working capital and long-term assets, capital structure, and cash flow.

Nordstrom's increased ROE was driven primarily by an improved ROA, which was boosted by increases in both profit margin (return on sales) and asset turnover. Value Line, an independent analysis firm, reports that much of the improvement at Nordstrom came from better inventory management, which is supported by the significant decrease in the days of inventory ratio. Better inventory management also reduced the chance that markdowns were needed to sell it, which in turn helps explain the improved gross margin. Nordstrom was also able to push down SG&A expenses, further enhancing profit margin, and the additional cash flow generated by the higher profit margin and reduced working capital allowed Nordstrom to continue to grow (consistently large capital expenditures) while reducing its debt. Nordstrom was also able to pay dividends and buy back a considerable amount of common stock, and still report lower capital structure leverage, which was used more effectively for the benefit of the shareholders (higher common equity leverage). There is no doubt that Nordstrom has clearly outperformed Saks across the board.

With respect to the industry comparison, Nordstrom's ROE and ROA performance significantly exceeded that of the industry, which in turn exceeded that of Saks. On profit margin, Saks reported about the industry average, while Nordstrom again reported much higher performance. Gross margin is higher than the industry median for both companies, which is not surprising given that both are high-end apparel retailers that mark up their goods well above industry norms. Both companies turn their assets over more slowly than the industry median, but for Nordstrom this is largely due to the fact that it offers credit to its customers (via a Nordstrom credit card), which is relatively unusual in the industry. Like most of the industry, Saks carries no receivables. On perhaps the most important metric for a retailer, inventory turnover (in days), Nordstrom clearly outperforms the industry and Saks is much slower. Both Saks and Nordstrom carry more debt than the industry median, but both companies are publicly traded and much larger than the average company in the industry, which offers them more access to debt capital. Saks' interest coverage ratio seems dangerously low, however, compared to both Nordstrom and the industry. The current ratio for Saks is much higher than the industry median, while its quick ratio is much lower—more evidence that Saks is carrying a large inventory balance.

This example clearly shows how financial statement analysis can be useful. It can be used to evaluate not only a company's overall performance, but also the underlying reasons. Managers at Saks can use the analysis to identify where actions need to be taken and managers at Nordstrom can use the analysis as a benchmark for further improvement. Indeed, financial statement analysis provides a powerful tool to assess a company's past performance. In the next chapter, we discuss how this tool can be used as a starting point for the assessment of future performance, and ultimately the value of the firm.

▶ GLOBAL PERSPECTIVE: WORKING CAPITAL MANAGEMENT (excerpts from *CFO Magazine*, September 2006, with selected tables appended)

How Low Can It Go?

Asked to explain his company's success at driving down working-capital levels, Qualcomm CFO William Keitel demurs, saying, "You can always do better."

He's not being humble so much as capturing the dominant theme for working capital over the past several years. In 2005, for the fourth consecutive year, the 1,000 largest publicly traded companies in the United States managed to reduce the amount of money they had tied up in working capital as a percentage of sales. As indicated in Figure 4-8, data compiled for *CFO* by Hackett-REL, the Total Working Capital Practice of The Hackett Group, indicates that days working capital (DWC) for the average company shrank by 5.6% last year, following a 3.6% decline in 2004. Excluding the auto industry (which can skew results because of the huge lending arms the major players operate), the average decline last year was 4.0%, versus 2.5% in 2004. This was far better than the performance in Europe, where the average large company's DWC declined just 0.5%.

While many companies are riding this wave of success, the courses they have charted vary considerably. Some have achieved reductions by improving customer communication, others by adjusting their collections processes, and yet others by tying incentive compensation more closely to a successful reduction in working capital.

That approach, says Hackett-REL president Stephen Payne, may become more common. Not only has the rate of improvement jumped markedly between 2004 and 2005, he says, but the trend will continue "for at least the next few years." The reason is a stronger focus on working capital and free cash flow by the analyst community. That, Payne argues, has translated into "an increasing number of companies adding a cash-flow-based component to the variable compensation of executives, which will ensure that the focus continues."

▶ SUMMARY

This chapter provides a comprehensive discussion of financial statement analysis. By carefully decomposing ROE into its components, we demonstrate how financial statements can be used to analyze value creation. Indeed, all managers should be able to see where their actions fit into that decomposition. Everyone in an organization plays some role in value creation, the ROE decomposition helps to show where. The ROE decomposition, however, does not address cash flow directly. We demonstrate how an analysis of the cash flow statement adds further insights into the ROE analysis.

	DSO	% change	DSI	% change	DPO	% change	DWC	% change
Airlines								
Southwest Airlines	12.4	−10%	7.2	−6%	25.2	7%	−5.6	nm
Continental Airlines	16.8	−4%	6.5	−17%	27.6	−2%	−4.2	44%
Skywest	3.7	−58%	9.1	−15%	12.6	−30%	0.2	nm
Delta Airlines	18.5	11%	3.9	−20%	13.4	0%	8.9	10%
UAL	17.6	−17%	4.1	−22%	12.5	−6%	9.2	−30%
Northwest Airlines	17.6	18%	7.8	12%	10.2	−45%	15.3	nm
Sector Median (U.S.)	**15.2**	**10%**	**6.5**	**−14%**	**16.5**	**−13%**	**5.3**	**115%**
Alitalia (Italy)	10.6	−33%	3.0	−11%	40.8	−4%	−27.2	15%
Ryanair (Ireland)	5.6	11%	7.7	−15%	25.2	9%	−11.9	31%
Air Berlin (Germany)	8.0	9%	1.0	5%	18.4	−15%	−9.4	−30%
Air France-KLM (France)	42.8	−2%	5.8	−21%	34.7	−5%	13.9	−4%
Finnair (Finland)	29.0	1%	8.8	−13%	19.3	0%	18.6	−5%
Easyjet (U.K.)	28.2	−15%	0	—	1.8	−70%	26.4	−3%
Sector Median (Europe)	**27.7**	**−3%**	**6.0**	**−15%**	**27.6**	**−8%**	**6.1**	**3%**
Commodity Chemicals								
Lyondell Chemical	33.7	−4%	35.8	−8%	29.2	12%	40.3	−16%
Georgia Gulf	48.2	0%	31.4	2%	32.5	−4%	47.1	5%
Arch Chemical	51.2	−1%	48.1	−2%	48.8	−6%	50.5	4%
Minerals Technologies	67.5	9%	43.6	4%	22.5	1%	88.6	9%
Du Pont De Nemours	53.5	4%	65.0	8%	29.3	9%	89.2	5%
A Schulman	57.4	−4%	59.4	−13%	26.0	−7%	90.9	−10%
Sector Median (U.S.)	**49.1**	**−1%**	**42.8**	**−7%**	**29.6**	**7%**	**62.3**	**−9%**
Celanese (Germany)	59.5	−23%	29.4	2%	44.4	−14%	44.4	−18%
Solvay (Belgium)	69.6	1%	47.5	−10%	52.2	5%	64.9	−10%
Lenzing (Austria)	42.9	−7%	48.0	−2%	24.7	7%	66.2	−8%
DSM (Netherlands)	60.3	6%	69.9	11%	43.7	11%	86.5	8%
EMS-Chemie (Switzerland)	69.7	−1%	64.1	−23%	31.2	−11%	102.5	−14%
Bayer (Germany)	69.4	−1%	73.4	−1%	26.3	−5%	116.4	0%
Sector Median (Europe)	**60.5**	**−1%**	**52.8**	**−2%**	**32.2**	**−5%**	**81.2**	**0%**
Food Producers								
Dean Foods	30.1	0%	13.2	0%	19.3	−3%	24.1	2%
General Mills	33.6	1%	33.7	−4%	36.9	−2%	30.4	−1%
Tyson Foods	17.0	0%	28.9	2%	13.5	3%	32.5	0%
McCormick	52.0	−12%	48.4	−4%	27.9	−1%	72.5	−11%
Hershey	42.2	25%	46.1	0%	12.7	3%	75.6	12%
Conagra Foods	32.4	−3%	65.5	−1%	20.5	−13%	77.4	2%
Sector Median (U.S.)	**31.9**	**4%**	**42.6**	**4%**	**19.9**	**−9%**	**54.6**	**9%**
Danone (France)	42.1	−1%	17.6	−1%	50.8	13%	8.9	−42%
LDC (France)	39.9	−4%	12.9	2%	39.7	−9%	13.1	22%
Nutreco (Netherlands)	42.3	11%	24.2	−39%	48.4	19%	18.1	−51%
Suedzucker (Germany)	38.1	13%	133.8	−9%	66.9	3%	105.0	−10%
Barry Callebaut (Switzerland)	52.4	2%	80.2	−10%	24.4	−1%	108.3	−6%
Danisco (Denmark)	59.4	−13%	106.2	−5%	22.0	−13%	143.6	−7%
Sector Median (Europe)	**43.1**	**4%**	**38.9**	**2%**	**33.2**	**5%**	**48.7**	**2%**

DSO: Days Sales Outstanding
DIO: Days Inventory Outstanding
DPO: Days Payables Outstanding

DWC: Days Working Capital
nm: Figure not meaningful

Figure 4-8. Working capital metrics across industries: U.S. vs. Europe
Source: CFO magazine, September 2006

Silicon Laboratories Inc. Financial Statements

Silicon Laboratories Inc.
Consolidated Balance Sheets
(in thousands, except per share data)

	December 30, 2006	December 31, 2005
Assets		
Current assets:		
Cash and cash equivalents	$ 68,188	$100,504
Short-term investments	318,104	263,206
Accounts receivable, net of allowance for doubtful accounts of $548 at December 30, 2006, and $1,088 at December 31, 2005	49,701	56,883
Inventories	40,282	23,132
Deferred income taxes	13,330	11,505
Prepaid expenses and other	14,102	9,670
Total current assets	503,707	464,900
Property, equipment, and software, net	43,321	32,584
Goodwill	78,224	62,877
Other intangible assets, net	21,970	14,838
Other assets, net	39,773	25,863
Total assets	$686,995	$601,062
Liabilities and Stockholders' Equity		
Current liabilities:		
Accounts payable	$ 36,396	$ 43,846
Accrued expenses	27,929	16,129
Deferred income on shipments to distributors	22,234	17,273
Income taxes	15,063	18,348
Total current liabilities	101,622	95,596
Long-term obligations and other liabilities	16,691	7,418
Total liabilities	118,313	103,014
Commitments and contingencies		
Stockholders' equity:		
Preferred stock—$0.0001 par value; 10,000 shares authorized; no shares issued and outstanding	–	–
Common stock—$0.0001 par value: 250,000 shares authorized: 54,802 and 54,530 shares issued and outstanding at December 30, 2006, and December 31, 2005, respectively	5	5
Additional paid-in capital	373,655	335,284
Deferred stock compensation	–	(1,105)
Retained earnings	195,022	163,864
Total stockholders' equity	568,682	498,048
Total liabilities and stockholders' equity	$686,995	$601,062

Silicon Laboratories Inc.
Consolidated Statements of Income
(in thousands, except per share data)

	Year Ended		
	December 30, 2006	December 31, 2005	January 1, 2005
Revenues	$464,597	$425,689	$456,225
Cost of revenues	208,217	193,904	206,320
Gross profit...	256,380	231,785	249,905
Operating expenses:			
Research and development	121,707	101,222	78,056
Selling, general, and administrative	102,358	72,553	65,164
In-process research and development............................	3,200	–	–
Operating expenses	227,265	173,775	143,220
Operating income	29,115	58,010	106,685
Other income (expense):			
Interest income...	13,745	8,285	3,054
Interest expense..	(872)	(322)	(311)
Other income (expense), net	744	(332)	2,148
Income before income taxes....................................	42,732	65,641	111,576
Provision for income taxes	11,574	18,135	34,883
Net income	$ 31,158	$ 47,506	$ 76,693
Net income per share:			
Basic...	$ 0.56	$ 0.89	$ 1.49
Diluted	$ 0.54	$ 0.86	$ 1.39
Weighted-average common shares outstanding:			
Basic...	55,346	53,399	51,471
Diluted	57,201	55,485	54,983

Silicon Laboratories Inc.
Consolidated Statements of Cash Flows
(in thousands)

	Year Ended		
	December 30, 2006	December 31, 2005	January 1, 2005
Operating Activities			
Net income	$ 31,158	$ 47,506	$ 76,693
Adjustments to reconcile net income to cash provided by operating activities:			
Depreciation and amortization of property, equipment, and software	16,243	17,712	16,191
Loss (gain) on disposal of property, equipment,and software	712	124	(2,174)
Amortization of other intangible assets and other assets	4,989	2,818	3,315
Stock compensation expense	39,400	7,274	4,237
Acquired and in-process research and development	3,200	13,687	–
Additional income tax benefit from employee stock-based awards	13,044	4,615	6,766
Excess income tax benefit from employee stock-based awards	(7,402)	–	–
Changes in operating assets and liabilities:			
Accounts receivable	7,182	(13,891)	4,887
Inventories	(16,933)	15,273	(4,341)
Prepaid expenses and other assets	(7,768)	(13,119)	(1,602)
Accounts payable	(5,098)	15,829	(10,689)
Accrued expenses	9,951	(4,195)	9,073
Deferred income on shipments to distributors	4,961	3,737	2,010
Deferred income taxes	(7,021)	(3,521)	(3,645)
Income taxes payable	(3,335)	10,141	(4,456)
Net cash provided by operating activities	83,283	103,990	96,265
Investing Activities			
Purchases of short-term investments	(404,664)	(385,552)	(638,337)
Sales and maturities of short-term investments	349,766	350,816	541,746
Purchases of property, equipment and software	(29,772)	(20,377)	(20,508)
Proceeds from the sale of property, equipment, and software	2,032	266	4,464
Purchases of other assets	(6,477)	(17,458)	(6,328)
Acquisitions of businesses, net of cash acquired	(21,223)	(6)	(114)
Net cash used in investing activities	(110,338)	(72,311)	(119,077)
Financing Activities			
Proceeds from Employee Stock Purchase Plan	3,357	2,862	2,746
Proceeds from exercises of stock options	34,800	17,327	10,268
Excess income tax benefit from employee stock-based awards	7,402	–	–
Repurchases of common stock	(50,046)	–	–
Payments on debt	(774)	–	–
Net cash provided by (used in) financing activities	(5,261)	20,189	13,014
Increase (decrease) in cash and cash equivalents	(32,316)	51,868	(9,798)
Cash and cash equivalents at beginning of period	100,504	48,636	58,434
Cash and cash equivalents at end of period	$ 68,188	$100,504	$ 48,636
Supplemental Disclosure of Cash Flow Information:			
Interest paid	$ 631	$ 344	$ 254
Income taxes paid	$ 8,519	$ 6,622	$ 36,350
Supplemental Disclosure of Noncash Activity:			
Accrued other assets	$ –	$ 8,126	$ 2,902
Stock issued for acquisition of business	$ –	$ 18,980	$ 11,569

The accompanying notes are an integral part of these consolidated financial statements.

► CASE AND REVIEW QUESTIONS

Freescale Semiconductor and Texas Instruments—ROE Analysis

Freescale Semiconductor and Texas Instruments are two important players in the global semiconductor business. You have almost certainly used their products today if you drove in a car, used a cell phone, or watched a digital projector. Background information about each company, taken from company Web pages on August 1, 2005, follows.

You would like to know whether and how each company is creating value for its shareholders. You have gathered both companies' balance sheets and income statements for 2002 through 2004. (Some of the figures have been reclassified from the published data to simplify the analysis.) Use those data to prepare an analysis of each firm's ROE for 2003 and 2004. Break the overall ROE down by ROA, common equity leverage, and capital structure leverage. Break ROA into profit margin (operating return on sales) and asset turnover. Break the two leverage components into sub-ratios. You can use Figure 4-2 as a guide.

Freescale was the semiconductor business of Motorola until late 2004, when it was spun off as a separate company (Freescale raised considerable debt capital at the same time). As part of the initial public offering (IPO), certain costs at Motorola were allocated to Freescale. In some cases, for example, interest expense relative to reported long-term debt, unusual relationships arise. In today's complex business environment, analysts encounter such situations frequently. They delve into the notes to the financial statements or they contact the company investor relations professionals to clarify their analyses.

1. Comment on your findings. Which company is creating more value (on a percentage and on an absolute basis)? What trends do you see? What advice would you provide to each company's management?

2. In Freescale's offering document for their IPO, they described their business strategy and some of the actions they expect to take in the future. An edited extract from the document follows. Does your analysis indicate that Freescale is making progress in any of the areas? Do the initiatives seem well chosen in terms of their effect on value creation? How will they affect key ROE sub-ratios in the future?

   Our Strategy . . . is to be the embedded processing leader . . . by continuing to apply the following strategy:
   a. focus on large, high-growth market opportunities where we can apply our distinctive intellectual property and technology capabilities;
   b. continue to develop high value-added, proprietary products;
   c. continue to build upon our strong foundation of intellectual property;
   d. increase the breadth and depth of our customer relationships, including current competitors of Motorola; and
   e. evolve our asset-light strategy and continue to improve our manufacturing and operational efficiencies.

About Freescale Semiconductor Inc.

Freescale is a leading global semiconductor company focused on providing embedded processing and connectivity products to large, high-growth markets. We currently focus on providing products to the automotive, networking, and wireless communications industries.

According to industry data, in 2003, we held numerous leading market positions in the supply of semiconductor products to these industries.

- According to general industry data, we were the global market share leader for semiconductors for automotive applications, and had the second largest global market share for microcontrollers and embedded microprocessors.
- According to International Data Corporation (IDC), we were the global market share leader for communications processors. In addition, according to ABI Research, we were the global market share leader in radio frequency power products for the cellular base station market.
- According to general industry data, we had the fourth position overall for wireless communications application-specific standard products and we had the fourth largest global market share for digital baseband semiconductors for cellular handsets.

A common attribute of our success in each of these target industries is our ability to offer families of embedded processors. In their simplest forms, embedded processors provide the basic intelligence for electronic devices and can be programmed to address specific applications or functions. Examples of our embedded processors, include microcontrollers, digital signal processors, and communications processors.

Since we began our operations in 1953 as the semiconductor products sector of Motorola, Inc., we have been an innovator and pioneer in the global semiconductor industry. We are responsible for a number of significant innovations that have had a meaningful impact on the industry. For example, we have developed key product categories, such as communications processors, microcontrollers, solid-state acceleration sensors, and cellular semiconductors and modules.

Our global customer base comprises more than 10,000 end customers, including more than 100 leading original equipment manufacturers that we serve through our direct sales force, as well as several thousand other end customers that we reach through a network of distributors. Approximately 22,000 full-time employees in more than 30 countries service and support these customers.

Freescale Semiconductor Inc.
Income Statement ($ millions)

	Year Ended December 31			Common Size			Percent Change	
	2004	2003	2002	2004	2003	2002	2003–2004	2002–2003
Net Sales	$5,715	$ 4,864	$ 5,001	100.0%	100.0%	100.0%	17.5%	−2.7%
Cost of sales	$3,575	$ 3,451	$ 3,763	62.6%	70.9%	75.2%	3.6%	−8.3%
Gross Margin	2,140	1,413	1,238	37.4%	29.1%	24.8%	51.5%	14.1%
Operating expenses								
Research and development	965	1,005	993	16.9%	20.7%	19.9%	−4.0%	1.2%
Sales, general, and administrative	799	649	604	14.0%	13.3%	12.1%	23.1%	7.5%
Non-recurring Items	110	63	1,156	1.9%	1.3%	23.1%	74.6%	−94.6%
Operating Income	266	(304)	(1,515)	4.7%	−6.3%	−30.3%	−187.5%	−79.9%
Additional income/expense items	51	100	1	0.9%	2.1%	0.0%	−49.0%	9900.0%
Earnings before interest and tax	314	(204)	(1,514)	5.5%	−4.2%	−30.3%	−253.9%	−86.5%
Interest expense	51	115	167	0.9%	2.4%	3.3%	−55.7%	−31.1%
Earnings before tax	263	(319)	(1,681)	4.6%	−6.6%	−33.6%	−182.4%	−81.0%
Income tax	52	47	86	0.9%	1.0%	1.7%	10.6%	−45.3%
Equity earnings—unconsolidated subsidiary	(3)	–	–					
Net Income	$ 211	$ (366)	$ (1,767)	3.7%	−7.5%	−35.3%	−157.7%	−79.3%

Freescale Semiconductor Inc.
Balance Sheet ($ millions)

	As at December 31st			Common Size		
	2004	2003	2002	2004	2003	2002
Current Assets						
Cash and cash equivalents	$2,374	$ 87	$ 44	35.9%	2.0%	0.9%
Net receivables	664	347	444	10.0%	7.8%	8.7%
Inventory	787	1,027	819	11.9%	23.1%	16.0%
Other current assets	176	228	112	2.7%	5.1%	2.2%
Total Current Assets	4,001	1,689	1,419	60.4%	38.0%	27.7%
Long-term assets						
Long-term investments	50	132	217	0.8%	3.0%	4.2%
Fixed assets	2,207	2,357	3,226	33.3%	53.0%	62.9%
Goodwill	222	220	220	3.4%	4.9%	4.3%
Intangible assets	47	28	19	0.7%	0.6%	0.4%
Other assets	95	23	24	1.4%	0.5%	0.5%
Total Assets	6,622	4,449	5,125	100.0%	100.0%	100.0%
Current liabilities						
Accounts payable	1,090	693	802	16.5%	15.6%	15.6%
Short-term debt/current portion of long-term debt	0	27	130	0.0%	0.6%	2.5%
Other current liabilities	71	19	35	1.1%	0.4%	0.7%
Total Current Liabilities	1,161	739	967	17.5%	16.6%	18.9%
Long-term debt	1,250	2	14	18.9%	0.0%	0.3%
Other liabilities	249	104	114	3.8%	2.3%	2.2%
Deferred liability charges	26	48	6	0.4%	1.1%	0.1%
Total liabilities	2,686	893	1,101	40.6%	20.1%	21.5%
Shareholders' Equity	3,936	3,556	4,024	59.4%	79.9%	78.5%
Total Liabilities and Shareholders' Equity	$6,622	$4,449	$5,125	100.0%	100.0%	100.0%

About Texas Instruments Incorporated

Texas Instruments Incorporated (TI) (NYSE: TXN) is a global semiconductor company and the world's leading designer and supplier of real-time signal processing solutions. The company's businesses also include sensors and controls, and educational and productivity solutions. Headquartered in Dallas, Texas, TI has approximately 36,000 employees worldwide with corporate, sales, and manufacturing facilities in more than 25 countries across Asia, Europe, and the Americas.

Founded more than 70 years ago, TI began taking actions in 1996 that transformed the company into a corporation focused on making semiconductors for the signal processing markets that have fed the wireless and mobile Internet revolution. This focus, along with a series of acquisitions, divestitures, and other actions has made TI one of the best-positioned semiconductor companies today.

Over the past few years, TI has continued to invest for the future, develop new technologies, and increase its financial strength. The company has exited from the recent market downturn in a better position than ever before and has just begun to tap the potential that real-time signal processing technology will bring to the world of electronics. As information any time, anywhere becomes increasingly pervasive through the mobile Internet and broadband connections move to and through the home, TI stands to benefit from the increased importance of signal processing, a technology which is tied to the company's strengths in digital signal processors (DSP) and analog. Together, they are the enablers for many of the electronics industries fastest growing market segments. Specifically, the company's growth in the future will be positively influenced by three end-market trends:

- digital cell phones transition from voice-only to high-speed multimedia devices;
- a rapidly growing broadband subscriber base around the world and the need to distribute broadband capability through the home; and
- consumer electronics transition to digital technology—a wide range of products that deliver information, entertainment, and connectivity anywhere the user goes.

In addition to its silicon technology for these markets, TI adds software and systems expertise to provide customers the power to differentiate their products.

Texas Instruments Inc.
Income Statement ($ millions)

	Year Ended December 31			Common Size			Percent Change	
	2004	**2003**	**2002**	**2004**	**2003**	**2002**	**2003–2004**	**2002–2003**
Total Revenue	$12,580	$9,834	$8,383	100.0%	100.0%	100.0%	27.9%	17.3%
Cost of revenue	6,954	5,872	5,313	55.3%	59.7%	63.4%	18.4%	10.5%
Gross Profit	5,626	3,962	3,070	44.7%	40.3%	36.6%	42.0%	29.1%
Operating expenses								
Research and development	1,978	1,748	1,619	15.7%	17.8%	19.3%	13.2%	8.0%
Sales, general, and administrative	1,441	1,249	1,163	11.5%	12.7%	13.9%	15.4%	7.4%
Operating Income	2,207	965	288	17.5%	9.8%	3.4%	128.7%	235.1%
Add'l income/expense items	235	324	(577)	1.9%	3.3%	−6.9%	−27.5%	−156.2%
Earnings before interest and tax	2,442	1,289	(289)	19.4%	13.1%	−3.4%	89.4%	−546.0%
Interest expense	21	39	57	0.2%	0.4%	0.7%	−46.2%	−31.6%
Earnings before tax	2,421	1,250	(346)	19.2%	12.7%	−4.1%	93.7%	−461.3%
Income Tax	560	52	(2)	4.5%	0.5%	0.0%	976.9%	−2700.0%
Net Income	$ 1,861	$1,198	$ (344)	14.8%	12.2%	−4.1%	55.3%	−448.3%

Texas Instruments Inc.

Balance Sheet ($ millions)	As at December 31st			Common Size		
	2004	2003	2002	2004	2003	2002
Current Assets						
Cash and cash equivalents	$ 2,668	$ 1,818	$ 949	16.4%	11.7%	6.5%
Short-term investments	3,690	2,511	2,063	22.6%	16.2%	14.1%
Net receivables	1,696	1,451	1,217	10.4%	9.4%	8.3%
Deferred taxes	554	449	545	3.4%	2.9%	3.7%
Inventory	1,256	984	790	7.7%	6.3%	5.4%
Other current assets	326	496	562	2.0%	3.2%	3.8%
Total Current Assets	10,190	7,709	6,126	62.5%	49.7%	41.7%
Long-term assets						
Long-term investments	264	1,600	1,938	1.6%	10.3%	13.2%
Fixed assets	3,918	4,132	4,794	24.0%	26.6%	32.7%
Goodwill	701	693	638	4.3%	4.5%	4.3%
Intangible assets	418	169	185	2.6%	1.1%	1.3%
Other assets	359	581	380	2.2%	3.7%	2.6%
Deferred asset charges	449	626	618	2.8%	4.0%	4.2%
Total Assets	16,299	15,510	14,679	100.0%	100.0%	100.0%
Current liabilities						
Accounts payable	1,914	1,763	1,512	11.7%	11.4%	10.3%
Short-term debt/current portion of long-term debt	11	437	422	0.1%	2.8%	2.9%
Total Current Liabilities	1,925	2,200	1,934	11.8%	14.2%	13.2%
Long-term debt	368	395	833	2.3%	2.5%	5.7%
Other liabilities	589	628	777	3.6%	4.0%	5.3%
Deferred liability charges	354	423	401	2.2%	2.7%	2.7%
Total liabilities	3,236	3,646	3,945	19.9%	23.5%	26.9%
Stockholders' equity						
Total Equity	13,063	11,864	10,734	80.1%	76.5%	73.1%
Total Liabilities and Shareholders' Equity	$16,299	$15,510	$14,679	100.0%	100.0%	100.0%

▶ APPENDIX 4A: SAKS AND NORDSTROM FINANCIAL STATEMENTS

Saks, Incorporated (NYS: SKS)

As Reported Annual Balance Sheet Scale (U.S. Dollar)	1/29/2005 thousands	1/31/2004 thousands	2/01/2003 thousands
Cash and cash equivalents	$ 257,104	$ 365,834	$ 209,568
Retained interest in accounts receivable			267,062
Merchandise inventories	1,516,271	1,451,275	1,306,667
Other current assets	127,082	162,893	93,422
Deferred income taxes, net	178,558	63,161	41,806
Total current assets	2,079,015	2,043,163	1,918,525
Property and equipment, net	2,046,839	2,080,599	2,143,105
Goodwill and intangibles, net of amortization	323,761	325,577	316,430
Deferred income taxes, net	166,364	121,859	148,805
Other assets	88,100	83,671	52,491
Total assets	4,704,079	4,654,869	4,579,356
Accounts payable	378,394	319,216	273,989
Accrued expenses	468,896	401,719	416,024
Accrued compensation and related items	71,831	69,404	55,049
Sales taxes payable	13,184	24,187	44,849
Current portion of long-term debt	7,715	151,884	4,781
Total current liabilities	940,020	966,410	794,692
Long-term debt	1,346,222	1,125,637	1,327,381
Other long-term liabilities	333,420	240,654	190,011
Common stock	14,012	14,183	14,496
Additional paid-in capital	2,116,301	2,105,925	2,131,091
Accumulated other comprehensive income (loss)	−86,818	−71,610	−69,158
Retained earnings (accumulated deficit)	40,922	273,670	190,843
Total shareholders' equity	2,084,417	2,322,168	2,267,272
Total liabilities and shareholders' equity	$4,704,079	$4,654,869	$4,579,356

Saks, Incorporated (NYS: SKS)

As Reported Annual Income Statement Scale (U.S. Dollar)	1/29/2005 thousands	1/31/2004 thousands
Net sales	$6,437,277	$6,055,055
Cost of sales	3,995,460	3,762,722
Gross margin (loss)	2,441,817	2,292,333
Selling, general, and administrative expenses	1,614,658	1,477,329
Property and equipment rentals	203,451	201,651
Depreciation and amortization	229,145	221,350
Taxes other than income taxes	164,067	149,094
Store pre-opening costs	4,520	4,832
Impairments and dispositions	31,751	8,088
Operating income (loss)	194,225	229,989
Interest expense	114,035	109,713
Gain (loss) on extinguishment of debt	–	10,506
Other income (expense), net	4,048	109
Income (loss) before income taxes	84,238	109,879
Provision (benefit) for income taxes	23,153	27,052
Net income (loss)	$ 61,085	$ 82,827

Nordstrom, Inc. (NYS: JWN)

As Reported Annual Balance Sheet Scale (U.S. Dollar)	**1/29/2005** **thousands**	**1/31/2004** **thousands**	**1/31/2003** **thousands**
Cash and cash equivalents	$ 360,623	$ 476,224	$ 208,329
Short-term investments	41,825	—	—
Accounts receivable, net	645,663	633,858	759,262
Investment in asset-backed securities	422,416	—	—
Retained interest in accounts receivable	—	272,294	—
Merchandise inventories	917,182	901,623	953,112
Current deferred tax assets	131,547	—	—
Prepaid expenses	—	49,750	40,261
Prepaid expenses and other current assets	53,188	—	—
Other current assets	—	121,681	111,654
Total current assets	2,572,444	2,455,430	2,072,618
Land, buildings, and equipment, net	1,780,366	1,724,273	1,761,544
Goodwill, net	51,714	56,609	40,355
Trade name, net	84,000	84,000	100,133
Other assets	116,866	145,376	121,726
Total assets	4,605,390	4,465,688	4,096,376
Notes payable	—	286	244
Accounts payable	482,394	512,035	414,754
Accrued salaries, wages, and related benefits	287,904	333,428	260,562
Other current liabilities	354,201	—	—
Income taxes payable	115,556	—	—
Income taxes and other accruals	—	196,967	188,986
Current portion of long-term debt	101,097	6,833	5,545
Total current liabilities	1,341,152	1,049,549	870,091
Long-term debt, net of current portion	929,010	1,227,410	1,341,826
Deferred lease credits		377,321	383,100
Deferred property incentives, net	367,087		
Other liabilities	179,147	177,399	129,302
Common stock	552,655	424,645	358,069
Unearned stock compensation	−299	−597	−2,010
Retained earnings	1,227,303	1,201,093	1,014,105
Accumulated other comprehensive earnings	9,335	8,868	1,893
Total shareholders' equity	1,788,994	1,634,009	1,372,057
Total liabilities and shareholders' equity	$4,605,390	$4,465,688	$4,096,376

Nordstrom, Inc. (NYS: JWN)

As Reported Annual Income Statement Scale (U.S. Dollar)	1/29/2005 thousands	1/31/2004 thousands
Net sales	$7,131,388	$6,491,673
Cost of sales and related buying and occupancy	4,559,388	4,213,955
Gross profit	2,572,000	2,277,718
Selling, general, and administrative expenses	2,020,233	1,943,715
Operating income	551,767	334,003
Total interest expense	88,518	100,518
Less interest income	7,929	5,981
Less capitalized interest	3,161	3,585
Interest income (expense), net	−77,428	−90,952
Other income, including finance charges, net	172,942	155,090
Earnings before income taxes	647,281	398,141
Income taxes	253,831	155,300
Net earnings	$ 393,450	$ 242,841

CHAPTER 5

Return on Equity, Value Creation, and Firm Value

ANALYSIS CHALLENGE: HOW MUCH IS THAT COMPANY WORTH?

You just completed a detailed strategic and financial analysis of a competitor, who has great products and appears to be very profitable. You learn that the owners are considering selling the company. Confident that together your two firms could be a leader in the marketplace, you might be interested in an acquisition. Yet, buying even a great company at the wrong price could be devastating. How much should you be willing to pay?

We pay special attention to return on equity (ROE) because it is computed from values on the financial statements and can be linked directly to management's primary goal: creating shareholder value. Chapter 4 described a framework that links ROE to its determinants—capital structure leverage, common equity leverage, and return on assets (ROA), as well as ROA's determinants—profit margin and asset turnover. In that chapter, we showed how effective management of sales and expenses, working capital, long-term assets, and capital structure can boost ROE. In this chapter, we link ROE and value creation to the value of a firm's common shares. By doing so, we draw linkages between management's decisions, the company's financial statements, and its market value.

Figure 5-1 illustrates these linkages. The results of management's operating, investing, and financing decisions are represented on financial statements, prepared in accordance with generally accepted accounting principles (GAAP). Financial ratios can be computed from the values on these statements to assess the return to the shareholders (ROE), changes in ROE across time, and other financial metrics (return on assets, profit margin, asset turnover, common equity leverage, and capital structure leverage) that help to explain the changes in ROE. Comparing ROE to the cost of equity (defined in Chapter 1) determines whether shareholder value has been created, which, in turn, is reflected in the market value of the company's equity securities (common shares). We reiterate that the relationship among ROE, cost of capital, and value creation is long term. That is, management can create value for shareholders in the long run—even if the ROE in the current period is less than the cost of capital—as long as the current deficiency is offset by positive results in future periods. The valuation model we describe in this chapter makes that clear.

In the next section, we discuss how the value of a company's common shares is determined and we describe a model that expresses the value of a company's equity securities

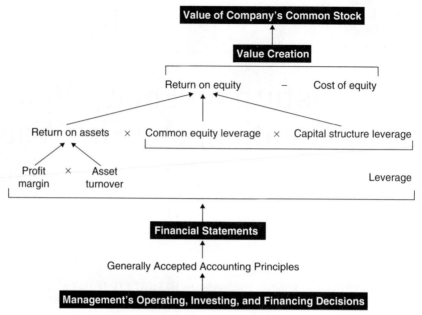

Figure 5-1. Management Decisions, Financial Statements, and Firm Value

in terms of *future* value creation and ROE. We then describe the steps an analyst should complete to place a value on the common shares of a company, and illustrate the process by using it to estimate the value of a share of Nordstrom, a company whose financial statements were analyzed in Chapter 4. We then compare the estimated price to the actual price, and discuss the implications of the difference.

Although this chapter describes how a firm's market value can be estimated, which can be used to determine whether common stocks are under- or overpriced, its real value is not in showing you how to "beat the market." The process we describe involves assumptions, predictions, and a variety of judgments that are virtually impossible to verify, leaving great uncertainty around any estimate of market value that we derive. The real value of this chapter lies in the identification of how management's decisions and the firm's financial statements link to value creation and firm value. What areas of management are keys to the success of the firm, how do they relate to each other, and what metrics are available to track and motivate management success? These are the questions that this chapter is primarily designed to address.

INSIGHT: THESE IDEAS ARE NOT JUST FOR SECURITY ANALYSTS ...

Although our discussion is set in the context of security valuation, the same issues arise in many contexts within a firm. For example, a manager might be interested in estimating the value of a business unit or division being considered for sale. Similarly, potential business acquisitions need to be priced, and managers can use these techniques to estimate the effects on firm value of alternative business strategies. Indeed, understanding linkages between business decisions and firm value is fundamental to sound management.

▶ A MODEL OF FIRM VALUE BASED ON ROE AND VALUE CREATION

The economics, finance, and accounting literatures have established that the theoretical value of a firm's common shares is equal to the present value of the expected future returns produced by the shares, which is represented by Expression 1.[1]

Expression 1

$$V_0 = \sum_{t=1}^{n} \frac{\text{Expected Future Returns}_t}{(1 + r_e)^t}$$

This expression means that the estimated value of a firm's common shares at time 0 (V_0) is equal to the sum of the annual returns that the equity investment is expected to produce over the life of the firm (n), each discounted by 1 plus the return required by the shareholders, given the firm's level of risk (r_e)—that is, the cost of equity. This expression can also be represented as shown in Expression 2.

Expression 2

$$V_0 = \frac{\text{Expected Return}_1}{(1 + r_e)^1} + \frac{\text{Expected Return}_2}{(1 + r_e)^2} + \frac{\text{Expected Return}_3}{(1 + r_e)^3} + \cdots$$

The expected returns to the shareholders can be expressed in any of several ways. For example, they can be dividends paid to the shareholders, and they can also be expressed in terms of cash flows or earnings. More recently, analysts, consultants, and managers have expressed them in terms of return on equity (ROE). Although expressing the expected returns in different ways leads to slightly different forms of the model, if applied correctly, they all lead to the same value. Expression 3 shows expected returns in terms of ROE. We use this formula because ROE links directly to value creation, the primary goal of management.

Expression 3

$$V_0 = SE_0 + \frac{(ROE_1 - r_e) \times SE_0}{(1 + r_e)^1} + \frac{(ROE_2 - r_e) \times SE_1}{(1 + r_e)^2} + \frac{(ROE_3 - r_e) \times SE_2}{(1 + r_e)^3} + \cdots$$

V_0, on the left side of Expression 3, represents the current value (at time zero) of all the firm's outstanding common shares. The right side begins with SE_0, the current dollar value of shareholders' equity (the shareholders' total investment in the firm, equal to contributed capital plus earned capital) and adds to that the returns to the shareholders expected in the future, each discounted for the time value of money. Note that the numerator of each return expression ($[ROE_n - r_e] \times SE_{n-1}$) is equal to the dollar value of the shareholder value creation expected in each future period—that is, the extent to which ROE exceeds the cost of equity multiplied by the shareholders' investment at the beginning of each period. This expression of value creation was introduced back in Chapter 1 (See Figure 1-5, Method 2). In essence, the value of a firm is equal to the shareholders' investment plus management's expected ability to create value for the shareholders in the future.

Note the key roles in Expression 3 played by stockholders' equity (SE), measured by the balance sheet; ROE (net income/stockholders' equity), measured by the income statement and balance sheet; and the cost of equity (r_e), which must be estimated (see

[1] A discussion of present value is found in Appendix A of the text.

Chapter 1). Consider also the potential importance of the determinants of ROE (return on assets, capital structure leverage, common equity leverage, profit margin, asset turnover, and other financial ratios), all of which are constructed from the financial statements. Indeed, Expression 3 highlights the close linkage between the measures produced by the financial statements and the market value of the firm.

In previous chapters, we indicated the importance of generating returns that exceed the cost of capital in the long run. Expression 3 makes it clear that to evaluate management's value creation efforts, we cannot assess only whether current period ROE exceeds the cost of capital. Although that might indicate successful value creation, Expression 3 highlights the relationship between value (V_0) and *future* returns that exceed the cost of capital. The expression also shows that value creation can take place even when ROE is less than the cost of capital in a given period. What is important is whether that negative return is more than offset by positive returns in other periods.

INSIGHT: INTERPRETING V_0

The term V_0 can be interpreted in several ways. First, it can be interpreted as the market value of the firm. In the case of a public company, the value can be found by taking the market price of the common stock times the number of shares outstanding (i.e., the market capitalization of the firm). In that case, the observed V_0 can be used to infer what the market thinks about future returns and cost of capital.

Alternatively, V_0 can be treated as the "intrinsic value" of the company. That is, based on one's estimates of future returns and cost of capital, V_0 then represents what the market price "should be."

► MARKET-TO-BOOK RATIOS

Expression 3 also clearly illustrates the difference between the firm's market value (V_0) and its book value (SE_0). If the firm is expected to create no value for the shareholders in the future ($ROE_n = r_e$), market value will equal book value; if the firm is expected to destroy value in the future ($ROE_n < r_e$), market value will be less than book value; and if the firm is expected to create value in the future ($ROE_n > r_e$), market value will exceed book value. Consequently, the difference between a firm's market value and its book value is a measure of the extent to which the market believes that shareholder value will be created (or destroyed) in the future.

Computing the market-to-book ratio for a firm is straightforward as long as the firm's shares are publicly traded. All one needs is the market price of the firm's common shares, the number of common shares outstanding, and the shareholders' equity section of the balance sheet. As of January 29, 2005, for example, Nordstrom common shares traded at approximately $24 each. Approximately, 278 million common shares were outstanding, and shareholders' equity as reported on the January 29, 2005 balance sheet was approximately $1.8 billion. The calculation of the market-to-book ratio is provided below.

$$V_{1/29/05} / SE_{1/29/05} = \$6.672 \text{ billion} / \$1.8 \text{ billion} = 3.71$$

$$\$6.672 \text{ billon} = \$24/\text{common share} \times 278 \text{ million common shares outstanding}$$

As the computation shows, the value of Nordstrom as of January 29, 2005, as determined by the stock market, was $6.672 billion, which is 3.71 times larger than the balance sheet's measure of the shareholders' investment ($1.8 billion). In terms of the ROE valuation model, stock market investors expect that Nordstrom's management will create considerable value in the future by generating ROEs that exceed Nordstrom's cost of equity.

ANALYSIS EXAMPLE: INTERPRETING A SAMPLING OF MARKET-TO-BOOK RATIOS

The market-to-book ratios, as of November 10, 2005, of selected companies are presented below:

| Microsoft | 5.94 | Dell | 12.72 | Iron Mountain | 4.40 |
| General Motors | 0.62 | Weis Markets | 1.86 | Lucent | 26.99 |

The measures are quite varied. Interpreting them in light of Expression 3 is informative. Microsoft's ratio (5.94) suggests that the market expects the company to generate considerable value beyond what is reported in the shareholders' equity section of its balance sheet. At 12.72, Dell's stock price reflects even greater expectations about future growth. Iron Mountain, a document storage company, falls below Microsoft but well ahead of Weis Markets (4.40 vs. 1.86). Weis Markets, a grocery chain, is in a very competitive industry. Its ROE is in the 10% range (probably close to its costs of capital) and its growth is steady but slow. The stock market recognizes that it will create value in the future, but not a huge amount. At 26.99, does the market think Lucent will create tremendous value or achieve remarkable levels of growth? In this case, the market-to-book ratio is high because book value is particularly low. Recent large losses and restructurings left Lucent with a very small shareholders' equity, driving the ratio up. General Motors has a market-to-book ratio less than 1.0. This unusual result is indicative of the financial problems that the company faces. Recent talk of a bankruptcy filing and large unfunded health care and pension obligations do not bode well for the company, suggesting that future ROEs may be less than GM's cost of capital (or even negative) and could be pushing the stock price down.

In the next section, we discuss and illustrate how a firm's intrinsic value (V_0) can be estimated using the ROE-based valuation model. Comparing this estimate, computed using Expression 3, to the actual market value can help to determine whether the market price of a firm's common shares is under- or overvalued. More important, however, is that working through this process will identify key variables that must be measured and managed to promote the success of the firm.

▶ USING THE ROE VALUATION MODEL TO ESTIMATE FIRM MARKET VALUE

To use Expression 3 to estimate the market value of a firm, you must estimate the firm's future ROEs and book values (stockholders' equity), and its cost of equity. These estimates can then be plugged into Expression 3, and the resulting market value estimate can be compared to the firm's current market value (number of outstanding common shares multiplied by the market price per share) to assess whether the firm's shares are over- or undervalued. In general, overvalued shares should be sold or avoided, and undervalued shares should be acquired or held. In the Nordstrom case above, for example, if your application of Expression 3 estimates that on January 29, 2005, that Nordstrom's market value is below $6.672 billion, its January 29, 2005 market value, Nordstrom shares should be avoided or sold; if the market value estimate is above $6.672 billion, it should be purchased or held.

ANALYSIS CHALLENGE: HOW MUCH IS THAT COMPANY WORTH? (REVISITED)

The valuation model we describe is equally applicable to private firms. That is, the owner of a private firm could use estimates inferred from analyses of similar public companies and knowledge of their own firm's expected performance to estimate the value of their firm.

A manager faced with a potential acquisition could estimate the value of the combined enterprise and compare that value with the value of the firm without the target company. The difference in value represents the maximum price that the manager should be willing to pay to make the acquisition.

Expression 3 shows that estimating the market value of a firm (V_0) requires a current balance sheet, an estimate of the firm's cost of equity (r_e), and predictions of the ROEs that management will generate in the *future*. The balance sheet provides a measure of the shareholders' investment (SE_0), a method of estimating a firm's cost of equity is described in the appendix to Chapter 1, and future amounts for shareholders' equity (SE_n) can be computed once the ROEs are predicted by simply adding net income for the year to the shareholders' equity balance at the beginning of the year.[2] Consequently, a key element to a meaningful estimate of what the market price of a company's common stock should be is accurately predicting future ROE.

Predicting Future ROE

Predicting the ROEs that a firm will generate in the future is a challenge, and although the financial statements play an important role, they must be used in the appropriate manner. First, financial statements report on past events. Although many of the estimates that underlie measures on the balance sheet are supported by management's beliefs about the future (e.g., we will be able to collect X dollars of our receivables in the future), the financial statements are not forecasts, per se. Second, the fact that financial statement values must be reasonably objective requires that many items relevant to the value of a company are not reported on the financial statements (e.g., human resources, market values of certain assets and intangibles, and knowledge) because they cannot be reliably measured. And finally, management may be biased when it prepares the financial statements, which is discussed in detail in Chapter 6 of this text. Consequently, any attempt to predict future ROEs should take these steps:

- Assess the business environment;
- Read and study the financial statements and notes;
- Assess the level and direction of management's reporting bias; and
- Analyze the level and determinants of historical ROE.

Assess the Business Environment

To forecast future returns, the first step is to learn about the company, its industry, and how the company and industry relate to the overall economy. What industry is the company in, who are the major players and competitors, and is it easy or difficult for outside firms to enter the industry? What is the nature of the company's operations, and what strategy is the

---

[2]Dividends are assumed to be zero in the ROE valuation model. Assuming no dividends simplifies the calculation, and it can be shown algebraically that the value of the firm is unaffected by whether earnings are paid out to the shareholders in the form of dividends or reinvested in the firm if we assume that the reinvested earnings earn exactly the required return.

company using to generate profits within its industry? What are the relationships between the company and its suppliers and customers, and who holds the bargaining power? Finally, when the overall economy booms or falls into recession, how are the company's sales and profits affected? How quickly do the company's sales and profits change when the indices of overall economic activity change? An astute analyst addresses these questions before reviewing the financial statements. The answers provide a forward-looking perspective on the company and create a useful context in which to interpret the financial statements. They can also help target key items on the financial statements for closer examination.

One way to quickly gain a sense of a company's operations and how its future prospects are viewed by other experts is to access investment services such as Moody's (http://moodys.com), Value Line (http://valueline.com), Dun & Bradstreet (http://smallbusiness.dnb.com), and Standard & Poor's (http://www.spglobal.com). These information sources provide extensive analyses of the operations and financial position of many companies, as well as ratings of the risks of their outstanding debts.

Read and Study the Financial Statements and Notes

With an understanding of the company's business environment, the financial statement information can be meaningfully studied. This involves (1) reading the audit report; (2) identifying significant transactions; and (3) reading the income statement, balance sheet, statement of cash flows, statement of shareholders' equity, and notes.

The audit report serves as the accounting profession's "seal of approval," stating whether, and to what extent, the information on the financial statements fairly reflects the financial position and operations of the company. It also provides an assessment of the condition of the company's internal controls. After reviewing the financial records of the company, the auditor usually renders a standard audit report, which states that all necessary tests were conducted in concluding that financial statements conform to generally accepted acccounting principles (GAAP), they fairly reflect the company's financial position and results of operations, and the internal control system can be reasonably relied upon. In such cases, the reader can be reasonably assured that the information in the statements is credible. However, the audit report is not an investment recommendation; it only informs financial statement readers that the data can be relied upon. Departures from the standard audit report should be examined closely. For example, when companies are in dire financial straights, the audit report may draw attention to the fact that the financial statements were prepared assuming that the firm is a going concern, but that the assumption is in doubt—suggesting that impairments and restructurings, or even bankruptcy, may be on the horizon.

RED FLAGS: THERMA-WAVE, INC.—GOING CONCERN MODIFICATION TO THE AUDITOR'S OPINION

Therma-Wave develops, manufacturers, markets, and services process control metrology systems used in the manufacture of semiconductors. When Therma-Wave issued its fiscal 2006 annual report on Form 10-K, the audit report contained the following paragraph:

"The accompanying consolidated financial statements have been prepared assuming that the Company will continue as a going concern. As discussed in Note 1 to the con-

solidated financial statements, the Company has suffered recurring net losses and negative cash flows from operations. These factors raise substantial doubt about the Company's ability to continue as a going concern. Management's plans in regard to these matters are also described in Note 1. The consolidated financial statements do not include any adjustments that might result from the outcome of this uncertainty."

(continues)

RED FLAGS: THERMA-WAVE, INC.—GOING CONCERN MODIFICATION TO THE AUDITOR'S OPINION (*continued*)

The message is clear. This is a company in financial trouble. Note 1 explains the challenges facing the company and several post-year-end steps that they have taken to reduce costs and gain financial flexibility. It is up to the reader of the financial statements to evaluate the likelihood that the changes are effective.

In May 2007, the company was purchased by KLA-Tencor Corporation.

Users should also make special note of significant transactions, such as major acquisitions, the discontinuance or disposal of a business segment, unresolved litigation, major write-downs of receivables or inventories, plant closings (often called restructurings), offers to purchase outstanding shares (tender offers), extraordinary gains or losses, and changes of accounting methods. Such items, normally discussed in the notes, can have an important effect on the future direction of the company and may distort the financial statements, making it more difficult to both assess the company's current financial position and predict its future performance.

 ## ANALYSIS CHALLENGE: MANAGEMENT LABELS LINE ITEMS. YOU SHOULD EVALUATE THE LABELS FOR YOURSELF.

Although management might provide a label for a given event or transaction, or GAAP may require a particular classification, we encourage analysts to assess the underlying economics for themselves and come to their own conclusion about what is recurring or nonrecurring, ordinary or extraordinary, and so on. A solid understanding of the underlying business model and industry economics helps interpret trends and predicts future results.

The financial statements should be reviewed in total, but it is important to target items key to the success of the company's operations. Identifying these items is one of the goals of understanding the company's business environment. For example, success for companies in the retail industry, such as Wal-Mart, Home Depot, and Nordstrom, depends on the quality of inventory management. Consequently, inventory, accounts payable, and cost of goods sold—and the related notes—are particularly important accounts for these companies. Performance in the financial services sector (e.g., HSBC Holdings and Merrill Lynch) depends on successful investment and receivables (i.e., loan) management, indicating that the accounts related to these assets are especially important. Software developers, such as Microsoft and SAP, and pharmaceuticals, such as Merck and Novartis, invest heavily in research and development. Integrated oil and gas companies such as ExxonMobil, Royal Dutch Shell, and British Petroleum need to generate funds for exploration and for maintenance and expansion of refining capacity. In sum, when reading financial statement information, savvy users recognize that the nature of the company's operations dictates where the analysis should be focused. Gaining adequate understanding of the key business measures is imperative if past ROE is to be well understood and future ROE predicted.

Public companies in the United States and many other countries provide a narrative description of the results of their operations and their financial position. Called Management's Discussion and Analysis (MD&A), it also provides forward-looking information about management's plans for capital expenditures and other initiatives that are helpful for understanding past results and predicting ROEs.

Assess the Level and Direction of Management's Reporting Bias

Management has an incentive to use discretion in the preparation of the financial statements to depict the financial condition and performance of the company in a self-serving light. Financial statement readers should assess whether management has acted upon its incentive, and estimate the direction and magnitude of its effect on the financial statements before attempting to use financial statement information to predict future ROEs. Managers who practice strategic reporting may be attempting to conceal negative news, which by itself would not bode well for the future. Furthermore, strategic reporting may create misleading trends in the financial information that should be adjusted for when predicting future ROEs. In general, such practices tend to mask the link between the financial statements and the true economic condition and performance of the company. Chapter 6 is devoted to this concept, called earnings management. The better users understand earnings management, the better they will be able to see through that "mask."

Analyze the Level and Determinants of Historical ROE

In Chapter 4, we introduced the ROE model (Figure 4-2), and described how figures on the financial statements can be used to construct financial ratios that measure past ROE and its determinants. Understanding these value drivers is critical in the assessment of future ROEs. How has the company created or destroyed value in the past? Has ROA (profit margin multiplied by asset turnover) been the primary value driver, or has leverage played the key role? Where in the ROE model are the company's strengths and weaknesses compared to its competitors and its industry? How will the stated and anticipated plans of the managers lead to future ROEs? Answers to these questions, in combination with a solid understanding of the nature of the company and its business environment and the level and direction of earnings management, help establish a strong foundation for predicting future ROEs, a key variable in estimating a company's value.

DRILLING DOWN: ESTIMATING ROE COMPONENTS

$$\text{ROE} = \frac{\text{Net income}}{\text{Common equity}} = \frac{\text{NI} + \text{Interest expense}}{\text{Sales}} \times \frac{\text{Sales}}{\text{Assets}} \times \frac{\text{Assets}}{\text{Common equity}} \times \frac{\text{NI}}{\text{NI} + \text{Interest expense}}$$

Estimating future ROEs can be done at the component level, too. The advantage of doing so is that managers can bring their knowledge of economic fundamentals and management's strategies to bear.

For example, if a company was earning a particularly high level of return on sales, one might predict that profitability would decline as new competitors entered the market. Understanding the barriers to entry faced by potential entrants helps determine the time period until profits hit normal levels. Similarly, one could ask how future profitability will be affected by choosing to close a plant today or entering a strategic partnership.

Asset turnover levels can be benchmarked across time and companies, within an industry and outside the industry. Fixed asset turnover may be limited by current technology, but forward-looking firms might improve the ratio through outsourcing. That, in turn, may impact operating profit levels.

Financial and capital structure leverage are likely to be affected most by the firm's debt policies, cash flow, and investment opportunities. Management's Discussion and Analysis, a section in the annual report, often provides insights into how these may change in coming periods.

Incorporating ROE Predictions into the Valuation Model

The valuation model in Expression 3 requires annual ROE predictions indefinitely into the future. To simplify this task, the time horizon over which predictions are made can be divided into two segments as illustrated in Expression 4.

Expression 4

$$V_0 = SE_0 + \frac{(ROE_1 - r_e) \times SE_0}{(1 + r_e)^1} + \frac{(ROE_2 - r_e) \times SE_1}{(1 + r_e)^2} + \frac{(ROE_3 - r_e) \times SE_2}{(1 + r_e)^3} + \frac{(ROE_4 - r_e) \times SE_3}{(r_e - g)(1 + r_e)^3}$$

Book value |————————————Predictable forecast horizon———————————| Long-run forecast assumption

The term on the right side of Expression 4 (SE_0) is the book value of the company (shareholders' equity). The next terms, called the predictable forecast horizon, identify the time period over which the analyst believes reasonably accurate predictions can be made. Expression 4 defines this period as three years in length, but depending on the company and the situation, it could be shorter or longer. Normally, the longer the accurately predictable forecast horizon, the more likely the estimated market value accurately reflects the true value of the firm.

The final term, called the long-run forecast assumption, captures one's views about the long-run prospects for the firm. The numerator represents the expected level of value creation that the firm can sustain over its life, while the denominator represents the discount factor for the time value of money.

The denominator is divided into two terms. Dividing the numerator by $(r_e - g)$ generates the present value of an annuity that begins with the value created in year 4 (in this case) and grows at a constant rate, g. The growth rate (g) can be positive, negative, or zero, depending on what the user believes about the firm's ability to sustain value creation in the long run. Because the present value of that growing annuity is as of the end of year 3, it must be discounted back to the present (time 0). The second factor, $(1 + r_e)^3$, represents the discount from the end of year 3 (or beginning of year 4) to the present.[3]

Using the Valuation Model to Estimate Nordstrom's Market Value

To illustrate how the valuation model can be used to estimate Nordstrom's market value, consider the following information computed from Nordstrom's 2002–2005 financial statements. As of January 29, 2005, Nordstrom had approximately 278 million common shares outstanding, with a per share market price of approximately $24, leading to a firm market value (market capitalization value) of $6.672 billion (278 million × $24).

	2005	2004	2003	2002	4-year average
Return on equity	0.23	0.16	0.07	0.10	0.14
Return on assets	0.10	0.07	0.03	0.04	0.06
Capital structure leverage	2.65	2.85	3.07	3.02	2.90
Profit margin	0.06	0.05	0.02	0.03	0.04
Asset turnover	1.57	1.52	1.43	1.46	1.50

[3] When g exceeds the cost of equity, $(r_e - g)$ becomes negative. This makes little sense. As a practical matter, analysts extend the predictable forecast horizon to a point where g does not exceed the cost of equity and then use the formula to simplify the long-run forecast value calculation.

We estimate Nordstrom's cost of equity (r_e) to be 12% . Based on the summary data, which show recent improvements in ROE and ROA, and reduced levels of leverage, we predict that Nordstrom will generate an ROE of 0.20 over the next three years and maintain a 14% ROE indefinitely, with no growth in value creation in the long run. Of course, many more factors would need to be considered in this prediction, but based simply on an analysis of recent ROEs, a 20% ROE in the short run and 14% in the long run seems like a reasonable *starting* point. These assumptions lead to the following valuation for Nordstrom (all dollar amounts are in billions).

	Predictable forecast horizon			Long-run forecast assumption
$V_0 = \$1.8 +$	$\dfrac{(.20 - .12) \times \$1.8}{(1 + .12)^1}$ +	$\dfrac{(.20 - .12) \times \$2.2}{(1 + .12)^2}$ +	$\dfrac{(.20 - .12) \times \$2.6}{(1 + .12)^3}$ +	$\dfrac{(.14 - .12) \times \$3.1}{(.12 - .00) \times (1 + .12)^3}$
$V_0 = \$1.8 +$	$\$ .1286$ +	$\$ .1408$ +	$\$ .1486$ +	$\$ .3690$
$V_0 = \$2.59$				

This calculation shows that if Nordstrom generates a 20% ROE over the next three years and then maintains an annual ROE of 14% throughout the remainder of its life, and its cost of equity holds constant at 12%, the present value of the company's future shareholder value creation (along with the equity it has now) would be $2.59 billion dollars, or $9.32 per common share ($2.59 billion/278 million outstanding common shares), which is 1.44 times greater than its current book value ($1.8 billion). Note that shareholder value is created in each year of the 3-year predictable forecast horizon, but 47 percent $(0.3690/[0.1286 + 0.1408 + 0.1486 + 0.3690])$ of Nordstrom's estimated future value creation comes from its expected ability to create value in the long run.

► IMPLICATIONS OF DIFFERENCES BETWEEN ACTUAL
AND ESTIMATED MARKET VALUES

Interestingly, the actual January 29, 2005 market price for Nordstrom shares was $24 per share, more than 2.5 times the estimated value ($9.32). What does this mean? One interpretation is that the actual market value of Nordstrom common shares is currently overvalued, suggesting that investors should avoid (not buy but rather sell) Nordstrom shares. This conclusion rests on the assumption that the predictions used in the model for Nordstrom's ROE and cost of equity are more accurate than the predictions used by the investors in the stock market. This assumption is tenuous because we did not conduct a thorough investigation of the nature of Nordstrom's business; its business environment, competitive strategy, and industry; and the magnitude and direction of the management bias used in the preparation of the financial information we used to support our predictions.

Rather than jump to a conclusion that Nordstrom common shares are overvalued and the market is somehow wrong, perhaps it would be wise to focus instead on what we do know. We know, for example, that the stock market's expectations seem more optimistic than ours with respect to ROE (which we estimated at 20% in the short run and 14% beyond with no growth) and/or the cost of equity (which we estimated at a constant 12%). The market seems to expect either higher ROEs, a lower cost of equity, and/or growth in the long-run forecast assumption.

ANALYSIS CHALLENGE: WHY IS OUR VALUE SO DIFFERENT?

Why might the market hold a different expectation from ours? Does it expect Nordstrom's profit margin to soar or asset turnover to accelerate? Has there been a change in the com- pany's tax rates, or does the market expect a more effectively leveraged Nordstrom in the future? When values are so dif- ferent, analysts should ask why.

We can gain insights into the market's expectations with respect to Nordstrom's ability to create value by working backwards and asking two questions: (1) Given a 12% cost of equity, what level of ROE would Nordstrom have to sustain indefinitely in the future to create a per share market price of $24? and (2) Given a 20% ROE for three years and a 14% ROE thereafter, what cost of equity would have to be assumed to create a per share market price of $24? Both questions can be answered by using the valuation formula.

Question 1 can be answered by setting V_0 to $6.672 billion ($24 per share × 0.278 billion shares), cost of equity (r_e) to 12%, growth (g) to zero, and then solving the valuation equation for ROE. The answer is approximately 29%, which means that, given a cost of equity of 12%, the market believes that Nordstrom can generate an ROE of 29% indefinitely. This information may be useful for management because it establishes a benchmark for what would be required to increase the market price of Nordstrom shares. Nordstrom's managers should ask themselves how they can achieve higher levels of ROE. If management can communicate to the stock market how those actions can generate an ROE of more than 29%, it should be able to increase the market price of Nordstrom stock and the market value of the firm. However, generating a 29% ROE indefinitely is extremely unlikely, even for the very best firms. Consequently, it appears that the market may be estimating a cost of equity for Nordstrom that is smaller than the 12% we used. We address this possibility next.

To address Question 2, we set V_0 to $6.672 billion, ROE to 20%, growth (g) to zero, and solve the valuation equation for cost of equity (r_e). The answer is approximately 7.5%, meaning that, given a ROE of 20%, the market believes that Nordstrom's cost of equity is 7.5%.

Similar to the conclusion regarding a 29% ROE, a 7.5% cost of equity is relatively low even for the very best firms. The most likely case is that the market's valuation of Nordstrom reflects an expected ROE somewhere between 20% and 29%, and a cost or equity (r_e) somewhere between 7.5% and 12%. In any event, this analysis shows that the market appears to be very bullish about Nordstrom. Long-term ROEs in the 20%–30% range and cost of equities in the 7%–12% range would be considered optimistic for virtually any firm.

GOVERNANCE CHALLENGE: YOUR STOCK PRICE SEEMS HIGH ...

If the market price of your company's shares is far ahead of management's beliefs about what a reasonable price is, what should be done? On the one hand, you might think it is cause for celebration. The overpriced stock can be used as valuable currency to make acquisitions. You might think it is an opportune time to raise capital by issuing new shares. On the other hand, one must ask why the market's expectations are out of line. Is the company's disclosure policy misleading the market? Should management acknowledge that the price appears high? Is it ethical to sell shares knowing that they are overpriced? How happy will your new owners be when they realize they paid too much? If expectations are later aligned and the price falls, will the company be subject to litigation for not having informed the market earlier? What damage will a fall in stock price do to the company's reputation? Reputation in the capital markets is only the beginning. Litigation affects a firm's ability to recruit top talent in the labor market and cannot help but harm their position in product markets, too.

Perhaps the most important conclusion of this backward-looking analysis is that Nordstrom's stock market price reflects the expectation of a relatively large difference between ROE and r_e throughout Nordstrom's life, a difference that leads to a large difference between the firm's market value ($6.672 billion) and its book value ($1.8 billion). This observation highlights the importance to management and the shareholders of maximizing the difference between ROE and r_e. Increasing the market's expectation of this difference by a small amount could have a significant positive impact on the firm's share price and market value. How can this expectation be influenced? By doing and communicating. "Doing" means taking actions that create more value. "Communicating" means telling the story in a credible fashion, and financial reporting plays an important role in that endeavor.

► USING FINANCIAL STATEMENTS TO ASSESS THE VALUE OF NON-U.S. FIRMS

U.S. investors are showing increasing interest in foreign securities traded on foreign markets. Such securities often provide returns that exceed those available in U.S. markets, and holding foreign stocks can help reduce an investor's risk by diversifying the investment portfolio to include securities of companies from more than one country. In most cases, the choice to buy or sell a foreign security is based on financial information provided by the investee company, presenting the investor with the challenge of analyzing and interpreting financial statements prepared according to non-U.S. accounting (often international reporting standards) and business norms.

We have already discussed some of the differences between U.S. GAAP and International Financial Reporting Standards (IFRS). An investor who uses information from the financial statements to guide trading in foreign securities certainly should attempt to reconcile these differences if meaningful comparisons are to be made among the selection of international investments. As U.S. GAAP and IFRS continue to converge, reconciling them will become a less onerous task. However, such reconciliations are not sufficient by themselves to achieve meaningful comparisons. Since accounting statements are products of the social, economic, legal, and cultural environments in which they are prepared, differences across these environments further complicate the interpretation of any adjusted financial statements. In other words, not only must the financial statements of IFRS and U.S. GAAP companies be reconciled, but the resulting numbers can only be interpreted and compared if one understands the different business environments in which the two companies operate.

Studies have shown that understanding the institutional, legal, and cultural environment is as important as adjusting financial statements for differences in accounting methods. For example, Japanese and Korean firms, in general, carry much higher debt/equity ratios than their U.S. counterparts. Does that mean that they are more highly leveraged and riskier? Not necessarily. The relationship between a firm and its bank and the nature of the capital markets in Japan and Korea differ remarkably from that in the U.S. Local banks backed by the government are the primary providers of capital, and in many ways, the banks have more of an equity relationship with their client firms, while government support significantly reduces the risk of loan default or anything resembling bankruptcy. Consequently, after adjusting the financial statements for different accounting methods, Japanese and Korean firms may appear on the surface to be more highly leveraged and more risky, but in substance, they may not be. They are simply products of a different business environment.

▶ SUMMARY

Management's success depends on whether it creates value for the shareholders, defined as generating ROEs that exceed the cost of equity in the long run. A company's share price reflects expected value creation because it is determined by the market's expectation of the difference between ROE and the cost of equity. The determinants of ROE include return on assets (ROA), profit margin, asset turnover, common equity leverage, and capital structure leverage. By properly managing these determinants, management can increase ROE and the market's expectation of ROE, as well as reduce r_e and the market's expectation of r_e. These actions should increase the value of the firm.

▶ CASE AND REVIEW QUESTIONS

Weis Markets and Chicago Rivet—Valuation

1. Use the valuation model presented in Chapter 5 to estimate the value of Weis Markets, Inc. (WMK) and Chicago Rivet & Machine Co. (CVR). (The model is reproduced below.) You should estimate the model's inputs based on an analysis of relevant financial ratios from past periods. That is, calculate prior ROEs, assess their determinants, establish trends, and estimate future ROEs, book values, and growth rates. A brief description of each firm, provided by Yahoo Finance, follows.

Expression 4

$$V_0 = SE_0 + \frac{(ROE_1 - r_e) \times SE_0}{(1 + r_e)^1} + \frac{(ROE_2 - r_e) \times SE_1}{(1 + r_e)^2} + \frac{(ROE_3 - r_e) \times SE_2}{(1 + r_e)^3} + \frac{(ROE_4 - r_e) \times SE_3}{(r_e - g)(1 + r_e)^3}$$

Book value |————————Predictable forecast horizon————————| Long-run forecast assumption

Note that the growth rate you use, g, reflects the growth rate of the numerator of the final term in Expression 4. Use a cost of equity for Weis and CVR of 0.10 and 0.12, respectively.[4]

[4]These estimates can be validated by using the capital asset pricing model, described in the appendix of Chapter 1. Yahoo! Finance lists Weis Markets' stock beta as 0.84 and Chicago Rivet's as −0.15. CVR's beta seems unrealistically low. A review of its competitors' betas suggests that a figure on the order of 1.2 is more appropriate.

Weis Markets, Inc., engages in the retail sale of food and pet supplies in the United States. The company's retail food stores sell groceries, dairy products, frozen foods, meats, seafood, fresh produce, floral products, prescriptions, deli/bakery products, prepared foods, fuel, and general merchandise items, such as health and beauty care, and household products. Weis also offers services, such as third parties providing in-store banks, laundry services, and takeout restaurants. As of December 31, 2005, the company owned and operated 82 retail food stores, leased and operated 75 retail food stores, and owned and operated a chain of 31 pet supply stores. Weis Markets was founded by Harry and Sigmund Weis in 1912. The company is based in Sunbury, Pennsylvania.

Chicago Rivet & Machine Co. engages in the manufacture and sale of rivets and rivet setting machines, primarily in North America. It operates through two segments: Fasteners and Assembly Equipment. The Fasteners segment engages in the manufacture and sale of rivets, cold-formed fasteners and parts, and screw machine products. The Assembly Equipment segment manufactures automatic rivet setting machines, automatic assembly equipment, and parts and tools for such machines. This segment also engages in the leasing of automatic rivet setting machines. The company offers its products through employees and independent sales representatives to the manufacturers of automobiles and automotive components. CVR was founded in 1920 and is headquartered in Naperville, Illinois.

2. As of July 15, 2006, Weis Markets' shares traded at a market-to-book-value ratio of 1.72. The corresponding figure for CVR was 0.93. Explain in economic terms why the companies' market-to-book ratios are so different.

WEIS MARKETS (WMK)

Year Ended:	12/31/2005	12/25/2004	12/27/2003	12/28/2002	12/29/2001
Net Sales	$2,222,598	$2,097,712	$2,042,499	$1,999,364	$1,971,665
Cost of Sales	1,636,137	1,548,210	1,505,926	1,471,479	1,457,002
General & Administration Expenses	506,900	477,317	465,952	448,478	451,723
Total Operating Expense	2,143,037	2,025,527	1,971,878	1,919,957	1,908,725
Operating Income	79,561	72,185	70,621	79,407	62,940
Investment Income	3,408	1,617	1,220	879	9,860
Other Income	16,337	13,801	16,363	14,400	9,047
Net Income Before Taxes	99,306	87,603	88,204	94,686	81,847
Provision for Income Taxes	35,885	30,412	33,628	35,537	31,792
Net Income	$ 63,421	$ 57,191	$ 54,576	$ 59,149	$ 50,055
Cash/Equivalents	$ 69,300	$ 58,234	$ 73,340	$ 3,929	$ 3,255
Securities	23,210	16,212	17,207	43,510	28,675
Accounts Receivable	38,376	36,058	34,111	30,188	26,530
Inventories	179,382	165,044	173,552	182,832	169,952
Prepaid/Other	6,076	4,970	3,987	3,980	8,294
Income Tax Recoverable	0	1,729	0	0	3,395
Deferred Taxes	4,359	3,003	4,793	0	0
Total Current Assets	320,703	285,250	306,990	264,439	240,101
Long-Term Assets	467,784	463,232	437,325	452,260	464,084
Total Assets	$ 788,487	$ 748,482	$ 744,315	$ 716,699	$ 704,185
Total Current Liabilities	$ 157,034	$ 147,378	$ 144,685	$ 149,502	$ 137,770
Total Long-Term Debt	0	0	0	0	25,000
Deferred Taxes	27,596	29,404	24,182	14,765	16,051
Total Liabilities	184,630	176,782	168,867	164,267	178,821
Total Equity	603,857	571,700	575,448	552,432	525,364
Total Liabilities & Shareholders' Equity	$ 788,487	$ 748,482	$ 744,315	$ 716,699	$ 704,185
Shares of Common Stock Outstanding	27,020	27,033	27,140	27,194	27,203

CHICAGO RIVET (CVR)

Year Ended:	12/31/2005	12/31/2004	12/31/2003	12/31/2002	12/31/2001
Revenues	$39,761	$39,233	$38,191	$43,013	$40,443
Cost of Revenue	34,060	30,955	30,744	32,427	31,256
Selling/Admin.	6,723	6,041	6,280	6,675	6,440
Total Operating Expense	40,783	36,996	37,024	39,102	37,696
Operating Income	(1,022)	2,237	1,167	3,911	2,747
Interest Income	148	64	72	84	145
Gain from Demutualization	257	0	0	0	0
Interest Expense	0	0	−23	−80	−260
Sale of Equipment	0	0	11	31	43
Other, Net	14	14	16	16	16
Net Income Before Taxes	(603)	2,315	1,243	3,962	2,691
Provision for Income Taxes	(206)	792	425	1,357	899
Net Income	$ (397)	$ 1,523	$ 818	$ 2,605	$ 1,792
Cash/Equivalents	$ 4,731	$ 5,464	$ 5,530	$ 2,204	$ 4,693
CDs	1,005	805	455	3,158	178
Receivables, Net	5,370	4,868	4,549	4,995	3,995
Inventories	5,972	6,242	5,233	6,090	6,051
Prepaid/Deferred.Tax	0	0	602	581	607
Deferred Income Taxes	560	554	0	0	0
Other	232	219	219	278	336
Total Current Assets	17,871	18,152	16,588	17,306	15,860
Long-Term Assets	10,052	11,147	11,550	12,782	13,819
Total Assets	$27,922	$29,299	$28,138	$30,088	$29,679
Total Current Liabilities	3,031	2,931	2,569	4,432	4,244
Long-Term Debt	0	0	0	0	1,633
Deferred Taxes	1,313	1,551	1,580	1,547	1,429
Total Liabilities	4,344	4,482	4,149	5,980	7,306
Total Equity	23,578	24,817	23,989	24,109	22,373
Total Liabilities & Shareholders' Equity	$27,922	$29,299	$28,138	$30,088	$29,679
Shares of Common Stock Outstanding	966	966	966	966	967

CHAPTER 6

Earnings Management

ANALYSIS CHALLENGE: CAN I TRUST THE NUMBERS?

Enron, WorldCom, Parmalat, Royal Ahold, Nortel, Tyco—the list goes on. We've heard the names and seen the demise of a once highly trusted public accounting firm. Can the num- bers really be trusted? Are the temptations to deceive just too great?

Management has access to information about a company's financial condition, performance, and future not available to outsiders (e.g., shareholders, customers, suppliers, and the general public). Much of this information is released when management periodically reports (Forms 10-K and 10-Q, and annual reports, etc.) to shareholders. Management must use considerable judgment in the disclosure and measurement of the economic events reported in the financial statements. That discretion can enhance the transparency of its reporting or make it more difficult for financial statement users to ascertain the true financial condition and performance of the company. In Chapters 7, 8, and 9, we cover the accounting for operating, investing, and financing activities. In this chapter, we provide an overview of the significant judgments that management makes in arriving at those accounting decisions. The later chapters examine these judgments in more detail.

The expression "earnings management" refers to cases when management uses its reporting discretion to produce financial statements that place management's performance in a particular light, often reducing the ability of the financial statements to fairly represent the financial performance and condition of the company. Extreme forms of earnings management (e.g., intentional financial misrepresentation) constitute fraud, but in the overwhelming majority of cases, earnings management is practiced within the boundaries of generally accepted accounting principles (GAAP), which, by its nature, allows much management judgment and discretion.

Managers are not inherently unethical, and they do not use every opportunity to exploit the investors and creditors who provide the company with capital. Indeed, it is in management's long-term best interest to report truthfully and without bias. Solid reporting reputations can lower a company's cost of capital and can expand its access to capital markets—especially when times are tough. It is well known, however, that many managers choose accounting methods, make estimates, and structure transactions that report their performance and financial position in ways that protect and further their personal interests.

166

Educated users of financial reports are on the lookout for signs of that behavior so that they can appropriately interpret the reported results.

ROE, VALUE CREATION, AND HIGH-QUALITY REPORTING

Value creation = Return on equity − Cost of equity

In a November 3, 2005, *The Wall Street Journal* article, "Samsung Reaches Out to Investors," writer Evan Ramstad discusses how Samsung Electronics enhanced its investor relations activities and reached out to the capital markets outside Korea. Noting that, historically, Samsung's management rarely met with investors and, when it did, spoke in vague generalities, Ramstad wrote, "Investors penalize the company's shares for the reduced access to management and transparency in reporting. Its stock has a price/earnings ratio of around 13 for next year's earnings, well below that of Intel, Nokia, and other large electronics and components makers."

A reputation for high-quality reporting can increase value creation by both increasing ROE (lower interest expense) and reducing the cost of equity. Stated another way, a reputation for managing earnings decreases management's credibility, which in turn leads investors to assess a higher cost to both debt and equity capital.

▶ INCENTIVES TO MANAGE EARNINGS

Management is often under significant pressure to ensure that net income achieves or exceeds certain benchmarks, such as last year's net income, budgeted net income, their own forecasts or those of analysts who follow the company, and industry performance metrics. Managers are fully aware that their financial statements are used by individuals inside and outside the company to evaluate and influence their actions, and that their future wealth is tied to financial accounting numbers. Management's performance is measured in the financial statements, and management compensation, for example, is often directly tied to reported profits, return on equity, and/or stock prices. In addition, debt covenants regularly include conditions, expressed in terms of financial accounting numbers, which constrain management behavior. Simply put, management's well-being is linked to the financial statements, creating incentives to use any discretion it has in the preparation of the statements to make its performance look as good as possible.

We acknowledge these realities, but we do not condone the practice of earnings management. We view the practice as costly to the effective management of the firm and potentially value destroying. In this chapter, we describe common forms of earnings management. The objective is not to provide you with a laundry list of tools to use; rather, we want you to be aware of how earnings are managed so that you can identify it, decipher it, and make more informed use of reported financial data.

We also recognize the argument that just as managers are aware that others are using the financial statements to evaluate them (providing incentives for earnings management in the first place), these same financial statement users are aware of the incentives and consider them as they write contracts, choose performance measures, and evaluate the managers. Some people argue that earnings management is simply a rational reaction by managers who believe that users of their reports expect that the reports have been managed. They argue that properly constructed contracts are the solution to the problem. That viewpoint has merit, but fails to recognize the enormous costs that this "cloak and dagger" behavior engenders, and the fact that contracts cannot cover every conceivable outcome. We believe that there is much merit to "telling it like it is"—the approach that we advocate.

INSIGHT: IT'S NOT JUST ABOUT OUTSIDERS ...

Although many discussions of earnings management and accounting misbehavior focus on external financial reporting, the very same "bag of tricks" is used to obfuscate internal reporting. Just as investors need to keep their eyes open for the possibility that someone is misleading them, company managers need to do the same. The manager of a business unit or division with authority over multiple operations will use accounting information to evaluate each one's performance; judge the managers; and decide who to promote, where to allocate resources, and where to send more help. Allocating resources within an organization requires the same vigilance over the reporting process necessary in external capital markets.

And there are controls in place that limit earnings management ...

Plenty of opportunities exist for management to exercise discretion in its financial reporting judgments. But managers do not have carte blanche to make up whatever data they choose. In addition to the moral arguments against just plain lying, formal controls that limit earnings management include internal and external auditing, securities regulations, and the threat of litigation—both civil and criminal—for failing to play by the rules. Informal controls include the role of the business press in breaking stories about questionable reporting and the role of security analysts in sharing their views about a company's reporting reputation.

▶ COMMON FORMS OF EARNINGS MANAGEMENT

Although the expression "earnings management" contains the word "earnings," it does not necessarily involve managing the earnings number per se. It can involve managing balance sheet accounts only, or even the statement of cash flows. Also, earnings management is not always practiced to make management's performance look better in the current period. Sometimes, management has incentives to understate performance. Earnings management assumes several different forms, practiced by management in different situations.

Overstating Operating Performance

In certain situations, managers simply attempt to devise a more favorable picture by overstating the performance of the company in the current period. This goal can be achieved by accelerating the recognition of revenue or deferring the recognition of expenses, both of which immediately boost net income and assets (or reduce liabilities). Young, fast-growing, aggressive companies sometimes use this strategy to help attract investment capital, and it also happens in situations where companies face financial difficulties that they wish to conceal.

Understating Operating Performance

Two well-known earnings management practices actually understate performance in the current period: taking a bath and creating hidden reserves.

Taking a Bath

When a company experiences an extremely poor year, managers have incentives to choose income-decreasing accounting methods and use conservative estimates or judgments (e.g., recognize an accounting loss, accelerate accrued expenses, and defer recognizing revenue) that, in turn, further reduce the company's operating performance and financial condition in that year. These incentives are often engendered by performance-based compensation contracts that set performance floors. Results below the floor are not rewarded. Those above are eligible for performance-based compensation. This strategy, called "taking a bath," enables companies to further understate performance in years that already are very poor, in the hope that the understatement may be less obvious. Moreover, the methods used to understate performance in the current year will naturally reverse themselves in future years, artificially boosting future measures of financial performance and creating the impression that the company is rebounding from the difficult year more quickly than it actually is. For example, overstating the write-down of slow-moving inventory in a given year means that the gross margin at the time of its eventual sale will be larger—giving the impression of better inventory and cost management in that later period. Accelerating expenses in a year when a performance plan's floor won't be met means that later periods—now unshackled from the burden of those expenses—are more likely to exceed the minimum and make management eligible for bonuses.

Creating Hidden Reserves and Smoothing Performance

The same contracts that set performance floors to determine bonus eligibility often set performance ceilings beyond which better performance is not rewarded. This leads to incentives for management to use very conservative accounting methods, and make estimates and judgments that lower earnings in years of otherwise extremely strong performance. Again, performance-based compensation contracts are at play; but environments that demand continuous improvement ("your target for next year is 10% more than last year's performance") create the same incentives. An accounting strategy, called "creating hidden reserves," helps management to "smooth" reported earnings over time, creating the impression of gradual, consistent, improving performance. Understating performance in the current period ensures that reported earnings in that period are not too high and, in addition, the natural reversal of the methods used to reduce current net income artificially boosts reported earnings in future periods when the company's actual performance may be less impressive. For example, overestimating the size of the future liability for warranty costs lowers current period earnings and allows managers the leeway to reverse the liability ("Oh my gosh, that liability is way too big, we'd better fix that!") in a later period when performance needs a boost.

ANALYSIS CHALLENGE: HIDDEN RESERVES, CONSERVATISM, PRUDENCE, AND JUST PLAIN LIES

Over a long period of time, accounting practices have emerged that encourage, or even require, conservative financial reporting. But conservatism is not the same as deliberate understatement. Delaying the recognition of revenue due to uncertainty about a transaction is conservative. Deliberately recording liabilities that do not exist or overstating ones that do is not conservative financial reporting. It is a lie, pure and simple. And when the deliberately overstated and misleading liability is reversed later, unless the reversal is clearly disclosed, management is once again lying about their performance. And as they say, two wrongs don't make a right.

"Hidden reserves" are not really hidden, they are just poorly labeled overstated liabilities or understated assets. In some countries, notably in continental Europe, there is a tendency to argue that these reserves are simply the result of prudent reporting. That is a controversial view elsewhere because it leads to the belief that it is OK to understate profits in good years and accepts the reversal of the reserves in poor years. By smoothing performance over time, managers lead unsuspecting financial statement readers to think that either the underlying economics of the business are more stable than they actually are or that the managers are particularly adept at managing in a volatile environment—neither of which is especially true. Sophisticated analysts also bear a cost. They need to estimate the setting up and the timing of the unwinding of the reserves. As they are unable to do that without detailed knowledge about the reserves, they realize that they face information risk, which makes their job more difficult. It also lowers their assessments of the company's value by increasing the cost of capital.

Performance-based compensation and a desire to reduce the volatility of reported earnings are not the only reasons that management may prefer to report lower earnings. Companies operating in industries that face accusations of unfair levels of profits (e.g., oil and gas companies, large drug companies, and companies with monopoly pricing power) have incentives to put a damper on reported profits to avoid costly political or societal regulation. Another example is the case of management buyouts. In a management buyout, firm insiders buy out the public shareholders and take the company private. The insiders—who may have influence over financial reporting decisions—have incentives to make the company appear less profitable, thus reducing the buyout price. Similarly, firms engaged in anti-trust disputes or anti-dumping litigation will argue that they are not earning excessive profits or have been harmed by the dumping behaviors of their competitors. In both cases, incentives to report lower earnings exist. Finally, to the extent that a firm can bolster its position in an income tax dispute by arguing that it made the same (income-decreasing) reporting for accounting purposes, incentives exist to report weaker performance.

Off-Balance-Sheet Financing

Managers have been known to structure financing transactions and choose certain accounting methods so that debt need not be reported on the balance sheet. By avoiding the recognition of debt, such activities, called "off-balance-sheet financing," make the reporting company appear less reliant on leverage, and therefore less risky. A well-known article published in *Forbes* once noted, "The basic drives of man are few: to get enough food, to find shelter, and to keep debt off the balance sheet." As we will see in Chapter 9, off-balance-sheet liabilities cannot exist without off-balance-sheet assets. As such, the practice leads to both an understatement of leverage *and* an overstatement of asset efficiency (understatement of assets) by artificially pushing up the asset turnover ratios.

INSIGHT: (AGAIN) IT'S NOT JUST ABOUT OUTSIDERS . . .

It is not just external users of the financial statements that can be misled by earnings management activities. Artificially creating the perception of strong or weak performance sends a signal to managers throughout the organization to change their behavior. Purchasing managers place orders on the grounds that demand is up, marketing managers extend brands that appear to be doing better than they actually are, and human resource managers alter their hiring processes when performance is strong. The opposite takes place when performance appears weak. None of these actions is likely to create value for the owners of the firm if the actions are based on misleading performance measures.

▶ HOW MANAGERS USE ACCOUNTING JUDGMENTS TO MANAGE EARNINGS

Figure 6-1 describes a framework that illustrates the general areas where management can exercise discretion in the preparation of the financial statements. When addressing the question of "how to account for an event," management must first decide whether the event created a material (significant) financial effect on the company. If the answer is "yes," management then determines how much detail must be disclosed on the financial statements as opposed to recognized in the notes. If the event is disclosed on the face of the financial

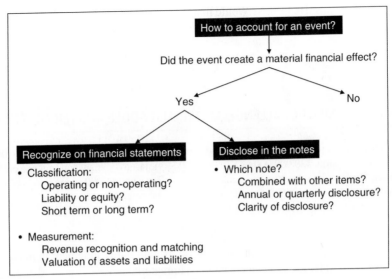

Figure 6-1. Framework for Earnings Management

statements, management must decide how to classify the event, as well as how to measure its financial effect. The remainder of the chapter is organized to highlight these four decisions: (1) materiality, (2) recognition versus disclosure, (3) classification, and (4) measurement.

Materiality Judgments

Financial statements are not exact and the concept of materiality has evolved in financial reporting. It states that transactions dealing with amounts large enough to make a difference to financial statement users need to be accounted for in a manner consistent with the principles of financial reporting. The magnitude of some transactions is so small that the method of accounting has no meaningful impact on the financial statements; these transactions are referred to as immaterial. Management is allowed to account for them as expediently as possible. Paper clips have useful lives that extend beyond the current period, but their costs are not capitalized!

Although materiality is a pragmatic concept, it poses a measurement and disclosure challenge because it requires judgment that can differ considerably among investors, creditors, managers, auditors, and others. What exactly is too small to make a difference and to whom? Unfortunately, few useful guidelines exist for what is—and is not—material, leaving the decision largely in the hands of management and the auditor. For many years, companies used quantitative methods to determine materiality (e.g., 5% of net income), but recently, the Securities and Exchange Commission (SEC) issued a statement (Staff Accounting Bulletin No. 99, "Materiality") eliminating that practice, requiring instead the use of qualitative analysis.

In determining materiality qualitatively, the size of the item is always considered, but whether it would affect the decision of an investor or creditor is often unclear. An amount too small to make a difference on the financial statements of a large company could be quite significant on the financial statements of a smaller one. The nature of the item is also important. A small adjustment to the inventory account, which directly affects cost of goods sold, the gross margin, and net income, may be more significant to financial statement users than large adjustments to accounts in the shareholders' equity section of the balance sheet. What about a small adjustment to reported net income that allows a company to just achieve its earnings forecast, or just beat last year's earnings number, or barely report positive profits? Would that be considered immaterial? Finally, the user must be considered. A creditor's definition of material may differ from that of an investor.

MEASUREMENT CHALLENGE: MATERIALITY DOES MATTER TO LENDERS

You might be indifferent as to whether appliance and electronics retailer Best Buy earns $30,000,000 or $30,001,000 in a given quarter. But you might care very much whether they lost $500 or reported a profit of $500. Because debt contracts often allow lenders to renegotiate debt terms when a company incurs a loss, losing $500 might be all it takes to violate a covenant and trigger a costly change in the contract. The same $1,000 swing makes a big difference depending on the context!

Management can exercise its materiality judgment in many different ways. Items considered by management to be immaterial may be expensed directly to the income statement, even in cases where, theoretically, they should be capitalized as assets and depreciated over their useful lives. Such a choice could help management to "take a bath" or build "hidden reserves." Items considered immaterial may be concealed by burying them in catch-all accounts on the financial statements instead of separately disclosing them. A loss on the sale of an investment, for example, might be included with other items in a miscellaneous non-operating expense account on the income statement to conceal the results of a poor management decision. Information items of potential importance may not be disclosed at all in the notes on the basis of subjectively determined immateriality. Management, for example, could choose not to disclose a missed interest payment, which may be a sign of serious financial problems, arguing that the amount is too small to make a difference. In essence, management can use its judgment of what is—and is not—material to manage earnings, making it more difficult for financial statement users to ascertain the financial performance and position of the reporting company.

GOVERNANCE CHALLENGE: YOU ARE ON THE AUDIT COMMITTEE ...

As a member of the company's audit committee—a subcommittee of the board of directors—you are charged with selecting the external auditor and discussing with them whether the company's financial statements are in accordance with GAAP and whether the management's reporting choices are appropriate. In your discussions with the auditors you should ask about any immaterial items encountered during the audit. What was their nature? How were they resolved? Who decided they were immaterial? Are items, individually considered immaterial, actually material when grouped together?

Recognition vs. Disclosure Judgments

Once management has decided that the financial effect of an event meets the materiality threshold, it must decide how to report the event in the financial statements. In some cases, GAAP allows management to choose note disclosure or financial statement recognition. Until recently, for example, companies were allowed to report the expense associated with employee stock option compensation either on the income statement as an expense or in the notes as a disclosure only. The overwhelming majority of companies chose the note disclosure option, probably because reporting the expense on the income statement lowered reported net income. Managers also argued that the stock option expense computation was unreliable. A recent accounting standard now requires income statement recognition.

IS EXPENSING STOCK OPTIONS PUTTING A DENT IN EARNINGS?

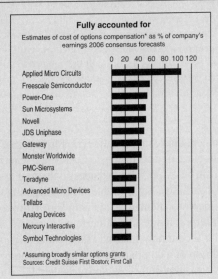

Fully accounted for

Estimates of cost of options compensation* as % of company's earnings 2006 consensus forecasts

*Assuming broadly similar options grants
Sources: Credit Suisse First Boston; First Call

With a new rule requiring employee stock options to be expensed, firms that use them will report lower earnings. Those firms had always been required to report the pro forma effect of the options in the notes to the financial statements. In theory, then, no one should have been fooled. However, research suggests that market prices did not fully consider the costs.

What sort of change will the new rule bring? An October 27, 2005, article in *The Economist* reports that Credit Suisse First Boston conducted a study showing that firms in the semiconductor industry would see forecasted profits fall 23% in 2006 if current levels of options were granted. And, as the accompanying chart shows, the effect varied widely across companies. The article went on to say that many firms were planning to report both GAAP earnings and pro forma earnings that excluded the costs. Whether market participants continue to ignore the expense remains to be seen. Given the changes in stock-based compensation programs that many firms have initiated, it appears that managers believe that market participants will not ignore the costs.

Accounting for liabilities contingent on the occurrence of a future event (e.g., unresolved litigation) presents management with another difficult decision. Should it accrue a possible liability (recording an income statement expense and balance sheet liability) or simply disclose its existence and nature in the notes? Here, the effect on net income can be huge, but whether to accrue it depends on whether the liability is probable and estimable, both of which are subject to considerable management discretion. Accruing such liabilities could represent management's attempt to "take a bath" or build a hidden reserve; simply disclosing them could keep reported net income from falling below an important benchmark.

When management decides to record the financial effect of an event on the financial statements, it must subjectively decide how much detail to include on the face of the financial statements versus in the notes. Property, plant, and equipment, for example, often appears on the balance sheet as a single item with a dollar amount net of accumulated depreciation. Breakdowns of the property, plant, and equipment categories and related accumulated depreciation are then disclosed in the notes along with descriptions of the depreciation methods, estimated useful lives of the assets, and other material information. The issue of how much detail to include in the financial statements versus the notes is relevant to almost every financial statement account (revenues, expenses, assets, liabilities, and dividends), and—absent a particular rule—management is allowed much leeway in the area as long as all material information is disclosed somewhere on the financial statements or in the notes. Management can practice earnings management by burying information items it wishes to de-emphasize in the notes, forcing financial statement users to dig to find them. Consequently, financial statement users should extend their analyses beyond the financial statements themselves, and include a close scrutiny of the notes.

MEASUREMENT (AND DISCLOSURE) CHALLENGE—SEGMENT DATA

Under current U.S. GAAP, companies are required to present key balance sheet and income statement data about each of their business segments. These data permit readers of the financial statements to glean insights into how a company's various business units are doing. Several measurement and disclosure issues arise. First, although management may have the data, they may not want to share it with competitors. Second, by combining segments strategically for reporting purposes, they may be able to manage reported segment performance in a way that puts the best face on the overall situation. This can be accomplished through the subjective allocation of shared costs across business units.

Pro Forma Reporting

An interesting and controversial management disclosure is called pro forma ("as if") reporting. Many companies report both earnings measured according to GAAP and what they label "pro forma earnings." These earnings are, in theory, helpful to readers if they are used to shed light on one aspect or another of reported earnings. For example, by highlighting truly one-time items and removing them from the income statement in arriving at pro forma earnings, management helps users more clearly interpret the results of current operations and better predict future results. Similarly, particular accounting rules may fail to unambiguously capture the financial performance and condition of a company, a problem that can be clarified by pro forma earnings adjustments. Pro forma reporting could be presented by management to undo the distortions generated by accounting rules that may not fit the situation.

Unfortunately, sometimes pro forma reporting is used to cast performance in a more favorable light. Research shows that the pro forma adjustments vary across time and across firms, rendering comparisons more difficult. Furthermore, they tend to be biased in favor of income-increasing adjustments. Finally, similarly labeled items (e.g., EBITDA, or earnings before interest, taxes, depreciation, and amortization) are measured differently across firms and even within firms across time. This, of course, can lead to inadvertent "apples to oranges" comparisons. Consequently, pro forma reporting, though potentially useful, is another vehicle for earnings management. Prudent readers of pro forma disclosures view pro forma data skeptically and come to their own conclusions about how to use the disclosures.

Classification Judgments

Classification is an important feature of financial statements, providing useful signals to financial statement users about the financial performance and condition of the company. The income statement, for example, contains two broad classification categories: operating and non-operating. Operating items are normal to business operations and occur frequently; non-operating items are unusual to business operations and/or occur infrequently. Assets and liabilities on the balance sheet are divided into current and non-current classifications. Current assets are expected to be converted into cash within the current operating cycle or one year, whichever is longer; current liabilities are expected to be discharged with current assets. The right side of the balance sheet is divided into two broad categories: liabilities and shareholders' equity. Liabilities represent obligations of the company and shareholders' equity represents the investment of the shareholders. The statement of cash flows includes three classifications: operating, investing, and financing cash flows, each of which refers to a distinct and important company activity.

High-quality financial statement analysis relies on proper classification. Financial ratios, such as return on equity (ROE), return on assets (ROA), profit margin, asset turnover, and capital structure leverage are only as useful as the classifications on which they are based. The effectiveness of debt covenant conditions or management compensation arrangements, both of which are often expressed in terms of financial ratios, also depends on proper classification. As is the case with most accounting issues, classification requires judgments provided by management—judgments that can be used to manage earnings.

MEASUREMENT CHALLENGE—OPERATING AND NON-OPERATING

Accounting standard-setters worldwide have spent considerable time and effort trying to arrive at a well-accepted classification scheme for reporting economic events. They have tried to define usual and unusual, core and noncore, recurring and nonrecurring, as well as other categories and have been stymied each time. The bottom line is that it is unlikely that a single classification scheme will ever meet the needs of all companies and all financial statement users. The solution is to require extensive and transparent disclosures by companies and for users to be prepared to tailor the data to suit their individual needs.

Operating vs. Non-Operating

Consider a case where a company has experienced a material loss from an activity that may—or may not—be considered operating. Perhaps the activity involved the sale or write-down of an investment by a diversified company that maintains an active portfolio of such investments, but generates most of its revenue from the sale of manufactured goods. Here, management may be able to use its discretion to disclose the loss in either the operating or non-operating sections of the income statement. Management could practice earnings management by judging the loss to be non-operating, which might keep operating income from falling below an important benchmark. Operating income is the measure most heavily relied on by financial statement users and most frequently found in management compensation contracts.

ANALYSIS CHALLENGE: GAINS AND LOSSES ON DISPOSAL OF FIXED ASSETS

When enterprises dispose of their fixed assets, the proceeds on the sale rarely equal the book value of the assets, resulting in a reported gain or loss on disposal of fixed assets. Accounting researchers Catherine Schrand and Beverly Walther discovered that companies tended to highlight losses through separate line-item disclosure, increasing the likelihood that analysts would remove them when making comparisons across periods (and enhance the chance that a favorable performance trend would emerge). Gains, on the other hand, were more likely to be lumped into "other items" categories, reducing the chance that they were adjusted for. The lesson for financial analysts—Pay attention to disclosure strategies!

Schrand, Catherine M., and Beverly R. Walther, 2000. "Strategic Benchmarks in Earnings Announcements: The Selective Disclosure of Prior-Period Earnings Components," *Accounting Review* 75, 151–177.

DRILLING DOWN—HOW SHOULD MANCHESTER UNITED'S PLAYER TRADING GAINS AND LOSSES BE TREATED?

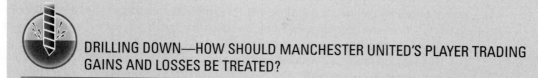

$$\text{ROE} = \frac{\text{Net income}}{\text{Common equity}} = \frac{\text{NI} + \text{Interest expense}}{\text{Sales}} \times \frac{\text{Sales}}{\text{Assets}} \times \frac{\text{Assets}}{\text{Common equity}} \times \frac{\text{NI}}{\text{NI} + \text{Interest expense}}$$

We reviewed the financial statements of Manchester United PLC in several cases in Chapter 2. We explore them further in Chapter 8. One of the items that Man United reports on the income statement is the gains and losses from player trading activities. These gains and losses are separated from what is labeled operating profit on the income statement. Does this make sense?

Yes, the gains and losses are difficult to predict because they vary from year to year, and the timing of player sales is at management's discretion. But isn't the acquisition, development, and eventual disposal of the players central to running a football (soccer) club?

When examining the components of profit margin (return on sales), users should focus on the profitability of operations with and without these kinds of gains and losses. Ignoring them completely ignores their important contribution to the long-run financial performance of the firm. By clearly separating their effects and through detailed note disclosure, Manchester United enables users to conduct such analyses. Simply because a company labels something "operating profit" does not mean that users have to view it that way.

Judgment is also required when classifying cash flows as operating or non-operating (investing or financing) on the statement of cash flows. Some companies, for example, classify cash flows from short-term debts in the operating section, while others classify them as financing cash flows. Similarly, cash flows from the purchase and sale of investments under certain circumstances can be classified either in the operating or investing sections of the statement of cash flows. Given that investors look closely at the operating section of the statement of cash flows when assessing the financial performance, management may be tempted to practice earnings management by using its judgment to classify cash flows to boost cash flows from operating activities.

RED FLAGS—DELPHI AND CASH FLOW MANAGEMENT

When managers think that cash flows are important performance measures focused on by outside users of the financial statements, they have an incentive to manage those measures. Auto parts manufacturer Delphi structured certain inventory transactions at the end of each fiscal quarter to bolster its cash flows. The company "sold" inventories of scrap and unusable equipment to companies that held it for short periods and then resold the inventories and equipment (at a higher price) back to Delphi. Delphi reported the initial "sales" and cash collections as operating cash flows, enabling them to meet or beat quarterly earnings expectations and report especially healthy operating cash flows.

The economics of the arrangement, however, do not involve sales, cost of sales, and the accompanying operating cash flows. Rather, Delphi was engaging in financing transactions. The company was essentially borrowing against its inventory and equipment. The higher repurchase price was nothing more than a way to pay the interest on the loan. By reporting the transactions as it did, Delphi temporarily boosted operating cash flows and concealed its financing activities.

On October 5, 2005, a *Wall Street Journal* article, "Delphi Executives Named in Suit over Inventory-Sales Practices," reported, "Delphi's senior management was so pleased with the inventory practices that a vice president of logistics once distributed a companywide memo praising the program and telling others to copy it ... Managers were also told to visit the plants where the inventory had been sold to 'learn from their methods.'" Now the practice is being reviewed in a securities-fraud investigation by the SEC and a criminal probe by the Department of Justice.

Liability or Equity?

Management's disinclination to report liabilities can influence how it structures and accounts for financing transactions. For example, management may choose to finance a project by issuing securities that contain characteristics of both debt and equity. By classifying these "hybrid" securities in the shareholders' equity section of the balance sheet, management can enjoy the benefits of the additional funds without having to increase the company's leverage ratios. Consequently, financial statement users should closely examine the terms of all securities that contain elements of both debt and equity to ascertain for themselves whether the securities should be classified as debt or equity. Of course, such an examination cannot be conducted unless the terms of the securities are clearly disclosed.

Short-Term or Long-Term?

Managers can also practice earnings management by using judgment in the classification of current vs. noncurrent assets and liabilities. Including assets in, and excluding liabilities from, the current section of the balance sheet can make the reporting company look more solvent and less risky (e.g., higher current ratio). Well-known examples where management relies heavily on judgment include the proper classification of restricted cash, prepaid expenses and deferred revenues, receivables, accrued payables, and debt subject to refinancing. In each case, management can influence important metrics of financial performance and condition by subjectively determining whether the item in question meets the criteria for current classification.

Measurement Judgments

The steps involved in initially measuring the values of assets and liabilities involve many significant management judgments. These judgments directly impact the timing of revenue recognition and the reporting of expenses, providing opportunities for earnings management. Furthermore, assets and liabilities are often subject to periodic revaluation, another subjective management task that can lead to earnings management.

Applying the Matching Principle

The matching principle states that expenses incurred to generate revenues are matched against those revenues in the period when the revenues are generated. The result of the revenue-expense match is net income for the period. Thus, two issues are of primary importance in the measure of net income: (1) the timing of revenue recognition, and (2) the method used to match expenses against the revenues.

Revenue Recognition.   Revenues and the related receivables are recognized when the four criteria of revenue recognition (discussed in Chapter 3) are met. Establishing exactly when this occurs, however, is difficult and subjective, giving management leeway in determining when and how a sale—and the associated receivable—are recorded. Revenue recognition practices differ across industries and across companies within industries. Some companies recognize revenue when goods are shipped; others when customers are invoiced; others still when cash is received; and, in certain cases, revenue is recognized when orders are received. Financial statement users must realize that, even within the guidelines of GAAP, managers can use discretion to speed up or slow down the recognition of revenue, which has a direct impact on reported profits. This concern is particularly important for transactions occurring near the end of an accounting period. Recognizing a receivable and a revenue on December 30 instead of January 2, for example, can significantly affect important financial metrics, such as ROE, ROA, profit margin, and asset turnover in both periods.

RED FLAGS—REVENUE RECOGNITION

A well-known revenue recognition red flag is when receivables increase faster than sales, which leads to an increase in days sales outstanding (DSO, or the average collection period). Why is this a red flag? It might simply reflect a large sale at the end of the period, or it might be due to employee turnover problems in the collections department—both of which are temporary and innocuous reasons for the increase in DSO. But savvy analysts realize from experience that when companies are aggressive in their revenue recognition and sales practices, the period over which their receivables remain outstanding naturally lengthens. Late December sales might have been achieved by offering extended payment terms—sales that might be more properly viewed as "pre-selling" January products. As such, January sales will be lower. Products shipped before customers place orders should not be recognized as sales in the first place, but if they are, customers are unlikely to pay promptly. In extreme cases, completely fictitious sales simply have no customer at the other end, causing the receivables balance to balloon.

High-profile revenue recognition debacles include Computer Associates, where their books were kept open for so-called 35-day months. The company backdated sales documents and pressured customers to take more product than they needed (and allowed customers to return unused items). FLIR Systems shipped products to customers who had not ordered the goods, and misclassified goods shipped on consignment as sales. Gateway sold computers to very high-credit-risk customers and did not make a provision for uncollectible receivables (despite the fact that internal analyses indicated that 50% of the sales would not be collected). In all of these cases, receivables grew faster than sales.

These practices are not without cost. When employees see that management is flouting the rules, it tells them that they, too, can play games—it's part of the corporate culture. When customers realize that a supplier places tremendous pressure on its people to meet sales targets, they will hold out until the very end of a period, knowing that sales discounts and generous payment terms are likely forthcoming. When companies ship products that customers have not ordered, the sales send a signal to the manufacturing department that demand is high. Manufacturing, in turn, orders raw materials, runs overtime shifts, and hires new workers—all to meet nonexistent demand. So, who really gains by playing games with revenue recognition?

Matching Expenses against Revenues. In one way or another, all costs incurred by a company are designed to create benefits (revenues) for the company. These costs can be divided into two categories based on the expected timing of those revenues: (1) expenses—costs considered to generate revenues only in the current period (or, alternatively, costs having no expected future benefits), and (2) assets—costs expected to generate revenues (or inflows of net assets) in future periods. Expenses are matched against (subtracted from) the revenues recognized in the current period on the income statement of the current period; assets are placed on the balance sheet and their costs are matched as expenses against (subtracted from) future revenues on the income statements of future periods as the assets are consumed. This process requires two important judgments from management: (1) should a cost incurred in the current period be expensed or capitalized (treated as an asset)?, and (2) if the cost is capitalized, how should it be allocated to future periods?

Expense or Capitalize? The proper accounting treatment for most costs incurred by a company is straightforward. Employee compensation, advertising and insurance costs, taxes, and selling and administrative costs, for example, are considered to benefit only the current period and therefore are treated as expenses. Research and development costs, although some may benefit future periods, are to be expensed according to U.S. GAAP. That rule argues that the future benefits cannot be measured with sufficient reliability for the costs to qualify as assets. Inventory purchases, investments in other companies, and investments in producing assets are treated as assets and placed on the balance sheet because they are expected to benefit future periods. However, in a number of cases, management uses considerable judgment in deciding whether a cost should be expensed or capitalized, and the effects on the measure of assets, liabilities, and current and future net income can be significant, introducing the possibility of earnings management.

RED FLAGS—CAPITALIZING COSTS AT WORLDCOM

WorldCom rented access to other telecom networks so that it could complete the calls its customers made. It arranged to rent the lines for extended periods. Unfortunately, when business slowed down, they had rented far more capacity than needed. Although the monthly rental fees should have been considered expenses (there was no future benefit in January to having rented lines the previous December), the company capitalized some $3 billion in line costs, calling them capital expenditures. The effect was to delay recognition of significant expenses, continue to report profits in periods that the firm was actually losing money, and dupe investors and creditors into thinking that company was in relatively good shape. Along with some other creative accounting in areas like restructuring reserves (hidden reserves), the company was able to—for a time—perpetuate the biggest fraud in U.S. business history.

The cost of this fraud to shareholders and bondholders is well known. But many other, less obvious costs arose due to the earnings management at WorldCom. Jobs were lost, employee reputations were tarnished, and local suppliers who counted on being paid for goods and services never received payment. Employees at other companies suffered, too. For a while, WorldCom was held out to be a model company—a company that showed everyone how it could be done. When AT&T could not keep up (How could they? The benchmark was not real.), it engaged in massive restructuring, cutting thousands of jobs.

For example, costs incurred in the manufacture of inventory or the acquisition of a major fixed asset can be difficult to classify. Under GAAP, all costs required to get inventory into sellable condition or producing assets into usable condition should be capitalized and included in the cost of the inventory or producing asset. Applying this guideline can be very subjective. How should overhead costs (e.g., the president's salary) be allocated to the cost of an item of inventory? What portion of the interest on funds borrowed to finance the construction of a new facility should be allocated to the cost of the new facility? In developing a mineral property, when should costs be attributed to the property? When do operations (and amortization of capitalized costs) begin? Such costs have to be either capitalized or expensed—a difficult question to answer, giving management an additional way to manage reported earnings.

Another situation where management exercises considerable judgment is the accounting treatment for expenditures incurred on property, plant, and equipment assets after being placed into service. Should these costs be capitalized as betterments, or expensed as maintenance? For example, if a company spends millions of dollars on a facility to both repair and upgrade it, should these costs be capitalized or expensed? How should customer acquisition costs be treated? Management, in the best position to know the correct treatment, is aware also that expensing the costs would reduce net income in the current period, while capitalizing them would not affect current net income, but reduce future net income amounts.

Yet another measurement challenge arises when one company (parent) purchases another company (subsidiary). To prepare the consolidated balance sheet, the purchase price paid by the parent to the shareholders of the subsidiary must be allocated to the acquired assets and liabilities of the subsidiary with the remaining amount assigned to an asset called "goodwill." This allocation process is highly subjective because the amounts assigned to the subsidiary's assets and liabilities are based on their fair market values, which, in many cases, are very difficult to estimate. This process presents another opportunity for earnings management because the final allocation leads to values for acquired assets that are accounted for differently in the future, which can significantly affect future income amounts. The cost allocated to inventory will be converted to cost of goods sold when the inventory is sold; the cost allocated to property, plant, and equipment will be depreciated over their useful lives; and the cost allocated to goodwill will not be amortized, but will be subject to possible write-down in the future.

RED FLAGS: ALLOCATING FAIR VALUES IN AN ACQUISITION

When companies allocate the purchase price of an acquisition to the assets and liabilities acquired, considerable judgment is required. One particularly challenging area is the valuation of intangibles. Items like customer lists and patents are not easy to value. Assigning a value to in-process research is even tougher, representing a ripe area for abuse: In-process R&D (IPR&D) must be valued, but a quirk in the accounting rules requires that the value assigned be immediately expensed. Some companies have used that opportunity to assign a large value to IPR&D and label it a one-time expense. In doing so, they avoid reporting expenses in future periods. There is less

remaining purchase price to allocate to other assets and thus, when those assets are consumed, future performance appears better.

Again, these practices can be very costly. Managers who are assigned assets with lower costs will make selling and production decisions based on those values. If they are working with distorted input values, they are more likely to make poor decisions. When the assets are later replaced at higher prices, managers may have trouble passing on those costs to customers who have been conditioned to believe the products or services are more affordable.

Allocating Capitalized Costs to Future Periods. Once a cost is capitalized and an asset is placed on the balance sheet, the cost is normally converted to expense in future periods. The conversion process is different for different assets. The cost of inventory, for example, is carried on the balance sheet until it is sold, at which time the cost is converted to cost of goods sold on the income statement. Although this process involves no significant management estimates, the amount of the cost allocated to the cost of goods sold depends on the inventory cost flow assumption (first in, first out [FIFO]; last in, first out [LIFO]; and weighted average), a choice made by management. We discuss this further in Chapter 7.

The cost of producing assets, such as property, plant, and equipment and intangible assets with determinable lives is converted to expense over the useful lives of the assets. This process involves significant and very subjective estimates by management, including the useful lives of the assets, the salvage values at the end of the estimated useful lives, and a formula for how much cost should be converted to expense in each year of the assets' useful lives (e.g., straight-line and accelerated methods). Once again, management makes these estimates, which can have significant effects on important financial measures of the company's performance and condition. We discuss this further in Chapter 8.

RED FLAGS—CHANGES IN ESTIMATES, METHODS, AND AUDITORS

When management makes material changes to accounting estimates or methods, it is required to disclose those changes and their effects on reported results. Prudent analysts ask whether the changes are designed to enhance the relationship between the financial statements and the underlying economics or to advance management's individual interests.

When management switches audit firms, another red flag is raised. Was it done to obtain a better price, or to shop for an auditor whose opinion about an accounting choice coincides more closely with its own? Did the auditor fire the client? Answers to these questions provide further insight into the quality of the company's financial reporting.

Valuation of Assets and Liabilities

Determining whether revenue recognition criteria have been met, choosing appropriate cost allocation methods, and deciding whether to capitalize or expense costs all affect when revenues and expenses are recorded and matched. In addition, management must also ensure at the end of each period that balance sheet assets and liabilities are properly valued. Market values of assets and liabilities change constantly, and in some cases balance sheet values must be adjusted to reflect these changes. Again, these adjustments often rely heavily on management's judgment and they can significantly affect important metrics of financial performance and condition.

Asset Valuation.   Regardless of the revenue recognition method or cost allocation procedure used, the balance sheet values for assets should not exceed their economic values. That is, assets should not be reported at amounts above their "expected future economic benefits." Making that determination involves a variety of subjective judgments. Managers can enhance the usefulness of the financial statements by making accruals that clarify the underlying economics. But unscrupulous managers could use the opportunity to distort key measures of performance and financial position.

Short-term investments, for example, are carried on the balance sheet at market value. If management classifies the investments as trading securities, it has little control over reported income; changes in the market values of trading securities are reflected on the income statement whether management holds or sells the securities. (We discuss this further in Chapter 8.) If, on the other hand, management classifies the investments as available for sale, which is much more common, market value changes are reflected on the income statement only if the securities are sold, not if they continue to be held. Market value changes of available-for-sale securities are reflected in the shareholders' equity section of the balance sheet and are considered part of comprehensive income. Thus, if management wishes to manage earnings using short-term investments, it can classify the investments as available for sale and influence reported net income by choosing at the end of each period which securities to sell. Selling appreciated securities would boost reported income; selling depreciated securities would depress reported income.

RED FLAGS—CHERRY PICKING AND DISCLOSURE MANAGEMENT

"Cherry picking a securities portfolio" is an expression used to describe strategically timing security sales to report a particular performance result. For marketable securities classified as available for sale, the actual economic gain or loss on the securities (which occurs when market prices change) is reported in comprehensive income when it takes place. Net income, however, only reflects the gains and losses when the securities are actually sold. So, by selling a few winners or a few losers, net income can be increased or decreased at management's discretion. Careful analysts will be on the lookout for cherry picking—especially at firms with large securities portfolios.

One place to look for the effect is in the statement of comprehensive income. Many companies place that information within the statement of changes in shareholders' equity. Others bury it in the notes. More transparent companies place it in a separate performance statement. The statement reports the gains and losses as they take place economically and reverses out the effects of previous economic gains and losses that happen to pass through the income statement in the current period.

Accounts receivable and inventory require end-of-period adjustments. Together, subjective estimates concerning future uncollectibles, as well as judgments concerning when to write off past-due receivables, can boost or depress reported income in a given year. Similarly, applying the lower-of-cost-or-market rule to inventory requires management to annually identify overvalued inventory for possible write-down, a subjective judgment that can be used to "take a bath" or build a hidden reserve. Delaying accruals for uncollectible receivables and obsolete inventories serves to increase reported income.

One of the most significant accounting judgments made by management at the end of a period involves restructurings and impairments of property, plant, and equipment. Companies sometimes choose to discontinue operations in certain areas or product lines, which often involves future plant closings and employee layoffs over several years. The costs associated with these activities are normally estimated in advance, leading to a significant write-off of impaired property, plant, and equipment and a large accrued expense/liability for costs associated with closing facilities (e.g., employee severance packages). The effect on the income statement is usually referred to as a "restructuring charge," and quite often very little immediate cash outflow is associated with the event. Thus, a huge expense ends up on the income statement—an expense resulting from a very subjective management estimate.

RED FLAGS—RESTRUCTURING RESERVES

When restructuring activities take place, the reported expense is generally accompanied by asset write-downs and accruals for liabilities. Savvy analysts look to note disclosures about the content of those liability accruals. If management purposefully accrues too much, it will have built up hidden reserves that can be reversed to boost income in future periods. What appears to be a miraculous manage-

ment turnaround may be nothing more than the reversal of an accrual.

After several years of poor performance and changes in management, Nortel Networks appeared to have turned the corner in 2003. Indeed, tens of millions of dollars were paid to executives as part of a "return to profitability" incentive arrangement.

In April 2004, the company's CEO and several other executives were fired when it emerged that the turnaround was more a function of creative accounting than managerial prowess. The company deliberately overstated losses in prior periods and set up accruals that were too large—knowing they would later be reversed into income—virtually assuring a turnaround on paper. In August 2004, seven more finance executives were terminated for cause.

The lawsuits were not far behind and they continue to this day.

Of course, this sequence of events did little to encourage customers to stake their information technology needs on Nortel products, making it even more difficult for the next set of managers to turn things around.

Liability Valuation. Like the valuation of assets, the valuation of liabilities can be subject to management's judgment. Notable examples include the timing and amount of end-of-period accruals for expense liabilities, lease accounting, and the equity method of accounting for investments.

We mentioned that the accrued portion of restructuring costs, leading to an income statement expense and a balance sheet liability, requires significant estimates by management. This same concept, fundamental to accrual accounting, applies to a variety of situations where future costs must be estimated and accrued. Consider, for example, the timing and amount of end-of-period accrued expense liabilities for items such as warranties, employee compensation costs, unresolved litigation, and postretirement costs. These items are clearly considered expenses, but some question exists about their measurement and when they should be recognized—and they all require estimates about the future. By understating these estimates, management can boost reported earnings, and by overstating these estimates, management can "take a bath" or build a hidden reserve. Management is in the best position to make these estimates because they know more about their business than anyone, making it difficult for auditors to raise a meaningful challenge at the time that the estimates are made.

ANALYSIS CHALLENGE: DEALING WITH OFF-BALANCE-SHEET ITEMS AT STANDARD & POOR'S

Standard & Poor's is a debt rating agency. In their financial analyses, S&P adds a variety of off-balance-sheet items back onto companies' balance sheets. These include operating leases, the debt of joint ventures and unconsolidated subsidiaries, guaranteed debt, contingent liabilities, and factored or securitized receivables. They do this to gain a complete picture of a company's obligations and cash needs. The ratings agency explains in their Corporate Ratings Criteria that some of the adjustments are complex and less precise. Nonetheless, the firm strives for completeness in their analyses.

A form of off-balance-sheet financing can occur when companies choose to lease, instead of purchase, assets used in the business. Depending on the terms of the lease contract (e.g., which party holds the risks and benefits of ownership), the lessee can be considered the owner of the property, at one extreme, or simply a renter at the other extreme. According to GAAP, if the contract terms indicate that the lessee is effectively the owner, the lessee company must treat the lease as a capital lease—book both an asset and a liability on its balance sheet—and the periodic lease payments reduce the principle of the liability and cover the interest cost. If the terms indicate that the lessee is only a renter (i.e., lessor is the owner), the lessee company can treat the lease as an operating lease—report no asset or liability—and the lease payments are treated as rent expense on the income statement. Management normally prefers operating lease treatment because it avoids having to recognize what is often a large asset and liability on the balance sheet, and it will practice earnings management by using judgment to structure the lease terms so that operating lease treatment can be justified—sometimes even in cases where the lessee company possesses many of the features of property ownership. Savvy analysts estimate the off-balance-sheet leased assets and lease liabilities and add them back to the balance sheet when they conduct their analyses. We examine this in more detail in Chapter 9.

Another form of off-balance-sheet financing occurs when companies use the equity method of accounting. As we will see in Chapter 8, the equity method is used when companies purchase "significant interests" (usually defined as between 20% and 50% of the outstanding voting stock) in other companies, referred to as affiliates. When the purchase is made, the cost of the investment is included in the noncurrent asset section of the investor's balance sheet, which is increased and decreased as the affiliate company records profits and pays dividends, respectively, by an amount proportional to the investor's equity interest.

In reality, an investment in the 20%–50% range sometimes represents more than a significant interest in the affiliate; in some cases (e.g., widely diffused ownership by others, and other forms of influence over management and the board of directors), it can effectively constitute a controlling interest. In such cases, the investor (parent) company should consolidate all the revenues, expenses, assets, and liabilities of the investee (subsidiary) company into its financial statements. However, the difference between a "significant" and a "controlling" interest is a matter of judgment, and management can avoid reporting liabilities by making an investment of less than 50%, and choosing not to consolidate the accounts (i.e., use the equity method), despite having effective control. In this way, the parent company need not include the liabilities of the affiliate on its balance sheet, which may help the parent to keep its reported leverage ratios from growing too large.

WHERE ARE THE REGULATORS?

At this point, you might be asking where the oversight is. We have described a long list of areas where considerable judgment takes place in arriving at financial statement data and we have argued that readers of financial statements need to maintain a healthy dose of skepticism in using the data because managers have been known to act in their own self-interest.

Accounting standard-setters recognize these problems and attempt to craft accounting principles and rules that lead to high-quality reporting. A recent debate centers on a desire for U.S. standard-setters (i.e., the Financial Accounting Standards Board [FASB]) to move away from detailed rules toward so-called principles-based standards. The challenge with such standards lies in implementing them. Companies, auditors, and regulators all like the idea of principles. But they also like guidance on implementation so that they can determine whether the principles are appropriately applied. This, understandably, gives rise to rules.

As soon as rules are written (or even contemplated), Wall Street players move into high gear, looking for ways to circumvent the spirit of the principles while meeting the rules. Tremendous resources are put to bear on the task—resources far greater than those at the disposal of regulators and standard-setters. In the end, the standard-setters tend to opt for extensive disclosures as a means of ensuring transparency. That highlights the need for financial statement users to be willing to read and analyze the notes and not just the financial statements themselves.

1. Revenue Recognition
   a. Accelerate or defer recognition of revenue, especially near the end of the accounting period.

2. Matching Expenses against Revenues
   a. Capitalize or expense costs?
      (1) Estimate overhead allocation to manufactured inventory;
      (2) Estimate capitalized interest;
      (3) Capitalize or expense postacquisition expenditures; and
      (4) Allocate purchase cost to assets acquired via acquisition.
   b. Allocate capitalized costs to future periods.
      (1) Choose inventory cost flow assumption (LIFO, FIFO, or average); and
      (2) Estimate useful lives and salvage values, and choose allocation methods for productive assets.

3. Asset Valuation
   a. Choose to hold or sell securities classified as available for sale;
   b. Estimate uncollectible accounts receivable;
   c. Apply lower-of-cost-or-market method to inventory; and
   d. Estimate asset impairment write-down associated with restructuring.

4. Liability Valuation
   a. Estimate accrued restructuring costs;
   b. Estimate costs of other accruals (e.g., warranties, employee compensation, contingent liabilities, and postretirement costs);
   c. Structure lease transactions to allow operating lease treatment; and
   d. Use equity method to keep affiliate liabilities off the balance sheet.

Figure 6-2. Measurement Judgments by Management

Measurement Judgments: Summary

Figure 6-2 organizes and summarizes the examples that we discussed of how management uses measurement judgments to manage earnings. While the examples do not represent a comprehensive list, they include a variety of often-used methods and certainly illustrate the considerable influence that management has over the financial statements.

► "REAL" EARNINGS MANAGEMENT

As we have shown, managing earnings through judgments concerning materiality, recognition vs. disclosure, classification, and measurement involves choosing between, or pushing the bounds of, acceptable accounting practices. Here, management has to consider the possible reaction of auditors and/or regulators, who might disagree with management's choices and require correction, better disclosure, or restatement of the results. Earnings management is practiced in another way, however, where there is little risk of intervention from auditors or regulators. This method is called "real" earnings management because it deals with the management of real business transactions, rather than the management of how to account for those transactions.

Real earnings management involves managing business transactions to achieve a desired reporting result. Cutting back or delaying expenditures for research and development (R&D) or advertising, for example, boosts reported earnings in the current period by reducing expenses. Such a strategy could enable a company to achieve an important benchmark in that period. Delaying inventory purchases at year end decreases reported inventory levels, perhaps below levels that the company normally holds, giving the impression of better inventory management. But those delayed purchases may come at the price of lost discounts or additional operating risks. Offering special incentives to increase sales or collect receivables right before year end may boost profits and cash flow from operations in the current period. Although such actions might not be questioned by the company's auditor or regulators, they may not be in the best interest of the shareholders for at least two reasons. First, real earnings management causes management to deviate from their normal business decisions, which could hurt the company. Pharmaceuticals that cut back on R&D may be boosting current earnings at the expense of discovering a new and profitable drug. Second, like other forms of earnings management, real earnings management can mislead shareholders and other financial statement users by making current earnings less indicative of future earnings.

▶ EARNINGS MANAGEMENT AND VALUE CREATION: SUMMARY

Now that we know about earnings management, what can we do about it, and how does it relate to shareholder value creation? We argue that management's success depends on whether it has created value for the owners. An important role of financial statements, therefore, is to provide information that can be used by investors, creditors, and other parties (including managers at the firm) to assess value creation—the extent to which ROE exceeds the cost of equity. We have also described metrics that serve as determinants of ROE, including capital structure leverage and ROA, as well as the determinants of ROA, profit margin, and asset turnover.

These metrics are constructed from the classifications and values reported on the financial statements, and their ability to accurately measure value creation and its determinants depends on the extent to which the numbers reported on the financial statements represent what they are purported to represent. The measures of revenues and expenses must accurately represent the benefits derived in a given period and the costs required to derive them. Assets, liabilities, and shareholders' equity on the balance sheet must accurately represent expected economic benefits owned or controlled by the company and able to generate future revenues, the company's existing obligations, and the shareholders' investment in the company, respectively.

To the extent that management engages in earnings management, measures of value creation and its determinants based on values reported on the financial statements are less useful. They less accurately indicate how much shareholder value management created and why. They also distort the information that decision makers within the firm use to allocate resources and make operating decisions. Earnings management serves to conceal the truth about actual performance, actual financial condition, and actual risk.

Savvy financial statement users can improve their interpretations of value creation assessments by better understanding how and when managers use their discretion to manage earnings. Under what conditions does management use its discretion to over- or understate reported net income, and how is it done? How and why do managers practice off-balance-sheet financing? How can the financial statements provided by managers be adjusted to more accurately represent the company's financial performance, financial condition, and risk? Thoughtful answers to these questions can significantly improve one's interpretation of the financial statements, and improve decisions based on that interpretation.

▶ A GLOBAL PERSPECTIVE ON EARNINGS MANAGEMENT

Throughout history, most of the capital in Japan and much of Western Europe was provided by large banks. Representatives from these banks sat on the boards of directors of many of the major companies in these countries and, accordingly, had direct access to many of the internal reporting documents. The need for an extensive financial reporting system that focused on useful information for external users was less than in the United States and other countries where equity ownership was both more important and more widely diffused. For years, the financial reporting requirements in these countries were relatively unstructured and oriented toward the needs of creditors instead of equity holders. Financial reports that evolved were very much at the discretion of management and very conservative, containing intentional asset understatements and liability overstatements—presumably to reduce the chance that banks would grant loans that eventually went unpaid. By deferring revenues and accelerating expense recognition, such conservative reporting also reduced the demand for dividends, another feature reducing the risk faced by the banks.

The situation is changing as companies in these countries seek greater amounts of equity capital and with the adoption of International Financial Reporting Standards (IFRS). Old practices die hard, however, so there is still much evidence of conservatism and earnings management. In general, IFRS allows management more choice and requires less disclosure than U.S. GAAP, which could lead to more earnings management. Consider, for example, the balance sheet of Novartis, discussed at the end of Chapter 2, prepared on the basis of IFRS. A large portion of what we would call the shareholders' equity section contains reserves of various kinds, and a number of the liabilities are referred to as "provisions." While it is impossible to know definitively in the absence of complete disclosure, these sections could easily contain discretionary adjustments made by management to revalue certain assets and/or liabilities that influence earnings. Interestingly, the management of these kinds of reserves is actually encouraged in some countries. Swiss federal law, for example, encourages management to (1) carry assets at less than historical cost, and (2) set up hidden reserves through excessive depreciation or liability write-ups. Some argue that such discretion enables management to better ensure the continued prosperity of the enterprise through income smoothing—recording conservative adjustments in good years and ignoring them in poor years. We are not convinced.

▶ CASE AND REVIEW QUESTIONS

WorldCom, Inc.—Earnings Management

The story of WorldCom, Inc., the largest bankruptcy in U.S. history, is by now well known. Fortunes were lost, reputations left in tatters, and jail sentences are being served. It is worth looking back at events that preceded the downfall for clues that might have exposed the troubles earlier.

1. Review the WorldCom financial statements that follow. These are the originally reported financial statements that were filed with the SEC for 2001. Is the company profitable? Are they in a healthy financial position? How is the company paying for the significant growth it has experienced over the past years?

2. Read the article, "Accounting Spot-Check Unearthed a Scandal in WorldCom's Books," which appeared in the June 27, 2002, edition of *The Wall Street Journal*. The article indicates that WorldCom improperly capitalized $3.1 billion of "line costs" as assets. What are line costs? Why should they not be considered assets? That is, why is it more appropriate to treat the costs as expenses?

3. In a statement to the SEC, WorldCom revealed details of the improperly capitalized amounts in 2001: $771 million in the first quarter, $610 million in the second quarter, $743 million in the third quarter, and $931 million in the fourth quarter. Assume that

WorldCom planned to depreciate these capitalized costs over the midpoint of the range for transmission equipment as disclosed in Note 1 to their financial statements. Further assume that depreciation begins in the quarter that assets are acquired (or costs capitalized). Calculate the depreciation expense for these costs for 2001. By how much did capitalizing the line costs affect reported net income for 2001? Is that amount material?

4. Figure 6-2 recaps a number of common forms of earnings management. Use that list to identify areas in WorldCom's financial statements that you would investigate further if you were a member of the company's audit committee and you were informed of potential fraud or earnings management.

5. Read the article, "Extreme Makeover," which appeared in *CFO* magazine in July 2004. The article recaps the aftermath of the WorldCom meltdown. Describe some of the incentives and opportunities to engage in earnings management that existed at the company. What remedies could be put in place to avoid them in the future (or at other companies)? What checks and balances exist to limit the amount of earnings management, and, in the case of WorldCom, outright fraud?

WorldCom, Inc., and Subsidiaries
Consolidated Statements of Operations
(in millons, except per share data)

	For the Years Ended December 31,		
	1999	**2000**	**2001**
Revenues..	$35,908	$39,090	$35,179
Operating expenses:			
Line costs...	14,739	15,462	14,739
Selling, general, and administrative........................	8,935	10,597	11,046
Depreciation and amortization..............................	4,354	4,878	5,880
Other charges...	(8)	–	–
Total...	28,020	30,937	31,665
Operating income...	7,888	8,153	3,514
Other income (expense):			
Interest expense...	(966)	(970)	(1,533)
Miscellaneous..	242	385	412
Income before income taxes, minority interests, and cumulative effect of accounting change.................................	7,164	7,568	2,393
Provision for income taxes..................................	2,965	3,025	927
Income before minority interests and cumulative effect of accounting change..........................	4,199	4,543	1,466
Minority interests..	(186)	(305)	35
Income before cumulative effect of accounting change..........	4,013	4,238	1,501
Cumulative effect of accounting change (net of income tax of $50 in 2000)............................	–	(85)	–
Net income..	4,013	4,153	1,501
Distributions on mandatorily redeemable preferred securities and other preferred dividend requirements...........	72	65	117
Net income applicable to common shareholders................	$ 3,941	$ 4,088	$ 1,384
Net income attributed to WorldCom group before cumulative effect of accounting change..............	$ 2,294	$ 2,608	$ 1,407
Cumulative effect of accounting change.......................	$ –	$ (75)	$ –
Net income attributed to WorldCom group.....................	$ 2,294	$ 2,533	$ 1,407
Net income (loss) attributed to MCI group before cumulative effect of accounting change..............	$ 1,647	$ 1,565	$ (23)
Cumulative effect of accounting chance.......................	$ –	$ (10)	$ –
Net income (loss) attributed to MCI group...................	$ 1,647	$ 1,555	$ (23)

	Pro Forma		
Earnings (loss) per common share:			
WorldCom group:			
Net income attributed to WorldCom group before cumulative effect of accounting change:			
Basic...	$ 0.81	$ 0.91	$ 0.48
Diluted...	$ 0.78	$ 0.90	$ 0.48
Cumulative effect of accounting change.......................	$ –	$ (0.03)	$ –
Net income attributed to WorldCom group:			
Basic...	$ 0.81	$ 0.88	0.48
Diluted...	$ 0.78	$ 0.87	$ 0.48
MCI group:			
Net income (loss) attributed to MCI group before cumulative effect of accounting change:	$ 14.32	$ 13.61	$ (0.20)
Basic...	$ 14.32	$ 13.61	$ (0.20)
Diluted...	$ –	$ (0.09)	$ –
Cumulative effect of accounting change.......................			
Net income (loss) attributed to MCI group:			
Basic...	$ 14.32	$ 13.52	$ (0.20)
Diluted...	$ 14.32	$ 13.52	$ (0.20)

The accompanying notes are an integral part of these statements.

WorldCom, Inc., and Subsidiaries
Consolidated Balance Sheets
(in millions, except share data)

	December 31, 2000	December 31, 2001
ASSETS		
Current assets:		
Cash and cash equivalents.	$ 761	$ 1,416
Accounts receivable, net of allowance for bad debts of $1,532 in 2000 and $1,086 in 2001	6,815	5,308
Deferred tax asset.	172	251
Other current assets	2,007	2,230
Total current assets	9,755	9,205
Property and equipment:		
Transmission equipment.	20,288	23,814
Communications equipment.	8,100	7,878
Furniture, fixtures, and other	9,342	11,263
Construction in progress.	6,897	5,706
	44,627	48,661
Accumulated depreciation	(7,204)	(9,852)
	37,423	38,809
Goodwill and other intangible assets	46,594	50,537
Other assets.	5,131	5,363
	$ 98,903	$ 103,914
LIABILITIES AND SHAREHOLDERS' INVESTMENT		
Current liabilities:		
Short-term debt and current maturities of long-term debt.	$ 7,200	$ 172
Accrued interest.	446	618
Accounts payable and accrued line costs	6,022	4,844
Other current liabilities	4,005	3,576
Total current liabilities	17,673	9,210
Long-term liabilities, less current portion:		
Long-term debt.	17,696	30,038
Deferred tax liability.	3,611	4,066
Other liabilities	1,124	576
Total long-term liabilities	22,431	34,680
Commitments and contingencies.		
Minority interests.	2,592	101
Company obligated mandatorily redeemable and other preferred securities	798	1,993
Shareholders' investment:		
Series B prefrred stock, par value $0.01 per share; authorized, issued and outstanding: 10,693,437 shares in 2000 and none in 2001 (liquidation preference of $1.00 per share plus unpaid dividends).	—	—
Preferred stock, par value $0.01 per share: authorized: 31,155,008 shares in 2000 and 30,967,637 shares in 2001, none issued	—	—
Common stock:		
WorldCom, Inc., common stock, par value $0.01 per share; authorized: 5,000,000,000 shares in 2000 and none in 2001; issued and outstanding: 2,887,960,378 shares in 2000 and none in 2001	29	—
WorldCom group common stock, par value $0.01 per share; authorized: none in 2000 and 4,850,000,000 shares in 2001; issued and outstanding: none in 2000 and 2,967,436,680 shares in 2001.	—	30
MCI group common stock, par value $0.01 per share; authorized: none in 2000 and 150,000,000 shares in 2001; issued and outstanding: none in 2000 and 118,595,711 in 2001.	—	1
Additional paid-in capital	52,877	54,297
Retained earnings	3,160	4,400
Unrealized holding gain (loss) on marketable equity securities	345	(51)
Cumulative foreign currency translation adjustment.	(817)	(562)
Treasury stock, at cost, 6,765,316 shares of WorldCom, Inc., in 2000, 6,765,316 shares of WorldCom group stock and 270,613 shares of MCI group stock in 2001	(185)	(185)
Total shareholders' investment	55,409	57,930
	$ 98,903	$ 103,914

The accompanying notes are an integral part of these statements.

WorldCom, Inc., and Subsidiaries
Consolidated Statements of Cash Flows
(in millons)

	For the Years Ended December 31,		
	1999	**2000**	**2001**
Cash flows from operating activities:			
Net income	$ 4,013	$ 4,153	$ 1,501
Adjustments to reconcile net income to net cash provided by operating activities:			
Cumulative effect of accounting change	–	85	–
Minority interests	186	305	(35)
Other charges	(8)	–	–
Depreciation and amortization	4,354	4,878	5,880
Provision for deferred income taxes	2,903	1,649	1,104
Change in assets and liabilities, net of effect of business combinations:			
Accounts receivable, net	(875)	(1,126)	281
Other current assets	143	(797)	164
Accounts payable and other current liabilities	692	(1,050)	(1,154)
All other operating activities	(403)	(431)	253
Net cash provided by operating activities	11,005	7,666	7,994
Cash flows from investing activities:			
Capital expenditures	(8,716)	(11,484)	(7,886)
Acquisitions and related costs	(1,078)	(14)	(206)
Increase in intangible assets	(743)	(938)	(694)
Decrease in other liabilities	(650)	(839)	(480)
All other investing activities	1,632	(1,110)	(424)
Net cash used in investing activities	(9,555)	(14,385)	(9,690)
Cash flows from financing activities:			
Principal borrowings (repayments) on debt, net	(2,894)	6,377	3,031
Common stock issuance	886	585	124
Distributions on mandatorily redeemable and other preferred securities and dividends paid on other equity securities	(72)	(65)	(154)
Redemptions of preferred stock	–	(190)	(200)
All other financing activities	–	(84)	(272)
Net cash provided by (used in) financing activities	(2,080)	6,623	2,529
Effect of exchange rate changes on cash	(221)	(19)	38
Net increase (decrease) in cash and cash equivalents	(851)	(115)	871
Cash and cash equivalents at beginning of period	1,727	876	761
Deconsolidation of Embratel	–	–	(216)
Cash and cash equivalents at end of period	$ 876	$ 761	$ 1,416

The accompanying notes are an integral part of these statements.

WorldCom, Inc., and Subsidiaries
Notes to Consolidated Financial Statements (Continued)
December 31, 2001

(1) The Company and Significant Accounting Policies—(Continued)

Our equity in Embratel's loss for 2001 is included in miscellaneous income/(expense) in the accompanying consolidated financial statements.

Fair Value of Financial Instruments:

The fair value of long-term debt and company obligated mandatorily redeemable and other preferred securities is determined based on quoted market rates or the cash flows from such financial instruments discounted at our estimated current interest rate to enter into similar financial instruments. The carrying amounts and fair values of these financial instruments were $25.7 billion and $25.3 billion, respectively, at December 31, 2000, and $32.2 billion and $32.9 billion, respectively, at December 31, 2001. The carrying values for all our other financial instruments approximate their respective fair values.

Cash and Cash Equivalents:

We consider cash in banks and short-term investments with original maturities of three months or less as cash and cash equivalents.

Property and Equipment:

Property and equipment are stated at cost. Depreciation is provided for financial reporting purposes using the straight-line method over the following estimated useful lives:

Transmission equipment (including conduit)	4 to 40 years
Communications equipment	5 to 10 years
Furniture, fixtures, buildings, and other	4 to 39 years

We evaluate the recoverability of property and equipment when events and circumstances indicate that such assets might be impaired. We determine impairment by comparing the undiscounted future cash flows estimated to be generated by these assets to their respective carrying amounts. In the event an impairment exists, a loss is recognized based on the amount by which the carrying value exceeds the fair value of the asset. If quoted market prices for an asset are not available, fair market value is determined primarily using the anticipated cash flows discounted at a rate commensurate with the risk involved. Losses on property and equipment to be disposed of are determined in a similar manner, except that fair market values are reduced for the cost to dispose.

Maintenance and repairs are expensed as incurred. Replacements and betterments are capitalized. The cost and related reserves of assets sold or retired are removed from the accounts, and any resulting gain or loss is reflected in results of operations.

We construct certain of our own transmission systems and related facilities. Internal costs directly related to the construction of such facilities, including interest and salaries of certain employees, are capitalized. Such internal costs were $625 million ($339 million in interest), $842 million ($495 million in interest), and $858 million ($498 million in interest), in 1999, 2000, and 2001, respectively.

The Wall Street Journal

June 27, 2002

PAGE ONE

Accounting Spot-Check Unearthed a Scandal in WorldCom's Books

By JARED SANDBERG, DEBORAH SOLOMON, and REBECCA BLUMENSTEIN

Staff Reporters of THE WALL STREET JOURNAL

NEW YORK—It all started a few weeks ago with a check of the books by Cynthia Cooper, an internal auditor for **WorldCom** Inc. The telecom giant's newly installed chief executive had asked for a financial review, and her job was to spot-check records of capital expenditures.

According to people familiar with the matter, Ms. Cooper soon found something that caught her eye. In quarter after quarter, starting in 2001, WorldCom's chief financial officer, Scott Sullivan, had been using an unorthodox technique to account for one of the long-distance company's biggest expenses: charges paid to local telephone networks to complete calls.

Instead of marking them as operating expenses, he moved a significant portion into the category of capital expenditures. The maneuver was worth hundreds of millions of dollars to WorldCom's bottom line, effectively turning a loss for all of 2001 and the first quarter of 2002 into a profit.

Ms. Cooper contacted Max Bobbitt, the head of WorldCom's auditing committee, setting in motion a chain of events that resulted in Mr. Sullivan's firing late Tuesday. The company said that it had turned up $3.8 billion of expenses that were improperly booked and will now be restated.

Even in a season when one giant company after another has been laid low by accounting scandals, WorldCom's disclosure stands out. The coming financial restatement will almost certainly be one of the largest in corporate history—more than six times that of Enron Corp. More important, it offers the clearest warning sign yet of the ease with which telecom companies, operating on the frontiers of accounting amidst a huge speculative excess, could manipulate their books to inflate their earnings.

President Bush himself called for a full investigation into the spiraling scandal, calling the accounting irregularities "outrageous."

The loss of trust by investors, customers, and financial institutions has been profound. Shareholders have lost more than $2 trillion, and more than 500,000 telecom workers have lost their jobs.

"There was so much pressure on companies to continue to grow and support those share prices," says Charles H. Noski, who is a vice chairman of **AT&T** Corp. and its former chief financial officer. AT&T hasn't come under fire for its accounting, although its stock has tumbled amid the general industry malaise. "People are going to try to figure out how do you know enough to trust what corporations are telling investors. There is an overhang on the market now."

Stock markets around the world reacted swiftly Wednesday to a growing sense of unease that, like WorldCom itself, much of the explosive, double-digit growth of the stock market boom may have been a mirage. The Dow Jones Industrial Average fell 6.7 points. **Qwest Communications International** Inc., a big Denver telecom company under investigation by the Securities and Exchange Commission for alleged accounting irregularities, saw its stock fall nearly 60% Wednesday, to $1.79 a share. The company has denied wrongdoing.

For WorldCom, the development could well spell the end of the nation's No. 2 long-distance company, which sells to consumers under the MCI brand name. WorldCom's banks said they wouldn't immediately act on debt covenants that could allow them to call their loans. But people familiar with the matter said a bankruptcy-court filing remains an option. Nasdaq halted trading in WorldCom's stock all day Wednesday. It currently stands at 83 cents, far from its high of $64.50 in 1999.

The SEC Wednesday filed civil fraud charges against WorldCom, saying the company "falsely portrayed itself as a profitable business." The U.S. Justice Department has launched a probe that could result in criminal charges, according to people familiar with the situation. These people said WorldCom and Mr. Sullivan could potentially face charges, including securities fraud, bank fraud and mail fraud.

Andrew J. Graham, Mr. Sullivan's attorney, said he wouldn't comment. But people familiar with Mr. Sullivan say he firmly believes he didn't do anything wrong.

Brad Burns, a spokesman for WorldCom, declined to comment on the SEC charges, but said the company is "very focused on serving our customers, working with our bank lenders, and ensuring our employees that we'll get through these difficult times."

WorldCom had already been reeling under a heavy debt load and declining revenues. In April, the board ousted the long-time chief executive, Bernard J. Ebbers, in part because of a controversy surrounding a $408 million loan WorldCom extended to him to cover margin calls on loans secured by company stock. Since then, its new chief executive, John Sidgmore, has been trying to hold off a financial crisis and restore investor confidence.

(continues)

Accounting Spot-Check Unearthed a Scandal in WorldCom's Books (*continued*)

Internal Investigation

At this point, it's unclear whether anyone else at WorldCom knew what Mr. Sullivan was doing. The company has launched an internal investigation and is trying to determine who knew what and when. WorldCom has hired William McLucas, an SEC former enforcement chief who assisted in an internal probe of Enron's accounting, to help in the WorldCom investigation. One of the people under scrutiny is Mr. Ebbers, a close confidant of Mr. Sullivan. The two men shared an adjoining office at their Clinton, Miss., headquarters.

Mr. Ebbers couldn't be reached for comment, and his attorney didn't have any immediate comment.

What is clear is that over the past five quarters as the market softened, Mr. Sullivan undertook an aggressive approach to the company's way of accounting for one of its biggest expenses.

This happened just as WorldCom's acquisition machine was grinding to a halt. Mr. Ebbers had cobbled together his empire from modest roots as a long-distance reseller and motel owner in Mississippi. Mr. Sullivan became a trusted ally after Mr. Ebbers acquired his company, Advanced Telecommunications Corp., in 1992. The two executives worked in tandem as WorldCom, then known as LDDS, acquired dozens of companies, seemingly springing out of nowhere to snag MCI Communications Corp. in 1998. WorldCom's double-digit growth rates helped it win a takeover battle for MCI, trumping a bid by GTE Corp.

But by early 2001, the growth had started to slow. The booming telecommunications market was beginning to falter from a glut of capacity after a frenzied investment in fiber-optic networks. Suddenly, it found it had too much capacity. It had signed multibillion-dollar contracts with third-party telecommunications firms such as Baby Bells to ensure it would be able to complete calls for its customers. An appraisal commissioned by WorldCom showed that roughly 15% of these costs weren't producing revenue, according to a WorldCom insider.

CREATIVE ACCOUNTING

By booking certain costs as a capital expense, WorldCom was able to boost its bottom line. A look at how the company conducted such accounting in 2001.

WorldCom's accounting

❶ Accounts $3.1 billion in 'line costs,' including telecom access and transport charges, as capital expenditure.

❷ Plans to amortize $3.1 billion over a period of time, possibly as much as 10 years.

❸ Reports net income of $1.38 billion for 2001.

Expense

Capital Expense	Operating Expense
Amortization	Cost of Business
Higher Net Income	Lower Net Income

Generally accepted accounting principles

❶ The $3.1 billion 'line-cost' expense is booked as an operating expense.

❷ The entire $3.1 billion would have been counted as a cost of business for that quarter.

❸ Net income for 2001 would have been a loss, amount to be determined.

Mr. Sullivan made an important decision, says a person familiar with his thinking. Instead of reducing profits by those costs whenever WorldCom issued results in 2001, Mr. Sullivan would spread those costs to a future time when the anticipated revenue might arrive.

He was in a murky area. One of accounting's most basic rules is that capital costs have to be connected to long-term investments, not ongoing activities.

According to WorldCom, the company transferred more than $3.8 billion in "line-cost" expenses to its capital accounts. WorldCom hasn't provided more detail about what those costs included, or what portions of their line costs were improperly capitalized. But line costs, according to the company's most recent annual report filed with the SEC, consist principally of access charges and transport charges. WorldCom's "line costs" totaled $8.12 billion in 2001, according to the company's income statement.

While companies can capitalize some costs like installation and labor, the magnitude of WorldCom's capitalization appears to be far beyond its industry peers.

A person familiar with the matter says Mr. Sullivan didn't appear to have realized any personal financial gain from his strategy. At WorldCom's peak in 1999, his shares were worth more than $150 million, and he currently owns about 3.2 million shares. But he hasn't sold any WorldCom stock in nearly two years, according to Thomson Financial/Lancer Analytics, a data service.

Mr. Sullivan never attempted to cover up the aggressive accounting method, the person familiar with the matter says. Details are spelled out clearly enough in internal company documents, this person says, that "other people had to see it unless they were blind." Still, Arthur Andersen, WorldCom's auditor at the time, said it wasn't consulted or notified about the capitalized expenses.

The CFO capitalized costs in amounts ranging from $540 million to $797 million each quarter. When April results came out this year, though, he began to doubt whether some of his revenue projections related to the line costs would be realized. In May, according to people familiar with his thinking, Mr. Sullivan was contemplating taking a charge. On May 23, the board was notified that a charge would include the line costs, but didn't signal how much it would be, a person familiar with the matter said.

Then in early June, Ms. Cooper called Mr. Bobbitt, chairman of the board's audit committee, notifying him that she had found suspect entries in the books.

Mr. Bobbitt had been under fire for months for his controversial role in extending Mr. Ebbers the $408 million personal loan from WorldCom. He quickly notified the newly hired accountants, KPMG LLP, of the discrepancy. The firm set to work.

Two weeks ago, KPMG came to WorldCom's offices in Washington and told the committee there was a problem. The investigation continued through the week and last Thursday the audit committee met at KPMG's Washington offices to ask Mr. Sullivan and company controller David Myers to justify their accounting treatment. Mr. Sullivan, according to people familiar with the situation, gave an impassioned defense of his decision, saying that since WorldCom wasn't receiving revenue, he could defer the costs of leasing the lines until they produced revenue. But KPMG officials weren't satisfied, citing accounting rules that clearly dictate that the costs of operating leases can't be delayed. The KPMG partner in charge of the WorldCom account, told Mr. Sullivan that he couldn't "get past the theory" but gave him the weekend to produce a so-called white paper that would set out his justification, a person close to the matter said.

Accounting experts say the rules are clear on what costs can be capitalized and what has to be expensed. "If the amounts being paid out are going to have created a long-lasting asset, then the costs depreciate and can be amortized over several years," says Carr Conway, a former SEC official and senior forensic accountant with Dickerson Financial Group in Denver. Unless the asset is going to generate value in future years, the cost for it can't be capitalized, he adds.

Weekend Huddle

Mr. Sullivan spent the weekend huddled with his team in Clinton, Miss., reviewing documents and constructing the white paper. But it wasn't going well. "He was becoming increasingly pessimistic" that he would have enough time to satisfy KPMG, said one person familiar with the matter.

At a board meeting Monday night at WorldCom's offices, Mr. Sullivan again made his case. A national practice specialist at KPMG said, however, that the issue was "an open-and-shut case," said one person who attended. "The KPMG people left no door open." After asking Mr. Sullivan to leave the room, board members concluded at the meeting that they would have to restate earnings. The meeting ended without a vote, which was postponed until Tuesday when Mr. Sullivan was fired and Mr. Myers was asked to resign.

Through it all, Mr. Sullivan was "very calm and articulate," says one person who attended the meetings. "He handled himself very well, though you could tell he was pained." As far as the board members, added another person, "most people were absolutely flabbergasted."

In a speech Wednesday, Mr. Sidgmore tried to make the most out of a bad situation. "We want to make clear that WorldCom reported itself in this matter and moved swiftly to do so," he said. "We turned ourselves in, in other words."

Write to Jared Sandberg at jared.sandberg@wsj.com, Deborah Solomon at deborah.solomon@wsj.com, and Rebecca Blumenstein at rebecca.blumenstein@wsj.com.

CFO.com
Extreme Makeover

How Robert Blakely and an army of accountants turned fraud-ridden WorldCom into squeaky-clean MCI.
Joseph McCafferty, *CFO* Magazine
July 1, 2004

Robert Blakely had yet to accept the job as CFO of WorldCom, Inc., when CEO Michael Capellas called on the evening of April 10, 2003. Creditors of the bankrupt telecommunications giant were meeting with Capellas and his team in New York the following day, and he wanted Blakely by his side. On the table: how to settle some $35 billion in outstanding debt. Blakely, who would already be in town for a meeting of the trustees of Cornell University, agreed to come—after, that is, he and Capellas hammered out an employment contract in the morning.

But the next day, bad weather delayed Capellas's flight from Washington, D.C. "There was no way we could talk," says Blakely. "By the time [Capellas] arrived, all the senior creditors were there." The fact that he wasn't formally on the payroll didn't keep the CFO-in-waiting from rolling up his sleeves and starting negotiations, which quickly grew acrimonious. "Basically, it was hand-to-hand combat all day," recalls Blakely.

At 11:30 a.m., he and Capellas slipped out of the negotiations to work through the remaining points of Blakely's employment contract. At noon, "We shook hands and I said, 'Yep, I'm on board,'" says Blakely.

They returned to the fray. Finally, by 8:30 in the evening, the WorldCom team had convinced 90 percent of the creditor groups to exchange most of their bonds for shares of stock in the reorganized company.

For the new CFO, that first 12-hour day was a harbinger of things to come. Raising WorldCom from the ashes of the biggest fraud—and bankruptcy—in U.S. corporate history, to emerge in April 2004 as the rechristened MCI Inc., boasting a clean set of books and a mere $5 billion of debt, would require many more 12-hour-plus days. Restating the company's financials, a chore that began before Blakely's arrival, would take more than a year and a half to complete. Internal controls had to be overhauled, new directors named, and a new set of corporate-governance policies adopted. Even though the fraud directly involved fewer than 50 employees, every one of the company's 50,000 workers worldwide had to undergo ethics training. And somehow, while all this was being done, the business had to keep moving forward.

The 62-year-old Blakely brought badly needed turnaround experience to WorldCom. In the late 1990s, the CFO led Houston-based Tenneco Inc., a $13 billion energy conglomerate, through a massive restructuring. Later, he made major improvements to internal controls and risk management at Lyondell Chemical Co., another Houston company. But nothing could have prepared him adequately for WorldCom, which declared bankruptcy in July 2002, not long after the disclosure of the fraud that drove CFO Scott Sullivan and CEO Bernard Ebbers from the company (see "Fall and Rise," at the end of this article). (Full disclosure: Both Blakely and Sullivan were recipients of *CFO* Excellence awards.) "No one has that kind of turnaround experience," says Blakely, "because it has never been done before."

That challenge was enough to lure Blakely out of retirement, where racing high-performance motorcycles apparently didn't provide enough of an adrenaline rush. "What intrigued me about [WorldCom] was that it was an opportunity to pull everything together that I had learned in my career," he says. "I don't like stable situations. Some might say that I'm a crisis junkie."

The Mother of All Audits

It was easy for Blakely to indulge his habit at WorldCom. Even with the majority of creditors on board, the most difficult tasks required to exit bankruptcy still lay ahead. Hardest of all was restating results for three years—2000, 2001, and 2002—and filing audited financial statements. Not only was $11 billion of fraud cooked into the books, but years of shoddy record-keeping and incompetent accounting clouded nearly every entry.

Blakely and his finance team hoped they could complete the audit by July 2003, three months after he was hired, but it took nearly that long just to size up the task. "It was more complex than anyone imagined," he says. Eventually, the team realized they had to reconstruct the financial statements from scratch. "I went back to Michael [Capellas] and told him that it looked more like July 2004 than July 2003," says Blakely. But it would have to be done faster: bankruptcy court judge Arthur Gonzalez had already set February 28, 2004, as the deadline for emerging from bankruptcy.

Reinforcements were needed. WorldCom already had 500 to 600 employees working full-time on the restatement, as well as 200 to 300 staffers from KPMG, the company's auditor. WorldCom turned to Deloitte & Touche for more help, and the accounting firm responded with some 600 professionals, culled from offices across the country. At the peak of the audit work, in late 2003, WorldCom had about 1,500 people working on the restatement, under the combined management of Blakely and five controllers.

The finance team started with the billing systems and reran all the revenue, deciding on the proper accounting. Then it redid all the cash applications and rebuilt the income statements from there. It also reassessed every acquisition Ebbers had made since 1992 in the course of transforming an obscure long-distance start-up into a global communications powerhouse—12 major deals and several smaller ones, worth $70 billion. "In some instances, we had to go back and reconstruct records to decide whether or not pooling of interest was the proper accounting at the time," says Blakely. In all, they found, WorldCom had overvalued several acquisitions by a total of $5.8 billion.

The difficulty of the audit work was compounded by the sorry state of WorldCom's records. In some instances, Post-it® notes were attached to journal entries in lieu of proper documentation. The FBI had taken documents that had to be tracked down and retrieved. In the end, Blakely's team made more than 3 million new or revised entries.

But even with Deloitte's help, WorldCom couldn't finish the audit before Judge Gonzalez's February 2004 deadline. It was forced to request a 60-day extension. "To bring [the audit] to closure was devilishly hard, because it's so complex. It just kept going on and on," says Blakely.

Finally, on March 10, Blakely's team finished a version of the 10-K restatement that would serve as a foundation for future financial statements. MCI executives planned a signing ceremony for March 11, at a previously scheduled meeting of the board. But later on the 10th, company personnel and KPMG discovered two significant errors in the deferred tax balances, which rippled through about 100 pages of the 192-page document. Dave Schneeman, vice president of general accounting, and Jim Renna, vice president of controls and remediation, led a small team that worked through the night to make the necessary fixes.

"I called at midnight, and they said they were making progress," says Blakely. "I called again at 6:00 a.m. the next day, and they said they had just finished, and I cried," he admits.

To WorldCom's investors, the story told by the restated results was a real tearjerker. Sullivan and Ebbers had claimed a pretax profit for 2000 of $7.6 billion; the reality, according to the restatement, was a loss of $48.9 billion (including a $47 billion write-down of impaired assets). For 2001, WorldCom had reported a pretax profit of $2.4 billion; the restatement showed a pretax loss of $15.6 billion. For the year 2002, the company was $9.2 billion in the red, pretax.

Blakely claims WorldCom's restated 2002 10-K is the most complex document ever filed with the Securities and Exchange Commission. He calls it "my Mount Everest" and keeps a copy, signed by the major participants, in a glass-door cabinet next to his desk. The audit, he says, "is the hardest thing I have done in my career." Total cost to complete it: a mind-blowing $365 million.

Hush Money

The audit provided new insights into the nature and the magnitude of the fraud at WorldCom. In fact, the same complexity that made the audit so difficult was one reason the fraud was able to go undetected for so long. As a result of Ebbers's acquisition spree, WorldCom had also acquired a slew of accounting systems that were integrated loosely, if at all. By Blakely's reckoning, there were 60 billing platforms and more than 20 accounts-receivable systems. The numbers rolled up from the various operating units to the company's former headquarters in Clinton, Mississippi. There, it was easy for accounting staffers to simply change the numbers.

"It was a very low-tech fraud in a sense," says Richard Breeden, a former SEC chairman and MCI's court-appointed corporate monitor. "If [a WorldCom employee] didn't like the figure he got, he just changed it." He says it was not unknown for accountants at headquarters to come to the office and find Post-it® notes on their computer monitors telling them to change numbers. Breeden says that in some quarters, imaginary revenue was added to the books using consolidated entries in big, round numbers that "didn't even *look* real."

Breeden also describes a command-and-control structure with a lot of power concentrated at the top. In his report of recommended reforms, he noted that Ebbers ruled with "nearly imperial reign." "The attitude at the company was that orders were to be followed, and it was clear that anybody that didn't would be fired," says Breeden. Along with the big stick came a few carrots. A generous stock-option plan was supplemented by a $238 million "employee-retention program" that was dipped into and doled out at the discretion of Ebbers and Sullivan. "It was basically a slush fund to give out quiet money," says Breeden. Sullivan wrote personal checks for $10,000 to some employees, he says, and gave $10,000 more to their wives.

Breeden and Blakely say that the fraud involved fewer than 50 people, mostly those who rolled up the financial statements in Clinton. When managers at operating units saw the consolidated financials, they were surprised how well the rest of the company seemed to be doing when the numbers they reported were so poor.

Dennis Beresford, a former chairman of the Financial Accounting Standards Board who now chairs MCI's audit committee, led one of two internal investigations into the fraud. He's convinced that everyone involved has been removed from the company. Beresford says WorldCom asked about 50 executives in the finance department to leave after the investigation showed they either took part in the accounting fraud or should have known about it. "We had too many people who looked the other way," he says.

In March, Sullivan agreed to plead guilty to securities fraud, conspiracy, and giving false statements to regulators. Those crimes could carry a sentence of up to 25 years in prison under federal sentencing guidelines, but Sullivan hopes to get less in exchange for his testimony in the trial against Ebbers that is scheduled to begin in November. Former controller David Myers and accounting executives Betty Vinson and Troy Normand have also pleaded guilty and are cooperating with authorities.

(continues)

Extreme Makeover (*continued*)

[Ebbers eventually received a 25-year jail sentence; Sullivan, 5 years; Myers, 1 year and 1 day; Vinson, 5 months in prison and 5 months of house arrest; and Normand, 3 years of probation.]

Do the Right Thing

Impressive as it was, cleaning up the fraud wasn't enough to restore the confidence of WorldCom's customers; Blakely had to make sure that nothing remotely like Sullivan's manipulations could ever happen again. In July 2003, WorldCom's largest customer, the federal government, had barred it from bidding on federal contracts while it reviewed whether the company should be placed on an "excluded parties" list. "Getting that [ban] lifted was the highest priority," says Blakely. "If the government doesn't want to do business with you, why should anyone else?"

The two main concerns identified by the General Services Administration, which administers the list, were controls and ethics. Indeed, KPMG, which succeeded Arthur Andersen as WorldCom's auditor, had identified 96 control issues, and a separate assessment by Deloitte zeroed in on several other "high risk" areas. With help from both accounting firms, Blakely's finance team put together a "heat map" that listed high-priority risk areas, and then went about fixing them. The solutions included adding basic checks and balances such as segregation of duties among finance staffers, limited access, and documented policies. The company then implemented a much more stringent, and inclusive, policy for closing the books. "It is impossible to completely eliminate the possibility of fraud," says Blakely. But, he says, the hundreds of added controls will greatly diminish the chances of it reoccurring.

MCI was also forced to implement what is likely the most stringent set of corporate-governance practices ever adopted. As part of WorldCom's $750 million cash and stock settlement with the SEC, it agreed to accept all the recommendations of the court-appointed monitor. Breeden's 150-page report on corporate governance, "Restoring Trust," lists 78 recommendations, including the separation of the CEO and chairman roles, and the required removal of one board member each year to make room for a new director. "Some [of the requirements] go beyond what is reasonable," contends Beresford. "But we have no choice but to accept them."

As for ethics training, MCI put the entire company of 50,000 employees through a course designed for it by professors at New York University's Stern School of Business. In addition, 90 executives attended a two-day ethics program at the University of Virginia's Darden School. Not surprisingly, MCI is trying to keep ethics in the foreground. Large banners proclaiming the company's "guiding principles" festoon the halls of its Ashburn, Virginia, headquarters. They include such mottos as "Everyone should feel comfortable to speak his or her mind" and "Do the right thing." The principles are also printed on the back of employee security badges.

All these measures were enough to convince the government that MCI had reformed. Last January, it lifted the debarment just in time for the renewal of a contract worth as much as $400 million.

There would be more to celebrate. On April 20, the company emerged from bankruptcy, officially taking the name MCI Inc., with its debt slashed from $41 billion to $5.8 billion, and with $6 billion in cash reserves. Its stock was scheduled to begin trading again on Nasdaq this month. "A lot of people didn't think we could get it done," says Beresford. "It took a Herculean effort to get to that point." (Not to mention the $800 million in fees MCI spent during its sojourn in Chapter 11, for lawyers, accountants, appraisers, tax experts, and other consultants.)

But the work on the controls isn't finished. Like most companies, MCI is busy documenting its controls in compliance with Section 404c of the Sarbanes–Oxley Act. More than 60 people are working on the project, and PricewaterhouseCoopers is providing outside assistance. "We've still got a long summer ahead to get to where we need to be," says Blakely.

Was It Worth It?

Right now, MCI is trailing the field. "They are third in a race of three," says Muayyad Al-Chalabi, managing director of San Francisco-based telecom research firm RHK Inc. Compared with archrivals AT&T and Sprint, MCI has lower margins, pays more (as a percentage of total revenues) to other carriers in access fees, and has the fastest-declining revenues (17 percent in the past year alone, year over year). "I don't know if MCI was worth saving," says Al-Chalabi.

The company will also have to fend off competition from Baby Bells like Verizon and SBC Communications, which are looking to provide enterprise telecom services to small-and mid-size businesses—a key customer base for MCI. And another setback came in June, when a federal court ruled that Baby Bells no longer had to lease access to their local networks to the likes of MCI at deep discounts, increasing MCI's cost to provide consumer long distance.

In May, MCI announced a $388 million loss for the first quarter of 2004, compared with a $52 million profit for Q1 2003. The company said it would cut 7,500 jobs, or 15 percent of its workforce. But Al-Chalabi says reducing head count alone won't solve MCI's problems. He points out that the company has a patchwork of networks left over from the acquisitions—the same problem that plagued the finance department—which impedes its efforts to obtain operating efficiencies. "They have a thousand or more systems that all need to be supported," says Al-Chalabi. "That increases the number of suppliers they have to deal with, and there is a lot of duplication in the systems."

All of these factors have fed speculation that MCI will put itself up for sale, likely to one of the Baby Bells. Yet Al-Chalabi notes that these potential buyers can already buy long-haul capacity very cheaply, without buying the MCI cow. Also, he says,

"The Baby Bells still have huge amounts of debt. I'm not sure they are in a position to do a big purchase right now." That could be bad news for MCI. "I don't think they can stand alone with the current trend," says Al-Chalabi. "They'll either be part of another company, or they'll have to dramatically change their ways."

MCI isn't ruling out a sale. But Blakely, who admits that the industry is in rough shape, thinks that the company can stand on its own. He is quick to point out that it generates $300 million in positive cash flow each quarter. A large portion of Internet traffic flows over MCI's network, and the company still has more than 20 million customers. Blakely says MCI will be profitable in the second half of this year.

Focusing on the future is a luxury MCI hasn't had for a long time. At a recent board meeting, Dennis Beresford noticed something he calls "astonishing": "The conversation was almost entirely about the operations of the business." That hadn't happened since he was elected to the board in July 2002, he says. "Just to be able to sit around and talk about strategy is wonderful."

Joseph McCafferty is news editor of CFO.

Fall and Rise

1985: Bernard Ebbers becomes CEO of long-distance provider Long Distance Discount Service (LDDS).

1995: LDDS acquires telecom provider Williams Telecom Group (WilTel) for $2.5 billion and changes its name to WorldCom.

1998: WorldCom's $40 billion acquisition of MCI is the largest merger in corporate history at the time.

1999–2000: WorldCom and Sprint, the nation's third-largest long-distance company, agree to merge. The deal is later blocked by antitrust regulators and abandoned.

March 2002: WorldCom receives a request for information from the Securities and Exchange Commission on accounting procedures and loans to officers.

April 2002: WorldCom CEO Ebbers resigns as the SEC probe intensifies. Vice chairman John Sidgmore takes over.

June 2002: CFO Scott Sullivan is fired. The SEC formally charges the company with fraud.

July 2002: WorldCom files for Chapter 11 bankruptcy, the largest ever filed in terms of outstanding debt. Former Salomon Smith Barney analyst Jack Grubman admits to attending WorldCom board meetings.

August 2002: Sullivan and former controller David Myers are arrested and charged with securities fraud.

November 2002: Former Compaq chief Michael Capellas is named CEO of WorldCom.

April 2003: 90% of creditors agree to WorldCom's reorganization plan. Robert Blakely is named CFO.

May 2003: WorldCom settles charges with the SEC and agrees to pay $750 million in fines and retribution.

October 2003: Bankruptcy court judge Arthur Gonzalez approves WorldCom's reorganization plan.

March 2004: Sullivan pleads guilty to criminal charges. Ebbers is formally charged with fraud. WorldCom files its restated 2002 10-K, which includes a write-down of $80 billion in goodwill, assets, and property.

April 2004: WorldCom exits bankruptcy and changes its name to MCI.

7

CHAPTER

Operating Transactions— Revenues, Expenses, and Working Capital

RECAP: WHAT GOES WITH WHAT?

$$\text{ROE} = \frac{\text{Net income}}{\text{Common equity}} = \frac{\text{NI} + \text{Interest expense}}{\text{Sales}} \times \frac{\text{Sales}}{\text{Assets}} \times \frac{\text{Assets}}{\text{Common equity}} \times \frac{\text{NI}}{\text{NI} + \text{Interest expense}}$$

As we discuss the income statement and working capital, remember the relationships among these accounts.

- Receivables are generated from sales and lead to cash flow from operations as customers pay.

- Inventory is purchased from suppliers on account, creating accounts payable. When inventory is sold, the cost of goods sold is recorded. When suppliers are paid, cash flow from operations is reduced.

- Prepaid expenses (e.g., for insurance) arise when suppliers are paid in advance and cash flow from operations is reduced. When the assets are

used up, selling and administrative expenses are recorded.

- Accrued expenses and liabilities are recorded when services (e.g., wages or utilities) are received and consumed (creating selling and administrative expenses). When the liabilities are paid, cash flow from operations is reduced.

From this brief recap, you can see the relationships among the income statement (profitability), the balance sheet (working capital management and asset turnover), and statement of cash flows (solvency). All three need to be properly managed to create value.

In this chapter, we begin with the income statement and a description of how its various categories (revenues, expenses, gains, and losses) help us measure and evaluate past value creation and predict future value creation. We then turn to the measurement and management of key operating working capital items such as receivables, inventories, and payables. Along the way, we demonstrate how measuring these balance sheet items affects income measurement and the statement of cash flows.

Operating transactions involve managing the activities related to the sale of goods and services and the operating working capital (Current operating assets − Current operating liabilities) required for those activities. The results of these activities are reflected on the

201

income statement, the working capital section of the balance sheet, and the operating section of the statement of cash flows. Effective income statement (sales and expenses) management is measured by profit margin, and effective working capital management is reflected in asset turnover and the company's solvency measures. Recall from Chapter 4 that profit margin multiplied by asset turnover equals return on assets (ROA), a direct determinant of return on equity (ROE), and a company's need for solvency depends on the level of its capital structure leverage, another direct determinant of ROE.

▶ INCOME STATEMENT: DISCLOSURE AND PRESENTATION

Figure 7-1 illustrates an income statement that comprises five major categories. In general, as one moves from the top to the bottom of the income statement, the events become increasingly less important to the normal and recurring operations of the business. The

XYZ Company Income Statement For the period ending December 31, 2008		
Sales		$ 850
Less cost of goods sold		350
Gross profit		500
Operating expenses:		
Wages and salaries	$ 25	
Advertising	10	
Insurance	20	
State and local taxes (non-income taxes)	30	
Utilities	50	
Depreciation	100	
Miscellaneous	150	385
Net operating income		115
Other revenues	40	
Less other expenses (including interest, net)	25	15
Net income from continuing operations before tax		130
Less income tax expense		40
Net income from continuing operations		90
Income on disposal of segment (net of tax)		10
Net income before extraordinary items		100
Extraordinary loss (net of tax)		5
Net income before change in accounting method		95
Cumulative effect of change in accounting method (net of tax)		3
Net income		$ 98
Earnings per share (100 shares outstanding):		
Net income from continuing operations		$ 0.90
Disposal of business segment		0.10
Extraordinary items		(0.05)
Change in accounting method		0.03
Total earnings per share		$ 0.98
Fully diluted earnings per share		$ 0.96

Figure 7-1. Income Statement

categories are useful because they help users determine the extent to which items on the income statement (1) reflect actual changes in the company's wealth occurring during the period, and (2) whether the item can be expected to persist in the future. These items, through their effect on profit margin, can indicate whether management has actually created value for the stockholders in the past and can be expected to create value in the future.

Operating Revenues and Expenses

Operating revenues and expenses refer to asset and liability inflows and outflows related to the acquisition and delivery of the goods or services provided by a company. They are considered usual and frequent. The term "usual" refers to the normal operations of the business. If a company is in business to sell furniture, for example, usual revenues come from furniture sales. Automobile dealerships, on the other hand, are in business to sell and service automobiles. They own office furniture, but inflows generated from selling it would not be considered usual. The term "frequent" refers to how often the revenue is generated or the expense is incurred. Revenues and expenses are considered frequent if they are expected to recur in the foreseeable future. They are not "one-shot," unpredictable events. For many companies, the sale of a fixed asset or a long-term investment, which can generate either a gain or a loss, is a transaction that tends to occur infrequently.

Other Revenues and Expenses

The section of the income statement headed "other revenues and expenses" contains revenues and expenses related to a company's secondary or auxiliary activities. Interest expense, interest revenue, gains and losses on asset disposals, restructuring expenses, litigation gains and losses, losses due to employee strikes, income from the rental of excess warehouse space, and other similar items are generally found in this section. The key feature about the items in this section is that they are "unusual or infrequent, but not both."

INSIGHT: THE INCOME STATEMENT, VALUE CREATION, AND VALUATION

We learned earlier that value creation takes place when, over the long run, a company's ROE exceeds its cost of equity capital. Not all value creation, however, is created equal. One-time, nonrecurring activities may boost ROE so that it exceeds the cost of equity, but have little impact on the market value of the firm because they have little to do with future value creation. Recall from Chapter 5 the model that links *future* value creation to the market value of the firm. Frequent, recurring activities, on the other hand, can have implications for both past and future value creation, and therefore firm value. Classified income statements help users determine which items should be included in their assessments of future value creation.

Interest Expense, Net

Although interest is certainly important and recurring, with the exception of financial institutions, it is not directly related to the acquisition and sale of a company's goods and services. Interest is a cost of financing, not a cost of operating. Many companies report interest expense net of interest and investment income, which arises when firms have marketable securities and other financial investments in interest-bearing or dividend-paying securities. To obtain a sense of the interest rate or return, one can compare interest expense to the level of interest-bearing debt, and interest and investment income to the company's financial investments.

Disposal of a Business Segment—Discontinued Operations

A business segment is defined as a separate line of business, product line, or class of customer involving an operation independent from a company's other operations. Diversified companies consist of many independent segments. The sale or discontinuance of any one of these segments is referred to as a disposal of a business segment and the related financial effects are disclosed separately on the income statement.

Extraordinary Items

Extraordinary items are defined as material events of a character significantly different from the typical, customary business activities of an entity, which are not expected to recur frequently in the ordinary operating activities of a business. In other words, extraordinary items are "both unusual and infrequent." Depending on the nature of a company's operations, extraordinary items could include gains and losses from terminating pension plans, gains and losses from litigation settlements, and losses resulting from casualties such as floods and earthquakes. Accounting standards issued by the Financial Accounting Standards Board (FASB) and the International Accounting Standards Board (IASB) generally restrict the sorts of items that can be labeled extraordinary. For example, the IASB maintains that extraordinary items are income or expenses resulting from events or transactions that are clearly distinct from the entity's ordinary activities and not expected to recur frequently or regularly. Very few items are treated as extraordinary.

ANALYSIS CHALLENGE: BEAUTY IS IN THE EYE OF THE BEHOLDER—AND SO IS THE DISTINCTION AMONG RECURRING, UNUSUAL, EXTRAORDINARY, AND OTHER!

It is impossible to set rules to cover the categorization of every possible revenue or expense. Consequently, savvy readers of financial statements take management's categorizations as guidance but not gospel. In other words, they ask themselves about the underlying economics of the item and use the information based on their needs. What is non-operating or non-recurring to one analyst may be just the opposite to another. Use your own judgment in interpreting the categorizations.

Standard-setters get into the act, too!
It's not just managers that decide how events are categorized. In an attempt to achieve consistency, sometimes standard-setters like the FASB's Emerging Issues Task Force (EITF) weigh in. After the September 11, 2001, terrorist attacks, the EITF took the position that, though clearly large in magnitude, a terrorist attack was not an extraordinary event. They took the same position with Hurricane Katrina, which led to the evacuation of New Orleans and large parts of the Gulf Coast of the United States in August 2005. These positions are based primarily on the nature of the events and not the magnitude of their effects. Secondarily, they also reflect the difficulty in identifying the direct and indirect costs associated with the events.

Changes in Accounting Methods

Consistency in measurement helps to maintain the credibility of accounting reports, enabling investors, creditors, and other interested parties to make more meaningful comparisons and to identify more easily the trends in a company's performance over time. In Chapter 3, we explained that once a company chooses an acceptable method of accounting, it continues to use that method from one year to the next. If a company can convince its auditors, however, that the environment in which it operates has changed and another accounting method is now more appropriate, it can voluntarily change the accounting method and still be in conformance with generally accepted accounting principles (GAAP). When a company voluntarily changes an accounting principle, it is required to restate its prior financial statements to reflect the change. For companies that report income statements across three years, each comparative statement will be restated and the earliest one will also include a line for the cumulative effect (net of tax) of the change on net income up to the start of that period.

When accounting standard-setters change the rules, they provide guidance about how companies can make the transition to the new rule. Normally, the financial statements must be retroactively restated, which includes a line item on the income statement adjusting income in the period of the change. Sometimes, however, standard-setters require that mandatory accounting changes are made prospectively, meaning that the change need only be reflected in future periods. That happens when the cost of obtaining the data needed to make the restatement is judged to exceed its potential benefit.

Disclosure of Income Taxes

Income taxes are disclosed in two different ways on the income statement. The first income tax disclosure immediately follows net income from continuing operations (before tax). It represents the tax expense resulting from all revenues and expenses except for those listed below it on the income statement. Dividing the income tax expense by net income from continuing operations (before tax) leads to the firm's effective income tax rate, which is used in many of the computations involved in the ROE model discussed in Chapter 4. The effective tax rate is also disclosed in notes to the firm's financial statements.

The remaining items (disposal of business segments, extraordinary items, and changes in accounting methods) are all disclosed net of tax. In other words, each of these items is disclosed on the income statement after the related income tax effect has been removed.

Earnings-Per-Share Disclosure

Generally accepted accounting principles (GAAP) require that earnings per share be disclosed on the face of the income statement and that per-share amounts associated with (1) net income from continuing operations (after tax), (2) disposals of business segments, (3) extraordinary items, and (4) changes in accounting methods be disclosed separately. An additional disclosure, called diluted earnings per share, is also required for companies that have the potential for significant dilution. Many companies, for example, have outstanding options to purchase their common stocks or bonds that can be converted to common stocks in the future. If and when these options and conversion privileges are exercised, the number of outstanding common shares will increase, which, in turn, will dilute the ownership interests of the existing common stockholders. The calculation of diluted earnings per share reflects these possibilities by essentially increasing the denominator of the earnings-per-share ratio, thereby reducing its value. The extent of potential dilution, as measured by the difference between diluted and unadjusted (basic) earnings per share, can be useful information for existing or potential shareholders who are concerned with maintaining the value of their investments.

Pfizer's 2004 to 2006 income statements are reproduced in Figure 7-2. Note how each of the categories (other than extraordinary items) appear on their income statements, permitting investors and analysts the opportunity to better evaluate past performance and predict future results.

Consolidated Statements of Income
Pfizer Inc. and Subsidiary Companies

(millions, except per common share data)	YEAR ENDED DECEMBER 31,		
	2006	2005	2004
Revenues	$48,371	$47,405	$ 48,988
Costs and expenses:			
Cost of sales[a]	7,640	7,232	6,391
Selling, informational, and administrative expenses[a]	15,589	15,313	15,304
Research and development expenses[a]	7,599	7,256	7,513
Amortization of intangible assets[a]	3,261	3,399	3,352
Acquisition-related in-process research and development charges	835	1,652	1,071
Restructuring charges and acquisition-related costs	1,323	1,356	1,151
Other (income)/deductions—net	(904)	397	803
Income from continuing operations before provision for taxes on income, minority interests, and cumulative effect of a change in accounting principles	13,028	10,800	13,403
Provision for taxes on income	1,992	3,178	2,460
Minority interests	12	12	7
Income from continuing operations before cumulative effect of a change in accounting principles	11,024	7,610	10,936
Discontinued operations:			
Income from discontinued operations—net of tax	433	451	374
Gains on sales of discontinued operations—net of tax	7,880	47	51
Discontinued operations—net of tax	8,313	498	425
Income before cumulative effect of a change in accounting principles	19,337	8,108	11,361
Cumulative effect of a change in accounting principles—net of tax	–	(23)	–
Net income	$19,337	$ 8,085	$ 11,361
Earnings per common share—basic			
Income from continuing operations before cumulative effect of a change in accounting principles	$ 1.52	$ 1.03	$ 1.45
Discontinued operations	1.15	0.07	0.06
Income before cumulative effect of a change in accounting principles	2.67	1.10	1.51
Cumulative effect of a change in accounting principles	–	–	–
Net income	$ 2.67	$ 1.10	$ 1.51
Earnings per common share—diluted			
Income from continuing operations before cumulative effect of a change in accounting principles	$ 1.52	$ 1.02	$ 1.43
Discontinued operations	1.14	0.07	0.06
Income before cumulative effect of a change in accounting principles	2.66	1.09	1.49
Cumulative effect of a change in accounting principles	–	–	–
Net income	$ 2.66	$ 1.09	$ 1.49
Weighted-average shares—basic	7,242	7,361	7,531
Weighted-average shares—diluted	7,274	7,411	7,614

[a] Exclusive of amortization of intangible assets, except as disclosed in Note 1K, "Amortization of Intangible Assets, Depreciation, and Certain Long-Lived Assets."

See Notes to Consolidated Financial Statements, which are an integral part of these statements.

Figure 7-2. Pfizer Inc. Income Statements

▶ WORKING CAPITAL

Managing operating activities involves maintaining a proper level of working capital (Current assets − Current liabilities). Working capital provides a company with much-needed liquidity (if the current assets are liquid), but it also requires costly financing via either long-term debt or equity (see Figure 2-4). Maintaining the appropriate balance between the need for (unproductive) liquid assets and adequate inventory, and the costs of financing working capital is an important part of value creation. If working capital is too high, asset (e.g., receivables and inventory) turnover ratios will put downward pressure on return on assets. In addition, the excess working capital needs to be financed, leading to more-than-necessary financing costs. If working capital is too low, the company may not be adequately meeting its customers' needs or its solvency position may be insufficient to support the level of capital structure leverage.

Our focus here is on current *operating* assets and liabilities. We cover current non-operating assets (e.g., short-term investments) in Chapter 8 and non-operating liabilities (e.g., current portion of long-term debt and notes payable) in Chapter 9. Current operating assets (normally including cash, accounts receivable, inventory, and prepaid expenses) are defined as assets intended to be used or converted into cash within one year or the company's operating cycle, whichever is longer. A company's operating cycle is the time it takes the company to convert its cash to inventory (to purchase or manufacture inventory), sell the inventory, and collect cash from the sale. In other words, the operating cycle is the time required for a company to go through all of the required phases of the production and sales process. The relative size of current assets differs significantly across companies in different industries. For example, current assets as a percentage of total assets vary from an average of 32% in the telecommunications industry to more than 80% for certain retailers and financial institutions.

Current operating liabilities are obligations expected to require the use of current assets or the creation of other current liabilities. Examples include accounts payable and accrued liabilities for operating items (e.g., wages and utilities) and unearned revenue. The relative size of current liabilities also varies across companies from different industries. Financial institutions, for example, use current liabilities (often in the form of deposits) as their most important source of financing.

▶ CASH

The cash account is the first asset listed in the current asset section of the balance sheet. It consists of coin, currency, and checking accounts, as well as money orders, certified checks, cashiers checks, personal checks, and bank drafts received by a company. Companies use a number of different titles to describe the cash account, most commonly "cash" or "cash and cash equivalents." Cash equivalents are short-term investments with original maturity dates of 90 days or less. A common example is a certificate of deposit that can be converted to cash immediately. Three issues concerning cash are particularly important to managers: (1) restrictions, (2) management, and (3) control.

Cash Restrictions

In general, cash presents few problems from a reporting standpoint. There are no valuation problems because cash always appears on the balance sheet at face value. The only reporting issue is whether there are restrictions on its use. Restrictions placed on a company's access to its cash are typically imposed by creditors to help ensure future interest and principal payments. As part of a loan agreement, for example, a creditor may require that a certain amount of cash be held in escrow—that is, controlled by a trustee until the debtor's existing

CROCS, INC.
CONSOLIDATED BALANCE SHEETS
(in thousands, except share and per share data)

	December 31, 2006	December 31, 2005
ASSETS		
Current assets:		
Cash and cash equivalents	$ 42,656	$ 4,787
Restricted cash	2,890	–
Short-term investments	22,325	–
Accounts receivable, less allowance for doubtful accounts of $1,690 and $566, respectively	65,588	17,641
Inventories	86,210	28,494
Deferred tax assets	3,690	1,939
Prepaid income tax	4,715	–
Prepaid expenses and other current assets	9,617	3,492
Total current assets	$ 237,691	$ 56,353

Cash and Cash Equivalents—Cash and cash equivalents represent cash and short-term, highly liquid investments with maturities of three months or less at date of purchase. The company considers receivables from credit card companies to be cash equivalents. The carrying amounts reflected in the consolidated balance sheet for cash and cash equivalents approximate fair value due to the short maturities.

Restricted Cash—Restricted cash represents cash commitments for certain purchase obligations. The classification of restricted cash on the consolidated balance sheet as current or noncurrent is dependent on the duration of the restriction and the purpose for which the restriction exists.

Figure 7-3. Crocs, Inc., Cash and Restricted Cash Disclosures

liability is discharged. Banks sometimes require that minimum cash balances be maintained on deposit in the accounts of customers to whom they lend money or extend credit. These amounts are called compensating balances. Cash held in escrow and compensating balances are examples of cash amounts that a company owns but cannot immediately use. In effect, they increase the cost of borrowing.

If material, restricted cash is separated from the general cash account on the balance sheet, and the restrictions are clearly described either on the balance sheet itself or in the footnotes. If the restricted cash is to be used for the payment of obligations maturing during the period of the current assets, the separate "restricted cash" account is appropriately classified as a current asset. If it is to be held for a longer period of time, it should be classified as noncurrent.

Figure 7-3 reproduces balance sheet and note disclosures of cash and restricted cash at footwear maker Crocs, Inc.

GLOBAL MANAGEMENT INSIGHT

Having lots of cash does not mean that a company has free access to it. In addition to the restrictions just described, there may be challenges in using the cash from one subsidiary to pay the bills of another. The problem is exacerbated when the funds are scattered across countries and currency transfer restrictions exist, explaining why companies sometimes report both cash balances *and* short-term bank borrowing.

Cash Management

Proper cash management requires that enough cash be available to meet the needs of a company's operations, yet too much is undesirable because idle cash provides no return and loses purchasing power during periods of inflation. Maintaining a proper balance is a challenge. On one hand, enough cash must be available so that a company can meet its cash obligations as they come due. Purchases are often made in cash, and payments on accounts payable and short-term loans require cash. Wages, salaries, and currently maturing long-term debts must be honored in cash. A little extra cash is normally desirable in case of unforeseen cash needs. However, cash over and above the amount needed should be put to good use: to reduce debt, to be invested in income-producing assets, or to be returned to shareholders as dividends.

INSIGHT: CASH BUDGETS

Cash management decisions often are based on the information provided by the accounting system. One useful tool for cash management, an output of the accounting system, is a cash budget—a report projecting future cash inflows and outflows used to assess future cash operating needs, and whether additional borrowing or equity issuances are necessary. This report is generated and used internally and normally is not available to shareholders, investors, creditors, and other parties outside a company. It contains information about future projections that cannot be objectively verified and audited.

Many companies manage their cash balances by maintaining lines of credit—loan agreements that allow them to borrow up to a maximum amount on demand. These companies manage their credit lines by borrowing what they need when they need it, and then paying the balance down when excess cash becomes available. A large, unused line of credit is normally considered a sign of solvency.

INSIGHT: HAVING A LINE OF CREDIT VS. DRAWING ON IT

Although access to a line of credit is viewed as a positive signal of solvency, actually drawing on it is not always viewed favorably. In 2000, for example, Xerox began drawing down a $7 billion backstop credit line because operating problems caused its stock to plunge, shutting it out of the commercial paper market, an important source of financing for large, healthy companies. Stephen Gresdo, managing director of a hedge fund and cofounder of bankstocks.com, commented, "It's usually not a good sign when a company draws down a [backup] line of credit. It's a last resort."

"Xerox Debt Worries Put Banks on Firing Line," Eileen Kinsella 12/04/00 7:29 PM ET, URL: http://www.thestreet.com/stocks/banking/1198176.html

Cash Control

The control of cash is an important task and the company's accounting system plays a key role. Cash control is a special concern for businesses such as grocery stores, movie theaters, restaurants, financial institutions, retail stores, department stores, and bars, which process frequent cash transactions. There are two aspects to cash control: record control and physical control.

Record control refers to the procedures designed to ensure that the cash account on the balance sheet reflects the actual amount of cash in the company's possession. Problems of record control arise when many different kinds of transactions involve cash, and it is difficult to record them all accurately. Proper control of cash records requires that all cash receipts and disbursements be faithfully recorded and posted. Periodically, the dollar amount of cash indicated in the cash account should be checked against and reconciled with the cash balance indicated on the statement provided by a company's bank.

Physical control of cash refers to the procedures designed to safeguard cash from loss or theft. Problems of physical control arise because it is universally desired and easily concealed and transported. Cash embezzlement by a company's employees is always a threat. Separation of duties is an important part of a well-controlled system. It requires that employees responsible for recording cash transactions should not also be responsible for the physical control of the cash.

▶ ACCOUNTS RECEIVABLE AND REVENUE RECOGNITION

Accounts receivable can be a major part of a company's working capital. Trade receivables arise when revenues are recognized before cash is received. In terms of the basic accounting equation, an asset (receivable) is increased and revenue, which appears on the income statement, increases net income and, ultimately, retained earnings. When cash is received later, the accounts receivable on the balance sheet is removed and cash is increased.

MECHANICS: REVENUE AND RECEIVABLES—BASIC JOURNAL ENTRIES AND T-ACCOUNTS

Accounts Receivable (+A)	$	
Sales (R, +RE)		$

To record sales on account.

Cash (+A)	$	
Accounts Receivable (−A)		$

To record the collection of accounts receivable.

A useful tool for account analysis is the T-account (See Appendix 3A). A T-account is a graphic representation of the activity in an account. Debit balances appear on the left side and credits on the right. Opening and ending balances are shown and the periodic activity is entered. The following T-account assumes that a company began the year with ac-

counts receivable of $100. During the year, products were sold for $3,000. The company collected $2,940 of receivables and, thus, ended the year with a balance of $160 of accounts receivable.

Accounts Receivable

Beginning Balance	$ 100		
Sales	3,000		
		$2,940	Collections
Ending Balance	$ 160		

Revenue Recognition

REVIEW: REVENUE RECOGNITION CRITERIA

In Chapter 3, we outlined the four criteria that need to be met in order to recognize revenue. They are (1) persuasive evidence that an arrangement exits, (2) delivery has occurred or services have been rendered, (3) the seller's price to the buyer is fixed or determinable, and (4) collectibility is reasonably assured.

Receivables arise when revenue is recognized prior to cash collection, begging the question of when revenue should be recognized. We discussed the criteria for revenue recognition in Chapter 3, but literally hundreds of accounting rules exist that cover revenue recognition and some are conflicting. This diversity arose over time as various authoritative bodies (FASB, American Institute of Certified Public Accountants (AICPA), Securities and Exchange Commission (SEC), and industry groups) issued pronouncements on revenue recognition in response to specific situations. The current situation is better described as a collection of practices than a set of rules. Standard-setters in the United States and internationally are presently working on a joint, comprehensive standard.

FREESCALE SEMICONDUCTOR, INC.—EXCERPTS FROM THEIR 2005 REVENUE RECOGNITION POLICY

Revenue Recognition: The company recognizes revenue from product sales when title transfers, the risks and rewards of ownership have been transferred to the customer, the fee is fixed or determinable, and collection of the related receivable is reasonably assured, which is generally at the time of shipment. Sales with destination point terms, which are primarily related to European customers where these terms are customary, are recognized upon delivery.

Revenue for services is recognized ratably over the contract term or as services are being performed.

Distributor Sales: Revenue from sales to distributors of the company's products is recognized when title transfers, the risks and rewards of ownership have been transferred to the customer, the fee is fixed or determinable, and collection of the related receivable is reasonably assured, which is generally at the time of shipment.

Multiple Elements: Revenues from contracts with multiple elements are recognized as each element is earned, based on the relative fair value of each element, and when there are no undelivered elements that are essential to the functionality of the delivered elements and when the amount is not contingent upon delivery of the undelivered elements.

Managing Receivables

In our credit-oriented economy, transactions that give rise to accounts receivable make up a significant portion of total business transactions. Restaurants and grocery stores carry relatively small levels of receivables because their customers normally pay with cash, personal checks, or bank cards such as MasterCard, Visa, and American Express. Department stores, such as JCPenney and Sears, carry larger portions of short-term receivables because they issue their own charge cards, which their customers use extensively. Many professional services and certain manufacturers carry large receivables because they bill clients and customers, and often do not receive final payment for several months.

Often backed by oral rather than written commitments, accounts receivable represent short-term extensions of credit normally collectible within 30 to 60 days. These trade credit agreements are referred to as open accounts. Often many such transactions are enacted between a company and its customers, and it is impractical to create a formal contract for each one. Open accounts typically reflect running balances, because at the same time that customers are paying off previous purchases, new purchases are being made. If an account receivable is paid in full within the specified 30- or 60-day period, no interest is charged. Payment after this period, however, can be subject to a significant financial charge. Customer credit card arrangements with department stores, like Sears and JCPenney, and oil companies, like ExxonMobil and BP Amoco, are common examples of open accounts.

Receivables turnover (Sales/average accounts receivable) measures how quickly a company's customers pay their bills or the extent of the company's investment in accounts receivable, which requires costly financing. Receivables turnover is a key metric of value creation for companies that extend credit because it can be a significant component of asset turnover, a determinant of ROA, which is a determinant of ROE.

Valuing Receivables on the Balance Sheet

The key factor in valuing accounts receivable on the financial statements is the amount of cash the receivables are expected to generate. Although the face value of the receivable represents a starting point, there are a number of reasons why it may not represent the actual amount of cash ultimately collected. Many companies, for example, offer cash discounts, allowing customers to pay lesser amounts if they pay within specified time periods. Other accounts receivable may produce no cash at all because customers simply refuse to, or cannot, pay (bad debts), or choose to return previously sold merchandise (sales returns). Each of these issues must be considered when placing a value on accounts receivable on the balance sheet.

INSIGHT: VENDOR FINANCING

Some companies offer credit terms extending beyond 30–60 days. Whether to expand business by offering financing or just to offer a more competitive package, companies that offer extended credit terms must manage and account for long-term receivables. These receivables are generally treated as outstanding loans, initially recorded at the present value of the contractual cash inflows (see the Appendix at the end of this book for a discussion of present value). As payments are received, a portion is considered interest revenue and a portion serves to reduce the outstanding receivable.

The valuation base for accounts receivable is not the face amount of the receivables, but rather the net realizable value, an estimate of the cash expected to be produced by the receivables. In the next section, we discuss only bad debts. Cash discounts tend to be relatively small, and sales returns, although important for many companies, are accounted for in a manner very similar to bad debts.

Accounting for Bad Debts (Uncollectibles)

In an ideal world, all receivables would be collected, and there would be no need to consider bad debts. However, accounts that are ultimately uncollectible are an unfortunate fact of life, and companies must act to both control them and estimate their effects on the financial statements.

Controlling bad debts is a costly undertaking for many companies. The creditworthiness of potential customers can be checked by subscribing to credit-rating services such as Dun & Bradstreet, Moody's, or Standard & Poor's. Companies create and maintain collection departments, hire collection agencies, and pursue legal proceedings. Each of these alternatives can improve cash collections, but at a cost. In the extreme, management can institute a policy requiring that all sales be paid in cash, but that approach would reduce sales revenue. For most companies, then, bad debts are an inevitable cost of everyday operations that must be considered in the management of accounts receivable.

From an accounting standpoint, bad debts reduce the cash expected to be collected from accounts receivable, reducing the value of accounts receivable on the balance sheet. Bad debt losses also represent after-the-fact evidence that certain sales should not have been recorded, since the fourth criteria of revenue recognition (i.e., cash collection is assured) was not met for those sales. As a result, both accounts receivable and sales or fee revenue (and net income) are overstated if bad debts are ignored. Proper accounting for bad debts, therefore, involves two basic adjustments: (1) an adjustment to reduce the value of accounts receivable on the balance sheet and (2) an adjustment to reduce net income.

The allowance method is used to account for bad debts. This method involves three basic steps: (1) the monetary amount of expected bad debts is estimated at the end of the accounting period; (2) based on that estimate, a charge to income (e.g., reduce revenue or create an expense) is recognized on the income statement and an allowance account, which is subtracted from gross accounts receivable on the balance sheet, is adjusted; and (3) when the bad debt actually occurs (i.e., when the specific uncollectible accounts are identified and written off), both accounts receivable and the allowance account are reduced.

To illustrate, suppose that during its first year of operations, DIY-Depot had credit sales of $20,000 and a balance in accounts receivable of $6,000 as of December 31.

1. **Estimate bad debts.** After reviewing the relevant information, DIY-Depot's accountants estimate that 2.5% ($500) of its credit sales, on average, are normally not collected.

2. **Recognize a charge to income on the income statement and balance sheet.** On December 31, the following adjustment would be made to the income statement and balance sheet.

    Reduce net income by $500 by reducing revenue or creating an expense; increase the accounts receivable allowance account, which is subtracted on the balance sheet from gross accounts receivable, by $500. This adjustment reduces both net income (and retained earnings) and current assets by $500. The accounts receivable portion of the December 31 balance sheet would appear as follows.

Accounts receivable	$6,000
Less allowance	(500)
Net accounts receivable	$5,500

3. **Bad-debt write-off.** On January 18 of the following year, DIY-Depot is notified that ABM Enterprises has declared bankruptcy and will not be able to pay the $200 it owes to DIY-Depot. Both accounts receivable and the allowance account

on the balance sheet are reduced by $200. Note that this write-off entry has no effect on the balance sheet and income statement. In our example, net accounts receivable before and after the write-off is $5,500 ($6,000 − $500 = $5,800 − $300). Also, although the bad-debt write-off can be initiated by a specific event (e.g., bankruptcy of a customer), more commonly, at year end companies review their outstanding accounts receivable and make a judgment about which accounts to write-off. Typically, the older and/or inactive accounts are carefully reviewed and considered for write-off. Because write-offs require judgment, sometimes they need to be reversed when customers ultimately pay. In such cases, the cash receipt is recorded and the allowance account is restored by the amount of the collection.

An important part of understanding accounting for bad debts involves the realization that the estimate and the write-off are focused at two different levels. The estimate is normally based on the level of credit sales during the past year (e.g., bad debt expense is estimated as 1% of credit sales) or the year-end balance in accounts receivable (e.g., 2% of accounts receivable are estimated as uncollectible). It is focused at a global level. Actual write-offs, on the other hand, often are focused at the specific customer level (e.g., the $200 balance in the Smith account is written off). Not surprisingly, the estimates rarely match the write-offs. If the mismatch is relatively small, it is normally ignored. If it grows too large or seems to be biased (consistently wrong in the same direction), the estimating procedure may need to be modified because accurate information about the cost of selling on account and the value of the asset base are relevant to both the management of those activities and the evaluation and prediction of value creation.

RECEIVABLES—ALLOWANCE AND WRITE-OFF JOURNAL ENTRIES

Bad-Debt Expense (E, −RE) $
   Allowance for Doubtful Accounts (−A) $

To record the allowance for doubtful accounts and bad-debt expense.

Allowance for Doubtful Accounts (+A) $
   Accounts Receivable (−A) $

To record the write off of an account receivable (a receivable previously written off that is later deemed collectible would result in a journal entry that reverses these debits and credits).

The following T-accounts assume that a company began the year with accounts receivable of $10,000. During the year, products were sold for $30,000. The company collected $28,500 of receivables. At the end of the previous year, management estimated that $175 in receivables would not be collected. During the current year, they identified $150 in accounts that would not be collected and wrote them off, removing the balance from both the gross receivables account and the allowance account. Finally, an analysis of the ending

balance of gross receivables indicates that $140 is unlikely to be collected. Therefore, the company records a bad-debt expense of $115 and adjusts the allowance account accordingly.

Accounts Receivable, Gross

Beginning Balance	$10,000		
Sales	30,000		
		$28,500	Collections
		150	Write-Offs
Ending Balance	$11,350		

Allowance for Doubtful Accounts

		$ 175	Beginning Balance
Write-Offs	$ 150		
		115	Bad Debt Expense
		$ 140	Ending Balance

TEST YOUR KNOWLEDGE: MEASURING RECEIVABLES

Your company began operations on January 1, 2007. The company reported the following selected items in its 2008 financial report:

	2008	2007
Gross Sales	$1,400,000	$1,500,000
Accounts Receivable, gross	600,000	650,000
Actual Bad Debt Write-Offs	22,000	10,000

You estimate bad debts at 2% of gross sales.

Analyze the activity in the allowance for doubtful accounts T-account, and comment on whether the bad-debt expense has been sufficient to cover the write-offs.

Accounts Receivable Control and Aging Schedules

Maintaining control over outstanding accounts receivable is an important part of effective management. Because large receivable balances require costly financing, receivables should be collected as quickly as possible, and bad debts should be held to a minimum. Aging schedules help companies control bad debts in a number of significant ways.

An aging schedule maintains control over accounts receivable by categorizing individual accounts in terms of the length of time each account has been outstanding. It can lead to better bad debt estimates by applying different collection percentages to accounts of different ages (e.g., older accounts are more likely to be uncollectible). It can identify slow-moving accounts, thus directing collection efforts toward at-risk accounts (and pointing toward changes in how future orders from those accounts are treated), and an aging schedule can also be helpful in estimating how much money a company is losing in potential interest charges. Such information can be useful in deciding whether to offer cash discounts and in determining the appropriate terms for such discounts.

TEST YOUR KNOWLEDGE: MEASURING RECEIVABLES WITH AN AGING SCHEDULE

You gather the following data about gross receivables balances at the end of fiscal 2008, along with historical data on the collection of accounts. *(continues)*

TEST YOUR KNOWLEDGE: MEASURING RECEIVABLES WITH AN AGING SCHEDULE (*continued*)

	2008	Noncollection Probability
Current	€ 290 000	2%
1–45 days past due	€ 110 000	5%
46–90 days past due	€ 68 000	8%
More than 90 days past due	€ 40 000	15%

What balance should you report for gross receivables, the allowance for doubtful accounts, and net receivables at the end of 2008?

MEASUREMENT CHALLENGE—LOAN LOSS PROVISIONS AT CITIGROUP

Citigroup is a diversified provider of financial services. The company has a substantial portfolio of loans in its various lines of business. The excerpt below is from the 2006 annual report.

Allowance for Credit Losses

Management provides reserves for an estimate of probable losses inherent in the funded loan portfolio on the balance sheet in the form of an allowance for credit losses. In addition, management has established and maintained reserves for the potential losses related to the Company's off-balance-sheet exposures of unfunded lending commitments, including standby letters of credit and guarantees. These reserves are established in accordance with Citigroup's Loan Loss Reserve Policies, as approved by the Audit Committee of the Company's Board of Directors. Under these policies, the Company's Senior Risk Officer and Chief Financial Officer review the adequacy of the credit loss reserves each quarter with representatives from Risk and Finance staffs for each applicable business area.

▶ INVENTORY

Inventory refers to items held for sale in the ordinary course of business, and its relative importance varies considerably across different industries. Wal-Mart, Tesco, Carrefour, and General Electric, for example, carry huge inventories, while Citicorp and H&R Block carry none. Proper inventory management and accounting are critical for retail and manufacturing companies, whose performance depends significantly on the successful sale of their inventories.

Inventory turnover (Cost of goods sold / Average inventory) measures how quickly a company is moving its inventory, or the extent to which its investment in inventories requires costly financing. Inventory turnover is a key metric of value creation for retailers and manufacturers because it can significantly influence asset turnover, a determinant of ROA, which is a determinant of ROE.

Shareholders, creditors, managers, and auditors are all interested in the amount, condition, and marketability of a company's inventory. Shareholders are interested in future sales, profits, and dividends, all of which are related to the demand for inventory, and in the efficiency with which managers acquire, carry, and sell inventory. Creditors are interested in the ability of inventory sales to produce cash that can be used to meet interest and principal payments. Creditors may also view inventory as potential collateral or security for loans. Management must ensure that inventories are acquired (or manufactured) and carried at reasonable costs. Enough inventory must be carried and available to meet changing consumer demands; yet carrying too much inventory is costly because it must be controlled, protected, stored, insured, and financed. Auditors must ensure that the inventory dollar amount disclosed in the financial statements is determined using GAAP. The value and marketability of a company's inventory can also provide an indication of its ability to continue as a going concern.

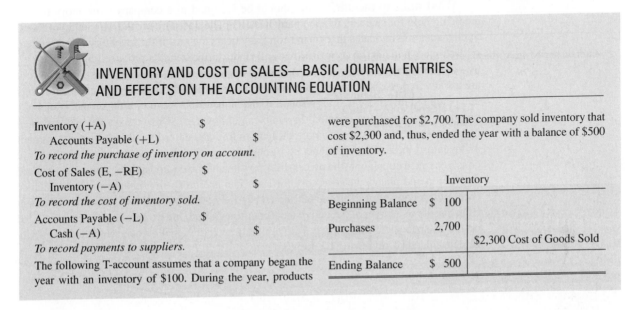

INVENTORY AND COST OF SALES—BASIC JOURNAL ENTRIES AND EFFECTS ON THE ACCOUNTING EQUATION

Inventory (+A) $
    Accounts Payable (+L) $
To record the purchase of inventory on account.

Cost of Sales (E, −RE) $
    Inventory (−A) $
To record the cost of inventory sold.

Accounts Payable (−L) $
    Cash (−A) $
To record payments to suppliers.

The following T-account assumes that a company began the year with an inventory of $100. During the year, products were purchased for $2,700. The company sold inventory that cost $2,300 and, thus, ended the year with a balance of $500 of inventory.

Inventory

Beginning Balance	$ 100	
Purchases	2,700	
		$2,300 Cost of Goods Sold
Ending Balance	$ 500	

ACCOUNTING FOR INVENTORY: FOUR IMPORTANT ISSUES

Figure 7-4 summarizes four important issues that must be addressed when accounting for inventory. At the top of the figure, the life cycle of inventory is divided into four segments.

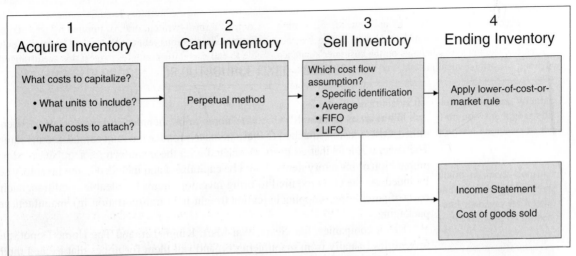

Figure 7-4. Accounting for Inventory: Four Important Issues

Inventory is (1) acquired, through purchase or manufacture, and then (2) carried on the company's balance sheet. It is then either (3) sold, or (4) remains on the balance sheet as ending inventory.

1. Acquiring Inventory: What Costs to Capitalize?

Inventory costs are capitalized because inventories are assets that provide future economic benefits. Determining the amount of capitalized cost involves two steps: (1) the number of units that belong in inventory must first be determined, and then, (2) costs must be attached to each unit.

What units to include? Units should be included in a company's inventory if they are being held for sale and the company has complete and unrestricted ownership of them. Such ownership indicates that (1) the company bears the cost if the inventory is lost, stolen, or destroyed, and (2) the company owns all rights to the benefits produced by the units.

In most cases, ownership is accompanied by possession; companies that own inventory are usually in possession of it. Under these circumstances, determining the number of units that belong in inventory is straightforward: the number of inventory units on the company's premises can simply be counted. In some cases, however, ownership is not accompanied by possession, and it becomes more difficult to find and determine the appropriate number of inventory units. Consignments and goods in transit are two common examples. In a consignment, a consignor (the owner) transfers inventory to a consignee, who takes physical possession and places the inventory for sale. The inventory should appear on the balance sheet of the consignor even though the consignee possesses it. When goods are in transit from a seller to a buyer at the end of an accounting period, the inventory should be included on the balance sheet of the party who at that time is the legal owner, which can normally be determined by reviewing the freight terms.

MEASUREMENT CHALLENGE—WHEN IS INVENTORY CONSIGNMENT INVENTORY?

Determining whether goods shipped to customers or distributors belong on the company's balance sheet can be tricky business; it is directly related to whether a sale has taken place.

As a general rule, if the risks and rewards of owning the inventory have been transferred, then a sale has occurred and the inventory belongs on the customer's balance sheet. If the arrangement is structured as a consignment, the "customer" is really only holding or displaying the inventory on the "vendor's" behalf. Thus, the risks and benefits of the inventory still reside with the vendor company, no sale has taken place, and the inventory remains on the vendor's books. Contract terms—written, oral, or implied by past actions—that include generous return policies and payments only on sale to end users, for example, suggest that the arrangement is a consignment.

What costs to attach? Once the items to be included in inventory have been determined, costs must be attached to these items to produce the total capitalized inventory cost. The general rule is that all costs associated with the manufacture, acquisition, storage, or preparation of inventory items should be capitalized and included in the inventory account. Included are the costs required to bring inventory items to saleable condition, such as the costs of purchasing, shipping in (called freight-in or transportation-in), manufacturing, and packaging.

Retail companies, like Sears, Wal-Mart, Kingfisher, and The Home Depot, purchase inventories (usually from manufacturers) and sell them for prices that exceed their costs.

Retailers provide a distribution service, rarely changing or improving the inventories they sell. As a result, the capitalized inventory cost for a retail operation consists primarily of only two components: (1) the purchase cost and (2) freight-in.

The operations of manufacturing companies, like IBM, General Electric, Honda, Procter & Gamble, Unilever, and Johnson & Johnson, on the other hand, are much more complex. These companies purchase raw materials and use processes involving labor and other costs to manufacture their inventories. The capitalized inventory cost therefore includes the cost of acquiring the raw materials, the cost of the labor used to convert the raw materials to finished goods, and other costs that support the production process. These other costs, called manufacturing overhead, include such items as indirect materials (e.g., cleaning supplies), indirect labor (e.g., salaries of line managers), depreciation of fixed assets involved in manufacturing, and utility and insurance costs.

The capitalized inventory costs of manufacturing operations include all costs required to bring the inventory to saleable condition. In this general respect, accounting for manufacturing operations is no different from accounting for retail operations. However, in manufacturing, costs that can be linked to the production process should be allocated to the inventory account. Therefore, manufacturing costs like depreciation, wages and salaries, rent, and insurance are often capitalized as part of the inventory cost and, accordingly, are matched against revenues (as part of cost of goods sold) when the finished inventory is sold.

2. Carry Inventory: Perpetual Method

Until recently, many companies, especially large retail and manufacturing operations, had difficulty maintaining a continuous record of inventory balances due to the speed with which inventories flowed in and out of the business. The number and variety of transactions were just too great to perpetually maintain an accurate count at a reasonable cost. Consequently, to prepare financial statements (i.e., compute the cost of goods sold and ending inventory), companies were forced to periodically disrupt operations and count their inventories.

Technology has dramatically reduced the cost of record keeping, and now most companies have computerized systems that maintain perpetual inventory balances. The bar code systems you see in major grocery stores (e.g., Safeway) and retailers (e.g., Target) are common examples. Although these systems do not eliminate the need to periodically count inventories, they offer a much greater level of control over inventories—a key element for the success of manufacturers and retailers.

The perpetual inventory method is very straightforward. Each time inventory is purchased, the inventory account is increased by the cost of the purchase, and each time inventory is sold, the account is decreased by the cost of the inventory sold. Accordingly, continual (perpetual) balances are maintained in the inventory and cost of goods sold accounts. At the end of the accounting period, though not necessary for the preparation of the financial statements, an inventory count is taken. The count provides an inventory amount that can be compared to the amount in the inventory account to ascertain whether actual inventory matches the company's perpetual inventory record.

To illustrate, if a company begins the year with 10 units of inventory, each with a cost of $5, and during the year, purchases 5 units at $5 each and sells 8 units at $10 each, the balance sheet and income statement would appear as follows.

Balance Sheet:

Beginning Inventory	+	Purchases	–	Sales	=	Ending Inventory
$50	+	25	–	40		$35
(10 u × $5/u)		(5 u × $5/u)		(8 u × $5/u)		(7 u × $5/u)

Income Statement:

Revenue	$80	(8 u × $10/u)
Cost of goods sold	(40)	(8 u × $5/u)
Gross profit	$40	

This method helps in the control of inventory by providing a balance that should be in the inventory account ($35 = 7 units × $5/u), which can be compared to the results of a physical inventory count. Suppose that a physical inventory count reveals only 6 units on hand. In this situation, the perpetual inventory method indicates a shortage, evidence of an inventory control breakdown that should be investigated and corrected by management. The shortage also requires the recognition of a $5 inventory loss, which reduces the balance in the inventory account (from $35 to $30), and is included as a loss (expense) on the income statement, reducing net income. Note that inventory misstatements directly affect both the balance sheet (inventory account) and the income statement (cost of goods sold).

TEST YOUR KNOWLEDGE: UNDERSTANDING CHANGING INVENTORY AND COST OF GOODS SOLD AMOUNTS

You gather the following data about inventories at a division of your company:

	2008	2007	2006
Beginning inventory	?	?	$ 2,312
Purchases	$9,170	?	$ 8,528
Goods available for sale	?	?	$10,840
Ending inventory	?	$1,931	?
Cost of goods sold	$9,285	$8,496	$ 8,749

Fill in the missing information.

3. Which Cost Flow Assumption?

When inventories are sold, the asset is used up and its benefits are realized. In using up the asset, the capitalized cost becomes an expense—cost of goods sold. Matching that expense with the revenue recognized from the sale provides an important performance measure: gross profit from sales. When that figure is expressed as a percentage of sales, it is called the gross margin.

An important and difficult question of inventory accounting involves how—at the point of sale—to allocate the capitalized inventory cost between the cost of goods sold, which goes to the income statement, and the ending inventory, which remains on the balance sheet. This choice affects both working capital and gross profit from sales. The examples so far assume that the cost of the sold inventory can be specifically identified, and in such cases the accounting is straightforward—the exact cost of the inventory sold is allocated to the cost of goods sold on the income statement and the cost of unsold merchandise remains in the inventory account on the balance sheet.

CARMAX, INC.—EXCERPTS FROM THEIR 2007 FINANCIAL STATEMENTS

CarMax, Inc. is the largest retailer of used cars in the United States. Inventory is a major asset and each car is different from the others. As a result, the company uses the specific identification method to account for its inventories. In its 2007 financial statements, they report:

(F) Inventory
Inventory is comprised primarily of vehicles held for sale or undergoing reconditioning and is stated at the lower of cost or market. Vehicle inventory cost is determined by specific identification. Parts and labor used to recondition vehicles, as well as transportation and other incremental expenses associated with acquiring and reconditioning vehicles, are included in inventory. Certain manufacturer incentives and rebates for new car inventory, including holdbacks, are recognized as a reduction to new car inventory when we purchase the vehicles. We recognize volume-based incentives as a reduction to cost of sales when we determine that the achievement of qualifying sales volumes is probable.

Because it is difficult for many companies to specifically identify the cost of sold inventory, generally accepted accounting principles allow managers to make one of three assumptions about the cost flow of the inventory items—averaging; first in, first out (FIFO); or last in, first out (LIFO). This choice can significantly affect net income, current assets, working capital, and other key metrics of performance through its effect on the allocation of inventory costs between the cost of goods sold and ending inventory. Importantly, this choice does not affect the total cost of goods sold that a firm reports across time, but it does affect the timing of the expense (cost of goods sold) recognition. That is, eventually, all costs of inventory flow through the income statement, but until all the inventory is sold, different costs reside on the balance sheet and income statements as a result of the cost flow assumption.

 DEFINITIONS—INTERPRETING THE TERMS FIFO AND LIFO

Although the terms FIFO and LIFO are commonly associated with inventory, they actually refer to the measurement of cost of goods sold. That is, cost of goods sold is measured on a first cost in, first cost out basis or a last (most recent) cost in, first cost out basis.

To illustrate and compare the three different cost flow assumptions, consider the following example. Figure 7-5 provides information about the inventory purchases and sales for Discount Sales Company over a two-year period. Following this information are calculations that track the information under three different cost flow assumptions: average cost (Figure 7-5a), FIFO (Figure 7-5b), and LIFO (Figure 7-5c).

In Figure 7-5, the inventory costs are increasing across time. The cost of the beginning inventory is $4 per unit; purchase costs are $7 per unit in Year 1 and $8 per unit in Year 2. Note in Figures 7-5 a, b, and c that inventory purchases in Years 1 and 2 are recorded in the same way across all three assumptions: $70 and $40 in Years 1 and 2, respectively. The

Description	Units	Unit cost	Total
Beginning inventory	3	$4	$12
Year 1			
Purchases	10	$7	$70
Sales	(8)		
Ending inventory	5		
Year 2			
Beginning inventory	5		
Purchases	5	$8	$40
Sales	(8)		
Ending inventory	2		

Figure 7-5. Inventory Activity for Discount Sales Company

Year 1:	Beginning inventory	12
	Plus purchases	70
	Less COGS	(50) *
	Ending inventory	32
Year 2:		
	Plus purchases	40
	Less COGS	(58)**
	Ending inventory	14

* 3 u × $4 = $12
10 u × $7 = 70
13 u $82

** 5 u × $6.31 = $32
5 u × $8.00 = 40
10 u $72

$6.31 = $82 / 13 u
$50.48 = 8 u × $6.31/u

$7.20 = $72 / 10 u
$57.60 = 8 u × $7.20

Figure 7-5a. Inventory (Average Assumption)

Year 1:	Beginning inventory	12
	Plus purchases	70
	Less COGS	(47) *
	Ending inventory	35
Year 2:		
	Plus purchases	40
	Less COGS	(59)**
	Ending inventory	16

* $47 = (3 u × $4/u) + (5 u × $7/u)
** $59 = (5 u × $7/u) + (3 u × $8/u)

Figure 7-5b. Inventory (FIFO Assumption)

Year 1:	Beginning inventory	12
	Plus purchases	70
	Less COGS	(56) *
	Ending inventory	26
Year 2:		
	Plus purchases	40
	Less COGS	(58)**
	Ending inventory	8

* $56 = 8 u × $7/u
** $58 = (5 u × $8/u) + (2 u × $7/u) + (1 u × $4/u)

Figure 7-5c. Inventory (LIFO Assumption)

differences in the assumptions relate to the different amounts attached to the cost of goods sold (COGS) when the outflow of the sold inventory is recorded.

Under the average assumption, a weighted average cost of the units available for sale is computed at the time of the sale. For example, at the time of the sale in Year 1, 13 units were available for sale—3 units at $4 and 10 units at $7, a weighted average (as illustrated in Figure 7-5a) of $6.31. This amount is multiplied times the number of units sold (8) to compute both COGS and the reduction in the inventory account. The same procedure is followed in Year 2, but note that the weighted average as of the date of the sale is different; it has risen to $7.20 per unit because the inventory purchase costs have risen.

TESCO PLC—EXCERPTS FROM THEIR 2007 FINANCIAL STATEMENTS

Tesco PLC of the United Kingdom is one of the world's leading retailers of food, nonfood, and retailing services. Tesco currently operates in China, the Czech Republic, Hungary, Japan, Malaysia, Poland, Republic of Ireland, Slovakia, South Korea, Thailand, Turkey, and the United Kingdom. In their 2007 annual report, they outline their inventory cost assumption:

Inventories

Inventories comprise goods held for resale and properties held for, or in the course of, development and are valued at the lower of cost and fair value less costs to sell using the weighted average cost basis.

Under the FIFO assumption, the oldest available inventory costs are used to compute COGS. That is, the cost of the first unit of inventory purchased is *assumed* to attach to the first unit of inventory sold. In Year 1, under the FIFO assumption, 3 of the 8 units sold were from the beginning inventory ($4 per unit), and the remaining 5 units were from the purchase in Year 1 ($7 per unit)—leaving an ending inventory ($35) comprising of 5 units at $7 per unit. In Year 2, 5 of the 8 units sold were assumed to have come from the remaining 5 units purchased in Year 1 ($7 per unit), and the other 3 units came from the Year 2 purchase ($8 per unit). The $16 ending inventory thus comprises 2 units at $8 per unit, all from the Year 2 purchase—the most current inventory costs.

GROUPE CARREFOUR—EXCERPTS FROM 2006 FINANCIAL STATEMENTS

The Carrefour Group of France is the second largest retailer in the world (after Wal-Mart of the United States). In their 2006 annual report, they explain their inventory cost assumption:

INVENTORIES

Inventories are valued at the most recent purchase price plus any additional costs, a method that is well suited to rapid inventory turnaround and does not generate a significant difference with the FIFO method. The cost price includes all costs that constitute the purchase cost of the goods sold (with the exception of foreign currency losses and gains) and also takes into consideration all the conditions obtained at the time of purchase and from supplier services.

In accordance with International Accounting Standards (IAS) 2, "Inventories," inventories are valued at their production cost or their net present value, whichever is lower.

The net present value is the estimated sales price less the additional costs necessary for the sale.

Under the LIFO assumption, the most current inventory costs are used to compute COGS. In Year 1, LIFO assumptions assigned all 8 units sold a cost of $7, the most recent purchase cost, leaving an ending inventory ($26) comprising of 2 units at $7 per unit and 3 units at $4 per unit. In Year 2, the 8 units sold were assumed to have come from three groups: 5 units from the most recent (Year 2) purchase, 2 units from the remaining units purchased in Year 1 ($7 per unit), and 1 unit from beginning inventory ($4 per unit). Year 2's ending inventory under LIFO ($8) is 2 units at $4 per unit—inventory costs from before Year 1.

WAL-MART STORES, INC.—EXCERPTS FROM THEIR 2007 FINANCIAL STATEMENTS

Wal-Mart Stores, Inc., of the United States is the world's largest retailer, with sales exceeding $348 billion for the year ending January 31, 2007. In their fiscal 2006 annual report, they explain their inventory cost assumption:

Inventories
The Company values inventories at the lower of cost or market as determined primarily by the retail method of accounting, using the last-in, first-out ("LIFO") method for substantially all of the Wal-Mart Stores segment's merchandise inventories. Sam's Club merchandise and merchandise in our distribution warehouses are valued based on the weighted average cost using the LIFO method. Inventories of foreign operations are primarily valued by the retail method of accounting, using the first-in, first-out ("FIFO") method. At January 31, 2007 and 2006, our inventories valued at LIFO approximate those inventories as if they were valued at FIFO.

Inventory Cost Flow Assumptions: Effects on the Financial Statements

Figure 7-6 compares the FIFO, average, and LIFO cost flow assumptions with respect to COGS, gross profit, and ending inventory for Years 1 and 2. Assume that Discount Sales Company sold its inventory for $10 per unit in both Years 1 and 2.

	FIFO	Average	LIFO
Year 1:			
Sales	$80	$80	$80
COGS	(47)	(50)	(56)
Gross profit	$33	$30	$24
Ending inventory	35	32	26
	FIFO	Average	LIFO
Year 2:			
Sales	$80	$80	$80
COGS	(59)	(58)	(58)
Gross profit	$21	$22	$22
Ending inventory	16	14	8

Figure 7-6. Financial Statement Effects of the Three Inventory Cost Flow Assumptions

Refer first to Year 1. FIFO gives rise to the largest gross profit ($33) and ending inventory ($35), while LIFO produces the lowest gross profit ($24) and ending inventory ($26). These differences arise because inventory costs are rising and LIFO uses the most current (highest) costs in computing COGS and allocates the oldest (lowest) costs to ending inventory. In general, in times of rising inventory costs, FIFO will give rise to higher net income and inventory numbers than LIFO. These differences reverse in periods when inventory costs decrease. The average assumption creates values between FIFO and LIFO in either case. In times of increasing inventory costs, using the FIFO assumption can boost important financial ratios, such as ROE, earnings per share, working capital, and the current ratio. Choosing LIFO, on the other hand, may value inventories at unrealistically low levels.

In Year 2, the situation is different. LIFO's COGS ($58) is actually less than FIFO's ($59), which means that gross profit is higher for LIFO ($22) than FIFO ($21) even though inventory costs increased. Although this result seems inconsistent with Year 1, it occurs because during Year 2, Discount Company sold more inventory items than it purchased, liquidating some of its inventory balance.

TEST YOUR KNOWLEDGE: INVENTORY COST FLOW ASSUMPTIONS

Watkins Corporation began operations on January 1, 2006. The 2006 and 2007 schedules of inventory purchases and sales are provided below.

2006:

Purchase 1	10 units @ $10 per unit	$100
Purchase 2	20 units @ $12 per unit	240
Total purchase costs		$340
Sales	15 units @ $30 per unit	$450

2007:

Purchase 1	10 units @ $13 per unit	$130
Purchase 2	15 units @ $15 per unit	225
Total purchase costs		$355
Sales	20 units @ $35 per unit	$700

Complete the following schedule and briefly discuss the tradeoffs associated with choosing an inventory cost flow assumption.

2006	FIFO	Weighted Average	LIFO	
Cost of goods sold				
Gross profit (Sales − COGS)				20
Ending inventory				

2007	FIFO	Weighted Average	LIFO	
Cost of goods sold				
Gross profit (Sales − COGS)				65
Ending inventory				

Observations about LIFO: Liquidations and LIFO Reserves

The LIFO assumption rarely matches the actual physical flow of the company's inventory items, and its use can create interesting phenomena that financial statement readers should consider. For example, in the illustration above, Discount Sales Company experienced a 3-unit inventory liquidation in Year 2—that is, it purchased only 5 units while selling 8 units. Under LIFO, the cost attached to these 3 units was only $18 ([2 units @ $7] + [1 unit @ $4]), $6 below the $24 (3 units at $8) that attaching current inventory costs would create. In effect, Discount "dipped into old LIFO layers" valued at old (lower) costs, and matched these costs against current sales. The liquidation of these inventories, while under the LIFO assumption ("LIFO liquidation"), boosted profits by $6 ($24 - $18). Under U.S. GAAP, in this situation Discount would be required to report that $6 of the total profits for the year was due to the LIFO liquidation. That disclosure is helpful to investors who want to distinguish "real" profits from profits due merely to the use of LIFO during a period over which inventories have been reduced.

Another helpful disclosure required under U.S. GAAP is that companies using LIFO must report in the footnotes what the value of their inventories would be if they used FIFO. In the illustration above—assuming that Discount was a LIFO user—it would report inventory on its balance sheet at the end of Years 1 and 2 of $26 and $8, respectively, but it would also be required to report in the footnotes that, under FIFO, its inventory would be $35 and $16. These disclosures are relatively easy for LIFO users because the FIFO value can be computed by simply multiplying ending inventory in units times the current cost of the inventory. The difference between ending inventory under FIFO and ending inventory under LIFO is called the LIFO reserve. The LIFO reserves for Discount for Years 1 and 2 are provided below.

	LIFO	FIFO	LIFO RESERVE
Ending inventory (Year 1)	$26	$35	$9
Ending inventory (Year 2)	8	16	8

This information is very useful for investors attempting to compare the performance levels of companies that use LIFO to companies that use FIFO. By definition, gross profit (LIFO) plus the change in the LIFO reserve is equal to gross profit (FIFO). Using the dollar values from Figure 7-6, the computation that converts gross profit (LIFO) to gross profit (FIFO) is provided below.

$$\text{Gross profit (LIFO)} + \text{(Change in LIFO reserve)} = \text{Gross profit (FIFO)}$$

$$\$22 \quad + \quad (\$8 - \$9) \quad = \quad \$21$$

INVENTORY—RESTATING LIFO INVENTORIES TO FIFO

Companies that use the LIFO cost flow assumption are required to provide information on what the value of the inventory is on a current cost (essentially FIFO) basis. The LIFO reserve reconciles the LIFO data to FIFO.

The T-accounts that follow demonstrate how one can estimate the cost of sales that would have been reported had a LIFO company used FIFO. Assume that the company reported a LIFO reserve of $500 at the beginning of the year and $575 at the end of the year.

Inventory, LIFO

Beginning Balance	$2,000	
Purchases*	7,500	
		$6,250 Cost of Goods Sold (LIFO)
Ending Balance	$3,250	

Purchases under LIFO are estimated by noting that Beginning inventory + Purchases − Cost of goods sold = Ending inventory. Purchases are identical under FIFO. Using the same equation but restating the LIFO beginning and ending balances to FIFO (by adding the reserve), we can solve for the FIFO basis cost of goods sold.

Inventory, FIFO

Beginning Balance	$2,500	
Purchases	7,500	
		$6,175 Cost of Goods Sold (FIFO**)
Ending Balance	$3,825	

**Note that COGS on a FIFO basis equals COGS on a LIFO basis less the change in the LIFO reserve (i.e. $6,250 − (575 − 500) = $6,175)*

INSIGHT: DOES THIS STUFF MATTER? IS THIS SOME SORT OF PARTY TRICK FOR ACCOUNTANTS?

As firms strive to enhance the efficiency of their supply chains and manage their inventory costs, they find ways to reduce inventory levels. If they've been using the LIFO inventory cost flow assumption and if their inventory unit costs have been rising, they face the possibility of recording substantial LIFO liquidation gains if inventory units are reduced. Those gains are unlikely to recur year after year and so investors and other users of the statements will want to factor that into their analyses of current performance and prediction of future results.

Consider General Motors in 2003. They use LIFO for most of their U.S. inventories and FIFO or average cost for the remainder. Even though overall inventories grew from $9.74 billion to $10.96 billion, the inventories under LIFO were "liquidated" (reduced) and a $200 million LIFO liquidation gain was reported. That might seem small in relation to the total inventory balance, but this nonrecurring item was very significant relative to operating income and the growth in operating income that year. The liquidation accounted for 7% of operating income and 22.5% of its year-over-year growth.

We look more closely at GM and its inventories in an end-of-chapter case.

Inventory Cost Flow Assumptions: Tradeoffs

When management chooses an inventory assumption, no requirement exists that the assumption reflect the *physical* flow of the inventory. Consequently, the cost of the inventory based on the assumption rarely reflects the actual cost of the inventory on hand. Choosing a cost flow assumption is largely independent of the actual physical flow of the inventory.

The tradeoffs involved in choosing an inventory cost flow assumption are divided into two categories: (1) income and asset measurement, and (2) economic consequences. Income and asset measurement refers to how well each assumption produces measures that reflect the actual performance and financial condition of a company. Economic consequences refer to the costs and benefits associated with using a particular assumption.

In terms of income and asset measurement, neither LIFO nor FIFO is clearly preferred. The LIFO assumption is a better application of the matching principle than FIFO because it allocates the most current purchase costs to the cost of goods sold, where they are matched against current sales in the determination of net income. Compared with LIFO, FIFO matches relatively old costs against current revenues.

FIFO, on the other hand, is generally viewed as producing a more current measure of inventory on the balance sheet. Ending inventory under FIFO reflects the costs of the most recent purchases; LIFO reports ending inventory in terms of older, less relevant costs. Using LIFO over a period of time, therefore, can give rise to ending inventory costs that are significantly outdated, and often understated.

In terms of economic consequences, if inventory costs (and quantities) are increasing, using the LIFO assumption gives rise to the lowest net income amount. During inflationary times, therefore, the LIFO assumption is an attractive alternative for use in the determination of a company's federal income tax liability, which is based on taxable income. Simply put, using LIFO saves tax dollars. U.S. federal income tax law includes a regulation (the LIFO Conformity Rule), stating that if a company uses the LIFO assumption for computing its tax liability, it must also use the LIFO assumption for preparing its financial statements. Companies that choose to use FIFO or average cost for reporting purposes may not use LIFO for tax purposes.

While LIFO usually brings about a lower tax liability than FIFO, it requires more bookkeeping procedures and is generally more costly to implement. Short-cut methods for estimating LIFO (dollar-value LIFO) have been devised to reduce the costs of maintaining LIFO records.

As illustrated earlier, "LIFO liquidations" can give rise to overstated net income amounts in years when inventory *levels* are cut back, and these can present problems by boosting tax liabilities, sometimes in years when operations are suffering. Many LIFO users allow such inventory liquidations to occur and bear these costs, but other companies intentionally avoid them by maintaining inventory purchases at levels sufficient to prevent inventory levels from diminishing. That practice avoids increased taxes, but at the same time, it can create other problems. It may not be the appropriate time to purchase inventory. For example, inventory costs may be at a seasonal high or significant discounts may not be available. Furthermore, such action does nothing to solve the problem associated with

LIFO's understated inventory valuation; it merely postpones a problem that grows worse with each passing year.

TEST YOUR KNOWLEDGE: INVENTORY COST FLOW ASSUMPTIONS

The following information was included in the footnotes of Caterpillar's 2006 annual report. The company uses the LIFO cost flow assumption for approximately 75% of its inventories, and reported a net income of $3,537 for 2006. The company's effective tax rate is 29% (dollars in millions).

	2006	2005
Inventories at current cost	$8,754	$7,569
Less adjustment to LIFO basis	2,403	2,345
Inventories on LIFO basis	$6,351	$5,224

1. Compute 2006 ending inventory for Caterpillar, assuming that it changed from LIFO to FIFO at the end of 2006.
2. Compute the accumulated income tax savings enjoyed by Caterpillar due to the choice of LIFO as opposed to FIFO.
3. Compute 2006 reported net income for Caterpillar, assuming that it changed from LIFO to FIFO several years before.

INTERNATIONAL INSIGHT: USING LIFO OUTSIDE THE UNITED STATES

LIFO is not allowed under International Financial Reporting Standards. The use of LIFO is mainly driven by its income tax benefits. U.S. tax laws are the exception in allowing the use of LIFO and in requiring the conformity between tax and accounting rules. That's one reason why many companies use a mix of inventory cost-allocation methods. They use LIFO for U.S. inventories and FIFO or average cost for their non-U.S. inventories.

Using FIFO can also create liquidity problems. In times of rising inventory costs, FIFO produces higher income than LIFO because it matches relatively old costs against current revenues. Because old costs are lower than current costs, FIFO creates "paper profits"— profits due to rising inventory costs instead of effective and efficient operations. Paper profits appear on the income statement, but they may not be repeatable. That is, the inventories sold will have to be replaced at higher current costs and unless the cost increases can be passed on through higher sales prices, future profits will suffer. Unfortunately, the inflated current-period profits are also used to determine a company's tax liability, which must be paid in cash. As a result, operating cash inflows may not be sufficient to cover the required cash outflows, and the company's liquidity position can suffer.

4. Ending Inventory: Applying the Lower-of-Cost-or-Market Rule

The inventory cost flow assumption determines not only the cost of goods sold, but also the capitalized cost allocated to ending inventory. Inventories on the balance sheet, however, are not necessarily carried at this dollar amount. Based on conservatism, ending inventory is valued at cost or market value, whichever is lower.

Applying the lower-of-cost-or-market rule to ending inventory is accomplished by comparing the cost allocated to ending inventory with the market value of the inventory. If the market value exceeds the cost, no adjustment is made and the inventory remains at cost. If the market value is less than the cost, the inventories are written down to market value. Such write-downs reduce the inventory balance on the balance sheet and reduce net income by recognizing an inventory write-down loss (expense) on the income statement.

PSA PEUGEOT CITROËN—EXCERPTS FROM 2006 FINANCIAL STATEMENTS

The following footnote was taken from the financial report of PSA Peugeot Citroën, a French automobile manufacturer that uses International Financial Reporting Standards. Note the allowance for obsolete inventory and inventory with a cost greater than market value.

Note 21. Inventories

(in millions of euros)	Dec. 31, 2006			Dec. 31, 2005			Dec. 31, 2004		
	Cost	Allowance	Net	Cost	Allowance	Net	Cost	Allowance	Net
Raw materials and supplies	€ 936	€(158)	€ 778	€ 876	€(142)	€ 734	€ 883	€(146)	€ 737
Semi-finished products and work-in-progress	793	(47)	746	752	(34)	718	821	(55)	766
Goods for resale and used vehicles	1,476	(137)	1,339	1,401	(121)	1,280	1,378	(116)	1,262
Finished products and replacement parts	4,123	(160)	3,963	4,315	(158)	4,157	3,943	(162)	3,781
Total	**€7,328**	**€(502)**	**€6,826**	**€7,344**	**€(455)**	**€6,889**	**€7,025**	**€(479)**	**€6,546**

Determining the market value of inventory can be very subjective, giving management much discretion when applying the lower-of-cost-or-market rule. Also, the lower-of-cost-or-market rule is often criticized because it treats inventory price changes inconsistently. Price decreases, based on difficult-to-determine market values, are recognized immediately, while price increases are not recognized until the inventory is sold in an objective and verifiable transaction.

► CURRENT LIABILITIES

Current liabilities are obligations expected to require the use of current assets, the creation of other current liabilities, or the provision of services. They normally include obligations to suppliers (accounts payable), short-term debts, current maturities of long-term debts, dividends payable to shareholders, deferred revenues (services yet to be performed or goods yet to be delivered that are expected to require the use of current assets), third-party collections (e.g., sales tax and payroll deductions), periodic accruals (e.g., wages and interest), and potential obligations related to pending or threatened litigation, product warranties, and guarantees. Current liabilities include a mix of operating and financing items, and the definition depends on when the obligation will be satisfied rather than the related activity (operating, investing, or financing).

Because they represent probable future outlays, determining the monetary amounts of all current liabilities involves an element of uncertainty. The relative degree of uncertainty gives rise to two current liability categories: (1) determinable and (2) contingent. Determining the amount of a determinable current liability is relatively straightforward; determining the amount of a contingent liability involves an estimate.

Determinable Current Liabilities

Determinable current liabilities include accounts payable, short-term debts, dividends payable, unearned revenues, third-party collections, and certain accrued liabilities.

Accounts payable, normally associated with inventory purchases, are amounts owed to others for goods, supplies, and services purchased on open account. They arise from frequent transactions normally not subject to specific, formal contracts between a company and its suppliers. These extensions of credit are the practical result of a time lag between the receipt of a good, supply, or service and the corresponding payment. The time period is usually short (e.g., 30 to 60 days) and is indicated by the terms of the exchange (e.g., 2/10, n/30; you can read this shorthand as "take a 2% discount if paid in 10 days, otherwise pay the full amount in 30 days").

Accounts payable turnover (Cost of goods sold / Average accounts payable) provides a measure of how quickly a company is paying its inventory suppliers, or the extent to which it is relying on suppliers as a source of financing. For retail and manufacturing companies especially, it can be an important component of value creation. Slowing payments to suppliers can provide a low-cost source of financing and can improve solvency, but slowing payments too much can damage business relationships with suppliers who may impose high financing charges on late payments, or pass the implicit financing on through higher prices.

REVIEW: THE CASH CONVERSION CYCLE

In Chapter 4, we introduced three key working capital turnover ratios: receivables turnover, inventory turnover, and accounts payable turnover. Dividing each one into the number of days in the period gives the days sales outstanding (DSO), the days of inventory outstanding (DIO), and the days of payables outstanding (DPO). DSO plus DIO less DPO defines the cash conversion cycle, an important metric that captures the efficiency of working capital management.

A liability is created when the board of directors of a corporation declares a dividend to be paid to the shareholders. **Dividends payable** are listed as current because dividends are usually paid within several weeks of declaration.

TEST YOUR KNOWLEDGE: DIVIDENDS AND PAYMENTS TO SUPPLIERS

• Merck & Co. declared dividends (dollars in millions) of $3,319 (2006), $3,339 (2005), and $3,329 (2004). The cash payments for dividends reported on the Statement of Cash Flows for the three years were $3,323 (2006), $3,350 (2005), and $3,311 (2004). Dividends payable at the end of 2005 was $830.

1. Briefly explain why dividends on the Statement of Stockholders' Equity do not equal dividends on the Statement of Cash Flows.

2. What kind of liability is dividends payable?

3. Calculate dividends payable at the end of 2006.

- The following information was taken from the 2006 annual report of Target Corporation (dollars in millions).

	2006	2005
INCOME STATEMENT		
Cost of goods sold	$39,399	$39,927
BALANCE SHEET		
Inventory	6,254	5,838
Trade accounts payable	6,575	6,268

1. Compute the inventory purchases made by Target during 2006.
2. How much cash did Target pay to its suppliers in 2006?

Recall that one of the primary criteria of revenue recognition is that the earning process must be complete before revenue can be recognized. If payments are received before contracted services are performed, an **unearned revenue**, **deferred revenue**, or **receipt in advance** liability is created because the company receiving the payments is under obligations that must be fulfilled. The liability is removed and revenue is recognized as the related services are performed or the relevant goods are delivered. If providing the related services or relevant goods is expected to require the use of current assets or be completed in the next operating cycle, the unearned revenue liability should be classified as current.

Unearned revenues arise from a number of different transactions: gift certificates sold by retail stores redeemable in merchandise, coupons sold by restaurants that can be exchanged for meals, tickets and tokens sold by transportation companies good for future fares, advance payments for magazine subscriptions, and returnable deposits. Airline companies normally receive payment before providing travel, giving rise to a relatively large current liability on their balance sheets—a liability that is removed as the travel is provided and the airline revenue is earned.

IRON MOUNTAIN INCORPORATED—EXCERPTS FROM 2006 FINANCIAL STATEMENTS

Iron Mountain, a company that we look at more carefully in a case at the end of Chapter 9, provides document storage services to companies. As evidenced by the current liability section of their balance sheet, customers pay the company in advance for that service. The company reports deferred revenues of $160.1 million at the end of 2006.

IRON MOUNTAIN INCORPORATED
CONSOLIDATED BALANCE SHEETS
(in thousands of dollars, except share and per share data)

	December 31,	
	2005	**2006**
LIABILITIES AND STOCKHOLDERS' EQUITY (excerpts)		
Current Liabilities:		
Current portion of long-term debt	$ 25,905	$ 63,105
Accounts payable	148,234	148,461
Accrued expenses	266,720	266,933
Deferred revenue	151,137	160,148
Total current Liabilities	591,996	638,647
Long-term debt, net of current portion	2,503,526	2,605,711
Other long-term liabilities	33,545	72,778
Deferred rent	35,763	53,597
Deferred income taxes	225,314	280,225

MECHANICS: DEFERRED REVENUES—BASIC JOURNAL ENTRIES AND EFFECTS ON THE ACCOUNTING EQUATION

Cash (+A)	$		Deferred Revenues (−L)	$	
Deferred Revenues (+L)		$	Sales (R, +RE)		$

To record the receipt of cash prior to revenue recognition.   *To record sales when the revenue recognition criteria have been met.*

Companies often act as collection agencies for government or other entities. The price paid for an item at luxury goods retailer Tiffany's, for example, includes sales tax, which Tiffany's must periodically remit to the proper government authority. Companies are also required by law to withhold from employee wages social security taxes, as well as an amount approximating the employee's income tax. These withholdings are periodically sent to the federal government. In addition to payroll tax deductions, companies often withhold insurance premiums or union dues, which in turn must be passed on to the appropriate third party. In each of these cases, a liability is created; the company receives or holds cash that legally must be paid to a third party. The liability is discharged when the cash payment is made. These **third-party collection liabilities** are usually considered current because payment is expected within the time period of current assets.

Income tax liability for a corporation is based on a percentage of taxable income in accordance with the rules stated in the Internal Revenue Code or other relevant tax laws. Most corporations are required by law at the beginning of each year to estimate their tax liabilities for the entire year and make quarterly tax payments based on these estimates.

Basing **compensation** on net income and/or share prices is a very popular way to pay executives and managers. Such payments represent a significant portion of the total compensation of virtually all upper-level executives in major U.S. corporations. Profit-sharing arrangements, which are also based on a measure of income, are commonly used to compensate employees at lower levels of the corporate hierarchy. Liabilities associated with incentive compensation plans must be accrued at year end because they are based on measures of performance (e.g., income or share prices) that cannot be determined until that time. They are listed as current on the balance sheet because they are typically distributed to employees early the following period, at which time, the liability is discharged.

INSIGHT: INCENTIVE COMPENSATION PLANS

Incentive compensation plans are popular because they induce managers and employees to act in a manner consistent with the objectives of the shareholders. By basing compensation on income or share prices, such plans encourage management to maximize these measures of performance. Keep in mind, however, that managers have incentives to influence the measure of income through operating, investing, and financing decisions; the choice of accounting methods;

estimates; assumptions; the timing of accruals; or even intentional misstatements. The SEC requires disclosure about executive pay in the annual proxy statement, which notifies shareholders of matters to be voted on at the annual shareholders' meeting.

Short-term debts (or short-term borrowings), a financing item, typically include short-term bank loans, commercial paper, lines of credit, and current maturities of long-term debt. Commercial paper, a means of providing short-term financing, represents short-term notes (30 to 270 days) issued for cash by companies with good credit ratings to other companies. A line of credit is usually granted to a company by a bank or group of banks, allowing it to borrow up to a certain maximum dollar amount, interest being charged only on the outstanding balance. Issued commercial paper and existing lines of credit are an indication of a company's ability to borrow funds on a short-term basis; thus, they are very important to investors and creditors who are interested in assessing solvency. Such financing arrangements are extensively described in the footnotes.

Long-term debts are often retired through a series of periodic installments. The installments (that is, the principal) to be paid within the time period that defines current assets (one year or the current operating cycle, whichever is longer) should be included on the balance sheet as a current liability—called **current maturities of long-term debts**. The remaining installments should be disclosed as long-term liabilities.

IRON MOUNTAIN INCORPORATED—CURRENT PORTION OF LONG-TERM DEBT

The current liabilities section of Iron Mountain's balance sheet lists $63,105 as the current portion of long-term debt. The noncurrent liabilities section lists the remaining portion ($2,605,711). Astute readers of the financial statements will read the notes to see whether some portion of that noncurrent debt is coming due relatively soon. Debt due in 13 months qualifies as noncurrent, but raises different liquidity issues than does debt due in 13 years. The bulk of Iron Mountain's long-term debt at December 31, 2006, matures after 2011.

Contingent Liabilities

Contingencies are defined in Statements of Financial Accounting Standards (SFAS) No. 5 as "existing conditions, situations, or sets of circumstances involving uncertainty as to possible gains or losses to an enterprise that will ultimately be resolved when one or more future events occurs or fails to occur." A common example is an existing lawsuit that will be settled in the future by court ruling. If the existing condition represents a possible increase in assets or decrease in liabilities, it is considered a gain contingency; if the existing condition represents a possible decrease in assets or increase in liabilities, it is considered a loss contingency and, in certain cases, gives rise to an accrued liability. Depending on the expected timing of the payment of the potential obligation, these liabilities can be classified as either current or long term.

Figure 7-7 illustrates the methods used to account for both gain and loss contingencies. Each is preceded by an initial event (e.g., filing of a lawsuit). The probability of the related gain or loss is then assessed, usually by experts in the area, and classified as either "highly probable," "reasonably probable," or "remote." Consistent with conservatism, contingent gains are never accrued (i.e., recorded on the financial statements) and are disclosed only when the probability of occurrence is high. Contingent losses, on the other hand, are disclosed and give rise to balance sheet liabilities and income statement expenses when the probability of the loss is high, and it can be estimated.

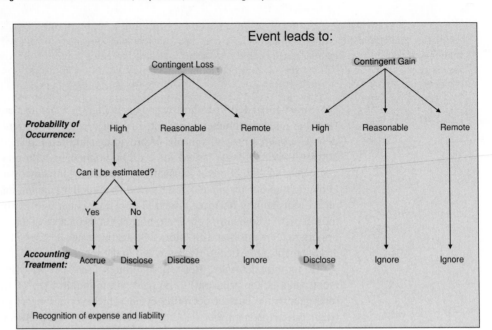

Figure 7-7. Accounting for Contingencies

Many contingent losses are considered highly probable, but the amount of the loss cannot be reliably estimated. In those cases, they are disclosed and described in the footnotes. The footnote sections of most major U.S. companies devote considerable space to possible loss contingencies associated with issues such as litigation, regulatory actions, guarantees of indebtedness, environment cleanup costs, and others.

MERCK AND CO., INC.—VIOXX LITIGATION DISCLOSURES

Major U.S. pharmaceutical company Merck and Co., Inc., is subject to a large number of lawsuits over its painkiller, Vioxx. In 2004, the company voluntarily withdrew the product and, in the process, incurred significant costs. Litigation continues in the case. To date, the company has won some cases and lost others. As the 2006 contingencies note (below) indicates, the company has not yet set up any liability for the lawsuits, other than to cover the cost of defending itself.

(Note: in late 2007, Merck announced a $4.85 billion out of court settlement to resolve U.S. Vioxx product liability lawsuits. The expense will appear in Merck's fourth quarter 2007 income statement.)

Voluntary Product Withdrawal

On September 30, 2004, the company announced a voluntary worldwide withdrawal of Vioxx, its arthritis and acute pain medication. The company's decision, which was effective immediately, was based on new three-year data from a prospective, randomized, placebo-controlled clinical trial, APPROVe (Adenomatous Polyp Prevention on Vioxx).

In connection with the withdrawal, in 2004 the company recorded an unfavorable adjustment to net income of $552.6 million, or $0.25 per share. The adjustment to pretax income was $726.2 million. Of this amount, $491.6 million was related to estimated customer returns of product previously sold and was recorded as a reduction of sales, $93.2 million was related to write-offs of inventory held by the company and was recorded in materials and production expense, and $141.4 million was related to estimated costs to undertake the withdrawal of the product and was recorded in marketing and administrative expense. The tax benefit of this adjustment was $173.6 million, which reflects the geographical mix of Vioxx returns and the cost of the withdrawal. The adjustment did not include charges for future legal defense costs (see Note 11). The Vioxx withdrawal process was completed during 2005 and the costs associated with the withdrawal were in line with the original amounts recorded by the company in 2004.

Contingencies and Environmental Liabilities *(excerpts)*

The company is involved in various claims and legal proceedings of a nature considered normal to its business, including product liability, intellectual property, and commercial litigation, as well as additional matters such as antitrust actions. The company records accruals for contingencies when it is probable that a liability has been incurred and the amount can be reasonably estimated. These accruals are adjusted periodically as assessments change or additional information becomes available. For product liability claims, a portion of the overall accrual is actuarially determined and considers such factors as past experience, number of claims reported, and estimates of claims incurred but not yet reported. Individually significant contingent losses are accrued when probable and reasonably estimable. Legal defense costs expected to be incurred in connection with a loss contingency are accrued when probable and reasonably estimable.

[The company provides extensive details about the Vioxx litigation to date, including cases dismissed and cases in process.]

Reserves

The company currently anticipates that a number of Vioxx product liability lawsuits will be tried throughout 2007. A trial in the Oregon securities case is scheduled for 2007, but the company cannot predict whether this trial will proceed on schedule or the timing of any of the other Vioxx shareholder lawsuit trials. The company believes that it has meritorious defenses to the Vioxx lawsuits and will vigorously defend against them. In view of the inherent difficulty of predicting the outcome of litigation, particularly where there are many claimants and the claimants seek indeterminate damages, the company is unable to predict the outcome of these matters, and at this time, cannot reasonably estimate the possible loss or range of loss with respect to the Vioxx lawsuits. The company has not established any reserves for any potential liability relating to the Vioxx lawsuits or the Vioxx investigations, including for those cases in which verdicts or judgments have been entered against the company, and are now in post-verdict proceedings or on appeal. In each of those cases, the company believes it has strong points to raise on appeal and, therefore, that unfavorable outcomes in such cases are not probable. Unfavorable outcomes in the Vioxx litigation (as defined below) could have a material adverse effect on the company's financial position, liquidity, and results of operations.

Legal defense costs expected to be incurred in connection with a loss contingency are accrued when probable and reasonably estimable. As of December 31, 2005, the company had a reserve of $685 million solely for its future legal defense costs related to the Vioxx Litigation.

During 2006, the company spent $500 million in the aggregate, including $175 million in the fourth quarter, in legal defense costs worldwide related to (1) the Vioxx product liability lawsuits, (2) the Vioxx shareholder lawsuits, (3) the Vioxx foreign lawsuits, and (4) the Vioxx investigations (collectively, the "Vioxx litigation"). In the third quarter and fourth quarter of 2006, the company recorded charges of $598 million and $75 million, respectively, to increase the reserve solely for its future legal defense costs related to the Vioxx litigation to $858 million at December 31, 2006. In increasing the reserve, the company considered the same factors that it considered when it previously established reserves for the Vioxx litigation. Management now believes it has a better estimate of the company's expenses and can reasonably estimate such costs through 2008. Some of the significant factors considered in the establishment and ongoing review of the reserve for the Vioxx legal defense costs were as follows: the actual costs incurred by the company; the development of the company's legal defense strategy and structure in light of the scope of the Vioxx litigation; the number of cases being brought against the company; the costs and outcomes of completed trials; and the most current information regarding anticipated timing, progression, and related costs of pretrial activities and trials in the Vioxx product liability lawsuits. Events such as scheduled trials, that are expected to occur throughout 2007 and into 2008, and the inherent inability to predict the ultimate outcomes of such trials, limit the company's ability to reasonably estimate its legal costs beyond the end of 2008. The company will continue to monitor its legal defense costs and review the adequacy of the associated reserves.

Many contingent losses *are* routinely accrued because they can be classified as highly probable and estimable. Examples include warranties and postretirement costs.

Warranties

In a warranty, a seller promises to remove deficiencies in the quantity, quality, or performance of a product sold to a buyer. Warranties are usually granted for a specific period, during which time the seller promises to bear all or part of the cost of replacing defective parts, performing necessary repairs, or providing additional services. From the seller's standpoint, warranties entail uncertain future costs. It is unlikely that all buyers will take advantage of the warranties granted to them, but enough of them do to consider the future costs highly probably and estimable.

Accounting for warranties involves estimating at the end of the accounting period the value of the future warranty costs associated with the sales made during the period. That amount is then accrued—creating a warranty liability on the balance sheet and a warranty expense on the income statement, which reduces net income. When the warranty costs are actually incurred in the future, the assets used up in the process (e.g., cash) and the warranty liability are both reduced, neither of which affects the income statement. Similar to the bad debt estimate discussed earlier in this chapter, actual warranty costs rarely equal the estimate. Such differences, however, are ignored unless they become too large or are biased (consistently over- or understated). In that case, an adjustment to the liability estimate is made, resulting in the recognition of additional expenses (or potentially the reduction of expenses). Unlike the case when accounting *methods* are changed, prior income statements are not restated for these changes in *estimates*.

MECHANICS: WARRANTIES—BASIC JOURNAL ENTRIES, T-ACCOUNTS, AND THE ACCOUNTING EQUATION

Warranty Expense (E, −RE) $
    Warranty Liability (+L) $

To accrue warranty liability (typically in the same period that the sale is recorded).

Warranty Liability (−L) $
    Cash (−A) $

To record the satisfaction of the warranty liability, in this case, via a cash payment.

The following T-account assumes that a company began the year with an accrued warranty liability of $100. During the year, products were sold and the estimated warranty cost of those products was $125. Actual payments under the warranty program during the period (for both current- and prior-period sales) were $85. The ending accrual for warranties is, thus, $140. Company management would evaluate whether that balance was appropriate after considering relevant information about product failures and warranty costs. If management deemed the expected future outlays to be greater than $140, they would accrue an additional amount of liability (with a corresponding expense). If, on the other hand, evidence supported accruing a liability less than $140, then the warranty liability account would be reduced (with a corresponding reduction in current-period expenses).

Warranty Liability

Warranties Paid	$85	$100 Beginning Balance
		125 Warranty Expense
		$140 Ending Balance

TEST YOUR KNOWLEDGE: WARRANTIES AND CONTINGENCIES

Agilent Technologies, Inc., a diversified technology company, provides warranties for products and services sold to customers. The company accrues warranty costs based on historical trends in warranty charges as a percentage of gross product shipments. The following information about the warranty liability account was taken from Agilent's 2006 annual report (dollars in millions):

	2006	2005
Beginning balance	$40	$52
Accruals	48	57
Settlements made during the period	(59)	(69)
Ending balance	$29	$40

1. Draw a T-account for warranty liabilities and record the activity disclosed above in that account, and ex-

plain how the entries represent an application of the matching principle.

2. Explain how Agilent could manage earnings through the methods used to account for its warranties.

Postretirement Costs

Postretirement costs include pensions and postretirement health-care benefits. They are promises by a company to make payments to, or on behalf of, retired employees, and often represent an important part of the employee compensation packages. Pension and postretirement health-care plans assume a number of different forms, determined by the negotiated contracts between firms and their employees. Under many plans, employees earn the right to receive postretirement payments as they complete years of service. Because these plans involve highly probable and estimable future obligations, financial accounting standards and the definition of a liability require that the costs be accrued as the employees earn their credits. As such, they are matched against the benefits produced by the employees' efforts that period. Similar to other accruals, an expense is recognized on the income statement and a liability appears on the balance sheet. The liability is reduced when the firm ultimately makes payments to, or on behalf of, the employees.

MEASUREMENT CHALLENGE—POSTRETIREMENT BENEFITS

Measuring postretirement benefits like pensions and health care is a major challenge. Companies need to estimate future salary levels and health-care costs, along with the life expectancies of employees and their eligible survivors. Then they need to choose appropriate discount rates to arrive at a present value for the liabilities. All of this needs to be done in a context where the legal liability of the contract (i.e., can it be amended without employee approval?) is uncertain. Standard-setters worldwide continue to struggle with how to best measure these costs and liabilities. Under U.S. GAAP and international standards, extensive disclosures are provided, permitting informed readers to assess the nature of these obligations.

► STATEMENT OF CASH FLOWS: OPERATING SECTION

Net cash from operating activities represents the difference between the cash inflows and outflows associated with the acquisition and sale of the company's inventories and services. It is disclosed in the operating section of the statement of cash flows, and reflects the cash receipts from sales and accounts receivable, as well as cash payments to employees and suppliers for the purchase of inventories, selling and administrative costs, taxes, and other operating activities. In the United States, companies are required to report interest paid as an operating cash flow. Under GAAP, the calculation of net cash from operating activities can be presented in either the direct or the indirect method. Both forms of presentation lead to exactly the same monetary amount for net cash from operating activities.

	Year Ended February 2, 2002	Year Ended February 3, 2001	Year Ended January 29, 2000
Cash flows from operating activities:			
Cash received from customers...	$ 166,829	$ 172,164	$ 157,130
Cash paid to suppliers and employees......................................	(157,384)	(222,239)	(170,806)
Interest and other income received...	174	213	91
Interest paid..	(3,788)	(3,450)	(2,619)
Income taxes paid..	(662)	(58)	(262)
Net cash provided by (used in) continuing operations...............	$ 5,169	$ (53,370)	$ (16,466)

Figure 7-8. Operating Section of Mayors Jewelers, Inc., Statement of Cash Flows (dollars in millions)

Direct Method

Under the direct method, the actual cash inflows from customers and the actual cash outflows associated with operating activities are listed directly on the statement. The difference between the cash inflows and outflows is net cash from operating activities. Although the FASB recommends this form of presentation and professional security analysts request it, it is rarely used. An example of the direct method format is shown in Figure 7-8.

Indirect Method

Under the much more common indirect method, net cash from operating activities is computed *indirectly* by beginning with net income, which appears on the income statement, and adjusting it for the differences between accruals (which underlie the measures of the revenues and expenses on the income statement) and cash flows. This method is illustrated in Figure 7-9, which was taken from DuPont's 2006 annual report.

Note the general format—net income for each of the three years (2004–2006) is adjusted by a variety of items, leading to cash provided by operating activities. The first two adjustments (depreciation and amortization of intangible assets) involve non-operating accounts added back to net income in the computation of cash provided by operating activities. In both cases, net income was reduced by an expense listed on the income statement that involved no cash outflow. To arrive at a measure of the cash produced by operating activities, these items must be added back to net income, which was computed on an accrual, not a

	2006	2005	2004
Cash from operating activities			
Net income	$ 3,148	$ 2,056	$ 1,780
Adjustments to reconcile net income (loss) to cash provided by operating activities:			
Depreciation	1,157	1,128	1,124
Amortization of intangible assets	227	230	223
Contributions to pension plans	(280)	(1,253)	(709)
Other special charges	(428)	(341)	1,020
Increase (decrease) in operating assets:			
Accounts and notes receivable	(194)	(74)	(309)
Inventories and other operating assets	(61)	211	569
Decrease in operating liabilities:			
Accounts payable and other operating liabilities	526	(406)	57
Accrued interest and income taxes	(359)	991	(524)
Cash provided by operating activities	$ 3,736	$ 2,542	$ 3,231

Figure 7-9. Operating Section of DuPont's Statement of Cash Flows (dollars in millions)

cash, basis. The second two adjustments (contribution to pension plans and other special charges) represent the opposite—operating items that used cash in the current period but did not affect net income. These items are subtracted from net income in the computation of cash provided by operating activities. For example, consider the "other special items" line. We can infer that in 2004, $1,020 of special charges (i.e., expenses) were reported on the income statement, over and above those paid in cash that year. In 2005, $341 more was paid in cash than was expensed on the income statement. Similarly, cash payments exceeded reported expenses by $428 in 2006.

The remaining adjustments describe the changes during the period in the working capital accounts—operating assets and operating liabilities. Increases in the operating assets (e.g., accounts receivable and inventory) are subtracted from net income in the computation of cash provided by operating activities because they represent growth in the assets during the period. Growth in accounts receivable, for example, means that sales revenues were recognized on the income statement faster than cash was being received from customers, putting downward pressure on cash flows from operating activities. Decreases in operating assets, on the other hand, are added to net income because lower levels of receivables and inventory, for example, suggest faster cash receipts from customers and smaller investments in inventory.

Decreases in operating liabilities are subtracted from net income in the computation of cash provided by operating activities because they indicate that liabilities are being discharged (via cash payments or the provision of services) faster than they are being created, which reduces cash provided by operating activities. Increases in operating liabilities have the opposite effect.

Net cash provided by operating activities is an important performance metric because it signals a company's ability to generate cash from operating activities—cash that can be used to acquire long-term investments, pay down long-term debt, and make payments to shareholders. Together, net income and net cash from operating activities provide information about the extent to which operating activities are being successfully managed, a requirement for value creation.

Understanding the reconciliation between net income and net cash from operating activities can be helpful when assessing how effectively working capital is being managed. If, for example, accounts receivable and inventories are growing at a faster rate than sales, management is forced to deal with a greater investment in current assets—an investment that requires costly financing and may be at greater risk of value loss through bad debts and inventory obsolescence. Such a situation may not promote value creation because it would put downward pressure on asset turnover, return on assets, and return on equity.

▶ SUMMARY

This chapter discusses operating transactions. The income statement, an important summary of operations, provides useful information about value creation and firm valuation. By classifying income into meaningful categories, it helps users evaluate whether value was created and identify the sources of that value creation. Furthermore, the categories help users assess whether earnings are persistent, leading to better predictions of future levels of ROE and value creation, and ultimately the value of the firm.

Analysis of the operating working capital accounts provides insight into the efficiency and solvency of the firm. Working capital needs to be financed with costly debt and equity. Maintaining an appropriate level of receivables and inventory and working with suppliers to manage payables is an important managerial activity. Receivables provide no return in and of themselves, but if customer credit is not available, profitable sales may be lost. Inventory is costly to hold, but some level is necessary to meet customer and/or manufacturing needs. Payables offer low-cost financing, but extending the payment time too long may lead suppliers to cut off shipments or raise prices. Managing the conflicting costs and benefits of holding net working capital is challenging, but it is an important determinant of value creation. If a given level of profitability can be maintained with less working capital, then costly financing needs can be reduced.

We also investigated several key operating measurement issues that require management judgment and can have a significant impact on the financial statements. For example, revenue recognition decisions, which directly affect reported levels of net income and accounts receivable, are based on considerable managerial judgment, especially in cases where the transfer of the benefits and risks of ownership are not obvious. We also saw that considerable judgment takes place when managers estimate the value of their receivables at each balance sheet date. Those judgments directly impact reported earnings through their effect on the bad debt expense. Inventory cost allocation choices, which affect the cost of goods sold and ending inventory, and the timing and measurement of contingent liabilities, which can give rise to large expenses and accrued liabilities, completed our discussion of working capital. Finally, we discussed cash flow from operations, how it differs from net income, and how it can help users better assess value creation.

▶ CASES AND REVIEW QUESTIONS

Freescale Semiconductor—Revenue Recognition

Freescale Semiconductor's revenue recognition policy reads:

Revenue Recognition: The company recognizes revenue from product sales when title transfers, the risks and rewards of ownership have been transferred to the customer, the fee is fixed or determinable, and collection of the related receivable is reasonably assured, which is generally at the time of shipment. Sales with destination point terms, which are primarily related to European customers where these terms are customary, are recognized upon delivery. Accruals are established, with the related reduction to revenue, for allowances for discounts and product returns based on actual historical exposure at the time the related revenues are recognized. Revenue for services is recognized ratably over the contract term or as services are being performed. Investment incentives related to government grants are recognized when a legal right to the grant exists and there is reasonable assurance that both the terms and conditions associated with the grant will be fulfilled and the grant proceeds will be received. Government grants are recorded as a reduction of the cost being reimbursed. Revenue related to licensing agreements is recognized at the time the company has fulfilled its obligations and the fee received is fixed or determinable, or is deferred. Revenues from contracts with multiple elements are recognized as each element is earned, based on the relative fair value of each element, on when there are no undelivered elements that are essential to the functionality of the delivered elements, and on when the amount is not contingent upon delivery of the undelivered elements. As a percentage of sales, revenue related to licensing agreements represented 2%, 3%, and 4% for the years ended December 31, 2004, 2003, and 2002, respectively.

Distributor Sales: Revenue from sales to distributors of the company's products is recognized when title transfers, the risks and rewards of ownership have been transferred to the customer, the fee is fixed or determinable, and collection of the related receivable is reasonably assured, which is generally at the time of shipment. In response to competitive market conditions, the company offers incentive programs common to the semiconductor industry. Accruals for the estimated distributor incentives are established at the time of the sale, along with a related reduction to revenue, based on the terms of the various incentive programs, historical experience with such programs, prevailing market conditions, and current inventory levels. Distributor incentive accruals are monitored and adjustments, if any, are recognized based on actual experience under these incentive programs.

1. In your own words, define "revenues." Explain how revenues are different from gains.

2. Describe what it means for a business to "recognize" revenues. What specific accounts and financial statements are affected by the process of revenue recognition?

3. In general, what incentives do company managers have to make self-serving revenue recognition choices?

4. Consider the following revenue recognition scenarios and answer the associated questions. Support your answers with reasoned arguments. Indicate where more information is required.

    a. In December 2004, Freescale contracted to provide services to an automobile manufacturer for a four-year period beginning February 1, 2005. The $50 million contract calls for annual payments of $12 million in monthly installments of $1 million. At the signing of the contract in December 2004, Freescale received a $2 million nonrefundable deposit to cover development costs. How much revenue will Freescale recognize in 2004? Provide a journal entry that records the receipt of the initial payment.

    b. On September 30, 2004, Freescale sold semiconductors and equipment to a small startup company. The contract states that the sales price is $15 million. The semiconductors and equipment have been installed, tested, and accepted by the customer. Because the customer is short of cash, Freescale's sales team agreed to provide vendor financing for the sale. The customer is scheduled to make the $15 million payment in full on September 30, 2006. That is the only payment that Freescale expects to receive for this sale. Assume that Freescale's cost of borrowing is 10% and a recent credit report indicates that the customer's is 15%. Provide the journal entries recorded by Freescale on September 30 and December 31, 2004, as well as September 30, 2006. Assume that Freescale prepares formal financial statements quarterly. As such, you should use the effective quarterly interest rate where necessary (see Appendix A: Time Value of Money for further guidance).

    c. At the end of December 2004, Freescale signed a $200 million contract to provide equipment, software, and services to a telephone handset manufacturer. By December 31, 2004, some of the equipment had been delivered and installed. Other equipment had been manufactured and shipped, but not yet received by the customer. Still other products are to be delivered over the following two fiscal years. All products contain a two-year warranty. Freescale has promised to maintain the products and provide software upgrades and a dedicated customer support team for a three-year period. How should Freescale recognize revenue on this contract?

    d. For the contract in part c, how would your answer change if you learned that there was a side agreement allowing the customer to return the products, no questions asked, through January 31, 2005? What if Freescale promised significant discounts on future purchases in return for signing the initial $200 million contract?

    e. How could Freescale manage its reported earnings through strategic revenue recognition choices for the contract in part c? What are the consequences of doing so? How might those consequences impact value creation at Freescale?

5. Assume that you are a member of Freescale's audit committee. Your role, in part, is to evaluate the appropriateness of the company's financial reporting policies and choices.

Each quarter, you meet with Freescale's external auditors and discuss financial reporting matters with them.

    a. What questions would you ask Freescale's external auditors to assure yourself that the company's revenue recognition policy was reasonable?

    b. What signs might indicate that a company aggressively recognizes revenue? By those standards, does Freescale recognize revenue aggressively? Refer to the Freescale financial statements included at the end of Chapter 4.

▶ ALCATEL—ACCOUNTS RECEIVABLE MEASUREMENT AND MANAGEMENT

Alcatel is a major global telecom company, headquartered in France and operating in more than 130 countries. Their 2002 financial statements, released as part of a press release reporting fourth-quarter and full-year 2002 results, appear on the pages that follow. They are prepared in accordance with French GAAP. All figures are in millions of euros (€). In 2006, Alcatel merged with Lucent Technologies to become Alcatel-Lucent.

1. Alcatel's balance sheet reports a balance for trade receivables and related accounts, net. What are the trade receivables net of?

2. If Alcatel anticipates that some accounts are uncollectible, why did the company extend credit to those customers in the first place? Discuss the risks that must be managed with respect to accounts receivable and vendor financing and how those risks affect value creation.

3. The balance in Alcatel's allowance for doubtful accounts (for trade receivables) was €1,092 at December 31, 2002, and €928 at December 31, 2001. Assume that Alcatel wrote off €115 of trade receivables as uncollectible during 2002. Create two T-accounts, one for gross trade receivables (that is, trade receivables before deducting the allowance) and another for the allowance for doubtful accounts. Analyze the change in both T-accounts between December 31, 2001 and 2002. Four journal entries are required to reconcile the two T-accounts: one to record sales, one to record the collection of trade receivables, one to record the write-off of trade receivables, and one to record bad debt expense.

4. In a February 5, 2003, *Wall Street Journal* article (Alcatel Allays Some Anxiety, Though Perils for Firm Persist). Chief Financial Officer Jean-Pascal Beaufret indicated that Alcatel collected its trade receivables in 104 days in 2002 (117 days in 2001). The average collection period for accounts receivable (called trade receivables at Alcatel) can be estimated using the following formula (the denominator is referred to as the accounts receivable turnover ratio):

$$\text{Average collection period} = \frac{365 \text{ days}}{\left[\dfrac{\text{Credit sales (annual)}}{\text{Accounts receivable}}\right]}$$

Confirm the figures reported by Alcatel's CFO using data for trade receivables from the press release. Assume that all sales are 'credit sales.' Use ending rather than average receivables balances. Comment on the trend. Provide possible reasons for the change. Is Alcatel managing its receivables effectively?

5. What was the average collection period for the fourth quarter of 2002? For the same period in 2001? You will have to adjust the average collection period formula so that it appropriately considers quarterly data. Comment on the trend and the relationship to the annual data.

6. Explain how managing receivables and working capital affects value creation.

ALCATEL

Consolidated Income Statements

(in millions of euros except per share information)

	Q4 2002 (unaudited)	Q4 2001* (unaudited)	2002	2001*	2000
Net sales	4,508	6,766	16,547	25,353	31,408
Cost of sales	(3,279)	(5,528)	(12,186)	(19,074)	(22,193)
Gross profit	**1,229**	**1,238**	**4,361**	**6,279**	**9,215**
Administrative and selling expenses	(647)	(893)	(2,862)	(3,773)	(4,136)
R&D costs	(562)	(713)	(2,226)	(2,867)	(2,828)
Income (loss) from operations	**20**	**(368)**	**(727)**	**(361)**	**2,251**
Interest expense on notes mandatorily redeemable for shares	(1)	–	(1)	–	–
Financial loss	(136)	(248)	(1,018)	(1,568)	(435)
Restructuring costs	(500)	(598)	(1,474)	(2,124)	(143)
Other revenue (expense)	(292)	(456)	(830)	(213)	623
Income (loss) before amortization of goodwill and taxes	**(909)**	**(1,670)**	**(4,050)**	**(4,266)**	**(2,296)**
Income tax	(62)	396	19	1,261	(497)
Share in net income of equity affiliates and discontinued operations	24	(16)	(107)	(16)	125
Consolidated net income (loss) before amortization of goodwill and purchased R&D	**(947)**	**(1,290)**	**(4,138)**	**(3,021)**	**1,924**
Amortization of goodwill	(147)	(185)	(589)	(1,933)	(576)
Purchased R&D	–	–	–	(4)	(21)
Minority interests	(25)	(23)	(18)	(5)	(3)
Net income (loss)	**(1,119)**	**(1,498)**	**(4,745)**	**(4,963)**	**1,324**
*Ordinary Shares (A)***					
Basic earnings per share	*(0.93)*	*(1.28)*	*(3.99)*	*(4.33)*	*1.25*
Diluted earnings per share	*(0.93)*	*(1.28)*	*(3.99)*	*(4.33)*	*1.20*
*Alcatel tracking stock (O) (Optronics division)****					
Basic earnings per share	*(1.06)*	*(1.52)*	*(3.86)*	*(1.47)*	*0.14*
Diluted earnings per share	*(1.06)*	*(1.52)*	*(3.86)*	*(1.47)*	*0.14*

* In order to make comparisons easier, restated income statements are presented to take into account significant changes in consolidated companies during the second half of 2001 and the first half of 2002.
** Net income per class A share for 2000 was restated to take into account the split by 5 of the nominal value of the class A shares approved at the shareholders' meeting of May 16, 2000.
*** For 2000, net income has been taken into account from October 20, 2000, issuance date of the class O shares.

Consolidated Balance Sheets at December 31

			(in millions of euros)
ASSETS	**2002**	**2001**	**2000**
Goodwill, net	4,597	5,257	7,043
Other intangible assets, net	312	472	504
Intangible assets, net	**4,909**	**5,729**	**7,547**
Property, plant, and equipment	8,236	9,698	11,941
Depreciation	(5,737)	(5,496)	(7,283)
Property, plant, and equipment, net	**2,499**	**4,202**	**4,658**
Shares in net assets of equity affiliates and net assets and liabilities of discontinued operations	306	799	1,152
Other investments and miscellaneous, net	975	1,169	3,327
Investments and other financial assets	**1,281**	**1,968**	**4,479**
TOTAL FIXED ASSETS	**8,689**	**11,899**	**16,684**
Inventories and work in progress	**2,329**	**4,681**	**7,415**
Trade receivables and related accounts, net	4,716	8,105	10,659
Other accounts receivable, net	4,037	6,851	5,160
Accounts receivable	**8,753**	**14,956**	**15,819**
Marketable securities, net*	716	490	443
Cash, net	5,393	4,523	2,617
Cash and cash equivalents*	**6,109**	**5,013**	**3,060**
TOTAL CURRENT ASSETS	**17,191**	**24,650**	**26,294**
TOTAL ASSETS	**25,880**	**36,549**	**42,978**

* Cash and cash equivalent as of December 31, 2002, includes in the marketable securities net line item, listed securities amounting to € 44 million. Without listed securities, cash and cash equivalent amounts to € 6,065 million as indicated in the consolidated statements of cash flows.

(in millions of euros)

LIABILITIES AND SHAREHOLDERS' EQUITY	2002		2001	2000*
	Before Appropriation	After Appropriation	After Appropriation	After Appropriation
Capital stock (Euro 2 nominal value: 1,239,193,498 class A shares and 25,515,000 class O shares issued at December 31, 2002; 1,215,254,797 class A shares and 25,515,000 class O shares issued December 31, 2001, and 1,212,210,685 class A shares and 16,500,000 class O shares issued December 31, 2000)	2,529	2,529	2,481	2,457
Additional paid-in capital	9,573	9,573	9,565	9,558
Retained earnings	(333)	(5,078)	(389)	4,719
Cumulative translation adjustments	(283)	(283)	(185)	(350)
Net income	(4,745)	–	–	–
Less treasury stock at cost	(1,734)	(1,734)	(1,842)	(2,023)
SHAREHOLDERS' EQUITY	**5,007**	**5,007**	**9,630**	**14,361**
MINORITY INTERESTS	**343**	**343**	**219**	**435**
OTHER EQUITY **Notes mandatorily redeemable for shares**	**645**	**645**	–	–
Accrued pension and retirement obligations	1,016	1,016	1,120	1,292
Other reserves (a)	3,301	3,301	4,154	3,005
TOTAL RESERVES FOR LIABILITIES AND CHARGES	**4,317**	**4,317**	**5,274**	**4,297**
Bonds and notes issued	5,325	5,325	5,969	4,972
Other borrowings	458	458	1,706	2,418
TOTAL FINANCIAL DEBT	**5,783**	**5,783**	**7,675**	**7,390**
(of which medium and long-term portion)	*4,687*	*4,687*	*5,879*	*5,577*
Customers' deposits and advances	1,482	1,482	1,693	1,560
Trade payables and related accounts (a)	4,162	4,162	5,080	6,393
Debts linked to bank activity	246	246	660	932
Other payables	3,895	3,895	6,318	7,610
TOTAL OTHER LIABILITIES	**9,785**	**9,785**	**13,751**	**16,495**
TOTAL LIABILITIES AND SHAREHOLDERS' EQUITY	**25,880**	**25,880**	**36,549**	**42,978**

(a) Accrued contract costs previously under the line "accrued contracts costs and other reserves" have been reclassified under the line "trade payables" (€ 650 million on December 31, 2000).

Consolidated Statements of Cash Flows

(in millions of euros)

	Nine months 2002 (unaudited)	Q4 2002 (unaudited)	2002	2001	2000
Cash flows from operating activities					
Net income (loss)	(3,626)	(1,119)	(4,745)	(4,963)	1,324
Minority interests	(7)	25	18	5	3
Adjustments to reconcile income before minority interests to net cash provided by operating activities:					
— Depreciation and amortization, net	739	271	1,010	1,279	1,189
— Amortization and depreciation of goodwill and purchased R&D	442	147	589	1,937	597
— Net allowances in reserves for pension obligations	8	(11)	(3)	41	24
— Changes in valuation allowances and other reserves, net	1,374	(16)	1,358	2,001	(32)
— Net (gain) loss on disposal of noncurrent assets	(413)	126	(287)	(943)	(915)
— Share in net income of equity affiliates (net of dividends received)	214	(26)	188	88	(47)
Working capital provided (used) by operations	**(1,269)**	**(603)**	**(1,872)**	**(555)**	**2,143**
Net change in current assets and liabilities:					
— Decrease (increase) in inventories	1,244	756	2,000	1,186	(3,330)
— Decrease (increase) in accounts receivable	3,103	333	3,436	1,407	(1,192)
— Decrease (increase) in advances and progress payments	3	107	110	(99)	74
— Increase (decrease) in accounts payable and accrued expenses	(1,038)	(46)	(1,084)	(925)	898
— Increase (decrease) in customers deposits and advances	(279)	106	(173)	153	424
— Increase (decrease) in other receivables and debts	136	170	306	(622)	(262)
Net cash provided (used) by operating activities (a)	**1,900**	**823**	**2,723**	**545**	**(1,245)**
Cash flows from investing activities					
Proceeds from disposal of fixed assets	236	44	280	182	107
Capital expenditures	(399)	(91)	(490)	(1,748)	(1,834)
Decrease (increase) in loans (b)	(720)	(119)	(839)	299	(962)
Cash expenditures for acquisition of consolidated companies, net of cash acquired, and for acquisition of unconsolidated companies	(206)	13	(193)	(743)	(834)
Cash proceeds from sale of previously consolidated companies, net of cash sold, and from sale of unconsolidated companies	797	16	813	3,627	1,579
Net cash provided (used) by investing activities	**(292)**	**(137)**	**(429)**	**1,617**	**(1,944)**
Net cash flows after investment	**1,608**	**686**	**2,294**	**2,162**	**(3,189)**
Cash flows from financing activities					
Increase (decrease) in short-term debt	(1,192)	(277)	(1,469)	(1,401)	(889)
Proceeds from issuance of long-term debt	–	645	645	1,744	2,565
Proceeds from issuance of shares	8	–	8	8	1,490
Dividends paid	(269)	(7)	(276)	(567)	(508)
Net cash provided (used) by financing activities	**(1,453)**	**361**	**(1,092)**	**(216)**	**2,658**
Net effect of exchange rate changes	(67)	(83)	(150)	7	(4)
Net increase (decrease) in cash and cash equivalents	**88**	**964**	**1,052**	**1,953**	**(535)**
Cash and cash equivalents at beginning of year	**5,013**	**5,101**	**5,013**	**3,060**	**3,595**
Cash and cash equivalents at end of year without listed securities	**5,101**	**6,065**	**6,065**	**5,013**	**3,060**
Operational cash flows (a) + (b) = Net cash provided (used) by operating activities + Decrease (increase) in loans (b)	**1,180**	**704**	**1,884**	**844**	**(2,207)**

▶ GENERAL MOTORS—INVENTORY MEASUREMENT AND MANAGEMENT

General Motors is one of the world's largest manufacturing firms. Inventories make up a sizeable portion of their asset base. Managing those inventories well can have a major effect on GM's ability to create value for their shareholders. Measuring those inventories can have a major effect on reported performance. GM's financial statements are provided on the following pages.

1. Refer to GM's 2003 balance sheet. What proportion of its assets are inventories? What proportion of its automotive assets are inventories?

2. Why does General Motors provide two distinct balance sheets?

3. Why do companies need to use cost-allocation methods to account for their inventories? GM's inventory footnote follows the financial statements. What inventory cost allocation methods does it use? Speculate as to why GM uses multiple methods.

4. Assume that the prices GM pays for inventory typically increase over time. Explain, in general terms, how the GM balance sheet would have been different had the company used only the FIFO method of inventory costing instead of the LIFO method. How would the income statement have differed? The statement of cash flows? What if prices typically *decrease* over time?

5. Set up *one* T-account for GM's total inventories (that is, combine the inventory accounts for this analysis). Enter the 2002 and 2003 ending balances in the T-account. Use information from the financial statements to recreate the activity that took place in the account during fiscal 2003 and answer the following questions. GM credits the total inventory account for the entire cost of goods sold. Note that the income statement line item cost of goods sold includes the labor and overhead needed to manufacture the equipment. Assume that the raw material costs represent half of the total cost of manufacturing the inventory.

   a. How much raw material inventory did GM purchase in fiscal 2003? Assume that raw material inventory was acquired in a single purchase. Provide the journal entry that GM made to record that purchase.

   b. Now set up a T-account for accounts payable. Enter the 2002 and 2003 ending balances in the T-account. Assume that accounts payable includes only inventory-related transactions and that all raw material is purchased on account. How much did GM pay its suppliers for inventory in fiscal 2003? Assume that the company made a single payment to all of its suppliers in fiscal 2003. Provide the journal entry that GM made to record that payment.

6. You would like to compare GM's operating performance and asset management to that of PSA Peugeot Citroën, a large French automaker. Peugeot uses FIFO for inventory purposes. Key data for PSA Peugeot Citroën's automotive operations include:

in millions of euros	2003	2002
Inventory, FIFO	6,660	6,167
Cost of sales (auto)	40,558	40,196
Net income (auto)	1,339	1,643
Total assets (auto)	36,055	35,289
Total liabilities (auto)	25,902	25,886
Owners' equity (auto)	10,153	9,403

Use those data and relevant data from GM's inventory note and financial statements to calculate each firm's ROE in 2003 and the average inventory holding period (or days sales in inventory) for 2003. Focus on GM's automotive operations. You will want to convert GM's LIFO inventories to a FIFO basis to make relevant comparisons.

$$\text{Average inventory holding period} = \frac{365 \text{ days}}{\left[\dfrac{\text{Cost of sales}}{\text{Average inventory}}\right]}$$

7. According to GM's inventory note, a LIFO liquidation occurred in 2003. Explain what this represents. What was the income statement effect of this event? Is the effect persistent? Is it material?

Consolidated Statements of Income

(dollars in millions except per share amounts) Years ended December 31,	2003	2002	2001
GENERAL MOTORS CORPORATION AND SUBSIDIARIES			
Total net sales and revenues (Notes 1 and 24)	**$185,524**	$177,324	$169,051
Cost of sales and other expenses (Note 5)	152,071	146,793	138,847
Selling, general, and administrative expenses	21,008	20,690	19,433
Interest expense (Note 16)	9,464	7,503	8,317
Total costs and expenses	182,543	174,986	166,597
Income from continuing operations before income taxes, equity income, and minority interests	2,981	2,338	2,454
Income tax expense (Note 11)	731	644	1,094
Equity income (loss) and minority interests	612	281	(138)
Income from continuing operations	2,862	1,975	1,222
(Loss) from discontinued operations (Note 2)	(219)	(239)	(621)
Gain on sale of discontinued operations	1,179	–	–
Net income	3,822	1,736	601
Dividends on preference stocks	–	(46)	(99)
Earnings attributable to common stocks (Note 20)	$ 3,822	$ 1,690	$ 502
Basic earnings (loss) per share attributable to common stocks			
$1⅔ par value			
Continuing operations	$ 5.10	$ 3.53	$ 2.21
Discontinued operations	$ 2.14	$ (0.16)	$ (0.42)
Earnings per share attributable to $1⅔ par value	$ 7.24	$ 3.37	$ 1.79
(Losses) per share from discontinued operations attributable to Class H	$ (0.22)	$ (0.21)	$ (0.55)
Earnings (loss) pet share attributable to common stocks assuming dilution			
$1⅔ par value			
Continuing operations	$ 5.03	$ 3.51	$ 2.20
Discontinued operations	$ 2.11	$ (0.16)	$ (0.43)
Earnings per share attributable to $1⅔ par value	$ 7.14	$ 3.35	$ 1.77
(Losses) per share from discontinued operations attributable to Class H	$ (0.22)	$ (0.21)	$ (0.55)

Reference should be made to the notes in the consolidated financial statements.

Supplemental Information to the Consolidated Statements of Income

(dollars in millions) Years ended December 31,

	2003	2002	2001
AUTOMOTIVE AND OTHER OPERATIONS			
Total net sales and revenues (Notes 1 and 24)	$155,831	$150,250	$143,173
Cost of sales and other expenses (Note 5)	143,464	138,359	130,158
Selling, general, and administrative expenses	11,863	11,749	12,430
Total costs and expenses	155,327	150,108	142,588
Interest expense (Note 16)	1,780	479	572
Net expense from transactions with Financing and Insurance Operations (Note 1)	232	296	435
(Loss) from continuing operations before income taxes, equity income, and minority interests	(1,508)	(633)	(422)
Income tax (benefit) expense (Note 11)	(869)	(378)	56
Equity income (loss) and minority interests	674	348	(68)
Income (loss) from continuing operations	35	93	(546)
(Loss) from discontinued operations (Note 2)	(219)	(239)	(621)
Gain on sale of discontinued operations	1,179	–	–
Net income (loss)—Automotive and Other Operations	$ 995	$ (146)	$ (1,167)

(dollars in millions) Years ended December 31,

	2003	2002	2001
FINANCING AND INSURANCE OPERATIONS			
Total revenues	$ 29,693	$ 27,074	$ 25,878
Interest expense (Note 16)	7,684	7,024	7,745
Depreciation and amortization expense (Note 12)	6,032	5,541	5,857
Operating and other expenses	8,529	8,306	7,308
Provisions for financing and insurance losses (Note 1)	3,191	3,528	2,527
Total costs and expenses	25,436	24,399	23,437
Net income from transactions with Automotive and Other Operations (Note 1)	(232)	(296)	(435)
Income before income taxes, equity income, and minority interests	4,489	2,971	2,876
Income tax expense (Note 11)	1,600	1,022	1,038
Equity income (loss) and minority interests	(62)	(67)	(70)
Net income—Financing and Insurance Operations	$ 2,827	$ 1,882	$ 1,768

The above supplemental information is intended to facilitate analysis of General Motors Corporation's businesses: (1) Automotive and Other Operations, and (2) Financing and Insurance Operations.

Reference should be made to the notes in the consolidated financial statements.

Consolidated Balance Sheets

(dollars in millions) December 31,

	2003	2002
GENERAL MOTORS CORPORATION AND SUBSIDIARIES		
ASSETS		
Cash and cash equivalents (Note 1)	$ 32,554	$ 20,320
Other marketable securities (Note 6)	22,215	16,825
Total cash and marketable securities	54,769	37,145
Finance receivables—net (Note 8)	173,137	134,643
Loans held for sale	19,609	15,720
Accounts and notes receivable (less allowances)	20,532	16,337
Inventories (less allowances) (Note 9)	10,960	9,737
Assets of discontinued operations	—	18,653
Deferred income taxes (Note 11)	27,190	39,767
Net equipment on operating leases (less accumulated depreciation) (Note 10)	34,383	31,026
Equity in net assets of nonconsolidated affiliates	6,032	5,097
Property—net (Note 12)	38,211	35,956
Intangible assets—net (Notes 1 and 13)	4,760	10,796
Other assets (Note 14)	58,924	14,176
Total assets	$448,507	$369,053
LIABILITIES AND STOCKHOLDERS' EQUITY		
Accounts payable (principally trade)	$ 25,422	$ 21,138
Notes and loans payable (Note 16)	271,756	200,168
Liabilities of discontinued operations	—	7,956
Postretirement benefits other than pensions (Note 17)	36,292	38,152
Pensions (Note 17)	8,024	22,679
Deferred income taxes (Notes 11 and 15)	7,508	6,523
Accrued expenses and other liabilities (Note 15)	73,930	65,344
Total liabilities	422,932	361,960
Minority interests	307	279
Stockholders' equity (Note 19)		
$1²/₃ par value common stock (outstanding, 561,997,725 and 560,447,797 shares)	937	936
Class H common stock (outstanding, 958,284,272 shares in 2002)	—	96
Capital surplus (principally additional paid-in capital)	15,185	21,583
Retained earnings	12,752	10,031
Subtotal	28,874	32,646
Accumulated foreign currency translation adjustments	(1,815)	(2,784)
Net unrealized gains (losses) on derivatives	51	(205)
Net unrealized gains on securities	618	372
Minimum pension liability adjustment	(2,460)	(23,215)
Accumulated other comprehensive loss	(3,606)	(25,832)
Total stockholders' equity	25,268	6,814
Total liabilities and stockholders' equity	$448,507	$369,053

Reference should be made to the notes in the consolidated financial statements.

Supplemental Information to the Consolidated Balance Sheets

(dollars in millions) December 31,

	2003	2002
ASSETS		
Automotive and Other Operations		
Cash and cash equivalents (Note 1)	$ 14,424	$ 12,162
Marketable securities (Note 6)	9,067	2,174
Total cash and marketable securities	23,491	14,336
Accounts and notes receivable (less allowances)	5,380	4,735
Inventories (less allowances) (Note 9)	10,960	9,737
Assets of discontinued operations	–	18,653
Net equipment on operating leases (less accumulated depreciation) (Note 10)	7,173	5,305
Deferred income taxes and other current assets (Note 11)	10,851	9,631
Total current assets	57,855	62,397
Equity in net assets of nonconsolidated affiliates	6,032	5,097
Property—net (Note 12)	36,071	34,135
Intangible assets—net (Notes 1 and 13)	1,479	7,453
Deferred income taxes (Note 11)	18,086	31,431
Other assets (Note 14)	42,262	1,461
Total Automotive and Other Operations assets	161,785	141,974
Financing and Insurance Operations		
Cash and cash equivalents (Note 1)	18,130	8,158
Investments in securities (Note 6)	13,148	14,651
Finance receivables—net (Note 8)	173,137	134,643
Loans held for sale	19,609	15,720
Net equipment on operating leases (less accumulated depreciation) (Note 10)	27,210	25,721
Other assets (Note 14)	35,488	28,186
Net receivable from Automotive and Other Operations (Note 1)	1,492	1,089
Total Financing and Insurance Operations assets	288,214	228,168
Total assets	$449,999	$370,142
LIABILITIES AND STOCKHOLDERS' EQUITY		
Automotive and Other Operations		
Accounts payable (principally trade)	$ 21,542	$ 17,919
Loans payable (Note 16)	2,813	1,994
Liabilities of discontinued operations	–	7,956
Accrued expenses (Note 15)	45,417	39,113
Net payable to Financing and Insurance Operations (Note 1)	1,492	1,089
Total current liabilities	71,264	68,071
Long-term debt (Note 16)	29,593	14,261
Postretirement benefits other than pensions (Note 17)	32,285	34,244
Pensions (Note 17)	7,952	22,633
Other liabilities and deferred income taxes (Notes 11 and 15)	15,567	13,734
Total Automotive and Other Operations liabilities	156,661	152,943
Financing and Insurance Operations		
Accounts payable	3,880	3,219
Debt (Note 16)	239,350	183,913
Other liabilities and deferred income taxes (Notes 11 and 15)	24,533	22,974
Total Financing and Insurance Operations liabilities	267,763	210,106
Total liabilities	424,424	363,049
Minority interests	307	279
Total stockholders' equity	25,268	6,814
Total liabilities and stockholders' equity	$449,999	$370,142

The above supplemental information is intended to facilitate analysis of General Motors Corporation's businesses: (1) Automotive and Other Operations, and (2) Financing and Insurance Operations.

Reference should be made to the notes in the consolidated financial statements.

Consolidated Statements of Cash Flows

(dollars in millions) For the years ended December 31,	2003	2002	2001
Cash flows from operating activities			
Income from continuing operations	$ 2,862	$ 1,975	$ 1,222
Adjustments to reconcile income from continuing operations to net cash provided by operating activities			
Depreciation and amortization expenses	13,978	11,865	11,764
Mortgage servicing rights amortization	1,602	3,871	948
Provision for financing losses	1,608	2,028	1,472
Other postretirement employee benefit (OPEB) expense	4,599	4,108	3,720
OPEB payments	(3,536)	(3,334)	(3,120)
VEBA contributions/withdrawals	(3,000)	(1,000)	1,300
Pension expense	3,412	1,780	540
Pension contributions	(18,168)	(5,156)	(317)
Retiree lump-sum and vehicle voucher expense, net of payments	923	(254)	(136)
Net change in mortgage loans	456	(4,715)	(4,615)
Net change in mortgage securities	236	(656)	(777)
Change in other investments and miscellaneous assets	1,741	1,335	180
Change in other operating assets and liabilities (Note 1)	792	4,477	(234)
Other	95	(842)	233
Net cash provided by operating activities	$ 7,600	$ 15,482	$ 12,180
Cash flows from investing activities			
Expenditures for property	(7,330)	(6,871)	(7,832)
Investments in marketable securities—acquisitions	(28,660)	(39,386)	(38,248)
Investments in marketable securities—liquidations	24,253	35,688	37,560
Net change in mortgage servicing rights	(2,557)	(1,711)	(2,075)
Increase in finance receivables	(149,419)	(143,024)	(107,566)
Proceeds from sale of finance receivables	107,505	117,276	95,949
Proceeds from sale of business units	4,148	–	–
Operating leases—acquisitions	(11,761)	(16,624)	(12,938)
Operating leases—liquidations	9,952	13,994	11,892
Investments in companies, net of cash acquired (Note 1)	(201)	(870)	(1,283)
Other	(1,422)	1,004	126
Net cash used in investing activities	(55,492)	(40,524)	(24,415)
Cash flows from financing activities			
Net increase (decrease) in loans payable	235	770	(21,740)
Long-term debt—borrowings	97,391	51,411	62,956
Long-term debt—repayments	(38,963)	(24,365)	(19,789)
Repurchases of common and preference stocks	–	(97)	(264)
Proceeds from issuing common stocks	–	62	100
Proceeds from sales of treasury stocks	60	19	418
Cash dividends paid to stockholders	(1,121)	(1,121)	(1,105)
Other	1,320	333	924
Net cash provided by financing activities	58,922	27,012	21,500
Net cash provided by discontinued operations	275	–	–
Effect of exchange rate changes on cash and cash equivalents	929	495	(96)
Net increase in cash and cash equivalents	12,234	2,465	9,169
Cash and cash equivalents at beginning of the year	20,320	17,855	8,686
Cash and cash equivalents at end of the year	$ 32,554	$ 20,320	$ 17,855

Reference should be made to the notes in the consolidated financial statements.

NOTE 9. Inventories

Inventories included the following for Automotive and Other Operations (dollars in millions):

	December 31,	
	2003	**2002**
Productive material, work in process, and supplies	$ 4,899	$ 4,803
Finished product, service parts, etc.	7,642	6,741
Total inventories at FIFO	12,541	11,544
Less LIFO allowance	1,581	1,807
Total inventories (less allowances)	$10,960	$ 9,737

Inventories are stated generally at cost, which is not in excess of market. The cost of approximately 92% of U.S. inventories is determined by the last-in, first-out (LIFO) method. Generally, the cost of all other inventories is determined by either the first-in, first-out (FIFO) or average cost method.

During 2003, U.S. LIFO-eligible inventory quantities were reduced. This reduction resulted in a liquidation of LIFO inventory quantities carried at lower costs prevailing in prior years compared with the cost of 2003 purchases, the effect of which decreased cost of goods sold by approximately $200 million, pretax.

CHAPTER **8**

Long-Term Producing Assets and Investments in Equity Securities

ANALYSIS CHALLENGE: HOW DOES OUTSOURCING AFFECT THE FINANCIAL STATEMENTS?

More and more companies outsource key operations. The reasons for doing so vary and include cheaper labor costs, avoiding large investments in fixed assets, the opportunity to take advantage of economies of scale in manufacturing, and divesting operations where the company does not have a competitive advantage.

How does this trend affect the financial statements? Does it really lead to value creation or are gains in efficiency offset by lower profit margins? What effects arise when plants are closed in domestic markets?

Return on assets (ROA) is a critical measure of performance. Along with leverage, ROA directly determines return on equity (ROE), the key to value creation. While increasing either ROA or leverage can boost ROE, increasing ROA is normally less risky. It involves getting more return (increasing profit margin or the return on sales) from fewer asset investments (quicker asset turnover), or simply being more efficient with your asset investments. In Chapter 7, we discussed current assets (cash, receivables, and inventory); in this chapter, we cover long-term investments in producing assets (property, plant, and equipment, and intangibles), as well as short- and long-term investments in equity securities (ownership investments in other companies). For many firms, these assets represent a large part of their overall investment in assets.

Asset investments make up the left side of the balance sheet—current and noncurrent (long-term) assets. Changes in the balance sheet values of these assets are reflected on the income statement (e.g., gains and losses on asset sales, and depreciation and amortization expense), and the cash outflows and inflows associated with the acquisition and sales of these assets are described in the investing section of the statement of cash flows.

LONG-TERM PRODUCING ASSETS, EQUITY SECURITIES, AND VALUE CREATION

$$\text{ROE} = \frac{\text{Net income}}{\text{Common equity}} = \frac{\text{NI} + \text{Interest expense}}{\text{Sales}} \times \frac{\text{Sales}}{\text{Assets}} \times \frac{\text{Assets}}{\text{Common equity}} \times \frac{\text{NI}}{\text{NI} + \text{Interest expense}}$$

Value creation takes place when a company's ROE exceeds its cost of equity. Managing working capital is an important activity affecting ROE; managing long-term producing assets and equity investments is important, too. Operating with fewer factories or making fewer investments, for example, means that a company needs less capital to finance a smaller asset base. Less capital translates into a lower return required for value creation.

▶ INVESTMENTS IN LONG-TERM PRODUCING ASSETS

Producing assets include land, fixed assets, natural resource costs, intangible assets, and deferred costs. Land includes the cost of real estate used in the operations of the company. Fixed assets, such as buildings, machinery, and equipment, are often situated on this real estate. Natural resource costs include the costs of acquiring the rights to extract natural resources. Such costs are very important in the operations of the extractive industries (e.g., mining, petroleum, and natural gas). Intangible assets are characterized by rights, privileges, and benefits of possession rather than physical existence. Examples include the costs of acquiring patents, copyrights, trademarks, and goodwill. Deferred costs represent a miscellaneous category of intangible assets, often including prepaid costs that provide benefits for a length of time that extends beyond the current period, organization costs, and other start-up costs associated with beginning operations (e.g., construction in process, property development costs capitalized prior to the start of production, and legal and licensing fees). Table 8-1 presents the noncurrent assets of Texas Instruments at December 31, 2006 and 2005. The bulk of the items relate to the physical assets used to manufacture and run the business, investments, and intangibles (many related to acquisitions that the company has made).

Producing assets provide the means to operate the business, providing benefits that extend beyond the current operating period. They are recorded on the balance sheet (i.e., capitalized) at cost, including any costs to bring the asset to usable condition. Over the period of their useful lives (if determinable), these costs are systematically converted to expenses (e.g.,

TABLE 8-1. Texas Instruments, Noncurent Assets

(dollars in millions)	2006	2005
Property, plant, and equipment at cost	$ 7,751	$ 8,374
Less accumulated depreciation	(3,801)	(4,644)
Property, plant, and equipment, net	3,950	3,730
Equity and other long-term investments	287	236
Goodwill	792	677
Acquisition-related intangibles	118	60
Deferred income taxes	688	243
Capitalized software licenses, net	307	342
Other assets	140	312

depreciation and amortization expenses), reducing net income on the income statement and generally being matched with the benefits that they help create. The cash outflows associated with the acquisition of these assets and the cash inflows associated with their disposition (e.g., sale or disposal) are found in the investing section of the statement of cash flows.

CAPITALIZE VS. EXPENSE—BASIC JOURNAL ENTRIES AND THE EFFECT ON THE ACCOUNTING EQUATION

When a company incurs a cost, whether paid in cash or still payable, accountants determine whether the cost qualifies as an asset or an expense. If the cost provides future economic benefits that can be objectively measured, it will be *capitalized* as an asset.

Asset (+A) $
   Cash (−A) or Payable (+L) $
To capitalize a cost as an asset.

If the benefits of the cost were already received and no future benefits exist, it will be *expensed*.

Expense (E, −RE) $
   Cash (−A) or Payable (+L) $
To record a cost as an expense.

Shareholders, investors, creditors, managers, and auditors are interested in the nature and condition of a company's producing assets because they represent the company's capacity to produce and sell goods and/or services. Planning and executing major capital expenditures for land, buildings, and machinery are some of management's most important concerns. Producing asset turnover (Sales/Average producing assets) measures how efficiently a company is managing its producing assets. If the ratio is relatively high, the company is generating large amounts of sales with a relatively small investment in producing assets, putting upward pressure on ROA and ROE. This metric is particularly important for companies that rely heavily on producing assets, such as heavy manufacturing, natural resource firms, and many service enterprises.

INSIGHT: PRODUCE OR OUTSOURCE FIXED ASSETS?

The fixed asset turnover ratio is defined as Sales / Average fixed assets. A sub-ratio of the total asset turnover ratio (i.e., Sales / Average total assets), this measure captures how efficiently a company uses its fixed assets to generate sales.

Different companies make different choices about their fixed assets. For example, some semiconductor companies choose to design and produce their own products. Others (fabless semiconductor companies) focus on design only and they outsource production, reducing their need for fixed assets. If both firms have the same sales levels, the fabless

companies will report higher fixed-asset turnovers. Whether they create more value will depend on how the higher efficiency (reflected in higher asset turnover) compares to the lower profitability (reflected in lower profit margin) due to the extra costs of outsourcing.

A similar issue arises in the hospitality business. Consider the two luxury hotel companies, Mandarin Oriental and Four Seasons. Mandarin Oriental owns and manages its hotels. Four Seasons manages, but chooses not to own, its properties.

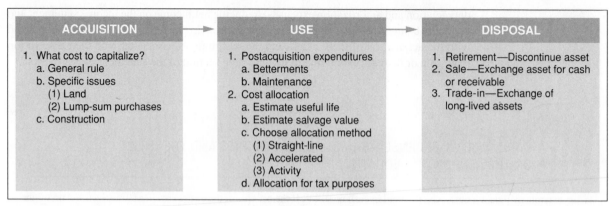

Figure 8-1. Accounting for Long-Lived Assets

▶ ACCOUNTING FOR PRODUCING ASSETS: AN OVERVIEW

As illustrated in Figure 8-1, important accounting issues must be addressed at three points during the life of a producing asset: (1) when the asset is acquired (purchased or manufactured), (2) while the asset is in use, and (3) when the asset is disposed of.

Acquisition: What Costs to Capitalize?

The acquisition cost of a producing asset is determined by either (1) the fair market value (FMV) of the acquired asset or (2) the FMV of what was given up to acquire the asset, whichever is more readily determinable. In most cases, the FMV of what was given up is used because cash, which by definition is at FMV, is normally given up in such exchanges. Furthermore, the capitalized cost includes all costs required to bring the asset into serviceable or usable condition and location. These costs include the purchase price of the asset and also costs like freight, installation, taxes, and title fees. For example, suppose that the purchase cost of a piece of equipment is $25,000, and it costs $2,000 to have it delivered, $1,500 to have it installed, and taxes and title fees total $500 and $300, respectively. The total capitalized cost of the equipment on the balance sheet would then be $29,300 ($25,000 + $2,000 + $1,500 + $500 + $300). The logic of adding the indirect costs to the cost of the asset itself lies in the definition of an asset. These costs serve to create the expected future benefits of the producing asset.

ACQUISITION OF PROPERTY AND EQUIPMENT—BASIC JOURNAL ENTRIES AND EFFECT ON THE ACCOUNTING EQUATION

Property and Equipment, cost (+A)	$	
Cash (−A)		$

To record purchase of fixed assets for cash (if the purchase was made with debt, a liability would be credited).

Applying these general rules involves judgment. Special cases arise, for example, when more than one asset is purchased at a single (lump-sum) price and when companies construct their own producing assets. In a lump-sum purchase, the total purchase cost must be allocated to the individual assets, which is normally done on the basis of subjectively determined FMVs. In the case of constructing a producing asset, all costs of materials, labor, and overhead used in the construction process must be included in the capitalized cost of the asset, which may also include interest costs incurred during the construction period on funds borrowed to finance the construction.

MEASUREMENT CHALLENGE—SELF-CONSTRUCTED ASSETS

When a company constructs its own assets, several unique accounting challenges arise. First, the entity needs to determine which costs are eligible to be capitalized. Direct material and labor seem obvious enough, but indirect costs are harder to identify with precision (e.g., the construction supervisor's wages should be included, but what about the salaries of the real estate development group charged with locating the property?). Furthermore, the construction period needs to be identified so that costs beyond that period are not added to the asset. This becomes more challenging when part of the asset begins to produce revenues prior to final completion (e.g., when a hotel begins taking guests prior to the end of all construction). Finally, during the construction period, only ultimately recoverable costs can be capitalized. If cost overruns take place or the expected benefits of a project decline, the entire cost of the asset may not be recoverable. In that case, certain costs should be converted to an expense. Companies deal with these challenges by monitoring fair values and developing accounting policies and procedures to be applied on a consistent basis.

Postacquisition Expenditures

Costs are often incurred subsequent to the acquisition or manufacture of a producing asset. Such postacquisition expenditures serve either to improve the existing asset or merely to maintain it. Costs incurred to improve the asset are called betterments, and costs incurred to repair or maintain its current level of productivity are classified as maintenance. The costs of betterments are capitalized and included on the balance sheet in the cost of the producing asset; maintenance costs are treated as expenses, immediately reducing net income on the income statement.

MEASUREMENT CHALLENGE—MAINTENANCE OR BETTERMENT?

The line between maintenance and betterment can be fuzzy. Consider the challenge faced by Canadian gold-mining giant Placer Dome. Property and equipment represents 47% of the company's $5.5 billion dollars in assets. They use dump trucks that haul more than 200 tons per load. When Placer Dome changes the oil in one of these trucks, the cost is expensed as maintenance. When a major overhaul of the engine is done, the company must determine whether the cost serves to extend the asset's life or otherwise improves the asset. If the overhauls are done every few months, it will make little difference to earnings whether the costs are expensed or capitalized. If the overhauls are done, say, once every three years, then expensing the costs immediately will understate current earnings (and overstate future earnings). The better policy, assuming that the costs are material, is to add the cost of the overhaul to property and equipment and depreciate it over the three-year period it benefits.

In order to be considered a betterment, a postacquisition expenditure must improve a producing asset in at least one of four ways:

1. Increase the asset's useful life over that which was originally estimated.
2. Improve the quality of the asset's output.
3. Increase the quantity of the asset's output.
4. Reduce the costs associated with operating the asset.

Betterments are usually infrequent and tend to involve larger dollar amounts. Maintenance expenditures fail to meet any of the criteria mentioned above, tend to be periodic, and tend to involve smaller dollar amounts.

GLOBAL ACCOUNTING INSIGHT—MAINTENANCE COSTS

Under U.S. generally accepted accounting principles (GAAP) and international financial reporting standards (IFRS), maintenance costs are considered expenses when they are incurred. Under German GAAP, the cost for maintenance is expensed if it is incurred within three months of year end—a policy that offers management an opportunity to manage earnings: Schedule maintenance for March 31 and the amount is expensed; schedule it for April 1 and it is not.

Although publicly traded companies in Europe must follow IFRS, private firms continue to follow their own local GAAP. Analysts reading these companies' statements need to be aware of the local earnings management opportunities.

Cost Allocation

Once the capitalized cost of a producing asset has been determined, it must be allocated over the asset's remaining useful life. As the expected economic benefits of the asset are realized, the asset is used up. Allocating the original cost serves to match the cost with the benefits produced by the asset. The allocation process requires three steps: (1) estimate a useful life, (2) estimate a salvage value, and (3) choose a cost allocation (depreciation or amortization) method.

DEFINITIONS: DEPRECIATION, AMORTIZATION, AND DEPLETION

The terms depreciation, amortization, and depletion are synonyms. All refer to means of allocating costs across time periods. Depreciation expense is used when allocating the cost of tangible assets. Amortization goes with intangibles and leasehold improvements. Depletion is associated with natural resources.

Estimating Useful Life and Salvage Value
Accurately estimating the useful life and salvage value of a producing asset is a challenge. An important consideration is the physical obsolescence of the asset. At what time

in the future will the asset deteriorate to the point when repairs are not economically feasible, and what will be the asset's salvage value at that time? It is virtually impossible to predict accurately the condition of an asset very far into the future, let alone predict the salvage value—the amount that can be recovered when the asset is sold, traded, or scrapped.

The problem of predicting useful lives and salvage values is complicated further by technological developments. The usefulness of a producing asset is largely determined by technological advancements, which could at any time render certain assets obsolete. Technical obsolescence, in turn, could force the early replacement of an asset that is still in reasonably good working order.

Generally accepted accounting principles provide no clear guidelines for determining the useful lives and future salvage values of producing assets. In practice, many companies assume the salvage value to be zero and estimate useful lives by referring to guidelines developed by the Internal Revenue Service. These guidelines, however, were established for use in determining taxable income and need not be followed in the preparation of the financial statements. Certain intangible assets, such as patents, trademarks, and copyrights, have legal lives, which establish a maximum value for the useful life estimate, but often the useful lives of these assets expire long before their legal lives. Consequently, management can use its discretion when estimating useful lives and salvage values. As long as the estimates are reasonable and are applied in a systematic and consistent manner, auditors generally allow much leeway in this area. A company's past experience with similar assets is a reasonable starting point for these estimates.

MEASUREMENT CHALLENGE—INDEFINITE-LIVED ASSETS

Some producing assets do not have determinable useful lives. Land, for example, is considered to have an indefinite useful life, as might a brand name purchased in the acquisition of another company. In such cases, the capitalized cost cannot be allocated over the estimated useful life because the useful life cannot be estimated. Accounting standards require that the cost of these assets remain on the balance sheet unless there is evidence that they have been "permanently impaired" or their value to the company has permanently diminished. When that happens, the balance sheet values of these assets are reduced and a loss is recognized on the income statement.

Cost Allocation Methods—Depreciation and Amortization
The useful-life estimate determines the period of time over which the cost of a producing asset is to be allocated. The capitalized cost less the salvage value is called the allocation base: the dollar amount of cost allocated over the asset's useful life. The cost allocation methods discussed in this section determine the rate of allocation or, in other words, the amount of allocation base converted to expense during each period of the asset's useful life. Three basic allocation methods are allowed under GAAP: (1) straight-line, (2) accelerated, and (3) activity.

DEPRECIATION OF PROPERTY AND EQUIPMENT—BASIC JOURNAL ENTRIES AND EFFECT ON THE ACCOUNTING EQUATION

Depreciation Expense (E, − RE) $

   Accumulated Depreciation (−A) $

To record depreciation expense on the fixed assets. (The accumulated depreciation account is a contra asset account. When netted against the property and equipment cost account, the result is net property and equipment—also known as the book or carrying value of the equipment.)

The following T-accounts assume that a company began the year with property and equipment, at cost, of $10,000.

During the year, the company bought $3,000 of new equipment. They sold equipment that originally cost $2,500. That equipment has an accumulated depreciation of $1,500. Both balances were removed when the equipment was sold (we look at disposals later in the chapter). During the year, they depreciated their property and equipment by $1,200. The company began with net property and equipment of $5,800 and ended with $6,000.

Property and Equipment, at cost

Beginning Balance	$10,000	
Capital Expenditures	3,000	
		$2,500 Cost of P&E sold
Ending Balance	$10,500	

Accumulated Depreciation

		$4,200 Beginning Balance
Acc Dep on P&E sold	$ 1,500	
		1,200 Depreciation Expense
		$4,500 Ending Balance

Why use a contra-asset account (accumulated depreciation)? Why not simply credit property and equipment for the depreciation? The answer lies in the information conveyed by the breakdown. Cost less accumulated depreciation provides a rough guide to the age of the equipment. If you observed two divisions of a company, each with $100,000 (net) of computers, you would know little about the relative age of the machines or the likelihood of capital expenditures in the coming year. If you learned that one division's net balance was made up of computers with a cost of $1,000,000 and accumulated depreciation of $900,000, you would know that those are older and more likely to be replaced than those of the other division with computers costing $110,000 and $10,000 of accumulated depreciation.

Straight-Line and Accelerated Methods. The straight-line method, which allocates an equal amount of cost in each year of an asset's useful life, is used by most companies to depreciate fixed assets and by almost all companies to amortize intangible assets with definite lives. It is popular for several reasons: (1) management believes that the asset provides equal benefits across each year of its estimated useful life, (2) it is relatively simple to apply, and (3) compared to accelerated methods, it tends to produce higher net income numbers and higher book values in the early years of an asset's life.

Under accelerated methods, greater amounts of the asset's capitalized cost are allocated (expensed) to earlier periods than to later periods. The most common accelerated method is called double-declining balance, which allocates costs to periods using the following formula: $[2 \times \text{Asset book value}] / \text{Useful life}$. Because the book value (cost less accumulated

Year	Straight-Line $(C - SV) / N$ Depreciation Expense	Accumulated Depreciation	Book Value	Double-Declining Balance $(2 \times BV) / N$ Depreciation Expense	Accumulated Depreciation	Book value
Cost			$15,000			$15,000
20X1	$2,400	$ 2,400	12,600	$6,000	$ 6,000	9,000
20X2	2,400	4,800	10,200	3,600	9,600	5,400
20X3	2,400	7,200	7,800	2,160	11,760	3,240
20X4	2,400	9,600	5,400	240	12,000	3,000
20X5	2,400	12,000	3,000	–	12,000	3,000

Key:
C = Cost = $15,000
SV = Salvage value = $3,000
N = Useful life = 5 years
BV = Book value = $15,000 – Accumulated depreciation
Note: 20X4 double-declining balance expense is $240, bringing ending book value to salvage value.

Figure 8-2. Straight-Line vs. Double-Declining-Balance Depreciation Expense

depreciation) decreases each year, the amount of allocated cost (i.e., the expense) also decreases each year. Theoretically, this method should be used for assets that generate greater benefits in the early periods of their useful lives. Practically, relatively few companies use this method (or other accelerated methods) for financial reporting purposes. However, accelerated methods are used by almost all companies when preparing reports for tax purposes because they result in lower taxable income amounts (and lower tax liabilities) in the early years of the asset's life.

To illustrate and compare the straight-line and double-declining-balance methods, assume that Dow Chemical purchased a storage tank for $15,000 on January 1, 20X1. The life and salvage value of the storage tank are estimated to be five years and $3,000, respectively. Figure 8-2 computes the depreciation expense amounts and book values under each method over the life of the asset.

The amount of depreciation under the straight-line method is constant across the five-year life, while under double-declining balance, the expense decreases as the book value decreases. Because the straight-line method gives rise to lower expense amounts in the early years, it gives rise to higher net income amounts in the early years. While this difference reverses in the later years of the asset's life, growing companies, by definition, tend to have more producing assets in the earlier years than in the later years of their useful lives. Consequently, the straight-line method normally gives rise to higher net income and book value amounts than double-declining balance.

COST ALLOCATION AT TEXAS INSTRUMENTS

More than one cost allocation method can be used by the same company. Texas Instruments uses an accelerated depreciation method to account for property and equipment, and the straight-line method for intangibles and software licenses. The following passage is an excerpt from the notes to their financial statements. Can you guess how the 150% declining balance method differs from double-declining balance?

"**Property, Plant, and Equipment, and Other Capitalized Costs:** Property, plant, and equipment are stated at cost and depreciated primarily on the 150% declining-balance

(continues)

COST ALLOCATION AT TEXAS INSTRUMENTS (*continued*)

method over their estimated useful lives. Fully depreciated assets are written off against accumulated depreciation. Acquisition-related costs are amortized on a straight-line ba-

sis over the estimated economic life of the assets. Capitalized software licenses generally are amortized on a straight-line basis over the term of the license."

Activity (Units-of-Production) Method. The activity method allocates the cost of a producing asset to future periods based on its activity. This method, sometimes called the units-of-production method, is used primarily in the mining, oil, and gas industries to allocate (deplete) the costs associated with acquiring the rights to and extracting natural resources, but it is also used in cases where it is more common to express the life of an asset in terms of its activity instead of years. The useful life of an automobile, for example, could be expressed in terms of miles driven instead of years. In periods when an asset is very active (e.g., production is high), a relatively large amount of the cost is allocated. In periods when the asset is less active, relatively fewer costs are allocated.

To illustrate, assume that a company purchases mining properties for $10 million in cash, and accurately estimates that the properties will yield 500,000 tons of ore. The company mines 100,000 tons during year 1; 250,000 tons in year 2; and 150,000 tons in year 3. The depletion expense and book value amounts over the three-year period are provided below.

	Calculation	Depletion	Book value
Year 1	$10,000,000 × (100,000 tons / 500,000 tons)	$2,000,000	$8,000,000
Year 2	$10,000,000 × (250,000 tons / 500,000 tons)	5,000,000	3,000,000
Year 3	$10,000,000 × (150,000 tons / 500,000 tons)	3,000,000	0

Of the three methods illustrated (straight-line, double-declining balance, and activity) activity normally provides the best application of the matching principle. It is the only method where the amount of the expense is directly determined by the activity of the asset, which should relate to the revenues (benefits) generated by the asset.

PLACER DOME—CAPITALIZING COSTS AND UNIT-OF-PRODUCTION METHOD OF COST ALLOCATION

Placer Dome spends considerable sums exploring for and developing mineral properties. Excerpts from a recent annual report explain how it determines which costs to capitalize and, for capitalized costs, how they are expensed.

"Exploration costs are charged against earnings as incurred. Significant costs related to property acquisitions, including allocations for undeveloped mineral interests, are capitalized until the viability of the mineral interest is determined. When it has been established that a mineral deposit is commercially mineable and a decision has been made to formulate a mining plan (which occurs upon completion of a positive economic analysis of the mineral deposit), the costs subsequently incurred to develop a mine on the property prior to the start of mining operations are capitalized. Capitalized

amounts may be written down if future cash flows, including potential sales proceeds, related to the property are projected to be less than the carrying value of the property. If no mineable ore body is discovered, capitalized acquisition costs are expensed in the period in which it is determined that the mineral property has no future economic value.

Costs incurred during the start-up phase of a mine are expensed as incurred. Ongoing mining expenditures on producing properties are charged against earnings as incurred. Major development expenditures incurred to expose the ore, increase production, or extend the life of an existing mine are capitalized."

Placer Dome was acquired by Barrick Gold Corporation in early 2006.

TEST YOUR KNOWLEDGE: PROPERTY, PLANT, AND EQUIPMENT

The condensed balance sheet as of December 31, 2007, for your company follows:

Assets		Liabilities and Shareholders' Equity	
Current assets	$40,000	Liabilities	$35,000
Land	50,000	Shareholders' equity	55,000
Total assets	$90,000	Total liabilities and shareholders' equity	$90,000

Revenues and expenses (other than amortization) are predicted to be $65,000 and $20,000, respectively, for 2008, 2009, and 2010. All revenues and expenses are received or paid in cash. On January 1, 2008, your company pays $40,000 cash for an item.

1. Assume that the company engaged in operating activities only during 2008, 2009, and 2010. Prepare income statements for 2008, 2009, and 2010 and the balance sheet as of December 31 for 2008, 2009, and 2010, assuming the $40,000 cash payment is treated in each of the following ways:
   a. Immediately expensed;
   b. Capitalized and amortized evenly over two years; and
   c. Capitalized and amortized evenly over three years.

2. Compute the total income recognized over the three-year period under each assumption.

3. What is interesting about the December 31, 2010 balance sheet prepared under all three assumptions?

Revising Estimates.   After using producing assets for several years, companies may find that their original estimates were inaccurate. In such cases, management should revise the estimates, and allocate the unallocated cost of the asset over the new remaining life. To illustrate, suppose that on January 1, 20X1, Singapore Airlines purchased aircraft for $11,000,000 and estimated the useful life of the aircraft and the salvage value to be 10 years and $1,000,000, respectively. If the company depreciated equal portions ($1,000,000) of the amount subject to depreciation ($10,000,000) each year, it would have recognized $5,000,000 of accumulated depreciation by the end of 20X5, and the aircraft would be reported on the December 31, 20X5 balance sheet in the following manner:

Aircraft	**$11,000,000**	
Less accumulated depreciation	**5,000,000**	**$6,000,000**

Assume that as of January 1, 20X6, management believes that the aircraft will actually be in service through 2015, 10 years beyond the present time, and 15 years from the date of acquisition (20X1). In other words, the company changed its original useful-life estimate from 10 to 15 years. At that point, Singapore Airlines would not restate the financial statements of the previous periods. Instead, it would simply depreciate the remaining depreciation base ($6,000,000 [Book value] − $1,000,000 [Salvage value]) over the remaining life of the aircraft (10 years). The amount of depreciation recognized on the 20X6 financial statements would be $500,000 ([$6,000,000 − $1,000,000] / 10 years).

Depreciating the book value of the asset over its remaining useful life, as of the date of the estimate revision, is known as treating the revision prospectively. That is, no "catch-up" entry is recorded and prior financial statements are not restated. Estimate revisions are not considered errors or changes in methods and, therefore, the financial statements as of the time of the revision are not in need of correction. Instead, the new information that led to the revision affects only the manner in which the aircraft is accounted for in the future. However, if the revision gives rise to a reported net income amount materially different from what would have been reported without the revision, the company is required to disclose the income effect of the revision in the footnotes.

CHANGING ESTIMATES: EXCERPTS FROM LA QUINTA CORP'S MARCH 31, 2005, FORM 10-Q

"During the three months ended March 31, 2005, we changed our estimate of the remaining useful life related to a hotel that is scheduled to be redeveloped beginning in the second quarter of 2005. The impact of the change in useful life during the three months ended March 31, 2005, was an increase in depreciation expense and net loss of approximately $2.4 million and $1.3 million, or $0.01 per share, respectively."

TEST YOUR KNOWLEDGE: CHANGING ACCOUNTING METHODS

Effective January 1, 2003, Zimmer Holdings changed the method it uses to account for handheld instruments used by orthopedic surgeons. Prior to that date the cost of these instruments was carried as a prepaid expense, and when used, the cost was converted to an expense as part of selling, general, and administrative expenses. The new method recognized these instruments as long-lived assets and the costs are now included in property, plant, and equipment, and depreciated over a five-year period using the straight-line method. The effect of the change was to increase reported earnings by $26.8 million.

Explain how this accounting change affected the basic accounting equation, and how it affects the computation of the current ratio and the fixed assets turnover ratio.

Disposal: Retirement, Sales, and Trade-In

Producing assets are acquired at cost, depreciated or amortized as they are used in the operation of a business, and eventually disposed of. The disposal can take one of three forms: retirement, sale, or trade-in. In all cases, the following procedures hold. The cost allocation (e.g., depreciation) is recorded up to the date of the disposal, the book value of the asset is removed from the books, and any receipt or payment of cash or other assets is recorded when the asset is disposed of. A gain or loss on the exchange is normally recognized in the amount of the difference between the book value of the asset given up and the value of the acquired assets, which is determined by either (1) the FMV of the assets given up or (2) the FMV of the assets received, whichever is clearly more evident and objectively determinable. Such gains and losses are usually reported in the "other revenues and expenses" section of the income statement.

Retiring Producing Assets

It is not unusual for companies to retire, close, or abandon their producing assets. Retirement can be due to obsolescence, the lack of a market for the asset in question, or closure by a regulatory body. In such cases, the original cost and accumulated depreciation of the asset are simply written off the books. No gain or loss is recognized if the asset is fully depreciated at the time of the retirement. A loss is recognized if the asset is not yet fully depreciated.

Assume, for example, that Ryanair, Europe's biggest low-cost carrier, retired two pieces of equipment. Item 1 was purchased for $10,000 and depreciated over eight years with no expected salvage value. At the time of its retirement, it was fully depreciated (i.e., accumulated depreciation was $10,000). Item 2 was purchased for $13,000 and was expected to have a $1,000 salvage value after its useful life of 12 years. At the time of its retirement, it was not fully depreciated—accumulated depreciation was only equal to $10,000.

No gain or loss would be recognized on the retirement of Item 1 because an asset with a book value of zero was simply abandoned. A $3,000 loss would be recognized on the retirement of Item 2 because the disposal of an asset with value on the balance sheet of $3,000 generated no proceeds for the company.

A highly subjective and controversial area of accounting involves the "permanent impairment" of a producing asset. Gains and losses are recorded when producing assets are disposed of. When the cost of an asset still in use exceeds its value, it is said to be impaired. We discussed this issue earlier in the context of producing assets with indeterminable lives (e.g., land and brand names). Generally accepted accounting principles require that when the value of an asset is permanently impaired, it should be written down. Recent guidelines are subject to judgment, leaving management much discretion over the amount and timing of such write-downs. Simply, it is very difficult to determine exactly when an asset has been permanently impaired and by how much. It is not unusual, for example, for companies to report huge losses on their income statements described as "restructuring charges," consisting, in part, of write-downs of producing assets judged to be permanently impaired.

MEASUREMENT CHALLENGE—MEASURING AND DISCLOSING IMPAIRMENTS

The procedure for identifying and measuring asset impairments varies depending on the type of asset. In each case, considerable judgment is needed. Under U.S. GAAP, once impairments are recorded, they are not reversed even if circumstances change. You can consider impairments as a special type of depreciation expense.

For assets with determinable useful lives, if circumstances suggest or management suspects that an asset may be impaired, the first step is to forecast the future cash flows associated with that asset (e.g., the benefits it will generate or the amount it could be sold for). Those cash flows are added up (i.e., not discounted) and compared with the book value of the asset. If the book value exceeds the undiscounted cash flows, an impairment *exists*. The impairment is *measured* as the difference between the discounted cash flows and the book value of the asset. By using undiscounted cash flows to *identify* an impairment, the threshold is high. By using the discounted cash flows to *measure* the impairment, the underlying economics are captured.

For assets (other than goodwill) with indefinite lives (generally land and intangibles), the fair value of the asset (e.g., the market value or potential selling price of the asset) is compared with its book value. If book value exceeds fair value, an impairment exists and is measured as the difference between the two values.

The excerpt that follows is from the March 31, 2005, Form 10-Q filed with the Securities and Exchange Commission (SEC) by La Quinta Corp.

"We regularly review the performance of long-lived assets on an ongoing basis for impairment as well as when events or changes in circumstances indicate that the carrying amount of an asset may not be recoverable. For each lodging asset held for use, if the sum of expected future cash flows (undiscounted and without interest charges) is less than the net book value of the asset, the excess of the net book value over La Quinta's estimate of fair value of the asset is charged to current earnings. We estimate fair value primarily (1) by discounting expected future cash flows or (2) based on expected liquidated sales proceeds, relying on common hotel valuation methods such as multiples of room revenues or per room valuations. For each asset held for sale, the carrying value is reduced, if necessary, to the expected sales proceeds less costs to sell by recording a charge [expense] to current earnings."

Selling Producing Assets

Accounting for the sale of a producing asset is exactly the same as accounting for its retirement, except that cash is received in the exchange. If the cash exceeds the book value of the asset, a gain is recorded on the transaction; if the cash is less than the book value of the asset, a loss is recognized.

Using the previous example, assume that Ryanair sold the same two pieces of equipment, each for $2,000. A gain of $2,000, increasing net income, would be recognized for Item 1 because an asset with a zero book value was sold for $2,000; and a loss of $1,000, decreasing net income, would be recognized for Item 2 because an asset with a book value of $3,000 was sold for only $2,000.

DISPOSING OF PROPERTY AND EQUIPMENT—JOURNAL ENTRIES AND EFFECT ON THE ACCOUNTING EQUATION

Cash (+A)	$ 2,000	
Accumulated Depreciation (+A)	10,000	
Property and Equipment, cost (−A)		$10,000
Gain on Disposal (Gain, + RE)		2,000
To record disposal of Item 1 for cash.		
Cash (+A)	2,000	
Accumulated Depreciation (+A)	10,000	
Loss on Disposal (Loss, −RE)	1,000	
Property and Equipment, cost (−A)		13,000
To record disposal of Item 2 for cash.		

Note that the debit to accumulated depreciation (in isolation) increases assets because the account is a contra asset.

Trading-In Producing Assets

In a trade-in, two or more noncash assets are exchanged, and cash is often also received or paid. The methods used to account for such transactions depend on whether the exchanged assets are similar or dissimilar. This text limits its coverage to exchanges of dissimilar assets, those of a different general type, that perform different functions, and/or are employed in different lines of business. The methods used to account for exchanges of similar assets are normally covered in intermediate accounting textbooks.

The accounting procedures followed when retiring or selling producing assets also apply when dissimilar assets are exchanged. In fact, selling a producing asset is exactly the same as trading it in for a dissimilar asset—cash. An accounting challenge arises, however, when accounting for exchanges of noncash assets, because it is difficult to determine the dollar amount at which the asset received should be valued on the balance sheet, making it equally difficult to measure the gain or loss recognized on the exchange. Determining the FMVs of either the assets received or given up in the exchange can be quite subjective. Often, industry publications or data obtained on recent transactions involving similar assets are consulted to determine the FMVs.

To illustrate the procedure, assume that SABMiller, an international brewer, exchanges a delivery truck with a book value of $8,000 (original cost is $67,000, accumulated depreciation is $59,000) for a new high-speed printer. The printer dealer agrees to accept the truck plus $12,000 in cash. The key to valuing the transaction involves estimating either the FMV of the receipt (printer) or the FMV of the payment (used truck plus $12,000 cash).

To this end, the accountant for SABMiller learns that recent sales of comparable printers have realized, on average, $16,000, and a publication of used truck prices indicates that the value of the truck is approximately $4,000.

Given these facts, there are two acceptable ways to value the printer on the balance sheet of SABMiller, each leading to the same result: (1) the FMV of the assets given up ($16,000 = $4,000 + $12,000), or (2) the FMV of the asset received ($16,000). Comparing the book value of the truck ($8,000) plus the cash payment ($12,000), both of which would be removed from SABMiller's books, with the value of the printing press ($16,000), which would be placed on the balance sheet, would give rise to a loss of $4,000 ($16,000 − $20,000) recognized on the exchange.

MEASUREMENT CHALLENGE—INTANGIBLE ASSETS

The bulk of our discussion of producing assets has centered on tangible assets like property and equipment. We discussed the capitalize vs. expense decision and cost-allocation methods. Similar reasoning applies to intangible assets purchased in arm's-length transactions. If objective evidence of future economic benefits exists and the purchase price can be reliably measured, then intangible assets belong on the balance sheet as assets. There are, however, some exceptions and, in general, internally developed intangible assets are not recognized.

For example, the intangible asset that relates to a customer list will be recorded as an asset if it is acquired in an arm's-length transaction, but not if it is developed internally, as the company's sales force establishes customer relationships. The cost of the former can be measured objectively. How would you measure the latter?

R&D costs present a particularly challenging issue. Under U.S. GAAP, all R&D costs are expensed as incurred. Under IFRS, a distinction is made between research (which by definition is difficult to associate with measurable benefits and thus expensed) and development costs. If the development costs can be associated with future benefits that the entity is expected to pursue or exploit, under certain conditions, they can be capitalized.

Standard-setters worldwide recognize the importance of measuring intangible assets, especially as economies generate more and more value from knowledge. However, they struggle with the tradeoff between information relevance and measurement reliability. Often, conservative reporting results and intangibles are not included on the balance sheet. Savvy readers look to the notes to the financial statements for supplementary data on, say, R&D spending, and to other sources, such as industry publications and press releases, for unaudited data that help them assess the economic value of the missing items.

TEST YOUR KNOWLEDGE: DISPOSALS OF PRODUCING ASSETS

The information below was taken from the 2006 annual report of Intel, a world-leading supplier of semiconductors and electronic products (dollars in millions).

	2006	2005
Property, plant, and equipment	$47,084	$44,132
Less accumulated depreciation	29,482	27,021
Depreciation expense	4,654	4,345
Investments in property, plant, and equipment	$ 5,779	$ 5,818

(continues)

TEST YOUR KNOWLEDGE: DISPOSALS OF PRODUCING ASSETS (*continued*)

1. From which of the financial statements was each figure taken?

2. Estimate the cost of property, plant, and equipment sold during 2006.

3. Estimate the accumulated depreciation associated with the property, plant, and equipment sold during 2006.

4. Assume that the property, plant, and equipment was sold during 2006 for $500 million cash. Estimate the gain or loss recognized on the sale. On what financial statement(s) would this amount appear?

▶ INVESTMENTS IN EQUITY SECURITIES

We reviewed the accounting for working capital and long-term producing assets and explored how investing in and managing these assets play a central role in value creation. These assets require financing, which has both an explicit (i.e., the interest cost of debt) and implicit (i.e., the cost of equity) cost that must be covered if shareholder value is to be created. Companies also make equity (ownership) investments in other companies and these investments must also earn a return that exceeds the cost of financing them.

Companies invest in equity securities of other companies for two primary reasons: (1) investment income in the form of dividends and share price appreciation, and (2) management influence, where the voting power of the purchased shares allows the investor company to exert influence or control over the board of directors and management of the investee company.

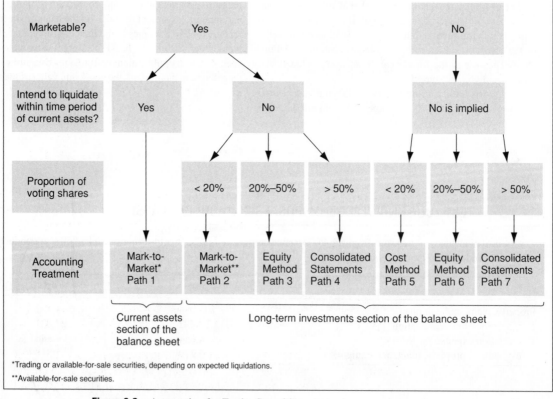

*Trading or available-for-sale securities, depending on expected liquidations.
**Available-for-sale securities.

Figure 8-3. Accounting for Equity Securities

Short-term equity investments facilitate cash management by providing investment income in the form of dividends and/or share appreciation, and allowing the company easy access to cash when needed. The primary motive behind long-term equity investments is influence over the investee company's operations and management. Most large, well-known U.S. companies are constantly involved in acquisitions, where they purchase all, or a majority (more than 50%) of, the outstanding common stock of other companies and then change these companies' operations and/or management. Companies can also exert influence over other companies by purchasing a significant portion, but less than a majority, of an investee's outstanding shares. The economics behind the different investments differs, and accounting rules are designed to capture these differences.

Figure 8-3 illustrates different investments in equity securities and the methods used to account them. Three questions must be answered before the appropriate accounting method can be determined: (1) Is the investment marketable?, (2) Does management intend to liquidate the investment within the time period of current assets?, and (3) What proportion of the voting shares has been acquired? Four different accounting treatments are illustrated, depending on the answers to these questions. The *cost* method is used if the securities are not marketable and the ownership percentage is relatively small (< 20%). *Mark-to-market* accounting is used for marketable equity securities if management intends to liquidate in the short term or holds a relatively small (< 20%) ownership percentage. The *equity method* is used if management has a "significant influence" over the investee company, which normally is established if the ownership percent is 20%–50%. Finally, *consolidated* financial statements are prepared if "control" is established, which normally involves holding more than 50% of the voting stock.

INVESTMENTS IN BONDS AND DEBT SECURITIES

Companies also invest funds in the bonds and debt securities of other entities. Like equity investments, bond investments are categorized into current and long-term investments based on management's intent and ability to hold them. Unlike equity investments, since there is no ownership claim with a bond, the percentage of the bonds that a company holds has nothing to do with the accounting. We discuss bonds in the next chapter when we discuss accounting for debt.

Cost Method

Some equity securities have no readily determinable market values. Equity securities in corporations whose securities are not publicly traded (i.e., closely held corporations or private companies), for example, may have restrictions on trading and therefore have no public market values. Relatively small investments (< 20%) in such securities, which by definition cannot easily be liquidated, are accounted for using the cost method. Investments in equity securities not readily marketable are listed on the balance sheet as long term because, by definition, they cannot be liquidated within the time period of current assets.

Applying the cost method is straightforward. Purchases are recorded at cost, including incidental costs of acquisition (e.g., brokerage fees), and the investment is carried on the balance sheet at cost while it is owned. Dividends are recorded as a receivable on the balance sheet and income on the income statement when declared. Disposals, when they eventually occur, increase the cash balance by the proceeds, remove the cost from the balance sheet, and give rise to realized gains or losses reflected on the income statement in the amount of the difference between the proceeds and the cost. Dividend income and gains and losses on these securities are usually reported in one of two places. Some companies report them as part of "other income." Others include them in "interest expense, net." In the latter case, analysis of returns on the investments and of interest costs requires disentangling the net interest figure into its component parts.

Assume, for example, that on January 1, 20X1, ABC Company paid $1,000 to purchase 1,000 shares of common stock in XYZ Company. The investment represented 5% of XYZ's outstanding voting shares. During the year, XYZ declared and paid to ABC a $100 dividend; in early January 20X2, ABC sold the shares for $1,200. Under the cost method, the balance sheet value of the investment throughout 20X1 and at year end would be $1,000. ABC would recognize dividend income on its 20X1 income statement of $100; a realized gain of $200 ($1,200 − $1,000) would appear on ABC's 20X2 income statement. The investing section of the 20X1 statement of cash flows would reflect a cash outflow of $1,000 and the investing section on the 20X2 statement would disclose a $1,200 cash inflow. The $100 dividend received in 20X1 would be an operating cash inflow.

INVESTMENTS IN EQUITY SECURITIES: COST METHOD—BASIC JOURNAL ENTRIES AND EFFECT ON THE ACCOUNTING EQUATION

Investments (+A) $
  Cash (−A) $
To record the purchase of equity securities (nonmarketable).
[No periodic mark-to-market adjustments are made.]

Cash (+A) $
  Investments (−A) $
  Gain on Sale of Investments (Gain, +RE) $
To record the sale of equity securities for a price greater than cost.

Cash (+A) $
Loss on Sale of Investments (Loss, −RE) $
  Investments (−A) $
To record the sale of equity securities for a price less than cost.

Under the cost method, the return on investment (ROI) computed from the financial statements for 20X1 would be 10% ($100 / $1,000). However, the actual ROI was 30% ($300 / $1,000) because the security both produced a dividend and appreciated in value. Because the investment could not easily be liquidated and its year-end market value was uncertain, based on the principle of objectivity, the cost method did not recognize the appreciation in value until the investment was actually sold in 20X2. The mark-to-market method, which is applied to marketable securities and discussed next, recognizes changes in the values of equity investments as they occur.

THE COST METHOD AND PERMANENT IMPAIRMENTS

Under the cost method, unrealized gains and losses on the investment are not recorded, with one exception. If, in management's view, the cost of the investment is permanently impaired, it should be written down. What sorts of evidence suggest a permanent impairment? A sustained series of losses, bankruptcy, loss of major customers, expiration of key patents or denial of approval for key pharmaceutical products, loss of access to capital, and other such events all indicate that an impairment may have occurred.

Mark-to-Market Method

Marketable equity securities that are either intended to be liquidated within the time period of current assets or constitute less than 20% of the outstanding voting stock are accounted for under the mark-to-market method. "Marketable" means that the security can be sold and converted into cash on demand. Stocks and bonds traded actively on the public stock exchanges usually meet this criterion because market prices exist, ensuring that they can be sold on short notice. Investments in marketable equity securities are listed on the balance sheet as current assets if management intends to liquidate them within the current asset time frame.

Under the mark-to-market method, investments in marketable equity securities must first be classified into one of two categories: (1) trading securities, or (2) available-for-sale securities. Trading securities are bought and held principally for the purpose of selling them in the near future with the objective of generating profit on short-term price changes. Financial services companies like JPMorgan-Chase or HSBC that run securities trading desks are likely to hold equity securities classified as "trading."

Investments in marketable equity securities not classified as trading securities are considered available-for-sale securities. Nonfinancial services companies like Dell and Advanced Micro Devices, which generally are not in the business of trading equity securities are likely to hold securities classified as "available for sale" (AFS). These firms tend to hold the securities as a means of earning a better return on excess cash. Trading securities are always listed in the current section of the balance sheet, while available-for-sale securities are listed as current or long term, depending on whether management intends to sell them within the time period of current assets.

ANALYSIS CHALLENGE: WHY IS THAT COMPANY TRADING SECURITIES?

If you observed a manufacturing firm holding substantial equity securities classified as "trading," a number of questions should arise. Does it make sense for the enterprise to be running a trading operation and do they have the requisite skills? The skill set for manufacturing is different than that for securities trading. Are adequate controls in place, and are adequate disclosures about the operations made? Given the unusual pairing of manufacturing and securities trading, you might also be wise to wonder about any other possible surprises.

In almost all respects, investments in trading and available-for-sale securities are accounted for in the same way. Purchases are recorded at cost; dividends, when declared, are recorded as a receivable on the balance sheet and income on the income statement. Consistent with the mark-to-market method, both are carried on the balance sheet at market value, a feature different from the cost method. Consequently, at the end of the accounting period, the balance sheet values of investments in both trading and available-for-sale securities are adjusted up or down to reflect current market prices. These changes in market prices give rise to unrealized (not yet cashed in) gains or losses that represent changes in the financial wealth of the company. However, these wealth changes are accounted for differently when the investment is classified as a trading security than for investments classified as available-for-sale securities.

For trading securities, the unrealized gains or losses are recognized and disclosed on the income statement in the amount of the price change. That is, unrealized gains and losses affect net income in the period when the value of the investment goes up or down, not in the period when the investment is sold. When trading securities are sold and the gains or losses are cashed in, only the price change in the current period is recognized on the income statement. All other price changes since the acquisition of the security have been recognized on past income statements.

INVESTMENTS IN EQUITY SECURITIES: TRADING SECURITIES—BASIC JOURNAL ENTRIES AND EFFECT ON THE ACCOUNTING EQUATION

Investments (Trading) (+A) $
   Cash (−A) $
To record the purchase of marketable securities (Trading).

Dividends Receivable (+A) $
   Investment Income (Gain, +RE) $
To record dividends declared on marketable securities (Trading).

[At each reporting date, the Trading securities are mark-to-market value.]

Investments (Trading) (+A) $
   Investment Income (Gain, +RE) $
To record unrealized gains on marketable securities (Trading).

Investment Loss (Trading) (Loss, −RE) $
   Investments (Trading) (−A) $
To record unrealized losses on marketable securities (Trading).

[At the time the securities are sold, the Trading securities are marked to market value, any remaining gain or loss is recorded, cash is received, and the securities are removed from the books.]

Cash (+A) $
   Investment Income (Gain, +RE) $
   Investments (Trading) (−A) $
To record the sale of marketable securities (Trading) with an additional gain since the last time they were marked to market.

Cash (+A) $
Investment Loss (Trading) (Loss, −RE) $
   Investments (Trading) (−A) $
To record the sale of marketable securities (Trading) with an additional loss since the last time they were marked to market.

HSBC: MARKETABLE SECURITIES CLASSIFIED AS TRADING

In their 2006 annual report, prepared using IFRS, international banking giant HSBC (Hongkong and Shanghai Banking Corporation) indicated

"(g) Trading assets and trading liabilities

Treasury bills, debt securities, equity shares and short positions in securities are classified as held for trading if they have been acquired principally for the purpose of selling or repurchasing in the near term, or they form part of a portfolio of identified financial instruments that are managed together and for which there is evidence of a recent pattern of short-term profit-taking. These financial assets or financial liabilities are recognised on trade date, when HSBC enters into contractual arrangements with counterparties to purchase or sell securities, and are normally derecognised when either sold (assets) or extinguished (liabilities). Measurement is initially at fair value, with transaction costs taken to the income statement. Subsequently, their fair values are remeasured, and all gains and losses from changes therein are recognised in the income statement in 'Net trading income' as they arise."

For available-for-sale securities, the unrealized gain or loss is not recognized on the income statement. Rather, the price change is considered a component of comprehensive income and reflected in the accumulated other comprehensive income account in the shareholders' equity section of the balance sheet and on the statement of shareholders' equity. In this way, the balance sheet reflects the market value of the securities, but net income does not reflect the price change. When the available-for-sale securities are sold, the entire realized gain or loss (difference between the cost of the investment and cash proceeds from the sale) is reported on the income statement. To avoid double counting, the accumulated unrealized price change in the shareholders' equity section of the balance sheet is reversed.

INVESTMENTS IN EQUITY SECURITIES: AVAILABLE-FOR-SALE (AFS) SECURITIES—BASIC JOURNAL ENTRIES AND EFFECT ON THE ACCOUNTING EQUATION

Investments (AFS) (+A) $
   Cash (−A) $
To record the purchase of marketable securities (AFS).

Dividends Receivable (+A) $
   Investment Income (Gain, +RE) $
To record dividends declared on marketable securities (AFS).

[At each reporting date, the AFS securities are marked to market value.]

Investments (AFS) (+A)   *Accumulate Other comprehensive income*
   AOCI* (+SE) $
To record unrealized gains on marketable securities (AFS). The unrealized gain flows directly to SE. It does not appear on the income statement and does not affect retained earnings.

AOCI (AFS) (−SE) $
   Investments (AFS) (−A) $
To record unrealized losses on marketable securities (AFS). The unrealized loss flows directly to SE. It does not appear on the income statement and does not affect retained earnings.

[At the time the AFS securities are sold, they are mark-to-market value, cash is received, the overall realized gain or loss is recorded on the income statement, the AOCI balance for the securities is reversed, and the securities are removed from the books.]

Cash (+A) $
AOCI (−SE) $
   Investment Income (Gain, +RE) $
   Investments (AFS) (−A) $
To record the sale of marketable securities (AFS) with a realized gain.

Cash (+A) $
Investment Loss (AFS) (Loss, −RE) $
   Investments (AFS) (−RA) $
   AOCI (+SE) $
To record the sale of marketable securities (AFS) with a realized loss.

*AOCI: Accumulated other comprehensive income (an owners' equity account).

AMD: MARKETABLE SECURITIES CLASSIFIED AS AVAILABLE FOR SALE

In their 2006 annual report, semiconductor firm Advanced Micro Devices, Inc., reported

Marketable Securities. The Company classifies its marketable debt and equity securities at the date of acquisition as either held to maturity or available for sale. Substantially all of the Company's investments in marketable debt and equity securities are classified as available for sale. These securities are reported at fair market value, with the related unrealized gains and losses included in accumulated other comprehensive income (loss), net of tax, a component of stockholders' equity. Realized gains and losses, and declines in the value of securities determined to be other-than-temporary, are in-

cluded in other income (expense), net. The cost of securities sold is based on the specific identification method.

The company classifies investments with a remaining time to maturity of more than three months as marketable securities. Marketable securities generally consist of money-market auction rate preferred stocks and debt securities, such as commercial paper, corporate notes, certificates of deposit, and marketable direct obligations of U.S. governmental agencies. Available-for-sale securities with a remaining time to maturity of greater than 12 months are classified as current when they represent investments of cash that are intended to be used in current operations.

The illustration that follows provides information about ABC Company's portfolio of equity securities over a three-year period. The events are accounted for under the cost method, as well as the mark-to-market method, as applied to both trading and available-for-sale securities. Under the mark-to-market method, the adjustment to market value at the end of the period is implemented not for each individual security, but at the portfolio level—an important distinction that simplifies the accounting method considerably. Figure 8-4 highlights the differences among the three approaches.

Assume that ABC Company acquired the following portfolio of equity investments on December 1, 20X1. Assume for simplicity that one share of each company was purchased, and prior to that date no equity securities were held.

White Company	$200
Green Company	300
Total portfolio cost	$500

As of December 31, 20X1, ABC held all investments and the current market prices were

White Company	$250
Green Company	100
Total portfolio market value	$350

During 20X2, ABC Company sold the share of White Company for $300. At the end of 20X2, the market value of Green Company was $175. In 20X3, the Green Company share was sold for $175.

	Balance Sheet				Equity			Income Statement
	Asset							
Method	**Equity Securities, cost**	**Unrealized Gain (Loss)**	**Book Value**		**AOCI**	**R/E**		**Investment Income**
Cost								
12/31/20X1	$500	n/a	$500		n/a	$ 0		$ 0
12/31/20X2	300	n/a	300		n/a	100		100
12/31/20X3	0	n/a	0		n/a	(25)		(125)
Trading								
12/31/20X1	$500	$(150)	$350		n/a	$(150)		$(150)
12/31/20X2	300	(125)	175		n/a	(25)		125
12/31/20X3	0	0	0		n/a	(25)		0
AFS								
12/31/20X1	$500	$(150)	$350		$(150)	$ 0		$ 0
12/31/20X2	300	(125)	175		(125)	100		100
12/31/20X3	0	0	0		0	(25)		(125)

AFS: Available-for-sale
AOCI: Accumulated other comprehensive income
R/E: Retained earnings
n/a: Not applicable

Figure 8-4. Effects of Equity Security Classification

Note in Figure 8-4 that the portfolio of securities was purchased for $500 and sold for a total of $475, giving rise to an overall loss in wealth of $25 over the holding period (December 1, 20X1–December 31, 20X3). All three approaches recognize the overall $25 loss, but do so in a different way across the three periods.

The cost method carries the investments on the balance sheet at cost and recognizes gains and losses on the income statement when the individual securities are sold (20X2 and 20X3); the mark-to-market method with trading securities carries the investments on the balance sheet at market value, and recognizes gains and losses on the income statement as price changes occur (20X1 and 20X2). The mark-to-market method with available-for-sale securities resembles trading securities in that it carries the investments on the balance sheet at market value, but resembles the cost method in that it recognizes the gains and losses on the income statement when the securities are sold (20X2 and 20X3). These features demonstrate that the fundamental difference across these methods involves balance sheet valuation and the timing (not the amount) of income recognition.

INSIGHT: INVESTMENTS IN MARKETABLE EQUITY SECURITIES AND COMPREHENSIVE INCOME

In Chapter 3, Figure 3–2, we defined comprehensive income as the change in the firm's equity during the period from all transactions except those with owners. The accounting for trading and available-for-sale (AFS) securities offers an opportunity to illustrate how comprehensive income and net income differ.

Consider trading securities. When the market values of trading securities change, the unrealized gains and losses are reported on the income statement as part of net income. Net income is added to retained earnings, and thus shareholders' equity is affected, too. On the other hand, if the same securities are classified as AFS, then the unrealized gains and losses are reported directly in the shareholders' equity section of the balance sheet (through the accumulated other comprehensive income account). They do not appear on the income statement until the AFS securities are sold and the gains and losses are realized.

In both cases, the change in shareholders' equity is the same. Because the market value changes are not due to transactions with owners, comprehensive income must be the same, too. Net income will differ, however, depending on how the securities are classified.

Assume that your company purchased securities at the beginning of 2007 for $100. By the end of the year, their market value increased to $110. They were sold in early 2008 for $125. The following table illustrates how net income and comprehensive income would be reported in 2007 and 2008.

	Trading		Available-for-Sale	
	Net Income	Comprehensive Income	Net Income	Comprehensive Income
2007				
Unrealized Gain	$10	$10	$ 0	$10
2008				
Realized Gain	15	15	25	15*
Total	$25	$25	$25	$25

*Realized gain of $25 less previously recorded unrealized gain of $10 (i.e., no double counting of comprehensive income).

TEST YOUR KNOWLEDGE: MARK-TO-MARKET ACCOUNTING

- The following information was extracted from the December 31, 2005, current asset section of the balance sheets of four different companies:

	Wearever Fabrics	Frames Corp.	Pacific Transport	Video Magic
Trading securities	$800,000	$490,000	$645,000	$210,000
Available-for-sale securities	130,000	40,000	250,000	85,000
Short-term equity invest.	$930,000	$530,000	$895,000	$295,000

There were no transactions in short-term equity securities during 2006, and as of December 31, 2006, the controllers of each company collected the following information:

	Wearever Fabrics	Frames Corp.	Pacific Transport	Video Magic
Trading securities	$820,000	$480,000	$625,000	$220,000
Available-for-sale securities	122,000	52,000	246,000	88,000
Short-term equity invest.	$942,000	$532,000	$871,000	$308,000

1. Compute the change in the wealth levels of each of the four companies due to the market value changes in their equity investments.

2. Compute the effect on 2006 reported income for each of the four companies due to the market value changes in their equity investments.

3. Explain why the answers to (1) and (2) are not the same.

- Biomet, Inc., provided the following disclosures in Note D of its 2006 annual report. It describes the company's investments in available-for-sale equity securities (dollars in thousands).

		Unrealized	
	Cost	Gains	Losses
2006	$19,307	$ 618	$ (541)
2005	22,288	1,099	(1,975)

1. Compute the fair market value of Biomet's available-for-sale equity portfolio for both 2006 and 2005.

2. What was the effect on the company's comprehensive income amount associated with its available-for-sale securities?

3. Assume that Biomet sold its entire portfolio of available-for-sale securities at the end of 2006. How much income would be realized on the sale?

- The *Capital Markets Report* (June 2000) suggests that Japanese banks, which carry large portfolios of short-term equity securities, are dreading the introduction of mark-to-market accounting. In the past, these investments have been carried on the balance sheet at cost or the lower of cost or market; thus, appreciated securities have not been written up to market value. The beauty of such a system, according to Japanese bank managers, is that it allows earnings to be managed by properly timing the sale of these securities because income is recognized only at the time of sale. Thus, a bank that had to absorb a particularly bad loan loss write-off could negate the income effects of that write-off by choosing to sell appreciated marketable securities. Immediately afterward, if the manager still wanted to hold the securities, they could be repurchased. This method of managing earnings disappears in a world of mark-to-market accounting because the income effects associated with appreciated securities is recognized when the price changes.

1. In your own words, explain how the mark-to-market system of accounting reduces the ability of bank managers to manage earnings.

2. While it seems that bank managers may not favor mark-to-market accounting, do you think that analysts would feel the same way?

3. Consider the methods used to account for available-for-sale securities. Can you think of a way in which managers might be able to manage earnings by properly timing the sale of available-for-sale securities? Explain.

Equity Method

Some companies exert significant influence on the operating decisions and management policies of other companies. That influence indicates a substantive economic relationship between the two entities and may be evidenced, for example, by representation on the board of directors, the interchange of management personnel between companies, frequent or significant transactions between companies, or the technical dependency of one company on the other. Significant investments in the equity securities (voting shares) of another company may also indicate significant influence and a substantive economic relationship. To achieve a reasonable degree of uniformity, the accounting profession concluded that an investment of 20% percent or more in the voting shares of another company represents a "significant influence," and that equity investments from 20% to 50% of the voting shares should be accounted for under the equity method.

The accounting procedures used to apply the equity method reflect a substantive economic relationship between the investor and investee (affiliate) companies. The equity investment, classified on the balance sheet as a long-term investment, is originally recorded at cost, but is adjusted at the end of each subsequent period for changes in the net assets (assets less liabilities) of the affiliate. As the balance sheet value of the affiliate increases or decreases (i.e., the affiliate grows or shrinks), so does the long-term equity investment account of the investor. Specifically, the value of the long-term investment on the investor's balance sheet is (1) periodically increased (decreased) by the investor's proportionate share of the net income (loss) of the affiliate and (2) decreased by all dividends transferred to the investor from the affiliate. In this way, the equity method acknowledges a close economic link between the two companies. Affiliate earnings and dividends, which indicate net asset growth and reductions, respectively, are reflected proportionately on the financial statements of the investor.

INVESTMENTS IN EQUITY SECURITIES: EQUITY METHOD—BASIC JOURNAL ENTRIES AND EFFECT ON THE ACCOUNTING EQUATION

Investments in Affiliates (+A)	$		Cash (+A)	$	
Cash (−A)		$	Dividends Receivable (A−)		$

To record the purchase of equity securities in an affiliated company (20%–50% ownership).

To record dividends received.

Dividends Receivable (+A)	$	
Investment in Affiliates (A−)		$

To record dividends declared on shares of an affiliated company.

Investments in Affiliates (+A)	$	
Equity Method Income (Gain, +RE)	$	

To record proportionate share of earnings of an affiliated company.

To illustrate, assume that on January 1, 20X1, American Electric Company purchased 40% of the outstanding voting stock of Masley Corporation for $40,000. During 20X1, Masley recognized net income of $10,000 and declared and paid dividends of $1,500 to American Electric. During 20X2, Masley recognized a net loss of $5,000 and declared and paid a $500 dividend to American Electric. The financial statement effects of these events, under the equity method, are illustrated in Figure 8-5.

Date	Balance Sheet Value	Income Statement—Earnings	Statement of Cash Flows
20x1			
1/01/x1	$40,000		$(40,000) (Investing)
Dividends	(1,500)		1,500 (Operating)
Earnings	4,000	$4,000*	
12/31/x1	$42,500		
20x2			
Dividends	$ (500)		$ 500 (Operating)
Earnings	(2,000)	(2,000)**	
12/31/x2	$40,000		
* $10,000 × 40%			
** ($5,000) × 40%			

Figure 8-5. Financial Statement Effects under the Equity Method

The initial cash payment for the investment is reflected in the investing section of the statement of cash flows, and dividend cash inflows from affiliates are included in the operating section. Furthermore, the investor's proportionate share of affiliate earnings is recognized on the income statement, but does not involve a cash inflow. Thus, the dollar amount of the effect on the income statement due to the relationship with the affiliate does not match the effect in the operating section of the statement of cash flows. In 20X1, for example, earnings were increased by $4,000, while operating cash flows were increased only by $1,500; in 20X2, earnings were decreased by $2,000, while operating cash flows were increased by $500. The use of the equity method is one of many important reasons why net income on the income statement differs from net cash flows from operating activities on the statement of cash flows.

JOINT VENTURES AND THE EQUITY METHOD

Joint ventures are a common way for many enterprises to enter new markets, share risks, gain access to technologies, and otherwise operate in partnership with other firms. By definition, in a joint venture neither party controls the venture. Key decisions are made jointly.

The accounting for investments in joint ventures follows the equity method. The investment is reported on one line of the company's balance sheet; the proportionate share of the joint venture's income is reported as investment income; dividends to the parties of the joint venture reduce the investment account; and additional contributions to the joint venture increase it.

Some analysts argue that using the equity method obscures important investment details by showing only one line on the asset side of the balance sheet. Under the equity method, for example, no portion of the joint venture's (or affiliate's) debt shows up on the investor's balance sheet, which could be a problem in cases where joint ventures (or affiliates) are highly leveraged. To address this problem, footnote disclosure of major classes of assets and liabilities for all of a company's joint ventures and affiliates is required.

The Coca-Cola example is illustrative. Although Coca-Cola's reported liability-to-equity ratio at December 31, 2005, is approximately 1.25, CCE—one of its major bottling investments—has a ratio of about 3.5. If Coca-Cola's 36% investment in CCE was accounted for on a proportionate basis, the liability-to-equity ratio would increase to 1.80. Total assets would increase as well. Although overall ROE would be unaffected, its components would be: ROA would fall and leverage would rise.

INSIGHT: EQUITY METHOD AND THE COCA-COLA COMPANY'S INVESTMENTS

The Coca-Cola Company has substantial investments in a number of bottling companies. The investments are sufficiently important that they are listed separately on the face of the company's balance sheet and they are described in more detail in the notes to their financial statements.

THE COCA-COLA COMPANY AND SUBSIDIARIES
CONSOLIDATED BALANCE SHEETS

December 31,	2006	2005
(in millions except par value)		
ASSETS		
CURRENT ASSETS		
Cash and cash equivalents	$ 2,440	$ 4,701
Marketable securities	150	66
Trade accounts receivable, less allowances of $63 and $72, respectively	2,587	2,281
Inventories	1,641	1,379
Prepaid expenses and other assets	1,623	1,778
TOTAL CURRENT ASSETS	8,441	10,205
INVESTMENTS		
Equity method investments:		
Coca-Cola Enterprises Inc.	1,312	1,731
Coca-Cola Hellenic Bottling Company S.A.	1,251	1,039
Coca-Cola FEMSA, S.A.B. de C.V.	835	982
Coca-Cola Amatil Limited	817	748
Other, principally bottling companies	2,095	2,062
Cost method investments, principally bottling companies	473	360
TOTAL INVESTMENTS	6,783	6,922
OTHER ASSETS	2,701	2,648
PROPERTY, PLANT, AND EQUIPMENT—NET	6,903	5,831
TRADEMARKS WITH INDEFINITE LIVES	2,045	1,946
GOODWILL	1,403	1,047
OTHER INTANGIBLE ASSETS	1,687	828
TOTAL ASSETS	$29,963	$29,427

TEST YOUR KNOWLEDGE: EQUITY METHOD ACCOUNTING

PepsiCo accounts for its investments in bottling operations under the equity method, and as of December 30, 2006, PepsiCo reported equity method investments of $3.69 billion on its balance sheet. Equity income on the income statement totaled $616 million, and PepsiCo received $137 million in dividends from its bottling operations during the year.

1. Assume that PepsiCo owns approximately 40% of the outstanding common stock of the affiliates. How much net income did the affiliates report for 2006?
2. What disclosure would one find in the operating section of PepsiCo's statement of cash flows?

Consolidated Financial Statements

A business acquisition occurs when an investor company acquires a controlling interest (more than 50% of the voting stock) in another company. If the two companies continue as separate legal entities, the investor company is referred to as the parent, and the investee company is called the subsidiary. In such cases, the parent prepares consolidated financial statements (including the income statement, balance sheet, statement of cash flows, and statement of owners' equity). Consolidated statements ignore the fact that the parent and the subsidiary are actually separate legal entities and, instead, treat the two companies as a single economic unit for reporting purposes.

Consolidated statements are prepared for financial reporting purposes only. The parent and the subsidiary maintain separate legal status. In many respects, they may continue to operate as relatively independent entities, and the subsidiary maintains a separate set of financial statements—perhaps following a different form of GAAP. For example, Dell Inc.'s French subsidiary may be required to follow French GAAP in its French regulatory filings. Only because the parent has a controlling interest over the subsidiary do professional accounting standards require that the financial condition of the two companies be represented to the public as one. In Dell's case, the French subsidiary's financial statements would be converted to U.S. GAAP prior to the consolidation.

A merger, or business combination, occurs when two or more companies combine to form a single legal entity. In most cases, the assets and liabilities of the smaller company are merged into those of the larger, surviving company. The stock of at least one company, usually the smaller one, is often retired, and it ceases to exist as a separate entity. Technically speaking, consolidated financial statements are not prepared after a merger because no parent/subsidiary relationship exists. At least one of the companies involved in the combination no longer exists. However, the financial statements of the surviving company reflect the assets and liabilities of the merged entities, including items that are recorded only when mergers and acquisitions occur.

Most business acquisitions and combinations consummate when cash and/or other assets (often shares) of the parent are paid to the shareholders of the subsidiary in exchange for the shares (which represent the assets and liabilities) of the subsidiary. These transactions are accounted for under the purchase method, where the assets and liabilities of the subsidiary are initially recorded on the balance sheet of the parent at FMV, and the difference between the purchase price and the net FMV of the subsidiary's identifiable assets and liabilities is recorded as goodwill.

To illustrate, assume that Mega Enterprises acquired 100% of the common voting shares of Littleton Company, whose balance sheet as of the date of the acquisition (12/31/X1) is provided below, by paying Littleton's shareholders $9,000 ($7,000 in cash and $2,000 in Mega common stock).

Littleton Enterprises Balance Sheet (12/31/X1)			
Current assets	$2,000	Current liabilities	$1,000
Noncurrent assets	4,000	Noncurrent liabilities	2,000
		Owners' equity	3,000
Total	$6,000	Total	$6,000

As you refer to Littleton's balance sheet, remember that the dollar amounts represent, for the most part, Littleton's historical costs. However, when Mega purchased all of Littleton's shares, it paid FMV for the company's equity. In other words, Mega is buying the assets and liabilities of Littleton (whether they appear on Littleton's balance sheet or not) at their FMVs.

Mega now has complete control over the assets of Littleton, and is responsible for its liabilities. Mega may choose to influence Littleton's operating, investing, and financing activities by reorganizing (possibly discontinuing) the company or allowing it to operate as a relatively independent subsidiary. In either case, accounting standards require that Littleton's assets and liabilities be consolidated with those of Mega—that is, for reporting purposes, Mega must prepare consolidated financial statements.

To prepare consolidated financial statements, Mega must first estimate what it received for its $9,000 payment to the shareholders, which can be divided into three categories: (1) the FMV of assets listed on Littleton's balance sheet; (2) the FMV of liabilities listed on Littleton's balance sheet; and (3) the FMV of assets and liabilities not listed on Littleton's financial statements (but for which Mega paid), which includes intangibles like trade names, patents, and customer lists that can be valued separately. It also includes an intangible asset called goodwill. All three categories of assets and liabilities will be used by Mega to generate returns. The $9,000 paid by Mega must be allocated across these three categories.

The first step in the allocation process is to estimate the fair market value of Littleton's assets and liabilities as of the date of the consolidation. Because accounting rules are conservative, many amounts on Littleton's balance sheet are not at FMV; rather, they are at (Littleton's) historical cost. Asset FMVs are normally appraised at a value higher than the amount indicated on the balance sheet, and as we discuss later in Chapter 9, liability FMVs can be either above or below the balance sheet value depending on the movement of interest rates since the liabilities were issued. Consequently, the balance sheet values of Littleton's assets and liabilities are not used on Mega's consolidated financial statements.

Assume that Littleton's assets and liabilities were appraised at $10,000 and $4,000, respectively. The allocation of the $9,000 payment and the effect on Mega's consolidated balance sheet would appear as below.

Allocation of $9,000 payment:

Fair market value of Littleton's assets	$10,000 (including separately identifiable intangibles)
Fair market value of Littleton's liabilities	(4,000)
Unallocated value	3,000 (this is considered the implied goodwill)
Total	$ 9,000

Effect on consolidated balance sheet:

Assets	=	Liabilities	+	Shareholders' equity
$10,000 (Littleton's assets)	=	$4,000 (Littleton's liabilities)	+	$2,000 (common stock)
3,000 (unallocated value)				
−7,000 (cash)				
$ 6,000	=		$6,000	

Overall, Mega's assets would be increased by $6,000; liabilities would be increased by $4,000; and shareholders' equity would be increased by $2,000. The liability increase equals the FMV of Littleton's liabilities because Mega is now required to pay them. The shareholders' equity increase reflects the common stock issued by Mega as partial payment for Littleton's stock. The net asset increase reflects increases due to the acquisition of Littleton's balance sheet ($10,000) and non-balance-sheet assets ($3,000), and the decrease in cash ($7,000).

MEASUREMENT CHALLENGE—ACQUISITIONS

In the case of acquisitions, an entire company is purchased and the purchase price must be allocated to the individual assets acquired and liabilities assumed. Statement of Financial Accounting Standard (SFAS) No. 141, "Business Combinations," provides guidance on the values to be assigned.

Depending on the type of asset in question, market values, appraised values, replacement values, and expected selling prices less reasonable profits are used. All of these require considerable judgment.

The $3,000 asset increase due to "unallocated value" represents Mega's payment for assets associated with Littleton's business over and above the FMV of the net assets acquired (including the identifiable intangibles) and are not reflected on Littleton's balance sheet. Mega will first determine whether there are any identifiable intangibles. Assuming that there are none, the remaining unallocated value is deemed to be goodwill.

Goodwill is a huge asset on the balance sheets of many well-known companies throughout the world—particularly companies whose growth stems from the acquisition of other companies. Figure 8-6 provides an excerpt from Pfizer's financial statements shortly after it acquired Pharmacia, a $56 billion acquisition. The residual amount is considered goodwill, which represents a substantial portion of the purchase price.

One way to view goodwill is that it represents the amount necessary (the "plug") to ensure that the acquisition is recorded in a way that maintains the balance of the accounting equation. There is, however, a more meaningful economic interpretation. Mega wanted to pay as little as possible for Littleton, and Littleton shareholders wanted Mega to pay as much as possible. After the negotiation dust settled, goodwill is the premium paid by Mega

Allocation of Pharmacia Purchase Price	
The purchase price allocation, finalized the early part of 2004, was based on an estimate of the fair value of assets acquired and liabilities assumed.	
(millions of dollars)	Amount
Book value of net assets acquire	$ 8,795
Less recorded goodwill and other intangible assets	1,559
Tangible book value of net assets acquired	7,236
Remaining allocation:	
Increase inventory to fair value	2,939
Increase long-term investments to fair value	40
Decrease property plant, and equipment to fair value	(317)
Record in-process research and level development charge	5,052
Record in-process intangible assets	37,066
Increase long-term debt to fair value	(370)
Increase benefit plan liabilities to fair value	(1,471)
Decrease other net assets to fair value	(477)
Restructuring costs	(2,182)
Tax adjustments	(12,947)
Goodwill	21,403
Purchase price	$55,972

Figure 8-6. Pfizer's Allocation of the Pharmacia Purchase Price

over and above the net FMV market value of Littleton's assets and liabilities, reflecting Mega's belief that Littleton's value to Mega exceeds the FMV of its individual assets and liabilities. Why did Mega pay $9,000 for a company that had net assets with an FMV of only $6,000 ($10,000 − $4,000)? Mega must believe that there is more to Littleton than simply its balance sheet assets and liabilities. Perhaps Mega believes that control over Littleton creates synergies that neither firm by itself was able to exploit, but together can be taken advantage of Perhaps Littleton has terrific employee or customer relations. Mega is willing to pay for that economic asset even though it is not reported as a separate intangible asset on Littleton's balance sheet. For whatever reason, Mega paid more for Littleton than simply the fair market value of its net assets, and that premium is captured on Mega's consolidated balance sheet in the goodwill account.

Consolidated income statements are, in principle, similar to consolidated balance sheets. Essentially, the revenues and expenses of the parent and subsidiaries are added together. During the year of an acquisition, only revenues and expenses from the date of acquisition onward are combined. The same is true for consolidated cash flow statements. Finally, in all consolidated financial statements, intercompany receivables and payables, revenues and expenses, and cash flows are eliminated to avoid double-counting them.

MEASUREMENT CHALLENGE—GOODWILL IMPAIRMENTS

Just because goodwill was recorded at the time of an acquisition doesn't mean that the value won't decline over time. If the synergies exist and produce benefits, the goodwill still exists. If not, the value may be impaired. Earlier, we discussed impairment expenses (charges) for tangible assets and for intangibles other than goodwill. The impairment test for goodwill, conducted at least annually, is a little different. Remember, goodwill was originally recorded as the difference between the purchase price of an acquisition and the fair value of the identifiable net assets. That is, it was a residual amount. To run the impairment test, management identifies and determines the fair value of each business unit that contains recorded goodwill and compares it to the fair value of the unit's assets and liabilities other than goodwill. The difference is "implied goodwill" of the business unit (again, a residual figure). If implied goodwill is greater than the book value (also known as the carrying value) of goodwill, then there is no impairment. If smaller, then the book value of the goodwill is written down to the implied value and an impairment charge (income statement expense) results.

BARRICK GOLD: ACQUISITION OF PLACER DOME

In their 2006 annual report, Barrick Gold Corporation provides detailed information about its acquisition of Placer Dome. It begins with a description of the transaction price, then the general principles of purchase method accounting. It follows with details of the valuation bases used to allocate the purchase price, and finally, Barrick Gold presents the allocation.

Accounting for the Placer Dome Acquisition
The Placer Dome acquisition has been accounted for as a purchase business combination, with Barrick as the account-

ing acquirer. We acquired Placer Dome on January 20, 2006, with the results of operations of Placer Dome consolidated from January 20, 2006, onward. The purchase cost was $10 billion and was funded through a combination of common shares issued, the drawdown of a $1 billion credit facility, and cash resources.

(*continues*)

BARRICK GOLD: ACQUISITION OF PLACER DOME (*continued*)

Value of 322.8 million Barrick common shares issued at $27.14 per share[1]	$ 8,761
Value of 2.7 million fully vested stock options	22
Cash	1,239
Transaction costs	32
	$10,054

1. The measurement of the common share component of the purchase consideration represents the average closing price on the New York Stock Exchange for the two days prior to and two days after the public announcement on December 22, 2005, of our final offer for Placer Dome.

In accordance with the purchase method of accounting, the purchase cost was allocated to the underlying assets acquired and liabilities assumed, based primarily on their estimated fair values at the date of acquisition. The estimated fair values were based on a combination of independent appraisals and internal estimates. We concluded that the excess of purchase cost over the net identifiable tangible and intangible assets acquired represents goodwill. Goodwill arising on the acquisition of Placer Dome principally represents the ability of the company to continue as a going concern by finding new mineral reserves, as well as the value of synergies that we expect to realize as a direct consequence of the acquisition of Placer Dome.

The principal valuation methods for major classes of assets and liabilities were:

Inventory	Finished goods and work in process valued at estimated selling prices less disposal costs, costs to complete, and a reasonable profit allowance for the completing and selling effort.
Building and equipment	Reproduction and/or replacement cost or market value for current function and service potential, adjusted for physical, functional, and economic obsolescence.
Proven and probable reserves and value beyond proven and probable reserves at producing mines	Multi-period excess earnings approach considering the prospective level of cash flows and fair value of other assets at each mine.
Development projects	Discounted future cash flows considering the prospective level of cash flows from future operations and necessary capital cost expenditures.
Exploration properties	Appraised values considering costs incurred, earn-in agreements, and comparable market transactions, where applicable.
Intangible assets	Value based on potential cost savings, price differential, discounted future cash flows, or comparable market transactions, as applicable.
Long-term debt and derivative instruments	Estimated fair values consistent with the methods disclosed in Note 19d.
Asset retirement obligations	Estimated fair values consistent with the methods disclosed in Note 20.

Summary Purchase Price Allocation

Cash	$ 1,102
Inventories	428
Other current assets	198
Property, plant, and equipment	
Buildings, plant, and equipment	2,946
Proven and probable reserves	1,571
Value beyond proven and probable reserves	419
Intangible assets (Note 15)	85
Assets of discontinued operations[1]	1,744
Other assets	347
Goodwill	6,506
Total assets	15,346
Current liabilities	669
Liabilities of discontinued operations[1]	107
Derivative instrument liabilities	1,729
Long-term debt	1,252
Asset retirement obligations	387
Deferred income tax liabilities	686
Total liabilities	4,830
Noncontrolling interests	462
Net assets acquired	$ 10,054

1. Includes operations that were sold to Goldcorp.

Severance Costs

Amounts recorded at acquistion	$ 48
Settlements in 2006	45
Amounts outstanding at December 31, 2006	$ 3

At acquistion, we recorded liabilities totaling $48 million that primarily relate to employee severance at Placer Dome offices that were closed during the year. We expect to pay all the outstanding amounts by second quarter 2007.

	2006	2005	2004
Operating Activities:			
Net income	$ 5,642	$ 4,078	$ 4,212
Depreciation and amortization	1,406	1,308	1,264
Restructuring and impairment charges	–	–	150
Bottling equity income, net of dividends	(479)	(411)	(297)
Other (net)	(485)	877	(275)
Net cash provided by operating activities	$ 6,084	$ 5,852	$ 5,054
Investing Activities:			
Capital spending	$(2,068)	$(2,486)	$(1,387)
Sales of property, plant, and equipment	49	88	38
Acquisitions and investments in noncontrolled affiliates	(522)	(345)	(64)
Cash proceeds from divestitures	355	217	52
Short-term investments:			
Purchases	(29)	(1,075)	(1,007)
Sales and maturities	2,046	84	38
Other	(25)		
Net cash used for investing activities	$ (194)	$(3,517)	$(2,330)

Figure 8-7. PepsiCo, Inc., and Subsidiaries Statement of Cash Flows (excerpts) (dollars in millions)

▶ INVESTING ACTIVITIES AND THE STATEMENT OF CASH FLOWS

Figure 8-7 includes excerpts from the statement of cash flows published by PepsiCo, Inc., as of December 31, 2006. In the operating section, depreciation and amortization are added back to net income in the computation of net cash provided by operating activities because they represent net income reducing expenses that involved no cash outflow. The $150 million add-back due to "restructuring and impairment charges" in 2004 is similar—an expense that involved no cash outflow. The subtracted dollar amounts associated with "bottling equity income, net of dividends" is the opposite phenomenon. Here, income recorded under the equity method increased net income, but the only cash inflow was associated with the dividends received from the bottling affiliates. As indicated on the statement, equity income exceeded dividends paid by the affiliates by $1.187 billion ($479 + $411 + $297) over the three-year period.

The investing section reports that PepsiCo spent almost $6 billion over the three-year period on capital expenditures, primarily property, plant, and equipment, and a little over $900 million on acquiring—and establishing a significant influence (noncontrolled affiliates) in—other companies. PepsiCo also sold a relatively small amount of property, plant, and equipment over the three-year period, and collected cash by divesting itself of (selling) significant investments, particularly in 2005 ($217 million) and 2006 ($355 million). It appears that PepsiCo also maintains a fairly large portfolio of short-term investments—having built it in 2004 and 2005 with sizable purchases (approximately $2 billion), and liquidating much of it (more than $2 billion) in 2006. Finally, the amount of cash generated by PepsiCo over the three-year period (almost $17 billion) far exceeded the amount of cash necessary to maintain its investing activities (slightly more than $6 billion). We see in the next chapter that over the three-year period, PepsiCo returned almost $14 billion to its shareholders through treasury stock purchases and dividends.

▶ SUMMARY

In this chapter, we covered investments in producing assets (fixed assets, natural resource costs, and intangible assets) and the equity securities of other companies. We discussed how these investments are reflected in the financial statements and how they should be managed to create shareholder value.

All costs incurred to prepare a producing asset for service are capitalized (treated as an asset on the balance sheet), and then the capitalized cost is periodically converted to expense (depreciation or amortization) over the useful life of the producing asset, if the useful life can be determined. If a producing asset is judged to be "impaired," its balance sheet value is reduced to its market value through an impairment charge, a noncash expense reflected on the income statement.

Short-term equity investments are carried on the balance sheet at market value, and if classified as "trading" securities, changes in market value are reflected on the income statement. If classified as "available-for-sale" securities, the income statement is not affected until the securities are sold. Long-term equity investments are accounted for under the equity method, where income and dividends recorded by the affiliate are reflected in the financial statements of the investor company, if the investment is large enough (e.g., 20%–50%) to constitute a "significant influence" over the affiliate. If the investment leads to "control" (e.g., more than 50%), the financial statements of the subsidiary are consolidated with those of the parent; if the parent paid a premium over and above the FMV of the subsidiary's net assets for the equity shares, goodwill is recognized on the consolidated balance sheet. Like other producing assets, goodwill is subject to an annual impairment test.

To create shareholder value, these investments must be managed to provide returns that exceed the costs of financing them. Key ratios constructed from accounting numbers indicating how well these investments are being managed include producing asset turnover (Sales / Average producing assets) and noncurrent asset turnover (Sales / Average noncurrent assets). These ratios directly affect total asset turnover (Sales / Average total assets). In addition, depreciation, amortization, and impairment charges associated with producing assets, as well as the income effects from short- and long-term equity investments, directly affect profit margins (return on sales). Finally, investment returns can be compared to the investment balance (Investment income / Average investments). Recall that total asset turnover multiplied by profit margin equals the ROA, which, in turn, drives the ROE—the key to value creation.

▶ CASES AND REVIEW QUESTIONS

Manchester United PLC—Investments in Players

Excerpts from the Manchester United PLC financial statements are presented on the following pages. The Manchester United football (soccer) club is one of the most well-known brands in the world of sports. One of its most important assets is its employees and, unlike most other companies, those players appear on the company's balance sheet as assets.

1. Based on your review of the accompanying financial statement excerpts, why does Manchester United carry football players on its balance sheet? Where do other player-related costs appear on the consolidated balance sheet?

2. Where does the cost of fielding a team appear on the company's income statement (consolidated profit and loss account)? That is, where do the player costs appear? Where do they appear on the consolidated cash flow statement?

3. Refer to Note 11a. Analyze the change in the balance of the net intangible assets balance. In doing so, explain how the gross intangibles balance changed, as well as the amortisation account (this account is akin to "accumulated amortization").

4. Refer to Notes 11b and 11c. These notes refer to individual players.
   a. Explain why homegrown players are reported on the balance sheet at a value of zero, despite being players on the "first team."
   b. Heinze was acquired from French club Paris Saint Germain. How much did Manchester United pay the French club for this player?
   c. How much amortization is attributable to Heinze in fiscal 2004? Estimate the amount for fiscal 2005.
   d. What are "unrecognized conditional assets and liabilities"? Where do they appear on the Manchester United balance sheets?

5. Note 11 refers several times to "transfer of asset held for resale." Note 31 explains this in more detail. Describe the nature of the event in question. What is the effect of the event on the balance sheet and income statement?

Manchester United Plc.
Consolidated profit and loss account (for the year ended 31 July 2004)

	Note	2004 £'000	2003 £'000
Turnover: Group and share of joint venture		**171,500**	174,936
Less share of joint venture		**(2,420)**	(1,935)
Group turnover	2	**169,080**	173,001
Operating expenses—other	3	**(139,170)**	(144,033)
Operating expenses—exceptional costs	4	**–**	(2,197)
Total operating expenses		**(139,170)**	(146,230)
Group operating profit before depreciation and amortisation of intangible fixed assets		**58,340**	55,072
Depreciation		**(6,591)**	(7,283)
Amortisation		**(21,839)**	(21,018)
Group operating profit		**29,910**	26,771
Share of operating loss in:			
—Joint venture		**(147)**	(407)
—Associates		**(11)**	(47)
Total operating profit: Group and share of joint venture and associates		**29,752**	26,317
Profit on disposal of associate		**173**	409
(Loss)/profit on disposal of players	11c	**(3,084)**	12,935
Profit before interest and taxation		**26,841**	39,661
Net interest receivable/(payable)	5	**1,066**	(316)
Profit on ordinary activities before taxation		**27,907**	39,345
Taxation	7	**(8,486)**	(9,564)
Profit for the year		**19,421**	29,781
Dividends	9	**(6,974)**	(10,391)
Retained profit for the year	23	**12,447**	19,390
Basic and diluted earnings per share (pence)	10	**7.4**	11.5
Basic and diluted adjusted earnings per share (pence)	10	**14.1**	14.3

Statement of total recognised gains and losses

	2004 £'000	2003 £'000
Profit for the financial year	**19,421**	29,781
Share of increase in joint venture reserves (Note 23)	**100**	–
Credit in relation to long-term incentive awards	**265**	208
Consideration paid for purchase of shares held by ESOP trust	**(231)**	(623)
Profit for the year and total recognised gains and losses in the year	**19,655**	29,366
Prior year adjustment (Note 1)	**(415)**	
Total gains recognised since last annual report	**19,240**	

The results for both the current and prior period derive from continuing activities.
The accompanying notes on pages 59 to 78 are an integral part of these financial statements.

Consolidated balance sheet (at 31 July 2004)

	Note	2004 £'000	2003 £'000 Restated (Note 1)
Fixed assets			
Intangible assets	11	78,233	55,299
Tangible assets	12	125,093	125,526
Loan to joint venture	13	1,000	1,000
Investment in associate	13	178	189
		204,504	182,014
Current assets			
Stocks	14	216	208
Debtors—amounts falling due within one year	15	39,487	30,756
Debtors—amounts falling due after more than one year	15	1,760	13,219
Intangible asset held for resale	31	1,382	11,941
Cash at bank and in hand		36,048	28,576
		78,893	84,700
Creditors—amounts falling due within one year	16	(44,635)	(50,202)
Net current assets		34,258	34,498
Total assets less current liabilities		238,762	216,512
Creditors—amounts falling due after one year	17	(8,795)	(2,391)
Provision for liabilities and charges			
Deferred taxation	19	(5,330)	(5,506)
Other provisions	19	(1,550)	–
Investment in joint venture:	19		
—Share of gross assets		260	375
—Share of gross liabilities		(4,760)	(4,641)
		(4,500)	(4,266)
Accruals and deferred income			
Deferred grant income	20	(856)	(1,011)
Other deferred income	21	(44,377)	(46,920)
Net assets		173,354	156,418
Capital and reserves			
Share capital	22	26,219	25,977
Share premium account	23	4,013	–
Other reserves	23	600	500
Profit and loss account	23	142,522	129,941
Equity Shareholders' funds	24	173,354	156,418

Consolidated cash flow statement (for the year ended 31 July 2004)

	Note	2004 £'000	2004 £'000	2003 £'000	2003 £'000
Net cash inflow from operating activities			58,769		57,939
Returns on investments and servicing of finance					
Interest received		1,169		316	
Interest paid		(112)		(167)	
Net cash inflow from returns on investments and servicing of finance			1,057		149
Taxation paid			(11,052)		(10,602)
Capital expenditure and financial investment					
Net proceeds from sale of players' registrations	11c	16,009		11,122	
Purchase of players' registrations	11c	(44,813)		(18,983)	
Proceeds from sale of tangible fixed assets		2,154		2,235	
Purchase of tangible fixed assets		(6,922)		(6,425)	
Net cash outflow from capital expenditure and financial investment			(33,572)		(12,051)
Acquisitions and disposals					
Proceeds from sale of investment in associated company		173		962	
Net cash inflow from acquisitions and disposals			173		962
Equity dividends paid			(11,927)		(8,131)
Cash Inflow before management of liquid resources and financing			3,448		28,266
Financing					
Issue of ordinary share capital		4,255		–	
Purchase of shares held through ESOP trust		(231)		(623)	
Net cash inflow/(outflow) from financing			4,024		(623)
Increase in cash in the year	25		7,472		27,643

Note to consolidated cash flow statement (for the year ended 31 July 2004)

Reconciliation of operating profit to net cash inflow from operating activities

	2004 £'000	2003 £'000
Net cash generated from operating activities		
Group operating profit	29,910	26,771
Depreciation charges	6,591	7,283
Amortisation of players' registrations	21,839	21,018
Credit in relation to long-term incentive awards	365	208
Profit on disposal of tangible fixed assets	(275)	(691)
Grants released	(155)	(183)
Increase in stocks	(8)	(12)
Increase in debtors	(285)	(5,357)
Increase in creditors and deferred income	787	8,902
Net cash inflow from operating activities	58,769	57,939

The accompanying notes on pages 59 to 78 are an integral part of these financial statements.

Financial statements
Notes to the financial statements (continued)

1 Accounting policies continued

Intangible fixed assets
The costs associated with the acquisition of players' registrations are capitalised as intangible fixed assets. These costs are fully amortised over the period covered by the player's initial contract.

Where a playing contract is extended, any costs associated with securing the extension are added to the unamortised balance at the date of the amendment and that book value is amortised over the remaining revised contract life.

Where a part of the consideration payable on acquiring a players registration is contingent on a future event, this amount is recognised once it is probable, rather than possible, that the event will occur and is amortised from the start of the year in which the contingent payment becomes probable. The total amount which is currently considered possible, but not probable, is disclosed in Note 28b.

Signing-on fees
Staff costs include signing-on fees payable to players representing part of their remuneration that are charged to the profit and loss account evenly over the period covered by the player's contract.

3 Operating expenses—other

	2004 £'000	2003 £'000
Operations excluding player amortisation and trading:		
Staff costs (Note 6)	76,874	79,517
Depreciation	6,591	7,283
Operating lease costs—land and buildings	1,169	754
Other operating charges	32,897	36,118
Auditors' remuneration: Audit services	81	60
Auditors' remuneration: Non-audit services	149	157
Grants released (Note 20)	(155)	(183)
Profit on disposal of tangible fixed assets	(275)	(691)
	117,331	123,015
Player amortisation and trading:		
Amortisation of players' registrations	21,839	21,018
	139,170	144,033
Auditors' remuneration for non-audit services comprised:		
Taxation advice	149	155
Taxation advice charged to loss on disposal of players	17	–
Other	–	2
	166	157

6 Staff Costs

The average number of employees during the year, including directors, was as follows:

	2004 Number	2003 Number
Players	69	68
Ground staff	90	90
Ticket office and membership	47	44
Catering	108	109
Administration and other	190	182
Average number of employees	504	493

The group also employs approximately 1,292 temporary staff on match (days (2003: 1, 330).
Particulars of employee costs, including directors, are as shown below:

	2004 £'000	2003 £'000
Wages and salaries	61,456	64,691
Bonuses	4,966	4,990
Social security costs	8,425	7,867
Other pension costs	2,027	1,969
	76,874	79,517

Details of directors' remuneration, together with interest in shares and share options, are given in the remuneration report on pages 46 to 52.

11 Intangible fixed assets

a)

Group	Transfer fee to other clubs £'000	Agents fees £'000	FAPL levy (net of refunds) £'000	Other costs £'000	Total £'000
Cost of players' registrations					
At 1 August 2003	80,229	6,060	2,528	482	89,299
Additions	44,008	5,501	1,122	17	50,648
Disposals	(7,049)	(400)	(352)	–	(7,801)
Transfer to asset held for resale	(6,471)	(730)	(157)	(10)	(7,368)
At 31 July 2004	**110,717**	**10,431**	**3,141**	**489**	**124,778**
Amortisation of players' registrations					
At 1 August 2003					34,000
Charge for the year					21,839
Provision for loss on disposal					1,893
Disposal					(5,201)
Transfer to asset held for resale					(5,986)
At 31 July 2004					46,545
Net book value of players' registrations					
At 31 July 2004					78,233
At 31 July 2003					55,299

11 Intangible fixed assets (continued)

b) Individual player contract status and asset values

Player	Date first contract commenced	Current contract expiry date	Cost 31.07.04 £'000	Charge in 2003/4 £'000	NBV 31.07.04 £'000	In creditors 31.07.04 £'000	Contingent payables[1] £'000
Acquired Players							
Bellion	Jul-03	Jun-07	2,812	703	2,109	100	–
Carroll	Jul-01	Jun-05	3,386	978	978	–	–
Djemba Djemba	Jul-03	Jun-08	3,456	691	2,765	175	665
Ferdinand	Jul-02	Jun-07	31,120	6,300	18,899	300	–
Fortune	Aug-99	Jun-06	1,575	31	60	–	–
Heinze	Jul-04	Jun-09	6,807	116	6,692	2,878	–
Howard	Jul-03	Jun-07	2,258	565	1,694	–	262
Keane	Jul-93	Jun-06	3,750	–	–	–	–
Kleberson	Aug-03	Jun-08	5,795	1,150	4,645	400	–
Lopez	Aug-02	Jun-05	1,498	499	499	–	–
Ronaldo	Aug-03	Jun-08	11,959	2,373	9,586	7,058	–
Saha	Jan-04	Jun-09	12,515	1,198	11,317	–	–
Silvestre	Sep-99	Jun-07	4,340	141	410	–	–
Smith	May-04	Jun-09	7,050	250	6,800	500	–
Solskjaer	Jul-96	Jun-06	1,500	–	–	–	–
Van Nistelrooy	Jul-01	Jun-08	19,791	3,023	9,333	1,339	–
Others (cost < £1m)			5,166	884	2,446	566	8,169
			124,778	**18,902**	**78,233**	**13,316**	**9,096**
Home-grown players[2]							
Brown		Jun-05	–	–	–	–	–
Fletcher		Jun-07	–	–	–	–	–
Giggs		Jun-06	–	–	–	–	–
Neville G		Jun-09	–	–	–	–	–
Neville P		Jun-09	–	–	–	–	–
O'Shea		Jun-06	–	–	–	–	–
Scholes		Jun-07	–	–	–	–	–
Disposals in the year							
Barthez			–	1,300	–	–	–
Forlan			–	1,637	–	186	–
			124,778	**21,839**	**78,233**	**13,502**	**9,096**

Notes:
[1] Contingent assets and liabilities are conditional upon playing appearances, new playing contracts or team performance (of either MUFC in relation to acquisitions or the buying club in relation to disposals). The conditional assets are recognised when all the conditions have been fulfilled; conditional liabilities are recognised once the payment becomes probable rather than possible.
[2] Players in first team squad at 31.07.04.

11 Intangible fixed assets (continued)

c) Player registration trading summary

Player registration disposals during the year

Player	Sale to Club	Unconditional proceeds receivable £'000	Conditional proceeds receivable £'000	NBV £'000	Other £'000	Profit and loss for year £'000	Cash flow in year £'000	Outstanding unconditional debtor £'000	Unrecognised conditional assets[1] £'000
Transfers out—prior years									
Beckham	Real Madrid	–	855	–	29	884	11,930	–	5,833
Cole	Blackburn Rovers	–	200	–	–	200	200	–	–
Stam	S.S. Lazio	–	–	–	–	–	–	12,000	–
Yorke	Blackburn Rovers	–	600	–	–	600	600	–	–
Others		–	–	–	368	368	181	150	–
Transfers out—current year									
Butt	Newcastle United	2,000	–	–	(500)	1,500	(250)	2,000	–
Veron	Chelsea	–	750	–	–	750	5,872	6,250	1,250
Contract terminations									
Barthez	Termination	–	–	(2,600)	(2,563)	(5,163)	(2,474)	–	–
Chadwick	Termination	–	–	–	(300)	(330)	(50)	–	–
Forlan	Provision for loss on disposal	–	–	(1,893)	–	(1,893)	–	–	–
		2,000	**2,405**	**(4,493)**	**(2,996)**	**(3,084)**	**16,009**	**20,400**	**7,083**

Player registration acquisition during the year

Player	From Club	Unconditional transfer fee £'000	Conditional transfer fees paid/ payable £'000	Agents fees £'000	FAPL Levy £'000	Other £'000	Total capitalised £'000	Cash flow in year £'000	Outstanding unconditional creditor £'000	Unrecognised conditional liability[1] £'000
Transfers In—prior years										
Bellion	Sunderland	500	200	–	(22)	–	678	2,303	100	–
Carroll	Wigan Athletic	–	500	–	25	–	525	525	–	–
Djemba Djemba	FC Nantes Atlantique	–	–	–	(84)	–	(84)	3,125	175	665
Ferdinand	Leeds United	–	1,500	–	14	–	1,514	2,339	300	–
Howard	Major League Soccer	–	–	–	(40)	–	(40)	702	–	262
Steele	Peterborough	–	400	–	9	–	409	409	–	–
Van Nistelrooy	PSV Eindhoven	–	–	1,202	–	–	1,202	331	1,339	–
Others (cost <£1m)		–	–	–	–	–	–	107	186	5,973
Transfer in—current year										
Heinze	Paris Saint Germain	5,983	–	525	299	–	6,807	3,929	2,878	–
Kleberson	Club Atletico Paranaense	5,000	–	680	115	–	5,795	5,395	400	–
Ronaldo	Sporting Lisbon	10,587	–	1,129	243	–	11,959	4,901	7,058	–
Saha	Fulham	11,500	–	750	265	–	12,515	12,515	–	–
Smith	Leeds United	6,000	–	750	300	–	7,050	6,550	500	–
Others (cost <£1m)		1,838	–	465	(2)	17	2,318	1,682	566	2,196
		41,408	**2,600**	**5,501**	**1,122**	**17**	**50,648**	**44,813**	**13,502**	**9,096**

[1] Contingent assets and liabilities are conditional upon playing appearances, new playing contracts or team performance (of either MUFC in relation to acquisitions or the buying club in relation to disposals). The conditional assets are recognised when all the conditions have been fulfilled; conditional liabilities are recognised once the payment becomes probable rather than possible.

11 Intangible fixed assets (continued)

d) Payments to agents during the year

Player	Agents payments creditor at 31.07.03 £'000	Agents payments capitalised to intangibles in the year £'000	Agents payments on disposals in the year £'000	Agents payments charged to P&L in the year £'000	Agents fees	
					Paid in year to 31.07.04 £'000	In creditors at 31.07.04 £'000
Djemba Djemba	350	–	–	–	175	175
Ferdinand	1,125	–	–	–	825	300
Fletcher[1]	–	–	–	100	100	–
Forlan	293	–	–	–	107	186
Heinze	–	525	–	–	100	425
Kleberson	–	680	–	–	280	400
Lopez	–	–	–	55	55	–
Miller	–	100	–	–	100	–
Pique	–	149	–	–	–	149
Ronaldo	–	1,129	–	–	1,129	–
Rossi	–	33	–	–	–	33
Saha	–	750	–	–	750	–
Silvestre	–	–	–	84	84	–
Smith	–	750	–	–	250	500
Van Nistelrooy	468	1,202	–	–	331	1,339
Veron	–	–	500	–	500	–
Others	74	183	–	–	245	12
	2,310	5,501	500	239	5,031	3,519

(1) Darren Fletcher was represented by Francis Martin who was a Director of Elite Sports Group Limited.

31 Post balance sheet events

Subsequent to the balance sheet date, the playing registration of Wayne Rooney has been acquired from Everton Football Club. The unconditional acquisition cost is £22,000,000, of which £10,500,000 is due after more than one year. Further conditional costs of £7,850,000 are payable dependent on Manchester United team success, the player signing a new contract, and international appearances by the player. Of this conditional amount, £3 million is guaranteed to Everton if the player stays with Manchester United until June 2007.

Further analysis is shown below:

	Transfer fee £'000's	Agent's fee £'000's	FAPL Levy £'000's	Total £'000's
Unconditional cost	20,000	1,000	1,000	22,000
Conditional cost	7,000	500	350	7,850
Total	27,000	1,500	1,350	29,850

The playing registration of Diego Forlan has been disposed of for a total consideration, net of associated costs, of £1,382,000. The associated net book value of the playing registration at 31 July 2004 was £3,275,000. As the transaction was in progress at the balance sheet date, a provision for the loss on disposal of £1,893,000 has been included in these accounts. The revised carrying value of the registration of £1,382,000 has been transferred from intangible fixed assets (Note 11) and reclassified as an intangible asset held for resale.

Italian Soccer Accounting—Depreciating Players and Amortizing Rights

Several short news articles follow. They describe a special law passed by the Italian government aimed at helping professional sports clubs in Italy appear more profitable. The law permits the amortization of player contracts over periods of up to 10 years.

1. Based on your reading of the articles, why is the 'Football Savior' law controversial?

2. What is meant by a 'true and fair view' of a company's financial position and results of operations? Why does this law violate that view?

3. Speculate on why European Union officials are stepping in over accounting matters.

4. A July 12, 2004, news article reported on EurActiv.com noted, "From next season, there will be a new UEFA [the European governing body for soccer] club licensing system, whereby clubs must meet various criteria to be eligible for UEFA's lucrative cup competitions. Many clubs are expected to struggle to meet some of the financial criteria." How might this affect the Italian government's interest in passing accounting laws?

5. Assume that you were analyzing the financial statements of Italian soccer powerhouse Juventus. If Juventus used the rules permitted under the "Football Savior" law, what changes would you make to their financial statements in order to obtain a clearer picture of the company's financial position and results of operations?

The Political Econnomy of Football

EU May Veto Italy's "Saviour" Law—6/11/03

The EU is threatening to veto Italy's so-called "saviour" law, which has helped to keep many cash-strapped football clubs afloat. It permits clubs to amortise the costs of player contracts over 10 years rather than the shorter life of the contracts. It now seems likely that Mario Monti and Fritz Bolkenstein, the EU competition and tax policy commissioners, respectively, are going to open formal investigations into the law. Mr. Monti is expected to find that the law violates EU state aid rules, while Mr. Bolkenstein is expected to rule that the accounting change violates EU and international norms. A final decision could be taken next Spring and according to the Financial Times could 'unmask the unusually incestuous relationships in Italy among owners, bankers, players, agents, and politicians.'

The prospect of EU action has sent many of Italy's football club owners into a panic. Rio Semeraro, president of Serie A club Lecce, claimed that 'It would be the bankruptcy of Italian football,' although others might think that it would be a much-needed wake-up call. Without the saviour law, AC Milan would have doubled its recently announced operating loss of €29.5m. Rome clubs Roma and Lazio each had losses topping €100m despite the law saving them tens of millions of euros. Both clubs have relied on backing from Capitalia, the Rome-based bank with political ties. Both teams have not paid full state taxes in years and owe players many months of back pay. Even Parma lost €35m.

The fact of the matter is that losses have been mounting for years, the result of rising salaries not matched by gate receipts or television income. Club owners have either ignored the problem or resorted to questionable financial and accounting methods, hence the saviour law. The day of reckoning may be at hand.

http://www.footballeconomy.com/archive/archive_2003_nov_06.htm

Press Releases

Commission asks Italy to change its rules on accounting by professional sports clubs ('Salva calcio')

Brussels, 7 July 2004

The European Commission has decided to ask Italy formally to change its "Salva-Calcio" law on financial reporting by professional sports clubs, including Serie A football clubs. The Commission believes that the legislation breaches EU accounting laws in that the balance sheets of a number of sport clubs fail to provide a true and fair view. The Commission's request takes the form of a "reasoned opinion," the second stage of EC Treaty infringement procedures (Article 226). Unless a satisfactory response is received within two months, the Commission may refer the case to the Court of Justice.

The effect of the February 2003 "Salva-Calcio" Act is that some professional sports clubs, especially major football clubs for which players' contracts are the biggest item of expenditure, may be able to submit accounts that underestimate their true costs in a given year, hide real losses, and give a misleading picture to investors.

In technical terms, the "Salva-Calcio" Act allows sports clubs to place in a special balance sheet item under assets, the capital losses arising from the decreased value of the rights to exploit the performances of professional players, as determined on the basis of a sworn expert valuation. This item is accounted for among the assets in the balance sheet and amortised. The "Salva-Calcio" Act specifies that companies opting for the special rules introduced by the Act, must proceed, for accounting and fiscal purposes, to amortise the balance sheet item in 10 yearly charges of equal amount, even if rights established by contracts with the players concerned last for, say, only two or three years.

The 4th (78/660/EEC) and 7th (83/349/EEC) Council Directives (Accounting Directives) on companies' annual and consolidated accounts require athletes' contracts, where treated as intangible assets, to be written off over their useful economic life, which generally would be the term of those contracts. The contract may not be written off over a longer period than the duration of the contract itself. In addition, the Accounting Directives provide that value attributed to fixed assets must be adjusted downwards to their real value on the balance sheet date if it is expected that the reduction in their value will be permanent. The Directives also set out the fundamental principle that financial statements should show a true and fair view of the companies' assets, liabilities, financial position, and profit or loss.

Therefore, the Commission believes that the "Salva-Calcio" Act breaches the Accounting Directives by allowing a number of athletes' contracts to be written off over a longer period than their useful economic life and by allowing sports clubs not to make value adjustments in respect of their contractual rights over professional athletes, even if those athletes have ceased to perform at the level expected from them, for example, through injury. Financial statements presented in such a manner cannot show a true and fair view and so depart from the "prudence principle" of the 4th Directive.

Though the Italian authorities have underlined that the "Salva-Calcio" Act was conceived as a "one off" measure, the Commission notes that it continues to affect the accounts of the sports clubs in question and that no measure has been up to now taken by the Italian authorities to put an end to these effects. In these circumstances, the Act is still in breach of the EU Accounting Directives.

http://europa.eu.int/rapid/pressReleasesAction.do?reference=IP/04/854&format=HTML&aged=0&language=EN&guiLanguage=en

Advanced Micro Devices and Intel—Fixed Asset Turnover

Advance Micro Devices, Inc., and Intel Corporation are two of the world's leaders in the design and manufacture of semiconductors. The two companies are fierce competitors. Currently, both own a number of chip fabs, where they produce their products. Intel is known for its leading-edge manufacturing capabilities. AMD, over the years, has stumbled in the manufacturing arena. Recent rumors suggested that AMD was considering a move to fabless. That is, they would concentrate on design and outsource production to sophisticated chip foundries.

1. What are the risks and benefits associated with owning semiconductor manufacturing facilities? How do they differ from the risks and benefits of a fabless strategy?

2. Perform an analysis of each company's ROE for 2005 and 2006, decomposing the measure using the following version of the DuPont model:

$$\text{ROE} = \frac{\text{Net income}}{\text{Common equity}} = \frac{\text{NI} + \text{Interest expense}}{\text{Sales}} \times \frac{\text{Sales}}{\text{Assets}} \times \frac{\text{Assets}}{\text{Common equity}} \times \frac{\text{NI}}{\text{NI} + \text{Interest expense}}$$

Which company is creating more value for its shareholders? How is that value being created? That is, explain how the elements of ROE differ across the entities.

3. Calculate the fixed-asset turnover ratio for each company. Which company is more efficient from an asset management perspective?

4. Each company's accounting policy for property and equipment is reproduced following their financial statements.
   a. Which company appears to be more conservative in their accounting policy?
   b. Use information from the notes and the balance sheets to estimate 2007 depreciation at AMD and Intel.
   c. By how much would your estimate of AMD's depreciation change if they followed Intel's depreciation policies? How would that affect ROE and its components?

5. If AMD were to go fabless, how would their financial statements change? Based on your answer, recalculate the company's ROE and its components for 2006. Assume that they had always been fabless.

Hints and Helps

AMD: In determining ROE to the shareholders, focuses on profits attributable to shareholders and total equity without minority interest. Consider minority interest on the balance sheet as a form of 'quasi-debt' and the minority interest on the income statement as a form of interest.
Intel and AMD: To get the most out of the data, use ending balance sheet values in lieu of averages.

Advanced Micro Devices, Inc., and Subsidiaries
Consolidated Statements of Operations

Three Years Ended December 31, 2006

	2006	2005	2004
	(in millions, except per share amounts)		
Net revenue	$5,649	$4,972	$3,924
Net revenue to related party (see Note 5)	–	876	1,077
Total net revenue	5,649	5,848	5,001
Cost of sales	2,856	3,456	3,033
Gross margin	2,793	2,392	1,968
Research and development	1,205	1,144	934
Marketing, general, and administrative	1,140	1,016	812
In-process research and development	416	–	–
Amortization of acquired intangible assets and integration charges	79	–	–
Operating income (loss)	(47)	232	222
Interest income	116	37	18
Interest expense	(126)	(105)	(112)
Other income (expense). net	(13)	(24)	(49)
Income (loss) before minority interest, equity in net loss of Spansion, Inc., and others and income taxes	(70)	140	79
Minority interest in consolidated subsidiaries	(28)	125	18
Equity in net loss of Spansion, Inc., and others (see Note 4)	(45)	(107)	–
Income (loss) before income taxes	(143)	158	97
Provision (benefit) for income taxes	23	(7)	6
Net income (loss)	$ (166)	$ 165	$ 91
Net income (loss) per common share:			
Basic	$ (0.34)	$ 0.41	$ 0.25
Diluted	$ (0.34)	$ 0.40	$ 0.25
Shares used in per share calculation:			
Basic	492	400	359
Diluted	492	441	371

Advanced Micro Devices, Inc., and Subsidiaries
Consolidated Balance Sheets

	December 31, 2006	December 25, 2005
	(in millions, except par value amounts)	
ASSETS		
Current assets:		
Cash and cash equivalents..	$ 1,380	$ 633
Marketable securities	161	1,003
Spansion senior subordinated notes (see Note 4)...............................	–	159
Total cash and cash equivalents and marketable securities.......................	1,541	1,795
Accounts receivable	1,153	818
Allowance for doubtful accounts..	(13)	(13)
Total accounts receivable, net	1,140	805
Inventories:		
Raw materials..	83	18
Work-in-process	545	225
Finished goods..	186	146
Total inventories	814	389
Deferred income taxes	25	93
Prepaid expenses and other current assets......................................	433	334
Receivable from Spansion (see Note 5)...	10	143
Total current assets	3,963	3,559
Property, plant, and equipment:		
Land and land improvements..	53	29
Buildings and leasehold improvements..	1,410	1,028
Equipment	5,202	3,310
Construction in progress...	672	1,121
Total property, plant, and equipment..	7,337	5,488
Accumulated depreciation and amortization......................................	(3,350)	(2,787)
Property, plant, and equipment, net...	3,987	2,701
Acquisition-related intangible assets, net (see Note 3)............................	1,207	–
Goodwill (see Note 3)...	3,217	–
Receivable from Spansion (see Note 5)	5	3
Investment in Spansion (see Note 4)...	371	721
Other assets..	397	304
Total assets	$13,147	$7,288

Advanced Micro Devices, Inc., and Subsidiaries
Consolidated Balance Sheets (continued)

	December 31, 2006	December 25, 2005
	(in millions, except par value amounts)	
LIABILITIES AND STOCKHOLDERS' EQUITY		
Current liabilities:		
Accounts payable	$ 1,336	$ 623
Accounts payable to Spansion (see Note 5)	2	233
Accrued compensation and benefits	177	227
Accrued liabilities	716	389
Income taxes payable	78	3
Deferred income on shipments to distributors	169	142
Current portion of long-term debt and capital lease obligations	125	43
Other current liabilities	249	162
Total current liabilities	2,852	1,822
Deferred income taxes	31	93
Long-term debt and capital lease obligations less current portion	3,672	1,327
Other long-term liabilities	517	459
Minority interest in consolidated subsidiaries	290	235
Commitments and contingencies (see Notes 14 and 17)		
Stockholders' equity:		
Capital stock:		
Common stock, par value $0.01; 750 shares authorized: shares issued: 553 on December 31, 2006, and 442 on December 25, 2005; shares outstanding: 547 on December 31, 2006, and 436 on December 25, 2005	5	4
Capital in excess of par value	5,409	2,800
Treasury stock, at cost (7 shares on December 31, 2006, and December 25, 2005)	(93)	(90)
Retained earnings	308	474
Accumulated other comprehensive income	156	164
Total stockholders' equity	5,785	3,352
Total liabilities and stockholders' equity	$13,147	$7,288

Property, Plant, and Equipment. Property, plant, and equipment are stated at cost. Depreciation and amortization are provided on a straight-line basis over the estimated useful lives of the assets for financial reporting purposes. Estimated useful lives for financial reporting purposes are as follows: equipment, two to six years; buildings and building improvements, up to 26 years; and leasehold improvements, the shorter of the remaining terms of the leases or the estimated economic useful lives of the improvements.

Intel Corporation
Consolidated Statements of Income

Three Years Ended December 30, 2006

(in millions, except par share amounts)	2006[1]	2005	2004
Net revenue	$ 35,382	$ 38,826	$ 34,209
Cost of sales	17,164	15,777	14,463
Gross margin	18,218	23,049	19,746
Research and development	5,873	5,145	4,778
Marketing, general, and administrative	6,096	5,688	4,659
Restructuring and asset impairment charges	555	–	–
Amortization of acquisition-related intangibles and costs	42	126	179
Operating expenses	12,566	10,959	9,616
Operating income	5,652	12,090	10,130
Gains (losses) on equity securities, net	214	(45)	(2)
Interest and other, net	1,202	565	289
Income before taxes	7,068	12,610	10,417
Provision for taxes	2,024	3,946	2,901
Net income	$ 5,044	$ 8,664	$ 7,516
Basic earnings per common share	$ 0.87	$ 1.42	$ 1.17
Diluted earnings per common share	$ 0.86	$ 1.40	$ 1.16
Weighted average common shares outstanding	5,797	6,106	6,400
Weighted average common shares outstanding, assuming dilution	5,880	6,178	6,494

Cost of sales and operating expenses for the year ended December 30, 2006, include share-based compensation. See Note 2: "Accounting Policies" and Note 3: "Employee Equity Incentive Plans."

Intel Corporation
Consolidated Balance Sheet

December 30, 2006, and December 31, 2005

(in millions, except par value)	2006	2005
Assets		
Current assets:		
Cash and cash equivalents	$ 6,598	$ 7,324
Short-term investments	2,270	3,990
Trading assets	1,134	1,458
Accounts receivable, net of allowance for doubtful accounts of $32 ($64 in 2005)	2,709	3,914
Inventories	4,314	3,126
Deferred tax assets	997	1,149
Other current assets	258	233
Total current assets	18,280	21,194
Property, plant, and equipment, net	17,602	17,111
Marketable strategic equity securities	398	537
Other long-term investments	4,023	4,135
Goodwill	3,861	3,873
Other long-term assets	4,204	1,464
Total assets	$ 48,368	$ 48,314
Liabilities and stockholders' equity		
Current liabilities:		
Short-term debt	$ 180	$ 313
Accounts payable	2,256	2,249
Accrued compensation and benefits	1,644	2,110
Accrued advertising	846	1,160
Deferred income on shipments to distributors	599	632
Other accrued liabilities	1,192	810
Income taxes payable	1,797	1,960
Total current liabilities	8,514	9,234
Long-term debt	1,848	2,106
Deferred tax liabilities	265	703
Other long-term liabilities	989	89
Commitments and contingencies (Notes 18 and 19)		
Stockholders' equity:		
Preferred stock, $0.001 par value, 50 shares authorized; none issued	–	–
Common stock, $0.001 par value, 10,000 shares authorized; 5,766 issued and outstanding (5,919 in 2005) and capital in excess of par value	7,825	6,245
Accumulated other comprehensive income (loss)	(57)	127
Retained earnings	28,984	29,810
Total stockholders' equity	36,752	36,182
Total liabilities and stockholders' equity	$ 48,368	$ 48,314

Property, Plant, and Equipment

Property, plant, and equipment, net at fiscal year-ends was as follows:

(in millions)	2006	2005
Land and buildings	$ 14,544	$ 13,938
Machinery and equipment	29,829	27,297
Construction in progress	2,711	2,897
	47,084	44,132
Less accumulated depreciation	(29,482)	(27,021)
Total property, plant, and equipment, net	**$ 17,602**	**$ 17,111**

Property, plant, and equipment is stated at cost. Depreciation is computed for financial reporting purposes principally using the straight-line method over the following estimated useful lives: machinery and equipment, 2 to 4 years; buildings, 4 to 40 years. Reviews are regularly performed if facts and circumstances exist that indicate that the carrying amount of assets may not be recoverable or that the useful life is shorter than originally estimated. The company assesses the recoverability of its assets held for use by comparing the projected undiscounted net cash flows associated with the related asset or group of assets over their remaining lives against their respective carrying amounts. Impairment, if any, is based on the excess of the carrying amount over the fair value of those assets. If assets are determined to be recoverable, but the useful lives are shorter than originally estimated, the net book value of the assets is depreciated over the newly determined remaining useful lives. See Note 11: "Restructuring and Asset Impairment Charges" for further discussion of asset impairment charges recorded in 2006.

Property, plant, and equipment is identified as held for sale when it meets the held-for-sale criteria of Statement of Financial Accounting Standards (SFAS) No. 144. "Accounting for Impairment or Disposal of Long-Lived Assets." The company ceases recording depreciation on assets that are classified as held for sale.

The company capitalizes interest on borrowings during the active construction period of major capital projects. Capitalized interest is added to the cost of qualified assets and is amortized over the estimated useful lives of the assets.

Porsche and Volkswagen—Equity Investments

The following articles describe the proposed acquisition by German sports car manufacturer Porsche AG of a substantial equity interest in fellow German automaker Volkswagen AG. Read the articles and answer the following questions. Assume that Porsche AG follows International Financial Reporting Standards.

1. Currently, Porsche has a 5% interest in Volkswagen. How does it account for that investment?

2. If Porsche is successful in raising its stake to 20%, how would the investment be accounted for?

3. The articles refer several times to corporate governance issues. What is corporate governance? What are the concerns about it in this case? Why are they concerns? What, if anything, does corporate governance have to do with shareholder value creation?

The Wall Street Journal

AUTOS

Porsche Sets Friendly Bid to Boost VW Stake to 20%, Prevent a Hostile Takeover

By MIKE ESTERL and STEPHEN POWER
Staff Reporters of THE WALL STREET JOURNAL
September 26, 2005; Page A3

FRANKFURT—**Porsche** AG said it plans to boost its stake in **Volkswagen** AG to 20% from less than 5% to prevent a possible hostile takeover of Volkswagen and secure the supply of components it buys from the company.

The friendly bid, valued at around €3 billion, or $3.6 billion, would make Porsche, of Stuttgart, Germany, the largest shareholder in Volkswagen, Europe's biggest automaker by unit sales.

Porsche Chief Executive Wendelin Wiedeking said the investment represents the "strategic answer" to the risk Porsche would face if Volkswagen were bought.

Volkswagen supplies Porsche with key components, including the body structure for the Porsche Cayenne, one of its most important models. The automakers also are developing gas–electric hybrid engines together.

The offer comes at a tumultuous time for Volkswagen, which has been struggling with high labor costs, strategic missteps, and a weak dollar that undercuts profit from exporting cars abroad. Volkswagen is on track to post a loss of as much as €900 million this year in North America for the second year in a row and is challenging its German unions to accept pay cuts or risk the loss of production to lower, wage parts of the world.

Volkswagen's shares soared in heavy volume last week amid rumors that an investor—possibly a hedge fund—was building a big stake in the Wolfsburg-based company.

Porsche said it was acting before European Union authorities move to overturn a rule that caps any VW shareholder's voting rights at 20%. The EU has pushed Germany to scrap the law, a step that could open the door to a hostile bid for Volkswagen.

The state of Lower Saxony, which has an 18% stake in Volkswagen, is supporting Porsche's bid, as is Volkswagen management.

The ties between Porsche and Volkswagen go back several decades. More than half of Porsche's stock and voting shares are owned by descendants of Ferdinand Porsche, a designer of Volkswagen's iconic Beetle. A grandson, Ferdinand Piech, is a former chief executive of Volkswagen and heads Volkswagen's supervisory board and holds a seat on Porsche's supervisory board.

Fears of increasing Anglo-Saxon influence at German corporations have been running strong in Germany lately. In the wake of a hedge-fund-led revolt at Deutsche Börse AG that scotched the company's bid for London Stock Exchange plc and led to the ouster of its chief executive, German Chancellor Gerhard Schröder called for global regulation of hedge funds, which are lightly regulated investment vehicles.

Volkswagen itself has seen a rise in the shareholdings of investors outside Germany. The proportion of Volkswagen shares held by foreign institutional investors rose to about 39% last year from 34% in 2003, according to the company's annual report. Its largest outside investor after Lower Saxony is now a U.S. investment-advisory firm—Brandes Investment Partners of San Diego—that reported an almost 11% stake earlier this year.

(continues)

Porsche Sets Friendly Bid to Boost VW Stake to 20%, Prevent a Hostile Takeover (*continued*)

One key question about Porsche's investment is how it will affect Volkswagen's move toward greater transparency and a corporate culture that is receptive to the views of profit-minded investors.

Under Chief Executive Bernd Pischetsrieder, Volkswagen has voluntarily agreed to disclose the salaries of the company's top executives, and has invited investment firms to Wolfsburg to explain the workings of the capital markets.

By contrast, Porsche's Mr. Wiedeking has criticized moves to require German corporations to disclose executive salaries and is among the fiercest opponents in Germany of Anglo–Saxon-style corporate governance.

Write to Mike Esterl at mike.esterl@dowjones.com and Stephen Power at stephen.power@wsj.com.

URL for this article: http://online.wsj.com/article/0,,SB112764691146051313,00.html

---

FT.com

Piech Looks to Retain the Family Cars

25 September 2005

Financial Times (FT.Com)

Ferdinand Porsche lies behind the creation of both Volkswagen and Porsche as carmakers.

After setting up his eponymous firm as a design company in 1931, Porsche was almost immediately mandated by Adolf Hitler to build a car for the people, or Volkswagen. The world-renowned Beetle was the result, and soon Porsche was helping in the construction of the new carmaker's headquarters in Wolfsburg.

Fast-forward 60 years and Porsche's grandson, Ferdinand Piech, stands behind another juncture between two of the great names of German carmaking. Porsche, in which Mr. Piech is one of the largest shareholders, wants to buy a fifth of the voting rights in VW, where Mr. Piech is chairman of the board.

"There is no doubt who is behind this: Piech," says someone who knows him well. "He talks fondly about VW and his grandfather." Because of his age, Mr. Piech would have to leave the VW board in 2007 anyway, the person continues. "He has sentimental feelings and he knows that would be the end of Porsche in VW. This links the two together."

But the co-operation between the two companies goes even deeper than family connections. In the 1950s, when Porsche was starting out, many of its cars used VW parts, and as it had no dealer network of its own, it relied largely on VW's.

Recently the co-operation has taken on a deeper aspect. The Porsche Cayenne, the sports utility vehicle that has become its biggest selling model, is largely manufactured by VW, based on its own Touareg off-roader.

The companies announced earlier this month that they would jointly develop petrol–electric hybrid motors for their SUV line-up and any other future models.

Porsche officials are also clear that buying a stake in VW will mean it becomes the luxury carmaker's "partner of choice." Alliances and joint ventures between companies are multiplying all the time as they look to share ever-increasing development costs.

VW has itself just unveiled plans to co-operate with Chrysler of the U.S. over a minivan for the American market.

Analysts think Porsche could start sharing more parts and processes with VW in a bid to reduce costs. It is launching a new fourth model, the Panamera, in 2009 for which it has estimated development costs at Euros 1bn ($1.2bn).

VW developed the Bentley Continental GT for a fraction of the price.

"Porsche needs someone to lean on. The two companies know each other well and in the long term it could make strategic sense," says Jurgen Piper, analyst at Bankhaus Metzler.

But there are some unquestionable differences between the carmakers. Porsche is the world's most profitable carmaker, but it sells less than 100,000 vehicles a year and is independent from outside shareholders as all its voting rights are held by the Piech and Porsche families.

VW, which has worked hard to cultivate a more shareholder-friendly image in recent years, is a sales behemoth, selling 5.1m cars last year, but it is losing money in its core VW brand.

This gulf has an impact on labour relations, one of the most important topics at VW.

Porsche is renowned for having a good relationship between workers and management, largely because it is so profitable that any problems that crop up are manageable.

VW, on the other hand, is hamstrung by high wage costs that lead its manufacturing costs to be 40 per cent higher than the competition.

Any attempts at tackling that, such as it is now trying with its new compact SUV, are hindered by the hugely political nature of the company.

An extraordinarily high 97 per cent of workers are members of the IG Metall union, while the government of Lower Saxony, the current largest shareholder with 18 per cent, has two board seats.

Optimists yesterday suggested Porsche could help VW with its labour problems but most see this as unrealistic.

If, as many suggested, Mr. Piech steps down early as chairman, then somebody from Porsche—perhaps its chief executive, Wendelin Wiedeking—could succeed him.

FT.com

Lex Live: Porsche/VW

26 September 2005

Financial Times (FT.Com)

Porsche Makes Nice Cars. Shame about Its Investment Strategy.

Resisting the current vogue to hand cash back to shareholders makes sense if there is a better use for the money. Unfortunately, Porsche's plan to acquire a 20 per cent stake in Volkswagen does not fit the bill.

Porsche says that the stake is the strategic answer to the risk of a hostile takeover. But VW has stated that current takeover defenses, expected to be dismantled in 2007, offer no real protection against the legal expertise of intelligent investment bankers. It is also not clear why Porsche, a highly desirable joint venture partner, needs to invest a quarter of its market capitalisation to protect co-operation agreements with VW. Porsche may be hoping to strike beneficial future deals. If so, the risk would remain that the priority of VW's largest investor might not be shareholder value.

With VW's shares at a three-year high and a recovery largely priced in, the timing leaves a lot to be desired. While Fiat might not be able to teach Porsche much about making cars profitably, the Agnelli family could tell it a thing or two about buying when the stock is unloved.

Family, not good governance, is at the heart of the VW deal. Ferdinand Piech, a grandson of Porsche's founder and one of its largest shareholders, is also VW's chairman. This cosy "German solution" does not bode well for the prospects of accelerated restructuring at VW. Porsche's investors, meanwhile, have received a lesson in the perils of non-voting stock. They can only watch as the company's cash pile heads off to a struggling, but no doubt delighted, VW. Rick Wagoner, General Motors' chief executive, is probably already checking to see if he is related to Mr. Piech.

CHAPTER **9**

Accounting for Financing Activities

ANALYSIS CHALLENGE: LEVERAGE AND OFF-BALANCE-SHEET FINANCING

When financial statement users analyze the leverage of a firm, they need to be sure they have a complete picture of the company's obligations. Debt contracts provide incentives for managers to structure transactions so that debt remains off the balance sheet, and guarantees, commitments, leases, and other arrangements can represent liabilities not reflected on the balance sheet. Prudent analysts pay special attention to these items in the notes to the financial statements.

Assessing value creation requires an examination of the financing sources of the business. Specifically, what is the value and cost of the company's debt, and what is the value and cost of the company's equity (contributed capital and earned capital)? Multiplying the cost of debt times the value of the debt, and adding to that the result of multiplying the cost of equity times the value of equity determines the amount that must be created through the company's investing and operating activities to create value for the shareholders. In this chapter, we cover how debt (long-term liabilities), contributed capital, and earned capital are measured on the financial statements. Recall that an estimate of the cost of debt (interest expense) is reflected on the income statement, but the financial statements do not provide an estimate of the cost of equity. We discussed and illustrated estimating the cost of equity in Chapter 1 and its appendix.

ROE, VALUE CREATION, AND FINANCING ACTIVITIES

$$\text{ROE} = \frac{\text{Net income}}{\text{Common equity}} = \frac{\text{NI} + \text{Interest expense}}{\text{Sales}} \times \frac{\text{Sales}}{\text{Assets}} \times \frac{\text{Assets}}{\text{Common equity}} \times \frac{\text{NI}}{\text{NI} + \text{Interest expense}}$$

Shareholder value creation takes place when a company's return on equity (ROE) exceeds its cost of equity capital. Financing activities have both direct and indirect effects on value creation. One direct effect is the use of leverage—the firm is using someone else's money to generate returns for the shareholders. However, that favorable direct effect is muted via the interest expense that accrues on liabilities and reduces ROE. An indirect effect arises as leverage increases: The more debt a company uses to finance its assets, the more likely it will be that lenders will charge higher interest rates, and the riskier the firm (and its common shares) becomes—a risk resulting in higher cost of equity capital.

▶ DEBT AND EQUITY DISTINGUISHED

Figure 9-1 summarizes the fundamental characteristics of debt and equity. When a company borrows money, it establishes a relationship with an outside party—a creditor or debtholder—whose influence on the company's operations is defined by a formal legal contract containing a number of specific provisions (e.g., maturity date [when the debt is to be paid back], interest rate, security [collateral] provisions, and covenant restrictions).

When a corporation raises capital by issuing stock, it establishes a relationship with an owner, often referred to as an equityholder, shareholder, or stockholder. Unlike debt, an equity relationship is not evidenced by a precisely specified contract. There is no maturity date because a shareholder is an owner of a company until it ceases operations or until the equity interest is transferred to another party. Dividend payments are at the discretion of the board of directors, and shareholders have no legal right to receive dividends until they are declared. In case of bankruptcy, the rights of the shareholders to the available assets are subordinate (secondary) to the rights of the creditors, who are paid in an order usually determined by the terms in the debt contracts. The shareholders receive the assets that remain. That is, a corporation's owners have a residual interest in the corporation's assets in case of bankruptcy or dissolution.

Shareholders, however, can exert significant influence over corporate management. Each ownership share carries a vote that can be cast in the election of the board of directors at the annual shareholders' meeting. The board, whose function is to represent the interests of the shareholders, declares dividends, determines executive compensation, has the power to hire and fire management, and sets the general policies of the corporation. In addition, certain significant transactions, such as the issuance of additional stock, often must be approved by a vote of the shareholders.

The economic differences between debt and equity dictate different accounting treatments. Debt is disclosed in the liability section of the balance sheet. The cost of debt comprises primarily tax-deductible interest, identified by the contract; however, contractual restrictions imposed on management can also represent significant, albeit less obvious and quantifiable, costs. Interest accrues on debt as time passes, increasing the firm's

Debt	Equity
Formal legal contract	No legal contract
Fixed maturity date	No fixed maturity date
Contractual interest	Discretionary dividend payments
Security in case of default	Residual asset interest
No direct voice in management: indirect influence through debt covenants	Vote for board of directors

These are basic characteristics. In practice, however, many different forms of these basic characteristics exist.

Figure 9-1. Characteristics of Debt and Equity

liabilities. As interest accrues, it is treated as an expense on the income statement. The cost of debt financing is thus matched against the benefits generated by the borrowed funds in the measurement of net income. When debt is paid off with an amount that differs from its book (balance sheet) value, a gain or loss is recognized on the transaction and reported on the income statement.

Equity is disclosed in the shareholders' equity section of the balance sheet. It provides a measure of the investment of the shareholders, a very important part of ROE and thereby a key element of value creation. Dividends paid to the shareholders are considered neither a cost of equity nor an expense of doing business, but rather a return of the owner's investment, normally in the form of cash. Thus, dividends do not appear on the income statement; instead, they reduce the shareholders' investment by reducing earned capital (retained earnings). When equity securities are bought back (in the form of treasury stock) at an amount that differs from its original issuance price, which appears on the balance sheet, no gain or loss is recognized on the transaction. Rather, it is treated as a return of the shareholders' original investment and contributed capital is reduced.

▶ RELATIVE RELIANCE ON DEBT AND EQUITY AS SOURCES OF FINANCING

Figure 9-2 illustrates the relative importance of liabilities (current and noncurrent), contributed capital, and retained earnings as sources of financing for 10 well-known companies representing five major industry groups. Overall, liabilities (with a few exceptions) are the primary financing source. Interest costs are tax deductible, reducing the cost of borrowing, and leverage is a popular way to provide returns to shareholders without using their capital.

Most of the firms appear to rely very little on contributed capital; in fact, for ExxonMobil and SUPERVALU, the percentage under contributed capital is negative, and for General Electric, Wendy's, Bank of America, and Merrill Lynch, the percentage is less than 5%. These companies are all well-established, successful firms that have repurchased large amounts of their outstanding shares (treasury stock) over the years at prices far exceeding the price at which the shares were originally issued. The companies relying heavily on

	Liabilities	Contributed Capital	Retained Earnings
Manufacturing:			
General Electric	0.83	0.03	0.14
ExxonMobil	0.48	−0.16	0.68
Retail:			
SUPERVALU	0.64	−0.02	0.38
Tommy Hilfiger	0.45	0.22	0.33
Internet:			
Amazon.com	1.07	0.65	−0.72
Cisco	0.27	0.63	0.10
General Services:			
SBC Communications	0.63	0.10	0.27
Wendy's	0.46	0.01	0.53
Financial Services:			
Bank of America	0.91	0.04	0.05
Merrill Lynch	0.95	0.02	0.03

Source: 2004 annual reports

Figure 9-2. Relative Importance of Liabilities, Contributed Capital, and Retained Earnings (percentage of total assets)

retained earnings as a source of financing (ExxonMobil, SUPERVALU, Tommy Hilfiger, SBC Communications, and Wendy's) have a history of profitability, choosing not to pay high levels of dividends.

Internet firms are somewhat unusual. In general, they have relied heavily on contributed capital because their (1) share prices were astronomically high when these firms were originally established in the mid- to late-1990s; (2) the speed of their growth created uncertainty about future risks, discouraging debt capital providers; (3) they had little collateral that could be used to secure loans; and (4) many were slow to show any profits. In fact, since its inception, Amazon has generated a large deficit, which has required significant debt financing. Interestingly, much of Amazon's debt includes features that permit holders to convert it into common shares.

Many companies, particularly in the United States, now finance their investments and operations by issuing "hybrid securities," which contain characteristics of both debt and equity. Examples include various kinds of preferred shares and bonds convertible to stock. Accounting for these issuances is difficult because they are neither clearly debt nor clearly equity, suggesting that they complicate the already difficult task of assessing value creation.

MEASUREMENT CHALLENGE: HYBRID SECURITIES

Under current U.S. generally accepted accounting principles (GAAP), accountants don't measure equity directly. They measure assets and liabilities and we define owners' equity as the difference between the two. The level of a company's equity is therefore a function of how the assets and liabilities are measured.

A major measurement challenge arises when firms issue hybrid securities—securities with features of both debt and equity. Examples abound and include mandatorily redeemable preferred shares and convertible bonds. Current directions in financial reporting strive to break the instruments into their debt and equity components. However, measurement challenges arise because the value of each component partially depends on the value of the other component!

▶ MEASURING THE VALUE OF DEBT

The Financial Accounting Standards Board (FASB) defines liabilities as "probable future sacrifices of economic benefits arising from present obligations of a particular entity to transfer assets or provide services to other entities in the future as a result of past transactions or events." The board commented further that all liabilities appearing on the balance sheet should have three characteristics: (1) they should be present obligations that entail settlements by probable future transfers or uses of cash, goods, or services; (2) they should be unavoidable obligations; and (3) the transaction or event obligating the enterprise must have already happened.

The liabilities listed on the balance sheet entail a variety of items. In Chapter 7, we discussed accounts payable, short-term debts, current maturities of long-term debts, deferred revenues, third-party collections, dividend payables, and contingencies (e.g., product warranties). In this chapter, we cover long-term contractual debt and deferred taxes.

Basic Definitions and Different Forms of Contractual Debt

When a company enters a debt contract, it is promising to make the future cash payments designated by the contract in exchange for some benefit. Such arrangements vary on two dimensions: (1) the timing of the contractual cash payments, and (2) the nature of the benefit received in the exchange. We cover two popular cash-payment timing variations (installment notes and interest-bearing notes) and two benefits received in the exchange (cash and noncash).

Installment Notes

In an installment note, periodic payments covering both interest and principal are made throughout the life of the contract. For example, a company may enter into an exchange in which it receives a benefit (e.g., cash, noncash asset, liability reduction, or service) and, in return, promises to pay $6,000 at the end of each of two years. The cash flows associated with this contract are

Interest-bearing Notes

Interest-bearing notes require periodic (e.g., annual or semiannual) cash payments (called interest payments) determined as a percentage of the face, principal, or maturity value (all synonyms), which must be paid at the end of the contract period. For example, a company may enter into an exchange in which it receives a benefit and, in return, promises to pay $1,000 per year for two years and $10,000 at the end of the second year. Such an obligation has a life of two years, a stated interest rate (or coupon rate) of 10% ($1,000 / $10,000), and a maturity, principal, or face value of $10,000. The cash flows associated with this contract are

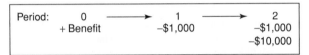

The benefits received in exchange for these obligations might be cash or noncash. Noncash benefits include assets (e.g., equipment, property, and securities), reductions in other debts (refinancing), and services (e.g., consultants). Figure 9-3 highlights four kinds of notes resulting from crossing installment and interest-bearing notes with cash and noncash benefits. Three of the four combinations represent very common forms of contractual debt financing. Item 1A represents a traditional bank loan where cash is borrowed and the debt is paid off in installments; 1B represents a lease arrangement where a noncurrent asset (e.g., equipment or property) is financed and payments are made in installments; and 2A represents a standard bond issuance where bonds with a stated interest rate and maturity are sold to the public for cash. Item 2B is less common, but could represent vendor financing for a piece of equipment (the noncash benefit) where small periodic payments are made, followed by a large balloon payment at the end.

Effective Interest Rate

All contractual debt contains an element of interest (the effective interest rate), whether or not it is stated in the contract. The effective interest rate is the actual (or economic) interest

---

1. Installment notes
   a. Cash benefit received (e.g., traditional bank loan)
   b. Noncash benefit received (e.g., lease arrangement)

2. Interest-bearing notes
   a. Cash benefit received (e.g., standard bond issuance)
   b. Noncash benefit received (e.g., vendor financing)

Figure 9-3. Four Kinds of Notes

rate paid by the issuer of the obligation (the borrower), and is determined by finding the discount rate that sets the present value of the obligation's cash outflows equal to the fair market value (FMV) of the benefit received in the exchange. When contractual obligations are exchanged for cash (1A and 2A in Figure 9-3), the cash amount received represents the FMV of the benefit received. In this case, determining the effective interest rate is straightforward. We know the present value of the cash inflow (the benefit received) and we know the amount and timing of the debt payments. The effective interest rate is the rate that equates the two.

When contractual obligations are exchanged for noncash items (1B and 2B), the FMV of the noncash items is determined through appraisals or some other means. Once that value is established, again we know the present value of the inflow and we know the amount and timing of the debt payments. Thus, we can determine the effective rate that equates the two.

The effective interest rate may or may not equal the interest rate stated on interest-bearing notes. For example, when bonds are issued (sold) at face value, the effective rate equals the stated rate. When bonds are issued at prices less than face value (discount), the effective rate is greater than the stated rate. When bonds are issued at prices greater than face value (premium), the effective interest rate is less than the stated rate. Understanding the effective rate of interest is important because it is used in determining the value of the debt on the balance sheet and in determining the cost of debt financing, both of which are important in assessing value creation. The Appendix at the end of the text covers present value and how the effective rate is computed.

INSIGHT: ANOTHER WAY TO THINK ABOUT BONDS

You can think of a bond as a series of post-dated checks. The amount and timing of the checks is set by the bond contract. For example, assume the contract described the bond as a 5-year, $1,000 bond, with a 9% coupon rate payable semi-annually. That description fully describes the checks that the bondholder will receive over the next five years. It is important to understand that the description does not say what a potential bondholder would pay to receive those checks—that is, what the market value of the bond is.

The description tells us that the bondholder will receive a check for $45 every six months for five years. That payment is determined by multiplying the face value of the bond by the coupon rate (here, $1,000 × 9% × ½). At the end of five years, an additional check for $1,000 will be received.

The economic, or market, value of those bonds at any given time is the present value of the remaining payments.

Although the description of the bond refers to a 9% interest rate, the effective interest rate that market participants charge will be a function of the risk related to the remaining checks at that time. If the company is very profitable and the risk of the checks not being paid is low, the effective rate may be less than 9%. On the other hand, if the company is facing bankruptcy, bondholders may view the checks as very risky investments and demand a high rate of return on their investment. Because the check payments can't be changed (they were determined by the bond contract) the market will discount those payments using a very high effective interest rate.

The bond contract determines the amount and timing of the checks. The market's perceptions of the riskiness of those checks determines their value when they are issued and subsequently.

Valuing Contractual Debt and Its Cost on the Financial Statements

Issuing notes and bonds are popular ways for major U.S. companies to raise cash. Both secured (backed by collateral) and unsecured notes and bonds are widely used. The issuance of notes normally involves only one or a small group of lenders (usually financial institutions), and notes take a variety of forms. Bonds are usually issued to raise large amounts of capital, often to finance expensive, long-term projects. They are normally sold to the public through a third party (called an underwriter), such as an investment banker or other financial institution, and represent an interest-bearing security requiring the issuer to make cash interest payments to the bondholder and a principal payment (usually in the amount of $1,000 per bond) when the bond matures, generally between 5 and 30 years from the date of issuance. After bonds are initially issued, they are often freely negotiable; that is, they can be purchased and sold in the open market. Both the New York and the American Security Exchanges maintain active bond markets.

The methods used to value notes and bonds on the balance sheet and their costs on the income statement involve basic rules applied at three points: (1) at issuance, (2) over the life of the debt, and (3) at retirement.

At Issuance

When an installment or interest-bearing note (or bond) is issued for cash or a noncash asset, both the asset account and the balance sheet liability are increased by the fair market value of the benefit (asset) received. For example, if an installment note is issued for cash (traditional bank loan), both the company's cash balance and the notes payable account are increased by the cash proceeds. If an installment note is issued for a noncash asset (e.g., equipment), both the equipment account and the note payable account are increased by the fair market value of the equipment. If bonds are issued for cash, both the company's cash account and the bonds payable account are increased by the amount of the cash proceeds. At issuance, the effective interest rate of the debt is established by finding the discount rate that sets the present value of the debt's future cash outflows equal to the fair market value of the benefit received.

Over the Life of Contractual Debt

The balance sheet value of contractual debt over the period of its life, whether an installment or interest-bearing note (or bond), is equal to the present value of the debt's remaining future cash outflows (principal and interest), discounted at the *effective interest rate established when the note was originally issued*. For example, if the contract underlying an installment note requires cash payments of $1,000 per year for 10 years beyond the balance sheet date, and the effective interest rate of the debt was computed to be 8% when the debt was issued, the balance sheet value of the debt is equal to $6,710 ($1,000 × 6.7108; see the Appendix).

The *interest expense* associated with contractual debt recognized on the income statement of a given period during the life of the debt is equal to the *effective interest rate, established when the debt was originally issued, multiplied by the balance sheet value of the debt at the beginning of the period*. For example, if the balance sheet value of the debt at the beginning of the period is $6,710, and the effective interest rate was established to be 8% when the debt was issued, the interest expense on the income statement is equal to $537 ($6,710 × 8%).

The **interest payments** during the period of the debt are set by the debt contract and may or may not equal the interest expense recognized on the income statement. When the payment equals the interest expense, the outstanding debt balance on the balance sheet remains unaffected; when the payment exceeds the interest expense, the debt balance is reduced; and when the payment is less than the interest expense, the debt balance is increased. The new debt balance is used to calculate the next period's interest expense.

Figure 9-4 illustrates the amortization of an installment debt where an asset with a fair market value of $6,710 is received in exchange for a promise to pay $1,000 per year for 10 years. The effective interest rate on the debt is 8%, computed at the time of issuance by finding the discount rate that equates the $6,710 (present value) with the ten $1,000 future installment payments.

Period	Beginning Value	Interest Expense	Payment	Repayment of Principal	Ending Value
Issue debt					$6,710
1	$6,710	$537	$1,000	$463	6,247
2	6,247	500	1,000	500	5,747
3	5,747	460	1,000	540	5,206
4	5,206	417	1,000	583	4,623
5	4,623	370	1,000	630	3,993
6	3,993	319	1,000	681	3,312
7	3,312	265	1,000	735	2,577
8	2,577	206	1,000	794	1,783
9	1,783	143	1,000	857	926
10	926	74	1,000	926	0

Note:
Debt contract specifies 10 payments of $1,000 to be made at the end of each period.
Effective interest rate at time of issuance is 8%.
Interest expense = Beginning value × 8%
Repayment of principal = Payment − Interest expense
Repayment of principal serves to reduce the value of the debt.

Figure 9-4. Debt Amortization Table

CONTRACTUAL DEBT—BASIC JOURNAL ENTRIES AND EFFECT ON THE ACCOUNTING EQUATION

Cash (+A)	$6,710		Interest Expense (+E, −RE)	$ 537
Long-Term Debt (+L)		$6,710	Long-Term Debt (−L)	$ 463
To record the issuance of debt.			Cash (−A)	$1,000

To record the first of 10 payments of $1,000. The payment covers interest and principal.

Note that the second journal entry will be recorded each period (using the appropriate figures from Figure 9-4). When the final payment is made, the book value of the debt will be zero.

INSIGHT: BONDS AS INVESTMENTS

In this chapter, we cover accounting for bonds as a source of financing. We've seen that the effective interest rate method is used to account for the debt. Companies not only issue bonds to raise funds, but they also invest in bonds. We covered accounting for investments in equity securities in Chapter 8. Now that we have explained the effective interest rate method, accounting for investments in bonds is straightforward.

There are three potential categories into which investments in corporate bonds can fall: trading, available-for-sale, and held-to-maturity. For all three categories, interest revenue is calculated using the effective interest rate method.

As with investments in equity securities, when bonds are held as *trading* assets, they are marked-to-market each period

(continues)

INSIGHT: BONDS AS INVESTMENTS (*continued*)

on the balance sheet and resulting unrealized gains and losses are reported on the income statement.

If the bonds are considered *available-for-sale*, again they are marked-to-market on the balance sheet, but unrealized gains and losses are included directly in equity as an element of "accumulated other comprehensive income." When the bonds are sold, realized gains and losses are reported as part of net income and the "accumulated other comprehensive income" is reversed.

The bonds are considered *held-to-maturity* investments if the company has the positive intent and ability to hold

them until they mature. The FASB lists a number of common reasons why bonds are sold prior to maturity (e.g., liquidity needs, other investment alternatives, and currency risks) and explains that selling prior to maturity for those reasons is evidence that the bonds should be classified as available-for-sale or trading. Held-to-maturity investments in bonds are accounted for using the effective interest rate method. Unrealized gains and losses are ignored. Thus, the accounting is simply the flip side of the accounting for bonds as debt.

At Retirement

When contractual debt is retired, the issuing company pays cash to the debtholders, and the debt is removed from the balance sheet. If the payment is made at the maturity date, the decrease in the company's cash balance will equal the decrease in the balance sheet value of the debt, and no gain or loss will be recognized on the transaction. If the debt is retired prior to maturity and the payment required to retire the debt does not equal the balance sheet value, a gain or loss will be recognized. If the payment exceeds the balance sheet value, a loss is recognized; if the payment is less than the balance sheet value, a gain is recognized. Such gains and losses, which appear on the income statement, are normally considered non-operating.

EARLY RETIREMENT OF CONTRACTUAL DEBT: BASIC JOURNAL ENTRIES AND EFFECT ON THE ACCOUNTING EQUATION

Assume the debt illustrated in Figure 9-4 is retired at the end of the third period for $5,389. From Figure 9-4, we see that the book value of the debt at that time is $5,206. Thus, the company will record a loss on early retirement of debt.

Long Term Debt (−L)	$5,206	
Loss on Early Retirement of Debt (Loss, −RE)	183	
Cash (−A)		$5,389

To record the retirement of debt at the end of period 3.

Note that the company had to pay a market price of $5,389 to retire a debt valued on its balance sheet at only $5,206. The discount rate that equates $5,389 to the seven remaining $1,000 payments is 7%, which is below the 8% effective rate established by the company when the debt was issued.

Differences between Book and Market Value

The balance sheet value (the book value) of debt and the related interest expense will equal the market value of the debt and market interest rates as long as the effective interest rate, established when the debt was issued, reflects the company's current financial condition and current market interest rates throughout the life of the debt. However, in most cases the company's financial condition and market interest rates change over the life of the debt, which in turn causes the effective interest rate and the market value of the debt to change. Over the life of contractual debt, therefore, its balance sheet value and related interest expense might not reflect current market values and rates.

Differences between how contractual debt and its cost are measured on the financial statements and its current market value introduce two important implications. First, if this difference is material, those interested in assessing value creation should adjust the balance sheet value of the debt and the interest expense to reflect current market values. Fortunately, GAAP requires that companies provide footnote disclosure of the market values of outstanding debt.

To illustrate the pro forma adjustment, assume that Company A has an outstanding interest-bearing note with a balance sheet value of $10,000 and an effective interest rate, established at issuance, of 10%. Interest expense on the income statement would be $1,000 ($10,000 × 10%). If the company discloses that the market value of the debt as of the balance sheet date is $10,500, perhaps because the company's financial condition has improved since the debt was issued and/or market rates have decreased, the current effective interest rate on the note can be computed, as described in the Appendix, by finding the discount rate that sets the present value of the debt's remaining cash outflows equal to its fair market value ($10,500). If this computation leads to a current effective interest rate of 9%, the value of the debt and interest expense on the financial statements should be $10,500 and $945 ($10,500 × 0.09), respectively.

FAIR VALUE OF FINANCIAL INSTRUMENTS AT GENERAL ELECTRIC

Statement of Financial Accounting Standard (SFAS) No. 107 requires that firms disclose the fair values of their financial assets and liabilities in the notes to their financial statements.

General Electric made the following disclosures in its 2006 annual report. (GE represents the manufacturing activities and GECS represents GE's Capital Services business.)

Note 27
Financial Instruments

	2006			2005		
		Assets (liabilities)			Assets (liabilities)	
December 31 (in millions)	Notional amount	Carrying amount (net)	Estimated fair value	Notional amount	Carrying amount (net)	Estimated fair value
GE						
Assets						
Investments and notes receivable	$ (a)	$ 494	$ 494	$ (a)	$ 573	$ 625
Liabilities						
Borrowings[b][c]	(a)	(11,297)	(11,204)	(a)	(10,208)	(10,223)
GECS						
Assets						
Loans	(a)	266,055	265,578	(a)	223,855	224,259
Other commercial and residential mortgages held for sale	(a)	7,296	7,439	(a)	6,696	6,696
Other financial instruments[d]	(a)	3,714	4,158	(a)	4,138	4,494
Liabilities						
Borrowings[b][c]	(a)	(426,279)	(432,275)	(a)	(362,069)	(369,972)
Investment contract benefits	(a)	(5,089)	(5,080)	(a)	(6,034)	(6,020)
Insurance—credit life[e]	2,634	(81)	(61)	2,365	(8)	(8)

(a) These financial instruments do not have notional amounts.
(b) Included effects of interest rate and cross-currency swaps.
(c) See note 18.
(d) Principally cost method investments.
(e) Net of reinsurance of $840 million and $292 million at December 31, 2006 and 2005, respectively.

The second important implication of differences between the financial statement value and market value of debt is that debt retired prior to maturity will give rise to an income statement gain or loss. For example, when **market interest rates decline,** companies often retire outstanding debt and refinance (issue new debt) at lower rates. Although this strategy is attractive because it reduces the cost of debt in the future (the new debt has a lower interest rate), the market value of the debt to be retired has risen, forcing the company to pay more than the debt's balance sheet value to repurchase it. Thus, as illustrated in the "at retirement" section above where the effective interest rate decreased from 8% to 7%, the company will recognize a loss on the retirement. The loss, which appears on the income statement, reflects the fact that the original debt carried a relatively high effective interest rate, putting the company at a competitive disadvantage—over the period of the debt—relative to other firms that were able to raise funds at lower rates.

RED FLAGS—GAINS ON EARLY RETIREMENT OF DEBT

When market interest rates rise, the market value of a company's existing debt will fall because the future debt payments become worth less as investors use higher discount rates to discount them. In essence, the economic value of the issuing company's debt obligations have decreased because for the period of the debt it has locked in lower-than-market interest rates. That economic gain will show up on the income statement *over time* as the company benefits from the low-priced debt. Interest expense will be lower than at firms that finance at the market rate.

The company could, however, recognize the economic gain right away if it were to retire the debt because the market value of the debt is lower than the book value. Would doing so create value? Not likely. Assuming the retirement was funded by issuing new debt, the gain on retirement would be completely offset by higher future interest costs.

Savvy financial statement analysts ask why the debt was refinanced, what benefits the company received by refinancing (does the new debt have a longer term? does the new debt have fewer restrictive covenants?), and whether the retirement was done simply to window dress the current period's performance.

TEST YOUR KNOWLEDGE: NOTES AND BONDS

The following questions offer you the chance to test your knowledge of notes and bonds.

• The following table was taken from the 2006 annual report of RadioShack.

Long term debt (in millions)

	2006	2005
Notes payable (interest 7.375%)	$350.0	$350.0
Notes payable (interest 6.95%)	150.0	150.0
Financing obligations	–	32.3

1. Briefly explain the transactions entered into by RadioShack during 2006. Which financial statements were affected?

2. Approximately how much interest expense was recognized in 2006 on the 6.95% notes?

3. If market interest rates rise during 2007, will the market value of RadioShack's outstanding debt increase or decrease? Why?

4. Assume that during 2007 RadioShack paid $160 million to retire the 6.95% notes payable. How much gain or loss would RadioShack have recognized on the transaction? Where in the financial statements would it be found?

- In October 1997, Hewlett-Packard issued zero-coupon bonds with a face value of $1.8 billion, due in 2017, for proceeds of $968 million.

  1. What is the life of these bonds?
  2. What is the stated interest rate on these bonds?
  3. Estimate the effective rate of interest on these bonds.

- During 2002, Southwest Airlines issued 10-year notes with a face value of $385 million. The stated interest rate on the notes was 6.5% and proceeds from the issuance approximated $380 million.

  1. Estimate the effective interest rate of the issuance.
  2. Compute the interest expense associated with this note recorded in 2002.
  3. Explain why the market paid less than $385 million for these notes.

Operating vs. Capital Leases

A lease is a contract granting use or occupation of property during a specified period of time in exchange for rent payments. Leases are a very popular way to finance business activities. Companies often lease rather than purchase land, buildings, machinery, equipment, and other holdings, primarily to avoid the risks and associated costs of ownership.

Operating Leases

In a pure leasing (or rental) arrangement, an individual or entity (lessor) who owns land, buildings, equipment, or other property transfers the right to use this property to another individual or entity (lessee) in exchange for periodic cash payments over a specified period of time. Normally, the terms of the lease are defined by contract, and over the period of the lease, the owner is responsible for the property's normal maintenance and upkeep. The lessee assumes none of the risks of ownership, and at the end of the lease, the right to use the property reverts to the owner. These types of agreements are called operating leases, and accounting for them is straightforward. The property is reported as an asset on the owner's balance sheet, and the periodic rental payments are recorded as rent revenue on the owner's income statement. If applicable, as in the case of a fixed asset, the capitalized cost of the property is depreciated by the owner. The lessee, on the other hand, recognizes no asset or liability, but simply reports rent expense on the income statement as the periodic rent payments are accrued.

OPERATING LEASES FOR THE LESSEE—BASIC JOURNAL ENTRIES AND THE EFFECT ON THE ACCOUNTING EQUATION

Rent Expense (+E, −RE)	$1,000	
Cash (−A)		$1,000

To record a $1,000 rent payment on an operating lease.

If the rent payment covered future periods, it would be treated as prepaid rent and expensed as time passed. If the lease agreement permitted a delay in making some lease payments, rent expense and rent payable would still be recorded (accrued).

Capital Leases

Many contractual arrangements, which appear on the surface to be leases, are actually purchases financed with installment notes, where the risks and benefits of ownership have been transferred to the lessee. The present value of the periodic lease payments, for example, may approximate the fair market value (FMV) of the property. It is also possible that the property may revert, or be sold at a bargain price, to the lessee at the end of the lease period.

Furthermore, the period of the lease may be equivalent (or close) to the asset's useful life. In effect, the lessee has actually purchased the property from the lessor and is financing it with an installment note (i.e., an asset has been received in exchange for an installment note payable). Such leases are referred to as capital (or finance) leases.

MEASUREMENT CHALLENGE—WHAT SORT OF LEASE IS IT?

Establishing whether the risks and benefits of ownership of an asset have been transferred to a lessee is a challenge, but it is at the heart of determining whether a lease is an operating lease or a capital lease. Well-intentioned managers may well interpret the same facts and circumstances and arrive at different conclusions. To establish consistency in lease accounting, U.S. GAAP lays out four bright-line rules for lease classification. If any one (or more) of the criteria are met, the lease is a capital lease. The rules are as follows:

1. Title passes at the end of the lease.

2. The lease contains a bargain purchase option.
3. The term of the lease is equal to or greater than 75% of the asset's estimated economic life.
4. The present value of the lease payments is equal to or greater than 90% of the fair value of the asset. The payments include the minimum lease payments and any guaranteed residual value, penalty for failure to renew, or bargain purchase option. The lessee's incremental borrowing rate is used unless the lessor is offering a lower rate (implicit in the lease payments).

CAPITAL LEASES—BASIC JOURNAL ENTRIES AND EFFECTS ON THE ACCOUNTING EQUATION (See Figure 9-4)

Asset under Capital Lease (+A) $6,710
    Lease Liability (+L) $6,710

To record the acquisition of an asset under a capital lease at its market value.
    The leased asset will be amortized (depreciated) over the shorter of the lease term or its estimated useful life.

Amortization Expense (+E, −RE) $671
    Accumulated Amortization (−A) $671

To record the periodic straight-line amortization of the leased asset over a 10-year estimated useful life.

Over the term of the lease, the $1,000 annual lease payments will cover the interest expense and reduce the lease liability. Interest expense is equal to the effective interest rate (8%) multiplied by the balance sheet value of the lease liability at the beginning of the period ($6,710).

Interest Expense (+E, −RE) $537
Lease Liability (−L) $463
    Cash (−A) $1,000

To record the first periodic lease payment.

According to GAAP, the lessee should account for a capital lease as if an amount equal to the FMV of the property was borrowed and immediately used to purchase the property. That is, both an asset and a liability, equal to the FMV of the leased property, should be recognized on the balance sheet at the beginning of the lease term. The leased asset should be amortized over the shorter of its useful life or the term of the lease (see Chapter 8), and the liability should be accounted for as an installment note as illustrated in Figure 9-4. The effective interest rate on the liability is established at the outset of the lease, the liability is carried on the balance sheet at the present value of the contract's future cash flows (discounted at the initial effective rate), and periodic interest expense should be computed by multiplying the effective rate times the balance sheet value of the liability at the beginning of the period. Similar to the previous discussion, if market interest rates change over the life of the lease contract, like any other contractual debt, the market value of the lease liability will diverge from the balance sheet value. That is, although the fair value of the lease liability changes, accounting for the lease does not change because the effective interest rate (at the inception of the lease) continues to be used.

RED FLAGS—LEASES AND OFF-BALANCE-SHEET FINANCING

Renting assets is a valuable way to obtain the use of an asset without bearing the risks and benefits of ownership. But when the rental agreements are such that the risks and benefits of ownership have been transferred, analysts should treat those assets as the company's and should consider the lease payments as debt. Capital lease treatment is designed to accomplish that. However, an entire industry has arisen with the purpose of helping companies lease assets under conditions that effectively transfer the risks and benefits of ownership, but still qualify, under GAAP, for operating lease accounting. That leads to potentially large missing assets and liabilities.

ROE analysis that doesn't consider the missing assets and liabilities runs the risk of overestimating asset turnover and underestimating leverage. We explore this issue in the Iron Mountain case at the end of the chapter.

Credit analysts like those at Standard & Poor's make explicit adjustments in their analyses, constructively capitalizing operating leases and treating them as capital leases. You should too. S&P's 2006 Corporate Ratings Criteria reads, in part,

Operating Lease Analytics

To improve financial ratio analysis, Standard & Poor's Ratings Services uses a financial model that capitalizes off-balance-sheet operating lease commitments and allocates minimum lease payments to interest and depreciation expenses. Not only are debt-to-capital ratios affected: so are interest coverage, funds from operations to debt, total debt to earnings before interest, taxes, depreciation and amortization (EBITDA), operating margins, and return on capital. This technique is, on balance, superior to the alternative "factor method," which multiplies annual lease expense by a factor reflecting the average life of leased assets.

The operating lease model is intended to make companies' financial ratios more accurate and comparable by taking into consideration all assets and liabilities, whether on or off the balance sheet. In other words, all rated companies are put on a more level playing field, no matter how many assets are leased and how the leases are classified for financial reporting purposes. (We view the distinction between operating leases and capital leases as artificial. In both cases, the lessee contracts for the use of an asset, entering into a debt-like obligation to make periodic rental payments.) The model also helps improve analysis of how profitably a company employs both its leased and owned assets. By adjusting the capital base for the present value of lease commitments, the return on capital better reflects actual asset profitability."

LEASE DISCLOSURES AT UNITED AIRLINES

UAL Corporation provides a list of its future minimum lease payments for assets under operating and capital leases. The note makes clear the importance of considering operating lease payments as obligations in analyses of leverage. Indeed, the obligations under capital leases are dwarfed by the off-balance-sheet operating leases.

At December 31, 2006, scheduled future minimum lease payments under capital leases (substantially all of which are for aircraft) and operating leases having initial or remaining noncancelable lease terms of more than one year were as follows:

(continues)

LEASE DISCLOSURES AT UNITED AIRLINES (*continued*)

(in millions)	Operating Lease Payments			Capital Lease Payments(a)
	Mainline Aircraft	**United Express Aircraft**	**Non-Aircraft**	
Payable during—				
2007	$ 358	$ 413	$ 507	$ 255
2008	351	409	484	321
2009	317	409	467	178
2010	307	380	453	441
2011	303	358	406	170
After 2011	1,239	1,117	3,464	698
Total minimum lease payments	$2,875	$3,086	$5,781	2,063
Imputed interest (at rates of 1.1% to 10.0%)				(603)
Present value of minimum lease payments				1,460
Current portion				(110)
Long-term obligations under capital leases				$1,350

(a) Includes non-aircraft capital lease payments aggregating $22 million in years 2007 through 2011, and United Express capital lease obligations of $15 million in both 2007 and 2008, $14 million in 2009, $13 million in 2010, $12 million in 2011, and $19 million thereafter.

INSIGHT: LEASING, PERFORMANCE EVALUATION, AND THE SALES FUNCTION

Lease accounting isn't just for accountants and analysts. Savvy sales managers understand that the way contracts are structured can provide them with an edge. Knowing what performance measures your customer is focused on permits you to craft arrangements that make the customer look good—and help you make the sale.

A customer whose performance is based on net income will be indifferent between operating leases and capital leases. Over the term of the lease, rent expense under the former will equal the sum of the interest and amortization expenses of the latter. A customer whose performance metric is operating income will likely prefer a capital lease: only amortization costs influence the measure. Interest will be excluded. A customer evaluated on the basis of EBITDA (earnings before interest, taxes, depreciation, and amortization) will find nirvana in a capital lease: neither the interest nor the amortization will affect the figure. The customer gets to use an asset and there is no effect on a key performance metric!

TEST YOUR KNOWLEDGE: LEASES

The following questions offer you the chance to test your knowledge of leases.
- As of January 31, 2007, Wal-Mart reported balance sheet total liabilities and total assets of $89.6 billion and $151.2 billion, respectively. In the footnotes, the company disclosed future operating lease payments of $10.4 billion.

Future capital lease payments of $5.7 billion were discounted to $3.8 billion and disclosed at that amount on the balance sheet.

1. Describe the difference between a capital lease and an operating lease.

2. Explain why a company might want to treat its leases as operating leases.

3. Compute the effect on Wal-Mart's total liabilities to total assets ratio if the company treats all its leases as capital leases. Assume that future operating lease payments are discounted at the same rate as future capital lease payments.

4. Explain how this kind of analysis may be useful to an analyst trying to compare the financial position and performance of two companies that rely heavily on leasing.

• Your Company acquired equipment on January 1, 2007, through a leasing agreement that required an annual payment of $30,000. Assume that the lease has a term of five years and that the life of the equipment is also five years. The lease is treated as a capital lease, and the market value of the equipment is $119,781. You use the straight-line method to depreciate fixed assets. The effective annual interest rate on the lease is 8%.

1. Compute the amounts that would complete the table that follows.

2. Compute rent expense for 2007–2011 if the lease is treated as an operating lease.

3. Compute total expense over the five-year period under the two methods and comment.

119,781/5 = 23,956

Date	Balance Sheet Value of Equipment	Leasehold Obligation	Interest Expense	Depreciation Expense	Total Expense
1/01/07	119,781	118,781	9		
12/31/07	95,825	95 825			
12/31/08					
12/31/09					
12/31/10					
12/31/11					

Deferred Income Taxes

The rules governing the computation of taxable revenues and deductible expenses for tax purposes, as specified by the Internal Revenue Service or other relevant tax authorities, differ from GAAP, which cover the measurement of revenues and expenses for computing financial accounting net income. These differences can be divided into two categories: permanent and timing differences. Permanent differences do not reverse themselves over time, but timing differences do. In the United States, premiums paid on life insurance policies covering key employees, for example, are not deductible for tax purposes, but they are treated as expenses for financial reporting purposes. Interest received on municipal bonds is not included in taxable income, but is recognized as revenue on a company's income statement. The different treatments for tax and financial accounting purposes in these two examples are considered permanent, because in neither case will the effect on income of the different treatments reverse itself. GAAP ignores these permanent differences.

Temporary differences between tax and financial reporting reverse themselves over time, and under GAAP, these differences can give rise to a deferred tax asset or liability. One of many common temporary differences occurs when a company depreciates its fixed assets using an accelerated method (larger amounts in early years and smaller amounts in later years) when computing taxable income, and the straight-line method (equal amounts each year) when preparing the financial statements. This very popular strategy causes taxable income to be less than accounting income in the early periods of the asset's life, but greater than accounting income in later periods as the difference reverses itself. Similarly, in early periods, the book value of the asset for tax purposes is lower than it is for financial reporting purposes. Over time, the two book values converge.

On the income statement, income tax expense is made up of two components: current and deferred income taxes. Computing the current portion of income tax expense is straightforward: It is simply the amount due to the various tax authorities for the period.

The deferred tax expense is measured as the change in the net deferred tax asset or liability position of the company. Thus, measuring deferred tax assets and liabilities each period has a direct effect on income tax expense each period.

Although deferred tax assets and liabilities are often discussed in terms of differences in how GAAP revenues and expenses differ from taxable income (i.e., taxable revenues and allowable deductions), measuring them takes an asset and liability approach. Often, the income statement approach and the balance sheet approach yield the same measurement, but when tax rates change or tax rules change, the income statement approach yields economically suspect figures.

To illustrate, suppose that Midland Plastics purchased a piece of equipment on January 1, 20X1, for $9,000. For tax purposes, Midland computes tax-deductible depreciation using an accelerated method that recognizes $6,000, $2,000, and $1,000 in years 1, 2, and 3, respectively, of the asset's useful life. For financial reporting purposes, the company uses the straight-line method and $3,000 of depreciation expense is recognized in each of the three years. Note that in both cases, the total deduction/expense is $9,000. What differs is the timing of the expenses and thus the pattern of book values of the equipment for GAAP and for tax purposes.

Because Midland used straight-line depreciation for accounting (GAAP) purposes and accelerated depreciation for tax purposes, in the first year, the net book value of the equipment will be higher for accounting than for tax purposes. In subsequent years, this difference will reverse. Although Midland reduced its current income tax obligation by using accelerated depreciation in year 1, in later years, they will report depreciation for accounting purposes with no corresponding tax deduction. In other words, the company has a deferred tax liability. The amount of the liability is the tax effect of the (cumulative) difference between what the company has expensed for accounting and for tax: in other words, the difference in the book value of the asset for accounting and for tax purposes times the tax rate.

To illustrate, refer to Figure 9-5. Assuming an income tax rate of 40%, Midland created a deferred tax liability in year 1 of $1,200 ($3,000 × 40%) by choosing accelerated instead

Year	NBV Tax	NBV GAAP		Difference	Tax Rate		Deferred Tax Liability	Deferred Tax Expense
Purchase	$9,000	$9,000	=	$ 0	× 40%	=	$ 0	
End of 20x1	3,000 −	6,000	=	3,000	× 40%	=	1,200	$1,200
End of 20x2	1,000 −	3,000	=	2,000	× 40%	=	800	(400)
End of 20x3	0 −	0	=	0	× 40%	=	0	(800)
Total	$9,000	$9,000		$ 0			$ 0	0

Deferred tax expense is equal to the change in the deferred tax liability. In 20x1, the increase in the liability leads to an expense. The decrease in the liability in each of 20x2 and 20x3 generates deferred tax benefits (i.e., reduces deferred tax expense). However, recall that in those years, the company will have fewer tax deductions and, thus, a higher current income tax expense.

Note that if the tax rate were to change, the ending deferred tax liability would change, too, resulting in a change in the deferred tax expense for that year. For example, if at the end of 20x2, the rate changed to 35%, the ending deferred tax liability would be ($2,000 × 35% =) $700, and thus the deferred income tax benefit for that year would be $500 (i.e., $1,200 − 700). The tax benefit is higher because the company now faces a lower tax rate.

Figure 9-5. Deferred Income Tax Liability and Expense

of straight-line depreciation for tax purposes. However, the deferred tax liability reverses itself in years 2 and 3 as accelerated depreciation drops below the straight-line and the book values converge. In year 2, it reverses by $400, and in year 3, by the remaining $800.

According to GAAP, this situation creates a liability in year 1 of $1,200 because future tax payments will be higher by $1,200, relative to what they would have been had Midland used the straight-line method for tax purposes. Consequently, a deferred tax expense and a deferred tax liability in the amount of $1,200 are recognized on the income statement and balance sheet, respectively, for year 20X1. The liability is removed as the difference reverses itself and the additional taxes are paid in years 20X2 and 20X3.

DEFERRED TAXES—BASIC JOURNAL ENTRIES AND EFFECTS ON THE ACCOUNTING EQUATION (See Figure 9-5)

Assume that Midland Plastics generated taxable income of $50,000 in 20X1. In arriving at that figure, they deducted $6,000 for depreciation (see Figure 9-5; the NBV of the equipment is $9,000 less $6,000). For financial reporting purposes, the deduction was only $3,000. The company faces a 40% tax rate. The following journal entries would be recorded:

Income Tax Expense, current (E, −RE)	$20,000	
Income Tax Liability (+L)		$20,000

To record the current portion of income taxes for 20X1 (taxable income times the tax rate).

Income Tax Expense, deferred (E, −RE)	$1,200	
Deferred Income Tax Liability (+L)		$1,200

To record the deferred portion of income taxes for 20X1 (the change in the deferred tax liability).

Continuing the example, assume that Midland Plastics generated taxable income of $60,000 in 20X2. In arriving at that figure, they deducted $2,000 for depreciation (see Figure 9-5). For financial reporting purposes, the deduction was $3,000. The company faces a 40% tax rate. The following journal entries would be recorded:

Income Tax Expense, current (E, −RE)	$24,000	
Income Tax Liability (+L)		$24,000

To record the current portion of income taxes for 20X2 (taxable income times the tax rate).

Deferred Income Tax Liability (−L)	$400	
Income Tax Expense, deferred (−E, +RE)		$400

To record the deferred portion of income taxes for 20X2 (the change in the deferred tax liability—because the liability decreased, a tax benefit is recorded).

Many U.S. companies report billions of dollars of deferred income tax liability on their balance sheets. These companies, mostly manufacturers, tend to be in heavily capitalized industries where huge investments have been made in property and equipment. Over the years, these companies have grown by consistently acquiring more property and equipment than they retired, and they use accelerated depreciation methods for tax purposes and the straight-line method for financial reporting. Consequently, they continue to create tax benefits that exceed the reversals, and the deferred income tax liability continues to accumulate. The liability would become smaller if the companies downsized by acquiring fewer fixed assets than they are retiring.

Deferred tax assets can also arise when companies record expenses and liabilities for accounting purposes prior to recording them for tax purposes. Deferred tax assets represent the future tax benefits that arise when a company reports taxable income before it reports that income for accounting purposes. Bad debt expense is an example. Companies accrue expected bad debt for accounting purposes, but deduct the expense for taxes only when the specific accounts are written off as uncollectible. Another major contributor to many companies' deferred tax asset balances is postretirement health benefits. These obligations are accrued (established as expenses and liabilities) when employees earn the benefits (as they work), but they are tax deductible only when the company pays the health costs (generally after they retire).

DRILLING DOWN—DECOMPOSING ROE

$$\text{ROE} = \frac{\text{Net income}}{\text{Common equity}} = \frac{\text{NI} + \text{Interest expense}}{\text{Sales}} \times \frac{\text{Sales}}{\text{Assets}} \times \frac{\text{Assets}}{\text{Common equity}} \times \frac{\text{NI}}{\text{NI} + \text{Interest expense}}$$

The DuPont model captures capital structure and interest in two places: the ratio of assets to common equity (capital structure leverage) and the ratio of net income to net income plus interest expense (common equity leverage). Each can be decomposed further.

First, we can estimate a company's average interest rate on outstanding debts. The ratio of interest expense to long-term interest-bearing debt provides the estimate. Check the cost of recent debt issuances (listed in the notes to the financial statements) for recent rates faced by the company.

Leverage can be decomposed into a variety of short- and long-term measures. We covered those measures in Chap-

ter 4, and they include the current ratio, the quick ratio, the long-term debt to equity ratio, and the interest coverage ratio.

Additional management activities related to leverage include the company's dividend and share buyback policies, their refinancing activities, their current access to the capital markets (what's the current credit rating?) and whether they have open lines of credit.

Savvy analysts and managers adjust the financial statements for off-balance-sheet obligations such as capital leases before computing ratios and conducting analyses.

INSIGHT: TAX LOSS CARRY FORWARDS AND DEFERRED TAX ASSETS

When companies report taxable losses, under many tax systems, they are permitted to refile prior income tax returns and deduct the loss or carry the loss forward as a deduction to be taken against future taxable income. When the loss is carried back, the company generates a tax benefit immediately by reducing their current income tax expense. When the loss is available to be carried forward, there is a potential future tax benefit: one that will be realized if the company generates taxable income in the future. That benefit is considered a deferred tax asset.

The deferred tax asset is calculated using the same method used in Figure 9-5. That is, the asset for tax purposes (the loss that can be deducted against future taxable income) is com-

pared with the asset on the balance sheet (in this case, there is no asset, so the value is zero) and the difference is multiplied by the tax rate expected to be in effect when the carryforward deduction is used. The deferred tax asset is the expected future tax savings that arose from the past losses. As with accounts receivable, the deferred tax asset is tested for recoverability each year. If evidence indicates that the carryforward will expire unused (perhaps the company expects to continue to report losses for tax purposes), then a valuation allowance must be recorded. The valuation allowance works just like the allowance for doubtful accounts discussed in Chapter 7.

Online movie subscription firm Netflix, Inc., reported substantial losses through 2004, generating a large deferred tax asset for its loss carryforwards. Because the company was unsure of its ability to use the losses against future taxable income, a valuation allowance offset the entire deferred tax asset. When the company turned profitable in 2005 and deemed the carryforwards useable, the valuation allowance

was reversed, leading to a very large tax benefit that year. The note that follows explains, first, why their tax rate was not the same as the statutory U.S. rate of 35%, then lists the deferred tax asset balances, and explains movements therein.

NETFLIX, INC.
NOTES TO CONSOLIDATED FINANCIAL STATEMENTS—(continued)
(in thousands, except share and per share data and percentages)

Provision for (benefit from) income taxes differed from the amounts computed by applying the U.S. federal income tax rate of 35% to pretax income as a result of the following:

	Year Ended December 31,		
	2004	2005	2006
Expected tax expense at U.S. federal statutory rate of 35%	$ 7,404	$ 2,917	$ 28,111
State income taxes, net of federal income tax effect	28	377	3,866
Valuation allowance	(3,816)	(35,596)	(16)
Stock-based compensation	(3,471)	(1,433)	(878)
Other	36	43	153
Provision for (benefit from) income taxes	$ 181	$ (33,692)	$ 31,236

The tax effects of temporary differences and tax carryforwards that give rise to significant portions of the deferred tax assets and liabilities are presented below:

	Year Ended December 31,	
	2005	2006
Deferred tax assets:		
Net operating loss carryforwards	$ 9,905	$ —
Accruals and reserves	3,880	3,109
Depreciation	10,841	1,393
Stock-based compensation	9,728	12,769
Other	647	1,564
Gross deferred tax assets	35,001	18,835
Valuation allowance against deferred tax assets	(96)	(80)
Net deferred tax assets	$34,905	$18,755

The total valuation allowance for the years ended December 31, 2005 and 2006 decreased by $39,083 and $16, respectively.

The Company continuously monitors the circumstances impacting the expected realization of its deferred tax assets. As of December 31, 2004, the Company's deferred tax assets were offset in full by a valuation allowance because of its history of losses, limited profitable quarters to date, and the competitive landscape of online DVD rentals. As a result of the Company's analysis of expected future income at December 31, 2005, it was considered more likely than not that substantially all deferred tax assets would be realized, resulting in the release of the previously recorded valuation allowance, generating a $34,905 tax benefit. In evaluating its ability to realize the deferred tax assets, the Company considered all available positive and negative evidence, including its past operating results and the forecast of future market growth, forecasted earnings, future taxable income, and prudent and feasible tax planning strategies. The remaining valuation allowance is related to capital losses, which can only be offset against future capital gains.

As of December 31, 2006, the Company had unrecognized net operating loss carryforwards for federal tax purposes of approximately $56 million, attributable to excess tax deductions related to stock options, the benefit of which will be credited to equity when realized. The federal net operating loss carryforwards will expire from 2019 to 2025, if not previously utilized.

TEST YOUR KNOWLEDGE: DEFERRED TAXES

The following questions offer you the chance to test your knowledge of deferred taxes.

Acme, Inc., purchased machinery at the beginning of 2007 for $50,000. Management used the straight-line method to depreciate the cost for financial reporting purposes and the double-declining-balance method to depreciate the cost for tax purposes. The life of the machinery was estimated to be four years, and the salvage value was estimated as zero. Revenue less expenses other than depreciation (for financial reporting and tax purposes) equaled $100,000 in 2007, 2008, 2009, and 2010. Acme pays income taxes at a rate of 35% of taxable income. Use Figure 9-5 as a guide for your analyses.

1. Prepare the journal entries to accrue income tax expense and income tax liability for 2007, 2008, 2009, and 2010. Indicate the balance in the deferred income tax account as of the end of each of the four years.

2. Assume that the tax rate was changed by the federal government to 20% at the beginning of 2009. Repeat the exercise in (1). Would it be appropriate to recognize a gain at the end of 2009 to reflect the tax rate decrease? Why or why not? If so, how much of a gain?

3. Assume that Acme purchased additional machinery at the beginning of 2008 and 2010. Each purchase was for $50,000, and each machine had a four-year estimated life and no salvage value. Once again, the straight-line depreciation method was used for reporting purposes and the double-declining-balance method for tax purposes. Repeat the exercise in (1), assuming a tax rate of 35%. Why is the deferred income tax account one of the largest liabilities on the balance sheets of many major U.S. companies?

▶ MEASURING THE SHAREHOLDERS' INVESTMENT

The shareholders' equity section of a corporate balance sheet consists of two major components: (1) contributed capital, which reflects contributions of capital from shareholders and includes preferred stock, common stock, and additional paid-in capital, less treasury

Contributed Capital:		
Preferred stock	$ 3,000	
Common stock	15,000	
Additional paid-in capital	80,000	
Less treasury stock	(8,000)	
Total contributed capital		$ 90,000
Earned capital:		
Retained earnings	120,000	
Accumulated other comprehensive income	5,000	
Total earned capital		125,000
Total Shareholders' Equity		$215,000

Note: This format differs slightly from that used by most U.S. companies. Normally, treasury stock is disclosed below retained earnings. However, that format confuses the distinction between contributed and earned capital. See, for example, the PepsiCo disclosure below. Repurchased preferred stock is listed immediately below the preferred stock account, but repurchased common stock is listed at the very bottom.

Figure 9-6. Shareholders' Equity Section of the Balance Sheet

stock; and (2) earned capital, which reflects the amount of assets earned and retained by the corporation, consisting essentially of retained earnings and accumulated other comprehensive income. An example of the owners' equity section of a corporate balance sheet appears in Figure 9-6, followed below by the shareholders' equity section from the 2006 and 2005 balance sheets of PepsiCo.

PepsiCo, Inc., and Subsidiaries, 2006 and 2005

PepsiCo, Inc., and Subsidiaries
December 30, 2006, and December 31, 2005

(in millions except per share amounts)	2006	2005
Preferred Stock, no par value	41	41
Repurchased Preferred Stock	(120)	(110)
Common Shareholders' Equity		
Common stock, par value 1²/₃¢ per share (issued 1,782 shares)	30	30
Capital in excess of par value	584	614
Retained earnings	24,837	21,116
Accumulated other comprehensive loss	(2,246)	(1,053)
	23,205	20,707
Less repurchased common stock, at cost (144 and 126 shares, respectively)	(7,758)	(6,387)
Total Common Shareholders' Equity	15,447	14,320
Total Liabilities and Shareholders' Equity	$29,930	$31,727

Preferred Stock

Preferred stock is so-called because preferred shareholders have certain rights not shared by common shareholders. These rights relate to the receipt of dividends and/or to claims on assets in case of liquidation. Stock preferred as to dividends confers the right to receive dividends before common shareholders. Normally, a specific annual dividend is paid to the preferred shareholders before any payments are made to the common shareholders, assuming that a dividend is declared by the board of directors. The remaining amount of the dividend is then paid to the common shareholders. The amount of the preferred annual dividend payment is normally expressed as either an absolute amount or as a percentage of an amount referred to as the par value of the preferred stock. Stock preferred as to assets carries a claim to the corporation's assets, in case of liquidation, with a higher priority than the claim carried by common stock. Most preferred stock carries both rights, but the exact characteristics and terms of preferred stock vary from one issue to the next.

Furthermore, preferred shares normally do not carry a right to vote in the election of the board of directors, and many contain a call provision that allows, or requires, the corporation to redeem (buy back) the shares for a specified price after a specified date. In these respects, preferred shares closely resemble debt. In fact, in some cases, the Internal Revenue Service has allowed corporations to deduct preferred dividends from taxable income because they were construed as interest for tax purposes.

DRILLING DOWN—HOW DO PREFERRED SHARES FIT IN?

$$\text{ROE} = \frac{\text{Net income}}{\text{Common equity}} = \frac{\text{NI} + \text{Interest expense}}{\text{Sales}} \times \frac{\text{Sales}}{\text{Assets}} \times \frac{\text{Assets}}{\text{Common equity}} \times \frac{\text{NI}}{\text{NI} + \text{Interest expense}}$$

Preferred stock is normally disclosed at the top of the shareholders' equity section, where it is located immediately below long-term liabilities. Issuing preferred stock is often desirable because management can raise what is essentially debt capital without increasing the liabilities reported on the balance sheet. That might serve to avoid violating covenants that restrict the amount of debt a company is allowed to issue. If the preferred stock carries no voting power, this strategy also raises capital without diluting the ownership influence of the existing shareholders. That might be important in a family-controlled business where the founder wants to share profits with children, but doesn't want to give up control over strategic matters requiring votes. Due to the "hybrid" character of preferred stock, financial statement users interested in computing ratios that involve distinctions between debt and equity (e.g., capital structure leverage) may find it more useful to treat it as a long-term liability and the dividend payments as interest. Occasionally, preferred stock is disclosed in the liability section of the balance sheet.

ROE to common shareholders can be calculated subtracting the preferred stock from total equity to arrive at common equity and subtracting the preferred dividends from net income (i.e., view them as a form of interest expense).

Common Stock

As a true equity security, common shares are characterized by three fundamental rights: (1) the right to receive dividends if they are declared by the board of directors; (2) a residual right to the corporation's assets in case of liquidation; and (3) the right to exert control over management, which includes the right to vote in the annual election of the board of directors and the right to vote on certain significant transactions proposed by management (e.g., large repurchases of outstanding shares and major acquisitions).

The value of the common stock issued by a corporation can be described in a number of different and sometimes confusing ways. *Market value* is the price at which the stock can be exchanged on the open market. This amount varies from day to day, based primarily on changes in investor expectations about the financial condition of the issuing company, interest rates, and other factors. The market prices of the common stocks of publicly traded companies must be disclosed in the notes to their financial reports. Market value is not a measure of the shareholders' investment, but rather a measure of the market's expectation about the company's ability to generate future returns.

The *book value* of a share of common stock is the book value of the corporation (i.e., assets less liabilities and preferred stock), as indicated on the balance sheet, divided by the number of common shares presently held by the shareholders. This value rarely approximates the market value of a common share, because the balance sheet, in general, does not represent a measure of the market value of the company. Recall from Chapter 5 that dividing the market value of a company's common stock by its book value (market-to-book ratio) provides a ratio that indicates the extent to which the market believes that the balance sheet reflects the company's true value. Ratios equal to 1 indicate that a company's net book value (as measured by the balance sheet) is perceived by the market to be a fair reflection of the company's economic value. More commonly, market-to-book ratios are somewhat larger than 1, indicating that in the opinion of market participants, the balance sheet is a conservative measure of the company's true value and that growth opportunities exist.

The ***par value*** (sometimes called "stated value") of a share of common stock has no relationship to its market value or book value and, for the most part, has little economic significance. At one time, it represented a legal concept, instituted by some states, intended to protect creditors; however, over time, the concept proved to be largely ineffective. It is not uncommon for corporations to issue either no-par common stock or common stock with extremely low par values.

Valuing Common and Preferred Stock on the Balance Sheet

Corporate annual reports contain three disclosures concerning the number of shares of preferred and common stock: authorized, issued, and outstanding. Authorized shares represent the number of shares a corporation is entitled to issue by its corporate charter. Additional authorizations must be approved by the board of directors and are often subject to shareholder vote. Issued shares have been sold to shareholders, and may or may not be currently outstanding due to treasury stock purchases. Outstanding shares represent the number currently held by shareholders, equal to issued shares less repurchased shares held in treasury.

The amount that appears in the preferred and common stock accounts on the balance sheet ($3,000 and $15,000 in Figure 9-6) is equal to the number of issued shares times their par value. When new shares are issued, if the market price of the newly issued shares exceeds the par value, which is almost always the case, the difference between the market price and the par value is disclosed in the additional paid-in capital account ("capital in excess of par" at PepsiCo).

For example, if 1,000 shares of preferred or common stock with a par value of $1 were issued for a per-share market price of $10, the company's cash balance would increase by $10,000 (1,000 shares × $10 per share); the preferred or common stock account would increase by $1,000 (1,000 shares × $1 par value per share); and the additional paid-in capital account would increase by $9,000 (1,000 shares × [$10 − $1 per share]). If the stock issued in the example had no par value, the entire $10,000 would be included in the preferred or common stock account.

ISSUING COMMON OR PREFERRED STOCK—BASIC JOURNAL ENTRIES AND EFFECTS ON THE ACCOUNTING EQUATION

Cash (+A)	$10,000	*To record the issuance of 1,000 shares of common or pre-*
Common or Preferred Stock (+CC)	$1,000	*ferred stock. The stock was issued for $10 per share and has*
Additional Paid in Capital (+CC)	$9,000	*a par value of $1 per share.*

Treasury Stock

Outstanding common stock is often repurchased and either (1) held *in **treasury***, awaiting to be reissued at a later date, or (2) retired. Repurchases of this nature normally must be authorized and approved by a company's shareholders and board of directors. Treasury stock carries none of the usual rights of common stock ownership. That is, while common shares are held in treasury, they lose their voting power and their right to receive dividends.

Companies purchase outstanding common shares, hold them in treasury, and reissue them for many reasons. By reducing a company's cash position and increasing the pro-portionate control of its existing shareholders, treasury stock buyback programs can be used to fend off possible takeover attempts. Some believe that purchasing treasury stock can increase the market price of a company's outstanding stock by reducing the number of outstanding shares, and signaling market participants that management is bullish about investing in its own stock. Another common reason is to support employee stock-based compensation (option) plans. Treasury shares have already been authorized, so it is rela-tively easy to reissue treasury shares as employees exercise their rights to purchase shares in accordance with company compensation plans. Treasury shares also are issued as payment when acquiring other companies. Finally, treasury stock purchases are often made to return cash to shareholders. In this sense, they resemble dividends, especially if the treasury stock purchase is proportionate across the shareholders. Many firms are reluctant to cut dividend levels once they are established. Share repurchases are considered more flexible in that respect.

Valuing Treasury Stock on the Balance Sheet

When a company purchases its own outstanding common stock and holds it in treasury, the cash balance is reduced and the treasury stock account, which represents a reduction of contributed capital, is increased by the number of shares purchased times the cost of each share. For example, if a company purchased 5,000 shares of its own outstanding stock for $20 per share, the cash balance would be decreased and the treasury stock account would be increased by $100,000 (5,000 shares × $20 per share). Because treasury stock is a contra-equity account, any increases in its balance serve to reduce overall equity.

TREASURY STOCK PURCHASES—BASIC JOURNAL ENTRIES AND EFFECTS ON THE ACCOUNTING EQUATION

Treasury Stock (−CC)	$100,000	*To record the purchase of 5,000 shares of common stock*
Cash (−A)	$100,000	*(i.e., treasury stock) at $20 per share.*

When a company reissues treasury stock, the cash account is increased and the treasury stock account is decreased by the number of shares reissued times the (re)issuance price. If the issuance price differs from the cost (balance sheet value) of the treasury stock, the difference is reflected in the additional paid-in capital account.

For example, assume that a company reissued 2,000 treasury shares, originally repur-chased for $10, for $15 per share. The cash balance would increase by $30,000 (2,000 shares × $15 per share); the treasury stock account would be reduced by $20,000 (2,000 shares × $10 per share); and additional paid-in capital would be increased by $10,000 (2,000 shares × [$15 - $10]). If instead the treasury shares were reissued for $5 (instead of $15) per share, the cash balance would only be increased by $10,000 (2,000 shares × $5 per share) and additional paid-in capital would be decreased by $10,000 (2,000 × [$5 - $10]).

TREASURY STOCK REISSUANCES—BASIC JOURNAL ENTRIES AND EFFECTS ON THE ACCOUNTING EQUATION

Cash (+A)	$30,000	
APIC (+CC)		$20,000
Treasury Stock (+CC)		$10,000

To record the sale of 2,000 shares of treasury stock. The stock was sold for $15 per share. The company had initially acquired it at $10 per share.
or
APIC = additional paid-in capital

Cash (+A)	$10,000	
APIC (−CC)	$10,000	
Treasury Stock (+CC)		$20,000

To record the sale of 2,000 shares of treasury stock. The stock was sold for $5 per share. The company had initially acquired it at $10 per share.

TEST YOUR KNOWLEDGE: TREASURY STOCK

The following questions offer you the chance to test your knowledge of treasury stock.

• The *Wall Street Journal* once reported, "Philip Morris Cos., in an aggressive move to boost its stock price, announced a $6 billion stock buyback plan and raised its quarterly dividend nearly 20%.... The announcement, which came after a regularly scheduled board meeting, raised the company's stock to a 52-week high.... Separately, rating agencies Standard & Poor's Rating Group and Moody's Investors Service Inc. confirmed their ratings on Philip Morris's debt. While both agencies said Philip Morris is continuing to generate strong cash flow, Moody's ... placed Philip Morris at the low end of its current rating level."

1. Explain how this announcement can increase the stock price of Philip Morris (now known as Altria Group), while at the same time reducing its credit rating.

• In a September 20, 2002, article entitled "Buybacks or Giveaways," *CFO.com* reported, "... large repurchase programs require a whole lot of capital. Critics of buybacks contend that companies can put their cash to better use. They also point out that investors are more likely to reward a company that attempts to grow its business—rather than artificially inflate its stock price." The article goes on to quote an investment banker as saying that "[stock repurchase programs] can be a sign that a company can't find anything better to do with its cash."

1. Describe some other uses for a company's cash. How could these uses benefit shareholders more than a stock repurchase?

2. Why might the stock market interpret a company's purchase of its own shares as a way to "artificially inflate" its stock price?

3. If the stock market is trading at very high levels, what risks do companies face with their stock repurchasing plans?

Stock Options

Stock options have become a very popular way to compensate executives. In addition to cash or other assets, many companies compensate executives by giving them the option to purchase equity securities at a fixed price over a specified period. For example, in fiscal 2005, Dell Inc. granted Michael Dell, the company founder and chairman of the board, options to purchase up to 400,000 shares of Dell Inc. stock. At the time of the grant, Dell shares were trading for approximately $33 per share. Michael Dell can exercise the options and purchase shares of the company for that same price any time within the next 10 years. If, within the 10-year period, Dell Inc.'s stock price increases to $45 per share, the executive can exercise the option by purchasing stock from Dell Inc. at $33 per share, which can then be sold for $45, creating an immediate $12 gain per share for the executive. If the company's stock decreases to $5 per share, the executive need not exercise the options. Companies consider stock options attractive because they require no cash payment when granted and motivate executives to maximize the company's share price and market value; executives consider them attractive because they have great upside potential with no risk of loss.

Economists and accounting standard setters have argued for years that issuing stock options is costly to companies, and stock option compensation expense should be recognized on the income statement. Industry has countered that placing a dollar value on stock options is highly subjective, suggesting that estimates of stock option compensation expense are too unreliable for placement on the income statement. New accounting standards have been issued in the United States, Statement Financial Accounting Standard (SFAS No. 123R), and internationally, International Financial Reporting Standard (IFRS 2), that require companies to include stock option compensation expense on the income statement. For many companies, especially in the high-tech industry where management is commonly compensated with stock options, estimates of stock option compensation can be very large. The stock options granted to Michael Dell in fiscal 2005 were estimated to be worth $4,196,000 at the grant date. Those granted to Kevin Rollins, then-CEO, had a grant date fair value of $14,412,000. The fair value of all options granted by Dell in fiscal 2005 was $812 million—none of which was reported as an expense (as SFAS No. 123R was not yet in effect). Had the options granted been expensed, net income would have dropped 27% from $3,043 million to $2,231 million.

MEASUREMENT CHALLENGE—VALUING EMPLOYEE STOCK OPTIONS

Coming up with a value for the stock options granted to employees is a major measurement challenge. Some people argue that the task is so difficult that it can't be done reliably. They argue that, given the difficulty, we should ignore the cost. Others argue that financial reporting requires many estimates and surely estimating the cost at $0 is wrong. We know the options have some value—just try taking them away from the employees

The measurement challenge exists because employee stock options often carry restrictions that ordinary traded options do not. For example, they may not be immediately exercisable, and they are generally not transferable and expire if an employee leaves the company. Valuing options for private companies involves finding comparable public firms and that can be challenging.

Measurement challenge or not, employee stock options should be treated as costs. As famous investor Warren Buffett eloquently opined in the *Washington Post* (April 9, 2002), "1) If options aren't a form of compensation, what are they? 2) If compensation isn't an expense, what is it? 3) And if expenses shouldn't go into the calculation of earnings, where in the world should they go?"

Under the new rules, the value of granted stock options must be estimated at the grant date, using an acceptable valuation formula. That grant date value is amortized over the vesting period of the options as stock option compensation expense on the income statement, reducing net income and ultimately retained earnings. At the same time, an equal amount will increase additional paid-in capital, reflecting that the shareholders' investment has been increased. In essence, the existing shareholders paid for the stock options by giving managers a right that may allow them to buy stock in the future at less than market prices.

EMPLOYEE STOCK OPTIONS—BASIC JOURNAL ENTRIES AND EFFECTS ON THE ACCOUNTING EQUATION

At the grant date, assume that 10,000 options were issued to employees. The strike price of the options (in this example, the current market price of the shares) is $10. The options vest over a three-year period and can be exercised for up to 10 years. The company has estimated the market value of the options to be $36,000 at grant date.

On the grant date, no entry is recorded, but footnote disclosure would be required.

Each year, one third of the options vest and the company records one third of the $36,000 cost:

Compensation Expense (+E, −RE) $12,000
    Additional Paid-In Capital, Options (+CC) $12,000
To record the vesting of one third of the options granted.

If the employees exercise all the options, the company records:

Cash (+A) $100,000
Additional Paid-In Capital,
    Options (−CC) $36,000
    Common Stock (+CC) $10,000
    Additional Paid-In Capital (+CC) $126,000
To record the exercise of 10,000 stock options. The strike price was $10 per share. The shares in this example are assumed to have a par value of $1 per share.

The shares are recorded at an amount equal to what the company received for them: $100,000 in cash and $36,000 in noncash wages (compensation).

If the options expire unexercised, the company records:

Additional Paid-In Capital, Options (−CC) $36,000
    Additional Paid-In Capital (+CC) $36,000
To record the expiration of 10,000 in stock options.

Note that even though the options expire unexercised, there is no adjustment to the compensation expense that was recorded over the vesting period.

Retained Earnings

Retained earnings is a measure of previously recognized profits that have not been paid to the shareholders in the form of dividends. As indicated in Figure 9-2, major U.S. corporations rely heavily on internally generated funds as a source of capital. This section discusses two factors that affect the retained earnings balance: (1) dividends and (2) appropriations.

Dividends
Dividends are proportionate distributions of cash or property to the shareholders of a corporation. They are declared by a formal resolution of the board of directors (usually quarterly), and the amount is usually announced on a per-share basis. Cash dividends, by far the most common, represent distributions of cash. Property dividends (dividends in kind) are distributions of property, usually debt or equity securities in other companies. Three dividend dates are important: (1) the date of declaration, when the dividends are declared by the board; (2) the date of record (the owner on that date receives the dividend); and (3) the date of payment, when the distribution is actually made.

When and how much of a dividend to declare depends on a number of factors, such as the nature, financial condition, and desired image of the company, as well as legal constraints. If dividends are to be paid in cash, the board of directors must first be certain that the corporation has sufficient cash to meet the payment. That requires a projection of the operating cash flow, including, for example, analyses of the company's current cash position, future sales, receivables, inventory purchases, and fixed-asset replacements. It is usually wise to make sure that the company's operating cash needs can be met before cash dividends are paid.

The goals of a corporation and the nature of its activities also have a bearing on dividend policy. Relatively young, fast-growing companies often adopt policies of paying no dividends, choosing instead to reinvest profits in growth opportunities. The shareholders receive their returns in the form of stock price appreciation. Many established companies pay quarterly dividends and often attempt to gradually, but consistently, increase them from year to year. This policy, which provides a consistent dividend while retaining some funds to finance available growth opportunities, tends to reflect an image of stability, strength, and permanence.

State laws and debt covenants can also limit the payment of dividends. In most states, the dollar amount of retained earnings less the cost of treasury stock sets a limit on the payment of dividends. In addition, the terms of debt contracts may further limit dividend payments to an even smaller portion of retained earnings.

Accounting for Dividends

When the board of directors declares a dividend (cash or property), on the date of declaration, a current liability (dividend payable) in the amount of the fair market value of the asset given up is created and the retained earnings account is reduced. The dividends payable account is removed from the balance sheet when the dividend is paid on the date of payment.

For example, assume that the board of directors declared a cash dividend of $5 per share on 1,000 outstanding shares. As of the date of declaration, a current liability (dividend payable) of $5,000 (1,000 shares × $5 per share) is created, and retained earnings is reduced by $5,000. At the date of payment, the current liability and the cash balance would both be reduced by $5,000.

DIVIDENDS—BASIC JOURNAL ENTRIES AND EFFECTS ON THE ACCOUNTING EQUATION

On date of dividend declaration,

| Retained Earnings (−RE) | $5,000 | |
| Dividends Payable (+L) | | $5,000 |

To record the declaration of $5,000 in dividends.

On the date of dividend payment,

| Dividend Payable (−L) | $5,000 | |
| Cash (−A) | | $5,000 |

To record payment of dividends.

Stock Splits and Stock Dividends

Corporations can distribute additional shares to existing shareholders by declaring either a stock split or a stock dividend. For practical purposes, there is little difference between the two. In both cases, the existing shareholders receive additional shares, and in neither case are the assets or liabilities of the corporation increased or decreased.

In a stock split, the number of outstanding shares is simply "split" into smaller units, which requires the corporation to distribute additional shares. A 2:1 stock split, for example, serves to double the number of outstanding shares, which requires that the company distribute an additional share for each common share outstanding. A 3:1 stock split triples the number of outstanding shares, which the company executes by distributing two additional shares for each one outstanding. In a 3:2 stock split, one additional share is issued for every two outstanding. No accounts on the financial statements are adjusted when a stock split occurs because no assets or liabilities are exchanged, and the capital structure of the company remains unchanged.

In a stock dividend, additional shares, usually expressed as a percentage of the outstanding shares, are issued to the shareholders. Large stock dividends have essentially the same effect as stock splits. Both a 100% stock dividend and a 2:1 stock split, for example, double the number of outstanding shares. Similarly, both a 50% stock dividend and a 3:2 stock split increase outstanding shares by 50%. Smaller stock dividends (e.g., 10%) increase the stockholdings of all shareholders by smaller amounts.

The methods used to account for stock dividends vary across companies. Accounting standards indicate that when a stock dividend is declared, retained earnings should be reduced, and contributed capital should be increased by the market value of the number of shares issued. But, in practice, not all companies follow these guidelines because very little economic justification exists for such accounting treatment—like stock splits, no assets or liabilities are exchanged and the company's capital structure remains unchanged. Yes, the shareholders now hold more shares, but their relative interest in the company is unchanged because the shares of all shareholders have been increased proportionately. Reducing retained earnings and increasing contributed capital for an event that has almost no economic significance blurs the distinction between earned and contributed capital. Fortunately, how a company chooses to account for stock dividends has no effect on the total shareholders' investment, an important part of assessing value creation.

Perhaps the most popular reason for declaring a stock split or a large stock dividend is to reduce the per-share price of the outstanding shares so that investors can more easily purchase them. Many managers believe that such an action encourages better public relations and wider stock ownership. Furthermore, company stock prices often appear to increase after a stock split is announced, consistent with the interpretation that the split signals investors that management believes that it can maintain the value of the stock in the future. Perhaps this signal provides investors with positive information about the company's prospects unavailable prior to the announcement.

The reasons for small stock dividends are unclear. Perhaps cash-poor corporations distribute stock dividends instead of cash dividends so that shareholders are at least receiving something, but this strategy could be interpreted as a publicity gesture. It may satisfy uninformed shareholders, who believe that they have received additional assets, but more likely, it signals financial problems. Finally, corporations may issue stock dividends to reduce retained earnings, placing a more restrictive limitation on future dividend payments, but how such a limitation benefits the company and its shareholders is not obvious.

RED FLAGS—REVERSE STOCK SPLITS

Sometimes companies engage in reverse stock splits. The Securities and Exchange Commission provides the following description, "... if you own 10,000 shares of a company and it declares a one for ten reverse split, you will own a total of 1,000 shares after the split. A reverse stock split has no affect [sic] on the value of what shareholders own. Companies often split their stock when they believe the price of their stock is too low to attract investors to buy their stock. Some

(continues)

RED FLAGS—REVERSE STOCK SPLITS (*continued*)

reverse stock splits cause small shareholders to be "cashed out" so that they no longer own the company's shares."

Another reason for a reverse split is to raise the price of a stock above $1.00 per share. A 1-for-10 reverse split of shares that trade at 12 cents per share brings the new share to $1.20. That is important for companies whose shares trade on stock exchanges that require minimum share prices above $1 (e.g., the New York Stock Exchange). When the only way to keep trading is to use a reverse split, that's a red flag. It suggests that management doesn't think operations are going to be successful enough in the short run to raise the stock price above the required minimum.

Appropriations of Retained Earnings

An appropriation of retained earnings is an agreement to restrict a portion of retained earnings from the payment of future dividends. It involves no asset or liability exchanges and has no effect on the company's capital structure. Such agreements are executed either at the discretion of the board of directors or in conformance with the terms of debt contracts, restricting dividend payments to free cash for special future needs (e.g., capital expansion and debt payments). Korean electronics giant Samsung Electronics provides a detailed description of the appropriations of its retained earnings. Some of these are required under Korean commercial law, others appear to be at the discretion of the company. In either case, the appropriations affect the level of dividends that Samsung shareholders can expect in the near term. We look at Samsung in more detail in an end-of-chapter case.

Accumulated Other Comprehensive Income

Accumulated other comprehensive income is equivalent to retained earnings in that it generally reflects changes in asset and liability values due to operating activities. Unlike retained earnings, however, these changes were not recognized as revenues or expenses on the income statement, and therefore did not affect net income. Changes in the values of investments in equity securities classified as available for sale increase or decrease accumulated other comprehensive income, but are not disclosed on the income statement (see Chapter 8). Changes in the values of assets and liabilities associated with translating the financial statements of certain subsidiaries expressed in foreign currencies to U.S. dollars for purposes of consolidation represents a second example. The accumulated other comprehensive income account can maintain a positive or a negative balance, depending on the direction of the changes in value. Increases in assets and decreases in liabilities increase accumulated other comprehensive income, while decreases in assets and increases in liabilities decrease the account. Importantly, these changes affect the measure of the shareholders' total investment and therefore affect the assessment of value creation.

▶ FINANCING ACTIVITIES AND THE STATEMENTS OF CASH FLOW AND SHAREHOLDERS' EQUITY

Figures 9-7 and 9-8 contain the financing section of the statement of cash flows and the statement of common shareholders' equity, respectively, for PepsiCo as of December 30, 2006. The statement of common shareholders' equity contains both a reconciliation of the shareholders' equity accounts, as well as a statement of total comprehensive income.

PepsiCo, Inc., and Subsidiaries Fiscal years ended December 30, 2006, December 31, 2005, and December 25, 2004 (in millions)	2006	2005	2004
Financing Activities			
Proceeds from issuances of long-term debt..	$ 51	$ 25	$ 504
Payments of long-term debt..	(157)	(177)	(512)
Short-term borrowings, by original maturity			
More than three months—proceeds...	185	332	153
More than three months—payments...	(358)	(85)	(160)
Three months or less, net..	(2,168)	1,601	1,119
Cash dividends paid..	(1,854)	(1,642)	(1,329)
Share repurchases—common..	(3,000)	(3,012)	(3,028)
Share repurchases—preferred...	(10)	(19)	(27)
Proceeds from exercises of stock options...	1,194	1,099	965
Excess tax benefits from share-based payment arrangements.....................	134	–	–
Net Cash Used for Financing Activities..	**$ (5,983)**	**$ (1,878)**	**$ (2,315)**

Figure 9-7. Statement of Cash Flows (Excerpts)

With respect to debt transactions, the financing section of the statement of cash flows shows that, over the three-year period, PepsiCo paid down its long-term debt—payments of $846 million ($157 + $177 + $512), exceeding proceeds of $580 million ($51 + $25 + $504) by $266 million. However, its short-term debt increased by more as total proceeds of $3,390 million ($185 + $332 + $153 + $1,601 + $1,119) exceeded payments of $2,771 ($358 + $85 + $160 + $2,168) by $619 million. Consequently, its overall debt position increased by $353 million, a relatively small amount given that total liabilities for PepsiCo at the end of 2006 was more than $14 billion.

Transactions affecting stockholders' equity are reflected on both statements (Figures 9-7 and 9-8). Concerning dividends, the dollar amounts on the two statements differ slightly because the statement of cash flows reflects dividends actually *paid*, while the statement of stockholders' equity reflects dividends *declared*. During 2006, PepsiCo reported net income of $5,642 million and declared total dividends of $1,921 million (34% of net income). This percentage is a bit below the percentage for 2005 (41%) and equal to the percentage in 2004 (34%).

During the three-year period, PepsiCo spent approximately $9 billion on treasury stock purchases, which when added to dividend payments of almost $5 billion, indicates that the company transferred almost $14 billion to its shareholders. The company reissued some of these treasury shares—$94 million ($31 + $31 + $32)—to employees who exercised their stock options, collecting approximately $3.258 billion ($1,194 + $1,099 + $965). Furthermore, compensation expense on stock options, which were reported on the income statement and increased capital in excess of par value, totaled $270 million (2006), $311 million (2005), and $368 million (2004).

On the statement of comprehensive income, the main difference between comprehensive income and net income is due to currency translations adjustments, necessary when the financial statements of PepsiCo's foreign subsidiaries (denominated in non-U.S. currencies) are consolidated with those of the U.S. parent. Positive adjustments occur when the non-U.S. currencies rise relative to the U.S. dollar and negative adjustments occur when the non-U.S. currencies fall against the U.S. dollar (assuming a net asset position for the subsidiary). Unrealized gains on securities are also reported, reflecting price increases on short-term investments held by PepsiCo classified as available for sale (see Chapter 8).

Consolidated Statement of Common Shareholders' Equity
PepsiCo, Inc., and Subsidiaries
Fiscal years ended December 30, 2006, December 31, 2005, and December 25, 2004

(in millions)	2006 Shares	2006 Amount	2005 Shares	2005 Amount	2004 Shares	2004 Amount
Common Stock...........	1,782	$ 30	1,782	$ 30	1,782	$ 30
Capital in Excess of Par Value						
Balance, beginning of year.........................		614		618		548
Stock-based compensation expense..........................		270		311		368
Stock option exercises[a]...............................		(300)		(315)		(298)
Balance, end of year................................		584		614		618
Retained Earnings						
Balance, beginning of year.........................		21,116		18,730		15,961
Net income................................		5,642		4,078		4,212
Cash dividends declared—common...........................		(1,912)		(1,684)		(1,438)
Cash dividends declared—preferred........................		(1)		(3)		(3)
Cash dividends declared—RSUs...............................		(8)		(5)		(2)
Balance, end of year................................		24,837		21,116		18,730
Accumulated Other Comprehensive Loss						
Balance, beginning of year.........................		(1,053)		(886)		(1,267)
Currency translation adjustment..................................		465		(251)		401
Cash flow hedges, net of tax:						
Net derivative (losses)/gains.................................		(18)		54		(16)
Reclassification of (gains)/losses to net income.....		(5)		(8)		9
Unamortized pension and retiree medical, net of tax....		(1,782)		–		–
Minimum pension liability adjustment, net of tax.........		138		16		(19)
Unrealized gain on securities, net of tax.....................		9		24		6
Other...		–		(2)		–
Balance, end of year................................		(2,246)		(1,053)		(886)
Repurchased Common Stock						
Balance, beginning of year.........................	(126)	(6,387)	(103)	(4,920)	(77)	(3,376)
Share repurchases.................................	(49)	(3,000)	(54)	(2,995)	(58)	(2,994)
Stock option exercises...............................	31	1,619	31	1,523	32	1,434
Other..	–	10	–	5	–	16
Balance, end of year................................	(144)	(7,758)	(126)	(6,387)	(103)	(4,920)
Total Common Shareholders' Equity........................		**$15,447**		**$14,320**		**$13,572**

	2006	2005	2004
Comprehensive Income			
Net income...	$ 5,642	$ 4,078	$ 4,212
Currency translation adjustment.................................	465	(251)	401
Cash flow hedges, net of tax.......................................	(23)	46	(7)
Minimum pension liability adjustment, net of tax.........	5	16	(19)
Unrealized gain on securities, net of tax.....................	9	24	6
Other...	–	(2)	–
Total Comprehensive Income.....................................	**$ 6,098**	**$ 3,911**	**$ 4,593**

(a) Includes total tax benefits of $130 million in 2006, $125 million in 2005, and $183 million in 2004.
See accompanying notes to consolidated financial statements.

Figure 9-8. Consolidated Statement of Common Shareholders' Equity

▶ THE RISE OF INTERNATIONAL CAPITAL MARKETS

U.S. capital markets are by far the largest in the world. As the world of business has become global, security exchanges outside the United States have become more and more important. The stock of JCPenney, for example, is traded not only on the New York Exchange, but also on exchanges in Antwerp and Brussels; General Electric is traded in New York, London, and Tokyo; Coca-Cola is traded in Frankfurt in addition to five different exchanges in Switzerland; and American Express stock is listed on no less than 15 stock exchanges, 11 of which are outside the United States. It is also true that many companies outside the United States list their equity securities on U.S. exchanges. A majority of Sony's equity is held in New York, and each year billions of dollars are raised through equity issuances on U.S. stock exchanges by non-U.S. companies. Indeed, a "world stock exchange" seems to be emerging.

The increasing level of international trading has important implications for accountants who must provide the financial reports necessary to support this investment activity. Each exchange, for example, has different reporting requirements, and issuing companies must prepare their financial statements and supporting disclosures in a manner that conforms to those requirements. To date, the requirements of the U.S. exchanges have been the most difficult to meet, which in turn has discouraged many companies from listing their securities on the U.S. exchanges and from raising funds in U.S. capital markets.

However, international accounting standards, as set by the International Accounting Standards Board (IASB), have become increasingly important because more and more non-U.S. exchanges are accepting them. Since 2005, all publicly traded companies in the European Union are required to use the IASB's International Financial Reporting Standards (IFRS). These are far more detailed than many EU companies are used to, and not all companies are pleased with the change. Investors stand to gain, however, as disclosures become more consistent and transparent. The SEC has recently allowed non-U.S. companies whose financial statements comply with IASB standards to list on U.S. exchanges. Indeed, the SEC recently invited public comment on a proposal to allow U.S. companies to file their financial statements in accordance with IFRS. Furthermore, convergence projects between the FASB and IASB are quicky removing differences in accounting standards. For now, managers raising capital and using financial data from customers, suppliers, and competitors around the globe should monitor and understand the key differences between U.S. GAAP and IFRS and how they affect financial reports.

▶ SUMMARY

This chapter examines the nature of debt and equity and how it is valued on the financial statements. Debt and equity represent important sources of financing and play important roles in value creation and its measurement. To create shareholder value, management must generate a return through operating (Chapter 7) and investing (Chapter 8) activities that exceeds the value of debt and equity multiplied by their respective costs (Chapter 9).

We began by describing the differences between debt and equity and introduced hybrid securities, which contain characteristics of each. We then covered several forms of contractual debt and the methods used to account for them based on the effective interest rate—the actual cost of the debt. A discussion of operating and capital leases followed, and the section on debt concluded with deferred tax liabilities and assets, which arise from timing differences between tax and financial accounting rules.

We then covered the nature of shareholders' equity and how to account for a variety of equity transactions—issuance of stock, purchase and reissuance of treasury stock, stock options, dividends (cash and stock, as well as splits), and appropriations of retained earnings. We concluded with reviews of PepsiCo's statement of cash flows (financing section) and statement of common shareholders' equity, and a discussion of international capital markets.

▶ CASES AND REVIEW QUESTIONS

Home Depot—Share Buybacks and Value Creation

Home Depot's 2006 financial statements are included in the end-of-chapter case in Chapter 1.

A July 2, 2007, article in the *Financial Times* reported that Home Depot would borrow funds to make a very large stock buyback. Read the article and answer the following questions.

1. Decompose Home Depot's 2006 ROE using the DuPont model specified below. As explained in Chapter 3, interest expense is net of related tax effects. Simplify the analysis by using ending balance sheet data where applicable. Is the company creating value for its shareholders?

$$\text{ROE} = \frac{\text{Net income}}{\text{Common equity}} = \frac{\text{NI} + \text{Interest expense}}{\text{Sales}} \times \frac{\text{Sales}}{\text{Assets}} \times \frac{\text{Assets}}{\text{Common equity}} \times \frac{\text{NI}}{\text{NI} + \text{Interest expense}}$$

2. Use information in the *Financial Times* article to restate your ROE analysis, assuming that Home Depot completed the share buyback at the beginning of 2006. Assume that interest on the incremental borrowing is charged at 8%. Discuss how ROE and its components change. Are the shareholders better off as a result of the change in capital structure?

FINANCIAL TIMES

2 July 2007

US groups borrow to pay out to investors.

By RICHARD BEALES and FRANCESCO GUERRERA

Some US companies are starting to take on more debt in order to pay it out to shareholders—a response to rampant leveraged buy-outs and activist investors.

The moves, while still unusual, could herald a gradual shift among publicly listed companies towards more aggressive capital structures.

Recent announcements include home improvement retailer Home Depot's intention to borrow $12bn (£6bn) to help finance a $22.5bn share buy-back and plans at Expedia, the online travel agent, to spend $3.5bn buying back 42 per cent of its shares—funding part of the buy-back with debt.

Tobias Levkovich, chief US equity strategist at Citigroup, said such announcements could be early indications of a change in attitude. "The bottom line is that managements are starting to look at this more aggressively," he said. "Shareholders, particularly in the large-cap world, are getting more frustrated."

He said even if the jittery credit conditions of recent weeks continued, making debt more expensive, companies could still afford to borrow more. "They're hurting their returns by being so under-levered," he said.

The latest round of borrowing is aimed at funding returns to shareholders rather than more traditional capital or research investment.

Edward Marrinan, head of credit strategy at JPMorgan, said that some recent moves to return cash to shareholders were aimed at staving off activist investors.

"Management understandably wants to retain as much control over their own company's destiny as possible," he said.

Home Depot's proposed buy-back is one of the largest in US corporate history.

Carol Tome, chief financial officer, told Wall Street analysts that increased indebtedness was justified to keep rewarding shareholders in the face of slower growth in profits and sales. She said. "As a maturing company, our financing strategy is evolving to one that facilitates capital distribution."

Ms. Tome said Home Depot, whose previous chief executive Robert Nardelli stepped down in January amid a controversy over his compensation and treatment of shareholders, would accept a downgrade by credit agencies as a result of its heavier debt load provided that it retained an investment grade rating.

In spite of such evidence, some analysts say the limited shift to gear up and reward shareholders with the proceeds will be restricted to specific cases where the threat of noisy activism or private equity attention has forced action.

Iron Mountain Incorporated—Financing Activities and Value Creation

Excerpts from the 2004 Iron Mountain Incorporated financial statements are presented on the following pages. Iron Mountain is a document storage and records-management company. Read the accompanying article, "Iron Mountain Is True to Its Name," that was published in the *Wall Street Journal*'s Tracking the Numbers column on September 23, 2004, and answer the following questions.

1. Decompose Iron Mountain's 2004 ROE using the DuPont model specified below. As explained in Chapter 3, interest expense is net of related tax effects. Is the company creating value for its shareholders? Simplify the analysis by using ending balance sheet data, where applicable. Evaluate the claim at the end of the article that Iron Mountain "earned a 5% return on capital over the past five years, which is under its 8.5% cost of debt."

$$\text{ROE} = \frac{\text{Net income}}{\text{Common equity}} = \frac{\text{NI} + \text{Interest expense}}{\text{Sales}} \times \frac{\text{Sales}}{\text{Assets}} \times \frac{\text{Assets}}{\text{Common equity}} \times \frac{\text{NI}}{\text{NI} + \text{Interest expense}}$$

2. In the *Wall Street Journal* article, concerns about Iron Mountain's debt load are raised. The ROE analysis you completed in the previous question captures the level of leverage in the next to last component and the after-tax cost of interest in the final component. Decompose those components further by calculating and interpreting the following ratios:
   - Overall Leverage
     - Total Debt to Equity
     - Long-Term Debt to Equity
   - Solvency
     - Current Ratio
     - Quick Ratio
   - Cost of Interest
     - Interest Expense to Long-Term Debt
     - Times Interest Earned

What is your overall assessment of Iron Mountain's common equity and capital structure leverage?

3. When companies lease assets, they must determine whether the leases are operating or capital leases. Operating leases are treated as rental arrangements. The lease payments are treated as rent expense and neither the leased asset nor the remaining lease payments appear on the balance sheet. On the other hand, capital leases are treated as purchases financed by the lessor. With a capital lease, at the time the lease is signed, the present

value of all lease payments (including any initial payments) is recorded as both a leased asset and a lease liability. Subsequently, the asset is amortized over the lease period and the lease liability is treated as an installment loan.

Because it is relatively easy to structure a lease agreement to obtain operating lease treatment, many analysts (e.g., Standard & Poor's credit analysts) routinely adjust the financial statements for the off-balance-sheet assets and liabilities. Companies are required to disclose their future operating lease payments in a note to the financial statements. Refer to Iron Mountain's commitments and contingencies note and determine the following amounts.

- Iron Mountain lists the lease payments it will make each year. Assume that each payment is made at the end of the respective year and that the payments labeled "Thereafter" are made evenly over six years (2010 to 2015). Determine the present value of the operating lease payments using a discount rate of 8.5%. That value is the estimate of the off-balance-sheet asset and liability for the operating leases.
- If the operating leases are capitalized, the leased assets will have to be amortized. Assume that the amortization period is 11 years. What would Iron Mountain record as lease amortization expense for 2005?
- If the operating leases had been capitalized, the lease obligation will accrue interest throughout the year. How much interest expense would Iron Mountain record on the leases in 2005?
- How does the total of the amortization and the interest expense (assuming that they had capitalized the leases) compare with the rent expense they will record in 2005 for the operating leases? Over the life of the leases, what will the overall relationship be?
- How does changing the accounting from operating lease to capital lease affect how lease payments are reported on the statement of cash flows?
- Based on the figures you calculated, develop a pro forma ROE analysis for Iron Mountain. To do so, assume that the data you estimated for year end 2004 and for 2005 can be applied to the 2004 figures. You'll need to restate net income before tax by removing rent expense and replacing it with amortization and interest. Recalculate the tax expense, assuming that the same average rate applies to the restated pretax earnings. Also, you'll need to add the capitalized leases to the asset figure. How does your analysis of ROE change when you capitalize the leases? Is the effect of off-balance-sheet financing significant at Iron Mountain?
- Review the company's statement of cash flows, and evaluate the CEO's claim that the business will have no trouble managing its debt and that if growth slows, "it will just gush cash."

13. Commitments and Contingencies

a. Leases

We lease most of our facilities under various operating leases. A majority of these leases have renewal options of five to ten years and have either fixed or Consumer Price Index escalation clauses. We also lease equipment under operating leases, primarily computers, which have an average lease life of three years. Trucks and office equipment are also leased and have remaining lease lives ranging from one to seven years. Total rent expense under all of our operating leases was $125,866, $134,371, and $163,564 for the years ended December 31, 2002, 2003, and 2004, respectively. There was $5,915 related to synthetic lease facilities included in rent expense for the year ended December 31, 2002. There was no such expense in 2003 and 2004. See Note 3.

Minimum future lease payments, net of sublease income of $2,715, $1,933, $1,375, $1,127, $912, and $1,546 for 2005, 2006, 2007, 2008, 2009, and thereafter, respectively, are as follows:

Year	Operating
2005	$ 151,166
2006	134,694
2007	118,604
2008	99,714
2009	83,201
Thereafter	490,302
Total minimum lease payments	$1,077,681

THE WALL STREET JOURNAL

September 23, 2004

TRACKING THE NUMBERS

Outside Audit

Iron Mountain Is True to Its Name

Document-Storage Firm Piles Up Companies, Debt To Be Industry's Biggest

By MOHAMMED HADI

DOW JONES NEWSWIRES

Eight years and billions of dollars have helped **Iron Mountain** Inc. buy rather than build its title: America's biggest document-storage and records-management company.

Since its initial public offering of stock in 1996, the 53-year-old Boston firm has gobbled up 112 companies across the U.S., South America, and Western Europe, boosting its revenue to an annualized $1.8 billion in the first six months of this year from $104.4 million in 1995. But that growth hasn't come without a price: $2.26 billion in long-term debt as of June.

Skeptics caution that this debt load leaves Iron Mountain too highly leveraged for it or investors' good. Indeed, the company's debt is almost twice its shareholder equity, or total assets minus liabilities. During the first half of 2004, the company spent $86 million, or about half its operating income, just to pay the interest on its debt. That is up 20% from $72 million spent in the first half of 2003. A downturn in business, or a broader move away from outsourcing paper-document storage, could affect Iron Mountain's ability to meet its financing needs.

Iron Mountain stores its clients' documents in warehouses dotted around the country. It started out by convincing companies to store documents in an old iron-ore mine in case of nuclear attack—thus the company moniker. Today the need for document storage is such a foregone conclusion in Corporate America that Iron Mountain's biggest competitor is the in-house records rooms of potential clients. Iron Mountain is also expanding its digital-storage business, but this is a fledgling operation whose revenue is small. In a nutshell, the company's making a play that the paperless office is still hypothetical, and there remains big money to be made storing hard copies of key documents for clients.

Being highly leveraged suits Chief Executive Richard Reese just fine. The recurring and predictable nature of the company's document-storage revenue, and the fact that Iron Mountain has more cash coming in than going out ensures that the company will be able to manage its debt, he says. "What everybody who really owns this stock for the long-term understands is that we can push hard on the growth, and if we pull the lever back, it will just gush cash," Mr. Reese says.

Investors seem to agree. Iron Mountain stock is up 25% this year and hit an all-time high of nearly $34 last week on the New York Stock Exchange. (Yesterday in 4 p.m. Big Board composite trading, the stock was down 9 cents to $33.41.) But at $34, the stock is trading at over 34 times Wall Street's 2005 earnings estimate of 99 cents a share.

Much of the company's revenue comes from recurring fees charged for documents already being stored, and about half of the company's revenue growth—excluding acquisitions—comes as current customers increase their business.

That consistency gives investors the security they need while they wait for management to "flip the switch and manage this business more for cash flow, and invest less," says Robert W. Baird analyst Timothy Byrne.

(*continues*)

Iron Mountain Is True to Its Name (*continued*)

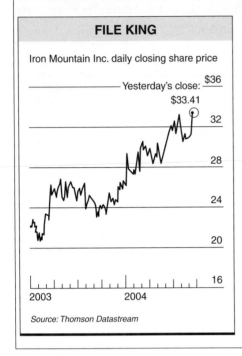

FILE KING

Iron Mountain Inc. daily closing share price

———————— Yesterday's close: $36

$33.41

32

28

24

20

16

2003   2004

Source: Thomson Datastream

Exactly when the company will start looking to extract cash and return it to shareholders in the form of a dividend or stock buyback is far from clear.

"We will give the cash back to them in time, but it's not going to happen in the near future," Mr. Reese says. "Why de-leverage if you can keep building the business?"

Mr. Reese adds that Iron Mountain is "looking for the point of no return," when the company's investments no longer add to the internal growth rate.

David Trainer, an analyst at research firm New Constructs LLC, however, reckons the company is already way past that point and has "too much capital generating too little cash." He says Iron Mountain earned a 5% return on capital over the past five years, which is under its 8.5% cost of debt.

Mr. Reese acknowledges that "if our cost of capital got too high and the opportunities for investment weren't there, we'd pull back," but he doesn't think that is the case at the moment.

The chief executive adds that Iron Mountain will naturally lower debt as its cash flow continues to increase. But operating cash flow fell slightly in the first half of 2004, to $129.7 million from $130.6 million in 2003's first half.

URL for this article:
http://online.wsj.com/article/0,,SB109589221803625392,00.html

IRON MOUNTAIN INCORPORATED
CONSOLIDATED BALANCE SHEETS
(in thousands, except share and per share data)

	December 31,	
	2003	2004
ASSETS		
Current Assets:		
Cash and cash equivalents	$ 74,683	$ 31,942
Accounts receivable (less allowances of $20,922 and $13,886, respectively)	279,800	354,434
Deferred income taxes	33,043	36,033
Prepaid expenses and other	84,057	78,745
Total Current Assets	471,583	501,154
Property, Plant, and Equipment:		
Property, plant, and equipment	1,950,893	2,266,839
Less accumulated depreciation	(458,626)	(617,043)
Net Property, Plant, and Equipment	1,492,267	1,649,796
Other Assets, net:		
Goodwill	1,776,279	2,040,217
Customer relationships and acquisition costs	116,466	189,780
Deferred financing costs	23,934	36,590
Other	11,570	24,850
Total Other Assets, net	1,928,249	2,291,437
Total Assets	$ 3,892,099	$ 4,442,387
LIABILITIES AND SHAREHOLDERS' EQUITY		
Current Liabilities:		
Current portion of long-term debt	$ 115,781	$ 39,435
Accounts payable	87,006	103,415
Accured expenses	234,426	234,697
Deferred revenue	107,857	136,470
Other current liabilities	39,675	1,446
Total Current Liabilities	584,745	515,463
Long-Term Debt, net of current portion	1,974,147	2,438,587
Other Long-Term Liabilities	24,499	23,932
Deferred Rent	20,578	26,253
Deferred Income Taxes	146,231	206,539
Commitments and Contingencies (see Note 13)		
Minority Interests	75,785	13,045
Shareholders' Equity:		
Preferred stock (par value $0.01; authorized 10,000,000 shares; none issued and outstanding)	—	—
Common stock (par value $0.01; authorized 200,000,000 shaires; issued and outstanding 128,362,881 shares and 129,817,914 shares, respectively)	1,283	1,298
Additional paid-in capital	1,033,643	1,063,560
Retained earnings	39,234	133,425
Accumulated other comprehensive items, net	(8,046)	20,285
Total Shareholders' Equity	1,066,114	1,218,568
Total Liabilities and Shareholders' Equity	$ 3,892,099	$ 4,442,387

The accompanying notes are an integral part of these consolidated financial statements.

IRON MOUNTAIN INCORPORATED
CONSOLIDATED STATEMENTS OF OPERATIONS
(in thousands, except per share data)

	Years Ended December 31,		
	2002	**2003**	**2004**
Revenues:			
Storage..	$ 759,536	$ 875,035	$ 1,043,366
Service and storage material sales..	558,961	626,294	774,223
Total Revenues.......................................	1,318,497	1,501,329	1,817,589
Operating Expenses:			
Cost of sales (excluding depreciation)..	622,299	680,747	823,899
Selling, general, and administrative..	333,050	383,641	486,246
Depreciation and amortization..	108,992	130,918	163,629
Merger-related expenses..	796	–	–
Loss (Gain) on disposal/write-down of property, plant, and equipment, net.......	774	1,130	(681)
Total Operating Expenses..	1,065,911	1,196,436	1,473,093
Operating Income..	252,586	304,893	344,496
Interest Expense, net..	136,632	150,468	185,749
Other Expense (Income), net..	1,435	(2,564)	(7,988)
Income from Continuing Operations Before Provision for Income Taxes and Minority Interest..	114,519	156,989	166,735
Provision for Income Taxes..	47,318	66,730	69,574
Minority Interest in Earnings of Subsidiaries..	3,629	5,622	2,970
Income from Continuing Operations before Discontinued Operations and Cumulative Effect of Change in Accounting Principle..	63,572	84,637	94,191
Income from Discontinued Operations (net of tax of $768)..	1,116	–	–
Cumulative Effect of Change in Accounting Principle (net of minority interest)......	(6,396)	–	–
Net Income	$ 58,292	$ 84,637	$ 94,191
Net Income per Share—Basic:			
Income from Continuing Operations before Discontinued Operations and Cumulative Effect of Change in Accounting Principle..	$ 0.50	$ 0.66	$ 0.73
Income from Discontinued Operations (net of tax)..	0.01	–	–
Cumulative Effect of Change in Accounting Principle (net of minority interest)....	(0.05)	–	–
Net Income per Share—Basic..	$ 0.46	$ 0.66	$ 0.73
Net Income per Share—Diluted:			
Income from Continuing Operations before Discontinued Operations and Cumulative Effect of Change in Accounting Principle..	$ 0.49	$ 0.65	$ 0.72
Income from Discontinued Operations (net of tax)..	0.01	–	–
Cumulative Effect of Change in Accounting Principle (net of minority interest)....	(0.05)	–	–
Net Income per Share—Diluted..	$ 0.45	$ 0.65	$ 0.72
Weighted Average Common Shares Outstanding—Basic..	126,977	127,901	129,083
Weighted Average Common Shares Outstanding—Diluted..	129,107	130,077	131,176

The accompanying notes are an integral part of these consolidated financial statements.

IRON MOUNTAIN INCORPORATED
CONSOLIDATED STATEMENTS OF SHAREHOLDERS' EQUITY AND COMPREHENSIVE INCOME
(in thousands, except share data)

	Common Stock Voting		Additional Paid-in Capital	(Accumulated Deficit) Retained Earnings	Accumulated Other Comprehensive Items	Total Shareholders' Equity
	Shares	Amounts				
Balance, December 31, 2001	126,441,473	$1,264	$1,006,415	$(103,695)	$(18,025)	$ 885,959
Issuance of shares under employee stock purchase plan and option plans, including tax benefit	1,132,963	11	13,369	–	–	13,380
Deferred compensation..................	–	–	243	–	–	243
Currency translation adjustment..........	–	–	–	–	3,378	3,378
Market value adjustments for hedging contracts	–	–	–	–	(16,391)	(16,391)
Net income............................	–	–	–	58,292	–	58,292
Balance, December 31, 2002	127,574,436	1,275	1,020,027	(45,403)	(31,038)	944,861
Issuance of shares under employee stock purchase plan and option plans, including tax benefit	788,445	8	18,240	–	–	18,248
Deferred compensation.................	–	–	(4,624)	–	–	(4,624)
Currency translation adjustment..........	–	–	–	–	16,466	16,466
Market value adjustments for hedging contracts	–	–	–	–	6,215	6,215
Market value adjustments for securities...........................	–	–	–	–	311	311
Net income............................	–	–	–	84,637	–	84,637
Balance, December 31, 2003	128,362,881	1,283	1,033,643	39,234	(8,046)	1,066,114
Issuance of shares under employee stock purchase plan and option plans, including tax benefit	1,455,033	15	33,450	–	–	33,465
Deferred compensation.................	–	–	(3,533)	–	–	(3,533)
Currency translation adjustment..........	–	–	–	–	14,669	14,669
Market value adjustments for hedging contracts	–	–	–	–	13,576	13,576
Market value adjustments for securities...........................	–	–	–	–	86	86
Net income............................	–	–	–	94,191	–	94,191
Balance, December 31, 2004	129,817,914	$1,298	$1,063,560	$133,425	$20,285	$1,218,568

	2002	2003	2004
COMPREHENSIVE INCOME:			
Net Income...	$ 58,292	$ 84,637	$ 94,191
Other Comprehensive (Loss) Income:			
Foreign Currency Translation Adjustments	3,378	16,466	14,669
Market Value Adjustments for Hedging Contracts, net of (tax benefit) tax provision of $(5,983), $2,268, and $4,955...	(16,391)	6,215	13,576
Market Value Adjustments for Securities	–	311	86
Comprehensive Income...	$ 45,279	$107,629	$122,522

The accompanying notes are an integral part of these consolidated financial statements.

IRON MOUNTAIN INCORPROATED
CONSLIDATED STATMENTS OF CASH FLOWS
(in thousands)

	Year Ended December 31,		
	2002	2003	2004
Cash Flows from Operating Activities:			
Net income	$ 58,292	$ 84,637	$ 94,191
Adjustments to reconcile net income to income from continuing operations before discontinued operations and cumulative effect of change in accounting principle:			
Income from discontinued operations (net of tax of $768)	(1,116)	–	–
Cumulative effect of change in accounting principle (net of minority interest)	6,396	–	–
Income from continuing operations	63,572	84,637	94,191
Adjustments to reconcile income from continuing operations to cash flows provided by operating activities:			
Minority interests in earnings of subsidiaries, net	3,629	5,622	2,970
Depreciation	104,176	123,974	151,947
Amortization (includes deferred financing costs and bond discount of $4,921, $3,654, and $3,646, respectively)	9,737	10,598	15,328
Provision for deferred income taxes	44,112	61,485	62,165
Loss on early extinguishment of debt	5,430	28,175	2,454
Loss on impairment of long-term assets	1,717	–	–
Loss (Gain) on disposal/write-down of property, plant, and equipment, net	774	1,130	(681)
(Gain) Loss on foreign currency and other, net	(5,773)	(28,961)	9,084
Changes in Assets and Liabilities (exclusive of acquisitions):			
Accounts receivable	(2,547)	(16,004)	(48,020)
Prepaid expenses and other current assets	(3,792)	6	(7,462)
Accounts payable	11,802	979	12,366
Accrued expenses, deferred revenue and other current liabilities	20,575	18,134	9,852
Other assets and long-term liabilities	1,536	(1,082)	1,170
Cash Flows Provided by Operating Activities	254,948	288,693	305,364
Cash Flows from Investing Activities:			
Capital expenditures	(196,997)	(204,477)	(231,966)
Cash paid for acquisitions, net of cash acquired	(49,361)	(379,890)	(384,338)
Additions to customer relationship and acquisition costs	(8,419)	(12,577)	(12,472)
Investment in convertible preferred stock	–	(1,357)	(858)
Proceeds from sales of property and equipment	7,020	11,667	3,111
Cash Flows Used in Investing Activities	(247,757)	(586,634)	(626,523)
Cash Flows from Financing Activities:			
Repayment of debt and term loans	(462,243)	(698,817)	(1,085,013)
Proceeds from borrowings and term loans	438,842	744,016	1,148,275
Early retirement of notes	(54,380)	(374,258)	(20,797)
Net proceeds from sale of senior subordinated notes	99,000	617,179	269,427
Debt (repayment to) financing and equity (distribution to) contribution from minority shareholders, net	(1,241)	20,225	(41,978)
Other, net	7,120	6,709	6,655
Cash Flows Provided by Financing Activities	27,098	315,054	276,569
Effect of Exchange Rates on Cash and Cash Equivalents	644	1,278	1,849
Increase (Decrease) in Cash and Cash Equivalents	34,933	18,391	(42,741)
Cash and Cash Equivalents, Beginning of Year	21,359	56,292	74,683
Cash and Cash Equivalents, End of Year	$ 56,292	$ 74,683	$ 31,942
Supplemental Information:			
Cash Paid for Interest	$ 133,873	$ 126,952	$ 177,005
Cash Paid for Income Taxes	$ 3,147	$ 8,316	$ 6,888

The accompanying notes are an integral part of these consolidated financial statements.

Samsung Electronics Co., Ltd.—Equity Transactions and Value Creation

Excerpts from the 2004 Samsung Electronics Co., Ltd., financial statements are presented on the following pages. Samsung, a Korean company, is one of the world leaders in memory chips, cell phone handsets, and flat panel displays. Read the accompanying article "Buyback Gives Samsung a Lift, But Rally May Be Short-Lived," that was published in the *Wall Street Journal*'s Heard in Asia column on September 17, 2004, and answer the following questions.

1. What is a share buyback? Why would Samsung buyback its own shares?

2. Refer to Samsung's statement of changes in shareholders' equity. How much did Samsung pay to buyback its own shares in 2004? Did the company reissue any of those shares?

3. On Samsung's balance sheet, the repurchased shares are labeled "Treasury Stock" and they are reported as a reduction in shareholders' equity. If Samsung owns these shares, why are they not treated as assets of the company?

4. Decompose Samsung's 2004 ROE using the DuPont model specified below. As explained in Chapter 3, interest expense is net of related tax effects. Is the company creating value for its shareholders? Simplify the analysis by using ending balance sheet data where applicable.

$$\text{ROE} = \frac{\text{Net income}}{\text{Common equity}} = \frac{\text{NI} + \text{Interest expense}}{\text{Sales}} \times \frac{\text{Sales}}{\text{Assets}} \times \frac{\text{Assets}}{\text{Common equity}} \times \frac{\text{NI}}{\text{NI} + \text{Interest expense}}$$

5. In the *Wall Street Journal* article, a number of references are made to actions that analysts believe Samsung should take or to events that will affect Samsung's performance. Identify three actions or events and explain how future ROE might be affected. That is, use the ROE model to pinpoint how returns and value creation will be affected by future events.

Hints and Helps

In determining ROE to the shareholders, focus on profit attributable to the common shareholders. To do so, you'll want to identify the portion of total equity that relates to common shareholders and the profit that flows to them. In terms of equity, consider minority interest on the balance sheet as a form of "quasi-debt" and remove it in arriving at common equity. Do the same for preferred stock. In terms of income attributable to common shareholders, net income is already adjusted for minority interest. However, you should subtract preferred dividends and treat them as though they were a non-tax-deductible interest expense. Note 21 to the statements (not included here) reveals that preferred dividends in 2004 were ₩210,586.

THE WALL STREET JOURNAL

HEARD IN ASIA

Buyback Gives Samsung a Lift, But Rally May Be Short-Lived

By HAE WON CHOI
Staff Reporter of THE WALL STREET JOURNAL
September 17, 2004; Page C16

SEOUL, South Korea—News of a big share buyback by Samsung Electronics Co. has put some spark back into its stock after a months-long slide. But analysts say they expect the rally will fizzle as the Korean company is confronted with a cloudy industry outlook.

On Monday, Samsung—which has a broad global shareholder base—announced plans to "stabilize" its share price by spending roughly two trillion won, or about $1.75 billion, to buy back about 2.7% of its shares. Its share price jumped 3.8% that day, to 475,000 won. Yesterday, Samsung edged up 2,000 won to close at 480,000 won—nearly 5% higher than where it ended Sept. 10, the last trading day before the buyback announcement.

Some analysts say they have mounting doubts about demand for many of Samsung's key products over the next two years. On Wednesday, Koo Bon Jun, a technology-stock analyst for **Citigroup** Inc.'s Smith Barney unit, downgraded Samsung to "hold" from "buy," writing that "the stock's upside is likely to be capped by weak industry fundamentals and slower earnings momentum" next year.

In his report, Mr. Koo said he expects profit margins in the company's cellphone business to shrink. The analyst, who set a 12-month price target of 515,000 won, also predicted that oversupply of liquid-crystal-display screens and computer-memory chips in 2005 will push down prices of those mainstay Samsung products.

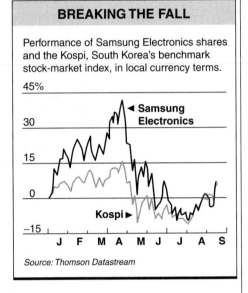

BREAKING THE FALL

Performance of Samsung Electronics shares and the Kospi, South Korea's benchmark stock-market index, in local currency terms.

Source: Thomson Datastream

Samsung is the world's largest manufacturer of dynamic-random-access-memory chips, or DRAMs, and a major player in cellphone handsets and LCD flat screens. Unlike many of its competitors, the company says it is still marching toward a record full-year profit despite recent price woes in the global market.

But some analysts fear that Samsung's financial performance can't remain so strong. And they say a stock buyback isn't the kind of strategic response they prefer.

"I think management at Samsung could be a bit more creative about spending the company's money," says Yu Chang Eyun, a technology analyst at BNP Paribas Peregrine Securities in Seoul. However, in spite of his view that Samsung should be putting some money into acquisitions, Mr. Yu still rates its shares "outperform."

Samsung accounts for 19% of the Korea Stock Exchange's total market capitalization, so movements of its shares can have a large impact on the whole market. Even after this week's surge, shares of Samsung are nearly 25% below their all-time high, on April 23, of 637,000 won.

Yesterday, the stock exchange said it was investigating allegations that Samsung violated fair-disclosure rules by leaking news of the buyback before it was reported to the exchange. Samsung declined to comment immediately.

Samsung, the third-largest maker of handsets after **Nokia** Corp. and **Motorola** Inc., has been on a dual buyback and investment binge. In the first half of this year, the technology company bought back 3.4% of its shares in a process that also cost about two trillion won. At the same time, it has announced plans to outspend rivals in upgrading facilities and technology, earmarking 8.9 trillion won for investment.

Analysts say that many investors would rather see companies using cash for buybacks than for acquiring businesses that might or might not provide a good return. Samsung's acquisition track record isn't the strongest. In the mid-1990s, Samsung bought U.S. computer maker AST Research, which later closed after continuing to suffer losses.

"Return on our own investment is so efficient that we would rather try to grow organically rather than through mergers and acquisitions," says Chu Woo Sik, head of Samsung's investor-relations team. "At the same time, we're always open to all growth opportunities."

However, some analysts believe Samsung isn't making as much effort as they would like to find new growth areas. They recommend that it spend even more lavishly on research and development to find more businesses that would cut its reliance on products that are basically becoming commodities.

There is another cloud on Samsung's horizon. The U.S. Department of Justice's continuing investigation of price fixing in the DRAM market is hanging over Samsung, which has acknowledged it is under investigation. The probe, started in 2002, centers on whether high-profile chip makers conspired to fix the price of DRAM chips sold in the U.S.

On Wednesday, **Infineon Technologies** agreed to plead guilty in U.S. court to a price-fixing charge. The German chip maker agreed to pay a $160 million fine, the third-largest criminal antitrust penalty ever imposed by the U.S. government. Infineon is also negotiating with five computer makers affected by the alleged price-fixing to reach settlements that are likely result in additional payments.

Samsung has said that it is "fully cooperating with authorities" and declined to elaborate.

DRAM chips are a pivotal part of personal computers and other electronics products, and Samsung ranks No. 1 in the global DRAM industry in revenue, with a market share of 30%.

Write to Hae Won Choi at haewon.choi@wsj.com.

URL for this article:

http://online.wsj.com/article/0,,SB109535781058519830,00.html

Samsung Electronics Co., Ltd., and Subsidiaries
Consolidated Balance Sheets
December 31, 2004 and 2003

(in millions of Korean won and in thousands of U.S. dollars (Note 3))

	2004	2003	2004	2003
Assets				
Current assets				
Cash and cash equivalents	₩ 3,129,614	₩ 4,125,700	$ 3,000,589	$ 3,955,609
Short-term financial instruments (Note 4)	4,978,491	4,969,380	4,773,242	4,764,506
Short-term, available-for-sale securities (Note 5)	2,784,977	2,717,275	2,670,160	2,605,249
Short-term, held-to-maturity securities (Note 5)	83,039	78,204	79,616	74,980
Trade accounts and notes receivable, net (Note 6)	6,774,392	6,315,442	6,495,103	6,055,074
Other accounts and notes receivable, net (Note 6)	1,143,424	910,052	1,096,284	872,533
Inventories (Note 7)	5,803,646	4,781,205	5,564,378	4,584,089
Short-term financing receivables, net (Note 8)	4,876,241	9,167,282	4,675,207	8,789,340
Prepaid expenses and other current assets	2,417,401	2,490,595	2,317,738	2,387,915
Total current assets	31,991,225	35,555,135	30,672,317	34,089,295
Property, plant, and equipment, including revalued portion, net (Note 11)	23,962,396	19,470,332	22,974,493	18,667,624
Long-term, available-for-sale securities (Note 9)	2,040,353	2,346,215	1,956,235	2,249,487
Long-term, held-to-maturity securities (Note 9)	967,319	2,032,648	927,439	1,948,848
Equity-method investments (Note 10)	3,057,769	2,810,686	2,931,706	2,694,809
Deferred income tax assets (Note 24)	676,813	633,676	648,910	607,551
Intangible assets, net (Note 12)	544,522	465,328	522,073	446,144
Long-term financing receivables, net (Note 8)	4,702,869	3,193,145	4,508,983	3,061,500
Long-term deposits and other assets (Note 13)	1,061,359	1,534,576	1,017,603	1,471,309
Total assets	₩ 69,004,625	₩ 68,041,741	$ 66,159,759	$ 65,236,567

Samsung Electronics Co., Ltd., and Subsidiaries
Consolidated Balance Sheets
December 31, 2004 and 2003

(in millions of Korean won and in thousands of U.S. dollars (Note 3))

	2004	2003	2004	2003
Liabilities and Shareholders' Equity				
Current Liabilities				
Trade accounts and notes payable	₩ 4,189,110	₩ 4,150,499	$ 4,016,405	$ 3,979,385
Short-term borrowings (Note 14)	7,101,220	7,250,955	6,808,456	6,952,018
Current maturities of long-term debt (Notes 15 and 16)	4,957,052	7,087,693	4,752,686	6,795,487
Other accounts and notes payable	3,433,149	3,849,574	3,291,610	3,690,867
Accrued expenses	3,940,213	3,676,140	3,777,769	3,524,583
Income taxes payable	1,550,192	967,539	1,486,282	927,650
Other current liabilities	936,647	1,038,112	898,036	995,311
Total current liabilities	26,107,583	28,020,512	25,031,244	26,865,301
Long-term debt, net of current maturities (Note 15)	5,445,429	8,953,619	5,220,927	8,584,483
Foreign currency notes and bonds (Note 16)	150,736	173,750	144,523	166,590
Accrued severance benefits (Note 17)	455,981	399,430	437,182	382,963
Deferred income tax liabilities (Note 24)	36,067	21,881	34,580	20,979
Other long-term liabilities	408,548	312,837	391,705	299,940
Total liabilities	32,604,344	37,882,029	31,260,161	36,320,256
Commitments and contingencies (Note 17)				
Shareholders' equity				
Capital stock (Note 1)				
Common stock	778,047	775,774	745,970	743,791
Preferred stock	119,467	119,467	114,542	114,542
Capital surplus	6,239,586	6,242,269	5,982,345	5,984,918
Retained earnings (Note 20)	30,576,954	24,415,681	29,316,351	23,409,090
Capital adjustments				
Treasury stock (Note 22)	(4,159,639)	(3,457,834)	(3,988,149)	(3,315,277)
Others (Note 23)	889,151	1,395,233	852,494	1,337,711
Minority interests	1,956,715	669,122	1,876,045	641,536
Total shareholders' equity	36,400,281	30,159,712	34,899,598	28,916,311
	₩ 69,004,625	₩ 68,041,741	$ 66,159,759	$ 65,236,567

The accompanying notes are an integral part of these consolidated financial statements.

Samsung Electronics Co., Ltd., and Subsidiaries
Consolidated Statements of Changes in Shareholders' Equity
Years Ended December 31, 2004 and 2003

(in millions of Korean won and in thousands of U.S. dollars (Note 3))

	Capital stock	Capital surplus	Retained earnings	Capital adjustments	Minority interests	Total	Capital Stock	Capital surplus	Retained earnings	Capital adjustments	Minority interests	Total
Shareholders' equity, January 1, 2004	₩ 895,241	₩ 6,242,269	₩ 24,415,681	₩ (2,062,601)	₩ 669,122	₩ 30,159,712	$ 858,333	$ 5,984,918	$ 23,409,090	$ (1,977,566)	$ 641,536	$ 28,916,311
Net income	–	–	10,789,535	–	–	10,789,535	–	–	10,344,712	–	–	10,344,712
Conversion of convertible bonds	2,273	46,995	–	–	–	49,268	2,179	45,058	–	–	–	47,237
Change in ownership interests, including new stock issuances by consolidated subsidiaries	–	(155,412)	–	–	–	(155,412)	–	(149,005)	–	–	–	(149,005)
Cumulative effects of changes in consolidated subsidiaries	–	–	–	(65)	630,004	629,939	–	–	–	(62)	604,031	603,969
Cash dividends	–	–	(1,596,282)	–	–	(1,596,282)	–	–	(1,530,472)	–	–	(1,530,472)
Disposal of treasury stock	–	45,535	–	114,551	–	160,086	–	43,658	–	109,828	–	153,486
Retirement of treasury stock	–	–	(3,025,129)	3,025,129	–	–	–	–	(2,900,411)	2,900,411	–	–
Acquisition of treasury stock	–	–	–	(3,841,485)	–	(3,841,485)	–	–	–	(3,683,111)	–	(3,683,111)
Loss on valuation of available-for-sale securities	–	–	–	(22,675)	–	(22,675)	–	–	–	(21,740)	–	(21,740)
Gain on valuation of investments using the equity method of accounting	–	–	–	(119,779)	–	(119,779)	–	–	–	(114,841)	–	(114,841)
Stock option compensation	–	20,318	–	(12,024)	–	8,294	–	19,480	–	(11,528)	–	7,952
Minority interests in losses of consolidated subsidiaries	–	–	–	–	(620,662)	(620,662)	–	–	–	–	(595,073)	(595,073)
Others	–	39,881	(6,851)	(351,539)	1,278,251	959,742	–	38,237	(6,569)	(337,046)	1,225,552	920,174
Shareholders' equity December 31, 2004	₩ 897,514	₩ 6,239,586	₩ 30,576,954	₩ (3,270,488)	₩ 1,956,715	₩ 36,400,281	$ 860,512	$ 5,982,346	$ 29,316,350	$ (3,135,655)	$ 1,876,046	$ 34,889,599

Samsung Electronics Co., Ltd., and Subsidiaries
Consolidated Statements of Changes in Shareholders' Equity
Years Ended December 31, 2004 and 2003

(in millions of Korean won and in thousands of U.S. dollars (Note 3))

	Capital stock	Capital surplus	Retained earnings	Capital adjustments	Minority interests	Total	Capital Stock	Capital surplus	Retained earnings	Capital adjustments	Minority interests	Total
Shareholders' equity, January 1, 2003	₩ 889,147	₩ 5,931,788	₩ 20,322,113	₩ (2,001,483)	₩ 1,179,781	₩ 26,321,346	$ 852,490	$ 5,687,237	$ 19,484,289	$ (1,918,967)	$ 1,131,142	$ 25,236,191
Net income	–	–	5,962,247	–	–	5,962,247	–	–	5,716,440	–	–	5,716,440
Conversion of convertible bonds	6,094	285,157	–	–	–	291,251	5,843	273,401	–	–	–	279,244
Change in ownership interests, including new stock issuances by consolidated subsidiaries	–	15,516	–	–	–	15,516	–	14,876	–	–	–	14,876
Cumulative effects of changes in consolidated subsidiaries	–	(14)	–	119	2,194	2,299	–	(13)	–	114	2,104	2,205
Cash dividends	–	–	(910,192)	–	–	(910,192)	–	–	(872,667)	–	–	(872,667)
Disposal of treasury stock	–	1,060	–	1,521	–	2,581	–	1,016	–	1,458	–	2,474
Retirement of treasury stock	–	–	(981,298)	981,298	–	–	–	–	(940,842)	940,842	–	–
Acquisition of treasury stock	–	–	–	(1,978,562)	–	(1,978,562)	–	–	–	(1,896,991)	–	(1,896,991)
Gain on valuation of available-for-sale securities	–	–	–	522,494	–	522,494	–	–	–	500,953	–	500,953
Gain on valuation of investments using the equity method of accounting	–	–	–	119,159	–	119,159	–	–	–	114,246	–	114,246
Stock option compensation	–	7,694	–	115,819	–	123,513	–	7,377	–	111,044	–	118,421
Changes in retained earnings of equity-method investees	–	–	20,413	–	–	20,413	–	–	19,571	–	–	19,571
Minority interests in losses of consolidated subsidiaries	–	–	–	–	(609,179)	(609,179)	–	–	–	–	(584,064)	(584,064)
Others	–	1,068	2,398	177,034	96,326	276,826	–	1,024	2,299	169,735	92,355	265,413
Shareholders' equity, December 31, 2003	₩ 895,241	₩ 6,242,269	₩ 24,415,681	₩ (2,062,601)	₩ 669,122	₩ 30,159,712	$ 858,333	$ 5,984,918	$ 23,409,090	$ (1,977,566)	$ 641,537	$ 28,916,312

The accompanying notes are an integral part of these consolidated financial statements.

Samsung Electronics Co., Ltd., and Subsidiaries
Consolidated Statements of Income
Years Ended December 31, 2004 and 2003

(in millions of Korean won and in thousands of U.S. dollars (Note 3))

	2004	2003	2004	2003
Sales (Note 27)				
Domestic	₩ 13,051,385	₩ 15,489,393	$ 12,513,313	$ 14,850,808
Export	68,911,624	49,328,063	66,070,589	47,294,404
	81,963,009	64,817,456	78,583,902	62,145,212
Cost of sales (Note 27)	52,952,682	42,252,493	50,769,590	40,510,540
Gross profit	29,010,327	22,564,963	27,814,312	21,634,672
Selling, general, and administrative expenses	17,249,581	16,268,736	16,538,429	15,598,021
Operating profit	11,760,746	6,296,227	11,275,883	6,036,651
Non-operating income				
Interest and dividend income	382,049	310,703	366,298	297,894
Foreign exchange gains	1,146,088	871,796	1,098,838	835,854
Gain on foreign currency translation (Note 29)	202,172	246,168	193,837	236,019
Gain on valuation of investments using the equity method (Note 10)	495,620	246,764	475,187	236,591
Others	662,878	627,096	635,549	601,243
	2,888,807	2,302,527	2,769,709	2,207,601
Non-operating expenses				
Interest expense	170,107	215,113	163,094	206,244
Foreign exchange losses	1,060,191	908,016	1,016,482	870,581
Loss on foreign currency translation (Note 29)	80,723	147,417	77,395	141,339
Impairment losses on investments	134,757	345,614	129,201	331,365
Others	827,617	553,034	793,497	530,234
	₩ 2,273,395	₩ 2,169,194	$ 2,179,669	$ 2,079,763

Samsung Electronics Co., Ltd., and Subsidiaries
Consolidated Statements of Income
Years Ended December 31, 2004 and 2003

(in millions of Korean won and in thousands of U.S. dollars (Note 3))

	2004	2003	2004	2003
Ordinary profit	₩ 12,376,158	₩ 6,429,560	$ 11,865,923	$ 6,164,489
Extraordinary income	–	–	–	–
Extraordinary loss	–	–	–	–
Income before income taxes and minority interests	12,376,158	6,429,560	11,865,923	6,164,489
Income taxes (Note 25)	2,207,285	1,076,492	2,116,285	1,032,111
Income before minority interests	10,168,873	5,353,068	9,749,638	5,132,378
Minority interests in losses of consolidated subsidiaries, net	620,662	609,179	595,074	584,064
Net income	₩ 10,789,535	₩ 5,962,247	$ 10,344,712	$ 5,716,442
Basic earnings per share (Note 26) (in Korean won and U.S. dollars)	₩ 67,916	₩ 36,376	$ 65	$ 35
Diluted earnings per share (Note 26) (in Korean won and U.S. dollar)	₩ 66,881	₩ 35,950	$ 64	$ 34

Samsung Electronics Co., Ltd., and Subsidiaries
Consolidated Statements of Cash Flows
Years Ended December 31, 2004 and 2003

(in millions of Korean won and in thousands of U.S. dollars (Note 3))

	2004	2003	2004	2003
Cash flows from operating activities				
Net income	₩ 10,789,535	₩ 5,962,247	$ 10,344,712	$ 5,716,442
Adjustments to reconcile net income to net cash provided by operating activities				
Depreciation and amortization	5,184,898	4,298,839	4,971,139	4,121,610
Provision for severance benefits	444,206	334,103	425,893	320,329
Loss on transfer of trade accounts and notes receivable	119,343	65,468	114,423	62,769
Bad debt expense	2,637,187	3,701,859	2,528,463	3,549,242
Compensation cost of stock options	71,693	124,633	68,737	119,495
Loss on foreign currency translation	80,723	147,417	77,395	141,339
Gain on foreign currency translation	(202,172)	(207,593)	(193,837)	(199,035)
Minority interest in losses of consolidated subsidiaries, net	(620,662)	(609,179)	(595,074)	(584,064)
Gain on valuation of investments using the equity method	(495,620)	(246,764)	(475,187)	(236,591)
Impairment losses on investments	(134,757)	345,614	(129,201)	331,365
Others	688,849	204,542	660,450	196,107
	18,563,223	14,121,186	17,797,913	13,539,008
Changes in operating assets and liabilities				
Increase in trade accounts and notes receivable	(673,376)	(528,666)	(645,615)	(506,871)
Increase in inventories	(1,311,935)	(525,950)	(1,257,848)	(504,267)
Increase in trade accounts and notes payable	61,005	1,198,981	58,490	1,149,550
Increase in accrued expenses	226,930	418,744	217,574	401,480
Increase (decrease) in income taxes payable	597,232	(456,259)	572,610	(437,449)
Payment of severance benefits	(250,184)	(153,222)	(239,870)	(146,905)
Decrease in financing receivables	536,191	1,404,869	514,085	1,346,950
Deferred income taxes	(30,885)	(508,984)	(29,612)	(488,000)
Others	(974,116)	(945,326)	(933,956)	(906,353)
Net cash provided by operating activities	₩ 16,744,085	₩ 14,025,373	$ 16,053,771	$ 13,447,143

Samsung Electronics Co., Ltd., and Subsidiaries
Consolidated Statements of Cash Flows
Years Ended December 31, 2004 and 2003

(in millions of Korean won and in thousands of U.S. dollars (Note 3))

	2004	2003	2004	2003
Cash flows from investing activities				
Net increase in short-term financial instruments	₩ 91,198	₩ (481,377)	$ 87,438	$ (461,531)
Proceeds from disposal of short-term, available-for-sale securities	4,307,147	3,203,960	4,129,575	3,071,870
Acquisition of short-term, available-for-sale securities	(4,672,698)	(3,897,062)	(4,480,056)	(3,736,397)
Net increase in other accounts and notes receivable	193,524	(119,151)	185,546	(114,239)
Proceeds from disposal of property, plant, and equipment	574,625	259,820	550,935	249,108
Acquisition of property, plant, and equipment	(10,497,204)	(7,700,754)	(10,064,433)	(7,383,273)
Proceeds from disposal of long-term, available-for-sale securities	922,257	2,396,519	884,235	2,297,717
Proceeds from disposal of long-term, held-to-maturity securities	584,437	480,725	560,342	460,906
Proceeds from disposal of equity-method investments	240,004	112,550	230,109	107,910
Acquisition of long-term, available-for-sale securities	(518,928)	(703,414)	(497,534)	(674,414)
Acquisition of long-term, held-to-maturity securities	(143,744)	(1,055,077)	(137,818)	(1,011,579)
Acquisition of equity-method investments	(161,047)	–	(154,407)	–
Others	897,858	(290,765)	860,842	(278,778)
Net cash used in investing activities	(8,182,571)	(7,794,026)	(7,845,226)	(7,472,700)
Cash flows from financing activities				
Net proceeds from (repayment of) short-term borrowings	(193,672)	(2,808,105)	(185,687)	(2,692,335)
Proceeds from long-term debt	3,224,434	6,682,166	3,091,500	6,406,679
Repayment of long-term debt	(2,123,112)	(221,929)	(21,081)	(212,779)
Repayment of current maturities of long-term debt	(6,622,079)	(5,434,340)	(6,349,069)	(5,210,297)
Payment of dividends	(1,596,282)	(910,192)	(1,530,472)	(872,667)
Acquisition of treasury stock	(3,841,484)	(1,978,562)	(3,683,110)	(1,896,991)
Others	1,513,280	98,557	(563,610)	94,494
Net cash used in financing activities	₩ (9,638,915)	₩ (4,572,405)	$ (9,241,529)	$ (4,383,896)

Samsung Electronics Co., Ltd., and Subsidiaries
Consolidated Statements of Cash Flows
Years Ended December 31, 2004 and 2003

(in millions of Korean won and in thousands of U.S. dollars (Note 3))

	2004	2003	2004	2003
Effect of exchange rate changes on cash and cash equivalents	₩ 125,577	₩ 50,753	$ 120,400	$ 48,661
Net increase (decrease) in cash and cash equivalents from changes in consolidated subsidiaries	(44,262)	57,374	(42,437)	55,009
Net increase (decrease) in cash and cash equivalents	(996,086)	1,767,069	(955,020)	1,694,217
Beginning of the year	4,125,700	2,358,631	3,955,609	2,261,391
End of the year	₩ 3,129,614	₩ 4,125,700	$ 3,000,589	$ 3,955,608

Whole Foods Markets, Inc.—Value Creation

Austin, Texas-based Whole Foods Markets is the world's leading retailer of natural and organic foods. It was founded in 1980 and now has 196 stores in North America and the United Kingdom. On the company Web site, they explain that they run their business with a focus on value creation. The value creation metric they focus on is Economic Value Added, a measure promoted by consulting firm Stern Stewart.

The EVA disclosure and Whole Foods Markets 2006 financial statements follow.

1. Explain how EVA, as used by Whole Foods Markets, ties in with the measure of value creation and the ROE model we use in this book.

2. Whole Foods provides details of its EVA calculation. Many of the figures are weighted averages. For example, the Total Assets figure is a weighted average of the total assets outstanding throughout the year, not a simple average of the beginning and ending total assets figure. The weighted averages are fairly close to the simple averages.

   Use the accompanying financial statements to remeasure EVA, assuming that you did not have access to the internal data that Whole Foods uses to calculate weighted averages. That is, use simple averages to calculate Whole Foods' EVA for 2006. Use the "Implied Goodwill" and "Other" figures that Whole Foods uses in its calculation of EVA capital. You will also have to estimate components of net operating profit after taxes (NOPAT). Do so using the figures reported on the Income Statement.

   Does your EVA estimate differ significantly from the one reported by Whole Foods?

Economic Value Added®

We use Economic Value Added ("EVA") to evaluate our business decisions and as a basis for determining incentive compensation. In its simplest definition, EVA is equivalent to net operating profits after taxes minus a charge for the cost of capital necessary to generate those profits. We believe that one of our core strengths is our decentralized culture, where decisions are made at the store level, close to the customer. We believe this is one of our strongest competitive advantages, and that EVA is the best financial framework that team members can use to help make decisions that create sustainable shareholder value.

We use EVA extensively for capital investment decisions, including evaluating new store real estate decisions and store remodeling proposals. We are turning down projects that do not add long-term value to the Company. The EVA decision-making model is also enhancing operating decisions in stores. Our emphasis is on EVA improvement, as we want to challenge our teams to continue to innovate and grow EVA in new ways. We believe that opportunities always exist to increase sales and margins, to lower operating expenses, and to make investments that add value in ways that benefit all of our stakeholders. We believe that focusing on EVA improvement encourages continuous improvement of our business.

Over 500 leaders throughout the Company are on EVA-based incentive compensation plans, of which the primary measure is EVA improvement. EVA-based plans cover our senior executive leadership, regional leadership, and the store leadership team in all stores. Incentive compensation for each of these groups is determined based on relevant EVA measures at different levels, including the total company level, the regional level, the store or facility level, and the team level. We believe using EVA in a multi-dimensional approach best measures the results of decisions made at different levels of the Company. We expect to continue to expand the use of EVA as a significant component of our compensation structure throughout the coming years.

The following table sets forth selected EVA information based on a 9% weighted average cost of capital and a 40% tax rate for the fiscal years ended September 24, 2006, and September 25, 2005 (in thousands):

	2006	2005
Net operating profit after tax (NOPAT)	$ 215,281	$ 165,579
Capital charge	150,871	139,793
EVA	64,410	25,786
Increase in EVA	$ 38,624	$ 8,203

The Company provides information regarding EVA as additional information about its operating results. EVA is a measure not in accordance with, or an alternative to, generally accepted accounting principles ("GAAP"). The Company's management believes that this additional EVA information is useful to shareholders, management, analysts, and potential investors in evaluating the Company's results of operations and financial condition. In addition, management uses these measures for reviewing the financial results of the Company and for budget planning and incentive compensation purposes. EVA is calculated by subtracting a charge for the use of capital (capital charge) from net operating profit after taxes ("NOPAT"). A reconciliation of GAAP net income to NOPAT follows (in thousands):

	2006	2005
GAAP net income	$ 203,828	$ 136,351
Provision for income taxes	135,885	100,782
Interest expense and other	19,088	38,832
Net operating profit before taxes (NOPBT)	358,801	275,965
Taxes (40%)	143,520	110,386
NOPAT	$ 215,281	$ 165,579

Capital charge is calculated by multiplying weighted average EVA capital by our weighted average cost of capital. A reconciliation of total net assets to ending EVA capital follows (in thousands):

	2006	2005
Total assets	$ 1,979,127	$ 1,696,953
Total liabilities	635,314	537,648
Net assets	1,343,813	1,159,305
Long-term debt and capital lease obligations	13,024	87,919
Implied goodwill (from pooling-of-interest transactions)	162,803	162,803
Other*	156,704	143,740
EVA capital	$ 1,676,344	$ 1,553,767

*Accumulated components of net income not included in NOPAT
— EVA® is a registered trademark of Stern Stewart & Co.

Whole Foods Market, Inc.
Consolidated Balance Sheets
(in thousands)
September 24, 2006 and September 25, 2005

Assets	2006	2005
Current assets:		
Cash and cash equivalents	$ 2,252	$ 308,524
Short-term investments—available-for-sale securities	193,847	–
Restricted cash	60,065	36,922
Trade accounts receivable	82,137	66,682
Merchandise inventories	203,727	174,848
Prepaid expenses and other current assets	33,804	45,965
Deferred income taxes	48,149	39,588
Total current assets	623,981	672,529
Property and equipment, net of accumulated depreciation and amortization	1,236,133	1,054,605
Goodwill	113,494	112,476
Intangible assets, net of accumulated amortization	34,767	21,990
Deferred income taxes	29,412	22,452
Other assets	5,209	5,244
Total assets	$ 2,042,996	$ 1,889,296

Liabilities and Shareholders' Equity	2006	2005
Current liabilities:		
Current installments of long-term debt and capital lease obligations	$ 49	$ 5,932
Trade accounts payable	121,857	103,348
Accrued payroll, bonus, and other benefits due team members	153,014	126,981
Dividends payable	–	17,208
Other current liabilities	234,850	164,914
Total current liabilities	509,770	418,383
Long-term debt and capital lease obligations, less current installments	8,606	12,932
Deferred rent liability	120,421	91,775
Other long-term liabilities	56	530
Total liabilities	638,853	523,620
Shareholders' equity:		
Common stock no par value, 300,000 shares authorized:		
142,198 and 136,017 shares issued, 139,607 and 135,908		
shares outstanding in 2006 and 2005, respectively	1,147,872	874,972
Common stock in treasury, at cost	(99,964)	–
Accumulated other comprehensive income	6,975	4,405
Retained earnings	349,260	486,299
Total shareholders' equity	1,404,143	1,365,676
Commitments and contingencies		
Total liabilities and shareholders' equity	$ 2,042,996	$ 1,889,296

The accompanying notes are an integral part of these consolidated financial statements.

Whole Foods Market, Inc.
Consolidated Statements of Operations
(in thousands, except per share amounts)
Fiscal years ended September 24, 2006, September 25, 2005, and September 26, 2004

	2006	2005	2004
Sales	$ 5,607,376	$ 4,701,289	$ 3,864,950
Cost of goods sold and occupancy costs	3,647,734	3,052,184	2,523,816
Gross profit	1,959,642	1,649,105	1,341,134
Direct store expenses	1,421,968	1,223,473	986,040
General and administrative expenses	181,244	158,864	119,800
Pre-opening and relocation costs	37,421	37,035	18,648
Operating income	319,009	229,733	216,646
Other income (expense):			
Interest expense	(32)	(2,223)	(7,249)
Investment and other income	20,736	9,623	6,456
Income before income taxes	339,713	237,133	215,853
Provision for income taxes	135,885	100,782	86,341
Net income	$ 203,828	$ 136,351	$ 129,512
Basic earnings per share	$ 1.46	$ 1.05	$ 1.06
Weighted average shares outstanding	139,328	130,090	122,648
Diluted earnings per share	$ 1.41	$ 0.99	$ 0.99
Weighted average shares outstanding, diluted basis	145,082	139,950	135,454
Dividends declared per share	$ 2.45	$ 0.47	$ 0.30

The accompanying notes are an integral part of these consolidated financial statements.

Whole Foods Market, Inc.
Consolidated Statements of Shareholders' Equity and Comprehensive Income
(in thousands)
Fiscal years ended September 24, 2006, September 25, 2005, and September 26, 2004

	Shares Outstanding	Common Stock	Common Stock in Treasury	Accumulated Other Comprehensive Income (Loss)	Retained Earnings	Total Shareholders' Equity
Balances at September 28, 2003	120,140	$ 423,297	$ –	$ 1,624	$ 320,055	$ 744,976
Net income	–	–	–	–	129,512	129,512
Foreign currency translation adjustments	–	–	–	856	–	856
Reclassification adjustments for losses included in net income	–	–	–	88	–	88
Change in unrealized gain (loss) on investments, net of income taxes	–	–	–	(515)	–	(515)
Comprehensive income	–	–	–	429	129,512	129,941
Dividends ($0.30 per share)	–	–	–	–	(37,089)	(37,089)
Issuance of common stock pursuant to team member stock plans	4,184	59,518	–	–	–	59,518
Issuance of common stock in connection with acquisition	478	16,375	–	–	–	16,375
Tax benefit related to exercise of team member stock options	–	35,583	–	–	–	35,583
Other	12	334	–	–	–	334
Balances at September 26, 2004	124,814	535,107	–	2,053	412,478	949,638
Net income	–	–	–	–	136,351	136,351
Foreign currency translation adjustments	–	–	–	1,893	–	1,893
Reclassification adjustments for losses included in net income	–	–	–	1,063	–	1,063
Change in unrealized gain (loss) on investments, net of income taxes	–	–	–	(604)	–	(604)
Comprehensive income	–	–	–	2,352	136,351	138,703
Dividends ($0.47 per share)	–	–	–	–	(62,530)	(62,530)
Issuance of common stock pursuant to team member stock plans	5,042	110,293	–	–	–	110,293
Tax benefit related to exercise of team member stock options	–	62,643	–	–	–	62,643
Share-based compensation	–	19,135	–	–	–	19,135
Conversion of subordinated debentures	6,052	147,794	–	–	–	147,794
Balances at September 25, 2005	135,908	874,972	–	4,405	486,299	1,365,676
Net income	–	–	–	–	203,828	203,828
Foreign currency translation adjustments	–	–	–	2,494	–	2,494
Change in unrealized gain (loss) on investments, net of income taxes	–	–	–	76	–	76
Comprehensive income	–	–	–	2,570	203,828	206,398
Dividends ($2.45 per share)	–	–	–	–	(340,867)	(340,867)
Issuance of common stock pursuant to team member stock plans	5,510	199,450	–	–	–	199,450
Purchase of treasury stock	(2,005)	–	(99,964)	–	–	(99,964)
Excess tax benefit related to exercise of team member stock options	–	59,096	–	–	–	59,096
Share-based compensation	–	9,432	–	–	–	9,432
Conversion of subordinated debentures	194	4,922	–	–	–	4,922
Balances at September 24, 2006	139,607	$ 1,147,872	$ (99,964)	$ 6,975	$ 349,260	$ 1,404,143

The accompanying notes are an integral part of these consolidated financial statements.

Whole Foods Market, Inc.
Consolidated Statements of Cash Flows
(in thousands)
Fiscal years ended September 24, 2006, September 25, 2005, and September 26, 2004

	2006	2005	2004
Cash flows from operating activities			
Net income	$ 203,828	$ 136,351	$ 129,512
Adjustments to reconcile net income to net cash			
provided by operating activities:			
Depreciation and amortization	156,223	133,759	115,157
Loss on disposal of fixed assets	6,291	15,886	5,769
Share-based compensation	9,432	19,135	–
Deferred income tax expense (benefit)	(15,521)	(27,873)	(682)
Tax benefit related to exercise of team member stock options	–	62,643	35,583
Excess tax benefit related to exercise of team member stock options	(52,008)	–	–
Interest accretion on long-term debt	460	4,120	7,551
Deferred rent	26,607	16,080	11,109
Other	693	1,317	(1,133)
Net change in current assets and liabilities:			
Trade accounts receivable	(17,720)	(2,027)	(19,158)
Merchandise inventories	(32,200)	(21,486)	(27,868)
Prepaid expenses and other current assets	(7,849)	(4,151)	(2,940)
Trade accounts payable	18,509	12,597	12,515
Accrued payroll, bonus and other benefits due team member	26,033	26,445	29,646
Other accrued expenses	129,886	38,023	35,279
Net cash provided by operating activities	452,664	410,819	330,340
Cash flows from investing activities			
Development costs of new store locations	(208,588)	(207,792)	(156,728)
Other property, plant, and equipment expenditures	(131,614)	(116,318)	(109,739)
Proceeds from hurricane insurance	3,308	–	–
Acquisition of intangible assets	(16,332)	(1,500)	–
Change in notes receivable	–	13,500	(13,500)
Purchase of available-for-sale securities	(555,095)	–	–
Sale of available-for-sale securities	362,209	–	–
Increase in restricted cash	(23,143)	(10,132)	(26,790)
Payment for purchase of acquired entities, net of cash acquired	–	–	(18,873)
Other investing activities	–	–	1,332
Net cash used in investing activities	(569,255)	(322,242)	(324,298)
Cash flows from financing activities			
Dividends paid	(358,075)	(54,683)	(27,728)
Issuance of common stock	222,030	85,816	59,518
Purchase of treasury stock	(99,964)	–	–
Excess tax benefit related to exercise of team member stock options	52,008	–	–
Payments on long-term debt and capital lease obligations	(5,680)	(5,933)	(8,864)
Net cash provided by (used in) financing activities	(189,681)	25,200	22,926
Net change in cash and cash equivalents	(306,272)	113,777	28,968
Cash and cash equivalents at beginning of year	308,524	194,747	165,779
Cash and cash equivalents at end of year	$ 2,252	$ 308,524	$ 194,747
Supplemental disclosures of cash flow information:			
Interest paid	$ 607	$ 1,063	$ 2,127
Federal and state income taxes paid	$ 70,220	$ 74,706	$ 60,372
Non-cash transactions:			
Common stock issued in connection with acquisition	$ –	$ –	$ 16,375
Conversion of convertible debentures into common stock, net of fees	$ 4,922	$ 147,794	$ 293

The accompanying notes are an integral part of these consolidated financial statements.

APPENDIX **A**

Time Value of Money

Financial accounting information is useful because it provides investors, creditors, managers, and other interested parties with measures of a firm's performance and financial condition. Concepts of valuation are important to the measurement process because values must be placed on the firm's transactions, the firm's assets and liabilities, and ultimately the firm itself. Understanding valuation is necessary for understanding successful management. Indeed, management endeavors to create shareholder value, which is reflected in the market value of the firm.

The economic value of an asset, liability, or entity is its present value, which is computed by forecasting the expected future cash inflows and outflows associated with the asset, liability, or entity and then discounting the cash flows using a rate of return (or "interest rate") that reflects the time value of money (i.e., a dollar in the future is worth less than a dollar at present). Financial accounting statements, as well as the notion of value creation, rely extensively on the concepts of present value and rate of return. Recall from Chapter 1, for example, that value is created if management generates a return on equity (rate of return on the shareholders investment) that exceeds the cost of equity (the rate of return expected by the shareholders), and in Chapter 5 we showed how the equity value of the firm is equal to the book value of equity today plus the present value of the shareholder value expected to be generated in the future.

This appendix covers the time value of money and the concepts of present value and rate of return. We note first that money has a price (interest), which gives it a time value— money held today has a greater value than money received tomorrow. We then introduce compound interest and proceed to work a number of examples that equate future cash flows to present values. We conclude with a discussion of rate of return, and the roles of present value and rate of return in the financial accounting system.

▶ INTEREST: THE PRICE OF MONEY

Money, like any other scarce resource, has a price. Individuals who borrow money must pay this price, and those who lend it receive this price. The price of money is called *interest* and is usually expressed as a percentage rate over a certain period (normally per year, but sometimes per month or per quarter). The dollar amount of interest is the result of multiplying the percentage rate by the amount of money borrowed or lent (*principal*). For example, a 10% interest rate per year on a principal of $100 will produce $10 (10% × $100) of interest after one year.

INSIGHT: TIME VALUE OF MONEY IN THE FINANCIAL STATEMENTS

Accountants use time value of money techniques in many places in the financial statements. We cover many of these in Chapters 7, 8, and 9. They include measuring revenue on long-term contracts, accruing interest income and expense, lease accounting, pension accounting, and the fair value estimates required when management assesses whether the firm's assets have been impaired.

▶ TIME VALUE

In an environment that charges interest for the use of money, would you rather have one dollar now or receive one dollar one year from now? If you choose to receive the dollar immediately, you could lend it, and it would grow to some amount greater than one dollar after a year has passed. Perhaps a bank would be willing to pay you interest for the use of that dollar. Therefore, in a world where money has a price, a dollar today is worth more than a dollar at some time in the future. The difference between the value of a dollar today and the value of a dollar in the future is called the *time value of money*. For example, if the interest rate is 10%, $1 placed in a bank today will grow to $1.10 ($1.00 × 1.10) in one year. In this example, the time value is $0.10 ($1.10 − $1.00).

Size of Time Value

Two basic factors determine the size of the time value of money: (1) the length of the period and (2) the price of money, or the interest rate. As the time period grows longer, the difference between the present value of a future cash amount and that cash amount itself grows larger. For example, $1.00 invested at a 10% interest rate grows to $1.10 ($1.00 × 1.10) in one year and $1.21 ($1.00 × 1.10 × 1.10) in two years, making the time value in this case $0.10 ($1.10 − $1.00) for one year and $0.21 ($1.21 − $1.00) for two years.

The second factor is obviously the price of money, or interest rate. If the interest rate is zero, the time value of money will be zero. Accordingly, as the interest rate gets larger, so does the difference between the value of a dollar today and the value of a dollar in the future. The higher the interest rate, the greater the time value of money. In the previous example, a 20% interest rate would give rise to a time value of money equal to $0.20 ($1.20 − $1.00) over one year and $0.44 ($1.44 − $1.00) over two years.

What determines the size of the interest rate? One component of the interest rate can be viewed as a rental fee for the use of money. Just as you pay rent for the use of someone else's apartment, you must also pay rent for the use of someone else's money. The lender needs to be compensated for delaying consumption and needs to protect themselves from the effect of inflation. In addition to the rental price of money, another important reason underlies why someone would prefer a dollar today to a dollar in the future: risk. That is, the future is uncertain. The possibility exists, for example, that a lender will never be repaid. Thus, interest rates cover not only the rental price of money (risk-free interest rate), but also a second component that reflects the level of uncertainty, or risk (risk premium). In the real world, therefore, the size of an interest rate is equal to the risk-free interest rate plus the risk premium. The risk-free rate is determined primarily by economy-wide factors (e.g., Federal Reserve Board policies, U.S. balance of payments, and the unemployment rate), and historically has averaged approximately 6%, ranging from 3% to about 9%. The risk premium depends more on the specific characteristics of the parties involved in the transaction, and can range from as little as 4%–6% for low-risk situations to 20%–25% or more in high-risk cases.

▶ TIME VALUE COMPUTATIONS

Computations involving the time value of money can be viewed from either of two perspectives: (1) the future value of a sum of money received today or (2) the present value of a sum of money to be received in the future. The following sections discuss these two perspectives.

Future Value

In our discussion of the time value of money, we showed that $1 invested at a given interest rate for a period of time will grow to an amount greater than $1. This dollar amount is called the future value.

Future Value—Simple Interest
As in the previous example, $1 invested at a 10% per year interest rate will grow to $1.10 ($1 × 1.10) at the end of one year. This $1.10 is referred to as the future value in one year of $1, given a 10% annual interest rate. In such a situation, an individual would be indifferent between receiving $1 now or $1.10 in one year. A simple interest calculation for one year is illustrated below.

Now	⟶	1 year
$1.00	⟶	$1.10

Future Value—Compound Interest
To compute the future value of $1 at the end of more than one period (say, two years), given a 10% interest rate, we use the notion of compound interest. That is, in the second year, the 10% interest rate is applied to both the original $1 principal and the $0.10 interest earned in the first year. In other words, we assume that the interest earned in a given period can be reinvested at the same rate for the next period. Here, the future value of $1 at the end of two years, given a 10% interest rate compounded annually, is equal to $1.21. An individual would be indifferent among receiving $1 now, $1.10 in one year, or $1.21 in two years, given a 10% interest rate compounded annually. The computation is depicted below.

Now	⟶	1 year	⟶	2 years
$1.00	⟶	$1.10	⟶	$1.21

Future Value—Table Factors
This same basic procedure could be used to calculate the future value of $1 for any number of periods in the future. After very many periods, though, this computation becomes quite time-consuming. Try, for example, to compute the future value of $1 in 40 years, given an 8% interest rate compounded annually. Fortunately, tables have been developed that

Periods (n)	2%	3%	4%	5%	6%
1	1.02000	1.03000	1.04000	1.05000	1.06000
2	1.04040	1.06090	1.08160	1.10250	1.12360
3	1.06121	1.09273	1.12486	1.15763	1.19102
4	1.08243	1.12551	1.16986	1.21551	1.26248
5	1.10408	1.15927	1.21665	1.27628	1.33823
6	1.12616	1.19405	1.26532	1.34010	1.41852
7	1.14869	1.22987	1.31593	1.40710	1.50363
8	1.17166	1.26677	1.36857	1.47746	1.59385
9	1.19509	1.30477	1.42331	1.55133	1.68948
10	1.21899	1.34392	1.48024	1.62889	1.79085

Figure A-1. Future Value of a Single Payment of $1

expedite these calculations. Table A-1, located at the end of this appendix,[1] is a future value table. It enables you to quickly compute the future value of any amount for any number of periods in the future. To compute a future value, first find the intersection of the interest rate and the number of periods. This amount is called the table factor. Then, multiply this table factor by the dollar amount. For example, find the table factor for a 10% interest rate and two periods. It equals 1.21. Multiplying this factor by $1 gives you the future value in two years of $1 invested at a 10% annual interest rate. Multiplying this factor by $20 gives you the future value in two years of $20 invested at a 10% annual interest rate.

Note that the table factor in this example (1.21) is equal to 1.10×1.10, or $(1.10)^2$. The general formula for the future value calculation is as

$$\text{Future value} = \text{PV}(1 + i)^n$$

where

$$\text{PV} = \text{Present value or money amount today;}$$
$$i = \text{periodic interest rate; and}$$
$$n = \text{number of periods.}$$

Figure A-1 illustrates the future value calculation of $1 invested at various rates for up to 10 periods.

The figure demonstrates three important points. First, it shows that the factors found on the future value table are nothing more than an individual interest factor $(1 + i)$ multiplied by itself for the number of periods $(1 + i)^n$. For example, the table factor for $n = 3$, $i = 5\%$ is 1.15763 ($1.05 \times 1.05 \times 1.05$).

Note also in Figure A-1 that as the interest rate gets higher, the time value of money is larger. Assume a present value of $100. In Period 3, for example, the time value of money at a 2% interest rate is $6.1 ($106.1 − $100); at 4%, it is $12.4 ($112.4 − $100); and at 6%, it is $19.1 ($119.1 − $100). Finally, as the period becomes longer, the time value of money becomes greater. These last two points illustrate the idea mentioned earlier that the magnitude of the time value of money is determined by two factors: (1) the size of the interest rate and (2) the length of the period.

---

[1]The factors in this table and in Tables 2, 3, 4, 5, and 6 are carried out to five digits beyond the decimal point. In our discussions, however, we sometimes round the factors to two or three digits beyond the decimal point to simplify calculations.

CALCULATOR BASICS: FUTURE VALUE

Most business calculators are able to solve time value of money problems. Although the particulars vary across models, in general, you enter the information that you know and solve for the missing variable. Cash inflows are positively signed. Outflows have negative signs.

To find the future value of €125 in four years, assuming a 12.25% interest rate, enter PV = 125, I = 12.25, and N = 4. Solve for FV and you'll get −198.45. The negative sign can be interpreted as if you borrow €125 today at 12.25% for four years, you will have to repay €198.45 at the end of the loan.

Future Value—Annuities

It often happens in business transactions that cash payments of equal amounts are made periodically throughout a period of time. Installment payments on loans, for example, are typically set up in this manner. A flow of cash payments of *equal* amounts paid at *equally spaced* periodic intervals is called an annuity. If these payments are made at the end of each period, the flow of payments is called an *ordinary annuity*, or an *annuity in arrears*. If these payments are made at the beginning of each period, the flow of payments is called an *annuity due*. Cash flows illustrating an ordinary annuity and an annuity due (both in the amount of $100 for five years) are provided below.

	Now	1	2	3	4	5
Ordinary annuity:	0	$100	$100	$100	$100	$100
Annuity due:	$100	$100	$100	$100	$100	0

The two annuities are equivalent except that an ordinary annuity has one payment at the end, whereas an annuity due has one payment at the beginning. Because money is worth more today than in the future, an annuity due is more valuable than an ordinary annuity.[2]

Computing the future value of an annuity involves computing the future value of each individual payment, and then adding up the individual future values. To simplify the process, Table A-2 (Future Value of an Ordinary Annuity) and Table A-3 (Future Value of an Annuity Due) at the end of this appendix provide the necessary table factors. To illustrate, the future values of an ordinary annuity and an annuity due of $100 for five years at a 10% interest rate are $610.51 ($100 × 6.10510) and $671.56 ($100 × 6.71561), respectively. Note that the annuity due grows to a larger amount because the first $100 payment grows to $161.05 ($100 × 1.61051) over the five-year period, while the last payment of the ordinary annuity ($100) does not grow at all, which explains the $61.05 ($671.56 − $610.51) difference.

	Now	1	2	3	4	5	(Future) value*
Ordinary annuity:	0	$100	$100	$100	$100	$100	$610.51
Annuity due:	$100	$100	$100	$100	$100	0	$671.56
*End of Period 5							

---

[2] Assuming equal cash flows, interest rates, and time periods.

CALCULATOR BASICS: ANNUITIES

Business calculators handle annuities as well. Consider our example of the annuity with five payments of $100 and a 10% interest rate.

Be sure to clear the time value of money memory before you start. Enter N = 5, I = 10, and PMT (i.e., payment) = 100. Most calculators default to an ordinary annuity assumption. Solve for the future value of the annuity by computing FV. You should obtain −610.51.

To determine the value of the annuity due, set the calculator to assume that the first payment occurs today. Often this is done by toggling a BGN (i.e., beginning) or DUE button between ordinary annuity and annuity due. Computing FV now tells us that the future value of the annuity due is −671.56.

Present Value

Present value is simply the "other side of the coin" of future value. Rather than asking about the future value of a current payment, we now focus on the question, "What is the present value of a future payment?" In the original example, we stated that $1 would grow to $1.10 after one year, given a 10% interest rate. This relationship can just as easily be stated in the opposite way. That is, $1 is the present value of $1.10 received one year in the future, given a 10% interest rate. As investors, we would be indifferent between $1 now (the present value) and $1.10 (future value) one year in the future. As managers, we should be willing to invest in projects where the present value of the expected cash inflows exceeds the present value of the expected cash outflows.

The computation of present value is exactly the reciprocal of the future value computation. Recall that the simple interest factor for the future value in one period is $(1 + i)$. The simple interest factor for present value is the reciprocal, $1/(1 + i)$. In the future value example presented earlier (1 year at a 10% interest rate), $\$1 \times (1 + 0.10)$ equaled $1.10, the future value. To compute the present value, we simply multiply $1.10 by $1/(1 + 0.10)$ to arrive at $1. The present value computation is illustrated as follows.

Now	⟵—————————	1 year
Present value		Future value
$1.00		$1.10

If the present value computation involves more than one period, just as in the future value case, the notion of compounding must be considered. The present value factor, once again, is simply the reciprocal of the future value factor, $1/(1 + i)^n$. More generally, we can rearrange our future value formula to arrive at the formula for the present value of a future lump-sum payment. That is,

$$\text{Future value} = \text{PV}(1 + i)^n$$

becomes

$$\text{Present value} = \text{FV}/(1 + i)^n = \text{FV}(1 + i)^{-n}$$

where

$$\text{FV} = \text{Future value or money amount received in the future;}$$
$$i = \text{periodic interest rate; and}$$
$$n = \text{number of periods.}$$

A two-period, 10% interest rate example follows:

Now	1	2
Present value	Future value (1)	Future value (2)
$1.00 ⟵	$1.10 ⟵	$1.21
$1.00 ⟵		$1.21

This example demonstrates that the present values of both $1.21 in two years and $1.10 in one year are equal to $1, given a 10% interest rate compounded annually. In this case, an investor would be indifferent among having $1 now, receiving $1.10 in one year, or receiving $1.21 in two years.

CALCULATOR BASICS: PRESENT VALUE

To find the present value of €125 in four years, assuming a 12.25% interest rate, enter FV = 125, I = 12.25, and N = 4. Solve for PV and you'll get −78.73. The negative sign can be interpreted as follows: If you lent €78.73 today at 12.25% for four years, you will receive €125 at the end of the loan.

Tables A-4, A-5, and A-6 at the end of this appendix include the table factors used in computing the present value of a single sum, an ordinary annuity, and an annuity due, respectively. To illustrate how to use these tables, consider the three-year ordinary annuity and the annuity due illustrated below.

	Now	1	2	3
Ordinary annuity	0	$100	$100	$100
Annuity due	$100	$100	$100	0

Given an 8% interest rate, the present value of both annuities can be computed by using Table A-4 (present value of a single sum), and simply adding up the present value of each individual payment as shown below.

Ordinary annuity =	$0 +	$100 × 0.92593 +	$100 × 0.85734 +	$100 × 0.79383
$257.71 =	$0 +	$92.593 +	$85.734 +	$79.383

Annuity due =	$100 × 1.00 +	$100 × 0.92593 +	$100 × 0.85734 +	$0
$278.33 =	$100.00 +	$92.593 +	$85.734 +	$0

The present value of the annuities can be computed more quickly by using Tables A-5 and A-6 as illustrated below. Note again that the present value of the annuity due exceeds that of the ordinary annuity because the third payment of the ordinary annuity is discounted over three years ($79.383 = $100 × 0.793830), which, when subtracted from $100, equals the $20.62 difference between the two present value amounts ($278.33 − $257.71).

$$\text{Ordinary annuity} = \$100 \times (\text{Table A-5 factor}; n = 3, i = 8\%)$$
$$\$257.71 = \$100 \times 2.57710$$

$$\text{Annuity due} = \$100 \times (\text{Table A-6 factor}; n = 3, i = 8\%)$$
$$\$278.33 = \$100 \times 2.78326$$

▶ AN ILLUSTRATION

You may quickly grasp the general concepts of future and present value, yet still have difficulty making the appropriate computations for a specific situation. The following example demonstrates how straightforward future and present value computations can be, and also how many different ways one can approach the same problem. We also introduce a concept we call equivalent value, which can be useful in understanding the time value of money.

Assume a $500, five-year, ordinary annuity at a 12% interest rate compounded annually as illustrated below. Figure A-2 shows that the future and present value of this payment stream can be computed in many different ways.

	Now	1	2	3	4	5
Ordinary annuity	0	$500	$500	$500	$500	$500

Can you follow each of the five methods shown? Note that each method brings you to a future value of $3,176 and a present value of $1,804. No matter how many different ways one tackles this problem, the same future and present values emerge.

▶ EQUIVALENT VALUE

To understand the concept of equivalent value, view the $500 annuity payments, the present value, and the future value as being "indifference" amounts. That is, in this example, an investor would be indifferent among a five-year, $500 ordinary annuity; $1,804 now; or $3,176 five years from now. These three payments are, in other words, equivalent in value. The idea of equivalent value is further illustrated in the fifth computation in Figure A-2. It involves two steps. We first compute the amount that would be equivalent to the five-year ordinary annuity if one lump sum were received at the end of Period 3 ($2,533). This amount is the equivalent value of this particular annuity at the end of Period 3. We then adjust this amount to present or future value by multiplying it by the appropriate table factor. Figure A-3 illustrates the equivalent values of the five-year ordinary annuity if lump-sum payments were made at the end of each of the five periods.

Figure A-3 shows that given a 12% interest rate compounded annually, an investor would be indifferent among the following seven payments:

1. A five-year, $500 ordinary annuity;
2. $1,804 now (present value);
3. $2,021 at the end of one year;
4. $2,262 at the end of two years;
5. $2,533 at the end of three years;

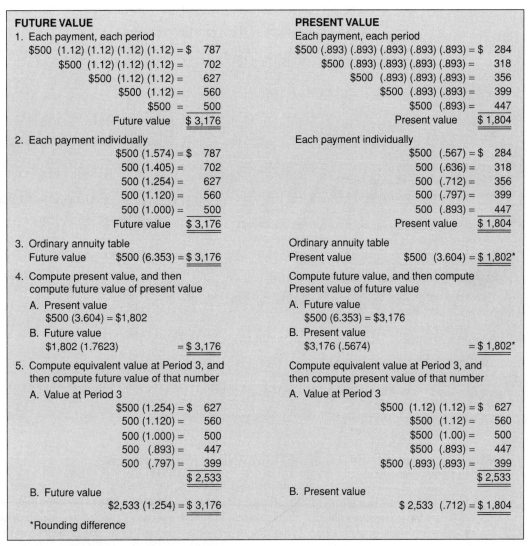

FUTURE VALUE

1. Each payment, each period

$500 (1.12) (1.12) (1.12) (1.12) = $ 787
$500 (1.12) (1.12) (1.12) = 702
$500 (1.12) (1.12) = 627
$500 (1.12) = 560
$500 = 500
Future value $ 3,176

2. Each payment individually

$500 (1.574) = $ 787
500 (1.405) = 702
500 (1.254) = 627
500 (1.120) = 560
500 (1.000) = 500
Future value $ 3,176

3. Ordinary annuity table
Future value $500 (6.353) = $ 3,176

4. Compute present value, and then compute future value of present value

A. Present value
$500 (3.604) = $1,802

B. Future value
$1,802 (1.7623)   = $ 3,176

5. Compute equivalent value at Period 3, and then compute future value of that number

A. Value at Period 3

$500 (1.254) = $ 627
500 (1.120) = 560
500 (1.000) = 500
500 (.893) = 447
500 (.797) = 399
$ 2,533

B. Future value
$2,533 (1.254) = $ 3,176

*Rounding difference

PRESENT VALUE

Each payment, each period

$500 (.893) (.893) (.893) (.893) (.893) = $ 284
$500 (.893) (.893) (.893) (.893) = 318
$500 (.893) (.893) (.893) = 356
$500 (.893) (.893) = 399
$500 (.893) = 447
Present value $ 1,804

Each payment individually

$500 (.567) = $ 284
500 (.636) = 318
500 (.712) = 356
500 (.797) = 399
500 (.893) = 447
Present value $ 1,804

Ordinary annuity table
Present value $500 (3.604) = $ 1,802*

Compute future value, and then compute Present value of future value

A. Future value
$500 (6.353) = $3,176

B. Present value
$3,176 (.5674)   = $ 1,802*

Compute equivalent value at Period 3, and then compute present value of that number

A. Value at Period 3

$500 (1.12) (1.12) = $ 627
$500 (1.12) = 560
$500 (1.00) = 500
$500 (.893) = 447
$500 (.893) (.893) = 399
$ 2,533

B. Present value

$ 2,533 (.712) = $ 1,804

Figure A-2.   Example Calculations

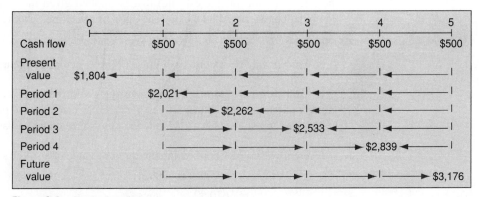

Figure A-3.   Equivalent Values

6. $2,839 at the end of four years; and

7. $3,176 at the end of five years (future value).

TEST YOUR KNOWLEDGE: PRESENT AND FUTURE VALUES

The following questions offer you the chance to test your knowledge of the time value of money.

- Assume an annual interest rate of 8% for each of the following independent cases. Compute the value at time 0 and the value at the end of the investment period for all the cash flows described.

a. $10,000 is invested and held for four years.

b. $2,000 is invested at the end of each year for eight years.

c. $5,000 is invested at the beginning of each year for three years.

d. $3,000 is invested at the end of each year for five years. The balance is left to accumulate interest for an additional five years.

e. A company will receive $25,000 at the end of seven years.

f. A company will receive $3,000 at the end of each year for two years.

g. A company will receive $4,000 at the beginning of each year for three years.

- Congratulations. You have just won the lottery. The lottery board offers you three different options for collecting your winnings:

1. You will receive payments of $500,000 at the end of each year for 20 years.

2. You will receive a lump-sum payment of $4,500,000 today.

3. You will receive a lump-sum payment of $1 million today and payments of $2,100,000 at the end of years 5, 6, and 7.

Assume that all earnings can be invested at a 10% annual rate. Which option should you choose and why?

▶ COMPUTING IMPLICIT RATES OF RETURN AND INTEREST RATES

In many business situations, it is helpful, or even necessary, to compute the expected or actual rate of return (or interest) generated by an investment (or note). Consider a company, for example, that plans to invest $1,000 in a project expected to generate $300 per year over a 5-year period. What rate of return is expected from that project? Similarly, consider a company that finances a piece of property with a fair market value of $100,000 by signing a note that requires annual cash payments of $20,000 for six years. What interest rate is the company paying on the note? These and similar questions can be answered by computing the rate of return (or interest rate) that is implied given the facts of the situation. Such computations are based on the present value computation, which can be viewed in terms of the following equation:

$$\text{Present value} = \text{Future cash flow} \times (\text{Table factor}; n = \text{years}, i = \text{interest rate})$$

So far, we have computed present values after being given a future cash flow, the number of periods (n), and an interest rate (i). For example, the present value of $1,000 to be received in five years at a 10% interest rate can be computed as

$$\text{Present value} = \$1,000 \times (\text{Table 4, present value of a single sum}; n = 5, i = 10\%)$$
$$= \$1,000 \times 0.62092$$
$$= \$620.92$$

Present value = Future cash flow × (Table factor; n = years, i = interest rate)
 $1,000   = $300   × (Table 5, present value of an ordinary annuity; n = 5, i = ?)

Rearranging,
Table factor = $1,000 / $300
Table factor =   3.33

On Table A-5, a 15% interest rate over a 5-year year period leads to a table factor of approximately 3.33.

Figure A-4. Computing an Implicit Rate of Return

However, a number of cases arise, similar to those mentioned above, where we wish to compute the interest rate (i) by either knowing—or having to estimate—the present value, the future cash flows, and the time period (n). Consider again the company that plans to invest $1,000 in a project expected to produce cash receipts of $300 per year (assume at the end of each year) for five years. In this case, the investment amount ($1,000) can be viewed as the present value, the future cash flow is a $300 ordinary annuity, and the time period (n) is five years. As illustrated in Figure A-4, the implicit rate of return (i) can be computed by first finding the table factor (3.33), and then finding that interest rate on that table where the period of time (five years) matches the table factor. The answer is approximately 15%.

In other words, if the company pays $1,000 for an investment that produces $300 at the end of each year for five years, that investment will generate a rate of return of approximately 15%.

CALCULATOR BASICS: IMPLICIT INTEREST RATES

To find the return that you would earn if you invested $1,000 today and received $300 per year at the end of the next five years, enter PV = −1,000, N = 5, and PMT = 300. Compute I (the interest rate or return) and you'll find that the return is 15.24%.

This sort of analysis can be very useful because the expected rate of return (about 15%) of the investment can be compared to the cost of the capital used to finance the investment to determine whether the investment is expected to create shareholder value. If the cost of capital is less than 15%, the investment is expected to create shareholder value and it should be undertaken; if the cost of capital is greater than 15%, the investment is not expected to create shareholder value and the investment should not be undertaken.

In a similar way, implicit interest rates can be computed on notes payable and receivable. Consider again a company that purchases a piece of property with a fair market value of $100,000, paying for it by signing a note payable requiring cash payments of $20,000 at the beginning of each year for six years. Figure A-5 illustrates the computation of the interest rate implicit in the note payable.

This computation means that the cost of financing the property is approximately 8%. As illustrated in Chapter 9, this form of analysis is useful when computing the interest expense

> Present value = Future cash flow × (Table factor; n = years, i = interest rate)
> $100,000 = $200,000 × (Table 6, present value of an annuity due; $n = 6$, $i = ?$)
>
> Rearranging,
> Table factor = $100,000 / $200,000
> Table factor = 5.00
>
> On Table A-6, an 8% interest rate over a 6-year year period leads to a table factor of approximately 5.00.

Figure A-5. Computing an Implicit Interest Rate

that appears on the company's income statement. In addition, the 8% cost of financing could be compared to the return expected from the $100,000 investment in the property to see whether the investment is expected to create shareholder value, which would occur if the rate of return on the investment is expected to exceed 8%.

INSIGHT: PAYMENTS, RATES, AND "PERIODS"

When using the tables or a business calculator, the number of "periods" (n) can refer to years, months, quarters, days, and so on. It is important to match the relevant periods and interest rates to the payments.

TEST YOUR KNOWLEDGE: IMPLICIT RETURNS

The following question offers you the chance to test your knowledge of the time value of money.
• Your company sells a building to a real estate developer in exchange for a note. The note specifies a lump sum of $300,000 to be paid 10 years in the future and annual payments (beginning today) of $2,000 at the beginning of each year for 10 years. Assume an annual interest rate of 10%.

1. Would you be wise to accept $110,000 now instead of the note? Why or why not?
2. At what interest rate would you be wise to accept the $110,000 instead of the note?

▶ TIME VALUE OF MONEY AND FINANCIAL REPORTING

We stated earlier that present value is the economic form of valuation. Investors, creditors, and managers use it to compare the values of alternative investments. Bankers, lawyers, and other decision makers use it to derive the terms of contracts such as mortgages, leases, pensions, and life insurance. Implicit interest rates and rates of return can be computed based on present value. Virtually any transaction that can be broken down into periodic cash flows utilizes the time value of money concept, which is covered in finance, economics, accounting, and other business courses. You may have already studied the time value of money, and you will probably see it again in the future. Its uses in business decision making and performance evaluation are limitless.

The study of financial accounting and its reliance on the time value of money concept is no exception. As you already know, financial accounting information is useful because it helps investors, creditors, and other interested parties evaluate and control the business decisions of management. Is management creating shareholder value and how can it be encouraged to do so? Such evaluation and control requires that financial accounting information be useful in assessing value: the value of entire companies, the value of individual assets and liabilities, and the value of specific transactions. Since present value is the economic form of valuation, financial accounting information must somehow reflect it to be useful.

However, a critical problem arises with the use of present value on the financial statements. Its calculation requires that both future cash flows and future interest rates be predicted. In the vast majority of cases, predicting the future cash flows associated with a particular asset or liability with a reasonable degree of confidence is almost impossible. For example, how would one go about predicting the future cash inflows and outflows associated with the purchase of a specific piece of equipment like an automobile? Moreover, accurately predicting interest rates has for years eluded even the best economists. Many people argue that the predictions that management must make to apply present value are simply too subjective for financial statements that are to be used by those outside the company. Auditors are unwilling and unable to verify such subjective judgments. The legal liability faced by both managers and auditors makes such verification potentially very costly.

For these reasons, although present value remains the goal of financial measurement, most of the valuation bases on the financial statements represent surrogate (substitute) measures of present value. Historical cost, fair market value, replacement cost, and net realizable value can all be viewed as surrogate measures of present value. These measures are valuable nonetheless because they can be used to estimate present values. These valuation bases are used primarily because present value is argued to be too subjective and unreliable for a system that requires auditors to verify financial statements prepared by management for shareholders and other outside interested parties. That view is slowly changing as techniques for measuring fair values are refined and markets develop where objective values can be obtained.

As discussed in Chapter 9, contractual agreements like notes receivable and payable meet the criterion of objectivity. Mortgages, bonds, leases, and pensions are other examples of contracts that underlie cash flows and thus remove much of the subjectivity associated with cash flow prediction. In these cases, implicit interest rates can be computed and these assets or liabilities can initially be valued at present value on the balance sheet. In recent years, even more areas explicitly or implicitly use present values. Financial instruments reported at fair values use present values. Asset retirement obligations involve taking the present values of estimated future cash flows. Allocating fair values in business acquisitions and combinations relies on present value estimates. Asset impairment charges incorporate the time value of money calculations. The list goes on.

In summary, there are two reasons why managers and financial statement users must understand the time value of money. First, present value is the economic form of valuation and is the standard against which all financial accounting measurements must be compared and evaluated. Understanding the time value of money is at the heart of understanding shareholder value creation—the goal of successful management. Second, in those cases where cash flow prediction is sufficiently objective (e.g., contracts), present value methods are used, and present values are actually incorporated into the financial statements. The balance sheet valuation of the assets and liabilities arising from such contracts results from the present value calculation. Given the relation between the balance sheet and the income statement, measuring assets and liabilities using present values inevitably means that earnings are affected, too.

TABLE A-1. Future Value of $1 (future amount of a single sum)

Periods (n)	2%	3%	4%	5%	6%	7%	8%
1	1.02000	1.03000	1.04000	1.05000	1.06000	1.07000	1.08000
2	1.04040	1.06090	1.08160	1.10250	1.12360	1.14490	1.16640
3	1.06121	1.09273	1.12486	1.15763	1.19102	1.22504	1.25971
4	1.08243	1.12551	1.16986	1.21551	1.26248	1.31080	1.36049
5	1.10408	1.15927	1.21665	1.27628	1.33823	1.40255	1.46933
6	1.12616	1.19405	1.26532	1.34010	1.41852	1.50073	1.58687
7	1.14869	1.22987	1.31593	1.40710	1.50363	1.60578	1.71382
8	1.17166	1.26677	1.36857	1.47746	1.59385	1.71819	1.85093
9	1.19509	1.30477	1.42331	1.55133	1.68948	1.83846	1.99900
10	1.21899	1.34392	1.48024	1.62889	1.79085	1.96715	2.15892
11	1.24337	1.38423	1.43945	1.71034	1.89830	2.10485	2.33164
12	1.26824	1.42576	1.60103	1.79586	2.01220	2.25219	2.51817
15	1.34587	1.55797	1.80094	2.07893	2.39656	2.75903	3.17217
20	1.48595	1.80611	2.19112	2.65330	3.20714	3.86968	4.66096
30	1.81136	2.42726	3.24340	4.32194	5.74349	7.61226	10.06266
40	2.20804	3.26204	4.80102	7.03999	10.28572	14.97446	21.72452

Periods (n)	9%	10%	11%	12%	14%	15%
1	1.09000	1.10000	1.11000	1.12000	1.14000	1.15000
2	1.18810	1.21000	1.23210	1.25440	1.29960	1.32250
3	1.29503	1.33100	1.36763	1.40493	1.48154	1.52088
4	1.41158	1.46410	1.51807	1.57352	1.68896	1.74901
5	1.53862	1.61051	1.68506	1.76234	1.92541	2.01136
6	1.67710	1.77156	1.87041	1.97382	2.19497	2.31306
7	1.82804	1.94872	2.07616	2.21068	2.50227	2.66002
8	1.99256	2.14359	2.30454	2.47569	2.85259	3.05902
9	2.17189	2.35795	2.55804	2.77308	3.25195	3.51788
10	2.36736	2.59374	2.83942	3.10585	3.70722	4.04556
11	2.58043	2.85312	3.15176	3.47855	4.22623	4.65239
12	2.81266	3.13843	3.49845	3.89598	4.81790	5.35025
15	3.64248	4.17725	4.78459	5.47357	7.13794	8.13706
20	5.60441	6.72750	8.06231	9.64629	13.74349	16.36654
30	13.26768	17.44940	22.89230	29.95992	50.95016	66.21177
40	31.40942	45.25926	65.00087	93.05097	188.88351	267.86355

TABLE A-2. Future Value of an Ordinary Annuity of $1

Periods (n)	2%	3%	4%	5%	6%	7%	8%
1	1.00000	1.00000	1.00000	1.00000	1.00000	1.00000	1.00000
2	2.02000	2.03000	2.04000	2.05000	2.06000	2.07000	2.08000
3	3.06040	3.09090	3.12160	3.15250	3.18360	3.21490	3.24640
4	4.12161	4.18363	4.24646	4.31013	4.37462	4.43994	4.50611
5	5.20404	5.30914	5.41632	5.52563	5.63709	5.75074	5.86660
6	6.30812	6.46841	6.63298	6.80191	6.97532	7.15329	7.33593
7	7.43428	7.66426	7.89829	8.14201	8.39384	8.65402	8.92280
8	8.58297	8.89234	9.21243	9.54911	9.89747	10.25980	10.63663
9	9.75463	10.15911	10.58280	11.02656	11.49132	11.97799	12.48756
10	10.94972	11.46388	12.00611	12.57789	13.18079	13.81645	14.48656
11	12.16872	12.80780	13.48635	14.20679	14.97164	15.78360	16.64549
12	13.41209	14.19203	15.02581	15.91713	16.86994	17.88845	18.97713
15	17.29342	18.59891	20.02359	21.57856	23.27597	25.12902	27.15211
20	24.29737	26.87037	29.77808	33.06595	36.78559	40.99549	45.76196
30	40.56808	47.57542	56.08494	66.43885	79.05819	94.46079	113.28321
40	60.40198	75.40126	95.02552	120.79977	154.76197	199.63511	259.05652

TABLE A-2. Future Value of an Ordinary Annuity of $1 *(continued)*

Periods (n)	9%	10%	11%	12%	14%	15%
1	1.00000	1.00000	1.00000	1.00000	1.00000	1.00000
2	2.09000	2.10000	2.11000	2.12000	2.14000	2.15000
3	3.27810	3.31000	3.34210	3.37440	3.43960	3.47250
4	4.57313	4.64100	4.70973	4.77933	4.92114	4.99338
5	5.98471	6.10510	6.22780	6.35285	6.61010	6.74238
6	7.52333	7.71561	7.91286	8.11519	8.53552	8.75374
7	9.20043	9.48717	9.78327	10.08901	10.73049	11.06680
8	11.02847	11.43589	11.85943	12.29969	13.23276	13.72682
9	13.02104	13.57948	14.16397	14.77566	16.08535	16.78584
10	15.19293	15.93742	16.72201	17.54874	19.33730	20.30372
11	17.56029	18.53117	19.56143	20.65458	23.04452	24.34928
12	20.14072	21.38428	22.71319	24.13313	27.27075	29.00167
15	29.36092	31.77248	34.40536	37.27971	43.84241	47.58041
20	51.16012	57.27500	64.20283	72.05244	91.02493	102.44358
30	136.30754	164.49402	199.02088	241.33268	356.78685	434.74515
40	337.88245	442.59256	581.82607	767.09142	1342.02510	1779.09031

TABLE A-3. Future Value of an Annuity Due of $1

Periods (n)	2%	3%	4%	5%	6%	7%	8%
1	1.02000	1.03000	1.04000	1.05000	1.06000	1.07000	1.08000
2	2.06040	2.09090	2.12160	2.15250	2.18360	2.21490	2.24640
3	3.12161	3.18363	3.24646	3.31013	3.37462	3.43994	3.50611
4	4.20404	4.30914	4.41632	4.52563	4.63709	4.75074	4.86660
5	5.30812	5.46841	5.63298	5.80191	5.97532	6.15329	6.33593
6	6.43428	6.66246	6.89829	7.14201	7.39384	7.65402	7.92280
7	7.58297	7.89234	8.21423	8.54911	8.89747	9.25980	9.63663
8	8.75463	9.15911	9.58280	10.02656	10.49132	10.97799	11.48756
9	9.94972	10.46388	11.00611	11.57789	12.18079	12.81645	13.48656
10	11.16872	11.80780	12.48635	13.20679	13.97164	14.78360	15.64549
11	12.41209	13.19203	14.02581	14.91713	15.86994	16.88845	17.97713
12	13.68033	14.61779	15.62684	16.71298	17.88214	19.14064	20.49530
15	17.63929	19.15688	20.82453	22.65749	24.67253	26.88805	29.32428
20	24.78332	27.67649	30.96920	34.71925	38.99273	43.86518	49.42292
30	41.37944	49.00268	58.32834	69.76079	83.80168	101.07304	122.34587
40	61.61002	77.66330	98.82654	126.83976	164.04768	213.60957	279.78104

Periods (n)	9%	10%	11%	12%	14%	15%
1	1.09000	1.10000	1.11000	1.12000	1.14000	1.15000
2	2.27810	2.31000	2.34210	2.37440	2.43960	2.47250
3	3.57313	3.64100	3.70973	3.77933	3.92114	3.99338
4	4.98471	5.10510	5.22780	5.35285	5.61010	5.74238
5	6.52333	6.71561	6.91286	7.11519	7.53552	7.75374
6	8.20043	8.48717	8.78327	9.08901	9.73049	10.06680
7	10.02847	10.43589	10.85943	11.29969	12.23276	12.72682
8	12.02104	12.57948	13.16397	13.77566	15.08535	15.78584
9	14.19293	14.93742	15.72201	16.54874	18.33730	19.30372
10	16.56029	17.53117	18.56143	19.65458	22.04452	23.34928
11	19.14072	20.38428	21.71319	23.13313	26.27075	28.00167
12	21.95338	23.52271	25.21164	27.02911	31.08865	33.35192
15	32.00340	34.94973	38.18995	41.75328	49.98035	54.71747
20	55.76453	63.00250	71.26514	80.69874	103.76842	117.81012
30	148.57522	180.94342	220.91317	270.29261	406.73701	499.95692
40	368.29187	486.85181	645.82693	859.14239	1529.90861	2045.95385

TABLE A-4. **Present Value of $1 (present value of a single sum)**

Periods (n)	2%	3%	4%	5%	6%	7%	8%
1	0.98039	0.97087	0.96154	0.95238	0.94340	0.93458	0.92593
2	0.96177	0.94260	0.92456	0.90703	0.89000	0.87344	0.85734
3	0.94232	0.91514	0.88900	0.86384	0.83962	0.81630	0.79383
4	0.92385	0.88849	0.85480	0.82270	0.79209	0.76290	0.73503
5	0.90573	0.86261	0.82193	0.78353	0.74726	0.71299	0.68058
6	0.88797	0.83748	0.79031	0.74622	0.70496	0.66634	0.63017
7	0.87056	0.81309	0.75992	0.71068	0.66506	0.62275	0.58349
8	0.85349	0.78941	0.73069	0.67684	0.62741	0.58201	0.54027
9	0.83676	0.76642	0.70259	0.64461	0.59190	0.54393	0.50025
10	0.82035	0.74409	0.67556	0.61391	0.55839	0.50835	0.46319
11	0.80426	0.72242	0.64958	0.58468	0.52679	0.47509	0.42888
12	0.78849	0.70138	0.62460	0.55684	0.49697	0.44401	0.39711
15	0.74301	0.64186	0.55526	0.48102	0.41727	0.36245	0.31524
20	0.67297	0.55368	0.45639	0.37689	0.31180	0.25842	0.21455
30	0.55207	0.41199	0.30832	0.23138	0.17411	0.13137	0.09938
40	0.45289	0.30656	0.20829	0.14205	0.09722	0.06678	0.04603
50	0.37153	0.22811	0.14071	0.08720	0.05429	0.03395	0.02132
60	0.30478	0.16973	0.09506	0.05354	0.03031	0.01726	0.00988

Periods (n)	9%	10%	11%	12%	14%	15%
1	0.91743	0.90909	0.90090	0.89286	0.87719	0.86957
2	0.84168	0.82645	0.81162	0.79719	0.76947	0.75614
3	0.77218	0.75131	0.73119	0.71178	0.67497	0.65752
4	0.70843	0.68301	0.65873	0.63552	0.59208	0.57175
5	0.64993	0.62092	0.59345	0.56743	0.51937	0.49718
6	0.59627	0.56447	0.53464	0.50663	0.45559	0.43233
7	0.54703	0.51316	0.48166	0.45235	0.39964	0.37594
8	0.50187	0.46651	0.43393	0.40388	0.35056	0.32690
9	0.46043	0.42410	0.39092	0.36061	0.30751	0.28426
10	0.42241	0.38554	0.35218	0.32197	0.26974	0.24718
11	0.38753	0.35049	0.31728	0.28748	0.23662	0.21494
12	0.35553	0.31863	0.28584	0.25668	0.20756	0.18691
15	0.27454	0.23939	0.20900	0.18270	0.14010	0.12289
20	0.17843	0.14864	0.12403	0.10367	0.07276	0.06110
30	0.07537	0.05731	0.04368	0.03338	0.01963	0.01510
40	0.03184	0.02209	0.01538	0.01075	0.00529	0.00373
50	0.01345	0.00852	0.00542	0.00346	0.00143	0.00092
60	0.00568	0.00328	0.00191	0.00111	0.00039	0.00023

TABLE A-5.   Present Value of an Ordinary Annuity of $1

Periods (n)	2%	3%	4%	5%	6%	7%	8%
1	0.98039	0.97087	0.96154	0.95238	0.94340	0.93458	0.92593
2	1.94156	1.91347	1.88609	1.85941	1.83339	1.80802	1.78326
3	2.88388	2.82861	2.77509	2.72325	2.67301	2.62432	2.57710
4	3.80773	3.71710	3.62990	3.54595	3.46511	3.38721	3.31213
5	4.71346	4.57971	4.45182	4.32948	4.21236	4.10020	3.99271
6	5.60143	5.41719	5.24214	5.07569	4.91732	4.76654	4.62288
7	6.47199	6.23028	6.00205	5.78637	5.58238	5.38929	5.20637
8	7.32548	7.01969	6.73274	6.46321	6.20979	5.97130	5.74664
9	8.16224	7.78611	7.43533	7.10782	6.80169	6.51523	6.24689
10	8.98259	8.53020	8.11090	7.72173	7.36009	7.02358	6.71008
11	9.78685	9.25262	8.76048	8.30641	7.88687	7.49867	7.13896
12	10.57534	9.95400	9.38507	8.86325	8.38384	7.94269	7.53608
15	12.84926	11.93794	11.11839	10.37966	9.71225	9.10791	8.55948
20	16.35143	14.87747	13.59033	12.46221	11.46992	10.59401	9.81815
30	22.39646	19.60044	17.29203	15.37245	13.76483	12.40904	11.25778
40	27.35548	23.11477	19.79277	17.15909	15.04630	13.33171	11.92461
50	31.42361	25.72976	21.48218	18.25593	15.76186	13.80075	12.23348
60	34.76089	27.67556	22.62349	18.92929	16.16143	14.03918	12.37655

Periods (n)	9%	10%	11%	12%	14%	15%
1	0.91743	0.90909	0.90090	0.89286	0.87719	0.86957
2	1.75911	1.73554	1.71252	1.69005	1.64666	1.62571
3	2.53129	2.48685	2.44371	2.40183	2.32163	2.28323
4	3.23972	3.16987	3.10245	3.03735	2.91371	2.85498
5	3.88965	3.79079	3.69590	3.60478	3.43308	3.35216
6	4.48592	4.35526	4.23054	4.11141	3.88867	3.78448
7	5.03295	4.86842	4.71220	4.56376	4.28830	4.16042
8	5.53482	5.33493	5.14612	4.96764	4.63886	4.48732
9	5.99525	5.75902	5.53705	5.32825	4.94637	4.77158
10	6.41766	6.14457	5.88923	5.65022	5.21612	5.01877
11	6.80519	6.49506	6.20652	5.93770	5.45273	5.23371
12	7.16073	6.81369	6.49236	6.19437	5.66029	5.42062
15	8.06069	7.60608	7.19087	6.81086	6.14217	5.84737
20	9.12855	8.51356	7.96333	7.46944	6.62313	6.25933
30	10.27365	9.42691	8.69379	8.05518	7.00266	6.56598
40	10.75736	9.77905	8.95105	8.24378	7.10504	6.64178
50	10.96168	9.91481	9.04165	8.30450	7.13266	6.66051
60	11.04799	9.96716	9.07356	8.32405	7.14011	6.66515

TABLE A-6.   Present Value of an Annuity Due of $1

Periods (n)	2%	3%	4%	5%	6%	7%	8%
1	1.00000	1.00000	1.00000	1.00000	1.00000	1.00000	1.00000
2	1.98039	1.97087	1.96154	1.95238	1.94340	1.93458	1.92593
3	2.94156	2.91347	2.88609	2.85941	2.83339	2.80802	2.78326
4	3.88388	3.82861	3.77509	3.72325	3.67301	3.62432	3.57710
5	4.80773	4.71710	4.62990	4.54595	4.46511	4.38721	4.31213
6	5.71346	5.57971	5.45182	5.32948	5.21236	5.10020	4.99271
7	6.60143	6.41719	6.24214	6.07569	5.91732	5.76654	5.62288
8	7.47199	7.23028	7.00205	6.78637	6.58238	6.38929	6.20637
9	8.32548	8.01969	7.73274	7.46321	7.20979	6.97130	6.74664
10	9.16224	8.78611	8.43533	8.10782	7.80169	7.51523	7.24689
11	9.98259	9.53020	9.11090	8.72173	8.36009	8.02358	7.71008
12	10.78685	10.25262	9.76048	9.30641	8.88687	8.49867	8.13896
15	13.10625	12.29607	11.56312	10.89864	10.29498	9.74547	9.24424
20	16.67846	15.32380	14.13394	13.08532	12.15812	11.33560	10.60360
30	22.84438	20.18845	17.98371	16.14107	14.59072	13.27767	12.15841
40	27.90259	23.80822	20.58448	18.01704	19.94907	14.26493	12.87858
50	32.05208	26.50166	22.34147	19.16872	16.70757	14.76680	13.21216
60	35.45610	28.50583	23.52843	19.87575	17.13111	15.02192	13.36668

Periods (n)	9%	10%	11%	12%	14%	15%
1	1.00000	1.00000	1.00000	1.00000	1.00000	1.00000
2	1.91743	1.90909	1.90090	1.89286	1.87719	1.86957
3	2.75911	2.73554	2.71252	2.69005	2.64666	2.62571
4	3.53129	3.48685	3.44371	3.40183	3.32163	3.28323
5	4.23972	4.16987	4.10245	4.03735	3.91371	3.85498
6	4.88965	4.79079	4.69590	4.60478	4.43308	4.35216
7	5.48592	5.35526	5.23054	5.11141	4.88867	4.78448
8	6.03295	5.86842	5.71220	5.56376	5.28830	5.16042
9	6.53482	6.33493	6.14612	5.96764	5.63886	5.48732
10	6.99525	6.75902	6.53705	6.32825	5.94637	5.77158
11	7.41766	7.14457	6.88923	6.65022	6.21612	6.01877
12	7.80519	7.49506	7.20652	6.93770	6.45273	6.23371
15	8.78615	8.36669	7.98187	7.62817	7.00207	6.72448
20	9.95011	9.36492	8.83929	8.36578	7.55037	7.19823
30	11.19828	10.36961	9.65011	9.02181	7.98304	7.55088
40	11.72552	10.75696	9.93567	9.23303	8.09975	7.63805
50	11.94823	10.90630	10.03624	0.30104	8.13123	7.65959
60	12.04231	10.96387	10.07165	9.32294	8.13972	7.66492

▶ CASES AND REVIEW QUESTIONS

Shoprite Holdings, Ltd.—Revenue Recognition

When companies sell products or services, they often do so "on account" or they provide vendor financing, permitting them to compete on both what they are selling (the product or service component) and the payment terms (the financing component). Financial accountants need to measure the revenue and, in some cases the revenue must be divided between these two components. When normal terms of trade call for, say, 30- or 60-day payment terms, time values are ignored on the grounds that the time period is too short, making the difference between present and future value immaterial—the financing component is judged to be quite small. In such cases, there is no need to recognize implicit interest, so all the revenue is attached to the product or service component of the transaction. When time periods are longer, however, the materiality argument no longer holds and financial reports must recognize revenue for both components.

Assume that South African retailer Shoprite Holdings, Ltd. sells furniture to a customer with a "sales price" of R2,000 under a "buy now, pay later" promotion. The terms of sale are that if the customer pays within one year, no interest will be charged. If the customer fails to pay on time, interest will accrue at 15% per year.

1. The company will record revenue in the amount of the present value of the sales price. What is that present value?

2. If the terms of the sale were that the customer was required to make four payments of R500 at the end of each of the next four years, how much revenue would Shoprite recognize at the time of the sale? How much interest revenue would the company record each year? How much total revenue would be recorded over the life of the arrangement?

E.ON AG—Asset Retirement Obligations

When companies purchase fixed assets that have substantial and estimable costs of retirement or disposal, they are required to accrue the present value of those costs at the time of the asset's acquisition. This is known as the asset retirement obligation. The costs are added to the value of the asset and a corresponding liability is recorded. The result is that the asset has a higher balance sheet value (and thus depreciation will be higher), the company's liabilities are higher (and the resulting debt ratios less favorable), and interest expense accrues on the liability each year until the asset is retired or disposed of.

E.ON AG, based in Duesseldorf, Germany, is one of the world's leading energy companies with core activities in power and gas. Assume that E.ON purchases a nuclear reactor from another energy company for €3 billion. The company expects to operate the facility for 20 years, at which time it will decomission the reactor. Estimated decommissioning costs are €500 million.

1. At what value will E.ON report the purchase of the reactor? Assume that the relevant discount rate is 9%.

2. After five years, what will the balance sheet value of the asset retirement obligation be?

3. If the company depreciates its reactors using the straight-line method, how much depreciation will it record each year? How much would be recorded if the asset retirement obligation was ignored? If the company ignored the costs until such time as they were actually paid, how well would the financial statements have measured performance and financial position over the course of the life of the nuclear reactor?

La Quinta Corporation—Asset Impairment Tests

Long-term assets are reported on the balance sheet at their acquisition cost along with the estimated asset retirement obligation, less any accumulated depreciation. That book value cannot exceed the value of the asset to the company. In other words, if conditions exist that suggest that the company will not be able to recover the book value of the asset through sale or use, then the asset's value is deemed to be impaired and needs to be reduced.

In Chapter 8, we described how U.S. hotel chain La Quinta Corporation deals with asset impairments:

"We regularly review the performance of long-lived assets on an ongoing basis for impairment, as well as when events or changes in circumstances indicate that the carrying amount of an asset may not be recoverable. For each lodging asset held for use, if the sum of the expected future cash flows (undiscounted and without interest charges) is less than the net book value of the asset, the excess of the net book value over La Quinta's estimate of fair value of the asset is charged to current earnings. We estimate fair value primarily (1) by discounting expected future cash flows or (2) on the basis of expected liquidated sales proceeds, relying on common hotel valuation methods such as multiples of room revenues or per room valuations. For each asset held for sale, the carrying value is reduced, if necessary, to the expected sales proceeds less costs to sell by recording a charge [expense] to current earnings."

The process involves two steps. In the first, the time value of money is ignored—cash flows are estimated and added up. If that undiscounted amount is less than the book value of the asset, the asset is deemed impaired. In that case, the second step arises—and measuring the impairment does involve taking the time value of money into account.

Assume that La Quinta owns a hotel with a book value of $3,000,000. Competition in the area has increased and room rates and occupancy levels have fallen, calling into question whether the asset's value is impaired. La Quinta's finance team estimates that future operating profits for the property will be $225,000 per year for the next 10 years.

1. Is the asset impaired? If it is, measure the impairment. Assume that La Quinta uses a discount rate of 11% for its impairment calculations.

2. Describe some of the practical challenges that managers face in testing for and measuring asset impairments.

3. Assume now that La Quinta's finance team estimates that the future profits from this property will be $325,000 per year for 15 years. Estimate the implicit rate of return that La Quinta is earning on the hotel. That is, determine the interest rate that equates the (pre-impairment) book value with the expected future cash flows.

Glossary

A

accelerated methods of depreciation   Accelerated methods of depreciation are used to depreciate fixed assets. Under these methods, more costs are allocated to earlier periods than are allocated to later periods. Examples include the double-declining-balance and sum-of-the-years'-digits methods. These methods are considered conservative since they recognize large amounts of depreciation in the early years of an asset's life.

accounting equation   The accounting equation is the basis for the four financial statements. It is a mathematical equation stating that the dollar value of a company's assets equals the dollar value of its liabilities plus the dollar value of its shareholders' equity. The balance sheet is a statement of this equation; transactions are recorded on the financial statements in a way that maintains the equality of this equation.

accounting period   An accounting period is the period of time between the preparation of the financial statements. Statements are often prepared monthly, quarterly, semiannually, or annually. Most companies report on a calendar-year basis, but for various reasons, some companies report on other 365-day cycles, called fiscal years.

accounts payable   Accounts payable are dollar amounts owed to others for goods, supplies, and services purchased on open account. They arise from frequent transactions between a company and its suppliers that are normally not subject to specific, formal contracts. These extensions of credit are the practical result of a time lag between the receipt of a good, supply, or service and the corresponding payment. Accounts payable are normally included on the balance sheet under current liabilities.

accounts payable turnover   *Cost of sales/Average accounts payable.* Accounts payable turnover measures how quickly, on average, accounts payable are paid to a company's suppliers. It reflects the number of times, during a given period, that these supplier accounts are turned over. Dividing this activity ratio by 365 changes it into an expression indicating how many days, on average, are required to pay off an account.

accounts receivable   Accounts receivable is a balance sheet account indicating the dollar amount due from customers from sales made on open account. It arises when revenues are recognized before receipt of the associated cash payment. Accounts receivable is normally included as a current asset, and for some companies, it can be quite large.

accounts receivable turnover   *Net credit sales/Average accounts receivable.* Accounts receivable turnover reflects the number of times a company's accounts receivables are recorded and collected during a given period. This ratio is often divided into 365 days, which indicates how many days, on average, receivables are outstanding—often referred to as the collection period.

accrual accounting   The accrual basis is a system of accounting that recognizes revenues and expenses when assets and liabilities are created or discharged because of operating activities. Accrual accounting differs from cash flow accounting, which reflects only cash inflows and outflows, and is the basis upon which the statement of cash flows is prepared. Statements prepared under accrual accounting, such as the income statement, are designed to measure earning power.

accruals   Accruals are accounting entries designed to ensure that the assets and liabilities created or discharged due to the operating activities of the current period are recognized as revenues or expenses on the income statement of that period. The recognition on the income statement occurs at a time different from the related cash flow, so a receivable or payable must be recorded on the balance sheet. Common examples include accrued payables, bad debts, warranties, and deferred revenues.

accrued payables   Accrued payables are obligations on the balance sheet that must be recognized at the end of each period because they build up over time. Accrued payables are normally included as current liabilities because they are expected to be paid with the use of assets presently listed as current on the balance sheet. Accrued payables normally include obligations associated with salaries, wages, interest, warranties, and taxes.

accumulated depreciation   Accumulated depreciation is a contra asset account on the balance sheet that reflects the dollar value of the total depreciation that has been previously recognized on the fixed assets up to the date of the balance sheet.

activity method   The activity method is a method of depreciating fixed assets or depleting natural resource costs that allocates the cost of the long-lived asset to future periods on the basis of its activity. This method is used primarily in the mining, oil, and gas industries to deplete the costs associated with acquiring the rights to and extracting natural resources. The estimated life under the activity method is expressed in terms of units of activity (e.g., miles driven, units produced, and barrels extracted) instead of years, as is done under the other common methods of depreciation (e.g., straight-line, double-declining-balance, and sum-of-the-years'-digits methods).

activity ratios   Activity ratios measure the speed with which assets or accounts payable move through operations. They involve the calculation of a number called turnover, which indicates the number of times during a given period that assets (or payables) are acquired, disposed of, and replaced. Dividing 365 by the turnover number produces the average number of days during the year that the assets (or payables) were carried on the balance sheet. Turnover is commonly calculated for accounts receivable, inventory, fixed assets, total assets, and accounts payable.

actuary   An actuary is a statistician who estimates risk for a wide variety of purposes, including the determination of insurance premiums, the funding of pension and health plans, and other purposes that involve assessing future demographic trends.

additional paid-in capital   Additional paid-in capital is included in the shareholders' equity section of the balance sheet and reflects capital contributions to the firm over and above the par value of issued common stock or preferred stock. It can also appear as the result of issuing stock dividends, stock options, and treasury stock, and is part of contributed capital.

aging schedule   Aging is a method of estimating and analyzing uncollectible accounts receivable that categorizes individual accounts on the basis of the amount of time each has been outstanding. Each category is then multiplied by a different uncollectible percentage, under the assumption that older accounts are more likely than new accounts to be uncollectible. This method is used primarily by management to identify and maintain control over uncollectible accounts receivables.

allowance method   The allowance method, under generally accepted accounting principles (GAAP), is the preferred method to account for uncollectibles and sales returns, both of which have a direct effect on the reported value of accounts receivable. The allowance method involves estimating the dollar amount of the uncollectibles or sales returns at the end of each accounting period and, based on that estimate, records an entry that reduces both net income and the balance in accounts receivable with a contra account called "allowance for uncollectibles."

amortization   Amortization is the systematic allocation of deferred charge (e.g., prepaid expense, fixed asset, bond discount or premium, deferred revenue, and intangible asset) over its life. Amortization is often used to describe the allocation of the cost of intangible assets to earnings, but

prepaid expenses and discounts and premiums on long-term receivables and payables are also amortized to earnings. Depreciation is the amortization of fixed assets, and depletion is the amortization of natural resource costs.

analytic review   Analytic review is an important part of financial statement analysis that focuses on whether balances in financial statement accounts deviate from expected levels and seeks to explain why such deviations occur. It includes analyzing common-size financial statements to identify relative changes in the sizes of financial accounts across periods, as well as comparing these changes in an effort to infer management actions.

annual report   An annual report is a document that a company publishes each year, containing the financial statements, a description of the company and its operations, an audit report, a management letter, footnotes to the financial statements containing supporting schedules, and other financial and nonfinancial information.

annuity   An annuity is a periodic cash flow of an equal amount over time. Bond interest payments, lease and rental payments, and insurance payments are examples.

appropriation of retained earnings   An appropriation refers to the act of making a portion of the retained earnings account unavailable for the payment of dividends. Such restrictions can be imposed contractually or voluntarily and are designed to ensure that cash is available in the future for some specific purpose.

asset   An asset is an item listed on the left side of the balance sheet that has been acquired by the company in an objectively measurable transaction and has future economic benefit—additional purchasing power, cash, or the ability to generate revenues.

asset depreciation range (ADR)   The asset depreciation range (ADR) system contains guidelines published by the Internal Revenue Service that define the minimum allowable useful lives and maximum depreciation rates for various kinds of long-lived assets. These lives are used when depreciating long-lived assets in the computation of taxable income.

asset impairment   An asset impairment occurs when the value of an asset is judged to be permanently reduced. See **asset retirement** and **restructuring charges.**

asset mix   Asset mix is the combination of assets listed on the balance sheet as of a given date. For example, the percentage of current assets, long-term investments, fixed assets, and intangibles to total assets can represent a company's asset mix. Common-size analysis across time can identify changes in a company's asset mix.

asset retirement   An asset retirement refers to the discontinuation of the use of a fixed asset.

asset turnover   *Sales/Average total assets.* Asset turnover measures how efficiently a company is using its assets to produce sales. A high ratio indicates that a company is producing a large amount of sales with relatively few assets. Asset turnover times profit margin equals return on assets, which is a direct determinant of return on equity.

audit   An audit is an examination conducted by an individual or entity, having no financial interest in the company (i.e., independent), to determine whether the financial statements of the company fairly reflect its financial condition, whether the statements have been prepared in conformance with generally accepted accounting principles (GAAP), and whether the company's internal control system is effective. The outcome of the audit is an audit report, or opinion letter, signed by the auditor, which states the extent of the auditor's activities and the conclusions.

audit committee   The audit committee is a subcommittee of the board of directors, made up entirely of nonmanagement directors, that works with management to choose the external auditor and monitor the audit so that it is conducted in a thorough, objective, and independent manner.

audit opinion   See **audit report.**

audit report   The audit report, which is written and signed by the external auditor, states whether, and to what extent, the information in the financial statements fairly reflects the financial performance and condition of the company. See **audit.**

authorized shares   Authorized shares refers to the number of shares of stock that a corporation is entitled to issue by its corporate charter, which is normally granted by the state in which the company is incorporated. Additional authorizations must be approved by the board of directors and are often subject to shareholder vote. Both preferred and common shares must be authorized before they can be issued.

available-for-sale securities   Available-for-sale securities refer to relatively small investments (less than 20% of the outstanding voting stock) in marketable equity or debt securities that are not considered trading securities. Available-for-sale securities are readily marketable, but are not intended to be sold in the near future—they can be listed as either current or noncurrent, depending on management's intention, and they are carried on the balance sheet at fair market value.

averaging assumption   In addition to first in, first out (FIFO) and last in, first out (LIFO), averaging is one of the three most common inventory cost flow assumptions. Under the average method, the cost of goods sold and the ending inventory are determined by computing a weighted average cost of the items sold and the items remaining, respectively.

B

bad debts   See **uncollectibles.**

balance sheet   The balance sheet is a financial statement that indicates the financial condition of a business as of a given point in time. It includes assets, liabilities, and shareholders' equity, and it represents a statement of the basic accounting equation. The assets and liabilities are divided into current and noncurrent classifications on the basis of liquidity, and comparisons of assets and liabilities often provide an indication of the company's ability to meet obligations as they come due (i.e., solvency).

bank reconciliation   A bank reconciliation is a document that lists items explaining the difference between the cash balance indicated in the company's ledger and the cash balance indicated in the company's bank statement. Differences between the two balances arise from outstanding checks, unrecorded deposits, and bank charges. Maintaining up-to-date bank reconciliations is one component of a good internal control system.

basic earnings per share   See **earnings per share.**

betterment   A betterment is a material expenditure made after the acquisition of a long-lived asset that improves the asset by increasing its life, increasing the quality or quantity of its output, or decreasing the cost of operating it.

"Big 4"   The four public accounting firms that audit most of the large companies in the United States are known as the Big 4. They are Deloitte & Touche, Ernst & Young, KPMG Peat Marwick, and PricewaterhouseCoopers.

board of directors   The board of directors is a group of individuals elected annually by the shareholders of a corporation to represent the interests of those shareholders. In addition to setting overall corporate policies, the board has the power to declare dividends, set executive compensation, and hire and fire management. The board also appoints and monitors the compensation and audit committees.

bond   Bonds are debt securities issued by an entity to a large number of investors to raise cash. The issuing company, in return, normally agrees to make cash interest payments to the bondholders until a specific future date (called maturity), usually 5 to 30 years in the future, at which time a large principal payment is made and the obligation is terminated. Companies issue bonds to raise large amounts of cash, and they are normally issued (sold) to the public through a third party (called an underwriter), such as an investment banker or financial institution. After bonds are initially issued, they are generally freely negotiable; that is, they can be purchased and sold in the open market.

bonds payable   Bonds payable represents a balance sheet liability reflecting the book value of bonds that have been previously issued and are presently outstanding. This liability is normally considered to be long-term, except for the portion that is due within the time period of current liabilities. Bonds payable are carried on the balance sheet at the present value of the future cash (interest and principal) payments specified by the terms of the bonds, discounted at the effective interest rate at the time of issuance.

book gain/loss   A book gain (or loss) is the difference between the value received (or given up) and the book value of the asset (or liability) disposed of. If, for example, an asset with a book value of $10,000 is sold for $12,000, a $2,000 book gain is recognized. Selling the same asset for $7,000 would create a book loss of $3,000.

book value   Book value is the value of an account, a company, or a share of stock as indicated by the balance sheet. It is often referred to as balance sheet value.

borrowing capacity   Borrowing capacity is the ability of a company to raise capital by issuing debt securities or other borrowings. Borrowing capacity is critical for successful businesses because debt financing is a method of raising much needed capital to support operations, invest in assets, or pay off outstanding debts.

business acquisition   In a business acquisition, a company (investor) acquires a controlling interest (51% or more of the voting stock) in another (investee) company. The investor company is called the parent, and the investee company is called the subsidiary; both companies normally continue to operate. The financial statements of the parent are prepared on a consolidated basis, where the assets, liabilities, income, and cash flows of the combined entity are included together. The financial statements of the subsidiary are unaffected.

business combination   See **merger.**

business environment   A business environment is the economic setting in which a company's operating, investing, and financing activities are conducted. The business environment consists of many items, most of which are not within management's control—including interest rates, market values of certain assets, competitive forces, the general state of the economy, changes in customer tastes and preferences, characteristics of the workforce, and government regulation.

business segment   A business segment is a separate line of business, production line, or class of customer representing an operation that is independent of a company's other operations. Many large companies have multiple lines of business, and if material, the assets, liabilities, revenues, and profits associated with these separate lines are disclosed in the footnotes to the financial statements.

C

call provision   A provision in a debt contract that allows the issuing company to repurchase outstanding debt (e.g., bonds) after a specified date for a specified price is a call provision. Call provisions protect issuing companies from situations where market interest rates drop significantly. In such cases, issuing companies can exercise their call provisions (repurchase the debt) and reissue debt at lower interest rates.

capital   Capital refers to funds (usually cash) generated by a company to support its operations. In a general sense,

capital can refer to funds produced through issuing either debt or equity securities, but the capital section of the balance sheet normally refers to owners' or stockholders' (shareholders') equity—sources of equity capital.

Capital asset pricing model   The cost of equity can be estimated using the capital asset pricing model, which expresses the return that an investor can reasonably expect on an equity investment (cost of equity) as a function of two factors: (1) the expected risk-free rate of return and (2) the expected risk premium associated with an investment in the firm itself.

capital lease   A capital lease is a lease treated as a purchase for that purposes of financial accounting. If, at the date of the lease agreement, a lease meets certain criteria, it is classified and accounted for as a capital lease by the lessee. Under a capital lease, the lessee is considered to have the economic ownership of the leased asset, which is financed through the periodic lease payments. The resulting accounting treatment recognizes both a balance sheet asset and a liability, which are initially placed on the books at the present value of the future cash payments, discounted at the effective rate of interest. The asset is then depreciated, and the effective interest method is used to amortize the liability as the lease payments are made.

capital market   Transactions involving the buying and selling of debt and equity investments are conducted in the capital market. This market includes the global stock and bond markets and the banking system.

capital structure   Capital structure refers to a company's financing sources: (1) borrowings or liabilities, (2) contributed capital, and (3) earned capital (primarily retained earnings). It is represented by the right side of the balance sheet: liabilities and shareholders' equity.

capital structure leverage   *Average total assets/Average shareholders' equity.* Capital structure leverage or financial leverage indicates the extent to which a company relies on debt financing. As the ratio increases (decreases), the amount of debt financing is greater (less). A ratio of 1:1 indicates that there is no debt in the company's capital structure. Capital structure leverage is a direct determinant of return on equity.

capitalization ratios   Capitalization ratios help analysts evaluate the capital structure of a company or, in general, the composition of the liability and shareholders' equity side of the balance sheet. They include (1) debt/equity, (2) debt ratio, (3) capital structure leverage, and (4) common equity leverage.

capitalize   To capitalize an expenditure means to place the cost of an expenditure on the balance sheet as an asset. Expenditures can either be expensed or capitalized.

cash conversion cycle   *Accounts receivable turnover (days) + Inventory turnover (days) − Accounts payable turnover (days).* This metric combines three turnover measures in a way that indicates the time period over which a company's major working capital requirements must be financed. As this measure increases, it indicates a longer time period, a greater working capital investment, and higher financing requirements. See **operating cycle.**

cash discount   When a good or service is sold on credit, the selling company wishes to collect the cash as soon as possible. To encourage prompt payment, many companies offer cash discounts on the gross sales price. Cash discounts specify that an amount of cash less than the gross sales price is sufficient to satisfy the obligation.

cash equivalent   Cash equivalents are securities that can be converted into cash in a very short time. Examples include commercial paper and other debt instruments with maturity dates less than three months in the future. Such items are often included in the definition of cash for the purposes of the balance sheet and the statement of cash flows.

cash flow   Cash flow is the movement of cash associated with a company's operating, investing, and financing activities. Cash flow involves inflows and outflows of cash, and a company's cash flow is considered to be strong if it can generate large amounts of cash relatively quickly. Cash flow is an important part of solvency, and an historical description of cash flow is provided by the statement of cash flows.

cash flow accounting   Cash flow accounting is a system that keeps a balance of cash and a record of cash inflows and outflows. The statement of cash flows is based on cash flow accounting.

cash flow from financing   Cash flow from financing activities represents cash generated during a particular period through a company's financing activities. These cash flows are disclosed in the financing section of the statement of cash flows and reflect cash flows associated with additional long-term borrowings and repayments, equity issuances and treasury stock purchases, and dividend payments.

cash flow from investing   Cash flow from investing activities includes cash inflows and outflows during a particular period from a company's investing activities. These flows are disclosed in the investing section of the statement of cash flows and reflect cash inflows and outflows associated with the acquisition and sale of a company's investments and long-lived assets.

cash flow from operations   Cash flows from operating activities include cash receipts and payments during a particular period associated with a company's operating activities. Also called net cash flow from operations, these flows are disclosed in the operating section of the statement of cash flows and can be computed and presented in either of two ways: (1) a direct method, which lists the cash flow effects of each income statement item, or (2) the more common indirect method, which arrives at cash from

operations by adjusting net income for differences between accruals and operating cash flows.

cash flow projection   Cash flow projection is the process of predicting the amount and timing of future cash inflows and outflows and plays an important role in financial statement analysis.

cash management   Cash management is the manner in which a company plans and executes the inflows and outflows of cash.

certificate of deposit   A certificate of deposit is a short-term bank obligation that pays a given rate of interest for a specified period of time, ending on the maturity date. Often interest penalties are assessed when cash is withdrawn prior to the maturity date.

certified public accountant   A certified public accountant (CPA) is an individual who has met a set of educational requirements to sit for the national CPA exam, passed the exam, and met the experience requirements of the states in which he or she practices. Certified public accountants must also pass an ethics exam, periodically participate in continuing education courses, and maintain their membership with the American Institute of Certified Public Accountants (AICPA). CPAs are empowered to sign audit reports.

classified balance sheet   A classified balance sheet is a balance sheet that is divided into classifications—including current assets, long-term investments, fixed assets, intangible assets, current liabilities, long-term liabilities, and shareholders' equity.

clean audit opinion   See **standard audit report.**

collateral   Collateral represents assets designated to be paid to a creditor in case of default on a loan by a debtor—often referred to as security on the loan. The balance sheet, which contains a listing of a company's assets, and the footnotes to the financial statements may help to identify various sources of collateral. Lenders often require that loans be backed by collateral as a way of reducing the cost associated with default.

collection period   See **accounts receivable turnover.**

commercial paper   Commercial paper is a fast-growing means of providing short-term financing; it represents short-term notes (30 to 270 days) issued for cash by companies with good credit ratings to other companies.

common equity leverage   (*Net income – Preferred stock dividends*)/(*Net income – Interest expense* [*1 – Tax rate*]). Common equity leverage measures the portion of the return to the shareholders relative to the return to all capital providers (shareholders and creditors). Higher levels of this ratio indicate that greater amounts of the return generated by the company are available to the shareholders, an indication of the effectiveness of the company's leverage.

common stock Common stock is a certificate that represents an ownership (equity) interest in a corporation, carrying with it the right to receive dividends if they are declared and the right to vote for the corporation's board of directors at the annual shareholders' meeting. It also carries with it the right to the assets of the corporation, but this right is subordinate to that of the corporate creditors. Issuing common stock is a popular way for corporations to raise capital.

common-size financial statements Common-size financial statements express dollar values as percentages of other dollar values on the same statement. On a common-size income statement, for example, expense items and the various measures of income (e.g., operating income and net income) are expressed as percentages of sales. On a common-size balance sheet, assets and liabilities are expressed as percentages of total assets (or liabilities plus stockholders' equity).

compensating balance Compensating balances are minimum cash balances that must be maintained in savings or checking accounts until certain loan obligations are satisfied. Compensating balances help financial institutions reduce the risks of default on outstanding loans by ensuring that at least some cash is available for scheduled loan payments.

compensation committee The compensation committee is a subcommittee of the board of directors charged with establishing the compensation packages of the company's officers. It is made up entirely of outside directors (not part of company management).

compensation contracts Compensation contracts specify the form and amount of compensation paid to the executives, managers, or employees of a company.

comprehensive income A measure of income that includes not only net income, but also other increases in a company's wealth not reflected on the income statement. Examples include unrealized price changes on available-for-sale securities and translation gains and losses related to the consolidation of foreign subsidiaries. A statement of comprehensive income, detailing the change in comprehensive income over a period of time, must be included in the financial statements.

conservatism Conservatism is an exception to the principles of accounting measurement stating that when in doubt, financial statements should understate assets, overstate liabilities, accelerate the recognition of losses, and delay the recognition of gains.

consignment A consignment is an agreement by which a consignor (owner) transfers inventory to a consignee (receiver) who takes physical possession and places the items up for sale. When the inventory is sold, the consignee collects the sales proceeds, keeps a percentage, and returns the remainder to the consignor.

consistency Consistency is a principle of accounting measurement stating that, although there is considerable choice among accounting methods, companies should choose a set of methods and use them from one period to the next. Consistency helps financial statement users to make useful comparisons across time.

consolidated financial statements Consolidated financial statements include a company's assets and liabilities, as well as the assets and liabilities of its majority-owned subsidiaries. See **business acquisition and merger.**

contingency A contingency represents an existing condition, situation, or set of circumstances involving uncertainty concerning a possible gain or loss for a company. The uncertainty will ultimately be resolved when one or more future events occurs or fails to occur.

contingent liability See **contingency** and **loss contingency.**

contra account A contra account is a balance sheet account that offsets another balance sheet account.

contributed capital Contributed capital represents that portion of the shareholders' equity section of the balance sheet of a corporation that reflects contributions from shareholders. It represents the amount of a company's assets that have been generated through issuances of stock (common and preferred), including the dollar amounts of both the stock and additional paid-in capital accounts. Treasury stock purchases reduce contributed capital because they represent returns of capital to the shareholders.

controlling interest Technically, a controlling interest is ownership of 51% or more of the outstanding voting stock of a company. In such cases, consolidated financial statements must be prepared. Control may be possible, however, with less than 51% of the stock. A significant influence on either the board of directors or operations of the company, especially in cases where the remaining ownership is spread across many entities, may also represent control.

convertible bonds Convertible bonds are bonds that can be converted to other corporate securities (usually common stock) during some specified period of time. Convertible bonds combine the benefits of a bond (guaranteed interest) with the privilege of exchanging it for stock (potential appreciation and dividends) at the holder's option. They are considered hybrid securities because they possess features of both debt and equity.

copyright Copyrights are exclusive rights granted by law to control literary, musical, or artistic works. They are granted for 50 years beyond the life of the creator. The cost of acquiring a copyright is capitalized on the balance sheet as an intangible asset and is normally amortized over its legal life, not to exceed 40 years.

corporate governance Corporate governance includes mechanisms that encourage management to report in good faith to—and act in the interest of—the shareholders. Effective corporate governance is critical for an effective financial reporting system. Components of corporate governance include financial information users and capital markets, contracts between management and debt and equity investors, financial reporting regulations and standards, independent auditors, boards of directors and audit committees, internal controls ensuring that the company is in compliance with financial reporting regulations, legal liability, professional reputation, and ethics.

corporation   A corporation is a legal entity, separate and distinct from its owners (shareholders), who annually elect a board of directors, which in turn represents the shareholders' interests in the management of the business. A corporation has an indefinite life, which continues regardless of changes in ownership. Shareholders of a corporation are usually free to transfer their ownership interests. In a corporation, the liability of the shareholders is limited to the dollar amount of their investments, and in this way, the corporate structure provides a shield that protects the personal assets of the shareholders from corporate creditors. Companies in need of large amounts of capital therefore normally take the corporate form.

cost   See **historical cost.**

cost expiration   Cost expiration is the process of converting a capitalized cost to an expense. Accounting entries recorded at the end of the period are often used to expire previously capitalized costs, which appear as assets on the balance sheet.

cost method   Under the cost method of accounting, assets are carried on the balance sheet at their original (historical) costs, and when an asset is sold, a gain or loss is recognized on the difference between the balance sheet value of the asset and the proceeds from the sale.

cost of capital   If a company has available cash, the cost of capital is the expected return foregone by investing the cash in a project rather than in comparable financial securities. If a company does not have available cash, it is the cost of acquiring the cash—that is, the cost of raising debt (effective interest) capital or the cost of raising equity capital (dilution). Value is created for the shareholders when the management of operations and investments creates a return that exceeds the cost of capital.

cost of debt   Because interest is tax deductible, the explicit cost of debt is equal to the annual debt-related interest expense times 1 minus the income tax rate (Interest expense $\times$ [1 – Tax rate]). Debt may have implicit costs as well, including covenant-imposed restrictions and security (collateral) requirements.

cost of equity   The cost of equity is the return that an investor can reasonably expect on an equity investment in a firm, or the return (expressed as a percentage) foregone by a firm's

shareholders, who have chosen to invest their funds in the firm instead of other equally risky investments. It can be estimated by the capital asset pricing model. Value creation, the key metric of management's success, is defined as the extent to which return on equity exceeds the cost of equity.

cost of goods sold   The cost of goods sold appears on the income statement, indicating the cost of inventory sold during the period. In retail companies, cost of goods sold consists primarily of the cost of acquiring the inventory; in manufacturing companies, cost of goods sold consists of material, labor, and overhead costs.

covenant   See **debt covenant.**

CPA   See **certified public accountant.**

credit quality   Credit quality refers to the likelihood that an individual or entity will pay an outstanding account in a timely manner. Customers or clients with high credit quality have a history of paying their obligations on time.

credit rating   A credit rating is an assessment by an independent agency of the risk associated with a company and especially its outstanding debts. Credit ratings are usually expressed in alphabetic and/or numerical grades (e.g., AA1), and credit-rating agencies include Standard & Poor's, Dun and Bradstreet, and Moody's Investors Service.

credit terms   Credit terms are the contractual terms associated with outstanding credit (accounts receivable and accounts payable) accounts.

creditor   A creditor is an individual or entity to which a company owes money or services or to which the company has an outstanding debt.

cumulative preferred stock   Cumulative preferred stock is a type of preferred stock with a cumulative feature, which means that when a company misses a dividend on cumulative preferred stock, the missed dividend becomes a dividend in arrears. Most preferred stock is cumulative.

current assets   Current assets are assets on the balance sheet expected to be converted to cash or expired in one year or the operating cycle, whichever is longer.

current cost   See **replacement cost.**

current liabilities   Current liabilities are obligations listed on the balance sheet that are expected to be paid with the use of the current assets listed on the balance sheet.

current maturity of long-term debts   This is a balance sheet current liability that represents that portion of a long-term liability due in the current period. This liability is expected to require the use of current assets.

current ratio   *Current assets/Current liabilities.* The current ratio is often used to assess a company's current asset management and its solvency position. It is normally an important part of financial statement analysis.

D

debenture   A debenture is an unsecured bond.

debt   Debt is a form of financing a borrowing that involves an obligation, stated in a formal contract, which indicates the time period of the obligation in addition to the amount and timing of the required cash payments. Often, the contract also identifies security (collateral) in the case of default and other provisions (debt covenants) normally designed to protect the interests of the lender.

debt covenant   A debt covenant is an agreement between a company's debtholders and its managers that often restricts the managers' behavior. These restrictions are usually designed to protect the debtholder's investment (that is, increase the likelihood of receiving the contractual debt payments on a timely basis), and they are often written in terms of numbers and ratios taken from the financial statements. Violating a debt covenant puts the issuing company (debtor) into technical default.

debt investment   A debt investment involves the purchase of a debt security or a loan of goods or services to another entity, with the expectation that some payment (principal and interest) will be received in return. Debt investments are usually backed by contracts that specify the terms of the arrangement—the maturity date interest and principal payments, security, and collateral, as well as other features that transfer risk from one party to the other (e.g., debt covenants and call provisions).

debt ratio   *Total liabilities/Total assets.* Assets are generated from three sources: borrowings, contributions from owners, and profitable operations not paid out in the form of dividends. The debt ratio reflects that portion provided by borrowings.

debt redemptions   See **redemption.**

debt/equity ratio   *Total liabilities (both current and noncurrent)/Shareholders' equity. (Note: Sometimes contractual debt only is used in the numerator.)* The debt/equity ratio indicates the extent to which a company can sustain losses without jeopardizing the interests of its creditors. Creditors have priority claims over shareholders, and in case of liquidation, the creditors have first right to a company's assets. From an individual creditor's standpoint, therefore, the amount of equity in the company's capital structure can be viewed as a buffer, helping to ensure that there are sufficient assets to cover individual claims. It also represents a measure of the extent to which a company is relying on leverage as a source of financing.

default   A default occurs when an individual or entity fails to make a contractual payment on a debt. See **technical default.**

deferred cost   A deferred cost is a miscellaneous category of assets listed on the balance sheet that often includes prepaid expenses extending beyond the current accounting period and intangible assets such as organizational costs, capitalized legal fees, and other start-up costs.

deferred income   See **deferred revenue.**

deferred income taxes   Deferred income taxes can appear in either the liability or asset section of the balance sheet—arising when companies recognize revenues and expenses for financial reporting and income tax purposes in different time periods. Deferred income tax liabilities (assets) arise in periods when temporary timing differences between tax and financial reporting cause taxable income to be different from net income on the income statement. Deferred tax liabilities (assets) represent expected increases (decreases) in taxes payable in future periods when these temporary timing differences reverse—at which time the deferred income tax liabilities (assets) are written off the books.

deferred revenue   Deferred revenue is a balance sheet liability reflecting services yet to be performed by a company for which cash payments have already been collected. Deferred revenues are also referred to as payments in advance, deferred income, and unearned revenues.

defined benefit pension plan   In a defined benefit pension plan, an employer promises to provide each employee with a specified benefit at retirement. This promise is difficult to plan for because the benefits are received by the employees in the future. The benefits must be predicted, and the employer must contribute enough cash to a pension fund so that the contributions plus the earnings on the fund assets will be sufficient to provide the promised benefits. See **defined contribution pension plan.**

defined contribution pension plan   In a defined contribution pension plan, an employer agrees only to make a series of contributions of a specified amount to a pension fund. These periodic cash payments are often based on employee wages or salaries, and each employee's percentage interest in the total fund is determined by the proportionate share contributed by the employer on the employee's behalf. Under this type of plan, the employer makes no promises regarding how much the employees will receive upon retirement.

depletion   Depletion is the amortization of the costs incurred to acquire rights to mine natural resources. For mining and oil and gas companies, such costs can be substantial, and these costs are normally depleted as the natural resource is extracted, using the activity method.

depreciation   Depreciation is the periodic allocation of the cost of a fixed asset to the income statement over the asset's useful life. Such allocation is necessary if the costs are to be matched against the benefits produced by the asset. For financial reporting purposes, management has much discretion over how depreciation is computed. For income tax purposes, there is much less leeway.

depreciation base   The depreciation (amortization) base is the portion of the cost of a long-lived asset subject to depreciation or amortization—capitalized cost less estimated salvage value.

depreciation expense   A depreciation expense is an item on the income statement—reducing net income—that reflects the depreciation recognized on a company's fixed assets during the period of time covered by the income statement. Depreciation is a cost expiration; it does not represent a cash outflow.

diluted earnings per share   Diluted earnings per share is a disclosure required by generally accepted accounting principles (GAAP) for companies that have the potential for significant dilution. This ratio, which must be disclosed on the face of the income statement, is computed by adjusting the earnings per share ratio for an estimate of the equity securities likely to be issued in the near future. Diluted earnings per share is less than earnings per share because the potential for additional equity issuances increases the denominator of the earnings per share ratio.

dilution   Dilution is the reduction in a shareholder's relative ownership interest due to the issuance of additional equity securities to others.

dilutive securities   Dilutive securities are outstanding securities that can lead to future equity issuances. Shareholders and potential shareholders should be aware of dilutive securities because when the options on dilutive securities are exercised, the equity positions of the existing shareholders are diluted. Examples include stock options and convertible bonds. Fully diluted earnings per share, which is a required disclosure under generally accepted accounting principles (GAAP), reflects the dilutive effects of these kinds of securities.

direct method   Under the direct method of presentation in the operating section of the statement of cash flows, the cash effects of the operating expenses are subtracted from the cash effects of the operating revenues in the computation of net cash from operating activities. This form of presentation is called the direct method because the cash inflows and outflows are taken directly from the cash account in the ledger—that is, they represent real cash flows.

direct write-off method   The direct write-off method of accounting for bad debts records bad debt expense and removes the outstanding receivable from the balance sheet at the point in time when a specific account is deemed uncollectible. This method of accounting for bad debts is normally considered unacceptable under generally accepted accounting principles (GAAP) because it does not attempt to record all expected bad debts in the same period in which the sales revenue is recorded, thereby violating the matching principle.

discount on bond payable   Discount on bond payable is a contra liability account representing the amount by which the face (maturity) value of a bond exceeds the present value of the bond's future cash payments, discounted at the effective rate of interest as of the date when the bond was issued. Such discounts are amortized over the remaining life of the bond issuance under the effective interest method, increasing periodic interest expense to reflect the fact that the bond was issued at a discount (that is, the proceeds at the initial bond issuance were less than the face value of the bond).

discount rate   Discount rate is used to describe the rate used in present value computations. To compute the present value of a future cash flow, for example, the cash flows are discounted at the discount rate, which reflects both the timing of the cash flows and the risk associated with receiving them. In this sense, the discount rate reflects the company's cost of capital—the cost of its debt and/or its equity.

dissimilar asset   Dissimilar asset is a classification of long-lived assets used in determining the proper method of accounting for long-lived asset exchanges. The methods used to account for exchanges of dissimilar assets are different from those used to account for exchanges of similar assets. When dissimilar assets are exchanged, book gains or losses are recognized on the transactions in the amount of the difference between the market value of that received and the market value of that given up. When similar assets are exchanged, book gains or losses are not recognized. Instead, the difference between the market value of that received and the market value of that given up serves to adjust (increase or decrease) the cost of the asset received in the exchange. See **trade-in.**

divestiture   A divestiture is the sale of an asset or investment and normally refers to the sale of a major equity interest in another company.

dividend yield   *Dividends per share/Market price per share.* Dividend yield indicates the cash return on the shareholders' investment. Recall that a return on an investment in common stock can come in two forms: dividends and market price appreciation. This financial ratio measures the size of the first. Dividend yields tend to be relatively small, especially for fast-growing companies that choose to pay little or no dividends.

dividends   Dividends are payments made to the shareholders of a corporation that provide a return on their equity investments. Dividends are declared by the board of directors and are normally paid in the form of cash, although dividends in the form of other assets and shares of stock in the company are not unusual.

dividends in arrears   Dividends in arrears are missed dividends on preferred stock with a cumulative feature. Dividends in arrears are not listed on the balance sheet as liabilities, but they must be disclosed in the footnotes to the financial statements, and they must be paid if and when the company declares a dividend.

double taxation   Double taxation is a phenomenon that occurs when corporate profits and dividends received by the shareholders are both subject to federal income taxes. Double taxation occurs because the Internal Revenue Service treats corporations and their shareholders as separate taxable entities. It is a major disadvantage of the corporate form of business.

double-declining-balance method   Double-declining balance is the most extreme form of accelerated depreciation. Each period, depreciation expense is computed by multiplying the book value of the depreciable asset (Cost – Accumulated depreciation) by two times the straight-line rate (1/estimated useful life). This conservative method recognizes large amounts of depreciation expense in the early periods of the asset's life and small amounts in the later periods. It is very popular for tax purposes.

DuPont (ROE) model   Using the DuPont (ROE) model to analyze financial ratios provides an important starting point for financial statement analysis. While there are a number of different forms of this model, all are designed to explain the changes in return on equity by breaking it down into the following components: profit margin, asset turnover, and leverage.

E

earned capital   Earned capital is a measure of the amount of a company's assets that have been generated through profitable operations and not paid out in the form of dividends. On the balance sheet, earned capital is part of the shareholders' equity section and comprises retained earnings and other accumulated comprehensive income.

earning power   Earning power is the ability of a company to generate profits and increase net assets in the future. Net income, especially the persistent components of net income, is considered an indication of earning power.

earnings   See **net income.**

earnings management   Earnings management refers to cases where management uses its discretion to produce financial statements that place management's performance in a particular light, often reducing the ability of the financial statements to fairly represent the financial performance and condition of the company. Earnings management can involve reporting discretion or the structuring of transactions to achieve certain reporting goals (called real earnings management).

earnings per share   *Net income/Average number of common shares outstanding.* Earnings per share or basic earnings per share is perhaps the best known of all financial ratios, largely because it is often treated by the financial press as the primary measure of a company's performance. According to generally accepted accounting principles (GAAP), earnings per share must appear on the face of the income statement and be calculated in accordance with an elaborate set of complex rules. See **diluted earnings per share.**

earnings persistence   Earnings persistence is the extent to which a particular earnings dollar amount can be expected to continue in the future and thus generate future cash flows. Earnings amounts with high levels of persistence are expected to continue in the future, while those with low levels of persistence are not.

earnings quality   Earnings quality refers to the extent to which net income reported on the income statement differs from true earnings. This difference is the result of two factors: (1) financial reports based on an objective application of generally accepted accounting principles (GAAP) are inherently limited and (2) management uses its subjective discretion to apply GAAP when preparing the statements (earnings management). Low earnings quality means that GAAP financial statements do not accurately reflect the company's true financial situation and/or management has used much of its discretion in preparing the financial statements.

economic entity assumption   The economic entity assumption states that the financial statements refer to entities that are distinct from both their owners and all other economic entities. This assumption is important in determining the methods to account for consolidated financial statements, investments in equity securities, and business segments.

economic value added   Economic value added (EVA) represents the extent to which a return generated by management exceeds the cost of the capital (debt and equity) invested to generate that return. See **value creation.**

effective interest method   The effective interest method is used to value long-term liabilities (e.g., bonds) and long-term notes receivable and the related interest charges, so that the book value of the note represents an estimate of the present value of the note's future cash flows. The future cash flows are discounted using the effective rate of interest as of the date the note was issued. The effective interest method is required under generally accepted accounting principles (GAAP).

effective interest rate   The effective rate of interest is the actual rate of interest on an obligation or receivable; it often differs from the stated interest rate. It is that rate which, when used to discount the future cash payments associated with the obligation or receivable, results in a present value equal to the fair market value of that which was initially exchanged for the obligation or receivable. Generally accepted accounting principles (GAAP) require that the effective interest rate be used to compute the periodic interest expense and revenue that appears on the income statement.

equity   Equity is an ownership interest. Equityholders in a company own common stocks that have been issued by that company. Two rights are associated with owning a common stock: (1) the right to vote for the board of directors at the annual shareholders' meeting, and (2) the right to receive dividends if they are declared by the board. The shareholders' equity section of the balance sheet represents the investment made by the equityholders in the company and is a measure of the assets that would remain for the equityholders after all liabilities have been paid.

equity investment   An equity investment is the purchase of an ownership interest (e.g., common stock) in a company.

equity issuance   An equity issuance is the sale of common shares (stock). Equity issuances raise funds—often large amounts—for a variety of reasons, including business acquisitions, investments in long-lived assets, payments on outstanding debt, or simply to support operations.

equity method   The equity method is used to account for equity investments in the amount of 20%–50% of the investee company's outstanding common (voting) stock. Such a significant influence on the investee company indicates a substantive economic relationship between the two companies and may also be evidenced, for example, by representation on the board of directors, the interchange of management personnel between companies, frequent or significant transactions between companies, or the technical dependence of one company on the other.

equity security   See **equity investment.**

ERISA   The Employment Retirement Income Securities Act passed by the U.S. Congress in 1974 requires employers to fund their pension plans at specified minimum levels and provide other safeguards designed to protect employees. See **defined benefit pension plan.**

escrow   Escrow is the state of an item (e.g., cash) that has been put into the custody of a third party until certain conditions are fulfilled. Damage deposits on rental agreements, for example, are often held in escrow until the end of the rental period.

exchange rate   The exchange rate is the value of one currency expressed in terms of another currency. Like the prices of all goods and services, the exchange rates among currencies vary from one day to the next. Companies that transact in more than one currency face the risks associated with fluctuating exchange rates, which can give rise to gains and losses—some of which are reflected on the financial statements. Hedging is a strategy that can be used to reduce such risks.

expense   An expense is the outflow of assets or the creation of liabilities in an effort to generate revenues for a company. Examples include the cost of goods sold, salaries, interest, advertising, taxes, utilities, depreciation, and others. Revenues less expenses is equal to net income—the income statement. While some expenses involve cash outflows, many do not; expenses can also be accrued (e.g., salaries, wages, and interest) or the result of cost expirations (e.g., depreciation and amortization).

expensed   Expensed means to treat an expenditure as an expense by running the account through the income statement and closing it to retained earnings. Expense items appearing on the income statement have been expensed.

external financing   External financing refers to the generation of funds to support operations and growth through the issuance of debt and/or equity, instead of retained earnings. Externally financed companies normally have capital structures with relatively large balances in debt and/or contributed capital.

extraordinary item   Extraordinary items appear on the income statement and represent the financial effects of events that are significantly different from the typical, customary business activities of an entity. Such events are not expected to recur frequently in the ordinary activities of the business. Extraordinary items are neither usual nor frequent.

F

face value   See **maturity value.**

fair market value   Fair market value is the dollar amount at which an item can be sold—exchanged for cash.

fees earned   See **service revenue.**

financial accounting   Financial accounting is a process through which managers report financial information about an economic entity to a variety of individuals who use this information for various decision-making purposes. The financial accounting process produces the financial statements and the associated footnotes.

financial accounting standards   In the United States, financial accounting standards represent the official statements of the Financial Accounting Standards Board (FASB) and its predecessor bodies, as well as the official statements from the Securities and Exchange Commission (SEC). The complete set of financial accounting standards currently in force comprise U.S. generally accepted accounting principles (GAAP). Many non-U.S. countries have their own financial accounting standards and International Financial Reporting Standards (IFRS) are also used by many non-U.S. firms. IFRS are established by the International Accounting Standards Board (IASB), successor to the International Accounting Standards Committee (IASC), which was formed in 1973 to develop worldwide accounting practices.

Financial Accounting Standards Board   The Financial Accounting Standards Board (FASB) is the professional body currently responsible for establishing financial accounting standards. The FASB consists of seven well-compensated, full-time individuals who have severed all ties from previous employers and represent many business backgrounds. Since 1973, this private-sector body has issued well over 100 statements of financial accounting standards, covering a wide variety of topics.

financial condition   Financial condition refers to the economic strength of a company as of a specific point in time. The balance is designed to measure financial condition.

financial flexibility   Financial flexibility refers to a company's capacity to raise cash through methods other than operations. Examples include short- and long-term borrowings, issuing equity, or selling assets. Financially flexible companies can readily borrow, issue equity, and/or sell liquid assets that are not essential to their operations.

financial performance   Financial performance refers to the economic success of a company over a specified time period. The income statement is designed to measure financial performance.

financial ratio analysis   Financial ratio analysis is one of several techniques used to analyze financial statements in an effort to assess earning power, solvency, and earnings persistence. Financial ratio analysis involves computing and analyzing ratios that use two or more financial statement numbers. These ratios are often divided into five categories: (1) profitability, (2) solvency, (3) activity, (4) capitalization, and (5) market ratios. The DuPont (ROE) model is used by many analysts to asses the determinants of return on equity (ROE), which is directly related to shareholder value creation (ROE − Cost of equity).

financial statement analysis   Financial statement analysis is the process of reading, studying, and analyzing the information contained in the annual report and other relevant documents to predict the future financial performance and condition of a company. Financial statement analysis involves assessing (1) earning power, (2) solvency, (3) earnings persistence, and (4) earnings quality.

financial statements   Financial statements are a summary of the financial condition and performance of a company, prepared by its management and, in some cases, reviewed by independent auditors. The financial statements consist of the income statement, balance sheet, statement of cash flows, statement of shareholders' equity, and related footnotes. The ability to read, understand, and interpret the financial statements is a key element of financial statement analysis.

financing activities   Financing activities are the activities of a company that affect its capital structure. They involve the collection of capital through equity or debt issuances and any related payments, such as dividends, debt payments, and treasury stock purchases.

first in, first out   First in, first out (FIFO) is a cost flow assumption used to value inventory and cost of goods sold. It assumes that the first items purchased are the first items sold. FIFO is one of three commonly used cost flow assumptions; last in, first out (LIFO) and averaging are the other two.

fiscal period assumption   The fiscal period assumption states that the life of an economic entity can be divided into fiscal periods and that performance can be measured over those periods. This assumption allows the measurement of income for a given period of time (quarterly or annually) and raises questions about how the benefits and costs of a company should be allocated across periods for financial accounting purposes.

fiscal year   Fiscal years end on dates other than December 31. Most companies report on a calendar-year (December 31) basis (e.g., seasonality), but for various reasons, some companies report on other 365-day cycles, called fiscal years.

fixed asset turnover   *Net sales/Average fixed assets.* Fixed asset turnover is a measure of how efficiently a company is using its fixed assets. For many companies, this activity ratio is an important component of asset turnover and, in general, financial ratio analysis. Asset turnover times profit margin equals return on assets—a direct determinant of return on equity.

fixed assets   Fixed assets, sometimes called property, plant, and equipment, is a category of long-lived assets, including buildings, machinery, and equipment.

FOB destination   An FOB (free on board) destination represents freight terms indicating that the seller is responsible for the sold merchandise until it is received by the buyer. Goods shipped FOB destination are considered owned by the seller until they reach their destination. See **FOB shipping point.**

FOB shipping point   FOB (free on board) shipping point describes freight terms indicating that the seller is responsible for the sold merchandise only to the point from where it is shipped. Goods shipped FOB shipping point are considered owned by the seller until they reach the designated shipper, at which time they become the responsibility of the buyer. See **FOB destination.**

footnotes   Footnotes are descriptions and schedules included in the annual report that further explain the numbers on the financial statements. The footnotes are audited by the independent auditor, and they are considered part of the financial statements.

forward contract   A forward contract enables the holder to buy or sell an asset or liability at a future date at a prespecified price. Forward contracts are also written to enable the holder to buy or sell currencies at a prespecified exchange rate. Companies enter into forward contracts often to hedge the risks of holding assets and/or liabilities denominated in foreign currencies.

freight-in   Freight-in, also called transportation-in, is the freight cost associated with purchased inventory.

frequent transactions   A frequent transaction is an operating transaction that affects the income statement and is expected to recur repeatedly in the foreseeable future. See **extraordinary item.**

G

gain contingency   A gain contingency refers to an event that leads to a possible future outcome involving an increase in assets or a decrease in liabilities. See **loss contingency.**

generally accepted accounting principles   Generally accepted accounting principles (GAAP) are the standards that guide the preparation of financial accounting statements in the United States. See **financial accounting standards.**

going concern   A going concern is an entity that is expected to exist into the foreseeable future. No financial problems indicating financial failure over the planning horizon are apparent. Going concern is an assumption that underlies the financial statements, and auditors are expected to qualify their audit reports if there is doubt about the ability of the audited company to continue as a going concern.

goods in transit   Goods in transit are between the buyer and the seller as of the end of an accounting period. See **freight-in, FOB destination,** and **FOB shipping point.**

goodwill   In general, goodwill often refers to items of value to a company that are not listed on the balance sheet. However, a goodwill account is often recognized on the balance sheet when a company purchases another company in a business acquisition for a dollar amount greater than the fair market value of the purchased company's net assets (Assets − Liabilities). This purchased goodwill is the difference between the purchase price and the fair market value of a purchased company's net assets; it represents the purchaser's assessment that the purchased company is worth more as a working unit than is indicated by the value of its individual assets and liabilities.

government accounting   See **nonprofit entity** and **not-for-profit accounting.**

gross margin   *Gross profit/Sales.* Gross margin measures the extent to which the selling price of sold inventory exceeds its cost.

gross profit   *Sales revenues − Cost of goods sold.* See **gross margin.**

H

hedging   Hedging is a strategy used by management to reduce the risk associated with fluctuations in the values of assets and liabilities.

hidden reserves   Hidden reserves refer to subjectively understated assets or overstated liabilities. Building hidden reserves is a reporting strategy used by management that allows it to "smooth" reported earnings from one period to the next. It is accomplished by subjectively recognizing accounting losses, normally in periods of high income, which reduces earnings in the current period and ensures that these losses are not recognized in future periods when reported earnings may be lower.

historical cost   Historical cost is the dollar amount incurred to acquire an asset (investment) or bring it to sellable (inventory) or serviceable (long-lived asset) condition. Historical cost is also referred to as original cost or, simply, cost.

human capital   Human capital refers to a company's human resources, including its workforce and management.

human resources   See **human capital.**

hurdle rate   See **cost of capital.**

hybrid security   Hybrid securities have characteristics of both debt and equity. Issuing these securities is becoming an increasingly popular means of corporate financing.

I

income   See **net income.**

income smoothing   Income smoothing is an expression used to describe a management practice where accounting discretion is used to maintain a smooth earnings stream across time. See **earning management** and **hidden reserves.**

income statement   The income statement is a financial statement, prepared on an accrual basis, indicating the performance of a company during a particular period (usually a quarter or a year). It consists of revenues minus expenses, leading to net income, an important indication of a company's earning power.

independent auditor   Independent auditors have no personal or financial interest in their clients. To ensure objective audits, the audit profession requires that auditors maintain complete independence from their clients when conducting audits.

indirect method   Under the indirect method, the operating section of the statement of cash flows contains a series of adjustments that reconcile net income with net cash from operations. This form of presentation is called the indirect method because net cash from operating activities is computed indirectly, starting with net income and then adjusting it for the differences between accrual and cash flow accounting.

industry   An industry is a classification of a group of companies based on the similarity of their operations, product lines, and/or customers. Three basic categories are manufacturing, retailing, and services (general and financial).

inflation   Inflation refers to the eroding of the purchasing power of a monetary unit over time. In an inflationary environment, a dollar at the beginning of a period of time will buy more goods and services than at the end of the period.

input market   The input market is where an entity purchases the inputs for its operations. Historical cost, which is used extensively on the balance sheet, represents the cost of a company's inputs (e.g., inventory and long-lived assets) when they were acquired previously. Replacement cost, which is used selectively on the balance sheet (e.g., lower of cost or market applied to inventory), represents the current cost of a company's inputs.

installment obligation   An installment obligation requires periodic payments covering both interest and principal. Installment obligations are normally represented in the long-term liability section of the balance sheet, but the current installment is often carried as a current liability.

intangible asset   Intangible assets are characterized by the rights, privileges, and benefits of possession rather than by physical existence. Also, they are normally considered to have a higher degree of uncertainty than tangible assets.

intention to convert   Intention to convert is a phrase that describes one of the criteria by which an investment in a security is classified in the current assets section of the balance sheet. For an asset to be listed as current, management must intend and be able to convert the investment into cash within the time period that defines current assets.

interest   Interest is the price, usually expressed as an annual percentage rate, associated with transferring (borrowing or lending) money for a period of time. See **stated interest rate, effective interest rate,** and **cost of debt.**

interest coverage ratio   See **times interest earned.**

interest-bearing obligation   Interest-bearing obligations are notes requiring periodic interest payments determined as a percentage of face value; notes with stated annual rates of interest greater than zero. Interest-bearing obligations differ from non–interest-bearing obligations, where no interest payments are made until the maturity date. Both interest- and non–interest-bearing notes (receivables and payables) are accounted for under the effective interest method.

interest rate swap   An interest rate swap is a contract that serves to exchange a fixed-interest obligation for interest payments at market rates. Such contracts are used to hedge the risk of holding fixed-interest debt. See **hedging.**

internal control system   The internal control system consists of procedures and records designed and followed by company personnel to ensure that (1) the company's assets are adequately protected from loss or misappropriation and (2) all relevant and measurable economic events are accurately reflected in the company's financial statements.

internal financing   Internal financing refers to the generation of funds to support operations and growth through profits instead of debt or equity capital. Internally financed

companies normally have capital structures with relatively large balances in retained earnings, usually a sign of financial strength.

Internal Revenue Code   The Internal Revenue Code contains the official federal income tax laws. The Internal Revenue Service monitors and enforces adherence to these laws.

Internal Revenue Service   The Internal Revenue Service is the government agency charged with monitoring and enforcing the payment of federal income taxes. See **Internal Revenue Code.**

International Accounting Standards Board (IASB)   The IASB is a private-sector body, based in Britain and successor to the International Accounting Standards Committee (IASC), formed in 1973. The IASB, which represents more than 100 countries, has issued a number of international financial reporting standards (IFRS) recognized as acceptable financial reporting by many of the major stock exchanges in the world, and may soon be accepted by the U.S. Securities and Exchange Commission (SEC).

international financial reporting standards (IFRS)   These are the financial reporting standards issued by the International Accounting Standards Board (IASB). These standards are considered as acceptable reporting in most of the stock exchanges throughout the world, and may soon be accepted by the U.S. Securities and Exchange Commission (SEC). Already, non-U.S. firms can file in the U.S. using IFRS-based financial statements.

Inter-period tax allocation   Inter-period tax allocation refers to the methods used to account for the timing differences that arise between tax and financial reporting across periods. It involves accounting for deferred income taxes.

Intra-period tax allocation   Intra-period tax allocation is the practice of disclosing the income tax effect of certain nonoperating items on the income statement or statement of retained earnings with the item itself. The income taxes associated with operating income are disclosed on the income statement in a single line item immediately below operating income. The effects on income of nonoperating items—such as disposals of segments, extraordinary items, changes in accounting principles, and prior-period adjustments—are disclosed on the financial statements' net of their income tax effects.

inventory   Inventory refers to items or products that are either available for sale in the normal course of business or support the operations of the business. See **merchandise inventory** and **supplies inventory.**

inventory turnover   *Cost of goods sold/Average inventory.* Inventory turnover measures the speed with which inventories move through operations. This activity ratio compares the amount of inventory carried by a company to the volume of goods sold during the period, reflecting how quickly, in general, inventories are sold. By dividing this ratio into 365 days, it can be converted to an expression indicating how many days it takes, on average, to turn over the inventory. For retail and manufacturing companies, this ratio is an important component of asset turnover, which, when multiplied by the profit margin, equals return on assets, a direct determinant of return on equity.

investing activities   Investing activities involve the management of a company's long-term assets. The investment activities of a given period are summarized in the investment section of the statement of cash flows, involving primarily purchases and sales of fixed assets and investments in equity securities.

L

land   Land refers to real estate held for investment purposes, usually appearing in the long-term investments section of the balance sheet. Land used in the operations of a business is considered a long-lived asset and is normally referred to as property. Land is carried at historical cost on the balance sheet, not fair market value, and is normally not subject to depreciation.

last in, first out   Last in, first out (LIFO) is a cost flow assumption used to value inventory and cost of goods sold. It assumes that the last items purchased are the first items sold. LIFO is one of three commonly used cost flow assumptions; FIFO (first in, first out) and averaging are the other two. See **LIFO conformity rule, LIFO liquidation,** and **LIFO reserve.**

lease   A lease is a contract granting use or occupation of property during a specified period of time in exchange for some form of payment, usually cash. Leases are a popular way to finance business activities. Companies often lease, rather than purchase, land, buildings, machinery, equipment, and other holdings, primarily to avoid the risks and associated costs of ownership. For purposes of financial accounting, leases are divided into two categories: operating leases and capital leases.

leasehold obligation   Leasehold obligations are the balance sheet liabilities associated with capital leases reported by the lessee. This liability is equal to the present value of the future payments associated with a capital lease, discounted at the effective interest rate existing at the original date of the lease. Leasehold obligations are listed on the balance sheet as long-term and are accounted for under the effective interest method.

leverage   Leverage involves borrowing funds and investing them in assets that produce returns exceeding the after-tax cost of the borrowing. In such cases, a company is managing its debt effectively and creating benefits for the stockholders, which should manifest themselves as increases in return on equity. Leverage, however, involves the commitment of future cash outflows, which increases the risk associated with the leverage company.

liability   A liability is a probable future sacrifice of economic benefits arising from present obligations of a particular entity to transfer assets or provide services to other entities in the future as a result of past transactions or events.

life of a bond   The life of a bond is the period of time from the issuance of the bond to the maturity date, at which time the face value is paid to the bondholders. See **bond.**

LIFO conformity rule   The LIFO (last in, first out) conformity rule is a federal income tax requirement stating that if a company uses the LIFO cost flow assumption to value inventory for tax purposes, it must also use the LIFO assumption when preparing its financial statements. Consequently, those companies that use LIFO to save taxes must report the LIFO cost of goods sold amount on the income statement, normally leading to lower reported net income values.

LIFO liquidation   A LIFO (last in, first out) liquidation occurs when companies that use the LIFO cost flow assumption have sales that exceed production. LIFO users must pay close attention to inventory levels because when inventory liquidations occur, abnormally high profits can be reported. This is due to matching inventory having old (often lower) costs against current revenues.

LIFO reserve   The LIFO (last in, first out) reserve is the difference between inventory reported under LIFO and inventory reported under FIFO (first in, first out). Under U.S. generally accepted accounting principles (GAAP), companies that use LIFO are required to report what inventory would have been had they used FIFO. The difference between these two amounts (the LIFO reserve) represents the accumulated amount by which net income reported by the LIFO user has been understated, relative to FIFO, since the adoption of LIFO. The increase (decrease) in the LIFO reserve over the current period, when added to (subtracted from) LIFO net income for that period, is equal to FIFO net income (before taxes) for that period.

line of credit   A line of credit is a borrowing arrangement granted to a company by a bank or group of banks, allowing it to borrow up to a certain maximum dollar amount, with interest being charged only on the outstanding balance.

liquidation   Liquidation is the process of selling assets for cash. When companies go through liquidation, they normally sell their existing assets for cash, which is used to pay off creditors in order of priority. Any remaining cash is distributed to the stockholders. Liquidation is also used to describe an inventory reduction, where sales in a given period exceed inventory production or acquisition. See, for example, **LIFO liquidation.**

liquidity   Liquidity is the speed with which an asset can be converted into cash. Assets on the balance sheet are listed roughly in order of liquidity. For example, current assets are considered to be more liquid than intangible assets. Of the current assets, cash is considered to be more liquid than accounts receivable, which is more liquid than inventory, which is more liquid than prepaid expenses.

listed company   A listed company has its equity shares listed on a public stock exchange. See **stock market** and **stock price.**

loan contract   A loan contract is a written agreement describing the terms of a borrowing arrangement, including the timing of cash payments (interest and principal), the maturity date, collateral (security) in case of default, and restrictions on the actions of management (called covenants).

loan covenant   See **debt covenant.**

long-lived assets   Long-lived assets are used in the operations of a business, providing benefits that extend beyond the current operating period. Examples include property, plant, and equipment, and intangible assets.

long-term debt   Long-term debt refers to obligations listed on the balance sheet, backed by formal contract, expected to be paid with the use of assets listed as non-current on the balance sheet. See **debt and liability.**

long-term debt ratio   *Total long-term liabilities/Total assets.* The long-term debt ratio reflects that portion of assets provided by long-term borrowings.

long-term investments   Long-term investments refer to assets on the balance sheet that are not intended to be sold in the near term, but rather are expected to generate benefits over a time period extending beyond that which defines current assets.

loss   A loss occurs when the expenses of a given period exceed the revenues. Loss also refers to a situation where an item on the balance sheet is exchanged for something with a value lower than the item's book value.

loss contingency   A loss contingency (or contingent loss) is an existing condition, situation, or set of circumstances involving uncertainty concerning a possible loss to a company that will ultimately be resolved when one or more future events occurs or fails to occur. See **contingency** and **gain contingency.**

lower-of-cost-or-market rule   The lower-of-cost-or-market rule is applied to accounting for inventories, which states that the balance sheet value of inventory will be its historical cost or its market value, whichever is lower.

M

MACRS   The Modified Accelerated Cost Recovery System is the set of rules defining the maximum amount of depreciation that can be recognized on a fixed asset for the purpose of determining taxable income in a given year. To determine this amount, a fixed asset is placed into one of eight categories, based on its estimated useful life as specified in the asset depreciation range (ADR) system.

Each of the eight categories is then linked with an allowable depreciation method.

maintenance expenditure   A maintenance expenditure is a postacquisition expenditure that serves to repair or maintain a fixed asset in its present operating condition.

management accounting   Management accounting systems produce information used for decisions within a company. Such systems produce reports that cover such areas as performance evaluation, production output, product costs, and capital budgeting. This information is not available to individuals outside the company.

management discretion   Management discretion refers to the latitude exercised by management when applying accounting methods. Management can choose from a variety of accounting methods, estimates, and assumptions when preparing the financial statements and still be within the guidelines defined by generally accepted accounting principles (GAAP). The financial statements are also influenced by the timing and execution of transactions planned in advance by management. By using its discretion in these ways, management can make choices that serve its own interest—choices that may or may not be in the best interest of the company's owners. This discretion also makes it difficult for analysts to ascertain a company's true financial condition and performance from the financial reports.

management letter   The management letter appears in the annual report and normally states that management is responsible for the preparation and integrity of the financial statements. While management letters differ from one company to the next, most contain references to generally accepted accounting principles (GAAP), ethical and social responsibilities, the quality and reliability of the company's internal control system, the independent audit, and the audit committee of the board of directors.

manufacturing company   Manufacturing companies acquire raw materials and, through a process, combine labor and overhead to manufacture inventory. Manufacturing companies are normally characterized by large investments in property, plant and equipment, and inventory.

margin   See **profit margin** and **gross margin.**

mark-to-market accounting   Under mark-to-market accounting, investments are carried on the balance sheet at their market values. Realized gains and losses are recognized on the income statement; unrealized gains and losses are reflected either on the income statement or in the stockholders' equity section of the balance sheet, depending on the classification of the investment. See **marketable securities.**

markdown   A markdown is a reduction in sales price normally due to decreased demand for an item. Markdowns are very common in the retail industry, especially at the close of the seasons. These discounts are designed to accelerate sales of old items (boosting inventory turnover), making room for new inventories.

market price The market price is the price at which an asset can be exchanged in the open (output) market as of a particular point in time. See **fair market value** and **stock price.**

market ratios The market ratios are the financial ratios that measure returns to common shareholders due to changes in the market price of the common stock and the receipt of dividends.

market share Market share is the proportion of the total market for a particular good or service held by a company. For example, if the total market for boys' tennis shoes is $50 million per year and Company A sells boys' tennis shoes valued at $5 million in a given year, Company A has a 10% market share. Market share and changes in market share measure how well a company is competing with other firms in a given market.

market value See **market price** or **fair market value.**

market-to-book ratio (*Number of outstanding common shares × Market price per share*)/*Net assets.* The market-to-book ratio indicates the extent to which the market believes that shareholders' equity on the balance sheet reflects the company's true market value.

marketable securities Marketable securities are investments that are readily marketable and intended to be sold within the time period of current assets. They are carried on the balance sheet at current market prices. See **short-term investments.**

matching principle The matching principle is a measurement principle of financial accounting which states that performance is measured by matching efforts against benefits in the time period in which the benefits are realized. Net income on the income statement is the result of matching expenses against revenues in the time period when the revenues are realized. The matching principle is applied by first recognizing revenues and then matching against those revenues the expenses required to generate them.

materiality Materiality is an exception to the principles of financial accounting which states that only those transactions dealing with dollar amounts large enough to make a difference to financial statement users need be accounted for in a manner consistent with generally accepted accounting principles (GAAP). The dollar amounts of some transactions are so small that the method of accounting has virtually no impact on decisions based on information in the financial statements. Such transactions are referred to as immaterial, and management is allowed to account for them as expediently as possible.

maturity date The maturity date is the date when a loan agreement ends. As of the maturity date, if all payments (interest and principal) have been made on the loan, the

associated debt is satisfied. For most bonds, the face value of the bond is paid to the holder on the maturity date.

maturity value The maturity value is the dollar amount written on the face of the note or bond certificate that is paid to the holder at the maturity date. Face value and par value are terms often used interchangeably with maturity value.

measurement theory Underlying the measurement of assets, liabilities, revenues, and expenses—the key components of the financial statements—is a theoretical framework consisting of assumptions, principles, and exceptions. The assumptions include economic entity, stable dollar, fiscal period, and going concern; the principles include objectivity, matching, revenue recognition, and consistency; and the exceptions include materiality and conservatism.

merchandise inventory Merchandise inventory represents items held for sale in the ordinary course of business. It is especially important to retail and manufacturing enterprises, whose performance depends significantly on their ability to market their inventory. Indeed, the demand for such companies' products is often the most important determinant of their success.

merger A merger is a business combination whereby two or more companies combine to form a single legal entity. In most cases, the assets and liabilities of the smaller company are merged into those of the larger company, and the stock of the smaller, merged company is retired.

misclassification Misclassification involves including a financial statement account in an inappropriate section of the financial statements.

mortgage A mortgage is a cash loan exchanged for an installment note that is secured by real estate. The mortgage gives the holder the right to take possession of the real estate in case of default.

mortgage payable A mortgage payable is a balance sheet account that indicates the outstanding obligation associated with a mortgage. Mortgage payables are included in the long-term liability section of the balance sheet, except for that portion expected to use assets presently listed as current. This portion is included as a current liability.

multinational corporation Multinational corporations have their home in one country, but operate and have subsidiaries operating within and under the laws of other countries.

multistep format Under a multistep format, the income statement is designed in a way that separates the cost of goods sold from operating expenses, highlighting gross profit. This format also separates the usual and frequent operating items from those that are unusual and/or infrequent, often referred to as other revenues and expenses or extraordinary items.

N

natural resource cost   Natural resource costs are the costs of acquiring the rights to extract natural resources. Natural resource costs, which appear in the long-lived asset section of the balance sheet, are quite large in the extractive industries (e.g., oil, gas, and mining), and they are normally depleted under the activity (units of production) method.

net assets   *Total assets − Total liabilities (Shareholders' equity)*. A company's net assets are also referred to as the company's book value, balance sheet value, and net worth.

net book value   Net book value is the dollar value assigned to an item on the balance sheet. When used in reference to an entire company, net book value is equal to net assets or stockholders' equity. The net book value of a company is also referred to as simply the company's book value, balance sheet value, shareholders' equity, and net worth.

net credit sales   *Gross sales on account − Estimate of sales returns and allowances.*

net earnings   See **net income.**

net income   Net income is the difference between the revenues generated by a company in a particular time period and the expenses required to generate those revenues. Net income is the "bottom line" of the income statement.

net of tax   To disclose an item net of tax on the income statement means to reduce its dollar value by the income tax effect associated with the item.

net operating income   *Operating revenues − Operating expenses*. It is also referred to as operating income.

net profit   See **net income.**

net realizable value   Net realizable value is the net cash amount expected from the sale of an item, usually equal to the selling price of the item less the cost to complete and sell it.

net sales   Net sales is equal to gross sales less an estimate of sales returns and allowances.

net worth   See **net assets** or **net book value.**

non–interest-bearing notes   Non–interest-bearing notes are debt instruments that do not require periodic interest payments determined as a percentage of the face value; the entire interest amount is paid at maturity. Non–interest-bearing notes have stated annual rates of interest equal to zero, but the effective (actual) rate of interest is greater than zero.

nonoperating items   Nonoperating items appear on the income statement below net operating income and are considered unusual and/or infrequent. Nonoperating items are considered less persistent than operating items.

nonparticipating preferred stock   Nonparticipating preferred stock, a common form, carries the right—if dividends are declared—only to an amount designated by the dividend percentage expressed in the terms of the preferred stock. Unlike participating preferred stock, there is no right to an additional dividend.

nonprofit entity   A nonprofit entity is an organization where the operations are not designed to make a profit. Rather, most nonprofit entities generate funds through contributions, user fees, or taxes and use these funds to achieve some organizational or social purpose. Nonprofit entities are also referred to as not-for-profit and/or government entities.

nonsufficient funds penalty   A nonsufficient funds penalty is an assessment charged by banks against their customers for writing checks that are not backed by adequate funds.

not-for-profit accounting   See **nonprofit entity.**

notes payable   Notes payable are obligations evidenced by formal notes. They involve direct borrowings from financial institutions, or other companies, and often are established to finance the purchase of long-lived assets. Notes payable appear on the balance sheet in either the current or long-term debt section.

notes receivable   Notes receivable are assets backed by formal loan contracts. They normally arise from issuing loans, the sale of inventory, or the provision of a service and are often listed in the long-term assets section of the balance sheet.

O

objectivity   Objectivity is a principle of financial accounting measurement stating that the values of transactions and the assets and liabilities created by them must be verifiable—that is, backed by documents and prepared in a systematic and reasonable manner.

obsolescence   Obsolescence, often referred to as physical obsolescence, is the state of an asset when repairs are no longer economically feasible.

off-balance-sheet financing   Off-balance-sheet financing is a reporting strategy designed to depict a company as less reliant on debt than it actually is. For example, managers have been known to structure financing transactions and choose certain accounting methods so that liabilities need not be reported in the liabilities section of the balance sheet.

open account   An open account is an informal credit trade agreement used in cases where frequent credit transactions are conducted and a running balance of the obligation or receivable is maintained. If payments are made regularly within reasonable time periods, interest charges are not usually assessed. An open account is normally used to describe the trade terms underlying accounts receivable and accounts payable.

operating activities   Operating activities are the activities of a company associated with the acquisition and sale of a company's products and services.

operating cycle   Operating cycle is the time it takes, in general, for a company to begin with cash, convert the cash to inventory (or a service), sell the inventory (or service), and receive cash payment.

operating expenses   Operating expenses are the costs incurred to generate operating revenues associated with the normal activities of a company. They are disclosed in the operating activities section of the income statement, leading to net operating income.

operating income   See **net operating income.**

operating lease   An operating lease is treated as a simple rental for financial reporting purposes, where the periodic lease payments are treated as an expense, and no asset or liability is recognized on the balance sheet. See **capital lease** and **off-balance-sheet financing.**

operating margin   Operating margin equals net operating income divided by sales. It indicates the number of cents of operating income earned from every dollar of sales.

operating performance   Operating performance represents a company's ability to increase its net assets through operating activities.

operating revenues   Operating revenues are revenues generated through the usual and frequent transactions of a company. They are disclosed in the operating activities section of the income statement, leading to net operating income.

operating transactions   Operating transactions are usual and frequent transactions involving the acquisition and sale of a company's inventories or services.

opinion letter   See **audit report.**

ordinary stock dividend   An ordinary stock dividend is a relatively small dividend paid in the form of a company's own equity shares. It is normally expressed as a percentage of a company's outstanding shares. For example, a 5% stock dividend declared by a company with 100,000 shares outstanding would involve the issuance of 5,000 (100,000 × 0.05) new shares to the shareholders. Under an ordinary stock dividend, the number of shares issued represents less than 25% of the number of shares outstanding before the issuance. Ordinary stock dividends are also just called stock dividends.

organizational forms   The most common forms of business organization are sole proprietorship, partnership, subchapter S corporation, and corporation.

original cost   See **historical cost.**

other gains and losses   Other gains and losses appear in the nonoperating activities section of the income statement and refer to transactions that are either unusual or infrequent, but not both. This section of the income statement is also called other revenues and expenses.

other revenues and expenses   See **other gains and losses.**

output market   The output market is the market where an entity sells the outputs from its operations. Fair market value, market price, and net realizable value are all output market values.

outstanding shares   Outstanding shares are shares of stock that have been issued and are presently held by shareholders. They have not been repurchased (as treasury stock) by the company.

overhead   Overhead refers to manufacturing costs that cannot be directly linked to particular products.

overstating financial performance and condition   Overstating financial performance and condition, sometimes called providing a favorable financial picture, is a reporting strategy in which management attempts to depict a more favorable picture of the financial statements by overstating the company's financial performance and condition.

owners' equity   Owners' equity refers to the section of the balance sheet that measures the results of the activities (contributions and withdrawals) of the owners of a partnership or sole proprietorship. See **shareholders' equity,** the term used to describe these activities for the owners (shareholders) of a corporation.

P

paper profits   Paper profits is an expression used to describe profits that appear on the income statement but do not reflect increases in a company's economic wealth. Paper profits can be created by cosmetic changes in accounting estimates, judgments, and methods. A quality-of-earnings assessment is designed to identify and remove paper profits from the financial statements.

par value   In the context of preferred stock, par value is often used in the determination of the amount of the annual preferred dividend payment. It also determines the dollar amount disclosed in the preferred stock account on the balance sheet. In the context of common stock, par value has little economic significance, but it is used to determine the dollar amount disclosed in the common stock account on the balance sheet.

parent company   Parent companies own controlling interests in other companies, called subsidiaries. The consolidated financial statements of the parent company include the financial statements of all subsidiaries under its control. See **business acquisition** and **merger.**

participating preferred stock   Participating preferred stock carries the right, if dividends are declared, not only to an annual dividend amount (determined by the dividend percentage expressed in the terms of the preferred stock), but also to a portion of the remaining dividend paid to the common stockholders. Most preferred stock is nonparticipating.

partnership   A partnership is an organizational form where two or more people agree, by means of a contract, on how the business is to be conducted and how the profits and losses will be shared. A partnership is not a legal entity; the partners are legally liable for each other's business activities and the partnership itself is not subject to federal income taxes. The partners, themselves, are taxed on their share of the partnership profit.

patent Patents are granted by the U.S. Patent Office and give the holders exclusive rights to use, manufacture, or sell a product or process for a period of 10 years. See **intangible asset.**

payments in advance See **deferred revenue.**

pension A pension is a sum of money paid to a retired or disabled employee, the amount of which is usually determined by the employee's years of service. For most large companies, pensions are an important part of the employees' compensation packages, and they are part of almost all negotiated wage settlements. There are two primary types of pension plans: a defined-contribution plan and a defined-benefit plan.

percentage-of-credit-sales approach The percentage-of-credit-sales approach is a method of estimating bad debts that multiplies a given percentage by the credit sales of a given accounting period. The percentage-of-credit-sales approach is a common method of estimating uncollectibles, used in conjunction with the allowance method, when accounting for accounts receivable.

perpetual method The perpetual method is a method designed to keep track of, and close control over, inventories. It maintains an up-to-date record, recording each purchase as it occurs and recording an inventory outflow at each sale. The perpetual method is becoming increasingly popular, especially with retailers, because it helps to maintain close control over inventories. Also, computer systems have dramatically reduced the cost of using this method. Bar code sensor systems, for example, are used to implement the perpetual method.

physical obsolescence See **obsolescence.**

portfolio A portfolio is a group of securities, investments, or assets held by an individual or company.

postacquisition expenditures Postacquisition expenditures refer to costs incurred subsequent to the acquisition or manufacture of a long-lived asset. They serve either to improve the existing asset (betterment) or merely to maintain it (maintenance expenditure).

postretirement costs Postretirement costs refer to health care and insurance costs incurred by employees after retirement. Most large companies cover a portion of such costs, and similar to pensions, such coverage is part of employee compensation and is earned over an employee's years of service.

preemptive right A preemptive right, which is attached to some equity shares, allows the holder to purchase a proportionate interest in any new equity issuance. It enables shareholders to maintain their relative equity interests, reducing the dilutive effect associated with a new issuance.

preferred stock Preferred stock is issued by companies to raise capital. It has special rights that make it a hybrid between debt and equity. These rights relate either to the receipt of dividends or to claims on assets in case of liquidation.

premium on bonds payable A bond premium is a financial statement account, included in the liabilities section of the balance sheet and added to the bond liability, representing the fact that the proceeds of a bond issuance exceeded the face value (i.e., the bonds were issued at an effective rate of interest greater than the stated rate of interest). Bond premiums are amortized over the life of the bonds, reducing interest expense. See **effective interest method.**

prepaid expenses Prepaid expense is an asset account that reflects payments for certain items (e.g., insurance and rent) before the corresponding service or right is actually used. Prepaid expenses are considered assets because they represent benefits to be enjoyed by the company in the future. For most companies, prepaid expenses are a relatively small, often insignificant, part of total assets.

present value Present value is a technique used to place a value, as of the present day, on a set of future cash flows. It is computed by discounting future cash flows at an interest rate that reflects a company's cost of capital.

price/earnings ratio *Market price per share/Earnings per share.* The price/earnings ratio (P/E) is a measure of the extent to which the stock market believes that a company's current reported earnings signal future cash inflows.

prime interest rate The prime interest rate is the rate charged by a bank to its best (lowest risk) customers.

principal Principal is the sum of money owed as a debt, upon which interest is calculated. In the case of a bond, the principal can be referred to as the face value, par value, or maturity value.

prior-period adjustment Prior-period adjustment refers to the financial effects of certain events that result in direct adjustments to the retained earnings account. They are relatively unusual and are disclosed on the statement of shareholders' equity, normally representing corrections of errors made in prior periods.

private company Private companies have equity shares that are not listed and traded on the public stock exchanges.

proceeds Proceeds refers to the amount of cash collected on a sale, a borrowing, a bond issuance, or a stock issuance.

production capacity Production capacity refers to the number of goods or services that a company can produce over a specified period of time given its resources. Production capacity tends to increase when (1) companies expand through business acquisitions and investments in long-lived assets and/or (2) companies increase the efficiency of their available resources. Companies act to increase production capacity when present capacity is insufficient to meet the existing and/or future demand for the company's products and services.

production efficiency   Production efficiency refers to the number of items produced (of a given quality) divided by the cost of producing those items. Companies are continually attempting to improve production efficiency by producing more high-quality output at lower costs.

pro forma financial statements   Pro forma financial statements are financial statements projected into the future.

Pro forma reporting   Pro forma reporting is a controversial management disclosure where management recalculates reported net income in a manner that it considers to be more meaningful. For example, by highlighting truly one-time items and removing them from the income statement in arriving at pro forma earnings, management may be helping users more clearly interpret the results of current operations and better predict future results. Pro forma reporting could also be presented by management to undo the distortions generated by accounting rules that may not fit the situation.

profit   See **net income.**

profit and loss statement   See **income statement.**

profit margin   See **return on sales.**

profitability   See **earning power.**

profitability ratios   Profitability ratios assess performance, normally measured in terms of some measure of earnings as a percentage of some level of activity or investment. Profitability ratios are designed to measure earning power and include return on equity, return on assets, earnings per share, return on sales (profit margin), and times interest earned.

property   Property is a long-lived asset account representing the real estate upon which a company's operations are conducted. It is not subject to depreciation and normally not held for sale in the normal course of business. It is carried on the balance sheet at historical cost.

property, plant, and equipment   See **fixed assets.**

prospectus   A prospectus is a document containing a set of pro forma financial statements and other relevant information (e.g., contractual terms of debt agreements) that is filed with the Securities and Exchange Commission (SEC) when a company issues equity or debt to the public.

proxy statement   A proxy statement is mailed to the shareholders of the company, inviting them to attend and vote for the board of directors at the annual shareholders' meeting. It also contains extensive information about the company and the compensation packages of the board of directors and management.

public accounting firms   Public accounting firms are concerned primarily with providing independent audits of financial statements prepared by companies. The result of

the audit is an opinion letter, signed by a certified public accountant (CPA), that provides a brief description of the auditor's procedures and responsibilities and states whether the statements present fairly the financial condition and performance of the company, are in conformance with generally accepted accounting principles (GAAP), and the internal control system is considered effective. In addition to auditing, public accounting firms also perform tax and business advisory services for their clients.

purchase method   Under the purchase method of accounting for business acquisitions, the assets and liabilities of the acquired company (subsidiary) are added to those of the parent at their fair market values as of the time of the acquisition. The difference between the purchase price and the fair market value of the subsidiary's assets is recorded as goodwill.

purchasing power   Purchasing power is the amount of goods and services a monetary amount can buy at a given point in time. See **inflation.**

Q

qualified audit report   A qualified audit report departs from the language in the standard audit report. The departure can be due to any of a wide variety of reasons—some of them are serious, others are not. See **audit report.**

quality of earnings   See **earnings quality.**

quick ratio   (*Cash + Marketable securities accounts receivable*)/*Current liabilities.* The quick ratio compares a company's highly liquid assets to its current liabilities, providing a measure of the portion of the current liabilities that could be paid off in the near future.

R

rate of return   See **return on investment.**

readily marketable   Readily marketable refers to how quickly an asset can be converted to cash. It is normally used in the context of short-term investments (marketable securities) and describes securities that can be sold, and converted into cash, on demand. Securities traded on the public stock exchanges are considered readily marketable.

realized gain or loss   A realized gain or loss occurs when an asset (liability) is exchanged for another asset (liability) with a market value that differs from the book value of the asset (liability) given up.

recognized gain or loss   A recognized gain or loss occurs when a gain or loss is recorded on the financial statements. All gains and losses disclosed on the income statement are recognized.

redemption   Redemption normally refers to the repurchase of outstanding debt (e.g., bonds) either before or at the maturity date. Depending on the terms of the debt, such repurchases can be at the option of either the issuing company or the debtholders, and the price of the repurchase can be prespecified or at the market price existing at the time of the transaction.

refinancing   Refinancing occurs when a company satisfies an outstanding debt by issuing another outstanding debt. A company may also refinance by first redeeming debt and then issuing new debt.

related party transaction   A related party transaction occurs when a company executes a transaction with an owner, an officer, or someone with a special interest in the welfare of the company. These transactions should be viewed cautiously by analysts because they may be designed to benefit the related party, often at the expense of the other stakeholders in the company.

replacement cost   Replacement cost is the current price that a company would have to pay in the input market to replace an existing asset while maintaining operations at the present level.

reporting strategies   Reporting strategies are policies used by management when choosing accounting methods, normally designed to achieve specific reporting objectives. There are four common strategies: (1) overstating financial performance and condition, (2) building hidden reserves, (3) taking a bath, and (4) off-balance-sheet financing.

residual interest   Residual interest represents the right of the common shareholders to receive corporate assets in case of liquidation, after the creditors and preferred shareholders, in that order, have received their shares. The shareholders' equity section of the balance sheet represents one rough measure of the value of the shareholders' residual interest.

restrictive covenant   See **debt covenant.**

restructuring charges   A restructuring charge is an expense or loss that appears on the income statement in a given year, reflecting anticipated future costs. Many companies restructure their operations, planning to close plants, lay off employees, and incur other related expenses, choosing to record a charge to income in a period prior to the time they actually close the plants, lay off the employees, etc.

retail company   A retail company purchases inventory and attempts to sell it for a price greater than its cost. Retailers purchase inventory from manufacturers or wholesalers and sell it to customers, providing primarily a distribution service, doing little to change or improve the inventory product.

retained earnings   Retained earnings is an account listed in the shareholders' equity section of the balance sheet, representing the dollar amount of the company's assets generated through prior profits and not paid out in the form of dividends.

retirement   In the context of business activities, retirement normally refers to either discontinuing the use of a fixed asset or purchasing outstanding debt.

return on assets   (*Net income + Interest expense* [*1 − Tax rate*])/*Average total assets.* Return on assets measures the returns to both the shareholders (net income) and the creditors (interest expense) on their total investment in the firm (average total assets). The cost of interest is reduced by (1 − Tax rate) because interest is tax deductible. Changes in this ratio can be explained by changes in return on sales and asset turnover; return on assets is a direct determinant of return on equity. See **DuPont model, financial statement analysis,** and **profitability ratios.**

return on equity   (*Net income − Preferred stock dividends*)/*Average stockholders' equity.* Return on equity compares the profits generated by a company to the investment made by the company's shareholders. Net income, which appears in the numerator, is viewed as the return to the company's owners, while the balance sheet value of shareholders' equity, which appears in the denominator, represents the amount of resources invested by the shareholders. Changes in this ratio can be explained by changes in return on assets, common equity leverage, and capital structure leverage. Value is created for the shareholders when return on equity exceeds the cost of equity.

return on equity from financial leverage   *Return on equity − Return on assets.* The difference between the two ratios measures the extent to which the return to the shareholders exceeds the return to all capital providers, including creditors. When return on equity is greater (less) than return on assets, it is a measure of the economic benefit (loss) to shareholders from financial leverage. When a company has no liabilities, then the return on equity will equal return on assets.

return on equity (ROE) model   See **DuPont model.**

return on investment   (*Market price*[*n − 1*] *− Market price*[*n*] *+ Dividends*[*n − 1*])/*Market price*[*n*]. Return on investment provides a measure of the pretax performance of an investment in a share of common stock. The numerator reflects the pretax return to the shareholder (market price appreciation and dividends), and the denominator reflects the amount of the shareholders' investment.

return on sales   (*Net Income + Interest expense* [*1 − Tax rate*])/*Net sales.* Return on sales provides an indicator of operating efficiency—increasing if operating expenses increase (decrease) at a slower (faster) rate than net sales. An efficient company, for example, will generate increased net sales with a constant level of operating expenses. Changes in this ratio can be analyzed by examining how the items on the income statement changed as a percentage of sales (that is, common-size income statement). Return on sales times asset turnover equals return on assets, a direct determinant of return on equity. See **profit margin.**

revaluation adjustment   Revaluation adjustments are designed to bring the dollar amount of certain accounts on the financial statements in line with the existing facts.

revenue   Revenue refers to inflows or other enhancements of assets of an entity or settlement of its liabilities (or a combination of both) during a period from delivering or producing goods, rendering services, or other activities that constitute the entity's ongoing major or central operations.

revenue recognition   Revenue recognition is a principle of accounting measurement that determines when revenue from the sale of a good or the provision of a service is entered into the financial statements. Revenue recognition is a critical question in the matching process because the expenses incurred to generate revenues should not be reflected on the income statement until the revenues are recognized. The sale of a good or provision of a service normally involves a series of steps—including ordering the good or service, producing it, transferring it to the customer, and receiving payment. The principle of revenue recognition helps to determine at which of these steps the revenue should be recorded in the books.

reverse account analysis   Reverse account analysis (also called T-account analysis) is a mechanical process that involves examining the activity in a given balance sheet account to acquire information not directly disclosed in the financial statements or footnotes.

risk   Risk refers to variation in the returns of a given investment. Risky investments are characterized by large fluctuations in their returns across time—providing large returns in some periods, while providing small, zero, or even negative returns in other periods. Risk, when applied to a potential borrower, refers to the probability of receiving timely interest and principal loan payments, sometimes called the risk of default. Equity and debt investors normally require larger expected returns to compensate for bearing additional risk.

risk premium   Risk premium refers to the percentage return on investment over and above the risk-free rate that reflects the level of risk associated with an uncertain investment. The risk-free rate plus the risk premium equals the expected rate of return that must be met before an investment will be accepted. In short, larger expected returns are necessary for higher-risk investments.

risk-free return   The risk-free return is the return provided by riskless securities (e.g., treasury notes and certificates of deposit). It varies across time due to macroeconomic factors such as economic activity, inflation, exchange rates, and monetary policy, but recently has been relatively low (4%–5%).

S

sales   Sales is a revenue associated with the sale of a good or product. Sales for a given period is computed by multiplying the number of items sold by the sales price, and it is typically the major revenue for manufacturers and retail companies.

sales growth   Sales growth is an important indicator of a company's performance over a period of time. It can be determined by comparing sales dollar amounts on the income statement across reporting periods. It normally reflects changes in customer demand for a company's goods or services—due to changing prices and/or quantities sold.

sales returns   Sales returns refer to recorded sales that are subsequently returned to the seller. The returns may be due to faulty merchandise and customer dissatisfaction; in a large number of cases, relatively open returns are part of normal business practices.

salvage value   Salvage value refers to the dollar value of a long-lived asset at the completion of its useful life. Salvage values must be estimated before long-lived assets are placed into service so that the depreciable base can be depreciated, or amortized, over the estimated useful life. Estimating salvage values is extremely subjective, so many companies assume them to be zero.

Sarbanes–Oxley Act   In an attempt to bolster corporate governance and restore confidence in the U.S. financial reporting system, this Act was passed by the U.S. Congress in 2002. It enacted sweeping changes in the responsibilities of management, financial disclosures, independence and effectiveness of auditors and audit committees, and oversight of public companies and auditors. The Act requires the principal executive and financial officers to certify that the financial reports have been reviewed, do not contain untrue statements or omit important information, and fairly present the company's financial condition and performance. It also places additional responsibilities on management and the auditor to ensure that adequate internal controls are in place to provide reasonable assurance that the financial records are complete and accurate. Management must also file an annual report on internal control over financial reporting, and the external auditor must attest to and report on management's assessment of internal controls.

secured note   Secured notes are formal promissory notes backed by assets (collateral) that are distributed to creditors in the event of default.

Securities and Exchange Commission   In 1934, the U.S. Congress created the Securities and Exchange Commission (SEC), a federal agency with the power to implement and enforce the Securities Act of 1933 and the Securities Exchange Act of 1934. The Securities Act of 1933 requires that companies issuing securities on the public security markets file a registration statement (Form S-1) with the SEC prior to the issuance. The Securities Exchange Act of 1934 states that companies with securities listed on the public security markets must (1) annually file audited financial reports with the SEC (Form 10-K), (2) file quarterly financial statements with the SEC (Form 10-Q), and (3) provide audited financial reports annually to the stockholders. The SEC is also currently active in establishing financial accounting standards.

security   See **collateral.**

service company   A service company provides a service, as opposed to a good, for its clients or customers. Service companies carry no inventories and do not recognize the cost of goods sold on the income statement. Service revenue or fees earned represent its main revenues. The service industry is normally divided into two groups: general services and financial services.

service revenue   Service revenue (also called fees earned) represents revenues from the provision of services. This account is normally found in the operating section of the income statement.

SG&A   SG&A refers to selling, general, and administrative expenses—often one of the most important expense categories on the income statement.

shareholder   Shareholders (also called stockholders) are individuals or entities that hold ownership interests in a corporation. These interests include (1) the right to vote in the elections of the board of directors, (2) the right to receive dividends if they are declared by the board of directors, (3) a residual interest in the corporation's assets in the event of liquidation, and, in some cases, (4) a preemptive right. *Stockholder* and *shareholder* are used interchangeably.

shareholders' equity   Shareholders' equity is the section of a corporate balance sheet that represents the shareholders' interests (or investment) in the corporation. It consists primarily of contributed capital and earned capital (Retained earnings + Other accumulated comprehensive income). The total dollar value of shareholders' equity also represents the company's net book value and its net worth.

short-term debt   Short-term debt refers to obligations on the balance sheet, backed by formal contract, expected to be paid with the use of assets presently listed as current on the balance sheet. Short-term debt is normally listed in current liabilities.

short-term investments   Short-term investments consist of investments in equity securities, bonds, and similar financial instruments that are both readily marketable and intended by management to be sold within the time period that defines current assets. Companies often purchase these kinds of securities to earn income with cash that would otherwise be idle for a short time. These investments are carried on the balance sheet at fair market value and, according to generally accepted accounting principles (GAAP) must be classified as either trading securities or available-for-sale securities.

similar asset   Similar assets are those that perform essentially the same function. See **trade-in.**

sole proprietorship   A sole proprietorship is considered to be a partnership with a single partner. It is not a legal entity and therefore not subject to federal income taxes. The sole proprietor is taxed and is personally liable for the activities of the business.

solvency   Solvency refers to a company's ability to meet debts as they come due. Assessing solvency is a very important part of financial statement analysis.

solvency ratios   Solvency ratios refer to financial ratios designed to measure a company's ability to meet its debts as they come due. The current and quick ratios are the two solvency ratios.

special-purpose entities (SPE)   These are entities created by a company solely to carry out an activity or series of transactions directly related to a specific purpose. The most common purposes include raising funds and transferring risk. The main accounting issue with SPEs concerns whether to consolidate the SPE into the financial statements of the creating company.

specific identification   Specific identification is a procedure used to value cost of goods sold and inventory. It is used when companies can specifically identify the inventory items acquired and sold during the period, as well as those that remain at the end of the period. In such cases, the actual costs of the items sold and retained can be allocated to the cost of goods sold and inventory, respectively.

stable dollar assumption   The stable dollar assumption states that the value of the monetary unit used to measure a company's performance and financial condition is stable across time; that is, the inflation rate is assumed to be zero. This assumption allows mathematical operations (addition, subtraction, multiplication, and division) to be performed on account values that are established at different points in time.

standard audit report   A standard audit report, often referred to as an unqualified report, states that the auditor was able to conduct an appropriate audit and render an opinion that the financial statements were prepared in accordance with generally accepted accounting principles (GAAP) and fairly reflect the financial performance and condition of the company, and the internal control system is effective. See **qualified audit report.**

stated interest rate   The stated interest rate is the annual rate of interest stated on the face of a formal promissory note or bond certificate. The stated interest rate times the face value determines the periodic interest payments.

statement of cash flows   The statement of cash flows is a financial statement that provides a summary of the activity in a company's cash account over a period of time. This statement divides cash activity into three categories: (1) operating, (2) investing, and (3) financing activities.

statement of retained earnings   The statement of retained earnings represents the portion of the statement of shareholders' equity that reconciles the balance in the retained earnings account at the beginning of an accounting period with the balance at the end of the period. It normally takes the following form: beginning retained earnings plus (minus) net income (loss) less dividends equals ending retained earnings. See **internal financing.**

statement of shareholders' equity   The statement of shareholders' equity is a financial statement included in the annual reports of major U.S. companies. It explains the changes in the accounts of the shareholders' equity section of the balance sheet during an accounting period. Generally accepted accounting principles (GAAP) requires that these changes be described somewhere in the annual report, and many companies include them in the footnotes.

stock   In the United States, the term stock normally refers to common or preferred stock. The expression "share of stock" is often used. On occasion, especially outside the United States (e.g., Great Britain), the term stock refers to inventory.

stock dividend   See **ordinary stock dividend.**

stock market   The stock market consists of a number of stock exchanges where equity securities are traded in a public forum. The New York Stock Exchange, the American Stock Exchange, and the Over-the-Counter (OTC) market are located in the United States and are the most active in the world. However, there are a number of other exchanges located in virtually all major cities outside the United States.

stock options   A stock option is an option to purchase common stock at a prespecified price during a specific time period.

stock price   Stock price is the market price of an equity security that has been previously issued and is presently listed on one of the public stock markets. Stock prices increase and decrease as investor expectations about a company change.

stock split   Stock splits are used by corporations to increase the number of shares outstanding and simultaneously reduce the market price. Stock splits are expressed in terms of a ratio that describes how the existing shares are to be divided. In a 2:1 split, for example, the existing shareholders each receive an additional share for every share owned. Consequently, the number of outstanding shares are doubled, and the market price per share is approximately cut in half. A 3:1 stock split effectively triples the number of outstanding shares, which the company executes by distributing two additional shares for each one outstanding. In a 3:2 stock split, one additional share is issued for every two outstanding.

stock split in the form of a dividend   Stock splits in the form of dividends are relatively large stock dividends where 25% or more of the outstanding stock is issued, as a dividend, to the existing shareholders. They are treated as stock splits.

stockholders   See shareholder

straight-line method   The straight-line method is a procedure for depreciating or amortizing long-lived assets that recognizes equal amounts of depreciation or amortization in each year of the asset's useful life. To compute straight-line depreciation for a given period, divide the depreciation base by the estimated useful life. This is the most common method for depreciating fixed assets and amortizing intangible assets.

subchapter S corporation   A subchapter S corporation is primarily the same as a corporation, with one important difference: It is taxed like a partnership. It is popular with many small businesses because it has the advantages of a corporation (e.g., stockholders are liable only up to the amount of their investment) without one of the major disadvantages (double taxation).

subsidiary   A subsidiary is a company with the majority of its common stock owned by another company, called the parent. Normally, the subsidiary prepares its own financial statements separately from the parent, but these statements are usually not available to the public because the shares of the subsidiary owned by the parent are no longer publicly listed. Under generally accepted accounting principles (GAAP) the parent must prepare consolidated financial statements.

sum-of-the-years'-digits method   The sum-of-the-years' digits is a method of accelerated depreciation that is less extreme than the double-declining-balance method. To compute depreciation for a given period, the depreciation base is multiplied by a ratio; the remaining estimated life serves as the numerator and the sum of the estimated life's digits serves as the denominator. This method recognizes relatively large amounts of depreciation in the early periods of an asset's life and smaller amounts in later periods.

supplies inventory   Supplies inventory refers to items available to support the operations of a business, such as office supplies and spare parts. Supplies inventory can be listed on the balance sheet under either current assets (e.g., office supplies) or long-lived assets (e.g., spare parts used to maintain long-lived assets). Supplies inventory is normally a relatively small asset on the balance sheet.

T

T-account analysis   See **reverse account analysis.**

takeover   In a takeover, an investor, group of investors, or another company purchases enough of the outstanding voting stock to gain a controlling interest (51% or more) in the acquired company. Takeovers are often classified as "unfriendly" (the existing board of directors and management are removed) or "friendly" (the existing board of directors and management are maintained). The threat of a takeover creates an important incentive for the board of directors and management to act responsibly and in the interest of the shareholders. Takeovers are accounted for under either the purchase or pooling-of-interests method.

taking a bath   Taking a bath is a reporting strategy that recognizes excessive losses or expenses in a single period. This strategy helps to ensure that future periods will show improved performance because losses and expenses recognized in the current period will not have to be recognized in the future.

tax accounting   Tax accounting systems produce information that is reported to the Internal Revenue Service and is used in the computation of the company's tax liability.

tax deductible   An expense is tax deductible if it is an allowable reduction (according to tax law) of taxable income—the dollar amount on which the tax liability is based. Many transactions are structured so that the related costs and expenses can be deducted for tax purposes.

taxable income   Taxable income is the number used to determine income tax liability. It is computed by subtracting tax-deductible expenses from revenues that must be included for tax purposes. Deductible expenses and includible revenues are determined primarily by the Internal Revenue Code. Taxable income normally differs from net income reported on the income statement, which is based on generally accepted accounting principles (GAAP).

technical default   In a technical default, a company violates the terms of a debt covenant. For example, a debt covenant may require that the company maintain a current ratio of at least 1.0. If the company allows the ratio to fall below 1.0, it is in technical default. Technical default normally leads to renegotiation of the debt terms and is normally a negative signal for the company.

technical obsolescence   Technical obsolescence is the state of an asset when technical advances have rendered its services no longer useful.

term loan   Term loans are paid in installments over a period longer than one year from the operating cash flow of a business.

times interest earned   *Net income before interest and taxes/Interest expense.* Times interest earned, also referred to as interest coverage, is a financial ratio that measures the extent to which a company's annual profits cover its annual interest expense. The profit number in the numerator should reflect the primary, recurring business operations of the company and should be calculated before income taxes because interest is deductible for tax purposes. The denominator—interest expense—can usually be found on the income statement.

trade-in   In a trade-in, an old asset (and usually cash) is exchanged for a new asset. The methods used to account for trade-ins depend on whether the assets in the exchange are similar or dissimilar.

trademark or trade name   Granted by the U.S. Patent Office, a trademark or trade name is a word, phrase, or symbol that distinguishes or identifies a particular enterprise or product. Trademarks last for a fixed period of time, but can be renewed indefinitely. See **intangible asset.**

trading securities   Trading securities are relatively small investments (less than 20% of the outstanding voting stock) in marketable equity (or debt) securities that are purchased and held principally for the purpose of selling them in the very near future with the objective of generating a profit on short-term price changes. Trading securities are always listed as current assets on the balance sheet and are carried at market value. Changes in the market prices of trading securities are reflected as income or loss on the income statement, normally in the nonoperating section.

transportation-in   See **freight-in.**

treasury notes   Treasury notes are obligations of the federal government that pay interest at a specified rate for a specific period of time, usually less than six months. These notes are very low risk, and companies often purchase treasury notes to temporarily earn interest with excess cash. Such investments are classified as short term on the balance sheet. The rate paid by treasury notes can also be used as a measure of the riskless rate of return. See **short-term investments.**

treasury stock   Treasury stock is previously issued stock that has been repurchased by the issuing company and held in the corporate treasury. It is often reissued at a later date.

U

uncollectibles   Uncollectibles, sometimes called bad debts, refer to outstanding accounts or notes receivable that will never be received. Under generally accepted accounting principles (GAAP), management is required to estimate the value of uncollectibles periodically and recognize an expense on the income statement, as well as reduce receivables on the balance sheet.

unearned revenue   See **deferred revenue.**

uniformity   Uniformity would be achieved if all businesses used the same accounting methods.

unqualified audit report   See **standard audit report.**

unrealized gain or loss   An unrealized gain or loss occurs when the market value of an asset (liability) on the balance sheet changes and no exchange has taken place. When the market value of an asset increases, for example, an unrealized gain occurs.

unsecured notes   Unsecured notes are formal, promissory notes (contracts) that are not backed by any form of security (collateral). For this reason, they tend to be high risk, but normally can only be successfully issued by strong companies. The presence of unsecured debt on the balance sheet of a company, therefore, is often a signal of financial strength; that company's creditors apparently have not required that the debt be secured by the company's assets. Unsecured bonds are called debentures.

useful life   The useful life of an asset is the estimated time period, or activity, over which a long-lived asset is expected to provide revenue-producing services. The estimated lives of intangible assets can be as long as 40 years, while fixed asset lives normally range from 3 to 30 years. The estimated useful life of an automobile may be more appropriately expressed in terms of miles driven (e.g., 150,000 miles), instead of years.

usual transactions   Usual transactions are part of the normal operating activities of a company. They involve the sale of a company's merchandise inventory or the provision of services expected in the normal course of business. If these transactions occur frequently, they are considered operating transactions and are disclosed as part of net operating income. If they occur infrequently, they are considered nonoperating items and classified as such on the income statement.

V

valuation base   Valuation base refers to the values (e.g., historical cost, replacement cost, fair market value, net realizable value, and present value) used to determine the dollar amount of an entity's assets and liabilities on the balance sheet.

value creation   Value creation is a key metric of management's success, defined as the extent to which return on equity exceeds the cost of equity. It can be computed as a percentage (Return on equity – Cost of equity) or as a dollar value (Net income – [Cost of equity × Average shareholders' equity]), and the market value of the firm can be expressed in terms of the book value of the firm plus the discounted future value creation. Value creation over time increases the value of the firm.

W

warranty   A warranty is an agreement by which a seller promises to remove deficiencies in the quantity, quality, or performance of a product sold to a buyer.

window dressing   Window dressing is a phrase used to describe the activity of managers who use accounting methods, judgments, and estimates or make operating decisions purely to make the financial statements appear more attractive to financial statement users.

working capital   *Current assets – Current liabilities.* Working capital measures the extent to which a company's current assets cover its current liabilities. It is viewed as a measure of solvency and is often used in debt covenants to ensure that the borrower maintains a sufficient buffer of current assets to current liabilities. Like the current and quick ratios, however, working capital is a relatively weak measure of a company's solvency position.

Index